"This is a textbook with a (major) difference: It generates excitement and builds confidence in its readers, even as it gives them vast amounts of information, beautifully presented and in readily comprehensible language. Beldman and Rhodes open windows into the ancient world in all its complexity and lay down clear paths through the almost infinitely varied landscape of modern biblical interpretation. With the skill of the best teachers, they anticipate the myriad questions that thoughtful students pose and address them with clarity and directness, not shying away from the most difficult theological conundrums but instead offering guidance for wrestling with them in good faith. A textbook this good could go a long way toward renewing the enthusiasm of those who teach Bible, and indeed raising up a new generation of wise readers and scholars for the church."

—**Ellen F. Davis**, Duke Divinity School

"This volume is a very readable and quite comprehensive guide to the Pentateuch. These first five books of the Bible are often not well understood, ignored as irrelevant, or reduced to simply prefiguring Jesus. How misguided! Beldman and Rhodes reveal the theological riches of the Pentateuch, which in many ways are foundational to Christian faith and germane to the mission of the people of God in the world today. A wonderful resource!"

—**M. Daniel Carroll R.**, Litfin Divinity School, Wheaton College (emeritus)

"How I wish I had had this book when I taught the Pentateuch years ago, and how I envy professors and students who will have the pleasure and benefit of having it as a textbook today! It is such a refreshing contrast to tedious introductions of old, with its interest-sustaining variety, exploring not only the what of the text's content but also how the different genres work and why these books matter theologically for disciples of Christ. The Pentateuch deserves such loving appreciation."

—**Christopher J. H. Wright,** Langham Partnership

"This latest addition to Baker Academic's Reading Christian Scripture series is, quite literally, outstanding: It stands out in a crowded market of introductions both to the Bible generally and to the Pentateuch specifically. It does so in a host of ways, including its design and its numerous sidebars, figures, and other helps that make this volume perfect for classroom use. It's also remarkably thorough. Hardly had an issue or question crossed my mind before I found Beldman and Rhodes addressing it. No stone is left unturned here, with the stones in question running from the ancient context right down to our present moment with its manifold concerns. Simply put, there is a great deal of information to be found in this book, but even more wisdom. The greenest of students and the most seasoned of scholars will learn much from this book."

—**Brent A. Strawn**, Duke University

"Beldman and Rhodes offer an accessible, theologically rich, visually engaging, and highly relevant resource for students and church leaders. They lay out the Pentateuch's grand design, address its many riddles and challenges, and guide readers toward a renewed understanding of God's revelation in these five books and of how we are to respond. I will use this valuable resource in my courses."

—**Chloe T. Sun**, Fuller Theological Seminary

"This textbook will jolt readers awake to the riches and depths of the Pentateuch. Beldman and Rhodes are engaging and reliable guides through the Torah's complex terrain. They don't shy away from the hard stuff, but they also help you rediscover familiar passages. What a gift to have this book!"

—**Matt Lynch**, Regent College

"This wide-ranging textbook on the Pentateuch is an excellent addition to the Reading Christian Scripture series. Beldman and Rhodes help readers contextualize the Pentateuch within God's larger story of Scripture, exploring the theological, literary, and social nature of the biblical text. Not shying away from the morally challenging dimensions of the Pentateuch, this book draws on the collective wisdom of the global church across history. This is particularly evident in chapters interspersed throughout the biblical survey that address important questions, such as how to read Old Testament narrative and poetry today, what to do with biblical law and ritual texts, and how to navigate violent Old Testament texts today. Even as Christians continue to disagree on these matters, Beldman and Rhodes provide a rich resource for Christian reflection. This textbook also exhibits a notable sensitivity to ethnic and cultural diversity that will serve many different communities in the body of Christ. Though fit for the classroom, this textbook puts the academic study of the Pentateuch in service of hearing the voice of the living God."

—**Andrew M. King**, Midwestern Baptist Theological Seminary and Spurgeon College

READING *the* PENTATEUCH *as* CHRISTIAN SCRIPTURE

• READING •
CHRISTIAN
SCRIPTURE

VOLUMES AVAILABLE

Reading the Old Testament as Christian Scripture
Mark S. Gignilliat and Heath A. Thomas

Reading the New Testament as Christian Scripture
Constantine R. Campbell and Jonathan T. Pennington

Reading the Pentateuch as Christian Scripture
David J. H. Beldman and Michael J. Rhodes

Reading Wisdom and Psalms as Christian Scripture
Christopher B. Ansberry

Reading the Prophets as Christian Scripture
Eric J. Tully

Reading the Gospels as Christian Scripture
Joshua W. Jipp

Reading Paul as Christian Scripture
Constantine R. Campbell

Reading the Later New Testament as Christian Scripture
Ruth Anne Reese and Madison N. Pierce

READING *the* PENTATEUCH *as* CHRISTIAN SCRIPTURE

A LITERARY, CANONICAL, AND THEOLOGICAL INTRODUCTION

DAVID J. H. BELDMAN
AND MICHAEL J. RHODES

Baker Academic
a division of Baker Publishing Group
Grand Rapids, Michigan

Published by Baker Academic
a division of Baker Publishing Group
Grand Rapids, Michigan
BakerAcademic.com

Printed in the United States of America

Library of Congress Cataloging-in-Publication Data
Names: Beldman, David J. H., 1977– author | Rhodes, Michael J., 1985– author
Title: Reading the Pentateuch as Christian scripture : a literary, canonical, and theological introduction / David J. H. Beldman and Michael J. Rhodes.
Description: Grand Rapids, Michigan : Baker Academic, a division of Baker Publishing Group, [2026] | Series: Reading Christian scripture | Includes bibliographical references and index.
Identifiers: LCCN 2026020981 | ISBN 9781540961051 cloth | ISBN 9781493455799 ebook | ISBN 9781493455805 pdf
Subjects: LCSH: Bible. Pentateuch—Criticism, interpretation, etc.
Classification: LCC BS1225.52 .B435 2026
LC record available at https://lccn.loc.gov/2026020981

Unless otherwise noted, italics in Scripture quotations have been added by the authors for emphasis.

Baker Publishing Group publications use paper produced from sustainable forestry practices and postconsumer waste whenever possible.

26 27 28 29 30 31 32 7 6 5 4 3 2 1

Contents

Acknowledgments

The Torah gives God's people our first glimpse of the countercultural family into which followers of Jesus have been welcomed by grace. As we come to the end of several years working together on these texts, we find ourselves in awe of the gracious gifts we have received from the family of God along the way.

Some of those gifts have come through our collaboration with each other. Dave is primarily responsible for the chapters on Genesis 12–50, Leviticus, and Numbers, along with "How to Read Old Testament Narrative and Poetry Today" and "How to Read Torah's Rituals Today." Michael is primarily responsible for the chapters on Genesis 1–11, Exodus, and Deuteronomy, as well as "How (and Why) to Read the Pentateuch Today," "How to Read Biblical Law Today," and "How to Read Violent Texts Today." While the project may appear to reflect a "divide and conquer" approach, in practice each of us has read, reread, critiqued, and strengthened the other's work throughout the process. We believe the result is a more unified and coherent book than either of us could have produced alone. We have been deeply blessed by the opportunity to learn from each other and to develop a deeper appreciation for each other's scholarship, instincts, and love for these magnificent texts.

We are deeply grateful to Jim Kinney, who approached Dave many years ago about writing for this series. We appreciate both his confidence and his encouragement throughout the process. We also want to offer special thanks to Brandy Scritchfield—for the many lunches at yearly acronym-fests, for her patience and encouragement, and especially for her genuine excitement about this book from beginning to end. We are equally grateful for the expert work of James Korsmo and the rest of the remarkable team at Baker Academic. Their editorial care, attention to detail, and painstaking work has made this book substantially better. Brandy and James: You have been brilliant and longsuffering. It has been a gift to work with such kindred spirits.

• • • • • • • •

I (Michael) would also like to thank the past and present staff and students of Carey Baptist College. Special thanks go to John Tucker and Andrew Picard, who encouraged me to take on this project; Glenn Melville, for forcing me to talk about the bizarre bloody bits of the Old Testament and thus helping me prepare for several chapters in this book; Siong Ng, Mei Ling Lee, and Anna Tovey, for providing outstanding library support; the students of my Pentateuch classes over the last few years, who read drafts of my chapters and provided invaluable feedback; and especially to my Māori colleagues and students, who opened my eyes to aspects of the Torah's vision of creation that I had completely missed. Ngā mihi nunui! You are all mentors and friends better than I deserve.

Thanks also go to the great cloud of scholarly witnesses whose friendship and encouragement have made all the difference for this project, including especially Ellen Davis, Matt Lynch, Mark Glanville, Peter Altmann, Trey Nation, Chris Wright, Danny Carroll, Carmen Imes, Michelle Stinson, Mark Catlin, Brent Strawn, Brian Kolia, and especially Dru Johnson (who got me into this mess in the first place!) and Robby Holt (who has been the best of mentors and models for what it means to be a theologian in service of the church).

Thanks are also due to the 4th of the 5th and Option 105 crews, especially those who gave feedback on portions of the book, including Marshall Teague, Griffin Pepper, Brandon Russell, Paul Norman, Andrew Novenson, Collins Harrison, and Jonathan Wilson.

I am immensely grateful for the love and support of my family. Special thanks go to Dad for reading and responding to several drafts; to Isaiah, Amos, Nova, and Jubilee, for inspiring me to wrestle with the Bible's "first burst of fire and light" more deeply for their sakes; and for my brilliant, beautiful bride, Rebecca, who is always my first, last, and best dialogue partner.

Finally, with deep gratitude, I would like to dedicate this book to my mentor, PhD supervisor, and friend Craig Bartholomew. Craig welcomed me into a community of theological readers and apprenticed me into a way of interpreting Scripture for the sake of the world. I am immensely, overwhelmingly grateful.

• • • • • • • •

I (Dave) would first like to thank my family. The years I worked on this book were marked by challenge and transition, and they navigated it all with tenacity and grace. We carry some bruises and scars from those years, but I am deeply proud of them and profoundly grateful to belong to this tribe. Leah, Luke, Jordyn, and Kate: I love you and thank God for you.

I am not sure this project would have been completed without the encouragement, support, sacrifice, and inspiration of my wife, Elsie. She believed I could pull this off at times when I was not at all sure I could. I also suspect there is no human being on the planet more excited about this book finally appearing in print. Elsie: Thank you, thank you, thank you!

I would also like to thank my students at Redeemer University, Missional Training Center, and Calvin Theological Seminary. My understanding and appreciation of the Pentateuch have been shaped profoundly through teaching in these contexts, and the engagement, questions, and pushback of students have sharpened my thinking over the years.

There are far too many scholar-friends and conversation partners to name individually, including many connected to the Scripture and Hermeneutics Seminar, whose encouragement sustained me throughout this work. I do, however, want to give special thanks to Daniel Lowery and A. J. Culp. Our almost-yearly retreats have become something close to sacred for me. I suspect the three of us have helped keep one another sane through more than a few difficult personal and professional seasons. Dan and A. J.: I love you guys and appreciate you immensely.

Finally, I would like to dedicate this book to the memory of Gordon Wenham, my PhD supervisor. News of Gordon's death in May 2025 came while I was writing my final chapters of this book. His memorial service was moving and reminded me afresh what a privilege it was to study under this giant in biblical studies and to know him personally. I remain deeply grateful not only for his scholarly guidance but also for his humility, generosity, pastoral care, and quiet faithfulness. I still remember participating in his thoughtful prayers during postgraduate seminars, traveling with him to Israel, and experiencing the kindness he showed my young family while we were living abroad.

Most days it feels audacious that I would attempt to write a textbook on the Pentateuch. For many years I assigned Gordon's own introduction to the Pentateuch to my students. It is my hope that the book Michael and I have written might, in some small way, honor Gordon's memory and continue the rich legacy he has left behind.

Visit www.bakeracademic.com/professors
to access study aids
and instructor materials for this textbook.

Abbreviations

Old Testament

Gen.	Genesis
Exod.	Exodus
Lev.	Leviticus
Num.	Numbers
Deut.	Deuteronomy
Josh.	Joshua
Judg.	Judges
Ruth	Ruth
1 Sam.	1 Samuel
2 Sam.	2 Samuel
1 Kings	1 Kings
2 Kings	2 Kings
1 Chron.	1 Chronicles
2 Chron.	2 Chronicles
Ezra	Ezra
Neh.	Nehemiah
Esther	Esther
Job	Job
Ps(s).	Psalm(s)
Prov.	Proverbs
Eccles.	Ecclesiastes
Song	Song of Songs
Isa.	Isaiah
Jer.	Jeremiah
Lam.	Lamentations
Ezek.	Ezekiel
Dan.	Daniel
Hosea	Hosea
Joel	Joel
Amos	Amos
Obad.	Obadiah
Jon.	Jonah
Mic.	Micah
Nah.	Nahum
Hab.	Habakkuk
Zeph.	Zephaniah
Hag.	Haggai
Zech.	Zechariah
Mal.	Malachi

New Testament

Matt.	Matthew
Mark	Mark
Luke	Luke
John	John
Acts	Acts
Rom.	Romans

1 Cor.	1 Corinthians
2 Cor.	2 Corinthians
Gal.	Galatians
Eph.	Ephesians
Phil.	Philippians
Col.	Colossians
1 Thess.	1 Thessalonians
2 Thess.	2 Thessalonians
1 Tim.	1 Timothy
2 Tim.	2 Timothy
Titus	Titus
Philem.	Philemon
Heb.	Hebrews
James	James
1 Pet.	1 Peter
2 Pet.	2 Peter
1 John	1 John
2 John	2 John
3 John	3 John
Jude	Jude
Rev.	Revelation

Bible Versions

AT	authors' translation
CEB	Common English Bible
ESV	English Standard Version
KJV	King James Version
NASB	New American Standard Bible
NET	The NET Bible (New English Translation)
NIV	New International Version
NLT	New Living Translation
NRSV	New Revised Standard Version
NRSVue	New Revised Standard Version updated edition

General

AD	*anno Domini*, in the year of the Lord
BC	before Christ
ca.	circa
cent.	century
cf.	*confer*, compare
e.g.	*exempli gratia*, for example
esp.	especially
i.e.	*id est*, that is

How (and Why) to Read the Pentateuch Today

The Bible's First Burst of Fire and Light

Why Bother with the Pentateuch?

Write down the first words or phrases that come to mind when you think of Genesis, Exodus, Leviticus, Numbers, and Deuteronomy. (Be honest!)

Why bother with the first five books of the Bible, commonly referred to as the Pentateuch or the Torah? Many Christians don't. How many of us have made New Year's resolutions to read the Bible cover to cover, only to falter at Exodus's blueprints for tabernacle construction and finally give up in the face of Leviticus's sacrificial regulations? Many stories from the Pentateuch are well known, but that doesn't mean they appear often in sermons. If your church uses the Revised Common Lectionary, Leviticus and Numbers show up only once every three years.[1]

Maybe we *shouldn't* bother with the Pentateuch. A "new atheist" like Richard Dawkins surely has the Pentateuch in mind when he claims that the "God of the Old Testament" is "jealous and proud of it; a petty, unjust, unforgiving control-freak; a vindictive, bloodthirsty ethnic cleanser; a misogynistic, homophobic, racist, infanticidal, genocidal, filicidal, pestilential, megalomaniacal, sadomasochistic, capriciously malevolent bully."[2] Nor are outsiders the only skeptical ones. When pastor Andy Stanley called Christians to "unhitch" the church "from the worldview, value system, and regulations of the Jewish Scriptures" in order to access the liberating message of God's love, grace, and forgiveness, the Pentateuch looms large in the background.[3] While most pastors might shy away from saying it quite so

> **THEOLOGICAL ISSUES**
>
> **God, Yahweh, Lord**
>
> In the Old Testament, God is referred to by several names and titles. The Hebrew word *elohim* simply means "god" or "gods." It can refer to the one Creator God or, in other contexts, to other spiritual beings. The personal name of Israel's God (see Exod. 3), however, is spelled with four Hebrew letters: *YHWH*, often pronounced "Yahweh." Because later Jewish tradition avoided speaking the divine name aloud, most English Bibles translate *YHWH* as "Lord," using small capital letters. In this book, we often use "Yahweh" to highlight God's covenant name and personal relationship with Israel. When you see "Lord" in small caps, it refers to that same divine name.

> **THEOLOGICAL ISSUES**
>
> **Talking About God**
>
> Following Scripture's lead, we use masculine pronouns for God. However, it is important to recognize (1) that God is neither "male" nor "female" but is instead beyond gender, and (2) that Scripture uses both masculine and feminine imagery to describe God (on feminine imagery for God, see the sidebar "Yahweh as Passionate Parent" in chap. 16).

openly as Stanley, many see these books largely serving as a foil, a tool to help us see the beauty of the "gospel" against the background of the harsh "law."

So why bother with the Pentateuch? Because *the Pentateuch is the critical launching pad and starting point for encountering God and God's ways with God's people and God's world*. The Pentateuch is like the big bang of the Bible: The entire universe of the scriptural story spins out and takes shape from these first explosive texts. The Torah introduces us to Yahweh, whose relentless commitment to live in his good world with his human image bearers and to corule that good world through those human image bearers drives the story of Scripture forward.

Just as some argue the vast and glorious complexity of the cosmos emerged from an initial explosion, so the entirety of Scripture bears witness to its fiery beginnings in the Pentateuch. In the Pentateuch we

- learn that God's cosmic rescue will take place through his work with Abraham's family;
- watch God's people come face-to-face with the God who is "slow to anger, and abounding in steadfast love and faithfulness" (Exod. 34:6);
- discover that Israel's relationship with Yahweh is a covenantal one, in which God graciously provides a good "law" that will enable his people to become a "priestly kingdom" for the sake of the nations (Exod. 19:6); and
- witness the formation of Israel through the wilderness wasteland as Yahweh guides, provides, protects, and corrects his people.

These themes echo across the Bible. Israel's songs celebrate the beauty and goodness of God's covenantal law. The Old Testament's prophets and storytellers look to the covenant to evaluate their community's common life, confront them for their failures, and help them understand their tragic experiences in light of their infidelity to God and God's way. In the New Testament, the story of Yahweh's relentless commitment to live in his good world alongside human image bearers and to corule that good world through them culminates in Yahweh coming as

Israel Museum / Wikimedia Commons / public domain

Figure 1.1. The De Castro Pentateuch, displaying the decorative opening page of Genesis (14th cent.)

Immanuel—"God with Us"—in Jesus. The Gospel writers describe Jesus's very life as a reenactment of Israel's story in the Pentateuch, complete with

- a sojourn in Egypt after his birth,
- a watery "exodus" at his baptism,
- time spent wandering in the wilderness, and
- a mountaintop sermon in which Jesus acts like a second Moses.

Jesus even gets some of his best teaching ideas *from* the Torah. His command to "love the Lord your God with all your heart, and with all your soul, and with all your mind" comes straight out of Deuteronomy (Matt. 22:37; cf. Deut. 6:5). "Love your neighbor as yourself" is a quote from Leviticus (Matt. 22:39; Lev. 19:18). Love your enemies? Exodus has that too (see Exod. 23:5). And "forgive us our debts, as we also have forgiven our debtors" is a one-sentence summary of a great deal of Torah teaching (Matt. 6:12). When the Pharisees ask Jesus to talk marriage and divorce, he opens the Pentateuch and starts interpreting (Matt. 19:1–12).

And it's not just Jesus. Luke alludes to Deuteronomy to explain the early church's communal sharing (Acts 4:34). Paul points to the Passover liturgy to explain the life of the church and to call the people to holiness (1 Cor.

5:6–8). John draws on the story of Cain to call us to love, and he alludes to the Torah's economic legislation to explain what love looks like (1 John 3:12, 17). The preacher of Hebrews makes sense of Jesus's death on the cross through the sacrificial world of Leviticus. Prick the Bible and it bleeds Pentateuch. Try to hum along with Scripture, and you find yourself singing a Torah tune.

Why bother with the Pentateuch? Because without it, we're liable to misunderstand the Father, Son, and Holy Spirit we encounter in the New Testament. These gritty, earthy, often messy texts show us Israel's God-guided attempt to farm, build, establish political norms, make love, worship, and raise children under the reign of the divine King and as participants in his mission. These texts can help us join up with God's mission and live under God's reign, as well.

How to Bother with the Pentateuch Well

None of this is to deny that reading the Pentateuch can be experienced as bewildering, boring, or even outright offensive. How do we read these books *well*? God's people have always wrestled with this question, and we don't have all the answers. Nevertheless, we offer three helpful principles.

1. Read the Pentateuch in Light of the Bible's Big Story

While we never want to allow the rest of the story to overwhelm our reading of the Pentateuch, reading the Pentateuch as Christian Scripture means reading Genesis through Deuteronomy as part of the Bible's grand, sprawling narrative. That narrative begins with God creating a good world to live in and creating human image bearers to corule that good world in fellowship with him. This image-bearing identity and job description means humans are called to be God's royal, priestly daughters and sons.

The biblical story continues through humanity's rebellion and Yahweh's subsequent work to get his cosmic plans back on track by calling Abraham's family to become a vehicle of God's blessings to the nations. One crucial way Abraham's family is to become this vehicle of blessing is by living as God's "kingdom of priests" (Exod. 19:6). In various ways, the Old Testament recounts how Israel ultimately failed to be fully faithful to this calling. But where Israel, like all humanity, proved faithless, God sent the faithful Israelite, Jesus of Nazareth, God-in-the-flesh. Jesus fulfills the promise of Israel and humanity by being *the* King, *the* Priest, *the* Son of God. At the cross, this Jesus became the sacrificial lamb whose "once

Figure 1.2. The Bible's big story

for all" self-offering "takes away the sin of the world" (Heb. 7:27; John 1:29). Through this Faithful One, the triune God dealt with the problem of human sin and rebellion, gathered a renewed people to be his vehicle of blessing to the nations, and launched them into the world to take his good news to every corner of the cosmos (see fig. 1.2).

The final chapter in the grand narrative portrays King Jesus returning to take up residence in his resurrected and renewed creation, living forever alongside humans who finally and fully live and reign with him forever and ever (Rev. 22:5).

In this book, then, we encourage you to consider how the Pentateuch sets the stage for, and indeed helps us understand, the biblical narrative that follows. We also encourage you to "read backward," considering how our understanding of the full sweep of the scriptural story affects the way we read Genesis through Deuteronomy.

2. Read the Pentateuch Theologically

Both the *subject* and *source* of the Pentateuch demand that we read theologically. In terms of the subject, the Pentateuch tells the story of God and God's ways in the world. In terms of the source, Christians maintain the Pentateuch is part of the Spirit-inspired Word of God. The God who speaks creation into existence, who enters creation as the Word made flesh, and who holds all creation in place by "the word of his power" (Heb. 1:3 ESV) speaks to us in Scripture—including the Pentateuch. If we accept this theological claim, we must embrace a theological reading.[4]

But what does reading theologically mean? Among other things, theological reading requires us to read in God's presence, trusting God's goodness, willing to be changed by our encounter, and appreciating the mystery that such an encounter entails.

Reading in God's presence. When we read the Bible academically, it's easy to treat the biblical text like a lifeless object to be examined. At worst, the tools of interpretation we learn in textbooks such as this one become scalpels, and the text becomes a dead corpse to be dissected.

For Christians, though, biblical texts are not dry, dusty relics that facilitate study. They are words coauthored by God that facilitate our present encounter with the Lord of heaven and earth. Scripture *speaks* as God's address to us today.[5] We bring the academic study of the Bible and all our tools of interpretation into the service of hearing God's voice. This means studying Scripture can itself be a spiritual discipline, but also that Scripture study ought to be woven together with other spiritual disciplines of prayer, meditation, communal discernment, worship, and more.

Trusting God's goodness. When we turn to the Torah, though, we find disturbing texts. The violence against women, pervasiveness of slavery, and depictions of Israel's future conquest of Canaan raise serious moral questions for us as readers. We cannot simply ignore these questions, not least because many Torah texts have been used to abuse women, the enslaved, Indigenous peoples, and others. Later in this book, we will offer some specific tools for thinking about such complex questions (see especially chaps. 8 and 13).

In approaching these issues, however, theological reading suggests we adopt a "hermeneutic of trust." Such an approach adopts "the posture of Jacob and refuses to let go of the text until it blesses us." This posture allows us to reject poor interpretations of the biblical text while remaining "patient with the text [itself] in the belief that when interpreted properly it will bring a blessing and not a curse."[6]

If we wrestle with the Torah like Jacob wrestled with God, we may walk away limping (Gen. 32:22–32). But we believe that such painful wrestling will eventually lead us to limp, like Jacob, with God into a new future amid the dawning light of a new day.

Willing to be changed. Theological reading calls us to trust the text but question specific interpretations of it, beginning with our own. To read theologically is to come ready to read the text "against ourselves." As Ellen Davis argues, Scripture suggests our relationship with God requires

> the discipline of regularly subverting that first impulse to read "for ourselves." . . . "And Joshua said to the people [at Shechem], 'You are witnesses *against your*

RECEPTION HISTORY

Trusting Scripture and Reading Alongside Others

Lisa Bowens explores the way Black American interpreters from the 1700s to the mid-twentieth century read Paul's texts. She argues that, by and large, they exemplified the "hermeneutic of trust": They "saw Scripture as God's sacred word and believed that it mattered for them, for their communities, and for the nation." They were suspicious of "white interpreters of the text, such as the slaveholders, proponents of slavery, and advocates of segregation, [but] not [of] the text itself." She quotes Fredrick Douglass:

> What do you do when you are told by the slaveholders of America that the Bible sanctions slavery? Do you go and throw your Bible into the fire? . . . Do you declare that a thing is bad because it has been misused, abused, and made bad use of? . . . No! You press it to your bosom all the more closely; you read it all the more diligently; and prove from its pages that it is on the side of liberty—and not on the side of slavery.[a]

own selves, that you yourselves have chosen for yourself the LORD, to serve him.' And they said, 'Witnesses.'" . . . This is paradigmatic for how we always stand before God when we read the covenantal text. We stand as potential witnesses against our own selves, as those who confess their own need and will to change, individually and (even more) as a community of faith.[7]

Appreciating the mystery. Finally, reading theologically means reading Scripture with an appreciation of the mystery and paradox that must exist whenever creatures try to speak faithfully about our Creator. Indeed, "mystery is the lifeblood of theological reflection" on Scripture because we stand "before God the incomprehensible One."[8] As Isaiah puts it, "As the heavens are higher than the earth, so are [God's] ways higher than [our] ways and [God's] thoughts than [our] thoughts" (Isa. 55:9).

At the same time, this incomprehensible One draws near to humanity and chooses to reveal himself to human creatures! As the Isaiah passage goes on to say, Yahweh's word does not return to him empty but accomplishes what God desires and achieves the purpose for which it was sent (Isa. 55:11). While we cannot know God exhaustively or completely—how could we!—we can know God partially and truly.

The implications for interpreting the Old Testament are tremendous. Because God speaks in language we can understand, theologians have argued that he accommodates himself to "our human language and condition."[9] As Calvin suggests, God accommodates "the knowledge of him to our feebleness. In doing so, he must, of course, stoop far below his proper height."[10]

One way the Old Testament accommodates us is by nearly always using metaphors to describe God.[11] Metaphors speak of one thing in terms of another: "Love is a rose," "God is a rock." Theologically speaking, our Creator can be described truthfully by reference to creation precisely because creation reflects the Creator's character; creation bears, to use another metaphor, the fingerprints of God. Yet because God is infinitely beyond creation and distinct from it, metaphorical language communicates only partial truth. Indeed, the key to all metaphors is the recognition that the two terms are alike in some ways but different in others.[12] Love is like a rose in its beauty and capacity for growth but unlike a rose in that you better not fertilize it with manure! This dynamic gives metaphoric language much of its power, because we must ponder the way the two terms are similar and dissimilar. We wonder, for instance, whether love, like a rose, has thorns.

THEOLOGICAL ISSUES

God *like* Us?

Many biblical metaphors for God are anthropomorphisms—that is, metaphors drawn from the *human* sphere. Because humans are made in God's image, human metaphors for God are particularly appropriate. Yet these, too, suggest both similarities and dissimilarities. When we read about God's "hands" and "feet," we learn something true about God, but probably *not* that Yahweh literally has hands and feet. When the Pentateuch describes Israel as Yahweh's "firstborn son," this does *not* mean that humanity is the product of a sexual relationship between Yahweh and some other being.

David Collection / Wikimedia Commons / public domain

Figure 1.3. Fifteenth-century Islamic miniature depicting Noah's ark by Hafiz-i Abru

So far, so good, but matters are even more complex. I can say truthfully that I love my children and God loves God's children. But does that word *love* mean exactly the same thing when describing human affection and God's divine affection? While there is a connection between the way we use the word *love* in these two contexts, the uses are not precisely the same. Divine love is exercised by a God whose ways are infinitely higher than ours.

Because God is Creator of all things, depictions of God drawn from creation truly "get at" something about God. However, because God is Creator *and not* creation, "God outdistances all our images" and "cannot finally be captured by any of them."[13] This is why the Bible offers so many different metaphoric depictions of God, some of which stand in tension with one another ("husband" and "judge," for instance). Like a photomosaic, each "image" depicts something true about God, but we glimpse far more when we step back and see how the images all hold together. Even then, though, the entire scriptural constellation of metaphors remains outdistanced by the reality of the triune God.

Consider an example: Genesis 6:6 tells us that God "regrets" having made human beings on the earth and that his heart is "deeply troubled" (NIV). Elsewhere Scripture seems to tell us that God does not change his mind, but the flood story depicts Yahweh seriously altering his prior proceedings with humanity based on this regret. This doesn't sound like the immutable, omniscient God.

What are we to make of this? Taking the depiction of God in the flood story as an example, some so emphasize God's otherness that they risk rejecting Scripture's own witness. They might say that while it *sounds* like Yahweh was "greatly troubled" and changed course, *we know* God is immutable and unchanging; God's troubled regret is just deeply metaphorical language so accommodated to our creatureliness that it doesn't tell us very much about God. However, this comes dangerously close to rejecting what

Scripture itself says, replacing biblical language with language derived elsewhere. It's also naive; all language about God, including words like *immutable*, involves accommodation.

At the other extreme, some read Genesis as describing a God who is so completely captured by "regret" that he is understood as constantly changing his mind, learning new things, discovering his own divine powerlessness to affect this or that outcome. In this case, we end up with a God who is "unsettled," "uncertain, indecisive, ambiguous, and conflicted."[14] This risks rejecting huge swaths of the biblical witness and ignores the way theological language is always accommodated. When Genesis tells us Yahweh regretted creating humanity, that must tell us something true about God, but it does not tell us that God's regretting is exactly like human regretting. What it means for God, who is the "Alpha and Omega," to regret creating humanity and what it would mean for us to regret having done so must be different.

Interpreters must wrestle with these mysteries, and different faith communities will settle in somewhat different places. Furthermore, we do not mean to suggest that everything about God is obscure! Our purpose here is simply to identify that this mysterious, paradoxical dimension of Scripture is a feature rather than a bug. To identify such dynamics in Scripture as "mysterious paradoxes" isn't just a fancy way of saying the Bible is irrational or contradictory. Mysterious paradoxes are part and parcel of everyday life, including even scientific study of the "natural world."

Consider one of the weirdest insights of quantum physics: the particle-wave duality of light. Scientists used to argue about whether light is a particle or a wave, given that particles and waves act differently. Today, quantum physics recognizes light acts like both a particle and a wave, and indeed, that light appears to act like one or the other based on whether or not a scientist is observing it![15] Quantum physics can describe this reality, but it cannot explain it. The best answer to the question of whether light is a particle or a wave requires scientists to make two seemingly contradictory statements. But the fact that it seems contradictory doesn't mean it isn't true. Nor, indeed, does it make the insight impractical; scientists have used quantum physics to help design and improve supercomputers, smartphones, and MRI machines.[16]

Apparent contradictions and mysterious paradoxes may seem embarrassing, but in both science and Scripture they can gesture toward deep truths and important breakthroughs. Yet when the Bible boldly declares in one text that God does not change his mind, only to declare with equal insistence in another that he has changed his mind, it's easy to either write this off as irrational or just pick the text we prefer and explain away or ignore

LITERARY NOTES

Tips for Reading the Pentateuch Wisely and Well

1. **Read slowly and reflectively.** Give the text time to shape your understanding and character. Let repeated readings deepen your understanding.
2. **Read in community.** Shared reading brings insights and challenges we might miss otherwise.
3. **Listen on the text's terms.** Pay attention to words, patterns, and structures. Let the Pentateuch speak in its own voice before importing outside assumptions.
4. **Read with imagination.** Enter the world of the text, picturing its settings, hearing its voices, and inhabiting its stories to better grasp their force.
5. **Seek wisdom for life.** Remember that these texts aim to shape God's people for holiness, justice, and worship in every area of life.

the others. But if we read with an appreciation of the mystery and paradox of human speech about God, we can see this as a kind of intentional doublespeak, a speaking twice in order to try to capture a paradox or mystery inherent in our limited understanding of the God who sits on high. Just as scientists must move forward accepting that light does act like a particle and a wave, Scripture calls us to receive and live into many truths that are rife with paradox and tension. To do otherwise is to reject the God who speaks through Scripture; after all, "the name the OT gives to a God whose ways are like mine is an idol."[17]

Reading theologically thus requires humility and trust. Such humble, trusting reading of the revealed mysteries of God leads us "further up and further in" to a life of praise.[18]

3. Read the Pentateuch Aware of the Worlds "In," "Behind," and "In Front of" the Text

Finally, paying attention to what interpreters refer to as the worlds "in," "behind," and "in front of" the text can help us read the Pentateuch well (fig. 1.4).

The world *in* the text refers to Scripture itself: the words and sentences, the stories, poems, and proverbs on the page. We believe the world *in* the text is primary in interpretation. Through our minds and imaginations, we enter the world of the text and inhabit it. When we speak of Scripture being authoritative, we refer to the text we have in front of us. Because of this, our focus will be on helping you engage the world of the text that is the Pentateuch.

The world *behind* the text refers to the people responsible for writing the text; this always includes an author or authors, but it may also involve editors and compilers who brought together oral traditions or previously authored bits of material and turned them into new stories, songs, poems, laws, or histories. The world behind the text also refers to the original audiences the authors intended to communicate to and the contexts within which those authors wrote and audiences listened. Such contexts include the messy social, political, religious, and economic dynamics that affected the way the message of Scripture was communicated and understood.

The world behind the text is important because, as the old adage goes, the Bible was written *for* us, but it wasn't originally written *to* us. The

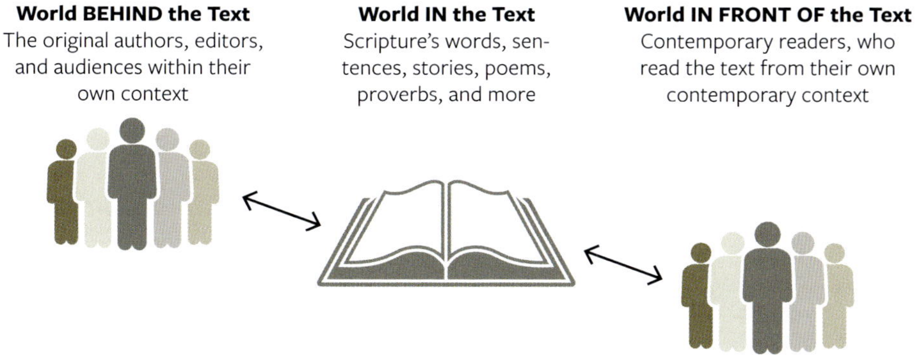

Figure 1.4. The three worlds of the text

world out of which the Pentateuch emerged was different from ours. Understanding the culture, economy, politics, and worldviews on offer in that ancient context can help us understand what the biblical authors were trying to say to their original audiences. Exploring the world behind the text is vital.

The world *in front of* the text is our world, the world of contemporary interpreters and their communities. We bring our assumptions and questions to the text and are called to live in response to what we discover there *in our own world*. Indeed, imaginatively inhabiting the world of the text through our study of Scripture allows us to consider our own world in front of the text in new ways.

HISTORICAL MATTERS

Source Criticism, Redaction Criticism, and the Documentary Hypothesis

Modern biblical scholarship has often focused on the "prehistory" of the Pentateuch. Such scholarship begins by noticing confusing aspects of the text. For instance, certain portions of the Pentateuch appear to prefer the divine name *Elohim* while others prefer *Yahweh*; Genesis 37:27 suggests Joseph's brothers sold him to Ishmaelites, while 37:28 suggests they were Midianites. Source and redaction critics explain these dynamics by arguing that much of the material in the Pentateuch existed prior to its incorporation into its present form. This earlier material was later gathered and edited by "redactors" who created the books we have today. They argue we can identify historical or theological tensions between these various sources. In its classic form, source criticism held that the Pentateuch came from four primary sources referred to as J, E, D, P, or the Yahwistic, Elohistic, Deuteronomist, and Priestly sources.

While source/redaction criticism *can* treat the Bible as a merely human book, it need not do so. Some biblical books were obviously compiled from earlier sources (e.g., Psalms, Proverbs), and there is no reason to think the author(s) of the Pentateuch did not draw on earlier material. If God inspires authors, God can inspire editors and collectors as well, and the Pentateuch itself does not make strong claims about authorship or publication date.

On the other hand, source/redaction criticism can be speculative and problematically circular ("We know this is from the Priestly source because priestly sources . . ."). There is no textual evidence for the alleged "sources"—nobody has ever dug up a copy of "P" or "J." Moreover, historical evidence suggests some of the criteria used to identify "contradictory" sources misunderstand ancient literature (see the discussion of the Kadesh inscription under "Three-World Reading, the Reliability of Scripture, and Questions from History" later in this chapter).

These challenges have generated a renewed interest in the "final form" of Scripture—namely, the Bible as we now have it. Where earlier scholarship identified problematic contradictions, more-recent scholarship suggests we see evidence of literary art. This book focuses on the final form, engaging questions about dating, sources, and redaction only when we consider it vital to do so.[b]

THEOLOGICAL ISSUES

Translating the Word

Andrew Walls and Kwame Bediako argue that Christian mission occurs as the good news of the incarnate God gets *translated* into every language and culture. Scripture itself demonstrates Yahweh "can inhabit" the language and thought worlds of all cultures.[c] When Deuteronomy 10:17 describes Yahweh using "indigenous" divine titles ("Lord of lords") and even a divine name ("the Great El") used by Israel's non-Israelite neighbors, the text creates a connection between Yahweh and the understanding of god among those neighbors (even while emphasizing many differences; see the sidebar "Melchizedek and Missiology" in chap. 5).[d] John's Gospel created a connection between the Jewish Messiah and the Greek idea of the *logos*.[e]

This process has continued ever since. By "using the indigenous methods of Greek intellectual discourse" to explore the significance of Jesus, the early church crafted creeds that captured new insights without abandoning original "Jewish categories."[f] The use of indigenous African names for God in modern Bible translation helped countless Africans discover that the God they met in Jesus answered the longings of their ancestors.[g] "Bible translation" thus "aims at releasing the word about Christ so that it can reach all aspects" of a culture, "so that Christ can live within that context, in the persons of his followers, as thoroughly at home as he once did in the culture of first-century Jewish Palestine."[h]

The danger is that our presuppositions and questions distort the text, that our world in front of the text overwhelms the world within the text. This is a real threat, but the solution cannot be to aim for a neutral, unbiased reading of Scripture. Our questions, concerns, identities, and self-understandings *do* affect the way we hear the Word, so it is better to acknowledge them honestly than to ignore them.

More positively and importantly, if our contexts make it harder for us to see some things in Scripture, they make it easier for us to see others. When interpreters from different contexts read together, we help each other see things we might have missed on our own. We can help one another hear the Word more faithfully in all of its fullness and begin to imagine how to live into that Word more faithfully today.

God has been and is at work in all three "worlds." God *acted* in the lives of the text's original authors, editors, and readers; God *ensures* that Scripture itself expresses his reliable word; and God *enables* us to hear his voice when we read (fig. 1.5).

An Example: Reading in Three Worlds

To help us think more carefully about this, let's consider how an awareness of the three worlds might affect our interpretation of Genesis 1–11. In Genesis 1:1–2:3, we discover a creation story in the *world in the text*. This immediately raises questions for us in *our world in front of the text*: How does this creation story compare to modern scientific stories of the world's origins from the perspective of natural history? This is our question, but it also involves questions about *the world behind the text*—namely, did creation "actually happen" this way?

Natural history or scientific accounts seek to offer what we might call a neutral, technical, newspaper-style description of the facts. Many people who are convinced the Bible is an outdated relic and committed to a particular natural history or scientific account of creation might find our questions easy to answer: Genesis offers a natural history that's obviously false based on what science says about the world. Some Christians respond by

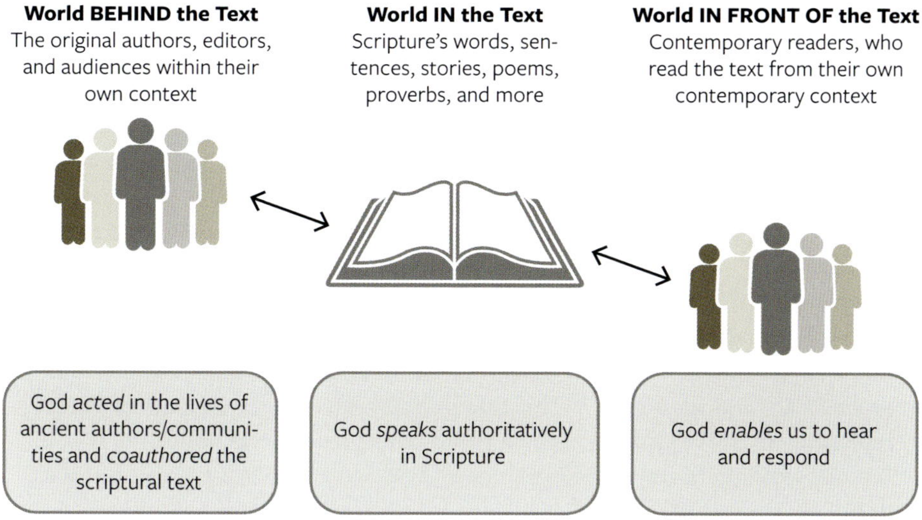

Figure 1.5. God's work in the three worlds of the text

agreeing with the claim that Genesis offers a natural history account of origins but then disagreeing with this conclusion. They look for alternate scientific evidence that the world came about precisely as Genesis describes it and argue that, as the Word of God, it speaks more clearly than unbelieving science. After all, science keeps changing, but God's Word stands forever!

If we consider the world behind the text, things get even more complicated. For instance, if we compare the Genesis creation stories to other ancient creation stories, we discover that Genesis appears to be arguing, debating, and dialoguing with those other stories. While people steeped in our natural history or scientific stories ask certain questions of Genesis, ancient readers might have been inspired by the text to ask quite different questions . . . and receive quite different answers.

The world behind the text also raises the question of genre and literary style, because

Workshop of Lucas Cranach / Wikimedia Commons / public domain

Figure 1.6. Creation illustration from Martin Luther's 1534 translation of the Bible we read differently depending on the type of literature we're reading.[19] If you open a book and read "Once upon a time, there lived a beautiful princess," what sort of story do you expect? A fairy tale, of course. And because you've read enough fairy tales to learn how they work, you will not expect the story to give you facts about an actual princess trapped in a tower. You may recognize that the fairy tale is trying to say something true. You may agree or disagree with what it's claiming. But you won't decide on the truthfulness of the tale based on whether it accurately depicts a recent kidnapping of golden-haired royalty. In other words, you will go looking for truth in that fairy tale differently than you will if you open a biology textbook that begins, "At each level of the biological hierarchy, we find a correlation of structure and function."[20] This opening suggests a different sort of literature altogether. We still expect it to try to tell us true things about the world. We still struggle through the evidence and decide whether we agree. But we decide on the truthfulness of the claims of this textbook's story differently than we would if it were a fairytale. We shift our expectations about how to evaluate the truthfulness of the text based on our understanding of its genre.

Bible readers navigate genre issues constantly. Because Jesus refers to his comments about the mustard seed as a parable, we are not bothered by the scientific fact that the mustard seed is not, after all, "the smallest of all the seeds on earth" (Mark 4:31). But we would be bothered by that line if we understood Jesus's statement to be within the genre of a botany textbook. On the other hand, when Paul argues that "if Christ has not been raised, your faith is futile" (1 Cor. 15:17), we understand him to be saying that if Jesus was not literally, physically, and bodily raised from the dead, then the gospel is a lie. The way we understand a text to be making a specific truth claim depends on our understanding of its genre.

Old Testament scholar V. Philips Long offers a helpful distinction between "truth values" and "truth claims."[21] The truth value of a text is whether it tells us something true about the world. Christians believe that every line of Scripture has a positive truth value; the Bible is always telling us the truth in this sense. But the truth claim is the type of truth the text conveys in order to communicate its truth value. So the parable about the mustard seed has truth value because it tells us the truth about the kingdom. On the other hand, because it is a parable rather than a scientific description, the parable does not make a truth claim about the scientific accuracy of the mustard seed's size; thus, its truth value does not depend on accepting that the mustard seed is (scientifically) the smallest seed in the garden.

The challenge is that most biblical texts don't tell us their genre, and we're unfamiliar with the various genres that would have been familiar to ancient readers. Part of our work as readers is to try to understand how ancient authors and readers might have understood the text we're reading in terms of genre and literary style. Would they have understood Genesis 1:1–2:3 as a natural history of creation's origins along the lines of a biology textbook? Would they have seen the truth value of these texts as depending on a truth claim that God created the world in a series of twenty-four-hour days, for instance? Or would they have understood the creation story differently? How does that change what it means for us to hear Genesis's creation story as God's truthful word?

Three-World Reading, the Reliability of Scripture, and Questions from Contemporary Science

To answer such questions about the truth claims and truth values of the Bible, in the chapters that follow we'll explore the world *behind* these texts, even while our focus will remain on the world *within* them. Nevertheless, because of how contentious the dialogue can be about the relationship between Genesis and science, perhaps it will help us to state a few things up front. First, humility is needed. Treating the Pentateuch as Scripture means trusting that the "book of the Bible" and the "book of creation" never finally contradict. Apparent contradictions mean we've misinterpreted Scripture, misinterpreted science, or perhaps both.[22]

Understanding biblical texts within their ancient context is complicated. There's just so much we don't know. We don't know when exactly Genesis was written, nor how it was edited. We don't know exactly when many of the other ancient stories we've discovered were written. We don't know exactly how *they* would have been interpreted. Likewise, any honest scientist will tell you that narrating a natural history of the world's origins is very complicated. Scientists admit that there's plenty we don't know.

We believe God could have created the world exactly as Genesis 1:1–2:3 narrates, reading Genesis 1:1–2:3 as a factual, neutral, historical account. If God can speak the world into existence and raise Jesus from the dead, we can't rule out the possibility that Genesis offers us a "scientific" depiction of the creative processes.

But even if all we had was Genesis 1–11 itself, we see significant evidence that these texts do not intend to offer us that kind of story. Consider the following:

- A reference to days, understood as twenty-four-hour periods, makes little sense prior to the creation of the sun (day 4).

- After depicting the heavens and the earth as being created in seven "days" in Genesis 1:1–2:3, Genesis 2:4 refers to the singular "day" when the "heavens and the earth" were created, and the rest of Genesis 2 proceeds to outline a creative process that is not easily reconciled with the previous account.
- Genesis identifies Cain's descendants as the "progenitors of all nomads and musicians, but they would've been cut off in the Flood." Likewise, the "Nephilim and warriors described in Genesis 6:1–4 exist before and after the Flood."[23]
- Genesis 10 suggests that language diversity occurred naturally as people spread out into various ecosystems, while Genesis 11 suggests language diversity occurred at Babel.

None of these challenges to reading Genesis as natural history come from new scientific discoveries or modern skeptics. Ancient peoples presumably associated days with the sun[24] and recognized that drowned descendants of Cain couldn't teach Noah's children to play the flute.

The issue of God's accommodating language comes into play as well. The Bible often *uses* ancient pictures of the world without necessarily *teaching* those pictures of the world.[25] In other words, the Bible may take for granted ancient ideas like the idea that the earth is flat, that it is part of

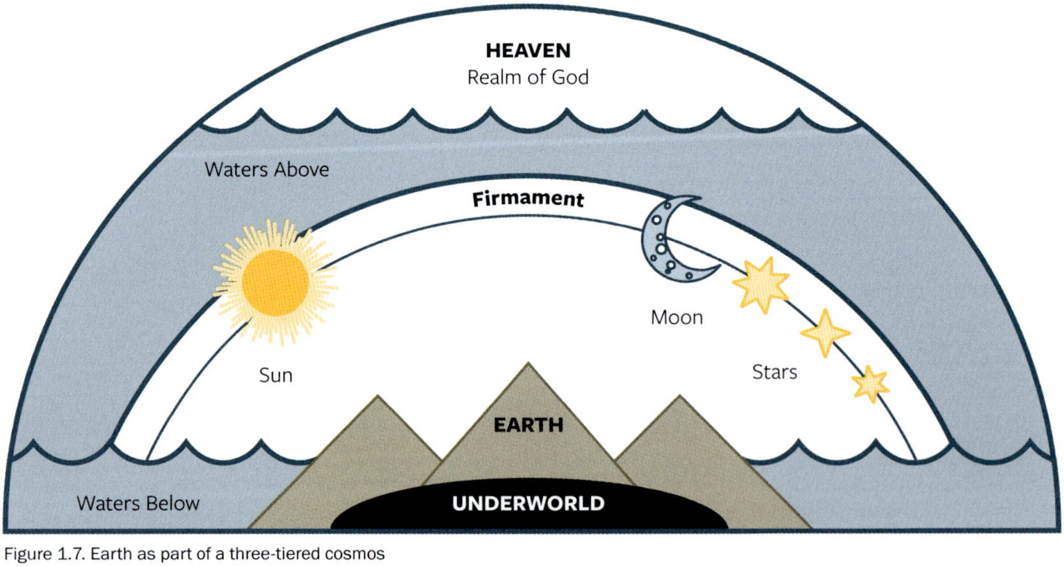

Figure 1.7. Earth as part of a three-tiered cosmos

Based on a figure from Ben Stanhope, *(Mis)interpreting Genesis: How the Creation Museum Misunderstands the Ancient Near Eastern Context of the Bible* (Scarab, 2018), 88.

a three-tiered cosmos, and that the sun moves across the sky (alternatively, the ancient authors may simply be using phenomenological and poetic language).[26] None of these ideas are scientifically true, but that is not a problem, because the truth value of these texts is not based on a truth claim about such scientific realities.[27]

Of course, those committed to reading Genesis 1–11 as natural history have a number of ways of resolving these and other issues. But their solutions rely on "filling in the gaps" of the biblical text with solutions that are not in the text itself. They *may* be right, but in light of how many obvious problems with understanding Genesis 1–11 as natural history must be solved by these sorts of solutions, we sense that if natural history is what Genesis 1–11 is trying to accomplish, it didn't do all that good of a job.

RECEPTION HISTORY

Calvin on Accommodated Astronomy

Speaking of differences between Genesis 1 and the astronomy of his day, the Reformer John Calvin argued, "The Holy Spirit had no intention to teach astronomy; and, in proposing instruction meant to be common to the simplest and most uneducated persons, he made use by Moses and the other Prophets of popular language."

LeFebvre unpacks Calvin's point: "God speaks to people within the cultural parameters of the age, including its pre-scientific understanding. . . . It is a mark of God's love and his desire to make his Word accessible to the simple that he always spoke within the cultural (if scientifically archaic) understandings of the age."[i]

We believe Genesis 1–11 tells us the truth about God, humanity, and the world without always offering us the kind of stories we'd expect from natural science or a history textbook. Perhaps Genesis offers something akin to a "major *theological* reinterpretation of traditional origin stories."[28] While these texts do not offer us "pure fiction," neither do they appear to offer us "simply history" as we might understand it; rather, they offer something "in between."[29] We see these texts as belonging to a different sort of genre than the one expected by those who try to explain what it means to have light and days prior to the sun's creation. This does not mean we dismiss the claims of Genesis 1–11 or take them less seriously. It does mean we should take these stories seriously on their own terms.

Let us state this as clearly as possible: We are committed to Scripture's authority and reliability. God coauthored these texts. We are not allowed to disregard them. They are determinative for our life as God's people. They are *true*. But we vigorously deny that these commitments require us to read these texts as literalistic natural history if we have good reasons for doubting that's the kind of reading the genre of the text demands.

Because we seek to focus on the world *in* the text, our hope is that Christians committed to reading Genesis 1–11 as science or natural history will still find a great deal in these pages to encourage and assist them. But our approach also means that Christians convinced the earth looks very old or that certain forms of evolution might be part of God's creative process need not give up their Bibles.

C. John Collins on Genesis 1–11

Old Testament scholar C. John Collins argues that "science as we think of it plays no role" in Genesis 1–11's "descriptions of the world," in part by comparing Genesis with what he believes are texts from the ancient world that *did* aim at something more akin to what we mean by science. He argues those texts represent a different kind of literature from that of Genesis.[j]

But he also compares Genesis 1–11 to the Sumerian King List, which identifies kings who reigned over enormous lifetimes before the flood and for short lifetimes afterward. He points out that scholars of these texts argue that they include a great deal of nonliteral imagery and symbolism (including those enormously long lifetimes), but that they also were understood as describing people who actually lived. Collins suggests that there is "history" here, but "history" that cannot be read in a "thoroughly literalistic fashion."[k]

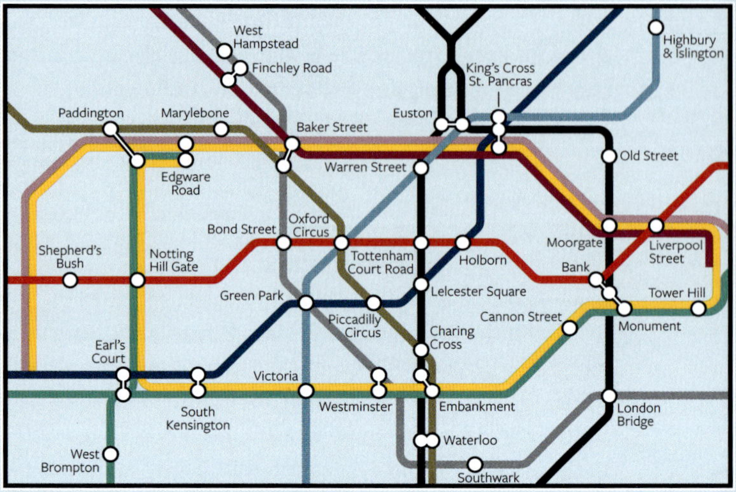

Figure 1.8. Map of the London Underground

Collins points to the map of the London Underground as a metaphor.[l] The map is trustworthy in that it helps people get where they need to go. Its lines and place names correspond to geographical realities. But the map distorts those geographical realities in numerous ways. *Indeed, doing so is part of how the map serves its purpose.* A person who tries to use it to walk from one of these places to the other will find it problematic, but nobody can fault the mapmaker for this frustration. The map requires us to use it the way it's meant to be used, not to force it to be used the way we want it to be used for our own purposes.

Three-World Reading, the Reliability of Scripture, and Questions from History

Genre questions are even more complicated as we move into the rest of the Pentateuch, not least because of the many genres we encounter: songs, poems, legal instructions, building projects, and lots of narratives. Many of these genres are interested in history. The exodus plays such a large role in the biblical narrative, for instance, that it seems to function similarly to Jesus's resurrection—if the people have *not* been liberated by Yahweh from Egypt, Torah faith may be useless![30]

Some argue ancient Israel was uniquely interested in history and was maybe even the first people to acknowledge its "decisive significance."[31] For instance, while ancient Near Eastern festivals seem to have been primarily interested in celebrating "mythic archetypes," Israel's festival calendar was based in the historical memory of Yahweh's liberation of Israel from Egypt.[32]

Many scholars question the reliability of the Pentateuch's historical depictions. Although trying to confirm the historicity of any text is complicated, we remain convinced of two truths.

1. Archaeology and other ancient historical studies do not *prove* the historicity of any particular aspect of the Pentateuch; nor do they disprove it. The limited, fragmentary nature of historical evidence and the difficulty of interpreting that evidence make conclusive "proofs" unlikely if not impossible.
2. Scholars have unearthed evidence demonstrating the *historical plausibility* of the Pentateuch's patriarchal and exodus narratives.[33]

Based on our hermeneutic of trust, we believe the Pentateuch reliably communicates what it's trying to communicate, including truths about historical facts. And because the Bible claims to be an authoritative word from the Lord of History, the truth value of some portions of the Pentateuch at least is connected to a truth claim that these events happened.

Nevertheless, genre issues remain important, because ancient cultures, including Israel, didn't "do" history the way we do. We tend to think of history writing as neutral, unbiased recounting of events. Philosophers of history point out that this does not reflect reality, since historians choose particular subjects, describe them from a certain perspective, and tell history out of specific motivations. Whether we accept that or not, it's abundantly clear that ancient history writing, at least, does not seek to offer an unbiased, neutral, recounting of "facts."

Consider a few examples. Genesis is filled with genealogies. These genealogies include people later Israelites clearly understood to have been historical. They are thus making truth claims about the existence of certain individuals and their relationship to others. But while in our culture, a genealogy "represents a line of descent for the purpose of identifying ancestors in their sequential order," in other cultures "sequential order was not a major concern. . . . The order was more representative of the relative significance of the various ancestors."[34] Such genealogies could also switch around the order to make a point or use age ranges for reasons besides recording the literal length of someone's life.[35]

This means that although a genealogy that eliminates names from the list would be making a false truth claim in *our* understanding of genealogies, that wouldn't have been the understanding of readers in the ancient world. When we notice that the genealogy in Genesis 10 includes seventy names, for instance, we may well be justified in thinking that seventy has a symbolic function. Early readers would not have thought the truth value of the text threatened by the discovery that Genesis 10 eliminates a few names in order to achieve such symbolism.

Or take the issue of dates. From our perspective, a "truthful" date is one that connects an event to its exact moment in time. If I say we met for dinner on November 29, and we met on November 30, my words are false. But there's strong evidence this isn't the way dates work in the Torah.

Absolute dating was relatively unusual in the ancient world. The fact that Exodus says the journey out of Egypt only takes three days and then gives dates that stretch it out over months makes it clear that Exodus isn't trying to deceive us; it's just doing something different with its history than we would. The specific dates given link the historical events to Israel's later celebration of festivals associated with those events. The Passover is said to happen on a certain date and then to be commemorated at a feast on that date going forward. Apparently, the Pentateuch added specific dates "to certain events for their liturgical remembrance, not as journalistic details."[36] In other words, even when the stories are obviously referring to events that actually happened, they aren't making the same sorts of truth claims modern history writing would.

Again, while this may strike us as problematic, it wouldn't have struck ancient readers that way. They could have recognized what these authors were doing and judged their truth claims with an intuitive awareness of how the different genres worked. For instance, one stunning example comes from the Kadesh inscriptions of Ramesses II. After winning a historic battle against the Hittites at Kadesh, the pharaoh commissioned "two differing, and even conflicting, accounts of the battle." He then had these differing accounts "*carved side by side at several monumental sites across Egypt*."[37] Apparently neither the pharaoh, nor the authors of these different accounts, nor their readers had any problem with two differing versions of the story. Presumably, they saw them as having distinct and complementary purposes that required somewhat different portrayals, even as both depicted and described events that actually happened.[38] Professor Joshua Berman describes premodern history as a form of "exhortation." Such exhortation includes references to historical events but also a strong theological agenda, as well as a literary artist's ability to craft a compelling narrative.[39]

We can think of examples of this today. The Broadway musical *Hamilton* was based on Lin-Manuel Miranda's extensive engagement with Ron Chernow's biography of Alexander Hamilton. Yet the use of hip-hop and R&B music, as well as the decision to choose Black cast members for many of the parts, was intentionally designed to create "a story about America then, told by America now."[40] Miranda told Hamilton's story in such a way that immigrants could see themselves in America's story, and every American could see their shared story *as* an immigrant story. This required a creative, artistic rendering of a historical narrative. It was precisely Miranda's desire to tell deep, meaningful truths about American life that drove

Figure 1.9. Ramesses II and chariot at the Battle of Kadesh

him both to stick close to the historical record *and* to freely and creatively adapt that historical record for his broader purposes.

When we read the stories of the Pentateuch, we often encounter references to historical events. But the transmission of historical facts is not the primary purpose of these stories. The primary purpose of these stories is to introduce us to the living Lord and invite us to walk in that Lord's ways. Miranda claims that the job of the artist is "to fall in love for a living"; the authors of the Pentateuch wielded their enormous artistic talents to help *us* fall in love with the God who stands as the central character in their stories. Many pentateuchal narratives depict historical events with all the free-wheeling artistry of a master storyteller and all the theological intention of a powerful preacher. What the Pentateuch chooses to focus on, the way it construes and interprets events, and the artistry used to bring all this together are driven by the desire to introduce us to God and to invite us to pledge our allegiance to him.

The complexity of understanding how the various subgenres of the Pentateuch communicate God's Word may seem bewildering. Again, it's worth remembering we can trust God to communicate faithfully through these texts. Indeed, Old Testament scholar Gordon Wenham suggests that the most helpful category for understanding the overall genre of Genesis through Deuteronomy is the traditional language of *torah*.[41] While *torah* is often translated "law," a better translation would be "instruction." Each of the Pentateuch's subgenres must be interpreted with an awareness of how these different kinds of literature work. But all these different types of literature are given to us by God as instruction, as guidance for living with God in God's world and in line with God's way.

Conclusion

We have considered *why* we ought to read the Torah and *how* to read it well. Now let's dive in! The chapters that follow are of two sorts. Twelve chapters dig deeply into the five books of the Pentateuch. We encourage you to read (or listen to a free audio version) to the portion of Scripture you're studying prior to reading the related chapter. This will allow you to use this textbook the way we've intended it to be used: as a tool to help you wrestle with these books, striving to hear in them God's generous address to us today. Interspersed with these longer chapters are a series of shorter chapters that outline specific tools for interpretation. These are designed to help you engage some of the Torah's trickier sections. In all of this, we invite you to prayerfully ask the risen Lord to speak to you by the Spirit through the Word.

LITERARY NOTES

You've Got Time for Torah!

You've got more time to read Torah than you think. According to Bible publisher Crossway, it would take less than fourteen hours to read the entire Pentateuch from start to finish.[m] And given the many freely available audio versions of the Bible, you can "read" the Torah while you're in the car, on a jog, making dinner, and more!

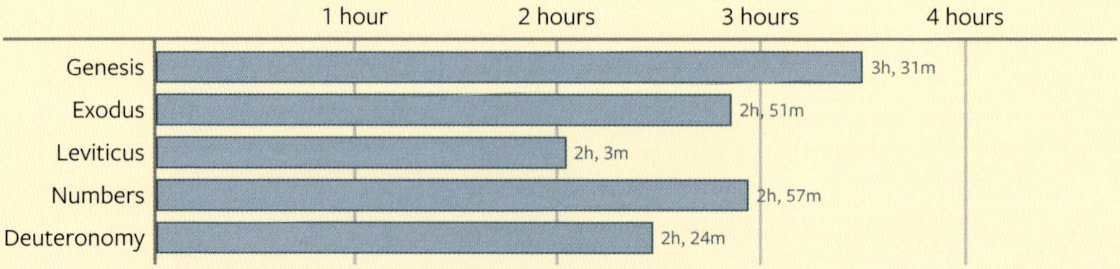

Figure 1.10. Approximate time it takes to read the books of the Pentateuch

Genesis 1–3

God's Good Creation, Humanity's Disastrous Rebellion

Orientation

If the Pentateuch is the metaphorical big bang of the Bible, then Genesis 1–11 is the first fiery burst of sound and light. Out of this explosion, the scriptural world spins out and takes shape. These chapters offer an essential starting point for glimpsing answers to life's big questions:

- Who is God, and what is God like?
- Who are we, what are we like, and why are we here?
- What's the world like?
- What's gone wrong?
- What, if anything, is God going to do about it?

Genesis 1–11 includes some of Christianity's most well-known stories. Adam and Eve, the Garden of Eden, and Noah and his ark have captured readers' imaginations for centuries. But that doesn't mean we find these stories easy to comprehend. We might even find them problematic. We need to listen to these first explosive, strange, startling stories afresh and wrestle with the questions they raise—not just because these texts are interesting (although they are!) but because they are *Scripture*. Here the fiery word of the living Lord burns hot, inviting us to grow deeper in our life with God in God's world.

Scholars sometimes refer to Genesis 1–11 as the primeval history. These stories are cosmic in scope. Even when they focus on individual figures, they do so out of a primary interest in humanity as a whole. You see this in the names: "Adam" simply means "human" in Hebrew; "Eve" basically means "the living."

By contrast, beginning in Genesis 11:10 and picking up in 12:1–50:26, Genesis zooms in on the story of Abraham's family on its way to becoming the nation of Israel. This creates something of a genre shift. The second section of Genesis offers a story of humans whose names and histories become part of Israel's origin story. In our view, these stories are presented as more historically grounded.[1]

Despite this basic division, Genesis remains deeply connected. This can be seen at the structural level through the use of genealogical material introduced with the Hebrew word *toledot* ("generations," "genealogy," or "descendants") at key moments. This structure serves a theological purpose, taking us on a journey from "the *toledot* of the heavens and the earth" (Gen. 2:4) to "the *toledot* of Jacob" (37:2). Genesis weaves the "family history" of Israel that dominates the Old Testament into the "family history" of the entire human family, and indeed creation itself.[2] Thus the cosmic possibilities and problems explored in creation and humanity's origin stories (Gen. 1–11) echo across the beginning of Israel's origin story (Gen. 12–50). While the first half of Genesis demonstrates God's commitment to rescue his good-but-rebellious creation, the second half reveals that God will conduct this rescue operation through Israel.

Genesis thus serves as the Pentateuch's prologue, introducing us to

- God's plan to live in his good world alongside human image bearers who corule that world with him;
- humanity's rebellion against that plan and the aftermath of that rebellion;
- God's decision to solve the problem of human rebellion through the family of Abraham; and
- the beginning stages of Abraham's family becoming a nation in the land of Egypt.

In this chapter, we explore Genesis 1–3.

Exploration

God Creates (Gen. 1:1–2:3)

READ GENESIS 1:1–2:3

Read the text as if you've never read it before. Consider the following: What does God do, say, and think/feel? What is said about humans? Where do you see nonhuman characters (besides God) acting?

THEOLOGICAL ISSUES

Creation Out of Nothing?

Some scholars and translations deny that Genesis depicts "creation out of nothing." While creation out of nothing isn't the focus of Genesis 1, the Hebrew text is compatible with that doctrine, which Scripture clearly teaches elsewhere (see Prov. 8:22–31; Col. 1:16).

The Bible wastes no time introducing its main character and what he's up to: "In the beginning God created the heavens and earth" (Gen. 1:1 NIV). In Hebrew, the verb "create" is *bara'*, and God is always the subject. Creation is something only God, *this* God, can do. Initially, the "earth was formless and empty" (1:2 NIV). The language suggests an uninhabitable, unformed environment, a dark, watery wilderness of a place.

Yet the Spirit of God is there, "hovering" like a bird over its young (see Deut. 32:11). God is present in this unformed, intimidating place, poised to act. The very first time we hear God's voice, it's to call into existence a world bursting with light and life, a world "formed to be inhabited" (Isa. 45:18).

God creates by speaking, separating, making, and setting. God names realms (day/night, sky, land/seas) and commissions creatures to participate in his creative process. God makes the sun and the moon that they might rule the day and night. God summons the "earth" to "put forth

Figure 2.1. *Genesis: Creation* by Baruj Salinas (2014)

Table 2.1. God's Creation in Genesis 1

Realms	Inhabitants
Day 1 (1:3–5) Light	Day 4 (1:14–19) Lights
Day 2 (1:6–8) Waters above (sky) Waters below	Day 5 (1:20–23) [Bird] life Marine life
Day 3 (1:9–13) Land	Day 6 (1:24–31) Land animals Humans

Source: Adapted from William P. Brown, *A Handbook to Old Testament Exegesis* (Westminster John Knox, 2017), 106.

vegetation" (Gen. 1:11), and the earth does "produce vegetation." The earth and the heavenly lights are here less like inert matter that God puts in motion and more like living characters that willingly respond to their Lord's commands by ruling and producing.

Then God blesses the creatures of sky and sea and commissions them to "be fruitful and increase in number" (Gen. 1:22 NIV). Through this blessing, God gives creation the power and capacity to flourish.[3] Even before the creation of humanity, God calls his creation good and invites members of the "community of creation"[4] to participate in his good purposes. And all of creation, from the sun, moon, and stars to the "great sea monsters" of the deep (1:21), responds in obedience.

The "formless and empty" world has become a set of ordered, diverse ecosystems exploding with life. Indeed, the orderliness of creation is a key to understanding the literary framework of the story. On days 1–3, God creates realms, while in days 4–6 he fills these realms with inhabitants (see table 2.1).

Some argue this orderliness is connected to Genesis 1 and 2's subtle suggestion that God created the world as a cosmic sanctuary.

LITERARY NOTES

Creating the Cosmic Sanctuary

The creation-as-sanctuary view has several important pieces of evidence:

- God rested on the seventh day. In the ancient world, gods rested in temples. Psalm 132:8 describes the temple as Yahweh's resting place.[a]
- Since temples (and palaces) often had gardens attached to them, the Garden of Eden in Genesis 2 may be understood as the "temple garden"[b] within the grander picture of creation as sanctuary.
- Genesis 1–2 uses language and imagery associated with Israel's sanctuaries. For instance, the word *ma'or* used to describe the heavenly lights is only used elsewhere in the Pentateuch to describe the lamps in the tabernacle,[c] cherubim only show up in the Pentateuch outside the Garden of Eden in relation to the tabernacle,[d] and the story of God creating the heavens and the earth in Genesis 1–2 corresponds to the story of Israel building the tabernacle in Exodus 39–40.[e]

This suggests Genesis 1–2 describes God creating the heavens and the earth as a cosmic sanctuary, an idea that shows up frequently elsewhere in the canon (see Job 38:1–7; Ps. 104:2–3; Isa. 66:1).

MADE IN GOD'S IMAGE: IT'S WHO WE ARE AND WHAT WE DO

Within this cosmic sanctuary, God gives humans a special role as those made according to the divine image (Gen. 1:26–27). Such language suggests humans have a God-given identity and job description as God's royal, priestly, family members.[5] First, Genesis explicitly connects the image with a royal identity and role. We can translate Genesis 1:26, "Let us make humankind in our image . . . *that they may rule*,"[6] and in the ancient world, kings were sometimes described as the "images" of the gods.[7]

Second, priests were also sometimes considered to be the "images" of the gods in the ancient world.[8] If the readers of Genesis understood creation as a sanctuary, they might expect that humanity's special role *inside* the sanctuary would be priestly. In Genesis 2:15, Yahweh puts humanity in the Garden of Eden "to work it and take care of it" (NIV). The Torah uses these same Hebrew words to describe how Israel's priests should "serve and protect" the sanctuary (Num. 3:7–8; 18:7). The priestly overtones of the image suggest that humanity would serve as mediators of God's presence to the whole creation.[9]

The sanctuary allusions in Genesis 1–2 suggest another kind of "image" found in sanctuaries: idols! Catherine McDowell argues the creation of the first humans in the Garden of Eden could remind ancient readers of the way newly crafted idol statues were ritually "enlivened" in Egypt and Mesopotamia. Thus humans may also be understood as living, breathing *idols* of God![10]

Finally, McDowell draws our attention to an important clue for understanding "image and likeness" language: the claim in Genesis 5:3 that Adam had a son "in his likeness, according to his image."[11] This is family language. For humanity to be created in God's image and likeness means that we were created as members of God's family. We share a kinship connection with God.

This is revolutionary. In the ancient world, when people talked about humans made in god's image, they were almost always talking about rulers like the men in figures 2.2 and 2.3. No other ancient text goes out of its way to clarify that both *women* and *men* are made in God's image.[12]

THEOLOGICAL ISSUES

"Let *Us* Make Humanity"?

Readers of Genesis have long debated how to understand God's reference to "us" in 1:26.

1. *The Creator could be speaking to the heavenly council or angels.* Note, however, that the verbs and pronouns that follow are singular: "God created [singular verb] humankind in his [singular pronoun] image" (Gen. 1:27). On this interpretation, then, these other members of the heavenly council are merely the "backdrop" for God's "deliberations."[f] The one Creator creates humanity in the Creator's image.
2. *The "us" refers to the Trinity.* While true theologically, it's unlikely this is how Genesis's early readers would have understood the phrase.
3. *The phrase "let us" may be a kind of royal plural*, a plural of majesty, as when an individual monarch sometimes refers to themselves using the "royal we."[g]

Figure 2.2. Assyrian relief depicting a royal lion hunt

Figure 2.3. Limestone bas-relief from Memphis, Egypt, 1290–1224 BC; in the Egyptian Museum, Cairo

ETHICS

Ignoring the Image

There is a long, tragic history of Christians arguing that women, Native Americans, Africans, people with disabilities, and others are not made in God's image, or at least not as fully made in God's image as others.[h] This is why it is crucial we recognize God's image as *both* an ineradicable, mysterious identity granted to any and every human *and* a vocation connected to that identity.

The good news is that Genesis's claim that humans are made in God's image has proved inspiring and liberating for Christians fighting for justice in all these same contexts. "Man is a child of God made in His image," Martin Luther King Jr. declared, "and therefore must be respected as such."[i] Indeed, for King, "the image of God [provided] the theological basis for black people's struggle for survival."[j]

Photo by Marion S. Trikosko / Library of Congress Prints and Photographs Division

Figure 2.4. Martin Luther King Jr. speaks at a press conference at the US Capitol about the Senate debate on the Civil Rights Act of 1964.

Genesis claims that every single person has an identity that gives them immeasurable worth and value as God's royal, priestly son or daughter. But this identity is also a job description, a vocation for humanity to embrace. If we want to grow in our understanding of what that job description entails, we might start by asking, What does *God* do in Genesis 1? How should God's work shape the way we see our work as those who bear God's image? In Genesis 1 alone, God makes, commands, names, and blesses; separates and makes distinctions; shows concern for the goodness, fruitfulness, and beauty of creation; engages the entire community of creation with generosity and care, not least by showing concern for its sustenance; and willingly collaborates with creation, joyfully inviting others—including animals, the earth, and the heavenly lights—to participate in his creation project.

To be made in God's image is to be invited into God's mission of blessing in his good world. God has created humans to be the sorts of beings who serve as conduits or vehicles of his blessing to "every square inch" of creation.[13]

ALL IN A WEEK'S WORK

Genesis 1 reports seven times that God saw that his creation was good (Gen. 1:4, 10, 12, 18, 21, 25, 31). These seven references invite us to share God's perspective.[14] There are other ways of viewing the world, then and now. People accustomed to thinking of creation as built for humans should recognize that God celebrates his creation before humans arrive on the scene; while Christians may often describe Genesis as teaching that God made the world *for humans*, Genesis simply does not say that. Moreover, humans might wonder whether "great sea monsters" have any place in a

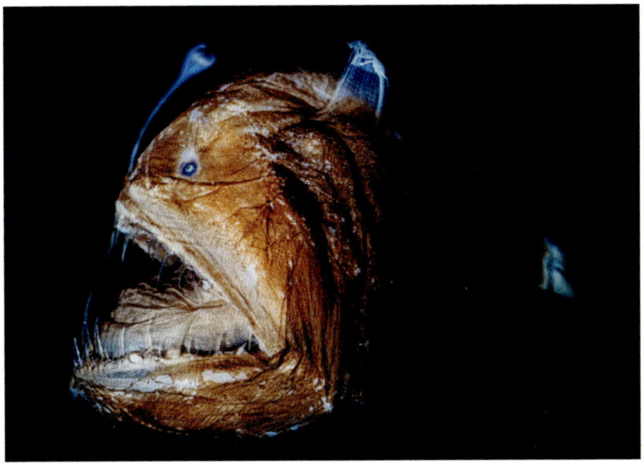

Kan Sukarakan / Shutterstock

Figure 2.5. This deep-sea anglerfish certainly looks like a monster!

good, well-ordered world. But Genesis invites us to share God's perspective on creation: It's all very good—even the wild and scary stuff.

Genesis also shapes us to see Sabbath rest as the culmination of creation. When the account says God rested on the seventh day, it doesn't refer to inactivity, exactly (Gen. 2:2–3). God makes the Sabbath "holy," or "set apart." In its ancient context, Sabbath rest likely refers primarily to God taking up residence in creation as creation's rightful king.[15] At the same time, God's institution of the Sabbath creates a "temple in time."[16] The world was built for worship; the rhythms of creation create a cadence of praise. Genesis 1 calls humanity to sync their lives with this created cadence.

READING GENESIS 1 IN DIALOGUE WITH OTHER ANCIENT ACCOUNTS

The truly eye-popping nature of God's goodness becomes clearer when we pay attention to other ancient creation stories. Because Israelites listening to Genesis would have known these (or similar) stories, they would have noticed similarities and differences.

For instance, like Genesis, the Babylonian creation myth Enuma Elish starts with waters, includes the creation of humanity, and culminates in the high god Marduk taking up residence in a newly built temple. But the differences are dramatic. Marduk is just one of many gods competing for control. The way he becomes the god worthy of his people's worship is by waging violent war against older divine beings, and especially Tiamat. This terrifying goddess represents the primordial Sea, and she comes to the battle backed by sea monsters. But Marduk "crushes her skull with his war club and scatters her blood into the wind. He splits her body in two. He uses half to make the heavens, and half to make the earth. The body of Tiamat seals out the primeval waters at the mountains of the horizons and from her eyes emerge the Tigris and Euphrates Rivers." Later, Marduk kills another god and "kneads [his] blood and bone into a savage"—that's us!—"who will do the work of the divine assembly." Such "savages" "set the divine assembly free to rest."[17]

A number of ancient texts share elements of this story, and especially the sense that the sea and its monsters represent watery chaos that threatens

ETHICS

When "Rule and Subdue" Becomes "Use and Abuse"

The command to humans to "rule and subdue" the earth and other creatures has often been taken as a license to use and abuse God's good world. But we need to interpret "rule and subdue" within the context of Genesis 1:1–2:3 itself. As bearers of God's image, humans are to exercise their royal "rule" in line with the Creator's own royal, collaborative, nonviolent rule.[k] Moreover, whatever "ruling and subduing" the animals means in Genesis 1, it apparently doesn't include eating them; right after calling humanity to exercise this rule, the text clarifies that God has given them the plants to eat (God explicitly permits eating meat later).[l] Finally, as we will see, Genesis 2 provides greater clarity in regard to humanity's task of "caring responsibility."[m]

the gods that the people worship.[18] Many likewise share a low view of humanity. Humans are slaves in a world created through violence. Indeed, chaotic, threatening violence is a permanent part of the created world. For Enuma Elish, both the earth and human beings are constructed out of corpses.

Genesis uses similar imagery to paint a dramatically different theological picture. The world is not created by the fighting or sexual antics of a host of divine beings but by the one Creator. This Creator does engage the dark waters of the sea during creation, but that sea is not an enemy. God himself creates the sea and even the great sea monsters—apparently, he *likes* sea monsters! Creation's wild inhabitants are part of God's good world, not a threat to it. Humans are royal family members rather than slaves, and the rest that God enjoys at the end of the creation story is not at the expense of humanity but shared with them. For ancient Israelites aware of those other ancient ways of seeing the world, Genesis 1:1–2:3 would be good news indeed!

Creation Up Close and Personal (Gen. 2:4–25)

READ GENESIS 2:4–25

Pretend you've never read this text before. Pay attention to God's words and actions. What do you notice?

Prefaced by an apparently complete creation account in Genesis 1:1–2:3, Genesis 2:4 appears to start over: "These are the generations of the heavens and the earth when they were created."[19] Whether this is a second, complementary creation account or a second look at the sixth day of creation as described in Genesis 1:24–31,[20] Genesis 2:4–25 gives us an "up close and personal" depiction of Yahweh Elohim's creation of the world, with a special focus on humanity. The creation of the first human being includes a wordplay: Yahweh makes the *'adam* (not yet a name) from the *'adamah* ("ground" or "dirt"). The Lord creates the "dirtling from the dirt" (2:7) in order to "work" or "serve" the dirt (2:5 AT).[21]

THEOLOGICAL ISSUES

Why Does Genesis 2 Use the Name "Yahweh"?

Genesis 1 refers to the Creator simply as Elohim ("God"). In Genesis 2:4 and following, however, the narrator introduces the name Yahweh Elohim ("the Lord God"). This signals to the audience that the Creator of all things is the same covenant Lord who will later reveal his name to Moses (Exod. 3) and liberate Israel from Egypt.

This supplements the picture painted in Genesis 1:1–2:3. Creation there is *good*, but that does not mean it is *perfect* in the sense that it is complete or static. Instead, creation is "a project in which God freely and graciously involves us."[22] Having created all things, Yahweh goes on to plant a garden within his good world and then gives humans a unique role in tending it. In light of the command that humanity rule and fill the earth, we might understand part of humanity's participation in the project as a spreading of Yahweh's garden pattern throughout the world.[23]

Genesis 2 clarifies the nature of humanity's ruling and subduing. Such language has been used to justify humanity's abuse of the world, but that is not what the text itself suggests. "Subduing" is undeniably strong language; perhaps it reminds us that, even in a good world, coruling with God takes courage and creative effort. But Genesis 2 specifies humanity's task as "working" or "serving" (*'avad*) and "caring for" or "preserving"[24] (*shamar*) the garden. Such verbs suggest tending and protecting, rather than using and exploiting, a picture that resonates with God's own gentle, collaborative rule in Genesis 1:1–2:3. Such rule involves responsible, loving service rather than dominating, self-serving exploitation.

RECEPTION HISTORY

When Ruling and Subduing Becomes "Dispossessing and Confiscating"

British colonialists often argued that Indigenous people had failed to cultivate their lands in line with Genesis 1:28's command to "rule and subdue." Andrew Picard, for instance, demonstrates that in Aotearoa New Zeland, colonialists reasoned that by "not cultivating their lands according to European ideals, indigenous communities were betraying the divine command and the land could be reclassified as 'waste land.' This reclassification changed indigenous land rights and opened the way for the land to be taken."[n] Genesis 1:28 was thus used to justify horrific acts of violent dispossession of Indigenous land around the world. Would that these colonialists had read Genesis 1:28's command to "rule and subdue" in line with Genesis 2:15's command that humanity "serve and protect" the garden!

THEOLOGICAL ISSUES

The Cultural Mandate

Genesis 1–2 offers humanity what some theologians refer to as the "cultural" or "creation" mandate, God's invitation to participate in the "unfolding of creation" through both care and cultivation in line with God's creative purposes. Economic, social, and cultural life, when pursued in line with God's way, are part and parcel of what it means to participate in the "ongoing creational work of God."[o]

Furthermore, Genesis 2 opens up new insights into *how* we dirtlings ought to fulfill our job description. Our human identity and job description are all gift: The breath that animates the dirtling is a gift; the garden space the dirtling is called to care for is a gift; Yahweh's presence with the dirtling is a gift. Even the tree of life is a reminder that the dirtling's day-to-day existence depends on Yahweh's ongoing grace.

God's gifts enable humanity's participation in the creation project. Even prior to humanity's sin and rebellion, these good gifts include God's law. Genesis 2:16–17 introduces Yahweh's first command: The dirtling must not eat from the tree of the knowledge of good and evil. God's commands are thus part of his good world.[25] The garden provides the dirtling with the ecological space needed to live as Yahweh's image bearer; the law provides the moral space within which to work out that vocation.

Genesis 2 also underscores the centrality of community to humanity's participation in God's creational project, and especially the community

Figure 2.6. This embroidery entitled *The Tree of Life* was created by a group of Roma women in 2016.

created through the marriage of a man and a woman. Because we read Genesis 1 before Genesis 2, we come to Genesis 2 knowing that men and women bear God's image equally and are equally entrusted with the task of filling and ruling God's world. By zooming in on a two-stage creation of humanity, Genesis 2 allows us to see how important the relationship between men and women is. Having beheld the goodness of his creation on seven occasions, in Genesis 2:18 Yahweh identifies something that is not good: for the dirtling to be alone.

So Yahweh decides to "make a companion [*'ezer*] for him who corresponds to him" (Gen. 2:18 NET). Many English versions translate *'ezer* in ways that make this first woman a subordinate, the "receptionist for the CEO, the cheerleader for the quarterback, or the nurse for the surgeon."[26] While the Hebrew root can refer to help, elsewhere in the Torah this is always a reference to *divine* help. Clearly the woman's status as "helper" does not imply subordination.[27] This "helper" "corresponds" to the dirtling; since *'ezer* carries notions of "strength, might, and valor," scholar Mary Conway suggests translating Genesis 2:18 as "I will create a strength/power equivalent to him."[28]

The language of correspondence also makes a strong statement about the way this man and woman are designed to fit, to correspond, in such a way that their life of mutuality makes their participation in God's mission possible. God's decision to make sexually differentiated humans enables these image bearers to do their God-given "ruling" and "filling" work.[29]

The dirtling receives the arrival of the woman with joy, breaking into poetry:

> "This is now bone of my bones
>   and flesh of my flesh;
> she shall be called 'woman [*'ishah*],'
>   for she was taken out of man [*'ish*]."

That is why a man leaves his father and mother and is united to his wife, and they become one flesh. (Gen. 2:23–24 NIV)

Both the bodily imagery and the Hebrew wordplay point to the unique intimacy of marital relationships.

The chapter ends with the statement that the dirtlings were "naked, and they felt no shame" (Gen. 2:25 NIV). Modern readers get the appeal. Nightmares of being naked in public are so common they show up in TV shows and films, and we are increasingly aware of the damaging effects of toxic shame. We long for the remarkable intimacy, the unguarded communion untouched by shame, experienced by these dirtlings.

For the Bible, though, nakedness means more than awkwardness about bodily exposure. It often refers to poverty and lack.[30] In Eden, the dirtlings are literally exposed, without resources to defend themselves. Yet, incredibly, this dangerous exposure becomes a gift because Yahweh has placed them in a "*subsistence farmer's paradise*."[31] The dependence and danger associated with "nakedness" is not experienced as leading to the "shame" associated with socioeconomic meltdown solely because of Yahweh's direct, generous provision. Such provision turns the exposure and dependence Israel later longed to avoid into a positive good. In the garden, the dirtlings discover the joy of a "holy insecurity."[32]

ETHICS

Problematizing Polygamy

We often wonder about the existence of polygamy in the Old Testament. However, if we recognize that Genesis 1–2 portrays the world as God designed it, not as we experience it, these texts make strong claims about the fundamental equality of men and women, about the deep mutuality within difference that allows them to fulfill their God-given tasks, and about Yahweh's vision for marriage as central to all of this. While the Torah describes polygamy, it doesn't recommend it. Indeed, the narrative depictions of polygamous relationships highlight the deep problems encountered by those who depart from the vision for the one-flesh relationship expressed in Genesis 2:24.

WikiArt / public domain

Figure 2.7. Painting of the Garden of Eden by Martiros Sarian (1904)

The First Image Bearers Rebel (Gen. 3)

READ GENESIS 3

In Genesis 3, the "craftiest" of the "wild animals" tricks the dirtlings into trying to become like God through eating from the forbidden tree, which appears "good for food and pleasing to the eye, and also desirable for gaining wisdom" (3:6 NIV). This catches us off guard. Humanity is *already* like God! And wisdom, knowledge, and "opened eyes" sound like worthy goals. But the serpent offers a path toward obtaining them by trusting another voice besides Yahweh's. In the Bible, "opening the eyes" is God's work (see Gen. 21:19; 2 Kings 6:17, 20; Isa. 42:7). Instead of listening to

Figure 2.8. *The Garden of Eden Serpent* by El Lissitzky (1916)

Yahweh's voice, these humans seek to have their eyes opened by listening to the crafty creature's voice.

The immediate result of their rebellion is that the joy of naked, dependent existence becomes a problem *they* must solve, a threat *they* must eliminate, a shame *they* must cover. God-given helplessness has become danger; existence has become burden.[33] Furthermore, the dirtlings' relationship with the Creator is shattered. His voice becomes a terror; they hide from his presence.

This relational breakdown is on full display in what follows. The man blames both the woman and God for his failures. The woman is more measured, simply identifying the snake's involvement. God's royal image bearers have been deluded by one of the very animals to whom they were called to mediate God's power and presence.

The cosmic curse consequences that result depict the world as we know it: a world of broken relationships with God, ourselves, other humans, and the rest of creation. Genesis 3 makes strong claims about the way the world got to be the way we experience it.

A CURSED SERPENT AND A LONG-TERM BATTLE

The fact that the curse on the serpent includes permanent, prolonged enmity between its offspring and humanity's suggests that we probably should see the snake as a representative of some darker evil.[34] As the story of Cain and Abel in Genesis 4 makes clear, humanity has "opened the doors to a dark power: now the doors will always be open, and humanity is daily to be exposed to attack."[35] Yet Yahweh's curse offers a glimmer of hope. While there will be perpetual war between "Team Serpent" and "Team Humanity," and while both will "strike" at each other, a strike aimed at the head of the snake represents a death blow. The enemy will wound; he will not finally win.[36]

This passage is often referred to as the *protoevangelium*, the "gospel beforehand," with the seed of the woman identified as the Messiah. Because the Hebrew word "seed" can refer either to an individual or a group, messianic interpretations of this text go back to at least the third century BC.[37] Yet while

> RECEPTION HISTORY
>
> **Playing the Blame Game**
>
> The dirtling begins the blame game, but interpreters often eagerly join in. In Milton's *Paradise Lost*, Adam is not present when Eve is deceived but recognizes that she has sinned with tragic consequences and eats the fruit anyway because he cannot bear to be parted from her.
>
> Genesis 3, however, says explicitly that the man was with her for the entirety of the serpent's speech. The serpent's verbs addressed to the woman are, as a Southerner would put it, "y'all" verbs rather than "you" (singular) verbs.

Genesis does tell the story of God's plans for humanity taking place through a particular "line" of promise, in the Old Testament, this is primarily a *corporate* hope. Genesis 3:15 thus likely highlights the way the hope of humanity is that Israel will be the seed that overcomes evil (note, too, that the only biblical use of the language of *protoevangelium* is in Gal. 3:8, where Paul writes that God "declared the gospel beforehand to Abraham, saying 'All the Gentiles shall be blessed in you'").

A CURSED VOCATION

Neither human is cursed as the serpent is,[38] but God's judgment on their rebellion includes painful childbirth, fractured relationships, and difficult work in dirt that is now cursed through their rebellion. There are several important aspects of this fallout.

First, Yahweh created humanity as creatures capable of mediating his blessing to others. Genesis 3 does not change that fundamental structure. Humans remain rulers and mediators. Through their rebellion, however, they become conduits of curses rather than blessings. Their rule now conveys dysfunction and strife to both animals (represented by the snake) and the earth itself. Creation goes awry *because* God gave humanity a particularly important role in his world, and they used their freedom and agency to rebel against that role.

Second, humanity's rebellion also creates a cataclysmic rupture between the human couple. The equality and mutuality of Genesis 2 give way to the battle of the sexes. Now the woman's desire will be for her husband, and he will "rule" over her (3:16). This fractured relationship is a result of human sin. While Genesis does not give us the last biblical word on men and women, it does give us the first several words. Those words include the strongest statement in the history of the world on the equality of men and women as made in God's image, a strong claim that men and women depend on each other for the fulfillment of humanity's God-given task, and a strong statement that male

CANONICAL CONNECTIONS

Protoevangelium Remixed

A primarily corporate reading of the "seed" nevertheless suggests a deep connection between this passage and Jesus. If this text is about the triumph of God's people over evil, the New Testament tells us that Israel accomplishes this triumph only through the faithful Israelite, Jesus of Nazareth. Paul even discusses this in terms of the promises made to "Abraham and to his seed" in Galatians 3:16 (NIV); Jesus is the *singular* seed of the Abrahamic promise. But through the work of the One, all of God's people likewise participate in Jesus's victory over evil. That's why Paul can also allude to Genesis 3:15 to describe the church's victory, writing, "The God of peace will shortly crush Satan under your feet" (Rom. 16:20). Even if the primary meaning of the "seed" in Genesis 3:15 is a human community that triumphs over evil, the New Testament reveals that this communal triumph only occurs through the work of the one Messiah (the individual seed), who destroys the power of Sin, Death, and the Devil.[p]

THEOLOGICAL ISSUES

The Risk and Reward of Being Created for Connection

Humans become who we are through relationship.[q] Our brains are wired to connect with others; infants begin imitating the facial expressions of their parents within the first hour of birth.[r] Anybody who has seen what a positive difference strong, healthy parents make for a child must surely celebrate the way God designed us to be the sorts of creatures capable of mediating blessing to others. Conversely, anybody who has seen the pain and suffering caused to people by parents who are abusive or absent knows that the very same creational structures that allow us to channel good gifts to others make it possible for us to become conduits of disaster as well.

CANONICAL CONNECTIONS

Glimpsing the Garden in Your Lover's Arms

Genesis 3 uses a rare word for "desire" to describe the problematic, one-sided desire of the woman for the man. This desire will be met by the man's attempt at mastery rather than by mutuality. But this disturbing marital picture is not the Old Testament's last word on such "desire." As Davis points out, that rare word for "desire" shows up in the woman's mouth in the Song of Songs.[5] This woman, whose voice dominates the Song and who openly celebrates a sexual relationship with her husband, declares, "I am my beloved's, and *his* desire is for *me*" (Song 7:10).

The curse of disordered desire and the breakdown between husband and wife is here overcome, at least for a moment, in the erotic life of these two starry-eyed lovers. It is a startlingly positive depiction of the possibilities of mutuality, delight, and embrace in the marriage bed, even for those who make love "east of Eden."

Figure 2.9. *Song of Songs* by April Aharon (2005)

dominance over women is the result of sin. It is an evil to be overcome rather than a created structure to be celebrated.

Finally, the results of humanity's rebellion make it difficult for humanity to do their God-given jobs. Procreation becomes painful and dangerous. Work becomes dangerous and difficult because of the cursed dirt. Worst of all, humans now face death.

WRESTLING WITH DEATH IN THE GARDEN AND BEYOND

The serpent told the woman that eating from the forbidden tree would not result in death (Gen. 3:4). This reference to death raises a number of questions. First, was the serpent right? After all, the dirtlings *don't* die "on the day" they eat the fruit, as God had said they would (2:17).

Some argue the story has nothing to do with the origins of human death at all.[39] This both stands in apparent contrast to Paul's words that death entered the world through one man (cf. Rom. 5:12) and ignores that Yahweh himself announces death as the consequence of eating the tree's fruit. Genesis 1–3 suggests humanity's relationship to death changes with their rebellion in dramatically negative ways.

This does not necessarily mean humans were created immortal by nature. The idea that humans are created out of the dust suggests mortality elsewhere (cf. Gen. 3:19; Ps. 103:14).[40] The implied need to return to the tree of life even in the garden could suggest as much. From this perspective, humans might have been created mortal yet destined for immortality as part of the triune God's unfolding creational project.[41]

But why don't the dirtlings *die*?[42] If humanity was created immortal, perhaps the loss of immortality is understood as death. If humanity was

Figure 2.10. The expulsion of Adam and Eve from the garden

created with the potential for immortality, perhaps they lose access to that possibility (see Gen. 3:22). Perhaps they experience a metaphorical death that involves diminished life.[43] Or perhaps Yahweh warns of physical death but chooses to show grace by delaying death or offering serious, but less deadly consequences.[44]

YAHWEH ACCOMPANIES HUMANITY IN THEIR "NEW NORMAL"

Regardless, Yahweh does not fully reject his dirtlings. Instead, he graciously chooses to accompany his image bearers and his wounded creation in their sin-shattered "new normal." Eve will still be the "mother of all the living" (Gen. 3:20 NIV). The children she brings into the world will be image bearers of God. That image may be marred, but it is not erased.

In a world prone to gendered competition and covered by soil that won't predictably produce fruit, the gift of "holy dependence" represented by nakedness becomes a threat. So before Yahweh executes judgment, he graciously provides the clothes the dirtlings pathetically failed to provide for themselves with the fig leaves.

Even their expulsion from the garden sounds a subtle note of grace. Yahweh says humanity has become "like one of us, knowing good and evil" (Gen. 3:22). They therefore need to be barred from the tree of life so that they do not live forever. These words are admittedly strange, but perhaps Yahweh recognizes that humanity could get what they wanted—new knowledge, eternal life—and that this would be terrible.[45] Perhaps limits on eternal life are necessary graces for humanity in our rebellious state.

By Genesis 3:24, the way back to the garden is shut. Humanity has been driven east, out into a world that suffers under the curse Adam and Eve have forced upon it. How Yahweh, humanity, and creation move forward in this tragic situation is the subject of the story as it continues in Genesis 4. As we will see, at every stage, Yahweh continues to accompany his rebellious human creatures, while also limiting "the force of evil, [keeping] it within bounds so that it may not reap its full harvest."[46]

THEOLOGICAL ISSUES

Wrestling with the Historical Adam and Eve

Genesis 1–3 may not offer an objective account of natural history, but it does make truth claims about the way the world is. These chapters may offer us an imaginative and poetic take on events, but it is an imaginative and poetic take on events that happened.

One question facing contemporary readers is whether the text requires us to see Adam and Eve as historical figures who are the biological ancestors of all human life. Many scientists argue both that the world is extremely old and that it is unlikely that the human species ever numbered less than the thousands.

This is a complex debate, and we are not competent to comment on the science. While we are concerned that this debate often distracts readers from the primary claims of the text, there are important issues here. We thus offer a few broad interpretive options or proposed scenarios that give us a way of "imagining the events" from a scientific perspective without "committing to the details of the picture." This can help us explore where and if Scripture might genuinely be said to conflict with specific scientific accounts.[t]

1. Perhaps the scientific claims mentioned above are simply wrong; the earth is six thousand years old (although perhaps God created it so that it appears to be old), and evolutionary science is completely misguided.
2. Perhaps the universe is extremely old, but God created biological life apart from evolutionary processes.
3. Perhaps the universe is extremely old, and God used evolutionary processes to create much of life on earth but intervened to create Adam and Eve uniquely.
4. Perhaps humanity as we know it evolved along the lines of evolutionary models, but God specially intervened to select an original human couple as the first true human image bearers. Their original rebellion changed the course of human history.
5. Perhaps Adam and Eve symbolize, or were representatives of, the initial community of humans who emerged through a God-ordained evolutionary process. God entrusted them with a uniquely human vocation and identity, and they rebelled (either collectively or through their representatives), eliminating the possibility of immortality offered by the tree of life and introducing curses into the dirt.

These are just a few possibilities, and there are many variations. Advocates of each explore the relationship between Genesis, science, and Christian theology, especially in relation to Jesus's and Paul's references to Adam and Eve. This range of options suggests it is possible to believe in an old earth and some kind of evolutionary creation account while still seeing Genesis as God's inspired, authoritative word. Each view has strengths and weaknesses. In our view, options 2–4 have the most to offer, yet this is a question that demands humility.

What we believe Genesis clearly teaches, and therefore ought to be embraced by all Christians is that

a. God made the entire cosmos good;
b. God created humans in God's image, entrusting them with an identity and role as corulers of God's world;
c. humanity rebelled against that job description, introducing a fundamental shift in creation (curses) and introducing the problem of sin and death (whether understood as a loss of immortality or as the loss of possibility of immortality).

Christians have nearly always accepted the "basic shape" of this story, even as their hypotheses about how this story fits with a scientific world picture have changed.[u] This shared story clearly paves the way to gospel hope: In Jesus, God will reclaim his good world.[v]

Living the Text: Becoming Citizens of God's Kingdom amid the Community of Creation

One of the many ways we might seek to live the text of Genesis 1–3 today is by allowing its stories to reshape the way we see creation. Westerners like ourselves often see creation as lifeless, inert "nature," a resource to be used for our own purposes. Likewise, many Western Christians read what Genesis says about humanity in a decidedly human-centered way; we see ourselves as both at the center of creation and very much set apart from it. When other cultures speak of Mother Earth or describe humans as closely related to the animals or other parts of creation, we often see this as animism or New Age paganism.

However, Indigenous scholar Danny Zacharias reads Genesis 1–2 from a Cree-Anishinaabe perspective. He points out that the earth *responds* to God's command in Genesis 1:12 ("Then God said, 'Let the earth put forth vegetation.' . . . The earth brought forth vegetation"), and Genesis 2:4 refers to the *genealogy* of the heavens and the earth and then places humanity within it.[47] This is often obscured in translation because, while *toledot* is usually translated "generations," "genealogy," or "descendants" throughout the rest of Genesis, English versions sometimes translate *toledot* as "account" in Genesis 2:4. Why? Because to some readers, it's *obvious* that "inert earth" cannot be a part of humanity's genealogy.

Indigenous readers might respond, Obvious to whom? When mainstream Western scholars write that "obviously, the inanimate heaven and earth cannot give birth to Adam"[48] or that God's command "Let the earth bring forth . . ." is "a command without an addressee,"[49] they are reading the biblical text through a cultural lens that may have led them to miss what the text actually says. (I [Michael] would like to express my gratitude to my Māori colleagues and students at Carey Baptist College, who have helped me begin to glimpse some of what I have been missing in these and other texts and who first drew my attention to these Western readings' failures to see what the text is saying.)

By contrast, Indigenous readers often relate to the idea of the earth responding to God's command or of humans somehow standing in the genealogy of the heavens and the earth. Māori biblical scholar Beverly Moana Hall-Smith points out that the concept of *whakapapa* "lies at the very core of what it is to be Māori." While *whakapapa* is often translated as "genealogy," she argues that it is "much more than that," identifying humans as "direct descendants of the heavens and earth."[50] Likewise, Māori theologian Wayne Te Kaawa observes that the notion of *whakapapa* "records, preserves, transmits and maps relationships between people *and the world* that they live in physically and spiritually";[51] he thus sees both the Māori worldview and the biblical text as creating a "genealogical link between land and humans."[52] For such readers,

THEOLOGICAL ISSUES

Human Rule Alongside Other Created Rulers

While readers often speak of Genesis establishing humanity as rulers over the entire world or all creation, this is misleading. Genesis speaks of the sun and moon as rulers before establishing humans as such, and there is no indication that humanity ought to exercise their royal vocation in relation to these heavenly lights. Indeed, humans and the rest of creation are simply beneficiaries of their ruling work. Moreover, while Genesis 1:26–28 calls humanity to exercise their royal vocation in relation to the earth, nowhere in the Bible are humans said to rule the seas.[w] Finally, if the "sea monsters" in Genesis 1:21 are not included in the category "fish of the sea" in 1:26–28—and no biblical text clearly identifies the Hebrew word for "sea monsters" with fish—they, too, represent wild aspects of creation not placed within the bounds of humanity's vocation (if that sounds strange, note that Job 41:1–10 describes at least one sea monster, Leviathan, as having no human ruler). Even in Genesis 1, then, humans are created rulers, but they are not the only created rulers, and the scope of their role has God-given limits.

it is easy to believe that Genesis describes humanity as somehow a part of the "genealogy" of creation.

Indigenous Christians can help those who hold a problematic view of creation as simply inert "stuff" avoid misreading Genesis and instead recognize the deeply relational way the text describes creation. Genesis 1–2 describes creation's relationship with God and its "kinship connection" with humanity in all sorts of ways. For instance, Zacharias points out that the human is made out of the dirt and so, by implication, are the rest of the land creatures (see Gen. 1:24). While Genesis 2 depicts God breathing the breath of life into the dirtling, Genesis 1:30 makes clear that all creatures created on the sixth day share this "breath of life" (see also Gen. 7:22; Ps. 104:29–30). Thus, while Genesis does set humans apart from nonhuman creatures in some ways, it also describes a deep kinship-like connection between humans, the earth itself, and our fellow nonhuman creatures in other ways.[53]

Earlier, we described humans serving as conduits of God's blessing to creation. And yet, the created world has a relationship with God that has integrity in and of itself, and the rest of creation also serves as a mediator or conduit of blessings to humanity. Bible scholars thus identify a three-way reciprocal relationship between God, humanity, and creation (see fig. 2.11).

Similarly, Māori Catholic theologian Pā Tate argues that when one "enhances one's relationship" with God, one's relationships with other humans and the rest of creation are "thereby also enhanced."[54] Or as Te Kaawa puts it in relation to the human community and the ecological community, "Humanity and the ground are co-partners created for companionship, mutual dependence and benefit. The disobedience of one inevitably affects the other. The ground plays a pivotal role in the continuing saga and is more than a setting or backdrop to a narrative; it is an active character with human-like qualities of its own."[55]

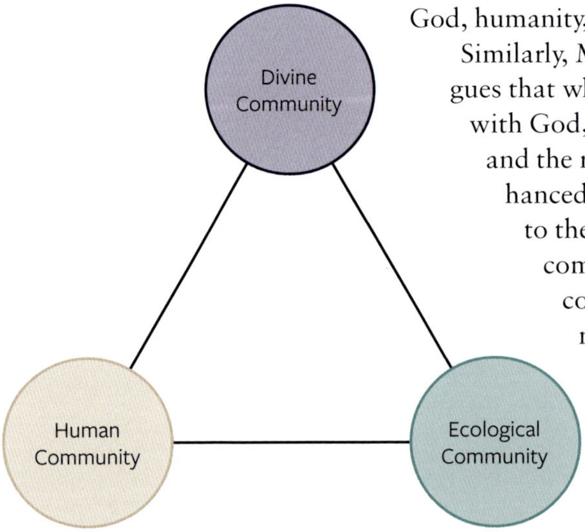

Figure 2.11. The community of creation

H. Daniel Zacharias, "GraceLand: The Land as Relational Gift in the Bible," *Journal of NAIITS* 17 (2020): 171.

This is precisely what we have seen in Genesis so far! Not only are humans created for a flourishing, reciprocal relationship with God and creation, their rebellion introduces corruption and suffering into the community of creation.

This is a far different picture of the world than most Western readers are used to. While we might not have a great answer for what this relational view of creation means "really" (or "ontologically," as a [Western] theologian might put it), this relational view of creation is everywhere in Scripture, and everywhere in a way that suggests we cannot write off descriptions of creation's role as a character in the drama as "merely" metaphorical.[56] It's not only that one day "all the trees of the field shall clap their hands" (Isa. 55:12); it's that the *heavens* are telling God's glory (Ps. 119:1), the *sun* "knows its time for setting" (Ps. 104:19), the *land* can "observe" the Sabbath (Lev. 25:2), *animals* can face the death penalty (Gen. 9:5), the *earth* can mourn because of God's judgment on human sin (Jer. 4:28), the *oceans* roar out praise to God in view of his coming just judgment (Ps. 96:11–13), the young *lions* roar to God that he might feed them (Ps. 104:21), Job expects the *wild beasts, birds, earth, and sea* to teach and instruct his friends about Yahweh's way in the world (Job 12:7–10), and so much more. And of course, Paul tells us that creation *groans* like a mother in childbirth, waiting for human resurrection (Rom. 8:22). Why? Because creation, *too*, will be resurrected, re-created into new creation! Surely here we see the "covenantal triangle" on full display—all creation waits for God to raise up humanity, because creation will share in that great re-creating liberation. As Te Kaawa puts it, "If Adam is in need of a saviour, then *Adamah* [the Hebrew word for land], from which Adam draws his identity, also shares in the need for a saviour."[57]

None of this makes creation equal to God or worthy of worship.[58] The Old Testament suggests that "everything is permeated by Yahweh's electric presence," but "without raising the universe to divine status."[59] To worship creation rather than Creator is idolatry, and the Torah wages war on such idolatry: "And when you look up to the heavens and see the sun, the moon, and the stars, all the host of heaven, do not be led astray and bow down to them and serve them" (Deut. 4:19). Even in Genesis 1, the sun and moon may go unnamed precisely to demote them from a place of worship.

Chris Wright's version of the covenantal triangle suggests that God's commands to Israel in relation to land and animals—which require Sabbath rest for the land, oxen to be able to eat while they work, and gleaning opportunities for wild animals, for instance—seek to shape Israel to become a community that recapitulates God's purpose for the community of creation within the promised land.[60]

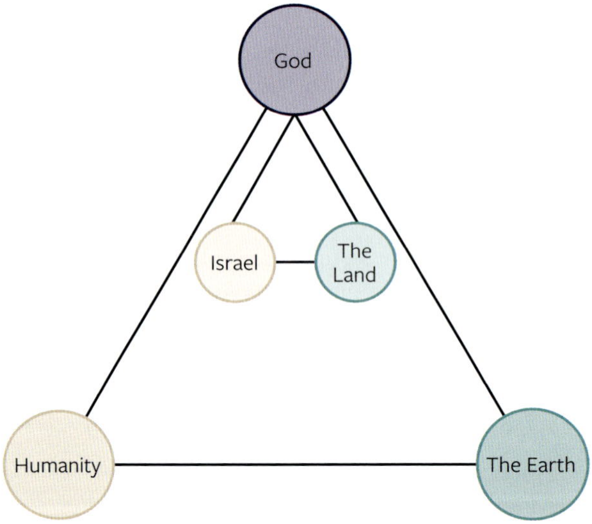

Figure 2.12. God's purposes for Israel and the world

The Bible's portrayal of creation thus invites Christians to imagine what it would mean to live as Jesus followers whose discipleship takes place within an "interconnected, interdependent" creation.[61] Such questions take on fresh urgency in light of contemporary ecological crises, including climate change, ocean pollution, deforestation, and a biodiversity crisis in which some 25 percent of all species on earth are "threatened with extinction."[62] As Old Testament scholar William Brown provocatively puts it, "Can a stream poisoned by toxic waste praise God? . . . Can the heavens adequately reflect God's glory when clouded by smog?"[63]

But Genesis's depiction of an interconnected, interdependent, responsive creation also invites us to read Scripture in conversation with others from differing cultural perspectives. Doing so may help us see aspects of God's Word that our cultural lenses make it hard for us to see and then join together in the work of "serving" and "caring" for the creational community into which Genesis welcomes us.

Genesis 4–11

The Avalanche of Sin and God's Persistent Grace

Orientation

Genesis 4–11 moves from the story of human rebellion and its immediate consequences to the broader fallout of that rebellion for God, humanity, and creation. Three major themes occur in almost cyclical fashion in these chapters.

1. **Humanity's rebellion unleashes the "avalanche of sin."**[1] The fallout from humanity's rebellion is swift and terrible, wreaking havoc on humanity and all creation.
2. **Yahweh accompanies his rebellious creation.** God generously accompanies his creation and his human image bearers in their rebellious state, doing whatever it takes to stick with the world he has made. Thus these stories demonstrate both Yahweh's just judgment on sin and his persistent grace toward his people and world. God's willingness to accompany creation in these chapters prepares us for the stunning revelation that Yahweh will accomplish his cosmic rescue plan primarily through one particular family (Gen. 12). Genealogies in Genesis 4–11 depict the "seed of promise" emerging from a particular line and lineage.
3. **The goodness of creation and human creatures persists.** If these first two claims are the major themes, a minor theme is that the goodness of creation persists. Creation is damaged but not destroyed. Likewise, the goodness of humanity's cultural engagement continues as well.

Exploration

The Avalanche Begins (Gen. 4)

■ READ GENESIS 4 ■

How do we see sin getting worse? Yahweh acting with judgment and grace? The goodness of creation persisting?

Despite the curses of Genesis 3, in Genesis 4 Adam and Eve become pregnant and bring children into the world. Eve joyfully celebrates participating in the process (4:1). Cain and Abel appear to find meaningful work and offer Yahweh some of the results. Maybe life east of Eden won't be so bad after all!

The good times don't last. For reasons that have puzzled commentators for centuries, Yahweh "looked with favor" on Abel's offering but rejected Cain's (Gen. 4:4–5). The best explanation seems to be that by emphasizing the way Abel brought the best portions, the narrator implies Cain did not.[2] Cain's anger leads to a conversation with Yahweh about *sin*—the first time the word appears in Scripture (4:6–7). Yahweh offers Cain an invitation: If he does what is right, even here, east of Eden, he can experience an acceptable relationship with God. But Yahweh also offers a warning: Sin is on the prowl, lying in wait for Cain like a deadly beast.[3] It isn't clear whether this image suggests sin is an "internal disposition or a power outside of persons that may afflict them (or both)."[4] What is clear is that the fallout from Genesis 3 includes a battle between humanity and sin.

Cain rejects God's warning and murders his brother. Don't let familiarity with the story shield you from the shock. We go from the dirtling's shout of joy at discovering human community in the *'ezer* "who corresponds to him" to the murder of the second son born out of that union by the first son, all in the space of two chapters.

Abel's blood "cries out" to Yahweh from the ground. As elsewhere in Scripture, an outcry against human injustice rises up to Yahweh and inspires him to intervene. Once again, human rebellion affects human relationships and the earth itself, which is again depicted as a character in the drama. The earth "opened its mouth to receive [Abel's] blood" from Cain's hand (Gen. 4:11 NIV). Cain, like his parents, serves as

CANONICAL CONNECTIONS

The Complexity of Sin

Christianity's account of sin is expansive and complex. Paul, for instance, describes sin as something we do (Rom. 2:12), a characteristic or identity (1 Tim. 1:9), and even as a hostile power that seeks to rule (Rom. 6:6), including through hostile structures, systems, and forces at work in the world (both spiritual and human; Eph. 6:12; 1 Cor. 2:6–8). The broad outlines of these three aspects of sin are all arguably present in the first few chapters of Genesis. In Jesus, we discover God's final and full answer to the complex problem of sin: forgiveness for sinful acts, new hearts purified from sinful dispositions, freedom from Sin's dark domination, and the establishment of the just and righteous kingdom of God.

Louvre Museum / public domain

Figure 3.1. Cain and Abel, ivory panel from the Cathedral of Salerno, Italy (ca. 1084)

a conduit of cursing to the earth, this time by forcing the earth into a kind of complicity with his violence.

The earth bites back. The land suffers by being forced into involvement with this unjust violence and is likewise involved in the judgment on Cain's actions.[5] Cain himself is cursed *from* the ground; the land will not "continue to *give its strength*" to Cain (Gen. 4:12 AT), and he will be forced to live as a restless wanderer on the earth. The sin-soaked journey eastward continues. This seems to represent an increased rupture in the relationship between the earth and humanity. "Interpersonal violence tears into the seamless fabric that links a human to his or her environment, and even threatens the order of creation itself."[6] (See fig. 3.2.)

Once again, however, we discover grace. While Cain deserves the death penalty, when he cries out to Yahweh, Yahweh graciously defends Cain by providing him with a mark of divine protection. Cain is exiled from Yahweh's presence yet mysteriously accompanied by Yahweh's generous provision.

Cain's line of descendants includes hopeful notes. His offspring build cities, raise livestock, invent new technologies, and create art/music. He remains an image bearer who participates in the cultural mandate. Yet Cain's violence and expulsion from God's presence cast a shadow. City building, art, and technology all participate in *both* creational goodness *and* the violence

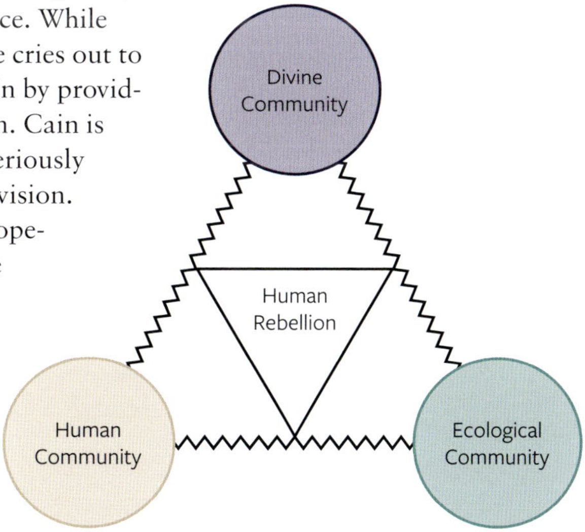

Figure 3.2. The community of creation

and creational devastation bound up in human rebellion. The art Cain's descendants create includes the violent, boasting poetry of humanity's first polygamist. Lamech not only takes two wives; he sings a song celebrating that he killed a young man for a slight (Gen. 4:23–24).

Lamech's violence mirrors Cain's and extends it. As with the previous stories of human dysfunction, it is accompanied by a hopeful note. Tellingly, that hope is identified not with Cain's line but with the emergence of a new line of promise from Adam and Eve. They have a son Seth, whom Eve identifies as a gift from God. At *this* time "people began to call on the name of Yahweh" (Gen. 4:26 AT).

Introducing the Line of Promise and Unexpected Problems (Gen. 5:1–6:4)

Genesis 5 gives "the book of the genealogy of Adam" from the creation of humanity "in the likeness of God" (5:1) through ten generations culminating in the birth of Noah's sons. By reiterating both humanity's high calling and identity and Yahweh's blessing, Genesis prepares us to see God's good purposes working in the world through the genealogy. It offers us something of a fresh start.[7]

With few exceptions, each element in the genealogy follows the same pattern. The drumbeat this repetition creates may suggest the meaningful, ordered progress of the human story within God's world.[8]

The exceptions to the pattern are equally instructive, however. Enoch "walked about with God, and was no more, for God took him" (Gen. 5:24 AT). The phrase "walked about" first appeared in the reference to Yahweh coming to "walk about" in Eden (3:8 AT). The verse points to the unique intimacy Enoch had with God, and his mysterious apparent avoidance of death. This is a tremendously optimistic note to sound amid the "avalanche of sin."

The same language of walking with God is used for Noah (Gen. 6:9). His name is related to the Hebrew word for "rest," and his father names him in the hope that "out of the ground that the Lord has cursed this one shall bring us relief from our work and from the toil of our hands" (5:29). Adam's and Cain's actions created an increasingly cursed ground and, by extension, increasingly painful work. Genesis 5 raises the question, Will God heal his creation through Noah?

Genesis 6:1–4, however, suggests the cosmos is falling apart. It begins with one of the strangest stories in Scripture. As humanity begins to increase, beautiful daughters attract the attention of "the sons of God." While some suggest these "sons of God" are humans, the most ancient and exegetically plausible interpretation is that they refer to corrupted spiritual beings of some kind.[9] The portrayal of these spiritual beings "seeing" something they identify as "good" and "taking" it intentionally echoes the language and sequence describing Eve taking the forbidden fruit. "Seeing" and "taking" are later used in a variety of contexts where men engage in sexual relationships with women who are not appropriate sexual partners (Gen. 12:14–15; 34:2; 2 Sam. 11:2–4; see also Judg. 14:1–3).[10] As biblical scholar Amy Kalmanofsky writes, "Like Eve, the divine sons transgress boundaries and take what is not rightfully theirs. . . . Genesis 6 continues Adam and Eve's troubled story and [suggests] that the daughters of humanity bear the burden of their ancestor's legacy."[11]

Genesis 6:4 connects the offspring of these dysfunctional sexual relationships between human women and semidivine beings with the famous Nephilim and "the heroes that were of old, warriors of renown." The strange events of 6:1–4 contribute to the dramatic increase in human violence that dominates the flood story that follows. Once again there is an escalation of evil and violence in the aftermath of human rebellion, with women perhaps implied as primary victims.[12] Once again, Yahweh intervenes to limit humanity's evil through judgment. This time, though, even the spiritual realm is caught up in the disorder associated with human rebellion.[13]

The Great Flood (Gen. 6:5–9:17)

The flood story plays a massively important role within Genesis 1–11. Unfortunately, overfamiliarity with the text can prevent us from grappling with its claims. To get a fresh perspective, it may help to start with an analogy.

PLACING THE FLOOD STORY IN CONTEXT

The Broadway musical *Wicked* tells the story of a brave young woman who uncovers an evil plot perpetuated by powerful people parading as the "good guys." It's a tale as old as time. But *Wicked* is also the story of *The Wizard of Oz* from the perspective of the "wicked" witch. Now, even if you aren't familiar with *The Wizard of Oz*, you can enjoy the music, set, and story of *Wicked*. But you'll miss some of the musical's message, because nearly every scene takes a shot at that other, more well-known way of telling the story. Or, to use a fancy scholarly word, *Wicked* is "polemical"; it confronts other ways of telling the story and seeing its characters.

The flood story in Genesis is also polemical. Long before Genesis was written, communities around the ancient world told stories of a large, cataclysmic flood.[14] Similarities between their stories and ours include (1) a divine being(s) sending the flood because of their displeasure with humanity, (2) a divine being(s) deciding to save one family from the flood by having them make an ark, and (3) members of the animal kingdom joining this family on that ark.[15] Even the "floor space" of the various "arks" have remarkable similarities.[16]

Early readers of Genesis would have heard the flood story in light of these other ways of telling the tale. "Everybody knows there was a flood," Genesis says, "but you haven't heard the *real* story yet." It's easy for us to miss this, though, because we're more familiar with the Genesis story than the other versions (we know *Wicked* better than *The Wizard of Oz*, in our analogy). To help us hear the Genesis story better, let's consider another ancient flood story that Genesis appears to be combatting: the Atrahasis epic.[17]

In the story of Atrahasis, the gods create humans to do the grunt work the gods and goddesses don't want to bother with. But the human slaves keep procreating, and their noise keeps the gods up at night. So the divine assembly sends plagues, drought, and famine to control the population and quiet things down. Each time, though, one of the gods, Enki, finds a way to help mortals survive. When the gods decide to send a flood to wipe

HISTORICAL MATTERS

The Flood and History

Because we believe Genesis does not offer a scientific description of natural history, we see the quest to prove there was a literal, worldwide flood as neither necessary nor helpful.[a] Nevertheless, the fact that so many cultures from so many different times and places tell stories of a catastrophic flood suggests that humanity really does carry memories of a massive flood event. The fact that these stories identify divine beings as ultimately responsible suggests that people tried to understand the event theologically. From this perspective, Genesis's flood story engages in theological battle over the nature of reality by offering a different account.[b] Once again, Genesis appears to offer a poetic, creative, theological depiction of events that actually occurred.

Julian / Adobe Stock

Figure 3.3. Mosaic of Noah's ark from the Kykkos monastery in Cyprus out humanity, Enki suggests to his friend Atrahasis that if *he* were a human, he'd start building a boat . . . a big one . . . say, right about now. Atrahasis gets the hint, builds the boat, and piles some animals on board.

Atrahasis isn't the only person with problems, though. The flood terrifies the gods and goddesses! "What were we thinking?" they moan. By cutting off humanity, they've cut off their food supply. The deities begin to waste away from hunger.

The story concludes with Atrahasis getting off the boat and making an offering to his nearly starved divinities, who "swarmed like flies around his sacrifice." Amid the squabbling between the gods that follows, the divine council finally comes up with a workable solution. They won't wipe out humanity, but they will limit their population by ensuring some women are barren and some newborns die young. That way humanity can provide for these divine beings without creating too much noise.

THE GENESIS VERSION: CREATION AND DE-CREATION

When we read Genesis 6:5–22, we immediately notice how different the catalysts for the flood are in these rival stories. Whereas the Atrahasis epic sees human fertility as obnoxious, Genesis portrays human procreation as part of God's blessing. The problem isn't the proliferation of people; the problem is the proliferation of evil. "Every inclination of the thoughts of the human heart" had become "only evil all the time" (6:5 NIV).

This is the "most shocking statement about human sinfulness in the whole Bible."[18] Human wickedness is directly connected to violence (Gen. 6:13), including both literal bloodshed and the structures of injustice and exploitation the prophets later describe with this same language (cf. Ezek. 45:9–10). Such violence is public enemy number one.[19] And once again, the problem extends beyond humans. "The earth was ruined before God," because "all flesh had ruined its way on the earth" (Gen. 6:11–12 AT). Humanity's ongoing mediation of cursing to creation has done seemingly irreparable damage to the very fabric of the world.

Many people see the flood as the irrational, angry act of a wrathful deity. Surprisingly, the text never mentions God's anger. But Genesis does draw our attention to how Yahweh feels: "Yahweh *regretted* that he had made humanity on the earth, and he was *deeply grieved* in his heart" (Gen. 6:6 AT). Elsewhere in Genesis, this language of grief describes the pain of childbirth (3:16) and the grief of Dinah's brothers when they hear she has been raped (34:7). The outpouring of the flood waters is preceded by the overwhelming grief of God. Yahweh's willingness to stick with creation comes at a cost.

TEARING DOWN THE HOUSE

Old Testament scholar Matthew Lynch suggests the flood is necessary because creation has become the equivalent of a house so consumed by termites that it must be torn down.[20] How might this metaphor help us understand the flood story? First, Genesis displays Yahweh as actively sending the flood (Gen. 6:7). The house must be torn down to the foundations. But Genesis also depicts Yahweh's actions as simply facilitating the natural consequences of human activity that are occurring already. This can be seen by noting the repeated uses of the verb "ruin" in the text: "God saw that all the earth was *ruined*, for all flesh had *ruined* its way on the earth. So God said to Noah, 'The end of all flesh has come before me. . . . Therefore, now *I* am going to *ruin* them and the earth'" (6:12–13 AT).

This portrays the flood as the natural, intrinsic end of humanity's destructive violence.[21] The termites are tearing down the house one way or another. Yahweh's judgment facilitates destruction already inherent in humanity's wickedness.

Getty Center / public domain

Figure 3.4. Fifteenth-century depiction of Noah's ark in an illuminated manuscript of the Bible

Second, the flood returns creation to the watery, unformed, great deep that had preceded God's work of fashioning creation (Gen. 1:2). The good news is that Yahweh's flood will not be the end of his commitment to the creation project. This act of de-creation paves the way for *new* creation. Yahweh tears down the termite-ridden house to build a new home.

REBUILDING THE HOUSE

Amid Genesis 6's depiction of Yahweh's "tear down" of creation, Noah finds "favor in the eyes of Yahweh" (6:8 AT). Yahweh calls this righteous one to participate in his new creation project, a calling that includes Yahweh establishing a covenant with Noah. This is the first time the Bible explicitly uses the language of covenant, a "formally confirmed agreement between two or more parties that creates or governs a relationship that does not exist naturally."[22]

Noah plays a special role within Yahweh's new creation purposes. He embodies the continuity between old and new creation, working to save representatives of the old creation and bring them into the new.[23] Yet as important as Noah is, the turning of the tide (pun intended) occurs when Yahweh "remembers" Noah (Gen. 8:1). Such "remembering" refers to God's action in line with promises previously made, often explicitly in relation to covenants (see Gen. 9:15; Exod. 2:24; Lev. 26:42). Just as the Spirit (*ruakh*) of God hovered over the flood waters prior to God's creative activity in Genesis 1, when God begins his postflood re-creating work, he sends a wind (*ruakh*) over the earth to drive back these same waters (Gen. 8:1).

BUT WHAT ABOUT THOSE WICKED HEARTS?

READ GENESIS 8:20–9:17

As you read, consider what changes between the preflood and postflood world.

Having received again the command to fruitfully fill the world after the flood (Gen. 8:15–17), Noah responds by worshiping through sacrifice. Yahweh accepts Noah's offering as a "pleasing aroma" (8:21 NIV). The creation project is back on track.

Or is it? What, after all, has changed? Yahweh recognizes that "every inclination of the human heart" remains wicked (Gen. 8:21 NIV). Yahweh has rebuilt the house, but termites remain a threat because the termites come with the human inhabitants God wants to help him run the household.

If humanity hasn't fundamentally changed, the gospel news is that God's relationship to the world has. Genesis 9 depicts Yahweh's fourfold commitment to accompany creation in a new way after the flood. These divine commitments sustain creation despite humanity's propensity to rebellion and violence. Humanity's "continued existence" is "to be understood in terms of the merciful forbearance of God toward those who do not deserve it: Life for both Israel and for the world is a gift of grace."[24]

First, God addresses the curse of the earth caused by humanity. After Noah's sacrifice, Yahweh "said in his heart: 'Never again will I curse the ground because of humans'" (Gen. 8:21 NIV). What this means, though, isn't exactly clear. The word for "curse" here is different than the word for "curse" in Genesis 3:17, and clearly, thorns, thistles, and sweaty work

Nationalmuseum / public domain

Figure 3.5. *Noah's Thank Offering* by Ester Almqvist

persist. Genesis 8:21 could refer to God's commitment not to destroy all life with a flood again or perhaps to God committing not to curse the ground further than he already had.[25] After all, the cursed-dirt problem has not remained static since Genesis 3:17; the earth has been increasingly corrupted ever since Cain made the cursed dirt worse. Noah's very name expresses the hope that there would be relief from the cursed dirt. Perhaps, then, God has actually rolled back effects of the cursed dirt associated with Cain.[26] Regardless, Yahweh commits to limit the effects of humanity's curse-causing violence and rebellion on creation.

Second, and relatedly, Yahweh commits to sustain creation despite human sinfulness. Yahweh will ensure the rhythms of "seedtime and harvest, cold and heat, summer and winter, day and night" endure (Gen. 8:22). Again, this requires Yahweh to defend creation from the full, unfettered consequences of human rebellion.[27] At the same time, Yahweh demonstrates his willingness to accompany humanity in their sinful state. Whereas humanity's care of the animals was intended to be benevolent, now the animals will fear humans; whereas previously plants were given to humanity for food, now animals are explicitly given as well (9:1–2).

This brings us to our third point: Yahweh limits "violence through law."[28] Going forward, Yahweh will demand a legal accounting for any being, human or animal, that takes the life of a human made in God's image. The legal language of this passage looks ahead to the law's concern with bloodshed. As scholar Leon Kass puts it, "The new world order takes human beings as they are, not as they might be. It does not try to obliterate their tendencies to wildness and violence; it tries, rather, to accommodate and restrain them by means of law."[29]

Fourth and finally, Yahweh graciously covenants with humanity and all creation to limit his own judgment. Perhaps the most powerful part of the flood story is this final piece of the puzzle. Yahweh ultimately accompanies his creation by establishing a covenant—a new, promissory relationship with all of humanity, every living creature, and the earth itself (Gen. 9:11). This cosmic covenant is Yahweh's commitment to stick with creation, no matter what. The sign of this covenant is that Yahweh hangs his weapon on the wall; the Hebrew word translated "rainbow" is the same as the word for "bow" as in "bow and arrows." Whereas covenants often involve an "If you do this, then I will . . ." dynamic, this covenant appears wholly unconditional. It "is an obligation that God assumes; it will be as good as God is, and so human beings can rest back in its promises."[30]

LITERARY NOTES

Animals in Covenant

God's covenant with the earth and every living creature provides further support for the claim that the earth and nonhuman creatures are characters in the drama of Scripture rather than "stuff" to be used and abused by humans. Hosea 2:18 declares that Yahweh will one day cut another covenant that involves humanity and the animal kingdom.

> In that day I will make a covenant
> for them
> with the beasts of the field, the
> birds in the sky
> and the creatures that move
> along the ground.
> Bow and sword and battle
> I will abolish from the land,
> so that all may lie down in safety.
> (Hosea 2:18 NIV)

The goal of this covenant, like the covenant of Genesis 9, includes an end to violence. Here we glimpse God's unrelenting commitment to restore the covenantal triangle of relationships between himself, humanity, and the rest of creation.

The flood story bears witness to Yahweh's commitment to costly, difficult grace. Yes, there is judgment here, but it is necessary judgment due to the expansiveness of human violence. The flood becomes an act of re-creation that inaugurates a new era of covenantal partnership between God and creation despite human sinfulness. Read in dialogue with the Atrahasis epic and other flood stories, this statement becomes even more powerful:

- In *their* flood story, capricious, bullying gods callously wiped us out because we made too much noise. In *our* flood story, Yahweh releases the flood with grief in his heart and only in response to such widespread human violence that creation was headed toward destructive chaos anyway.
- In *their* flood story, the "hero" survives because of one god's arbitrary preference, and humans are allowed to fill the world within limits only because the gods need them to get food. In *our* flood story, Noah is saved because of his righteous character and faithful obedience. Creatures are blessed with fertility not because the gods are hungry but because God refuses to give up on his beloved world.

CANONICAL CONNECTIONS

Looking to Another Noah

The reference to Noah's sacrifice tied to God's gracious renewal of creation reminds Christians of Jesus. Like Noah, Jesus was the uniquely righteous one amid a pervasively wicked people. Just as Noah passed through the waters of the flood, Jesus passed through the waters of baptism. Noah's forty days of watery judgment anticipate Jesus's forty days in the wilderness, where Jesus, like Noah, was even accompanied by wild animals (Mark 1:13).

While the covenant family was saved by entering Noah's ark, the new covenant family is saved by being united to Jesus himself, entering the "ark" that is his body. By his death, Jesus, like Noah, offers an effective sacrifice for the sake of others. God works through Noah to offer external law that limits violence and a partial resolution to the cursed dirt. God works through Jesus to fulfill the law by writing it on his people's hearts. When Jesus returns, he will rid the world of the curse altogether. "He comes to make his blessings flow, far as the curse is found!"[c]

- *Their* flood story ends with the gods bringing new evils on humanity. Some of the most painful human experiences, including infertility and infant mortality, are the gods' strategies to keep us in check. *Our* flood story ends with God putting the effects of human violence in check, and indeed putting in check his own willingness to destroy the world. In *their* flood story, human flourishing is restricted by divine violence. In *our* flood story, divine violence is willingly restricted to make human flourishing possible.

Because it is *this* kind of God at work in *this* flood story, the Bible's flood story becomes nothing less than good news. Yahweh will not abandon his plan to dwell in his good world alongside humans who bear his image and partner with him to corule that good world.

The World Goes Awry . . . Again (Gen. 9:18–29)

Noah, like a new Adam, gets to work in a garden. In a pattern that feels painfully familiar, Noah quickly makes a mess of things, getting drunk and lying naked in his tent. In this awkward situation, Ham somehow violates his father, leading Noah to curse Ham's son Canaan with perpetual slavery.

National Library of the Netherlands / public domain

Figure 3.6. *Shem and Japhet Cover Noah* by Marius Bauer, 1882–1914

But what did Ham do exactly? And why is his son Canaan the one that gets cursed? And how in the world could perpetual slavery be a legitimate consequence?

Interpreters have puzzled over these questions since ancient times.[31] Whether Ham's transgression is voyeurism, paternal incest, castration, or even maternal incest, it isn't pretty.[32] Given the rest of the biblical story, we're likely supposed to see here not only the ongoing wickedness that tears families apart but also a foreshadowing of Israel's future conflict with the Canaanites.

On the other hand, the curse "is emphatically not uttered by God; it is uttered by a hungover Noah."[33] As Old Testament scholar Amanda Beckenstein Mbuvi puts it, "As in Eden, the episode leads to cursing and ultimately to conflict, but in this instance, *Noah* is the author of both. He ordains a divided future for his sons and their descendants."[34] Indeed, by "consigning Canaan" to be a "slave of slaves" (Gen. 9:25), Noah mandates a form of subordination that, from the perspective of Genesis, is new in human history.[35] None of this means Ham was innocent. It does suggest Genesis does not approve of and likely even implicitly critiques Noah's response. Indeed, Genesis traces long-term conflict to this important moment.

Another Promising Start (Gen. 10)

Genesis 10 moves in a more promising direction. From the beginning, Yahweh intended for humanity to "fill the earth." Genesis 10's sprawling genealogy depicts this "filling" beginning in earnest, as the descendants of Noah's sons—Shem, Ham, and Japheth—"spread out" after the flood (10:5, 32). Their "spreading" generates diversity within the human family; as these brothers fill the earth, they become "peoples/nations, in their lands, with their own languages, according to their extended family groups, in their own peoples/nations" (10:5 AT). Obedience to Yahweh's command to fill the diverse ecological spaces of the world generates cultural, linguistic, political, and ethnic diversity. Humans quite naturally—better, *creationally*—develop diversity as they encounter, and then dwell within, the diverse ecosystems of God's world.

RECEPTION HISTORY

Racism and the Curse of Ham

Tragically, Noah and Ham's story became "the single greatest justification for Black slavery for more than a thousand years."[d] At a time when white supremacists argued science proved humanity was divided into distinct racial groups and that the white race was superior,[e] "Genesis 9:18–29 served as a proof-text and platform in the national debate regarding slavery. . . . It was cited in books, pamphlets, sermons, newspapers, and even in-floor proceedings of the US Senate." As one state senator said, "'This very African race are the descendants of Canaan . . . and are still expiating in bondage the curse upon themselves and their progenitors.'"[f]

Although Genesis 9:18–29 makes no reference to skin color, this racist reading often identifies the curse with blackness itself.[g] From this perspective, the story not only explained the division of humanity into "better" and "worse" races but also demonstrated the need to maintain "sharp distinctions between groups" to ensure "the blessing and curses of the biblical patriarch would be properly maintained."[h]

Contemporary science recognizes that "race" is not a biological category; "modern genetics shows that roughly 94% of human genetic variation is found *within* populations, whereas only 6% is *between* populations (or 'races')."[i] The white supremacist reading not only contradicts the science; it also fails as an interpretation of Genesis, which limits the curse to Canaan (not Ham and all his descendants), never mentions color, and describes an intrafamily conflict rather than the division of humanity into hard-and-fast "races."[j] Racist readings say less about Genesis and more about the "attempt to find authoritative grounding" for white supremacy.[k] Yet they also serve as a cautionary tale about the dangers of reading our own idolatries into the text and invite us to explore how Genesis might challenge our perspectives on human diversity.[l]

HISTORICAL MATTERS

Language and Ecology

Dru Johnson argues that Genesis 10 agrees with scientists who believe diverse human languages evolved primarily as humans moved into different ecosystems. Place thus shapes culture and language.[m]

Genesis 10 tells this story through genealogy. While, for many Western readers, genealogy is a form of science that catalogues "people according to precise biological relationships," both in the Bible and in many other cultures, genealogy is a form of storytelling. Genesis's genealogies thus "interpret the world,"[36] and Genesis 10 does so through a genealogy that appears to be unique in world literature.[37] Paying attention to Genesis 10's genealogical art reveals further insights.

First, many biblical genealogies are "linear," focusing on a single line of descent. But Genesis 10 is a "segmented genealogy." It "branches out into multiple lines of descent," emphasizing both vertical connections (i.e., connections back to Noah) and horizontal connections (i.e., kinship relations with extended family across the whole).[38]

Second, Genesis 10 maps relationships between groups, but there is no one overarching criteria for categorizing those groups. Indeed, references to "peoples/nations," "lands," "languages," and "extended family groups" suggest different criteria by which people might be categorized. Some scholars see this as evidence of sloppy genealogical work, but Mbuvi demonstrates that Genesis 10 draws deeply on the genealogical form to make a profound theological point. While the genealogy of Genesis 10 is traditionally referred to as the Table of Nations, Mbuvi argues this description is doubly misleading. "Table" leads us to expect something like the periodic table, "depicting groups neatly arranged in cells" based on a single criterion.[39] But others, such as Mbuvi and Crüsemann, demonstrate that Genesis 10 portrays "multi-layered collective identities which encompass many peoples."[40] Likewise, summarizing all the diverse groups as "nations" is problematic, because what we mean by "nation" only encompasses one layer of identity, whereas Genesis 10 speaks to many layers of identity.[41] By portraying all this diversity within a genealogy, the text portrays all these diverse peoples as family.

Third, Genesis 10's seventy names from across the known world of Israel's day suggest this is humanity's family tree,[42] and even Israel's worst enemies are part of the family. Just before the biblical story shifts to focus on God's particular call to God's chosen people, Genesis 10 emphasizes God's universal purposes for all humanity and their kinship connections with one another.

The Tower of Babel (Gen. 11:1–9)

READ GENESIS 11:1–9

As you read, ask yourself, *Why* do the people want to build the tower?

When we talk about the Tower of Babel, we often emphasize the people's problematic desire to "make a name for themselves" and build a "tower with its top in the heavens" (Gen. 11:4). Prideful humans resisting God's purposes is part of the story. But readers often miss the goal of that resistance: "Then they said, 'Come, let us build ourselves a city, and a tower with its top in the heavens, and let us make a name for ourselves; otherwise we shall be scattered abroad upon the face of the whole earth.'"

According to the builders themselves, their goal is to avoid the scattering that reflects God's creational purposes in Genesis 10. Given God's persistent commitment to corule his entire world through his image bearers, this self-preservation instinct puts "the rest of creation at risk."[43] Because Genesis 10 depicts humanity positively spreading out and experiencing cultural and linguistic diversification *as a creational result*, the tower builders' refusal to scatter may even be understood as a kind of forced cultural sameness: In those days, the "whole world had one language and a common speech" (11:1 NIV). Luis Pedraja goes so far as to argue that "the people of Babel were intolerant of cultural and linguistic diversity."[44]

Yahweh's response is both humorously ironic and extremely serious. On the one hand, he must "come down" to see this tower allegedly reaching the heavens. On the other hand, Yahweh "confuses" their languages so they are unable to pursue a society built on resistance to Yahweh's command to scatter.

This does not mean, contrary to a long history of interpretation, that language diversification itself is a curse, a fall from a "pristine Edenic language."[45] We cannot read the emergence of different languages after Babel as a "reminder of divine retribution on human pride"[46] in Genesis 11 because we've already seen such language diversification celebrated as a good generated by humanity's obedience to spread out in Genesis 10. While Genesis 11 depicts God interrupting the building project and scattering the people, read together with Genesis 10, the story depicts this as God facilitating the

HISTORICAL MATTERS

Imperial Echoes at the Tower of Babel

The story in Genesis 11 would have reminded Israelite readers of the woes of imperialism. The brickmaking would remind them of their enslavement in Egypt. The name "Babel" would remind them of the oppressive imperial city of Babylon. The homogenous language of the builders would remind them of the Assyrian Empire, which sought to dominate other nations by bringing "together deported peoples from all countries, [homogenizing] their language and [having] them work on one task, the building of the capital and the palace."[n] Babel thus "represents imperial civilization par excellence," and the story makes clear that the "imposed, artificial unity" of such imperial civilization is a "danger to the human race."[o] All those familiar with the underside of empire would have seen God's judgment on the Babel building project as good news.

LITERARY NOTES

Barring the Way to the Wrong Sort of Life

Yahweh's words about scattering the people because "nothing that they propose to do will now be impossible for them" (Gen. 11:6) closely echo Yahweh's words about barring Adam and Eve from the tree of life lest they eat of it and live forever. The connection is telling. You might think everlasting life is a good thing, but it becomes a serious evil if that life is lived in rebellion against God. You might think people working together on a common project is a good thing, but it becomes disastrous if that project rebels against God's plans. In both cases, God disrupts human rebellion for the sake of humanity and his larger mission.

LITERARY NOTES

Did Genesis Get the Order Wrong?

Careful readers may respond to Genesis 11:1's assertion that all people had one language with a "Wait, what? Didn't Genesis 10 already talk about how language diversification occurred as the families spread out?" This is another aspect of Genesis's theological artistry. If Genesis 11 *preceded* Genesis 10, the chronology might make more sense, but we would be forced to see human diversity as "the graceless Judgment of God."[p] The need to navigate such cultural diversity would then be understood as a regrettable part of life in a fallen world—as depicted in a meme a student showed me (Michael) that had "Some jerks decided to build this and now I have to learn 3 languages" splashed across the famous image of the Tower of Babel (see fig. 3.7).

By placing Genesis 10 first, however, Genesis tells a different story, a story "about the one creator-God and his distinct people *in the midst of a divinely intended diversity of cultures.*"[q]

Figure 3.7. *Turris Babel* by Athanasius Kircher (1679)

kind of scattering that ensures creation is "peopled everywhere by [God's] regents, who are attentive to all parts of creation."[47] God's judgment is "redemptive" and "restorative,"[48] an "act of liberation" that enables humanity to develop "diverse identities."[49]

The story ends ominously. Yes, humanity is spreading out and diversifying, but they don't *want* to, and the divisions that occur as they do are now bound up in divine judgment as well as creational norms. In a pattern we have detected repeatedly, Scripture (1) highlights the Creator's generous creational purposes, only to (2) show how humans made in God's image rebel against those purposes, before (3) tracing how God continues to partner with humanity amid their rebellion through acts of both *judgment* and *grace*. Here at the end of the tower story, the note of grace is quieter than before. The pattern is about to change. God is about to do a new thing.

Living the Text: Genesis and Cultural Diversity

Genesis 1–11 offers God's people a powerful picture of the one human family in all its diversity. Tragically, the church has often traded this vision for various forms of racism, nationalism, and ethnocentrism. One crucial way God's people can live these texts today is by allowing them to "talk back" to our problematic ways of imagining human unity and diversity.

For instance, white supremacy places all people on a racial ladder based on a set of categories associated with skin color. It has often treated those on the bottom rungs as less than human, while holding out the hope that some placed in the middle of the hierarchy might "move up" by becoming more like the people at the top. Those at the top "help" those lower down by helping them become as much like the white supremacist ideal as their inferior status allows. Indigenous people whose parents were beaten in missionary schools for speaking their mother tongues bear witness to the brutal inhumanity of such racism.[50]

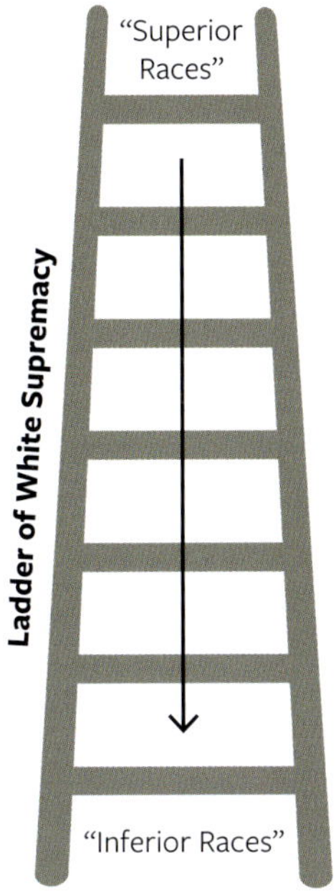

Figure 3.8. Ladder of white supremacy

Against this, Genesis claims that every human being is made in God's image, a member of the one human family tree. When we arrive at Genesis 10, the Old Testament text "most concerned with human diversity,"[51] the genealogy identifies the diversity of languages, cultures, ethnicities, and political groups that characterize the human family as a creational good.

From this perspective, colonialism's attempt to remake the world into the homogenous image of the colonial power was a rejection of God's purposes. It was the embrace of Babel. Given that 61 percent of the languages "spoken as a first language in 1795" are currently "doomed or extinct," with a new language dying every forty days, *Babel* may be an all too appropriate name for our age.[52]

Other Christians try to replace a white-supremacist worldview with a "color blind" approach. This fails to recognize the genuine diversity of human communities, downplaying or overlooking the beautiful distinctives that differentiate human groups from one another. Because such color blindness also ignores the fact that some groups have more power, it fails to notice the way color-blind "melting pots" require some groups to abandon the gifts of their diverse heritages in favor of a soup that looks suspiciously like the dominant cultural one. Whereas earlier generations *forced* people to abandon their languages and cultures, globalization and other homogenizing influences too often make cultural sameness simply the cost of doing business, or even the cost of joining "our" neighborhood, political group, or church.

HISTORICAL MATTERS

The Inappropriateness of Race in Relation to Genesis

While Genesis 10 offers at least four different categories by which to track human diversity, nowhere does it use *racial* classifications based on skin color. Indeed, the way Genesis 10 describes a gradual evolving diversity within one family due to geography undermines the artificial, pseudoscientific classification system that created categories like "white" and grouped individuals living in Ireland and individuals living in Russia together, even though they lack a shared "nation," "land," "language," or "extended family group."

Christians justify color blindness by pointing to the way Genesis places all humanity in one family tree; "we're all just people," after all. But this ignores the way Genesis celebrates the proliferation of languages, cultures, and ethnicities across that family tree. Because Genesis 10 suggests these differences emerge as people inhabit different geographies, something unique is lost when a single dominant culture or language from one place displaces or destroys the cultures and languages indigenous to another place. As both Indigenous Christians and Genesis itself remind us, lands matter, both in and of themselves and as spaces that cultivate and sustain diverse human communities.

There is yet another way Christians have failed to embrace Genesis's portrait of human unity and diversity. Sometimes God's people have tried to acknowledge the intrinsic dignity of all human beings and the goodness of human diversity. Failing to follow the logic of Scripture itself, however, they have then turned Scripture's vision of diverse human communities into a mandate for separate-but-equal ethnic ghettoes. For instance, the Tower of Babel story served as the cardinal text for Christians arguing for apartheid in South Africa.[53] Pro-apartheid Christians believed the Tower of Babel spoke a word about the goodness of human diversity and the danger of forced homogenization, but they then argued the text made both "diversity and segregation" part of God's good design.[54] Diverse human groups were such a good part of God's plan that they must be preserved *through* separation. Many forms of nationalism follow a similar logic, as do certain forms of racial or ethnic essentializing that occur across the ideological spectrum.

Mbuvi argues that such reasoning simply turns the racist hierarchical ladder on its side (see fig. 3.9).[55] Humans remain separated into hard-edged categories based on a single distinguishing criteria (nation, *volk*, language, etc.).[56] Once again, Genesis 10 resists this, because it does not offer tidy divisions between people based on one criterion; it does not give us a *table* of *nations*. Instead, it offers a family tree that depicts relationships across

Figure 3.9. Scripture's vision corrupted into cultural segregation

Family Tree

Figure 3.10. The family tree of nations

various lines of difference (language, location, nation, extended family group) that emerge as the one family spreads out into God's world. The picture is not of a ladder or table but of a tree that "develops its shape in response to the circumstances in which it grows."[57] The multiple ways Genesis 10 describes diversity suggest that attempts to categorize human diversity in only one way are reductive, and—if the Tower of Babel or the modern era are any evidence—dangerous.[58]

Genesis 1–11's vision of humanity and the people of God develops in powerful ways across the canon. While the Old Testament focuses on Israel, God's work with Israel is for the sake of the whole human family in all its beautiful and messy diversity (12:3). Furthermore, Scripture makes clear that what it means to be "Israel" is not something traceable through Ancestry.com. Canaanites like Rahab and Moabites like Ruth become a part of Israel's family tree and, indeed, become paradigmatic portraits of what it *means* to be God's people (see Matt. 1).

Scripture sometimes speaks of national and ethnic communities being subordinated to Israel as the representation of God's kingdom on earth. But over the course of the Old Testament, that theme begins to be transformed; not only will kings bring the wealth of their nations into Israel (Isa. 60:11), but God will take members of those nations "as priests and as Levites" in his kingdom (66:21). Even ancient foes like Assyria and Egypt will stand alongside Israel as a "blessing in the midst of earth," with the Lord declaring, "Blessed be Egypt my people, and Assyria the work of my hands, and Israel my heritage" (19:24–25). As all the families of the earth had creational value "in the beginning," so all the nations will participate in the glorious redemption of God at the end.

That's why Revelation alludes to Genesis 10's universal family tree at least four times to declare the good news that what God has done in Jesus is for the sake of "saints from every tribe and language and people and nation" (Rev. 5:9; see 7:9; 13:7; 14:6). When God's redeemed community gathers around God's throne, the human family is together at last, in one place, at the feet of the Lamb. They not only gather *from* all the peoples of the earth, but they bring the goodness that those peoples *created* and *became* as they lived in every corner of God's good earth with them. When they shout, "Salvation belongs to our God," each does so in their mother tongue. All creation looks forward to this coming intercultural cacophony of praise. God's kingdom does not demolish human diversity; it catches up all that is right and good and creational in such diversity and reclaims it for the Creator and King. Humanity in all of its diversity "will bring into [the city of God] the glory and the honor of the nations" (Rev. 21:26).

From this perspective, the oft-noted parallel between Babel and Pentecost becomes even more powerful. Safwat Marzouk argues Genesis 10–11 suggests that "God's vision for human communities is to move from being monocultural to becoming multicultural and multilinguistic communities."[59] God's plans thus involve the creation of intercultural communities in which "communication and interaction are possible not because one language dominates" or because differences disappear or are ignored but because members of God's family learn "to speak each other's languages."[60] As Willie Jennings notes, at Pentecost the Spirit celebrates the diversity of human communities by enabling the disciples to "speak in mother tongues of others."[61] Thus the unity of Pentecost is the opposite of the unity of Babel; a multitude of languages are preserved, and reconciliation occurs as God's people learn to share in the joy of connecting across diverse language groups. Yet Pentecost also points beyond Genesis 10 in the sense that the Spirit makes "communication possible. Those who were dispersed . . . are gathered again, not to reproduce uniformity, but to celebrate a unity in which diverse people can enrich one another by communication."[62]

This vision has massive implications for God's people today. Churches often fall into the traps identified above. Homogenous churches divide the body of Christ, while multicultural congregations can suppress differences, fail to celebrate genuine diversity, or force members of "minority" cultural, linguistic, or ethnic groups to become like "us."[63] We struggle to become intercultural communities that anticipate the final cacophony of praise. But when God's people begin to slowly and haltingly make our way toward the intercultural vision that runs from Genesis to Revelation, we discover the richness of life lived in the midst of God's incredibly diverse family, united by our love of the Lord and grateful for the surprising gifts he gives to *all* through *each*. Those who have worked the hardest to live into this bold vision bear witness to how difficult it is. But the good news is that the unity of the body of Christ amid the dizzying and delightful diversity of its members is "not an unattainable goal. It is the reality that" already "surrounds the Christian." Our job is to "*embrace it*."[64]

How to Read Old Testament Narrative and Poetry Today

The Weird and Wonderful World of Old Testament Literature

Whenever we start reading good literature (as opposed to, say, the instructions for the board game Monopoly), we are transported into another world: the world in the text. Sometimes, this world is foreign to our experience. In fantasy literature, for example, we encounter talking animals, make-believe creatures, magical places, and superhuman abilities. The best of fantasy literature causes us to suspend disbelief as we grapple with the deeper questions of human existence.

At other times, literature invites us to journey with ordinary people in extraordinary circumstances. William Golding's classic novel *Lord of the Flies* transports readers into a world of chaos and social disintegration that emerges when a group of British schoolboys are stranded on an island without adult supervision. In a similar dystopian vein, Suzanne Collins's *Hunger Games* imagines a future world where the tyrannical ruling elite force twenty-four child delegates from twelve districts to compete annually in a horrifying fight-to-the-death contest. These narratives aren't disturbing because they confront us with inconceivable worlds. Rather, they disturb us because they invite us to imagine conceivable worlds without social structures (*Lord of the Flies*) or with oppressive social structures (*Hunger Games*), and they expose and examine the darkness lurking in the hearts of humanity. In this, they summon us to consider just how *we the reader* might maintain our humanity in the most inhumane circumstances.

Wikimedia Commons / public domain

Figure 4.1. *Jacob's Family* by Giovanni Andrea de Ferrar (ca. late 1630s)

Similar to the best literature, the narrative and poetry in the Pentateuch function not to entertain or distract us from reality but to inspire us to live more fully into reality, to wrestle with the deep questions of life: What does it mean to be human? What is the nature of reality? Why are we here? What is the good life, and how do we live for the common good?

The literature we encounter in the Pentateuch can be strange and foreign to our twenty-first-century experience. Much of this is due to the historical and cultural differences between the ancient Near Eastern context of the Pentateuch (the world behind the text) and our context today (the world in front of the text). Few of us have any experience in a subsistence-based agrarian economic system (i.e., we do not grow and harvest our food on land just outside our door; we get our food in grocery stores); in a social system structured around tribes, clans, and households; in multigenerational households that may include polygamous relationships; in a religion involving animal sacrifice; or in a culture where life is precarious and violence and death are daily realities.

The Pentateuch's earliest readers would have resonated with these realities in ways that we do not. Yet, some dimensions of the Pentateuch would have struck even its earliest readers as confounding and beyond their normal experience: talking beasts (the serpent in Gen. 3 or Balaam's donkey in Num. 22), divine visitations and visions (e.g., Gen. 15; 18; 28; Exod. 3), supernatural events like the ten plagues (Exod. 7–11), the parting of the Red Sea (Exod. 14), miraculous healings (e.g., from fatal snake bites in Num. 21), fire-consuming or earth-swallowing divine judgments (Lev. 10; Num. 16), and so on. How are we to read and understand the weird and wonderful world of the Pentateuch?

We need reading strategies and methods that are appropriate to the Pentateuch's literary artistry, historical concerns, and theological intent. The Pentateuch contains many kinds of literature, and we will explore several in more detail in later chapters (e.g., law in chap. 8 and ritual texts in chap. 10). In this chapter, we focus on the broad categories of *narrative* and *poetry*.

We should keep a few things in mind as we examine characteristics and reading strategies specific to narrative and poetry. First, the primary mode of discourse in the Pentateuch is narrative. Genesis begins with the creation of the world, humanity's placement in it, and God's summons to humanity to be his partners in continuing to cultivate creation, and Deuteronomy ends with Israel poised to enter the promised land. The laws, genealogies, rituals, sermons, and poems of the Pentateuch are embedded within this grand narrative arc. This means we must attend not only to what the Pentateuch says but to how it tells its story.

As discussed in chapter 1, Old Testament narrative is grounded in real events and people, but it is not a neutral chronicle. It is crafted. The narrators are historians as well as artists and theologians, selecting, framing, and shaping the material in order to form Israel's moral imagination and identity. This is exactly what ancient readers would have expected storytellers to do, even with historical stories. While we sometimes see history writing as a neutral, unbiased presentation of the facts, they saw history writing as more akin to "exhortation."[1]

Second, if we hope to understand the true impact of the Pentateuch's literature, we must grasp the purpose of narrative and poetry. Since the Enlightenment, narrative and poetry have often been considered less "truthful" than logical propositions or empirical claims. The Bible resists this dichotomy. It insists that truth must be asserted as well as embodied, that knowledge must be both propositional and formational. Stories and poems shape us, not by arming us with abstract truths, but by placing us inside the drama of God's world and forming our instincts, desires, and sense of vocation within it.[2]

LITERARY NOTES

Ellen Davis on the True Stories in the Bible

"When we do theology, we tend to write an essay. We write a bunch of footnotes, we make a bunch of historical claims or philosophical claims, and we prove an argument. That's not the way the Bible does theology. . . . The Bible does that by telling stories that are true.

"There was actually a wonderful Roman historian [Tacitus] who said [about] the way stories tell truth: *They're not about something that happened once; they're about things that happen over and over and over again.* I think that's a rather useful way of thinking about how the Bible's stories are true."[a]

Biblical stories do more than report past events; they are carefully crafted to form identity. They invite their hearers to enter the world of the text, to wrestle with human complexity, moral ambiguity, divine purpose, and missional responsibility. In that sense, biblical narrative is prescriptive as well as descriptive. Reading slowly, imaginatively, and communally is essential, because these stories are not just about *them* but about *us*.

To read the Pentateuch faithfully requires analyzing its characters and plotlines, its rites and statutes, its imagery and parallelism, but it also means allowing these writings to analyze us, to probe our assumptions, stretch our imagination, and reorient our hearts. We will explore this in more detail in the sections that follow. The Pentateuch's stories and poems are a theological invitation to formation, crafting a people who can bear God's name for the blessing of the whole world.

Features of the Pentateuch's Narratives

There are several important literary characteristics or features of narrative in the Pentateuch. We briefly consider these in the sections below.

Setting and Theological Geography

Settings in the Pentateuch can carry theological and symbolic significance.[3] Descriptions of place and direction frequently signal more than geography; they can point to movement toward or away from God's purposes. For example, while "going down to Egypt" indicates a physical relocation, it may also hint at spiritual compromise or looming trouble.

> THEOLOGICAL ISSUES
>
> **Going Down to "Egypt"**
>
> In the biblical imagination, the geographical move of "going down to Egypt" is a theological symbol. Again and again, "Egypt" is a place of refuge that turns into bondage, provision that hardens into oppression, and power that opposes God's purposes. Abraham goes down to Egypt and emerges compromised (Gen. 12:10–20); Jacob's family finds food there but eventually becomes enslaved (Gen. 46–Exod. 1). Later kings will be warned not to trust Egypt's horses or alliances (Deut. 17:16; Isa. 31:1). "Going down to Egypt" becomes shorthand for turning to human strength instead of divine faithfulness.
>
> This symbolism makes the opening of the gospel story in Matthew a stunning reversal: Jesus is taken down to Egypt, not in rebellion, but in obedience (Matt. 2:13–15). The place of slavery becomes a sanctuary. The son is called "out of Egypt" (Matt. 2:15), just as Israel once was. This inversion does not erase Egypt's symbolic weight but fulfills it. It shows that God's redemptive purposes can pass through even the darkest geographies and return with resurrection light. "Egypt" remains a cautionary symbol, but it is also a canvas for divine grace.

Some settings operate as symbolic templates. The wilderness, for instance, is more than barren landscape. It is a place of testing, encounter, and formation. It recurs as a place of in-betweenness, where provision is sparse, dependence is learned, and God draws near (see the Living the Text section in chap. 14). Exile and sojourning similarly become theological motifs (Gen. 3:23–24; 4:12–16; 23:4; 47:9; Lev. 26:33; Deut. 28:36–37). Even everyday settings carry weight: The sheep-shearing

Figure 4.2. The wilderness

festival often cues scenes of indulgence and vulnerability (Gen. 31:19–21; 38:12–19; see also 1 Sam. 25); eastward movement typically suggests estrangement from God's blessing (Gen. 3:23–24; 4:16; 13:10–13; 29:1).

Readers who attend closely to location, movement, and spatial markers find that setting shapes a story's meaning. Biblical narrative invites us to see space and place as part of God's covenantal pedagogy: Where the story happens matters, because it is there that identity is tested, revelation is given, and God's purposes are at work.

Brevity and Sparseness

Pentateuchal narrative is compact, even terse.[4] Unlike modern novels that might dwell on the color of curtains or the precise weather on a given day, Hebrew narrative gives minimal physical description and rarely offers internal monologue. In this way, it's more like Hemingway than Dickens: lean, economical, and purposeful. Every word carries interpretive weight. Because these narratives avoid physical description, occasions when such detail is offered require close attention. For example, Esau's hairiness (Gen. 25:25; 27:11, 23), Sarah's beauty (12:11, 14), and Joseph's appearance (39:6) indicate a theological or narrative emphasis.

Because little is said, what is left unsaid often matters just as much. Gaps in the narrative (i.e., moments when motivations are unstated or logic seems to leap) are not editorial oversights. They are invitations to slow down, ask questions, and engage imaginatively. When the serpent asks Eve what God had said about the tree, she not only repeats God's instructions but adds to them by saying they weren't allowed even to touch the tree (Gen. 3:3). The narrator does not tell us what to think about this deviation; as a result, the narrative opens up space for readers to explore why Eve added that command. Or to take another example we've already considered, the narrative never explains why Cain's offering is rejected (4:3–5), a gap that invites readers to consider motive, heart, and response. When Noah curses Canaan (9:25), the narrative leaves both Ham's offense and the justice of Noah's response unresolved, inviting reflection rather than easy judgment. These stories demand that we observe carefully, ponder, and meditate.[5]

Reliable but Reticent Narrator

The biblical narrator is omniscient and trustworthy.[6] For instance, the narrator occasionally "lets us in on" the inner world of the characters, including God's inner deliberation (e.g., "Let us make humankind in our image," Gen. 1:26) or God's reasoning (e.g., behind calling Abraham in 18:17–19). These are insights that no human character witnesses, and only the narrator can grant access to the divine perspective.

However, while the narrator may know everything, they don't always reveal everything we might like them to. Biblical storytellers are reticent, deliberately reserved or restrained in what they choose to reveal. Direct commentary is rare. Moreover, unlike modern storytelling, the narrator does not often tell the reader how to feel or evaluate events. When the narrator does offer interpretive guidance, as in the ominous framing of Genesis 6:5 ("Every inclination of the thoughts of their hearts was only evil continually"), it should catch our attention.

More often, however, readers are left to infer meaning through characters' actions, narrative pacing, and dialogue. The narrator offers no overt critique of Abraham's repeated deceptions (Gen. 12; 20) or of Sarah's harsh treatment of Hagar (Gen. 16). Instead, the structure and consequences of the story, among other clues, guide the reader's judgment. This restraint invites us to enter the text as thoughtful participants, discerning what kind of life the narrative commends or critiques.

Dialogue and Behavior-Driven Characterization

The Pentateuch's primary mode of characterization is through what people say and do.[7] As Old Testament scholar Rachel Toombs notes, "Nearly every instance of understanding a person in the text comes by way of action or dialogue."[8] This means readers must actively discern, listening to speech, observing behavior, and tracing how both develop over time.

Wikimedia Commons / public domain

Figure 4.3. *Isaac Blessing Jacob* by Bartolomé Esteban Murillo (17th cent.)

Abraham's shifting tone across his encounters, Jacob's evolving interactions with God and with Esau and his sons, Rebekah's decisive scheming, Moses's oscillation between courage and fear, and Joseph's blend of generosity and manipulation all reveal complex characters. The spareness of physical description is offset by the richness of dialogue and interaction, as blessings, disputes, negotiations, and acts of deception or reconciliation carry the narrative forward and disclose God's ongoing work of relational and ethical formation. Biblical characters are not flat "heroes" or "villains" but complex people; their complexity is part of the good news for readers like us!

Patterns of Formation and Deformation

In their recording of events, the narratives of the Pentateuch portray moral and spiritual formation.[9] Across the generations a pattern recurs: Fear leads to self-preservation, which often takes the form of deception, manipulation, or abandonment. These deformation patterns repeat, from Abraham's lies about Sarah, to Jacob's grasping at blessing, to the brothers' betrayal of Joseph. But alongside these failures are slow-burning patterns of formation. Trust, courage, repentance, and reconciliation gradually emerge, often painfully and nearly always imperfectly, as God continues to work with flawed people.

The stories of the Pentateuch do not trace an upward arc of moral heroism but rather reveal the tension between covenantal calling and the gravitational pull of cultural accommodation and family dysfunction. Readers are invited to see how God forms individuals like Abraham, Jacob, or Joseph, and to see how God works across the generations to shape a people through their faithfulness and their failure. These recurring patterns and the subtle variations between them are essential to the Pentateuch's theological project: to form readers who recognize both the dangers of deformation and the hope of ongoing, patient transformation.

Narrative Pacing and Time Compression

Narrative tempo in the Pentateuch is typically rhetorical and/or theological.[10] Broad epochs can flash by in a sentence (e.g., "Then a new king arose over Egypt," Exod. 1:8 NIV), while a single year can take dozens of chapters (Exod. 19–Num. 10). Time slows down at moments of significance and covenantal importance (although Deuteronomy recalls Israel's long wilderness history, it unfolds over only a few days on the plains of Moab). This variation in pacing is intentional and signals readers to pay attention. The textual detail around events like the giving of the law at Sinai, the tabernacle's construction, or the death of key figures shows that something weighty is happening, often something central to Israel's vocation and identity. Theological gravity often shapes narrative tempo.

Repetition and Thematic Structuring

Repetition is a central meaning-making device in Hebrew narrative.[11] Repeated key words, phrases, motifs, and type-scenes form patterns of recognition and expectation. These include recurring narrative structures. For instance, many of Israel's "founding fathers and mothers" discover their spouses at wells, struggle with infertility before experiencing a divine breakthrough, and get into serious conflicts with their siblings. Repetition also includes structural refrains like "These are the generations of . . ." in Genesis.

CANONICAL CONNECTIONS

Betrothal at the Well: Subverting a Type-Scene

Biblical narratives often draw on familiar storytelling patterns known as type-scenes, recurring setups that create reader expectations. As Robert Alter has shown, one of the most recognizable is the betrothal at the well: A man travels to a foreign land, meets a woman at a well, water is drawn, hospitality is exchanged, and marriage follows. Classic examples include Isaac's servant and Rebekah (Gen. 24), Jacob and Rachel (Gen. 29), and Moses and Zipporah (Exod. 2). These scenes signal divine provision and covenantal union.[b]

According to New Testament scholar Craig Keener, when Jesus meets a Samaritan woman at a well in John 4, the Gospel writer may be evoking this Old Testament type-scene both to subtly answer the question the woman asks—Jesus *is* greater than "our ancestor Jacob" and offers something greater than the water of Jacob's well—and to play on the marital overtones of the type-scene. "The Son [pursues] this woman for the Father, perhaps as Abraham's servant pursued Rebekah for his master (Gen. 24:4)." Indeed, if John's readers were familiar with the image of "God's people as his bride," then perhaps what John shows us really is something of a "marriage," with the Samaritan woman representing the bride. Regardless, "what is most significant is that this woman becomes the first model of a worshiper in Spirit and truth that the Father sought."[c]

Figure 4.4. The woman at the well from a 1684 Arabic manuscript of the Gospels

Just as important as the repetition are the variations. When a pattern changes, it's often a clue that the author is making a point. For example, repeated deception scenes involving women and garments in Genesis echo and contrast with one another, inviting us to consider what's being revealed or critiqued (e.g., Gen. 27:1–46; 37:3–36; 38:1–30; 39:7–23). These repetitions create intertextual resonance across the Pentateuch and the rest of Scripture. The artful echo, development, and contrast also help form the theological imagination of the reader.

Plot and Narrative Movement

Biblical plots may appear straightforward, but their structures are usually multilayered. Consider the simplicity of pentateuchal narrative as it unfolds: A conflict sets the plot in motion, a response develops the plot, and a resolution brings it to completion. Yet beneath this surface lies deep theological and literary design. Plot in biblical narrative, as in any narrative, involves a sequence of events, but it also entails the arrangement of events to emphasize causality and meaning, to create tension, suspense, and development in service of a larger moral or theological purpose.[12]

Plot in the Pentateuch is often shaped by delayed resolution, narrative gaps, and retrospective reinterpretation. Details introduced late in a story, such as Joseph's emotional testing of his brothers or God's hidden hand in sending him to Egypt, can reframe earlier events and invite readers to look again. This kind of plotting trains theological attentiveness. What appears to be a narrative detour may be a key to understanding human and divine intention.

Moreover, plot in Hebrew narrative is deeply connected to character development. Actions, reactions, and choices form a dynamic interplay in which events both reveal and shape the moral and spiritual trajectory of characters. Rather than offering explicit moral commentary, the narrator often entrusts the plot with the task of forming readers' moral and theological discernment as they reflect on a character's actions.

The plot structures of the Pentateuch are as much about formation as resolution. They intend not only to recount what happened but to shape the reader's understanding of how God works—often slowly, unexpectedly, and through human weakness.

• • • • • • • •

Together, these multifaceted features of the Pentateuch's narratives help us understand how the stories are more than recordkeeping or morality tales. They are theologically shaped stories, designed to form covenant imagination. By attending to how these stories are told—their brevity, structure, character development, pacing, patterns, and plots—we become more attentive readers and hopefully more receptive hearers. These literary features serve the deeper goal of the text: to transform.

The Dynamic Relationship Between Narrative and Law

An important feature of the Pentateuch's narratives is how they intertwine with law. Far from functioning independently, narrative and law operate as a unified formation framework for a people called to live in alignment with God's purposes. Reading the Pentateuch well requires careful attention to this narrative-law dynamic.[13]

From its opening chapters, the Pentateuch presents God forming a covenant people, narrating their calling and formation while simultaneously instructing them through law. The narratives reveal covenant identity in process; the laws provide covenant instruction for communal life. If we imagine the various interpretative audiences, they all receive these narratives and laws together, hearing both the patriarchal stories and the covenant stipulations at Sinai as parts of a single formation project.

The Pentateuch's narratives frequently present complex and morally ambiguous situations that ancient readers would have evaluated through the lens of the law they were simultaneously receiving. Many Genesis narratives contain ethically questionable actions that appear to receive little or no narrative judgment: Jacob's deception of Isaac (Gen. 27), Judah's treatment of Tamar (Gen. 38), Reuben's sin with Bilhah (35:22), and repeated episodes of favoritism, deception, and exploitation. However, these stories were not told in isolation. The law provided Israel with the tools to evaluate such actions covenantally. For example, laws regulating false witness (Exod. 20:16; Deut. 19:16–21), sexual boundaries (Lev. 18; Deut. 22:13–30), family responsibilities (Deut. 25:5–10), and social justice (Lev. 25; Deut. 15) would have immediately cast these narrative episodes in a critical light. In this way, the law functions as a kind of interpretive commentary on the narratives, guiding readers to discern right from wrong within the covenant story.

LITERARY NOTES

When Narrative Actions Collide with the Law

Many troubling actions in Genesis receive little explicit narrative comment. However, Israel's earliest hearers would have immediately recognized these behaviors as violations of the covenantal ethic revealed in the law:

- Jacob deceives Isaac (Gen. 27), violating laws against false witness and deception (Exod. 20:16; Lev. 19:11–12).
- Judah wrongs Tamar (Gen. 38) by withholding Levirate responsibility; his actions are confronted by laws on family duty and justice for widows (Deut. 25:5–10).
- Reuben sleeps with Bilhah (Gen. 35:22), violating laws on sexual boundaries within the household (Lev. 18:8; Deut. 22:30).
- Episodes of favoritism and exploitation are challenged by commands for justice, equity, and protection of the vulnerable (Lev. 25; Deut. 15).

At its heart, this dynamic between narrative and law reflects God's covenantal pedagogy. God is forming a people, not recounting history or issuing abstract regulations. The patriarchal narratives show God calling, testing, disciplining, and shaping covenant partners who often stumble, but whom God patiently forms. The laws provide the concrete ethical and communal shape of covenant life toward which that formation is aimed. Narrative and law together reveal the type of people God is forming: a people who reflect his righteousness (*tsedaqah*) and holiness (*qodesh*) in every dimension of life.[14]

Thus, to read pentateuchal narrative rightly means going beyond what happens in a particular story to discern how God forms covenant identity through both story and instruction. The Pentateuch trains both ancient and contemporary people to live as faithful covenant partners who embody God's character and mission in the world.

Reading Hagar Well

Read Genesis 16 and 21 and use Hagar's story as a model for reading biblical narrative attentively.

- *Notice what happens to Hagar.* Who has power over her? How is that power used?
- *Listen for Hagar's voice.* What does she say (or not say), and how does that shape the story?
- *Attend to God's response.* What does God see, hear, name, or promise? Why does it matter that Hagar is the first person in Scripture to name God?
- *Read her story through the lens of Torah.* How do later laws about the sojourner, the vulnerable, and justice cast Abram and Sarai's treatment of Hagar in a different light (see, e.g., Exod. 22:21; 23:9; Lev. 19:33–34; Deut. 10:18–19; 23:15–16)?
- *Ask the formation question.* What does this story reveal about how we treat others when we have power and how God cares for us when we are vulnerable?

The Power of Poetry in Israel's Founding Story

Although the Pentateuch is primarily narrative, poetry appears at carefully chosen moments and functions as an essential instrument in Israel's formation. This poetry calls God's people to slow down, to feel as well as to think, and to have their imaginations shaped for life lived before the face of God and oriented toward the world.[15]

The Role of Poetry in Covenant Formation

From the very beginning, Israel was trained to inhabit its story. As Moses stands before the people on the plains of Moab in Deuteronomy, he calls the people to recall God's past acts so that those acts can shape Israel as a covenant people (Deut. 31:19–22; 32:1–43). Story, ritual, and song together are the means by which God forms his people into covenantal missional identity and vocation.[16] Poetry in particular carries unique power to sustain Israel's memory and covenant imagination across generations.

Poetry works differently than narrative, law, or other kinds of literature. While narrative recounts God's mighty acts and law defines covenant responsibilities, poetry enters the imagination, the affections, and the senses. It is one of God's chosen tools for shaping how his people feel, hope, fear, and desire. It forms covenant partners as those who not only know about God but whose hearts and imaginations are rightly ordered before him.

Figure 4.5. Miriam and the Song of the Sea

Like all poetry, the Pentateuch's poetry intends to evoke, invite, and unsettle. The information relayed by Israel's songs was not primarily for determining doctrine but for forming a community whose covenant life involved joy, lament, gratitude, repentance, and hope. A song like the Song of the Sea in Exodus 15 adds little to the "facts" of the story but rather retells the story in a compressed, poetic form filled with rich imagery and evocative language. Poetry trains the people to pray, to weep, to trust, and to hope as covenant partners shaped by God's character.

Where Poetry Appears in the Pentateuch

Poetry appears at significant hinge points throughout the Pentateuch. These poems often accompany covenantal transitions, moments of blessing, or responses to God's saving acts. The most prominent examples include Jacob's poetic blessings on his sons, which function as both benediction and prophetic forecast (Gen. 49); the Song of the Sea, celebrating God's deliverance and kingship after the Red Sea crossing (Exod. 15); Balaam's oracles, which paradoxically bless Israel despite Balak's curses (Num. 23–24); and the Song of Moses and the Blessing of Moses, which together serve as a covenantal capstone and final exhortation (Deut. 32–33).

These poetic interludes do not interrupt the Pentateuch's narrative. They intensify and reinforce it, providing an evocative lens for interpreting and responding to the surrounding stories. They offer a kind of covenantal

LITERARY NOTES

Poetry in the Pentateuch

While the Pentateuch is primarily narrative, poetry appears at crucial moments to intensify key theological themes. These poetic sections often serve as interpretive commentary within the larger covenantal story.

Location	Description
Gen. 1:27	Creation of humanity (brief poetic form)
Gen. 2:23	The man's exclamation upon meeting the woman
Gen. 4:23–24	Lamech's song of vengeance
Gen. 9:25–27	Noah's oracle about his sons
Gen. 27:27–29, 39–40	Isaac's blessings to Jacob and Esau
Gen. 49	Jacob's poetic blessings over his sons
Exod. 15:1–18	Song of the Sea (Moses and Miriam)
Exod. 15:21	Miriam's refrain
Num. 6:24–26	Priestly blessing
Num. 21:17–18	Song of the Well
Num. 21:27–30	Ballad of victory over Heshbon
Num. 23–24	Balaam's oracles
Deut. 32	Song of Moses
Deut. 33	Blessing of Moses

Poetic language is not confined to discrete poems like the ones in this list; it often appears within prose as a heightened mode of speech (e.g., Gen. 12:2–3; 24:60; 25:23; Num. 21:14–15; Deut. 7:10; 27:15–26; 28:3–6, 16–19). Other passages (e.g., Gen. 1:1–2:4 or Deut. 26:5–10) occupy the space between prose and poetry, reminding readers that the Pentateuch frequently communicates theological truth through heightened and image-rich language even in prose.

liturgy, calling Israel to inhabit the story at the level of the heart and imagination.

The Form and Features of Hebrew Poetry

While biblical poetry shares some general features with poetry across cultures, it has distinctive characteristics rooted in its ancient Hebrew setting.[17] Most scholars think the most notable structural feature of biblical poetry is *parallelism*: paired lines placed in close proximity that relate to one another in meaning and structure.

Recognizing parallelism trains readers to slow down and read for pattern, nuance, and flow of thought. It invites attention to how meaning is shaped between lines, not just within them. When readers attend to how poetic lines relate to one another, they become more alert to what the text emphasizes theologically, how it shapes emotion, and where it invites moral reflection. Understanding parallelism helps readers engage more reflectively, discerning the artistry of the text and the depth of what it reveals about God, humanity, and the world.

Hebrew poetry, like all poetry, is characterized by *brevity and economy of expression*. Articles, conjunctions, and even verbs are often omitted. This terseness requires readers to slow down, attend carefully to each word and image, and engage deeply with the text, even more so than with biblical narrative, which is also marked by brevity.

Poetry uses rich *figurative language*, requiring the imagination. Narrative can also use such language, but it is characteristic of poetry. Examples of figurative language include metaphor ("Judah is a lion's cub. . . . He lies down and crouches like a lion," Gen. 49:9 CEB), personification ("Heaven! Pay attention and I will speak; Earth! Listen to the words of my mouth," Deut. 32:1 CEB), and hyperbole ("Who can count the dust of Jacob; or number even a fourth of Israel?," Num. 23:10 NIV). These devices reveal truth that propositional language alone cannot.

Poems in the Pentateuch often use *structural devices and patterns* such as inclusios and chiasms to reinforce meaning and aid memorization. An inclusio frames a passage by repeating similar language or ideas at the beginning and end. Exodus 15:1–18, for instance, begins and ends by praising Yahweh as warrior and deliverer, highlighting his strength. A chiasm arranges ideas in a mirrored, inverted pattern (A-B-C-B′-A′) to highlight a central theme. Again, the Song of the Sea provides an example of this (Exod. 15):

A Praise for YHWH's triumph over the enemy (vv. 1–6)
  B YHWH's power and the destruction of Egypt (vv. 7–10)
    C YHWH's unique power and redeeming love (vv. 11–13)
  B′ Fear among the nations and Canaanites (vv. 14–16)
A′ YHWH will reign forever (vv. 17–18)

This structure centers on God's identity (v. 11: "Who is like you, O Lord?") and covenantal love, framing divine power in relational terms.

These literary structures communicate theological truths, embedding them deeply in the communal memory and imagination through symmetry, repetition, and rhythm.

The Formational Power of Poetry: Recovering Covenant Imagination

Today the church still needs this poetic formation, maybe now more than ever. In a

LITERARY NOTES

Three Basic Kinds of Parallelism?

Older discussions of Hebrew poetry often identified three main patterns of parallelism. These labels are not exhaustive, but they are still useful starting points:

Synonymous parallelism

Adah and Zillah, hear my voice;
  you wives of Lamech, listen to what I say (Gen. 4:23).

Antithetical parallelism

I will bless those who bless you,
  and the one who curses you I will curse (Gen. 12:3).

Synthetic (or developmental) parallelism

The scepter shall not depart from Judah,
  nor the ruler's staff from between his feet (Gen. 49:10).

As James Kugel and others note, many lines fit more than one category. Nonetheless, paying attention to how line B relates to line A is a key step in reading biblical poetry well.

More recently, however, scholars such as James Kugel and Adele Berlin have challenged the adequacy of these three categories.[d] Kugel famously proposed that biblical poetry tends to follow a more flexible pattern: "A, and what's more B." In this view, the second line does not simply repeat or oppose the first but may deepen, reframe, or advance it. Rather than seeing rigid types, it is better to view biblical parallelism as a dynamic literary device that invites reflection and enriches meaning through echo, variation, and surprise.

THEOLOGICAL ISSUES

Why the Church Still Needs Poetry

Biblical poetry reaches parts of us that propositions alone cannot touch. As James K. A. Smith and others note,[e] our deepest discipleship challenges are often imaginative, not informational—we may know what is true yet struggle to see or desire the world as Scripture describes it. Poetry works at that deeper register. It trains us to hope rightly, grieve truthfully, rejoice deeply, and name our longings before God. Songs like those in Exodus 15, Genesis 49, or Deuteronomy 32 immerse us in alternative worlds where God reigns, the vulnerable are remembered, and justice and mercy meet. Recovering biblical poetry, whether sung, prayed, or meditated upon, helps heal the church's imagination, and it anchors us in the story God is telling.

cultural moment where discipleship is often reduced to information transfer, biblical poetry reawakens the imagination. It helps God's people see the world truthfully and feel the weight of God's character—his justice, mercy, holiness, and covenant love. Poetry reminds us that faithfulness is about both right thinking and rightly ordered desire.

Praying a Pentateuchal Poem

Choose a short poem or selection from a poem (e.g., Exod. 15:1–6; Num. 6:24–26). Read it aloud slowly. Notice repeated words, images, and how lines relate. Rewrite one verse as a prayer for your community. Ask yourself, If I prayed this poem regularly, how might it reshape my view of God, myself, and the world?

Example: The Trickster Gets Tricked—the Jacob Cycle and Narrative, Poetry, and Moral Formation

The story of Jacob is among the most theologically rich and morally complex narratives in the Pentateuch. Jacob, unlike some idealized biblical figures, is cunning, self-interested, and deceptive. Yet he is also chosen. His story vividly illustrates the narrative strategies discussed in this chapter: ambiguity in characterization, repetition and reversal, embedded poetry, and theological formation through storytelling.

Tension is part of Jacob's story even before he is born. His mother Rebekah, long barren, miraculously conceives twins. But the pregnancy is painful and tumultuous, prompting her to cry out to God. The divine response comes in poetic form:

> Two nations are in your womb,
>   and two peoples from within you shall be divided;
> the one shall be stronger than the other,
>   the older shall serve the younger. (Gen. 25:23 ESV)

Figure 4.6. Scenes from the life of Jacob

Rijksmuseum / Donation from Antiquarian Bookshop Martinus Nijhoff / CC0

This brief oracle sets the interpretive frame for the Jacob cycle. It is stylized and rhythmic, likely a poetic or proverbial form, and it establishes key themes of reversal, struggle, and divine election. The shift into poetry signals the gravity and enduring significance of the moment, marking God's speech as a weighty, declarative pronouncement intended to be pondered, remembered, and repeated. The poetry invites the reader to slow down, reflect, and consider how the divine word will shape the story. We now expect conflict and the subversion of birth order in what follows.

Jacob is born grasping his brother Esau's heel, a detail that not only explains his name ("heel-grabber") but suggests that striving and manipulation will define him. The next several chapters reinforce this idea: Jacob exploits Esau's physical hunger to secure the birthright (Gen. 25:29–34), and with his mother's help, he steals the firstborn blessing by deceiving his blind father (Gen. 27). These stories are rich with dramatic irony, sensory imagery (touch, smell, taste), and multiple opportunities for confession that Jacob resists. Despite God's pronouncement, the narrative does not give easy moral validation for Jacob's deception. Instead, it invites critique. Why else would the storyteller emphasize Jacob's repeated lies, Isaac's suspicion, and Esau's anguished cry: "Bless me too, my father!" (27:34 NET)?

Jacob's story also encourages reflection in light of later Torah instructions. Jacob dishonors his father through deliberate deception, a clear violation of the principle later encoded in the Ten Commandments: "Honor your father and your mother" (Exod. 20:12). The Torah also contains laws against placing stumbling blocks before the blind or exploiting them in other ways (Lev. 19:14; Deut. 27:18), and it forbids bearing false witness or dealing falsely with one another (Exod. 20:16; Lev. 19:11). These echoes further underscore the moral weight of Jacob's actions, and they reinforce the ethical world of the Torah by dramatization instead of direct instruction.

The story takes a dramatic turn when Jacob himself, fleeing Esau's wrath, becomes the victim of deception. In Haran, he meets his match in his uncle Laban, who tricks him into marrying his older daughter, Leah, instead of the younger, Rachel (Gen. 28:15–30). The parallels to Jacob's earlier deceit are unmistakable: Just as Jacob took advantage of his father's impaired sight, Laban manipulates Jacob's inability to see clearly, perhaps due to veiling, darkness, or cultural custom. Both deceptions hinge on substituted identities, reversed expectations regarding birth order, and exploitation of vulnerability. The symmetry is also moral: The trickster is tricked. Moreover, later in Jacob's life, the patterns repeat *again*. His own sons deceive him using a garment and a slaughtered goat (Gen. 37:31–33), the very things Jacob once used to deceive Isaac. These thematic repetitions reinforce that the means Jacob used to secure blessing become the means of his own undoing. Narrative repetition becomes theological instruction.

What does all this teach us? By immersing us in the complexity of human motives, divine purpose, and relational fracture, the story of Jacob cultivates discernment. It also prompts us to reflect on God's mysterious election: God's purposes do not depend on human virtue, but neither are human actions without consequence. By attending to the literary features of the text—poetic speech, ambiguous characterization, symbolic repetition—we become better interpreters and, more importantly, wiser and better-formed readers of Scripture.

Conclusion: Reading Pentateuchal Narrative and Poetry Today

To read pentateuchal narrative and poetry well means attending carefully to their craft and opening ourselves to their power. These texts invite us to inhabit our own stories with covenantal imagination, to see ourselves not as autonomous individuals but as participants in a larger redemptive story. They remind us that God is still at work forming a people through story and song, shaping lives marked by trust, justice, mercy, and hope for the sake of the world.

Genesis 12:1–25:11

Discipleship into God's Way of Righteousness and Holiness

Orientation

The great Jewish rabbi and philosopher Abraham Joshua Heschel once said humanity is "called to responsible living and to be a partner of God in the redemption of the world."[1] The truth expressed here is foundational to biblical faith and finds its earliest roots in Genesis. As we begin our journey into Genesis 12–50, two aspects of Heschel's conception of humankind are worth highlighting: (1) ethics and (2) partnership.

Key to Genesis 12–50 are the distinctive *ethics* ("responsible living") that God's people are called to live out, and their *partnership* (covenant) with God for the "redemption of the world." These thirty-eight chapters include a range of material (mostly narrative but also genealogies and other types of literature) and unfold in three major sections that trace God's dealings with Abraham, Isaac, Jacob, and Joseph: Abraham (12:1–25:11), Jacob (including Isaac; 25:19–36:43), and Joseph (37:1–50:26). These sections illustrate how these individuals are formed in relationship with God (partnership) and how this relationship yields a distinctive way of life (ethic) for the sake of the world. In other words, God has a deliberate mission (to restore the world), and he binds himself to people and forms those people to be coconspirators in that mission of universal blessing. This is what God is doing in Genesis 12–50, and it is what he continues to do today. This is one reason these chapters deserve our attention.

While this orientation section introduces the whole of Genesis 12–50, the rest of the chapter centers on Abraham's story (12:1–25:11). The next chapter takes up the narratives of Isaac, Jacob, and Joseph (25:12–50:26).

The Literary Design of Genesis 12–50

Attentive readers can almost feel the transition from Genesis 1–11 to Genesis 12–50. The universal, mysterious, and fantastic quality of the stories in the primeval history gives way to narratives that are particular, deeply familial, and in many ways very ordinary. The narrative shifts its focus from all humanity or individuals as representatives of all humanity to a focus on specific people. However, this shift does not create two separate and distinct compositions; the sections are intricately interconnected, and neither can be properly understood without the other.

Fans of major movie franchises such as the Harry Potter films or the Marvel series may notice how the soundtrack returns again and again to familiar musical themes. These themes recur across different scenes and films, yet they are often subtly reworked through changes in melody, rhythm, harmony, or even key. The music remains recognizable, but its tone and emotional weight change as the story unfolds. Genesis is like that. Themes and motifs that chapters 1–11 introduce return in modified form again and again in chapters 12–50. To use another analogy, the whole of Genesis is like an intricately woven tapestry; threads that weave in and out of the later narratives trace back to the origin stories of Genesis 1–11. These threads are woven deeply into the fabric of Genesis as a whole, and they even weave beyond Genesis into the tapestry of the Pentateuch and the whole of Scripture.

Readers should attend carefully to several significant themes and motifs from Genesis 1–11 that carry into Genesis 12–50:

Covenant (*berit*). The special relationship that God forged with Noah, his family, and all creation continues, as God enters into relationship with Abraham, Isaac, Jacob, and Jacob's twelve sons.

Blessing (*barakh*). The universal blessing established at creation and threatened by human rebellion will now be channeled through God's special relationship with chosen individuals and families.

The human vocation. The divine plan for men and women bearing God's image to serve as corulers of God's good world is threatened by humanity's self-serving schemes, yet God continues to establish and defend the divine plan in his work with Abraham's family.

Human resistance. Humanity's rebellious attempt to "make a name" for themselves, rather than to receive the name God has determined to give to / make for them, continues in the story of Abraham and his descendants.

The persistence of God's presence. God's commitment to make his home in the world is reestablished in God's covenant to be with Abraham and his offspring.

However, Genesis 12–50 is not just about Abraham, Isaac, Jacob, and Joseph. Embedded in these narratives are accounts of others, both "insiders" and "outsiders" (e.g., Sarah, Melchizedek, Hagar, Laban, Rachel, Leah, Dinah, Judah, Tamar, and Potiphar and his wife). Genesis 12–50 gives space and therefore dignity to Ishmael and his line (25:12–18) and to Esau and his line (36:1–43). The inclusion of Ishmael, Esau, Lot, and various foreign kings and peoples in Genesis is a helpful reminder that, although they are not the immediate recipients of God's covenant partnership, they and the nations they represent are the ultimate goal of God's covenant with Abraham and his descendants. Thus, Genesis 12–50 represents not only the origin of God's people but also the origin of God's international and global plan of restoration that begins with Israel (i.e., Abraham and his descendants) but encompasses all families/nations of the earth (12:3; 18:18; 22:18; 26:4; 28:14).

The Timely Message of Genesis 12–50

Genesis 12 and the chapters that follow provide the answer to the mess that results from human rebellion (Gen. 3–11). The intention of God's promises to Abraham and his descendants "was to get the human project back on track after the disasters of the fall, the flood and the idolatrous Tower."[2] Genesis 12–50 suggests a way counter to the way of rebellion—self-determination, self-preservation, and other-destroying—that permeates Genesis 3–11. Indeed, such rebellion

CANONICAL CONNECTIONS

Patriarchs as Previews of Israel's History

Although the story of each patriarch in Genesis is unique, several recurring patterns bind their narratives together and anticipate Israel's later history.[a] For example, they

- must leave their homeland (12:1; 26:1–3; 28:10; 37:28);
- have strained relationships with their brothers/kin (13:7; 21:8–10; 27:41; 37:4);
- go down to or toward Egypt (12:10; 26:1–2; 37:28; 46:1–7);
- bear sons of whom the younger is favored (17:18–19; 25:23; 27:27–29; 37:3–4; 48:14–20; 49:8–12, 22–26);
- receive promises of children, land, and divine partnership (e.g., 12:1–3; 26:2–5; 28:13–15; 35:9–12); and
- are recognized by foreigners as recipients of divine blessing (21:21–22; 26:28–29; 30:27; 41:39–40).

Such connections are part of the literary design of Genesis 12–50 and deserve close attention. Comparison of this kind can also reveal intriguing differences.

Wikimedia Commons / public domain

Figure 5.1. *Hagar and Ishmael* by Carlo Maratti

LITERARY NOTES

The Structure of Genesis 12–50

Chapter 2 above, on Genesis 1–3, discussed the Hebrew word *toledot* ("These are the generations/accounts of . . ."). The word occurs frequently throughout Genesis 12–50, and if the placement of the *toledot* refrain is a clue to the structure of Genesis, then the following structure for Genesis 12–50 emerges:

The account of Abraham (11:27–25:11)
The account/genealogy of Ishmael (25:12–18)
The account of Isaac and Jacob (25:19–35:29)
The account/genealogy of Esau (36:1–37:1)
The account of Joseph and his brothers (37:2–50:26)

RECEPTION HISTORY

Adam and Abraham

Rabbi Levi said that Abraham "was worthy of being created before Adam, but the Holy One, blessed be he, reasoned: 'He may sin and there will be none to set him right. Hence I will create Adam first so that if he sins Abraham may come and set things right.'"[b]

shows up again and again in Genesis 12–50, as well. Nevertheless, this portion of Genesis provides a different way.

Scholar Leon Kass identifies this new way: "In a word, the new human way—the way of the Children of Israel, launched as a light unto the nations—is to be built on two related principles: the practice of *righteousness* in relations toward others, informed by the pursuit of *holiness* in relation to the divine. Both are grounded not in human reason or freedom but in the peculiarly human experience of awe and reverence, elicited by the mysteries of the world's order and power and especially by the voice of commanding moral authority."[3]

Righteousness (which includes justice) and holiness, *tsedaqah* and *qodesh*, are the new human way of being in the world. Righteousness/justice (*tsedaqah*) orients humans to a right relationship with other humans and the world, while holiness (*qodesh*) orients them to a right relationship with God. This new way is the way of comprehensive, global, and universal blessing. It is a way set against the miserable and self-serving way demonstrated in Genesis 3–11.

Careful readers should observe how the characters of Genesis 12–50 get discipled into the way of *tsedaqah* and *qodesh*. Yet Genesis 12–50 merely inaugurates this new way; its fulfillment lies beyond the book. God's righteous, just, and holy way is the bedrock of biblical faith, undergirding the Ten Commandments and identified by Jesus in the two great commandments that summarize all the Law and the Prophets (i.e.,

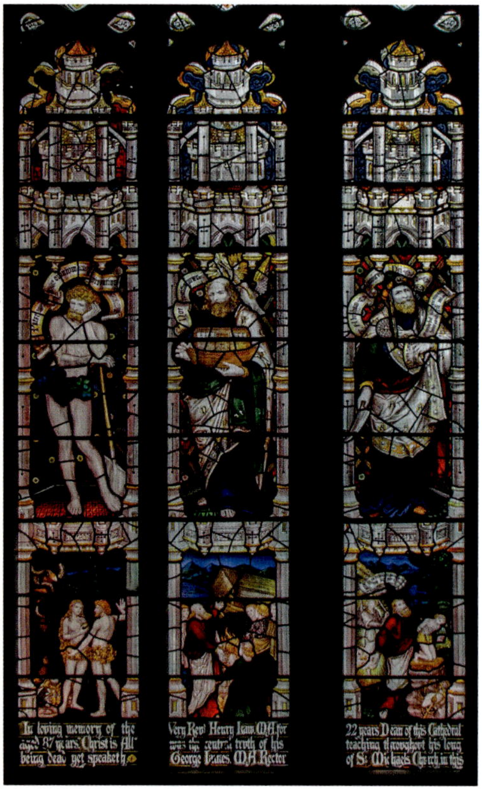

Figure 5.2. From Adam to Abraham. *God Our Saviour* by Kempe (1886) in the Gloucester Cathedral.

all of Scripture): (1) Love God and (2) love your neighbor (Matt. 22:36–40; Mark 12:28–31; Luke 10:25–27). Genesis, the book of "beginnings," offers a beginning of discipleship in the righteous and holy way of God.

This is easy to miss, in part because we misunderstand the nature of Genesis. We sometimes forget that the book was written long after the events it narrates, and the interests of the author are not merely historical. In narrating stories in which the patriarchs are discipled into this new way, the author makes a very contemporary claim for his audience: This new way was not just for the patriarchs and their communities. Genesis was "written for *our instruction*" (Rom. 15:4); it introduces us to *the* human way of existence. Genesis thus invites us to consider several questions:

- What does following the way of *tsedaqah* (righteousness/justice) and *qodesh* (holiness) look like in our context?
- How can we embody God's righteous, just, and holy way in our time and places?
- In what ways has our culture effectively discipled God's people in the twenty-first century into the way of fear, self-preservation, and name-making?
- What can we learn from the patriarchs and the challenges they faced in their contexts as we seek to follow this new way in ours?
- How does the good news of the biblical story disciple believers today in the way of Yahweh, which is the way of Jesus?

We will explore and reflect on these vital questions along the way and in the final section of this chapter. For now, let's observe how Yahweh partners with the first major character in Genesis 12–50 and disciples him into the way of *tsedaqah* and *qodesh*.

Exploration

READ GENESIS 12–25

Read the text straight through if you can. Note the various divine encounters and their settings, tones, and outcomes. Ask, What kind of person is Abraham becoming, and what kind of God is revealed?

The account of Abraham is the longest narrative in Genesis. At first glance, the various stories do not appear to make a coherent whole, but it is important to remember as we work through these narratives that God is setting out on a long path of restoration, one that begins with God's partnership with and formation of Abraham. Through Abraham and his descendants God works against the forces and effects of sin and rebellion in the world. That sin and rebellion, however, is not just out there in the world but also within Abraham himself and within his family. How will God work with Abraham, helping him on the new way of *tsedaqah* (righteousness) and *qodesh* (holiness) for the blessing of all families/nations?

The key to understanding the entirety of Abraham's story can be found in the seven encounters between God and Abraham, which have a chiastic arrangement:[4]

1. God asks Abraham to let go of country, kin, and father (12:1–3).
   2. God encourages Abraham to take initiative (12:7–8).
      3. God asks Abraham to walk (look at and stake out) a land he will never own (13:14–17).
         4. God asks Abraham to not be afraid; Abraham responds (15:1–21).
      5. God invites Abraham to walk with him in mutuality (17:1–22).
   6. Abraham takes initiative, hosting God, and God invites Abraham to talk with him (18:1–33).
7. God asks Abraham to let go of what is most precious, and the Abraham-God partnership is complete (22:1–18).

In these encounters, God makes promises to Abraham but also presents Abraham with increasingly difficult and costly challenges. As Abraham responds, his relationship and genuine partnership with God become progressively deeper and more meaningful.

First Divine Encounter (Gen. 12:1–3)

In the first divine encounter between Abram and God, God asks the patriarch to let go of his country, kin, and father. In this, he was to leave behind everything that would provide safety, security, and prosperity. In Abram's ancient Near Eastern culture, land, kin, and a father's house provide food, commodities for commerce, a social structure and safety net for relationships and stability, and an economic network for trade. God asks Abram to give this up. God's way seems counter to the way that seems wise to the world, but this is the pattern of the kingdom. Jesus will make similar demands on his followers: Leave your fishing nets and tax collecting, your family and fields, your self-reliant ways . . . and come follow me. Following God is costly.

Figure 5.3. *Abraham Leaves Haran* by Francesco Bassano il Giovane (1578)

However, even as Yahweh asks Abram to let go, he makes promises to Abram and his descendants. First, God will provide a land to replace the one Abram is leaving, though the location of this new home remains a mystery. Abram will have to step out in faith. Second, Yahweh promises to make him into a great nation and give him a great name. What kind of name would God give Abram—a descendant of Noah's son Shem, whose name literally means "name" and whose descendants built the Tower of Babel to "make a name" for themselves? Moreover, Abram is old and childless, and his postmenopausal wife is barren. How could he be the father of a great nation when he cannot even father a single child? "Let go of perceptions, Abram, and in faith take hold of my promises," urges Yahweh. Third, God promises to replace Abram's network of social/familial relationships with a lasting nexus of relationships of mutual blessing. The partners in this network of

LITERARY NOTES

Abram and Abraham: How Name Changes Signal Identity and Vocation

Readers may notice that Genesis refers to the patriarch first as Abram (Gen. 12–16) and only later as Abraham (Gen. 17). In Genesis 17:5 God renames him Abraham: "No longer shall your name be Abram, but your name shall be Abraham; for I have made you the father of a multitude of nations" (RSV). Shortly thereafter Sarai is renamed Sarah (17:15), and the covenant promise is explicitly bound to her as well (17:16). Name changes in the Pentateuch signal more than a new label; they mark a deepened covenant identity. Abram and Sarai become Abraham and Sarah as God binds his promise of worldwide blessing to this couple and their descendants.

Name changes often signal turning points in God's mission. Jacob becomes Israel (Gen. 32:28), and Hoshea is renamed Joshua (Num. 13:16). In each case, the new name reflects a renewed vocation within God's unfolding mission.

relationships are God, Abram, and everyone else—those who bless and curse Abram, whether family or foreigner.

All these promises are to serve a purpose, and Yahweh tells Abram what that is. We could paraphrase Genesis 12:1–3, "Let go of your grasp on human security and prosperity and I will (1) give you a land of your own, (2) make you into a numerous and prosperous nation, and (3) establish in you a relationship of mutual blessing. . . . And I'm doing this all *so that all families of the earth will be blessed*."

RECEPTION HISTORY

Biblical Israel and Contemporary Politics

God makes enormous promises to Abraham and his descendants. One challenging issue for reading the Old Testament *as Christian Scripture* is understanding the relationship between

- Israel in the Old Testament,
- the primarily Jewish Jesus movement of the New Testament period, and
- post–New Testament Judaism and the primarily gentile post–New Testament church.

On the one hand, the church has a long, devastating history of antisemitic hatred and violence toward Jews. This has often been fueled by what is sometimes called supersessionism. In some versions, this theological perspective claims that the "church" "replaced" or "superseded" the Jews. Tragically, such theology directly contributed to the horrors of the Holocaust. Not only does antisemitism violate Jesus's command to love one's neighbors; it ignores Romans 9–11, which speaks of enormous irrevocable promises to the "Israelites," God's people "according to the flesh" (9:3–4 ESV), and anticipates a "grafting in again" of members of Israel who have been cut off through their rejection of Jesus (11:17–36). For the New Testament, the church is not a gentile phenomenon that replaces the children of Abraham. Instead, "gentile believers were incorporated into biblical Israel, forming a new entity—the church—which stands in continuation with biblical Israel. The link between the two, the cornerstone, is Jesus Christ the Jewish Messiah."[c] Paul himself offers stern warnings to gentiles who exhibit pride toward Jewish people who have not accepted Jesus (11:17–24).

On the other hand, other Christians read Old Testament prophetic promises as predicting the establishment of the modern state of Israel. Modern-day Middle Eastern politics become signs of the eschaton, and part of the church's job becomes supporting this modern secular state of Israel. This is also misguided. Note the following biblical perspectives:

- Many of the prophetic promises of restoration were fulfilled in Old Testament Israel's return from exile under the Persians.
- The entirety of Old Testament prophecy is fulfilled in and through Jesus, and the New Testament draws on Old Testament prophecy to describe not the reestablishment of a Jewish state but the establishment of the new heavens and the new earth at Christ's return.
- There is only one group that the New Testament ever describes with the "holy nation" language the Old Testament uses for ancient Israel. That group is the church (1 Pet. 2:9–10). Again, this is not because the gentile church replaces Israel; it is because the church gathers both Jews and gentiles into the body of Jesus, who himself fulfills Israel's vocation.
- The idea that the establishment of a modern, secular Jewish state plays a unique theological role in salvation history ignores that Paul directly identifies "those who believe" in Jesus as the "children of Abraham" (Gal. 3:6–9 CEB).

As with supersessionism, reading Old Testament prophetic promises as predicting the establishment of the modern state of Israel has yielded bitter fruit. Because such Christians believe God is "on modern-day Israel's side," they have sometimes downplayed or ignored grievous injustice toward Palestinians, including Palestinian Christians. As Bob Dylan sings, "You don't count the dead when God's on your side."[d]

As a result, some Christians ignored or even supported the killing of tens of thousands of Palestinian civilians in Gaza during Israel's response to the October 7, 2023, terrorist attacks, for instance, and have actively supported Israeli settlers who have violently seized Palestinian land in the West Bank.

None of this is to say that contemporary conflicts in the Middle East have simple, straightforward solutions. But Christians must never claim God's unconditional support for any modern nation. Reading the Pentateuch *as Christian Scripture* requires us to reject both antisemitic interpretations and interpretations that equate the contemporary Israeli nation with God's prophetic promises to God's people. Both interpretations misunderstand the biblical text and have led Christians away from the love and justice God calls his people to extend to all their neighbors, and especially those who are suffering violence and injustice.

Many unanswered questions remain: Why did God single out Abram? How will God accomplish these things? How will this special relationship of blessing facilitate the divine blessing of all nations/families? What is clear is that God's restoration plan is in place. God mentions *blessing* five times in these short verses. This fivefold blessing provides an answer to the five instances of "curses" of Genesis 3–11.

Through this special relationship, Yahweh will partner with Abram and his descendants to make them a channel of blessing to all people and the whole of creation. A new way of being in the world has opened up, a way of life and blessing. This way is different than the death-dealing way of Cain, the violence of preflood humanity, and the arrogant resistance to God's plan at Babel, whereby individuals strive to determine their own name and greatness.

This first divine encounter begins with God asking Abram to go, and it ends with Abram obeying the call, without speaking a word in the text (Gen. 12:4). Abram, his wife, and his nephew pack up and travel to the land of Canaan, arriving at Shechem in the heart of Canaan (12:6).[5] The narrator then provides what seems to be an obvious and unnecessary piece of information: "At that time the Canaanites were in the land" (12:6). Of course, Canaanites are living in the land of Canaan! But this note signals a complication in Yahweh's promise to give Abram a land of his own. How will Abram possess this land when there are already people possessing it? He had been faithful in leaving country, kin, and father, but for what? A land already occupied? This cues Abram's second divine encounter.

LITERARY NOTES

Five Curses and Five Blessings

Genesis 3–11 traces the spread of human rebellion and its consequences. Within these chapters, the Hebrew root for "curse" appears five times:

- The serpent is cursed (3:14).
- The ground is cursed because of Adam (3:17).
- Cain is cursed from the ground (4:11).
- The ground is described again as cursed (5:29).
- Canaan is cursed (9:25).

The language of curse reverberates through Genesis 3–11, marking the deepening fracture between God, humanity, and the land. When God calls Abram in Genesis 12:1–3, the Hebrew root for "bless" appears five times in just two verses:

- "I will ***bless*** you" (12:2).
- "You will be a ***blessing***" (12:2).
- "I will ***bless*** those who ***bless*** you" (12:3).
- "In you all the families of the earth shall be ***blessed***" (12:3).

The symmetry is deliberate. The fivefold pattern of curse in Genesis 3–11 is met by a fivefold declaration of blessing in Genesis 12. Through Abraham, God announces his intention to answer curse with blessing and to restore what has been broken.

Second Divine Encounter (Gen. 12:7–8)

In a second divine encounter, Yahweh encourages Abram to take initiative. In Genesis 12:7–8 God "appeared" to the patriarch, though the narrator does not say what kind of appearance this is. Regardless, God's revelation is expanding in this developing partnership, and he gets straight to the point (only four words in Hebrew): "To your offspring I will give this

Figure 5.4. *Pharaoh Gives Sarah Back to Abraham* by Isaac Isaacsz (1640)

land" (12:7). God establishes here the promise of land, but with the caveat that Abram's descendant will receive it, not Abram. Still without speaking in the text, Abram responds by building an altar to Yahweh, "who had appeared to him."

Abram travels again and finds himself between two places: "House-of-God" (Bethel) and "Heap-of-Ruins" (Ai).[6] Is it possible that these two places represent for Abram a choice between two ways? On one side is a place of divine presence, which is the destination of the way of righteousness and holiness. On the other side is ruin and desolation, the worldly way of fear, self-preservation, and name-making, the way that leads to death and misery. In this place between two alternatives, Abram does two things: He builds a second altar to Yahweh and calls on Yahweh's name (Gen. 12:8). Then, he continues east.

Hardship often tests the strength and depth of one's discipleship, and now Abram encounters hardship. A severe famine tests the extent to which he has been discipled by the powers and principalities of his ancient Near Eastern context and to what extent Yahweh's countercultural way of righteousness and holiness has taken hold. Will Abram choose "House-of-God" or "Heap-of-Desolation"? The narrative has set a pattern of hardship-resulting-in-altar-building; will Abram now build another altar to Yahweh in response to hardship?

No, instead he goes to Egypt, where he speaks his first words in the Genesis narrative as he schemes to pass his wife off as his sister: "Please say that you are my sister so that it may go well for me because of you, and that I may live on account of you" (Gen. 12:13 NASB).[7] Abram fears that because of Sarai's beauty the men will kill him to take her if they know she is his wife. If they think she is his sister, they will still take her but spare Abram. Abram would live, but Sarai would be vulnerable to sexual assault. It seems Abram has been discipled into a way that sees blessing as a finite commodity: One person's well-being must come at the expense of another, typically the weak and vulnerable. In the face of adversity, Abram does not build an altar to Yahweh but reveals the depth of his allegiance to the way of the world: Sarai must suffer so Abram may live.

ETHICS

Descriptive or Prescriptive? Reading Ethically in Genesis

Old Testament narratives like Genesis 12–50 are rich with stories of God's people. But these followers, including the patriarchs, are not always models to follow. Their stories are descriptive, telling us what happened, not always what *should* happen. When Abraham lies, Jacob deceives, or Joseph manipulates, the text may not always explicitly pass judgment, but that doesn't mean it endorses their behavior. Instead, we must read carefully, asking, How does this action align with God's covenant purposes? What are the consequences? Ethical interpretation in Genesis requires careful discernment rather than mindless imitation.

Where does this way lead? Without a doubt it leads to "Heap-of-Ruin." Sarai's beauty attracts the pharaoh of Egypt, and she is taken into his harem. She is exploited by, alienated from, and abandoned by her husband. Adding to the depth of her misery, Pharaoh rewards Abram with riches. Not only does Sarai's sacrifice preserve Abram's life; in a demented twist it also greatly increases his wealth. However, God afflicts Pharaoh's house with "great plagues," and Pharaoh angrily returns Sarai and banishes Abram from Egypt. Abram returns to the land of promise, having received a costly lesson in the way of righteousness and holiness.

Before his third encounter with God, Abram displays some progress in his formation. Returning to that place between House-of-God and Heap-of-Ruin, Abram visits the altar he had constructed and again calls on Yahweh's name. Friction develops between his herdsmen and the herdsmen of his nephew Lot. Abram decides the best solution is to part ways. Instead of choosing the best land for himself, he allows Lot the choice of the best land. Having separated from Lot, Abram encounters God for a third time.

Third Divine Encounter (Gen. 13:14–17)

In this encounter God asks Abram to walk (look at and stake out) a land he will never own. Yahweh repeats his promise about land and descendants, this time with further specificity. Abram is to look in each direction. It is possible that from Abram's vantage point he could see all the way west to the Mediterranean and east to the Transjordan mountains, and all the way

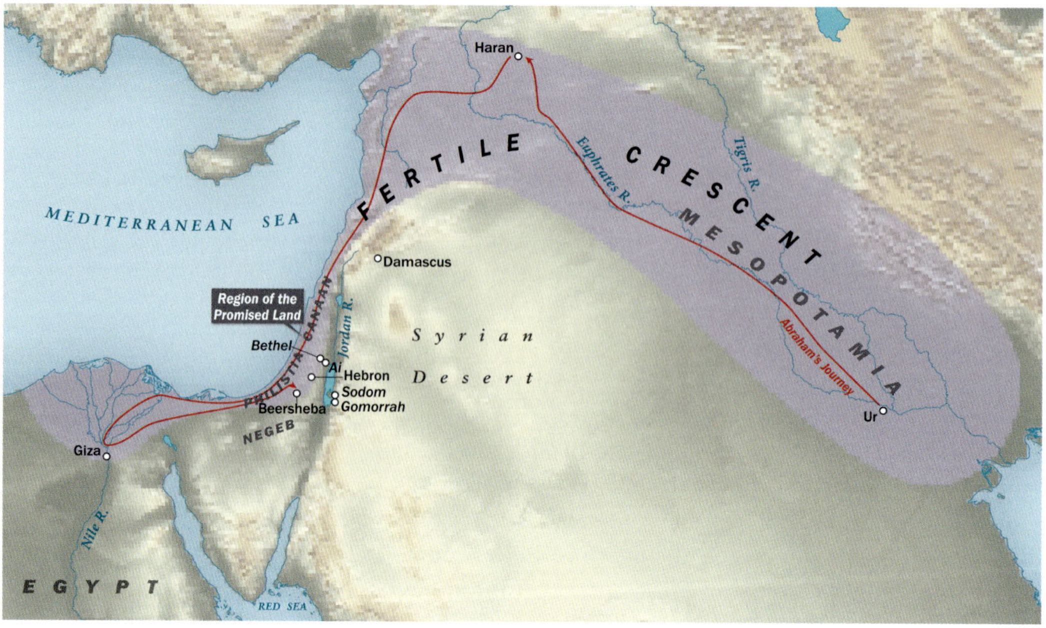

Figure 5.5. Key locations in Genesis

north to Mount Hermon and south to the Dead Sea.[8] God promises that Abram and his descendants will possess as far as he can see. Furthermore, the number of descendants Yahweh promises will be countless, as many as the dust of the earth.

Once again, God asks Abram to perform an act of faith: He is to get up and walk all around the length and breadth of the land. Abram is surveying the land not as an act of seizure or possession but as an expression of trust. Abram's walk can be understood as an embodied acceptance of the land as a divine gift. Even though the land will belong to his descendants instead of him, Abram's journey (which likely would have taken several weeks) demonstrates his faith that God will make good on his promises. Abram then moves to Hebron, where he builds another altar to Yahweh.

Before the fourth divine encounter, Abram intervenes militarily on behalf of Lot and the city-state Sodom, where Lot lived (Gen. 14). This account provides some noteworthy information. First, Abram is by no means a great nation, but his ability to muster 318 battle-ready men (14:14) suggests that his influence and greatness are increasing. Second, Abram is ready to mobilize for the sake of his kin, and by implication for the sake of Sodom. Third, Abram becomes an agent of salvation for Lot and all of Sodom, gaining him the gratitude and respect of Sodom and surrounding city-states (e.g., Salem). Fourth, as a result, Abram is recognized and blessed by Melchizedek, king of Salem, and the king of Sodom. Abram's desire for justice and peace contributes to the relationship of mutual blessing God promised in Genesis 12:1–3.

Fourth Divine Encounter (Gen. 15:1–21)

The complex of Abram stories pivots on this fourth divine encounter, in which God asks him not to be afraid and the patriarch responds. In every encounter so far, God has made promises to Abram, and in the first and third he has set Abram a challenge (leave his home; walk around Canaan). In this fourth encounter, both promise and command appear, but the command is not a tangible action. Rather, it touches something deep inside Abram. "Do not fear," says Yahweh (command; Gen. 15:1 NASB), "I am a shield to you; your reward shall be very great" (promise; 15:1). What does Abram fear that God should ask him to relinquish his fear? The timing of this command is peculiar because it comes right after Abram heroically rescued Lot (as well as five local kings) from an alliance of kings (see Gen. 14). Abram is not afraid to go into battle.[9] However, in Egypt fear drove him to take matters into his own hands, sacrificing Sarai for his own sake.

Abram may be afraid that God is not the kind of partner that will come through

Given in memory of Carl O. Schniewind / Art Institute of Chicago

Figure 5.6. *The Meeting of Abraham and Melchizedek* by Giovanni Battista Tiepolo (1719)

THEOLOGICAL ISSUES

Melchizedek and Missiology

Wherever the gospel has gone, God's people have argued about how to understand the relationship between the God revealed in Scripture and the traditions about a creator god found in many cultures around the world. Questions such as whether Bible translators can use Indigenous names for God in their translations raise the issue of whether and how local traditions about divine beings have any connection to the God and Father of our Lord Jesus Christ.

In relation to this question, Aboriginal pastor and theologian Graham Paulson observes that, in Genesis 14, Abram "respectfully acknowledges the name of the Creator used by the Indigenous priest Melchizedek. But he [also] joins this name to Israel's own name for God, [Yahweh]." Indeed, Abram shows respect for an Indigenous priesthood through Melchizedek.[e] The text thus creates a point of connection between the God who has entered a unique covenant relationship with Abram and the Indigenous understandings of El Elyon (God Most High). This does not imply that Genesis endorses every aspect of Canaanite theology! As Old Testament scholar Jerry Hwang argues, the Old Testament as a whole both presents Yahweh *as* El and Yahweh as *against* El.[f]

CANONICAL CONNECTIONS

A Priest in the Order of the King of Righteousness and Peace

In Genesis and beyond, Melchizedek offers a strange glimpse of the just and righteous way that God has called Abram to embrace. This mysterious priest-king's name literally means "king of justice/righteousness," while the place that he is king over (Salem) is related to the Hebrew word for peace. The New Testament author of Hebrews picks up on the meaning of Melchizedek's name and his mysterious appearance to argue that he foreshadows Jesus: "Without father, without mother, without genealogy, having neither beginning of days nor end of life, but resembling the Son of God, he remains a priest forever" (Heb. 7:2–3). Moreover, Jesus resembles Melchizedek because his priesthood does not come through "a legal requirement concerning physical descent, but through the power of an indestructible life" (7:16). Our righteous and just priest-king has thus become the guarantor of a new and better covenant, appearing "once for all at the end of the age to remove sin by the sacrifice of himself" (9:26). Such connections are part of the literary design of Genesis 12–50 and deserve close attention. Comparison of this kind can also reveal intriguing differences.

on his promises. God has said his promise of land will only be received by Abram's descendants, and Abram and Sarai are still childless (and not getting any younger). In this fourth encounter Abram speaks to God for the first time. What he says sounds like a challenge, questioning whether God will deliver on his promise of offspring (Gen. 15:2–3). His words may suggest that he is taking matters into his own hands and giving God a pass,[10] saying (with some bravado), "I've got this taken care of; a member of my household, Eliezer, will be my heir. What kind of reward, then, do you have to offer me?" Yahweh does not rebuke Abram but rather assures him that he will have a son and that his descendants will be as numerous as the stars. Abram trusts God (15:6), and "God likes it. God considers such trust a tribute to Abram's goodness of person, his righteousness, his merit."[11]

This is the first time we hear Abram and God talk to each other, and the dialogue continues in similar fashion around the subject of land. God reassures Abram about the land, and Abram asks how he can be sure he will possess it. Abram boldly questions God's promises of land, descendants, and, implicitly, God's relationship of mutual blessing. Maybe the fear that Abram has is that God will not do what he promised.

God responds with a striking and bloody covenant ceremony. At God's instructions, Abram takes several animals, cuts them in two, and arranges the pieces opposite one another, forming a grisly pathway between them. Normally in such rituals, the weaker party (Abram) would pass between the pieces, symbolically declaring, "May I suffer the fate of these animals if I break this covenant." But in this divine encounter, Abram falls into a deep sleep, and God alone, represented by a smoking fire pot and a blazing torch, passes between the divided animals. In doing so, Yahweh pledges that the fulfillment of his promise rests entirely on his own faithfulness, not on Abram's ability to keep the covenant. Before sealing the promise, God also tells Abram that his descendants will experience slavery and suffering before finally inheriting the land.

Abram is being formed into the way of righteousness and holiness, and his partnership with Yahweh is deepening. In this partnership there is room for being bold and wrestling with God. Even so, the way of fear, name-making, and self-preservation is difficult to give up. The story of Abram abandoning Sarai to Pharaoh shows the horrible consequences of following the way of the world; what follows the covenant ceremony

HISTORICAL MATTERS

Concubines, Surrogacy, and Cultural Compromise

In the ancient Near East, it was culturally acceptable for a barren wife to offer her female servant as a surrogate: a woman who would bear children on the wife's behalf. Legal texts like the Code of Hammurabi show that this practice aimed to preserve family lines and inheritance. In Genesis, Sarah gives Hagar to Abraham (Gen. 16), and Rachel and Leah later do the same with Bilhah and Zilpah (Gen. 30).

But while culturally sanctioned, these arrangements reflect desperation and distorted trust; they are human attempts to force God's promises rather than wait on his provision. The narratives highlight the relational pain, injustice, and rivalry that result, subtly critiquing these practices rather than endorsing them.

in chapter 15 does as well. Yahweh promised that Abram's heir would be his own offspring (Gen. 15:4), but when Sarai presents Abram with a scheme that he sleep with her servant to produce an heir, Abram "listened to the voice" of his wife (16:2). The scheme does produce a son, but it also produces tension and strife between Sarai and her servant Hagar (and eventually her son Ishmael), and between Sarai and Abram. Violence and alienation emerge. Although Ishmael will not be heir to the promises Yahweh made to Abram, Yahweh does meet Hagar and makes promises to her and her offspring.[12]

LITERARY NOTES

Genesis 16 as a Return to the Fall

Several verbal and thematic cues suggest that the story of Sarai, Abram, and Hagar deliberately echoes the fall narrative in Genesis 3. Sarai "takes" Hagar and "gives" her to Abram, and Abram "listens to the voice" of his wife (a phrase that only occurs here and in Gen. 3:17). Additionally, the plan is framed as a way to "build" Sarai a household, language reminiscent of Babel's self-trust as well as Eden's disobedience. As Gordon Wenham observes, the pattern is similar: Distrust of God's promise leads to human attempts to secure blessing on their own terms, and the result is relational fracture, blame shifting, and harm to the vulnerable. The parallels highlight how quickly the ancestral family reenacts the dynamics of the first fall whenever divine promises are grasped rather than received.[g]

Fifth Divine Encounter (Gen. 17:1–22)

The fifth divine encounter takes place thirteen years after Ishmael's birth, and in it God invites Abraham to walk with him in mutuality. In

RECEPTION HISTORY

Seeing Hagar, a Marginalized Matriarch

Though Hagar occupies only two chapters in Genesis (16 and 21), her legacy has echoed powerfully across centuries. An Egyptian slave, a surrogate mother, and a woman cast out into the wilderness—twice—Hagar stands as one of the most vulnerable figures in the patriarchal narratives. And yet, she is the only person in the Hebrew Bible to name God directly: "You are El-roi" ("the God who sees me"; 16:13). Her story is one of divine encounter and survival on the margins.

Hagar's reception history is as complex as her narrative. In Jewish interpretation, she is often portrayed as a foil to Sarah, sometimes negatively. In Islamic tradition, she is honored as a matriarch. Hagar (Hājar) is the mother of Ishmael, and her desperate search for water in the wilderness is ritually reenacted by millions of Muslims during the Hajj pilgrimage. For many Black theologians and womanist scholars, Hagar is a symbol of survival, resistance, and divine recognition. Delores Williams famously centered Hagar in her book *Sisters in the Wilderness*, interpreting her story as a paradigm for African American women's experience of oppression and divine care.[h]

In the biblical text, Hagar is used and cast aside by Abraham and Sarah. But she is not forgotten by God. Her wilderness encounters are moments of *divine attention and provision*, and her son Ishmael is granted a future and a nation. Hagar reminds us that God's covenantal care extends beyond the chosen line and that God sees, hears, and responds to those pushed to the edges.[i]

Figure 5.7. *Hagar* by Sarah Beth Baca (2019), watercolor and ink

HISTORICAL MATTERS

What Is Circumcision?

Circumcision is the removal of the foreskin from the male reproductive organ. In Genesis 17, God commands Abraham and his descendants to circumcise every male child on the eighth day as a "sign of the covenant" (Gen. 17:9–14; Lev. 12:3). Unlike some neighboring cultures, where circumcision marked adolescence, Israel practiced it in infancy as a sign of covenant belonging. This sign was permanent, embodied, and necessarily bloody. Like other covenant rituals in the Pentateuch, it marked the seriousness of belonging to a holy God.

For some readers, the practice may seem strange or unsettling. In its ancient context, however, it functioned as a visible and embodied reminder that Israel's identity and future rested not in human strength but in God's covenant faithfulness.

RECEPTION HISTORY

Rublev's Icon

Rublev's icon visualizes Genesis 18 through a trinitarian lens, reminding viewers that the God who visits Abraham is relational, hospitable, and mysterious. What if this story is not just about Abraham's faith but about how God chooses to be present—with intimacy, humility, and shared food?

State Tretyakov Gallery, Moscow / public domain

Figure 5.8. *The Trinity* (depicting the three angels and Abraham at Mamre) by Andrei Rublev (ca. 1411 or 1425–27)

this appearance, God reveals one of his names (El Shaddai, traditionally translated "God Almighty") to Abram and also gives Abram and Sarai new names. Although the relationship of mutuality is evident in the other divine encounters, this passage reinforces that mutuality by using an "As for me . . ." and "As for you . . ." formula (Gen. 17:4, 9).[13] God invites Abram to "walk with/before" him with integrity ("blameless") in the way that Enoch and Noah, and presumably Adam and Eve, did before him (5:22, 24; 6:9; 3:8). God confirms his everlasting covenant with Abram and his descendants and gives him the name Abraham because he will father many nations (17:4–5). Abraham is to show his trust by enacting the bloody rite of circumcision, which he and all his male household members undergo. Sarai, too, receives a new name, Sarah ("princess"), and her yet unborn son and Abraham's heir also receives a name (Isaac, "he laughs"). God will indeed bless Ishmael and make him fruitful and multiply, but it is through Isaac that God will establish the covenant of blessing. The reinforced partnership of mutuality between God and Abraham in this encounter will further deepen in the next divine encounter.

Sixth Divine Encounter (Gen. 18:1–33)

In this second-to-last encounter, Abraham takes initiative, hosting God, who then invites Abraham to talk with him. The encounter begins with Abraham welcoming three visitors. Readers know that this is Yahweh with two (heavenly) companions (Gen. 18:1), but whether Abraham initially realizes this is not known. Either way, Abraham has been formed

CANONICAL CONNECTIONS

Yahweh's Way

This chapter has emphasized that the patriarchs are being discipled into a countercultural "way" (the way of righteousness and holiness). Yahweh's interior dialogue in Genesis 18:17–19 explicitly references this notion. God has chosen Abraham and his household and children *so that* they might keep "Yahweh's way to do righteousness and justice" *so that* the Lord may bring blessing to all nations *through* Abraham and his family (18:18–19 AT).

into the kind of person who goes to great lengths to show generosity to strangers, embodying the relationship of mutual blessing that was part of his call. During the meal Abraham prepares, God reveals that Sarah will become pregnant and in about a year give birth to Isaac; at last, specific details about the promise of the heir!

Before the three visitors depart, Yahweh brings Abraham into his plans regarding the judgment on the wicked city of Sodom. In a beautiful dance of boldness and vulnerability, Abraham pleads with God for the salvation of Sodom on the basis of what is right and just. Yahweh doesn't just tolerate Abraham's repeated intercession; he invites and honors it. This is precisely the kind of exchange for which Yahweh has been discipling Abraham. In the end, Abraham's intervention is not enough to save Sodom, but he does secure the salvation of Lot and his family.

Discipleship is not a straight line, and old practices and patterns have a way of rearing their ugly heads. Abraham again sells out Sarah to save his own skin, and apparently this has been a regular practice beyond the Egypt incident (Gen. 20:13). Sarah ends up in the harem of King Abimelech of Gerar, but God prevents Abimelech from touching her (20:6). God tells Abimelech in a dream that he will die, but Abraham intercedes on the king's behalf. Abimelech returns Sarah to Abraham with a peace offering. Later, Abimelech recognizes the divine favor that Abraham receives and approaches Abraham to partner with him in a covenant relationship of mutual blessing, which Abraham does, living out what God intended for him (21:22–32).

Seventh Divine Encounter (Gen. 22:1–18)

In this final encounter between Abraham and God, God asks Abraham to let go of what is most precious, and the Abraham-God partnership is complete. This encounter is also the most perplexing. After all these years waiting for a child and after God had promised that Isaac would be the heir of God's blessing and covenant, God puts the whole partnership in the balance by asking Abraham to sacrifice Isaac. He asks the patriarch to trust him enough to put his future hope on the line. Will he relinquish the way of fear, self-preservation, and name-making for the way of Yahweh? "God is asking Abraham throughout the story to give up a way of being in the world. Abraham is being challenged to move beyond parochialism [what is good for him and his household and kin] in order to become a blessing to all families beyond his own family, to forfeit the desire to make his own name great—for the sake of the common good."[14]

Although Yahweh makes a request of Abraham as in other encounters, this is the first time he does not offer a promise with it.[15] The narrative develops by sharing the bare facts of Abraham's actions, leaving to the readers the task of imagining the characters' inner turmoil. Abraham obeys, packs his things, and leaves for Mount Moriah with Isaac and his servant. Isaac is confused but Abraham is resolute, trusting that God will provide (Gen. 22:7–8). In the moment before Abraham brings the knife down, Yahweh intervenes.

This narrative brings us back to the first divine encounter.[16] There Abraham was asked to leave country, kin, and father's household, and now he proves willing to relinquish "your son, your only son Isaac, whom you love" (Gen. 22:2, 12). Yahweh declares, "Now I know . . ." (22:12). The test

THEOLOGICAL ISSUES

The (Near) Sacrifice of Isaac

Like the author of Hebrews, many understand Abraham's act primarily in terms of faith or trust. Abraham believes that somehow, in the end, both he and Isaac will return from this ordeal, that God will provide a sacrifice or raise Isaac from the dead (Heb. 11:17–19; Gen. 22:5, 8).

Others emphasize Abraham's obedience. Scholar Jon Levenson explores this in light of ancient practices of child sacrifice, which were based on the idea that such sacrifices offered the very best to the god one worshiped. From this perspective, Abraham is the "knight of obedience" as well as a "knight of faith."[j] Against this ancient background, it is highly significant that this God does not desire child sacrifice (see Jer. 19:5); the story anticipates Israel's later understanding that the firstborn belonged to God but that God provided a way for the firstborn to be redeemed.

Another line of interpretation explores Isaac's age; while we might assume he is quite young, ancient Jewish interpreters placed him somewhere between fifteen and thirty-six. From this perspective, Isaac is a willing participant, an "archetypical martyr" who foreshadows the voluntary death of Jesus. Levenson suggests that both "Jewish and Christian systems of sacrifice" thus "come to be seen as founded upon a father's willingness to surrender his beloved son and the son's unstinting acceptance of the sacrificial role he has been assigned in the great drama of redemption."[k]

Yet another question is how to reconcile Abraham's vigorous protest to God over Sodom compared with his silence here. Ellen Davis sees the two stories as gesturing toward "what it is to serve prophetically in covenantal context: negotiating dual commitments to humanity and to God, from moment to moment discerning when to challenge God" and "when to submit in trust to the sometimes-inscrutable divine will."[l]

By contrast, J. Richard Middleton argues that Abraham does not fully pass God's test but should have raised his voice in psalm-like protest on behalf of Isaac.[m] Such theological ambiguity suggests the power of even this most difficult text to push us deeper into our understanding of God, the world, and the life of faith.

The William M. Ladd Collection, Gift of Herschel V. Jones, 1916 / Minneapolis Institute of Art

Figure 5.9. *The Sacrifice of Isaac* by Rembrandt (1655)

reveals Abraham's faith; it is evidence of his discipleship into Yahweh's way of righteousness and holiness. On the basis of this profound act of faith, God swears by himself that he will certainly do what he promised Abraham in their first encounter: "Because you have done this . . ." God will multiply and bless his descendants and in turn bless all nations of the earth (22:16–19).

The account of Abraham closes with two stories and a note about his death (including two genealogies). Chapter 23 recounts the death and burial of Sarah, a whole chapter in which Abraham engages with Hittite men to purchase a burial plot. Without negotiating, Abraham purchases the field of Machpelah for much more than it was worth. This is the first piece of land that Abraham owns in Canaan, a sort of down payment for the whole land that his descendants would inherit.

After burying Sarah, Abraham seeks a bride for Isaac (Gen. 24). He sends his oldest and most trusted servant back to his people's land. Through divine guidance, the servant finds Rebekah. With the blessing of her family, she returns to marry Isaac. The narrator concludes Abraham's story with the report of his death at the age of 175: "Abraham breathed his last and died in a good old age, an old man and full of years, and was gathered to his people" (25:8). Isaac and Ishmael reunite to bury their father, laying him to rest with Sarah in the cave at Machpelah (25:9–10).

Abraham was discipled into the way of righteousness and holiness and became a covenant partner with God for the purpose of mutual blessing. The legacy of Abraham is certainly as the father of the faith, but it is also as God's beloved friend (see 2 Chron. 20:7; Isa. 41:8; James 2:23). What about Abraham's descendants? Will their discipleship be any less bumpy? To what extend have they been discipled by the ways of the culture around them? What traps will ensnare them as they become friends and partners with God in his mission of blessing?

Living the Text

Covenant Faithfulness in Our Cultural Moment

Abraham's story isn't just a record of ancient wanderings and promises; it is a prophetic word for our time. At the heart of this narrative lies a vital question: What kind of people will trust God enough to bless others in a world defined by fear, control, and rivalry? Genesis 12–25 speaks to personal discipleship as well as to the church's public posture in a fractured age. It exposes the ways we grasp for safety and power, and it calls us to a slower, riskier, but more beautiful way of being in the world.

Faithfulness in an Age of Self-Preservation

Abraham's failures are often rooted in fear. He repeatedly protects himself by passing off Sarah as his sister, placing her in vulnerable and compromising situations. He is a man caught between the promise of God and the threats of the world, a man who sometimes chooses self-preservation over trusting partnership.

We live in a time when fear and self-preservation shape much of Christian witness. In response to cultural shifts, some churches retreat into defensiveness, drawing sharp boundaries to protect identity and doctrine. Others seek political influence as a way to guard their legacy or reclaim lost ground. In both cases, the goal is at best survival and at worst power, often at the expense of integrity, hospitality, or the vulnerable.

Genesis doesn't excuse Abraham's actions, but it does show us that faithfulness is forged in the tension between fear and trust. Abraham grows by learning over time to entrust himself and others to God's plan and provision. The world tells us to defend our turf and protect ourselves, but the Abrahamic path calls us to sacrificial trust—to give away power, to give away what is most dear, to give away ourselves. We, like Abraham, are called to be a blessing, even when it costs us most dearly.

Discipleship as Letting Go

"Go," God says. "Leave your country, your kindred, your father's house." From the start, the covenantal life requires relinquishment. Abraham is invited to walk away from the known into an uncertain future, trusting that what God offers is more enduring than what he's leaving behind.

The call to let go still confronts us today. Many of us live in cultures obsessed with control: strategizing, optimizing, and securing outcomes. Christian discipleship often gets co-opted by these same instincts: Build your platform, increase your numbers, protect your tribe, curate your brand. But Abraham's journey defies all of that. His life is defined by wandering. He pitches tents. He waits. He loses. He obeys, even when the next step feels unbearable. This is not failure. It is formation. Abraham's life displays the slow, disorienting process of becoming a covenant partner. He must let go of his homeland, as well as the illusion that he can secure God's promise by his own strength. Discipleship still requires the same—letting go of comfort, entitlement, and the idol of impact—in order to become the kind of people through whom God's promised blessing can move forward.

Figure 5.10. *Abraham's Journey from Ur to Canaan* by József Molnár (1850)

Ethical Formation in a Compromised Culture

The world of Genesis is morally complicated, and so is Abraham. His story is filled with ambiguous choices, fractured relationships, and hard consequences. He makes room for strangers and also exiles his own son. He receives divine promises and still takes matters into his own hands. He builds altars in trust and sells out his wife because of fear. Yet God remains committed to shaping him and accomplishing his purposes through him.

Abraham's journey reminds us that covenant formation is ethical formation. To follow God is to be changed, sometimes painfully, often slowly, into someone who reflects God's character. That includes learning to do justice, love mercy, and walk humbly with God (Mic. 6:8). It also includes naming failure, repenting from harm done, pressing into reconciliation, and making space for correction and growth.

Opposite instincts often plague today's church. We have too often prioritized institutional survival over moral integrity. We have excused failure in the name of fruitfulness. We have protected reputations while leaving the vulnerable exposed. Abraham's story doesn't let us get away with that. It insists that the covenant way involves becoming people who can mediate God's promises well. This means cultivating ethical resilience in a compromised culture. It means acknowledging where we have compromised our witness and doing the slow work of repair. It means refusing to spiritualize harm or excuse injustice in the name of tradition or truth or reputation. It means being at least as truthful about our own horrific failures as Genesis is about Abraham and Sarah's failures. And it means letting God's holiness and not our own metrics define what faithfulness looks like.

The Global Horizon of God's Covenant Purposes

From the very beginning, God's covenant with Abraham is outward facing: "In you, all the families of the earth shall be blessed" (Gen. 12:3). This global horizon is in the DNA of God's promise. The election of Abraham is not for exclusion but for expansion.

That calling plays out in surprising ways. Throughout the Abraham narrative, outsiders are not sidelined; they are seen, included, and sometimes blessed. Hagar receives a divine encounter. Ishmael is promised a future. Abimelech receives God's warning and blessing. Melchizedek is honored as a priest of the Most High. Even Lot is not forgotten. The covenant people are called to be a people for the sake of others.

This contrasts with the way many Christians today imagine what it means to be chosen. We are tempted to see our chosenness as a reason to separate—or to dominate. But Scripture reminds us that our election is never an excuse for superiority. It is a summons to service. To bear God's name is to bear God's concern for the nations, the outsiders, the unexpected heirs of promise. In our age of polarization, nationalism, and cultural gatekeeping, the Abrahamic vocation remains a corrective. The church is a conduit instead of a fortress, a people set apart to carry the blessing of God into every corner of the world.

Conclusion: Becoming a People of Promise

Genesis 12–25 offers a raw, beautiful invitation to become a different kind of people, to walk a path of discipleship characterized by righteousness and holiness. The path won't be perfect. It shouldn't be triumphant. But it should be faithful. Abraham's story maps a path of trust, surrender, ethical formation, and global calling. And it does so in a world not unlike ours: full of compromise, fear, and the temptation to secure blessing on our own terms. The church today needs this vision. We need to recover the slow courage of covenant faithfulness. We need to let go of fear and control. We need to be willing to wander, to wait, to be reshaped. Most of all, we need to remember who we are: not gatekeepers of a legacy, but stewards of a promise, called to live lives of righteousness and holiness for the sake of the world God so loves.

Genesis 25:12–50:26

Transmission of God's Way Through the Generations

Orientation

In Genesis 12–25, Yahweh calls Abraham out of a world marked by violence, scarcity, and self-exaltation to walk in a new way—a way of righteousness (*tsedaqah*) and holiness (*qodesh*), trusting God's promise and pursuing blessing for others rather than grasping for power or self-preservation.

Renata Sedmakova / Shutterstock

Figure 6.1. Modern fresco of scenes from Genesis in the church Chiesa di San Giuseppe Artigiano by Franco Vignazia (2019)

The last section of Genesis follows the next generations in that same process of formation (25:19–50:26). Isaac, Jacob, and Joseph each embody different responses to God's call, responses shaped in part by their circumstances, family systems, and personal ambitions. The text invites readers to observe how Yahweh remains faithful to his promises and how complicated and incomplete the formation of God's covenant partners can be. If the Abraham story centers on the founding of the covenant family, the stories of Isaac, Jacob, and Joseph explore what happens when that family begins to fracture—internally through favoritism, rivalry, and fear, and externally through the pressures of empire and cultural assimilation.

Isaac's story illustrates that we are all products of our families and their circumstances, that we bear and will repeat the disfunctions of our ancestors, but also that there is hope and that God is faithful in working his own story through our individual failures and victories. Jacob, whose name means "heel-grabber," struggles not only with others but with God himself. His name change to Israel signals a new identity, yet the old patterns of manipulation and fear do not easily fade. His life is a prolonged wrestling match—with his brother, his uncle, his wives, and with the God who both wounds and blesses. By contrast, Joseph's story is outwardly cleaner, marked by personal virtue, leadership skill, and a stunning rise to power in Egypt. Yet even here the narrative raises hard questions: What does it mean to flourish within empire? How do we discern when God's people have been co-opted by the powers they were meant to resist?

In Joseph's story, the central question comes into sharper focus: Can God's people remain faithful to the way of *tsedaqah* and *qodesh*, the way of trusting God and blessing others, when divine silence replaces direct encounter, when patterns of sin run in the family, and when the surrounding culture offers comfort, security, and control? Can the covenant truly be transmitted across generations?

Exploration

The Accounts of Isaac and Jacob (Gen. 25:19–37:1)

READ GENESIS 25:19–37:1

Read the text in one sitting if possible. How do Isaac and Jacob respond to tension, deceit, or danger? How do they learn, resist, or display Yahweh's way? Where do you see patterns repeating or breaking from Abraham's story?

ISAAC—LIKE FATHER, LIKE SON

Compared to Abraham, Jacob, and Joseph, Isaac doesn't get much airtime. Although he is present in Jacob's story (just as Jacob is in the story of Joseph and his brothers), only a single chapter is devoted to him (Gen. 26). Before this chapter, Isaac is born to elderly and barren parents, circumcised on the eighth day, and has a feast held for him on the day of his weaning, the same day his half-brother, Ishmael, and his mother, Hagar, are banished because of Sarah's spitefulness (Gen. 21). When he is likely a teenager and God asks Abraham to sacrifice him (Gen. 22), Isaac comes off as compliant, unafraid, and inquisitive. We might wonder what emotionally and psychologically it would do to a person to be bound by your own father, placed on an altar, and then watch as he raises a knife in the air to plunge into your body; we might also wonder to what extent this set the trajectory of his life and shaped his narrative in Genesis.

Fast-forward a few decades. At the age of forty, Isaac is unmarried and still grieving the death of his mother three years earlier (Gen. 24:67). His father, Abraham, puts forth all the effort to arrange his marriage to Rebekah. Isaac loves her, and this marriage provides him comfort after Sarah's death. At the death of Abraham, Isaac partners with Ishmael to bury Abraham (25:9).

The narrator then says Isaac prayed to God about Rebekah's barrenness, and God granted his request. Jacob and Esau are born twenty years after Isaac and Rebekah were married (Gen. 25:26). When the boys grow up, Isaac favors Esau because of the meat he provides by hunting, but Rebekah favors Jacob (25:28). All of this is the background to the single chapter devoted to Isaac (Gen. 26).

In Genesis 26, God appears twice to Isaac (26:1–5, 23–25). In the first encounter, Yahweh warns him not to go down to Egypt to flee a famine (like Abraham did). And God passes on to Isaac all the promises of blessing and the missional partnership that he had made with Abraham. Isaac obeys the divine command not to go to Egypt and settles in Gerar. However, he does not have to go to Egypt to repeat his father's folly. Like Abraham, Isaac tries to pass his wife off as his sister for fear of his own well-being (26:6–11; cf. 12:10–20; 20:1–18). However, he cannot keep his affections for Rebekah a secret, and Abimelech, king of the Philistines in Gerar, realizes they are married. Abimelech rebukes him for the lie and eventually sends him away because of the wealth and power he attains.

Isaac moves on and continues to repeat the actions of his father. He digs out wells that Abraham had previously dug, and the newly found water puts him at odds with the inhabitants of the land, so he leaves (Gen.

Zvonimir Atletic / Shutterstock

Figure 6.2. Marble relief of Esau selling his birthright to Jacob

26:12–22, 26–33; cf. Gen. 13). Yahweh then appears to him a second time. As he had told Abraham, he commands Isaac not to fear, and he repeats his commitment to be with Isaac and to multiply his offspring. Isaac repeats his father's actions: He builds an altar and calls on Yahweh's name. Another well is dug (26:24–25). Finally, King Abimelech returns to Isaac when he perceives that Yahweh has blessed him. He expresses his desire to enter into a covenant of mutual blessing with him. Isaac agrees. They celebrate, make their vows, and Abimelech returns to his land.

Beyond Genesis 26, Isaac moves in and out of the narratives of Jacob as a minor character, which contributes to the composite picture. His loss of sight (27:1) may symbolize his loss of control over his two independent sons. He shows favor to firstborn Esau, is tricked and manipulated by second-born Jacob, and finds himself doing damage control with his at-odds sons. The narrator does, however, give a fitting conclusion for a patriarch, highlighting his old age and the fullness of his days. Isaac is "gathered to his people." In the same way that Isaac reunited with his half-brother Ishmael to lay their father Abraham to rest, so Isaac's sons reunite to lay him to rest (35:29), bringing closure to his narrative.

ETHICS

Dry Wells and the Divine Way

Leon Kass reads Isaac's digging of his father's wells as a metaphor for passing on the "God-revering way of life" to one's descendants: "There is no guarantee that the wells fathers dig will be there for their sons. But if fathers maintain their relationship with God and teach their sons the way of the covenant, these can survive intact into the next generation, serving as a wellspring of moral and spiritual guidance to elevate and dignify human life."[a]

Commentators have been hard on Isaac, considering him passive and incompetent. One says, "Isaac appears to live out the rest of his days in a state of anticlimactic existential exhaustion, capable only of imitating elements of his father's life."[1] Paul Borgman agrees, considering him a "flop," an "incompetent son," acting in "foolishness," with an "inability to function well in the real world."[2] Although Walter Brueggemann thinks he is remembered through the texts of Genesis as "the precious son of a great father and the beguiled father of a scheming son," he regards Isaac as important for the purposes of Genesis: "The figure of Isaac is made the bearer of an important and distinctive theological perspective."[3] For Brueggemann, this important perspective brings together the promise/gift of divine blessing and the reality of great prosperity, judged by worldly standards (e.g., abundant harvest, great wealth). Abraham becomes prosperous through his partnership of blessing with Yahweh; the language used for Isaac's material prosperity in chapter 26 is excessive and repetitive. Prosperity seems to have passed from Abraham to Isaac, but what of instruction in the way of righteousness and holiness, the way of divine-human partnership? As the patriarchs pass down land titles, livestock, and other possessions, are they also passing down Yahweh's unique way of life and blessing? This concern will become important for Jacob's narrative as Jacob seems fixated on securing the material prosperity that seems bound up in covenant partnership with Yahweh rather than on that relationship itself.

JACOB—LIKE GRANDFATHER, LIKE/UNLIKE GRANDSON

There are obvious parallels between Abraham and Jacob. God singles out both to partner with him in his cosmic plan of bringing blessing to the world and is forming both into his way of righteousness and holiness. Both struggle with aspects of that call, both take matters into their own hands rather than waiting on God and pressing into God's way, and both find the formation process difficult and sometimes painful.

There are also differences between the two men. Abraham seems more honest on the whole and more respectable than Jacob. He can be bold like Jacob, but he is more frequently respectful, often deferring to others. Moreover, Abraham manifests a general kindness to others and shows a tendency to advocate for others.

Abraham seems focused on the *promise* of generational covenant partnership with God, but Jacob is preoccupied with the tangible and material *blessings* of the covenant for him and for his immediate family.[4] A careful reading of the Abraham narrative reveals that Abraham becomes wealthy quite quickly in terms of his historical context, especially in flocks, herds, and other livestock but in other ways too. Readers can sometimes overlook this because Abraham is preoccupied by other things, and especially the heir that would inherit the promises of God. By contrast, Jacob fixates on matters of fertility, prosperity, and security and will stop at nothing to manipulate those around him (including God!) to gain them. Only later in his formative process do these matters find their proper place within the framework of God's covenant partnership.

JACOB STRUGGLES WITH BROTHER, FATHER, UNCLE, WIVES . . . AND YAHWEH

The complex of stories involving Jacob can be viewed within a concentric framework that turns around conflict and resolution.[5] At the outer edges are the introduction and transition from Isaac's narrative to Jacob's (Gen. 25:1–26:35) and the conclusion and transition to the narrative that centers on Joseph and the brothers (34:1–36:43). Within that framework, the narrative begins with Jacob and Esau's conflict (25:19–34; 27:1–28:9), and it ends with reconciliation between the two brothers (33:1–20). Within this are two parallel accounts in which Jacob encounters and struggles with God, first at Bethel (28:10–22) and then at Peniel (32:22–32), and between those parallel accounts are Jacob's conflicts with Laban over his daughters (29:1–30) and then again over wages, which ends in reconciliation and covenant partnership (30:25–31:55). At the very center of the whole complex of stories is the conflict within Jacob's own family with his own wives, which results in the birth of Jacob's sons (and one daughter), the eventual heads of the tribes of Israel (29:31–30:24).

The origin story of Jacob and Esau is the origin story of two nations, Israel and Edom. Prophetic words from both Yahweh and Isaac seem to establish that these two men and their descendants are destined to be at odds. When Rebekah asks God about the struggling in her womb, he tells her it is the struggle of two nations and two peoples, and the older will serve the younger (Gen. 25:23). What Jacob could not accomplish at his birth (i.e., gaining the advantage of being firstborn), he accomplishes later through manipulation and trickery (see detailed discussion on this deception at the end of chap. 4). The words of Isaac—both when he blesses Jacob disguised as Esau and when he sends him to escape to Haran—contain words and phrases that establish Jacob as the recipient of the promises of the Abrahamic covenant and the bearer of the creation/cultural mandate to Adam (27:28–29; 28:1–4). However, Jacob has yet to hear from God that he will be God's covenant partner.

LITERARY NOTES

Structural Outline of Genesis 25–36

- A Introduction and transition (25:1–26:35)
  - B Jacob's conflict with Esau (27:1–28:9)
    - C Jacob encounters God at Bethel (28:10–22)
      - D Conflicts with Laban over his daughters (29:1–30)
        - E Birth of Jacob's children (29:31–30:24)
      - D′ Conflicts with Laban over wages, and then reconciliation and covenant partnership (30:25–31:55)
    - C′ Jacob encounters God at Peniel (32:22–32)
  - B′ Jacob's reconciliation with Esau (32:1–33:20)
- A′ Conclusion and transition (34:1–36:43)

Figure 6.3. *Jacob and Rachel at the Well* by François Lemoyne (1720)

LITERARY NOTES

Isaac's "Blessing" of Esau

Isaac has prophetic words of "blessing" for Esau too. Whereas Jacob will receive the "dew of heaven" and the "fatness of the earth" (Gen. 27:28), Esau will dwell away from those very things (27:39); whereas brothers and nations will serve Jacob (27:29), Esau will be subservient to his brother (27:40a). Isaac's words at the end of this blessing to Esau sound foreboding: "When you grow restless, you will tear off his yoke from your neck" (27:40b NET). Isaac's blessing does not seem like much of a blessing: His life and that of his descendants will involve struggle, sword, and servitude. Yet there is hope of liberation beyond the struggle. After years of exile, Jacob will return to land and family. Despite his fears, he makes amends with the brother he treated so badly. They do reconcile, and Jacob blesses Esau with generous gifts (32:13–15; 33:11).

The circumstances of Jacob arriving in Haran and meeting his future bride and his uncle Laban are recounted in Genesis 29. Jacob's first divine encounter functions as a transition between the stories of Jacob's struggle with Esau and his dealings with Laban and his marriage to Rachel and Leah. We will consider Jacob's struggle with Yahweh below, but at this point in the story, God meets Jacob on his journey from his father's household in Beersheba to Haran and confirms his covenant partnership with Jacob; he tells Jacob that the promises he made to Abraham and Isaac (land, descendants, blessing) and the purpose of the partnership (the blessing of all nations) will extend to Jacob (28:13–15). While we might expect Jacob to respond like his father or grandfather before him and build an altar to Yahweh, Jacob is undergoing his own formative process, being discipled by God into the way of righteousness and holiness. Unlike his ancestors but very much in line with his character in the story so far, Jacob tries to manipulate the circumstances and to make a deal. He vows that if God follows through on his end of the bargain—being with him, prospering him, and returning him to his father's land/household—"then Yahweh will be my God," and *then* he will repay God (28:20–22 AT). Jacob has yet to learn how to relinquish control, to embrace the covenant relationship and

HISTORICAL MATTERS

Marriage Customs in Genesis

Marriage customs in Genesis include arranged matches, parental negotiations, and marriage within the extended family. These may seem foreign to modern readers, but in the ancient world they were common and served practical ends: preserving family honor, protecting inheritance, and maintaining clan stability.

Genesis adds a further dimension to such customs: covenant. Decisions about Isaac and Jacob marrying within the family are not about ethnic purity but about preserving fidelity to Yahweh's promises. At the same time, the wider biblical story welcomes outsiders like Tamar, Rahab, Ruth, and others into the covenant line, showing that what ultimately matters is allegiance to Israel's God, not biological closeness.

recognize that his partnership with Yahweh is not transactional.

In Haran, Jacob discovers an individual whose trickster abilities match his own: his uncle Laban. Indeed, Laban's deception of Jacob is remarkably similar to the one Jacob orchestrated against his father, Isaac. First, Laban tricks Jacob into marrying Leah and then manipulates him into another seven years of labor for Rachel. Both men fulfill their end of the bargain, but this is not the end of the struggle between them, a struggle that will have long-term unintended consequences for Jacob's own family.

The story of Jacob marrying Rachel and Leah asks us to imagine the relational dynamic created by the situation: A man marries two sisters, one whom he loves and who is distinguished for her beauty, and the other whose only physical description is a brief and debated comment about her "soft" or "tender" eyes (Gen. 29:17), set in contrast to Rachel's beauty. Complicating the situation, Rachael is not able to bear children, while Leah is very fruitful in childbearing. Twenty-nine verses (29:31–30:24) tell the gut-wrenching story of the birth of Jacob's eleven sons and one daughter, a story of competition and striving that pulls two innocent female servants into the disfunction. (Leah bore seven children, Rachel one, Rachel's servant Bilhah two, and Leah's servant Zilpah two. Rachel later conceives and [as she dies] gives birth to another son, Benjamin.) This central section in the structure of Jacob's stories is one of the rare instances where Jacob seems a passive figure. What will be the fate of a household and children forged in such circumstances? This is a troubling beginning for the family that would become the twelve tribes of Israel.

With twelve children, Jacob appears to have secured a legacy through which his name will continue. He now sets his sights on land and seeks Laban's permission to return to his "home and country" (Gen. 30:25), along with some wages (sheep) from his labor. Laban and Jacob angle to get the upper hand against the other, and their conflict climaxes when Jacob determines to leave and secretly takes his family and possessions with him. The two parties narrowly avoid battle, but in the end Laban and Jacob part ways as covenant partners (Gen. 31).

Jacob has left behind the years of conflict and manipulation with Laban and begun his return journey toward Canaan. Though materially prosperous, he remains spiritually in process, carrying unresolved tension with his brother Esau and being prone to scheming self-preservation. The question now is whether his upcoming encounter with God at Peniel will reshape his identity for the road ahead.

The story of Jacob's departure from Laban is a reminder that his fourteen-plus years in Haran were an escape but not a final dwelling place. God's larger plan would develop back in Canaan with Jacob's descendants and family. In Genesis 31 God affirms Jacob's desire to return and promises his presence ("I will be with you"; 31:3, 5; see also 31:11–13). This chapter in Jacob's narrative is also a reminder that the larger plot is the development of God's covenant partnership with the patriarchs to form a people into the way of righteousness and holiness for the sake of all nations. Jacob seems to be discipled more by the way of self-preservation, scarcity, and self-interest. Two things are noteworthy in this regard. First, when the narrator tells of Jacob's stealthy departure from Laban, he refers to the latter as "Laban the Aramean." Leon Kass supposes this drives a deeper point: Jacob's return home marks a symbolic break from the "way of the world" and a movement toward the way of Yahweh.[6]

Bequest of Harry G. Sperling, 1971 / The MET

Figure 6.4. *Laban Searching for His Idols*, after François Boucher

Second, if this is correct, then Genesis 31:19 introduces a significant complication. Just as Jacob begins this pivotal journey, the narrator tells us that "Rachel stole her father's household gods." This is a telling moment. Even as Jacob moves to separate himself both literally and spiritually from Laban, "the Aramean," Rachel smuggles part of that old world along with them. Although Jacob may be "*separating* himself *from the Aramean* and his ways, Rachel—the text pointedly remarks—takes *her father's gods* and ways *with her* on her journey."[7] The idols of Laban represent more than household trinkets; they symbolize the persistence of the old way. This raises a sobering question: Can Jacob truly depart from the way of the world, his own habits of deceit and self-preservation included, if the gods of that world still travel with him?[8] Homecoming for Jacob means facing Esau and the consequences of Jacob's heel-grabbing ways. What path will

HISTORICAL MATTERS

Household Gods (*Teraphim*)

The "household gods" Rachel steals (Gen. 31:19) are called *teraphim* in Hebrew. These were small domestic idols associated with family religious practice in the ancient Near East. They were sometimes used for seeking guidance for the future and were later condemned by Israel's prophets as illegitimate or idolatrous objects (e.g., 2 Kings 23:24; Zech. 10:2). Some scholars think they may have been connected to inheritance rights. In Genesis 31, the episode underscores the tension between lingering attachment to such objects and the exclusive allegiance demanded by Israel's God.[b]

CANONICAL CONNECTIONS

Through the Waters

Throughout Scripture, water marks the threshold of transformation. Noah passes through the flood, Israel walks through the Red Sea, and the Jordan River becomes the entry point into the promised land. These crossings signal more than geography; they represent passage from an old identity to a new calling. When Jacob crosses the Jabbok River (Gen. 32:22), he passes through the waters as a deceiver. On the far bank, after a night of wrestling, he emerges wounded, renamed, and blessed as Israel. Later, Jesus steps into the Jordan, not to repent, but to enter Israel's story, going down into the waters as a sign of solidarity and surrender. In Christian baptism, we follow this same pattern: going down into the waters of death and rising into new life, clothed with a new identity in Christ.

Jacob follow as he anticipates encountering his brother?

The initial plan Jacob hatches has all the marks of his manipulating ways. First, he sends messengers to determine if Esau is coming in peace. They return with word that Esau is coming to meet Jacob with four hundred men. Second, Jacob assumes that Esau and his entourage are geared for battle and divides his flocks and herds and his household into two groups, supposing that if Esau attacks, the second group (which includes the people and possessions most precious to Jacob) could escape. Jacob does turn to God in prayer then, leveraging the promises God had previously made to him and stretching them slightly to his advantage. Jacob gets no answer from God, so he determines to lavish his brother with gifts in stages, hoping to pacify Esau with waves of offerings.

All of this looks very much like the old Jacob, the Heel-Grabber. He demonstrates the way of self-interest and self-preservation: manipulating God and human to serve himself and showing a willingness to sacrifice the well-being of others (his servants and those least valuable in his eyes) for his own advantage. However, on the eve of meeting Esau, Jacob will first come face-to-face with God, an encounter that will change him permanently.

That night, Jacob sends his family and possessions across the Jabbok River, but he remains behind. Alone with his thoughts and the uncertainty of what lay ahead, Jacob meets "a man" who wrestles with him through the night. The identity of the man, the nature of the wrestling, and other details of this story are mysterious. As Jacob realizes his competitor is more than human, he struggles all the more. Ultimately, as Heel-Grabber and the divine-human figure literally wrestle, Jacob must confront his own identity and his way of being in the world. After Jacob's opponent deals a blow that prevents Jacob from getting the upper hand and gives him a lifelong injury, he asks Jacob, "What is your name?" Many years earlier, Jacob had answered a similar question, asked by Isaac as Jacob took advantage of his blind father, deceiving him and usurping his brother. Then, he did not give his own name, but on this

Bequest of Harry G. Sperling, 1971 / The MET

Figure 6.5. *Vision After the Sermon* by Paul Gauguin (1888)

CANONICAL CONNECTIONS

A Wounded Ancestor and a Ritual Reminder

At the end of the account of Jacob's wrestling with God and God's divine blessing, the descendants of Jacob are called the "children of Israel" for the first time (Gen. 32:32 KJV). The same verse also records the Israelites' first dietary ritual: a lasting practice of not eating the tendon near the hip, where Jacob was struck.

This embodied habit reminded Israel that they descended from one who was wounded in his flesh in the process of becoming a faithful covenant partner. Jacob's limp marked him as one who had struggled with God and lived. His children carry that memory, not just in story, but in the very way they eat. It is a quiet ritual that tells them who they are: the people of the wounded wrestler, named by God.

occasion, on the eve of losing everything, he admits he is Jacob, Heel-Grabber. The divine visitor responds that it is time for Jacob to shed that name and that identity: He is Heel-Grabber no longer, but "Israel, because you have struggled with God and with humans and have overcome" (Gen. 32:28 NIV). Jacob names the place Peniel, "because I saw God face to face, and yet my life was spared" (Gen. 32:30 NIV).

The change in Jacob's name does not mean he will (or should) give up his struggling nature, but it does mean he needs to reorient that struggle in the service of God's new way. Tenacity and determination are necessary assets for following Yahweh's way and participating in his purposes in a world that will be at odds with those purposes.[9] To be the people of God, *Israel*, means to be a community that wrestles with their Creator. And yet, Jacob was brought to the limits of his striving and carried in his body the lasting mark of his struggle with God. As Kass notes, "The man who limps gets along only with the help of grace."[10]

Jacob's long night of wrestling and new name are a major turning point. He is renamed and reborn at the river, and he initially seems changed, taking a different approach to his encounter with Esau. Jacob approaches his brother first and with great humility and then brings out his wives with their children to meet Esau. Moved, Esau receives Jacob's gifts (a "blessing"; Gen. 33:11 KJV), and the brothers are reconciled.

But then Jacob refuses to travel together with Esau's party and says they will rendezvous with him at Seir in the south (Gen. 33:14). In fact, Jacob's intention was to travel west to Succoth to settle there. On the one hand, this separation may have been wise; even though the brothers reconcile, the prophecy at their birth was that the brothers represent two nations (Israel and Edom) and that they would be divided (25:23). Just as Jacob separated his family from the person and way of life of Laban, so it may have been wise to separate from Esau/Edom and the Edomite way. But that does not explain why he lies to Esau. Fear, especially for his family, is a theme that runs through the rest of Jacob's story, and perhaps it is fear that draws out Jacob's heel-grabbing, self-preserving ways here. As in the Christian way of being born again, so in the life of Jacob: Even a whole lifetime is too short to disciple us out of the old way of self-sufficiency and self-preservation.

So, is Jacob the Heel-Grabber or the Struggler-with-God-and-Humans? The answer is not straightforward. Three observations may help. First, after the encounter at the Jabbok River, God again appears to Jacob, commissions him with the cultural mandate (Gen. 35:11), and reaffirms the Abrahamic promises (35:11–12). Before doing so, God renames him Israel for a second time (35:10). In both renaming scenes, at the Jabbok and here, the divine figure declares that Jacob will no longer be called Jacob, but Israel.

Second, between these two naming episodes, the narrator exclusively refers to the patriarch as "Jacob" (over 25 times) and never as "Israel." The troubling story of Dinah falls in this in-between space. When his daughter is assaulted, Jacob remains disturbingly passive. Rather than seeking justice or defending her honor, he fades into the background. His sons take matters into their own hands, acting with brutal excess. Jacob fears that their actions will bring destruction on his household (Gen. 34:30). In this moment, he reflects the self-preserving instincts of his forebears—like Abraham and Isaac, who also sacrificed others' well-being for their own survival. Jacob's fear eclipses justice for Dinah. The narrator may be signaling that the name "Jacob" still fits; his transformation is incomplete.

Finally, in the remainder of Genesis (chaps. 35–50), the narrator begins to use both "Jacob" and "Israel" interchangeably, with "Israel" appearing more frequently. The shift suggests a complex and ongoing transformation. Jacob may have wrestled with God and received a new name, but he has yet to fully embody it.

TRANSITION FROM JACOB TO JACOB'S SONS

The cycle of stories around Jacob started with Jacob and Esau struggling with each other in the womb; it ends with the brothers reuniting to bury their father Isaac (Gen. 35:27–29). After Genesis 35, Jacob becomes a minor figure in the story of Joseph and his brothers. Two pillars signal the end of Jacob's story. After God appears to Jacob and changes his name for the second time, the patriarch sets up a pillar to commemorate the place where God met him twice, and he names it Bethel, "House of God"

(35:9–15; cf. 28:18–22). As Jacob leaves that place, his beloved wife Rachel gives birth to her second and Jacob's twelfth son, Benjamin. Rachel dies in childbirth, and Jacob erects a second pillar to mark her grave.

HISTORICAL MATTERS

Pillars and Sacred Memory

In the ancient world, pillars or standing stones marked encounters between heaven and earth. Jacob's pillars at Bethel (Gen. 28:18–22; 35:14–15) commemorate where God met him. Such stones served as visible witnesses to divine promise or covenant (cf. Exod. 24:4; Josh. 4:1–9). These tangible markers gave sacred memory a visible form: They turned a location into a testimony.

Just as the stories of Abraham and Isaac are separated by the genealogy of Isaac's brother Ishmael (Gen. 25:12–18), so the transition from the story of Jacob to Joseph and his brothers is marked by the genealogy of Jacob's brother Esau (36:1–37:1). These transition points indicate that (1) these stories of individuals are origin stories of peoples and nations and (2) God's covenant partnership with Abraham, Isaac, and Jacob (and sons) is oriented toward Yahweh's blessing for the nations (represented by Ishmael and Esau).

While we have focused on how God formed or discipled the patriarchs into his way of righteousness and holiness, these patriarchs were responsible for passing that way on to their children.[11] Yahweh declared that he had chosen Abraham to keep Yahweh's way of blessing *and* teach that way to his children (Gen. 18:19). The text provides few clues about how that transmission happened, and we may well ask how successful the patriarchs were in passing down God's new way.

This is an important question for at least three reasons in the final section of Genesis, chapters 37–50. First, not a single person in this fourth generation from Abraham encounters or hears a word from God. This is a noticeable shift from the previous narratives. God speaks to and/or encounters Abraham nine times and Jacob six times; even Isaac, who has only a single chapter devoted to his life, has two divine encounters. Joseph and his brothers will have to learn God's way of righteousness and holiness apart from direct divine visitation and divine instruction. The language of God's wisdom, spirit, and presence will be important in these chapters. However, the behavior of each of the twelve brothers raises questions about how well Jacob and his wives did at transmitting and discipling this generation into God's way of righteousness and holiness.

Second, while sibling rivalry was a part of Isaac's and Jacob's stories, such rivalries increase among Jacob's children. Simeon and Levi are shrewd and ruthless in avenging their sister's honor at Shechem (Gen. 34). Reuben, Jacob's firstborn, slept with Jacob's concubine after the death of Rachel (35:22), apparently seeking to usurp his father's authority and grasp his father's legacy.[12] Jacob does little to confront his sons in either circumstance, but he does pass on his own parents' problematic favoritism.

Figure 6.6. *Tamar* by Lidia Kozenitzky (2009)

As Jacob's story draws to a close, then, the complex dynamics of generational transmission come fully into view. Though God has remained faithful to his promises, the spiritual and moral formation of Jacob's children is uneven at best. In the next chapter of the patriarchs' story, the tension between God's way and other ways only intensifies.

Third, in this final section of the book, the narrator portrays significant moral ambiguity in its main character, Joseph. He is seventeen years old when his story begins in Genesis 37, and we can only surmise the formation he received in his first seventeen years regarding the way of Yahweh before he ended up in Egypt. However, clues in the text suggest that the way of Egypt, which will stand out in the Old Testament as a symbol of the way that Israel is meant to reject, also has a formative influence on Joseph's life and ethic. In the final analysis, Joseph offers *both* an example of moral/spiritual integrity *and* a cautionary tale about discipleship into the alluring way of imperial power and privilege.

Wrestling with a Difficult Story (Gen. 38)

After only one chapter, Genesis pauses the Joseph story to tell of Judah and Tamar. It feels like a digression—and a disturbing one. Yet this story is a turning point for Judah, who will later emerge as a changed man (see Gen. 44). Here he acts with selfishness and hypocrisy, while his daughter-in-law Tamar, though appearing to behave immorally, seeks justice within the social expectations of levirate marriage, the duty to produce an heir for a deceased husband (Deut. 25:5–10).

Read Genesis 38 slowly, paying attention to the narrator's restraint and use of irony.

Trace the contrasts: How do Judah and Tamar each act to secure a future? What motivates them?

Notice the irony: Who deceives whom, and to what end?

Watch for reversals: How does the story challenge assumptions about guilt, righteousness, and God's purposes?

Look for recurring motifs: What familiar Genesis themes (garments, goats, recognition, firstborn reversal) reappear here?

And now reflect, What does careful attention to this difficult story teach about God's mercy, human hypocrisy, and the surprising ways the covenant promise is carried forward?

The Account of Joseph and His Brothers (Gen. 37:2–50:26)

READ GENESIS 37–50

> Read this text as one continuous story. Note moments of reversal, trace Joseph's development, and ask, What kind of person does Joseph become, and what kind of God is at work behind the scenes?

THE DREAMER GOES TO EGYPT

Joseph's dreams launch and drive the plot of these last chapters. The context of his dreams is that of an old father having preferential love for and indulgence toward the son of his old age (Gen. 37:3). Before the dreams, which suggest Joseph will one day rise to authority over his parents and brothers, his brothers already resent him; the dreams only fuel their hatred. When presented with an opportunity to eliminate him, they seize it, first plotting to kill him but then deciding to sell him into slavery. Joseph experiences deep injustice in Egypt, first as a slave in Potiphar's household, where his integrity lands him in prison when he resists the seduction of Potiphar's wife. In prison, Joseph interprets dreams, demonstrating wisdom. Despite this, he is forgotten until Pharaoh has troubling dreams that lead to Joseph's release and elevation to second-in-command over Egypt. Through savvy decisions, Joseph saves Egypt and the surrounding peoples, including his own family, from a devastating famine. The story culminates in a powerful reunion and reconciliation with his brothers and ends with Joseph's recognition and declaration that God has transformed their harmful intentions into salvation and blessing (50:20).

The Joseph narrative brings some resolution and fulfillment of the promises made to Abraham's family. After Joseph reveals his identity to his brothers, Jacob is reunited with the son he had mourned as dead for decades. Encouraged by God, he relocates his entire household to Egypt (Gen. 46:2–4). Upon the family's arrival, Pharaoh provides Jacob and his sons with the best land in Goshen, securing their

> THEOLOGICAL ISSUES
>
> **"Bury Me in the Land"—Hope Beyond Egypt**
>
> Before they each die, Jacob and Joseph request that they not be buried in Egypt (Gen. 47:29; 50:25). Though they found provision and even honor in Egypt, they knew it was not their true home. Jacob's funeral is especially elaborate: forty days of embalming, seventy days of Egyptian mourning, and Pharaoh's full support for a grand procession to the family tomb at Machpelah. The Egyptians honor Jacob like royalty, an indication of Joseph's elevated status and his role in saving Egypt.
>
> But this honor also carries theological weight. Egypt may offer temporary security, but God's promises are rooted in Canaan. Even in death, the patriarchs look forward—to covenant fulfillment, to return. Joseph's dying request that his bones be carried out of Egypt (fulfilled in Exod. 13:19) echoes the same hope.
>
> These burial stories remind Israel—and us—that our true identity is not in power, place, or present comfort but in God's promises and presence. By insisting on burial in the land of promise, Jacob and Joseph declare that their story, and Israel's, will not end in Egypt. As Hebrews 11 notes, their final acts were expressions of trust that God would fulfill his promises, even beyond death.

well-being amid widespread famine. The aging Jacob blesses Pharaoh, embodying Israel's missional calling to be an agent of divine blessing even to foreign nations. Before his death, Jacob gathers his sons and pronounces blessings upon them. He also blesses Joseph's sons, Ephraim and Manasseh, making them heirs in the family line and including them in the covenant promises. Jacob's blessing establishes a foundation for Israel's continued growth into a great and numerous people. Jacob dies and is buried in the family's burial place in Canaan, as he had requested (47:29–31). Joseph, too, requests that his bones be carried back to Canaan one day, though Genesis ends by describing how Joseph is embalmed and placed in a coffin in Egypt.

JOSEPH'S DISCIPLESHIP: THE WAY OF YAHWEH OR THE WAY OF THE EMPIRE?

Joseph appears to be the most morally upright of the patriarchs, embodying Yahweh's way of righteousness (*tsedaqah*) and holiness (*qodesh*). Unlike his ancestors, he seems to resist the self-serving schemes, deceit, and manipulation that plague Abraham, Isaac, and Jacob (though he is adept at deceiving his brothers). Over the course of the narrative, Joseph repeatedly rises to positions of leadership and responsibility—whether as Potiphar's household manager, as overseer within the Egyptian prison system, or as Pharaoh's trusted advisor—an apparent demonstration of industriousness, discernment, and administrative wisdom (Gen. 39–41). When confronted with sexual temptation, he chooses the path of moral integrity, refusing the repeated advances of Potiphar's wife and choosing imprisonment rather than betraying his master or his God (Gen. 39). Even while unjustly imprisoned, Joseph acknowledges God's sovereignty in interpreting dreams (40:8; 41:16, 28, 32), a pattern that continues as he guides Pharaoh through the famine crisis (41:33–57). Beneath Joseph's external strength and restraint is tenderness for his brothers and longing for his family, especially evident as he repeatedly weeps in secret before revealing himself (42:24; 43:30; cf. 45:1–2). His forgiveness and reconciliation with his brothers culminate in a remarkable theological affirmation: What others intended for evil, God intended for good (50:20). Joseph appears to embody the kind of mature covenant partner Yahweh desires: formed in righteousness and wisdom to participate in God's redemptive mission to bless the nations.

Yet the narrator gives subtle clues that there is another, powerful formative influence on Joseph that runs counter to the way of Yahweh. It is in Genesis 47:13–26 that we most find reason to pause and even reread and reevaluate what has come before.

Let's begin in Genesis 45, which resolves the plot tension introduced in chapter 37: Joseph reveals his true identity to his brothers and, rather than exacting revenge, offers forgiveness and reconciliation. The family of promise then finds itself in unexpected circumstances in which the alluring world of empire is now open to them.[13] On the surface, this appears to be a providential answer to the devastating effects of the famine, a divinely orchestrated means of survival and flourishing (though earlier journeys to Egypt have warned us that easy solutions often conceal new forms of bondage). Yet before the narrative shifts toward the future in Genesis 48–50, it invites us to linger in the unresolved tension between family and empire, between the way of Yahweh and the way of scarcity, self-preservation, and name-making. As Brueggemann puts it: "In relation to these three themes [family, empire, and the tension between the two], we shall see, respectively, that *Jacob* functions as the mouthpiece for the promise tradition, *Joseph* demonstrates again his mastery of the Egyptian enterprise, and that *the brothers* are thrust into a dilemma between the faith of the fathers and the success of the 'dream brother' with the accompanying temptations of the empire."[14]

Is Brueggemann correct that Joseph is entangled in the Egyptian imperial vision? Now we come to Genesis 47:13–26, which is key to answering this question. The economic policies narrated in these verses certainly display Joseph's shrewd administrative skill, but they also serve as a lens through which the entire Joseph narrative must be reread and reevaluated, exposing subtle but clear ways in which Joseph has been shaped by the logic and practices of empire.

In Genesis 47:13–26 what begins as famine relief becomes an aggressive program of economic centralization. Joseph first acquires the Egyptians' money, then their livestock, and finally their land and even their very persons, transferring unprecedented wealth and control into the hands of Pharaoh. His program restructures Egyptian society, reducing citizens to a population of state-dependent tenant farmers—a form of economic state slavery—permanently altering the economic landscape in Pharaoh's favor. The narrator does not want us to miss the importance and summarizes: "So Joseph bought all the land of Egypt for Pharaoh, for all the Egyptians sold their fields, because the famine was severe on them. The land became Pharaoh's. As for the people, he made servants of them from one end of Egypt to the other" (47:20–21 ESV). Joseph also establishes a lasting statute requiring that one-fifth of all agricultural produce be paid as a tax to Pharaoh (47:23–26).

Alongside this social and economic reordering, Joseph privileges his own family, shielding them from servitude and settling them securely in Goshen,

Wikimedia Commons / public domain

Figure 6.7. *Joseph, Overseer of Pharaoh's Granaries* by Lawrence Alma-Tadema (1874)

with the best of Egypt's resources (Gen. 47:27). Moreover, one group of Egyptian people is conspicuously exempt from Joseph's economic reforms: the priests (47:22, 26). These details raise important questions: Why is the narrator keen for readers to know that the priests are uniquely privileged in Joseph's reorganization? What should we make of Joseph's social and economic policies more broadly? To answer these questions, we need to look back at Joseph's rise to power, now seen in light of the reforms that ultimately consolidate Pharaoh's control.

When the prisoner Joseph is finally remembered and interprets Pharaoh's dreams, he undergoes a dramatic transformation (Gen. 41:40–45). Pharaoh elevates him to the highest position of power in Egypt, second only to Pharaoh himself. Pharaoh gives him the signet ring, fine garments, a golden chain, and a royal chariot with criers demanding gestures of reverence. He gives Joseph an Egyptian name and arranges his marriage to an Egyptian woman from a prominent priestly family.[15] This calculated alliance aligns Joseph and his descendants with Egypt's religious and political elite, likely explaining the priests' exemption from his famine policies.

What does all this amount to? These details unmistakably establish that Joseph has undergone a process of "Egyptization." Brueggemann says, "The entire procedure (vv. 41–45) appears to be a proper Egyptian litany of installation. Joseph is now completely encapsulated in Egyptian reality. . . . He is fully Egyptian, easily accepting the role and authority of his new office."[16] According to my coauthor, Michael Rhodes,

> Joseph's rise to power has offered him ample opportunity to be discipled by Egypt in problematic ways. He struggles to maintain the countercultural identity and covenantal memory necessary to avoid political cooption. As a result, when his brothers show up, Joseph is *unrecognizable as a member of Abraham's family.* He looks like an Egyptian (Gen. 42:8), talks like an Egyptian (Gen. 42:23), and eats like an Egyptian (Gen. 43:32). . . . Small wonder, then, that when he first speaks with his brothers, although he *recognizes* them, the Hebrew who has become like Pharaoh (Gen. 44:18) "acted like a foreigner toward them" (Gen. 42:7 AT).[17]

The formative influence of Egypt on Joseph helps explain his later policies. Far from offering incidental details, Joseph's famine policies expose the degree to which his leadership, though undeniably effective, has been shaped by the structures of imperial power, blending shrewd administration with an underlying logic of consolidation, privilege, and assimilation. It may even be that Joseph's outer transformation is meant to reflect an inner formation that had already been taking root. Kass argues that the dream that begins the whole Joseph story—his brothers' sheaves of wheat bowing to his—offers an easily missed clue. The strangest feature of this, says Kass, is that the image is of *sheaves*! "What kind of shepherd dreams of sheaves of wheat? The imagery of the dream belongs to another place, to a more fertile place, where one man does indeed command obeisance from all around, namely, to Egypt."[18] It seems Joseph's Egyptian aspirations may be rooted very early in the story, and at the conclusion, Joseph's Egyptian dream has become a nightmare for the Egyptians.

Joseph is not without personal virtue; his integrity in Potiphar's house, his willingness to forgive his brothers, and his recognition of God's providence are rightly celebrated. But at least in the political arena, the Joseph narrative functions more as a cautionary tale about the dangers of power, privilege, and assimilation into empire. Throughout the lives of Abraham, Isaac, and Jacob, God disciples covenant partners to walk in the way of righteousness and holiness, calling them into hopeful dependence on his promises rather than fearful self-preservation and name-making. Joseph's story plays out differently.

RECEPTION HISTORY

Joseph: A Fourth-Generation Sellout?

Walter Brueggemann argues that Joseph sold out—that without a sense of moral dilemma, he "distanced himself from old covenantal dreams, trading them for the deep nightmare of the empire." The biblical tradition recognized Joseph's compromise, and that is why, according to Brueggemann, Israel confesses faith in "the God of Abraham, Isaac, and Jacob," and not in "the God of Joseph."[c]

Rather than being formed as a sojourner in dependence on God's provision, Joseph is steadily incorporated into the imperial machinery of Egypt, adopting its wealth, privilege, and ways. His famine policies concentrate power in Pharaoh's hands and create the very system of state servitude that will eventually enslave the Israelites. The text bids us to consider the unsettling possibility that the imperial complex that oppresses Israel in Exodus may be, in part, the long shadow of Joseph's compromised administration.

Conclusion (Gen. 48–50)

The final chapters of Genesis draw the patriarchal narratives to their conclusion while sharpening the tensions that will propel the story into Exodus. Jacob blesses Joseph's sons, Ephraim and Manasseh, incorporating them fully into Israel's future and ensuring Joseph's continued prominence in the covenant family (Gen. 48). His blessings of his twelve sons in Genesis 49 recall the fractured family story and anticipate the complex future of the tribes that will emerge.

Chapters 46–50 expose the unresolved tension between covenant and empire. When Joseph presents his brothers to Pharaoh, he counsels them to identify as shepherds, a vocation despised by Egyptians, so they might be permitted to settle apart in Goshen (Gen. 46:31–34). But when questioned, the brothers openly declare themselves sojourners (47:3–4), subtly claiming that Egypt is not their true home. Jacob makes this even more explicit, repeatedly demanding that his bones be taken back to Canaan, the land of promise (47:29–31; 49:29–32; 50:5–6). God's promise to multiply Abraham's descendants is partially fulfilled, but those descendants dwell under the provision and protection of empire, increasingly entangled in its wealth and power. Even Joseph's final request that his bones be returned to the land (50:24–25) is a quiet reminder that Israel's home remains elsewhere. Genesis closes with the people of promise secure but entangled, on the threshold of enslavement *and* of the deliverance that will define their story.

The tensions in Joseph's story are a fitting culmination to the entire patriarchal narrative. From Abraham's first call to leave home and trust God's promises to Isaac's and Jacob's struggles with fear, deception, and self-preservation, the family of promise has wrestled with how to live faithfully under God's covenant while navigating the threat and allure of surrounding powers. Genesis 12–50 ends with a lingering tension: Can God's people occupy places of privilege and power without being absorbed by the imperial forces they must resist, and still bear God's vocation to bless the nations with integrity? This question is as urgent for today's church as it was for the patriarchs.

Living the Text: Covenant Formation in the Shadow of Empire

In the stories of Abraham, Isaac, and Jacob, God forms covenant partners into his countercultural way of *tsedaqah* (righteousness) and *qodesh* (holiness), calling them to trust his promises rather than grasp for security, power, or self-preservation. These narratives offer enduring lessons for today about moral and spiritual formation, the transmission of covenant faith through family discipleship, and the ongoing vocation of God's people to be a blessing to the nations. In this final section, we consider the Joseph narrative, which pushes the same issues of formation into new and challenging territory, especially for God's people living in close proximity to political power and empire.

Food, Formation, and the Economy of God

An important theme in the Joseph story is food, but this is a narrative thread that runs throughout Genesis from its earliest chapters. Food plays a central role in the drama of creation, rebellion, and covenantal formation. Ellen Davis observes that "Genesis 1 is a theological statement about food, and at the same time it is an ecological statement."[19] God creates a world of abundant provision, a fruitful environment intended to sustain the life of all his creatures. In the first divine speech to humanity, God offers food as pure gift: "I give you every seed-bearing plant on the face of the whole earth" (1:29 NIV). Food, from the outset, is a symbol of God's abundant provision, human dependence, and the proper ordering of creation under God's care.

Yet it is precisely around food that humanity's rebellion takes place. The serpent entices Adam and Eve with the prospect of eating their way into life, knowledge, and autonomy: "You will not die; . . . you will be like God" (Gen. 3:4–5). Food becomes the source of a counterfeit promise, offering life apart from God and luring humanity into a grasping, self-determining posture. The result is not life but subjugation, toil, and death. As part of God's judgment, creation itself resists humanity's efforts: "Cursed is the ground because of you; through painful toil you will eat from it all the days of your life. . . . By the sweat of your brow you will eat your food" (3:17, 19 NIV). What begins as a rejection of God's provision leads to multilayered bondage: alienation from God, fractured relationships, painful labor within creation itself, and, as Genesis and Exodus unfold, economic, social, and political forms of slavery.

By the end of Genesis, this food dynamic takes on a profound and troubling form. In a world of famine and scarcity, Joseph, representing the

Figure 6.8. *Joseph Dwelleth in Egypt* by James Jacques Joseph Tissot (1900)

family of promise, is elevated by God's providence to a position of imperial power. He holds the keys to life and death as the administrator of Egypt's grain supplies. The critical question is whether Joseph's control over food will reflect the generous provision of the Creator or mirror the serpent's logic of grasping, control, and subjugation. Will the provision of food point to the life-giving generosity of God? Or will it become a tool of manipulation, power consolidation, and imperial oppression? The narrative affirms Joseph's personal faithfulness, yet the broader economic consequences of his policies introduce a moral complexity that the text does not resolve. It also leaves us, as readers, asking how God's people today navigate similar tensions when entrusted with resources, power, and the means of sustaining life.

The formation of the patriarchs was intended to resist the scarcity-driven, self-preserving mentality that took root in Eden. The serpent's economy, which continues to shape both their world and ours, says resources are scarce, more for one means less for another, fear leads to hoarding, and self-protection is the wisest course. But in God's economy, the dynamics of provision are radically different. A widow's handful of flour and jar of oil sustain her household throughout a three-year drought (1 Kings 17:8–16); another widow's jar of oil is multiplied to pay off debts and rescue her children from slavery (2 Kings 4:1–7).[20] A few loaves and fish, blessed and broken, feed multitudes with abundance left over (Matt. 14:13–21; 15:32–39; Mark 6:30–44; 8:1–10; Luke 9:10–17; John 6:1–15). The way of Yahweh calls his covenant partners to resist the logic of scarcity and embrace open-handed generosity, where blessing flows most fully in acts of provision for the vulnerable. Brueggemann says the end of Genesis urges the people of God to imagine that "there are alternatives to imperial modes of nourishment" (cf. Mark 8:15; John 6:35).[21]

Faithfulness in the Shadow of Empire

In his book *Just Discipleship*, my coauthor sharpens this dilemma by contrasting two ways God's people might engage political power, the Joseph Option and the Daniel Option: "Both the 'Daniel Option' and the 'Joseph Option' recognize that God's people can, at least on some occasions, use political power to seek the good of the communities to which they have been sent. Both agree with Jeremiah that, on such occasions, God's people find their 'welfare' in seeking the broader community's 'welfare' (Jer. 29:7). But in other ways, they differ substantially in terms of the overall approach to political advocacy."[22]

Joseph exercises political influence by more fully assimilating into Egypt's imperial structures. He accepts Pharaoh's elevation, takes on an Egyptian identity, marries into Egypt's priestly class, and implements economic policies that enrich Pharaoh while reducing Egypt's citizens to state-dependent servitude. His decisions privilege his family, securing their survival, but help build the very system that will later enslave Israel.

Daniel, by contrast, serves Babylon while deliberately resisting assimilation. He maintains covenantal distinctiveness while using his position to confront imperial injustice. Daniel directly calls Nebuchadnezzar to practice righteousness and show mercy to the oppressed (Dan. 4:27). As a result, Nebuchadnezzar experiences a humbling transformation, ultimately exalting the justice and sovereignty of Israel's God (4:34–37). Daniel's faithfulness not only leads to his survival but also brings about a partial reordering of imperial power toward justice.[23]

This contrast between Joseph and Daniel is not merely a question of ancient imperial politics; it reflects an enduring challenge for God's people in every generation. In a world where Christians often find themselves embedded within powerful institutions—political, economic, cultural, or educational—the question is not whether we serve, but how we serve. Like

Joseph, believers may gain positions of influence within systems shaped by self-interest, economic exploitation, and injustice. The temptation is to accommodate, to leverage power primarily for the protection of our own communities, or to justify compromise by appealing to the good we believe we are accomplishing.

Joseph's example also offers a warning for modern Christians who compartmentalize personal virtue from public witness. Joseph's commitment to sexual purity, his ethic of forgiveness, and his attribution of wisdom to God stand in tension with his assimilation into imperial economics and politics. The disjunction between his personal piety and his public policies exposes a faulty formation that, while preserving his family, has devastating consequences for Egypt and ultimately for Israel itself.

For God's people today, Daniel offers a more compelling model of covenantal faithfulness within compromised systems. Like Daniel, believers are called to serve without surrendering covenant identity, to resist assimilation, and to use positions of influence to advocate for righteousness and mercy, especially for the poor and oppressed. Faithfulness requires more than personal integrity; it demands the courage to speak truth to power, even at great personal cost. This is, ultimately, the way Jesus himself confronted the power structures of his own world, exposed their injustice, and embodied God's kingdom of justice and mercy, even to the point of death on a cross.

Exodus 1–18

The Liberating God Rescues His People

Orientation

Exodus is the salvation story of the Old Testament, the "gospel tract" of the First Testament. Here God formally introduces himself as Yahweh for the first time. Here God liberates brutally enslaved people and reveals himself as redeemer for the first time. Here the people receive the law for the first time and build their first proper sanctuary. And here, for the first time in Scripture, God's people explicitly worship him as *king*.

Exodus shapes the rest of Scripture. The story of Israel's deliverance from Egypt is referred to around 120 times in just the Old Testament.[1] When Israel enters Canaan, they pass through the waters again, not on the way out of the house of slavery but on their way into the land of promise. The prophets describe Israel's return from Babylonian exile centuries later as another exodus. Even Jesus passes through the exodus-like waters of baptism on the way to a wilderness testing and an eventual giving of the law on another mountain (Matt. 3:13–17). When Jesus chats with Moses and Elijah in a cloud of glory on the mountain of transfiguration, they speak of "his exodus" (*exodon*; Luke 9:31 AT). Jesus then suffers and dies during the Passover before making the greatest exodus of all in his resurrection. When John of Patmos sees a vision of the saints celebrating God's just judgment, they're singing Moses's song (Rev. 15:3–4). Listening to Exodus helps us hear the Spirit's song sung throughout Scripture.

HISTORICAL MATTERS

Dating the Exodus

As discussed in chapter 1, the truth value of a biblical text depends on the truth claims of that text. The truth value of the exodus is connected to the truth claim that Yahweh really did bring his people out of Egypt. Scholars who take the historicity of the book seriously debate whether the exodus occurred in the fifteenth or thirteenth century BC.[a]

LITERARY NOTES

The Structure of Exodus

Prologue (Exod. 1–2): Growth and bondage in Egypt[b]

Deliverance (Exod. 3–15): Out of Egypt and to the mountain of God

Covenant (Exod. 16–24): Called and equipped to be God's "treasured possession"

Life in God's house (Exod. 25–40): Plans for and challenges to dwelling with Yahweh

Structure

There are a variety of ways to understand the structure of Exodus. Walter Brueggemann and Tod Linafelt identify three major sections: deliverance, covenant, and presence.[2] L. Michael Morales argues God's people move through the waters, to the mountain, for life in God's house.[3] In these three-part structures, the first major section follows an initial prologue and establishes Israel's identity as God's liberated people. At the mountain, the people receive guidance on how to live into their identity as God's priestly kingdom. In the final section, the people receive instructions for creating a space for Yahweh to dwell among them and, after an initial major failure, build that space in line with God's instructions.

Others identify a "saga of Moses" that anticipates the "saga of Israel."[4] In Moses's saga, Moses is rescued through the waters, wanders in the wilderness, speaks with God amid the fire on a mountain, and receives instructions that culminate in worship. Each of these events in Moses's life anticipates Israel's journey in the rest of the book.

Whatever the structural specifics, the book clearly tracks a dramatic shift, evident in the repeated use of the Hebrew verb *'avad*, which means "to work" or "to serve." Related noun forms refer to service, a servant, or a slave. Exodus uses this language to describe the Egyptians enslaving God's people and making their lives bitter with hard service (Exod. 1:13–14). Yahweh liberates the people from this slave service to Pharaoh. But again and again, the book also declares that the goal of Israel's liberation from slave service to Pharaoh "is that they may serve" Yahweh (4:23; 7:16; 8:16, 20; 9:1, 13; 10:3).

English versions obscure this because they often translate *'avad* as "worship" rather than "serve" when describing Israel's relationship to Yahweh. Unfortunately this obscures some of the deep meaning of the book. Israel is liberated *from* harsh service as slaves to Pharaoh and liberated *for* joyful service to Yahweh as Yahweh's own servants. The book begins with God's people being forced to build storage cities for a cruel king who claimed to be god.[5] In the middle of the book, they get to know their divine liberator and discover why becoming *his* servants is good news. The book ends with God's people joyfully and willingly serving Yahweh by building a worship space for their divine king.

Structural Connections with the Pentateuch

Exodus is integrally connected to the rest of the Pentateuch. Repeated references to the exodus as the fulfillment of the promises to the patriarchs, as well as an early reference to Joseph (Exod. 1:8), closely connect the book with Genesis. One important implication is that Yahweh's decision to call Abraham *for the sake of the nations* should be kept in view throughout the book. Exodus is about Yahweh's ways with Israel *for the sake of the world*.

Given that the Pentateuch can be read as a biography of Moses, Exodus also links with Leviticus and the rest of the Torah by introducing the central (human) character of the story. Exodus also brings Israel to Mount Sinai, where they remain until Numbers 10:11. Thus the events at Mount Sinai arguably stand at the center of the Torah. More immediately, Exodus ends with the tabernacle constructed but so filled with Yahweh's glory that Moses cannot enter it. Leviticus begins by addressing how Israel might enter God's house.

Exploration

The Introduction (Exod. 1:1–2:22)

READ EXODUS 1:1–2:22

Consider what this text says about (1) God and (2) the female characters in the story. What questions does this raise?

Because of Joseph's rise to prominence, Egypt provided Jacob's family with a safe place to escape the famine at the end of Genesis. Exodus opens with Israel continuing to flourish there. By using language from Genesis 1 to describe their growth, Exodus 1:7 suggests God's creational, covenantal plans for Israel are beginning to be fulfilled: "The Israelites were fruitful and . . . multiplied."

The good times don't last. Exodus 1:8 reports that a new king "who did not know Joseph" takes over. This new king offers us a three-step master class in xenophobic oppression: (1) Create strong "us/them" identities, (2) use this difference to sow fear about whether "they" are really committed to "us," and (3) create an oppressive "solution" to the manufactured problem.

For Pharaoh, this is political business as usual: "Let's deal wisely with them . . ." (Exod. 1:10 NET). From a theological perspective, the Egyptians have taken their stand against Yahweh's creational, life-affirming

ETHICS

Exodus and Immigration Today

Danny Carroll points out the parallels between the experiences of the Israelites in Egypt and those of many immigrants today. Speaking of the Latino/a experience in the US, Carroll writes: "The trek here is hard, and life once they get to the United States can be full of long hours of work with low pay and few benefits. Perhaps they have left one Egypt for another. *Here the majority culture fears their numbers and their being different, although they want their labor.*"[c] Jorge Pixley suggests "pharaoh's fear is the fear of *every* oppressor, ancient or modern. The oppressed are necessary to do the dirty work no citizen wants to do, but they are feared and controlled as a potential enemy."[d] The Torah will repeatedly remind Israel of their oppression in Egypt so that they treat immigrants with compassion and care.

Dennis MacDonald / Shutterstock

Figure 7.1. Mexican migrant workers picking tomatoes

way.[6] But the more the Israelites are oppressed, the more they multiply. Their growing numbers cause the Egyptians to loathe them (1:12), leading to ever-more-ruthless oppression. This culminates in Pharaoh's infanticidal plan to kill all the Israelite males and the story of how those plans are thwarted, at least partially. In these opening chapters, we note three themes.

WHERE IS YAHWEH?

With one notable exception, God goes unmentioned in these opening stories. The allusions to Genesis 1 in the description of Israel's growth in Egypt make us wonder whether he's working behind the scenes. But given that God's actions are on center stage in the rest of Exodus, it's significant that the story doesn't start there. As readers, we wonder, *Where is God?* Perhaps the Israelites wondered the same thing.

WATCH OUT FOR THE WOMEN

While we may wonder where God is, we can't help but be struck by all the women in the opening chapters of Exodus. The first characters to confront Pharaoh aren't Moses and Aaron. They're Shiphrah and Puah, midwives who become some of the world's first practitioners of nonviolent resistance. When commanded to kill Israelite boys, they refuse and offer a crafty response instead. Their claim that they haven't been able to kill the boys because "the Hebrew women are not like the Egyptian women" is doubly deceptive (Exod. 1:19). On the one hand, Pharaoh is unlikely to know much about what happens in the delivery room. That's not a place powerful men tend to hang out.[7] On the other hand, the midwives play on Pharaoh's ethnic stereotypes: "*They* are not like *us*."[8]

In the only mention of God in these early chapters, God *sees* these midwives' deceptive liberation strategies and *rewards* them (Exod. 1:20–21). God recognizes they have resisted Pharaoh's deathly order because they fear God more than Pharaoh.

Moses's mother "follows a strategy similar to Shiphrah and Puah's, disobeying Pharaoh's decree that infant boys be cast into the Nile by feigning obedience to that same decree and 'casting' her infant boy into the Nile."[9] Moses's young sister then "takes her stand" along the river, much as Moses would later "take his stand" there to confront Pharaoh (Exod. 8:16).[10] Like the midwives, Moses's female family members subversively work for life in the face of death.

The daughter of Egypt's megalomaniacal despot finds baby Moses, pities him, and defies her father's order. Because of her courageous, disobedient action, Israel's future liberator is raised in Pharaoh's own house. Moses's sister helps bring this to pass by nudging Pharaoh's daughter toward saving the child's life. Carmen Imes suggests Pharaoh's daughter may have suspected the girl of getting Moses's own mother, so that these two "silently colluded in the fight against injustice."[11]

Pharaoh presumably tries to kill male children because he believes males pose a threat to his power. Ironically, Pharaoh is repeatedly outsmarted by a female "conspiracy of the compassionate."[12] Their wily, deceptive resistance work ensures that Israel's (human) liberator, Moses, survives. This "women's work" anticipates in microcosm what Yahweh himself does in macrocosm in the rest of Exodus.[13]

ETHICS

Harriet Tubman: "The Puah of Her People"

Harriet Tubman was an enslaved Black woman who escaped to freedom on the Underground Railroad. She repeatedly risked her life to return to the South and rescue dozens of others. Later she served as a Union spy. Known as "the Moses of her people,"[e] Tubman might equally well be referred to as "the Puah of her people." Like the midwives, she used craftiness, deception, and extreme courage to save lives under a horrendously oppressive regime.

National Portrait Gallery / Smithsonian Institution / CC0

Figure 7.2. Harriet Tubman (ca. 1885)

THEOLOGICAL ISSUES

God the Midwife

While the midwives' work in Exodus anticipates Yahweh's later deliverance, scholar Juliana Claassens observes that the book of Psalms goes further, describing Yahweh himself as a midwife: "The conviction that God is the God of life, who works ceaselessly to bring life into the world, forms the basis of the psalmist's prayer to the Deliverer God":[f]

> For you, O Lord, are my hope,
> my trust, O Lord, from my youth.
> Upon you I have leaned from my birth;
> it was you who took me from my
> mother's womb. (Ps. 71:5–6)

This provocative image of God as midwife powerfully captures "God's nurturing presence and saving power."[g]

NEW BEGINNINGS

These early chapters of Exodus introduce Moses. When Exodus says Moses's mother places him in a "basket," the Hebrew word is *tevah*, "ark." Moses's journey on dangerous waters in this life-saving "ark" helps us see the unfolding story as another instance of "new creation."

Things start humbly for Moses. His willingness to side with his Israelite kin against the Egyptians seems promising (Exod. 2:11–12). In the end, however, the Israelites reject him as a leader, and he barely escapes with his life. When he arrives at the well in Midian and rescues the daughters of Reuel from local shepherds, Zipporah identifies him as an

Figure 7.3. *Moses in the Bullrushes* by Henry Ossawa Tanner (1921), an early twentieth-century African American painter

Figure 7.4. *The Mother of Moses* by Simeon Solomon (1860)

Egyptian, raising questions about Moses's identity. Is he a prince of Egypt? An Israelite freedom fighter? Something else? Where does he belong?

Yahweh Acts (Exod. 2:23–4:31)

READ EXODUS 2:23–4:31

Consider what we as readers learn about Yahweh's character. What questions do these chapters raise?

THE TURNING OF THE TIDE

The tide turns in Exodus 2:23–25, but the definitive change does not come through politics as usual. The Israelites *cry out*, and "out of their slavery their cry for help rose up to God" (2:23 AT). The God-saturated language of 2:24–25 indicates Yahweh's response: "And God heard, . . . and God remembered. . . . And God saw . . . , and God knew" (AT).

These lines are theologically explosive. God only seemed to be absent, perhaps so the narrator could help us empathize with the Israelites' experience of wondering whether God had abandoned them.[14] But in these verses we are welcomed into the heart of Yahweh. No distant, hard-to-find, disengaged deity here. This God not only hears the cries and sees the oppression; he intimately knows the suffering of humans.

Moreover, this God will be faithful to his promises. The idea of remembering his covenant does not imply those promises had slipped God's mind but rather that God is now moving to act on them. Readers are filled with expectation: "The silence of God is about to be broken"![15] But how?

MOSES MEETS YAHWEH

Within the well-known story of Moses's encounter with Yahweh at the burning bush are several areas for reflection.

The burning bush. The symbolism of the burning bush could be read in multiple, perhaps complementary, ways. The fire could be a "symbol for the transcendent, awesome, and unapproachable" nature of God.[16] Or the "lowly bush" might represent Israel's frailty, with the fire symbolizing their oppression. Such an image suggests God's people will not be destroyed by their suffering.[17] Yet another interpretation emphasizes that in his willingness to enter creation in this way, "God made his presence lowly."[18] God condescends to the needs of his creatures in his desire to communicate with them.

ETHICS

The God Who Hears

Throughout the Bible, "Yahweh is a God who *hears* the cry of the oppressed and *responds* with justice."[h] In Genesis 18:20, Yahweh hears the "outcry" against Sodom and Gomorrah, whose men committed horrendous acts of sexual violence against vulnerable strangers (19:5) and who were remembered for refusing to help the poor despite great wealth (Ezek. 16:49). When Israel suffers at the hands of their national enemies and "cries out," Yahweh raises up deliverers (see, e.g., Judg. 3:9, 15; 6:7–8). Psalms gives Israel songs and prayers with which to lift their cries to Yahweh (e.g., Pss. 22:5; 107:13; 142:1).

But Yahweh also hears the outcries of oppression that occur within Israel. God warns the people that he will hear and forcefully respond to the cries of widows, orphans, and victims of unjust lending practices in their midst (Exod. 22:23–27). Such texts implicitly call God's people to imitate Yahweh in his hearing and responding to injustice, while explicitly warning them should they fail to do so.

RECEPTION HISTORY

The Burning Bush, Jesus, and the Virgin Mary

Some early Christians believed the burning bush prefigured Jesus's incarnation in the womb of the virgin Mary. As John of Damascus says, "The virgin bore Fire within her, yet was not consumed, when she gave birth to the light-bearing Benefactor."[i] This sixteenth-century Orthodox icon by Michael Damaskinos captures this visually by depicting Moses's interaction with a burning bush within which Mary and the incarnate Christ are seated. This image captures the mystery that God, in the bush and in the incarnation, inhabits creation without consuming it.

Figure 7.5. Orthodox icon by Michael Damaskinos (16th cent.)

Figure 7.6. *Study for Moses and the Burning Bush* by Henry Ossawa Tanner. Tanner, one of the first African American painters to achieve international acclaim, painted this piece after visiting the Sinai Peninsula.

Holy ground. The reference to "holy ground" (Exod. 3:5) is the first use of "holy" since Yahweh made the seventh day of creation "holy" (Gen. 2:3). Once again, it is Yahweh's presence and activity that makes something holy, set apart, suffused with God's own life and vitality. Such holiness, like fire, is both benevolent (bringing warmth and light) and dangerous (threatening to burn and kill).[19] Throughout the Torah, Yahweh's holiness will bless and burn the Israelites. The danger and delight of dwelling near Yahweh's holy presence—and of becoming holy to safely do so—are major themes and will be the driving focus of Leviticus.

God's name. The revelation of God's special name, Yahweh, to Moses has attracted intense debate. The Hebrew for Yahweh's self-revelation in Exodus 3:14 is *'ehyeh 'asher 'ehyeh*. The NRSV translates this as "I AM WHO I AM," but these words could also be translated "I will be who I will be," "I will be who I am," "I am who I will be," and so on.

The third-person form of the verb in Yahweh's self-revelation is *yihyeh* and typically means "he is" or "he will be." That verb gives us YHWH, the four-letter personal name Israel used in relationship with the one Creator God. Because later Jews were reluctant to say this name out loud, we cannot be sure exactly how it was pronounced, but *Yahweh* seems most likely. Traditionally, English Bibles translate Yahweh as "LORD," written with small capital letters.

CANONICAL CONNECTIONS

A "God with Us" Kind of God

Israel's special name for God resonates with Scripture's larger Immanuel, God-with-us story.[j] The Bible begins with God creating the universe as a sanctuary within which to dwell alongside human image bearers. The Bible ends with God taking up residence with those image bearers in a new heavens and a new earth. Between these two poles, we discover a God who walks with Abraham, shows up in Egypt, fills the tabernacle and temple with his glory, serves as a "little sanctuary" for his people in exile (Ezek. 11:16), comes to dwell among his people in the flesh at the incarnation, and sends his Spirit to fill his people while they await his return. This God, our God, is, was, and always will be "God with us."

But what does it *mean*? The name may point to Yahweh's unchanging character; God is and will always be who he has always been. Such a name would bring immense comfort to God's people. The God who made enormous promises to their fathers will be faithful.[20] It might also suggest Israel will discover who God is through what God does. "You want to know who I am?" Yahweh asks Moses. "Watch and see."

Intriguingly, immediately before and after revealing his name, God tells Moses "he will be" with him. In other words, the primary characteristic emphasized in Yahweh's climactic revelation of his name is that he will be with the Israelites. Whatever happens going forward, this God is a God who will always be with his people.

The calling. After a long speech emphasizing that *he* will come down and deliver his people, God suddenly tells Moses, "And now, go, and I will send *you* to Pharaoh. *You bring out my people*, the children of Israel, from Egypt!" (Exod. 3:10 AT). Here Yahweh weaves together his own action with Moses's action. God is the one coming down to liberate his people. Yet Moses is called to do the liberating work. Moses famously resists this calling, protesting that he just isn't the man for the job.

The contest. Yahweh clarifies that the Israelites will only be able to leave Egypt if Yahweh triumphs over Pharaoh. Yahweh's announcement sets the stage for the contest that plays out in Exodus 5–15 and that will culminate in the killing of the firstborn of Egypt in exchange for Yahweh's firstborn, Israel (4:23). Yahweh describes this as a difficult act of justice on an unrelenting oppressor (see below for further discussion). The language of Israel as Yahweh's firstborn son points to their unique relationship with God. Yet Craig Bartholomew reads this language as an invitation: "If [Yahweh] has one son he could have another, and . . . Egypt might also become a son of [Yahweh]."[21]

That Yahweh's judgment on Egypt is about justice can also be seen in the promise that the Israelites will leave Egypt with possessions they receive from their oppressors (Exod. 3:21–22).[22] Israel leaving Egypt laden down with valuable items anticipates Israel's later law that debt slaves be released and sent out with liberal provisions (Deut. 15:12–18). The "plunder" Israel takes from Egypt is not stolen goods; it is a form of reparation.

RECEPTION HISTORY

"Building for God with Gold from Egypt": Origen on the Plunder of the Egyptians

Writing in the first centuries of the Christian era, Origen suggested that the Israelites used the "plunder" of the Egyptians to build the "things which pertained to the service of God. For from the things which the children of Israel took from the Egyptians the vessels in the holy of holies were made."[k] For Origen, the story offers an illustration of the way Christians in his day could likewise use the "plunder" of their pre-Christian Greek culture, philosophy, and learning "for the worship and glorification of God."[l] Origen recognized this was a dangerous operation; "Egyptian gold and Greek materials are to be used for the glorification of God," as Andrew Walls puts it, "but it is necessary to watch out lest idols be manufactured in the process."[m] Nevertheless, Walls argues that Origen's willingness to "plunder" the riches of his culture and deploy the "gold" found there in the service of Christ, "building for God with gold from Egypt,"[n] is a model for Christians today, not least in Africa, Asia, and the Pacific. Believers who are "confident in the Scriptures, and yet at home in" their own cultural traditions can reclaim those traditions as treasures and materials for "the worship and glorification of God." Doing so will enable Christians from around the world to discover how to weave "the Christian faith into the fabric of" every culture and language under heaven.[o]

ETHICS

Reparations in Exodus

Matthew Schlimm makes a detailed argument that the "plundering" of the Egyptians is an act of reparation. A number of ancient Jewish and Christian interpreters read the text this way, suggesting that the Egyptians gave these goods in recompense for the Israelites' unpaid labor. Furthermore, the description of the Egyptians freely giving their goods sounds more like an offering of reparations than the plundering that occurs in war.

Recognizing this transaction as an act of reparation helps explain one of the puzzles of the text. While most English versions describe the Israelites "plundering" the Egyptians, the Hebrew verb nearly "always means 'deliver,' 'rescue,' or 'save.'" According to Schlimm, Exodus 3:22 and 12:36 suggest that these reparations worked both to repair the damage done to the Israelites and to rescue the Egyptians by making right the wrong they had done to the Israelites, thus helping them to avoid further judgment: "The Israelites rescue the Egyptians from God's ongoing judgment by asking for and receiving their valuables." As for the Egyptians, "In an act of significant sacrifice, they surrender their greatest valuables with no strings attached. They demonstrate concretely they are no longer going to exploit the Israelites. They give the Israelites the means to move forward not in destitution, but in prosperity."[p]

Exodus 4:21 introduces the idea that God will "harden" Pharaoh's heart during the contest. Few ideas offend modern readers more. If God hardens Pharaoh's heart, doesn't that make God responsible for Israel's and Egypt's suffering? Doesn't it let Pharaoh off the hook for his rebellion? Closer reflection on this language helps us understand this mysterious dynamic.

First, translations flatten out language related to Pharaoh's heart. The Hebrew text uses three different verbs to describe action taken on Pharaoh's heart. His heart is "strengthened," "made heavy," and "hardened." Because the "heart" is the center of a person's thinking, feeling, and willing in the Old Testament, a heavy or hardened heart is less capable of appropriate thinking, feeling, and willing. But the idea of "strengthening" a person's heart is different; it suggests encouraging a person in a path they have already chosen.[23] This is what Yahweh says he will do in Exodus 4:21. Like his infanticidal predecessor, Pharaoh is a wicked, Hitler-like tyrant who has brutally enslaved God's people; his heart is sick. Yahweh's strengthening of Pharaoh's heart in no way charts a new path for this brutal dictator. It is instead about "giving him the boldness or courage to do what he most desires."[24]

Second, Exodus 4:22–23 looks ahead to Yahweh's actions toward the end of the contest, but the language used of Pharaoh's heart during the contest complicates the timeline of this divine action (see table 7.1). In the first four plagues, Pharaoh himself is said to have a strong,

Table 7.1. Pharaoh's Heart in Exodus

Yahweh Acts	No Acting Subject Specified	Pharaoh Acts
"I will make strong his heart" (4:21)		
"But I will make hard Pharaoh's heart" (7:3)		
	"The heart of Pharaoh was strong" (7:13)	
	"The heart of Pharaoh is heavy" (7:14)	
	"Pharaoh's heart was strong" (7:22)	
		"Pharaoh did not take even this to heart" (7:23)
		"Pharaoh made his heart heavy" (8:15)
	"Pharaoh's heart was strong" (8:19)	
		"Pharaoh made his heart heavy" (8:32)
	"The heart of Pharaoh was heavy" (9:7)	
"Yahweh made strong the heart of Pharaoh" (9:12)		
		"He made his heart heavy" (9:34)
	"So the heart of Pharaoh was strong" (9:35)	
"I have made his heart heavy" (10:1)		
"But Yahweh made strong Pharaoh's heart" (10:20)		
"But Yahweh made strong Pharaoh's heart" (10:27)		
"Yahweh strengthened Pharaoh's heart" (11:10)		
"I will strengthen Pharaoh's heart" (14:4)		
"Yahweh made strong Pharaoh's heart" (14:8)		

Note: Scripture quotations are the authors' translation.

heavy heart or to make his own heart heavy. Only afterward is Yahweh said to "strengthen" or "make heavy" Pharaoh's heart (Pharaoh once again makes his heart heavy in 9:34–35).

While the text affirms Yahweh's sovereignty over the contest, it also places responsibility on Pharaoh himself. Pharaoh embraced evil repeatedly and resolutely, including by making his own heart heavy. Eventually,

Yahweh judges Pharaoh, in part by giving him over to his own wicked way. There is something quite commonsense about this; what feel at first like free choices to embrace sin gradually become more irresistible.

In the end, the Bible offers a nuanced account of God's sovereignty over Pharaoh's heart alongside an equally strong statement about Pharaoh's responsibility. "Pharaoh did it to himself, and Yahweh did it to him."[25] For the biblical writers, affirming both is theologically essential.

MOSES DISCOVERS THE DANGER OF LIFE WITH GOD AND IS RESCUED BY ANOTHER WOMAN

As Moses returns to Egypt to confront Pharaoh, Yahweh seeks to kill him on the way (Exod. 4:24–26). This is one of the strangest stories in Scripture, but it nevertheless makes several important theological points. First, life with Yahweh can be dangerous. Jacob learned this lesson in his wrestling match. Yahweh may be for his people, but that doesn't mean he can be presumed upon. This is the underlying conviction of Leviticus and will be evident throughout the Pentateuch, especially in the Passover.

Second, Moses has apparently chosen not to place the sign of the covenant on his son through circumcision. Perhaps this is what draws Yahweh's ire. Remember, Moses strenuously resisted God's command to go back to Egypt, agreeing only with great reluctance and after a lot of debate. If Moses is still on the fence, perhaps still wrestling with his conflicted Israelite-and-Egyptian identity, this story reminds us it can be dangerous to get near God if you haven't fully committed yourself.

Third, once again, Moses is saved by the heroic quick thinking of a woman. Shockingly, his female rescuer is a foreigner associated with a priestly family outside Israel, yet she knows how to properly perform circumcision. Here we glimpse how Israel's ethnic boundaries were porous. Inclusion in "Israel" was ultimately not about ethnicity but about identity and allegiance. Moses would later be challenged for having a wife who was not Israelite enough, but here he owes his life to his "outsider" bride.

Yahweh's Victory over Egypt (Exod. 5:1–15:21)

READ EXODUS 5:1–15:21

Read (or listen to) this text in one sitting, if possible. Consider what Yahweh says and does in these chapters. What do these texts reveal about God's character?

Exodus 5–15 recounts Yahweh's dramatic victory over Pharaoh. To understand this contest better, it's worth reflecting on the society, politics, and theology of Pharaoh's Egypt before considering the details of Israel's deliverance.

Jacques Descloitres, MODIS Rapid Response Team, NASA/GSFC

Figure 7.7. Satellite image of Egypt and the Sinai Peninsula

PHARAOH'S EGYPT

Egypt was the dominant superpower of the day. Much of its power was based in its ecology. Unlike the land of Canaan, which depended on rain for agricultural productivity, and unlike the enormous desert area around Egypt (see fig. 7.7), Egypt had an agricultural economy that thrived due to the relatively dependable waters of the Nile.[26] Because of their stable water supply, no people ate as well as the Egyptians for thousands of years.[27]

Such agricultural prosperity allowed Egypt to acquire enormous economic power. The ability to feed the hungry during years of distress enabled

The Yorck Project / Wikimedia Commons

Figure 7.8. Depiction of Egyptian slavery on an ancient Egyptian tomb

Egypt to develop the most "intensely centralized government in existence." That centralized government was also a military superpower.[28]

Historical records confirm what Exodus tells: Pharaoh's Egypt seriously oppressed the poor (see fig. 7.8). Massive building projects required enslaved laborers, and Egyptian texts recount the misery of those required to make bricks. We even have records of enslaved people being given enormous quotas for brickmaking that they regularly failed to meet.[29] Egypt also demanded oppressive taxes and forced labor from Canaan, the land to which Israel was headed.[30]

Egypt's Nile-backed power and prosperity influenced its theology. The ancient historian Herodotus claimed the Egyptians were more "excessively" religious than any other people.[31] They worshiped hundreds and even thousands of gods. Indeed, the pharaoh himself was understood as being a god.[32] Several pharaohs were worshiped during their lives, and Seti I is depicted in one temple scene as "making an offering to himself."[33]

Because of this royal theology, Egyptian life was grounded in "the absolute rule of the Pharaoh,"[34] who served as the "crucial lynchpin that held together . . . the disparate worlds of gods and [humanity]."[35] Part of the rationale for such a belief is that Pharaoh was seen as the one responsible for maintaining "order, truth, and balance" in both society and the created world.[36] He was, for instance, responsible for the Nile's seasonal flooding, as well as for overseeing Egypt's irrigation system. Such theology promoted a worldview in which complete obedience to the pharaoh was necessary for the social and ecological order to flourish.

Given this background, Exodus 5–15 depicts a contest between Yahweh the true God and Pharaoh the idolatrous false god, a contest centered in part on the question of which master will claim Israel's service. We see this in Pharaoh's first response to Moses's demand that Pharaoh release Yahweh's people: "Who is Yahweh, that I should listen to his voice and send Israel out? I do not know Yahweh!" (5:2 AT). Pharaoh is confident he has nothing to fear from Israel's God and brutally increases his subjugation of the Israelites. But because of "their broken spirit and their cruel slavery," the Israelites, too, wonder whether any victory over Pharaoh is possible (6:9).

TEN SIGNS AND WONDERS

Through Moses, Yahweh does indeed win a devastating victory over the false god Pharaoh. Central to Yahweh's contest with Pharaoh are the so-called ten plagues or "strikes." Nahum Sarna suggests all except the death of the firstborn could be attributed to natural phenomena, and some scholars suggest each plague follows from the previous one in a natural, causal succession.[37] Exodus, however, emphasizes Yahweh's direct, divine agency in executing these events and maintains that Pharaoh should see the "finger of God" in them (Exod. 8:19).

Notably, Exodus uses the language of "plague" rarely. More often it speaks of "signs" or "wonders."[38] Such "signs" communicate Yahweh's superiority over Pharaoh. The "signs" are public precisely because God seeks to make himself known to the ends of the earth.[39] Moreover, commentator Carol Meyers notes that the theme of the Egyptians coming to know Yahweh "recurs, increasing in scope" as the plagues go on, and thus ought to be understood as "the ultimate goal of the structured set of wonders."[40] Thus, by the end of the contest,

- Israel knows Yahweh is *their* God (6:7; 10:2);
- Egypt knows Yahweh (7:5; 14:18) is utterly unique (9:14); and
- Pharaoh (and his officials) know there is no one like Yahweh (8:10), that Yahweh is present in power in Egypt (8:22), that the whole earth belongs to Yahweh (9:29), and that Yahweh makes a distinction between Egypt and Israel (11:7).

Indeed, Yahweh's wonders cause his name to "resound through all the earth" (Exod. 9:16).

The signs also play a key role in forcing Pharaoh to free the Israelites; God's judgments get more severe as the plagues continue.[41] They also give the Egyptians an opportunity to repent. This can be seen most clearly in Yahweh's instructions to the Egyptians on how to protect themselves during the plague of hail (Exod. 9:13–19). Indeed, Moses's anger at Pharaoh when he warns him about the death of the firstborn is best understood as his frustration that Pharaoh's stubborn heart has forced this terrible catastrophe on the people.[42] When the Israelites later sacrifice an animal to "redeem" their firstborn, they explain to their children that they do so in memory of Yahweh's killing of the Egyptian firstborn (13:15). The terrible price of freedom is preserved in Israel's worship.

Exodus describes these "signs" as instruments of God's just judgment. While some may find the idea that Yahweh executes forceful, just

CANONICAL CONNECTIONS

Plagues Leading to Life

The book of Joshua suggests Yahweh's victory over Egypt did indeed cause his name to "resound through all the earth." Rahab has heard of Yahweh's victory over Egypt and understands what it means: "The Lord your God is indeed God in heaven above and on earth below" (Josh. 2:11). Based on this knowledge, Rahab becomes a Yahweh worshiper herself.

Isaiah looked ahead to a day when Yahweh would "strike" Egypt (a word used several times for the plagues in Exodus) as an act of grace. "The Lord will strike Egypt, striking and healing; they will return to the Lord and he will listen to their supplications and heal them" (Isa. 19:22). This remarkable text alludes to Yahweh's "smiting" Egypt at the exodus in the context of a passage that describes Egypt in Israel-like ways: "On that day Israel will be the third with Egypt and Assyria, a blessing in the midst of the earth, whom the Lord of hosts has blessed, saying, 'Blessed be Egypt my people, and Assyria the work of my hands, and Israel my heritage'" (19:24–25). Even Israel's archenemies will belong to the people of God!

retribution on the Egyptians problematic, we need to remember Egyptian pharaohs were brutal, infanticidal tyrants, and the Egyptians themselves had frequently been complicit in their regime. Egyptian citizens presumably obeyed Pharaoh's command to throw Israelite boys in the Nile; served as taskmasters over Israelite slaves; benefitted from Egyptian oppression; and, as best we can tell, never protested Pharaoh's murderous regime.[43] Pharaoh himself recognizes he and his people have sinned (Exod. 9:27). For readers who have experienced serious oppression, God's willingness to bring justice by any just means necessary is good news indeed.

There are other, mutually compatible ways of thinking about the ten signs. Exodus 12:12 describes the Passover as a passing of judgment on "all the gods of Egypt." This suggests the signs represent Yahweh's assault on the false divinities of Egypt:[44] It's a cosmic "Royal Rumble," with all the Egyptian gods in the ring. Yahweh turns the life-giving power of the divinized Nile to blood, blacks out the allegedly divine power of the sun, and smites Egypt's sacred cows.

Fretheim situates the meaning of the plagues within a theology of creation. Because Pharaoh was understood to be responsible for maintaining cosmic order, from an Egyptian perspective, resisting him could cause the world to fall into chaos. But for Exodus, it is Pharaoh who resists God's creational ways and Egypt that becomes "an embodiment of the forces of chaos."[45] The plagues, then, "are the effect of Pharaoh's anticreational sins upon the cosmic order writ large," and the world has "gone berserk" on Pharaoh's watch.[46]

THE PASSOVER

After introducing the final sign, Exodus 12–13 lingers over the death of the firstborn. Instead of moving immediately to the event's fulfillment, the narrative shifts to instructions for how Israel will structure their calendar and their worship around this event. From now on, a ritual reenactment of the tenth sign will mark the beginning of Israel's year. The rhythms of their calendar will remind them that their lives began at the exodus. This weaving together of historical narrative with liturgical instruction breaks down the barrier between remembering the past and worshiping in the present, between what God did for *them* and what God does for all of *us*.

Becoming a people. The Passover meal forever shapes the identity of God's people. When children ask why their parents celebrate the Passover, the parents respond, "It is because of what the Lord did for me when I came out of Egypt" (Exod. 13:8). Future generations are to give this same answer, including all those generations who were not literally enslaved in Egypt. As rabbinic teaching would later explain, "In each and every generation a person must view himself as though he personally left Egypt."[47] The elements of the feast enable each generation to ritually reenact the flight from Egypt. Such rituals shape the bodies and hearts of future generations to know, deep in their bones, that their lives depend on Yahweh's miraculous victory over evil (for more on how rituals work, see chap. 10).

This is central to Israel's worship and moral character. Theologically, Israel must worship and love Yahweh alone because he is the God who has been faithful to his promises and rescued them in their hour of need. Morally, the Torah regularly grounds Israel's ethics in their exodus experience. Furthermore, the way the Passover feast creates and forms this new community explains a beautifully inclusive dynamic at the heart of Exodus. The book repeatedly emphasizes the uniqueness of Israel. This is why Exodus 12:43 declares that "no foreigner shall eat" the Passover, but the very next verses clarify that any outsider who is circumcised *can* celebrate the Passover! The Passover belongs exclusively to Israel, but the door is flung open for outsiders to become Israelites. Through the Passover feast, foreigners can claim that their ancestors, too, were liberated by Yahweh. Indeed, when Israel leaves Egypt, Exodus 12:38 tells us that "a mixed crowd also went up with them." This "mixed crowd" refers to a number of non-Israelites who joined themselves to Israel, presumably including some Egyptians.[48] Anybody willing to side with Yahweh and follow him on the road out of Egypt can become a part of his family. What it means to be Israel is not primarily a matter of ancestry or ethnicity, but of allegiance.

Death and blood at Passover. Exodus presents the killing of the firstborn as a matter of just judgment and as necessary to convince Pharaoh to release Israel. But why is the bloody Passover ritual necessary for Israel's firstborn to avoid sharing the Egyptians' fate?

One way of understanding the original ritual is as a way for the Israelites to identify themselves publicly and openly as Yahweh's people. The Israelites have been largely passive throughout the plague cycle; now they are called to join the proceedings.[49] Perhaps it is in this sense that the blood on the door is "a sign for *you*" (Exod. 12:13). Yet the blood also serves as a sign for Yahweh that functions similarly to the sign of the bow after the flood; when Yahweh sees it, he will turn from judgment.

Blood is no arbitrary symbol; the Passover meal is part of a sacrifice to Yahweh. Therefore, the sacrificial animal is killed so the people can eat it—it's

THEOLOGICAL ISSUES

The Gravitational Pull of God's People

One way the nations find blessing through Israel is by joining themselves to Israel. This happens throughout the Bible. In major covenant ceremonies, immigrants and refugees are invited to pledge their allegiance to Yahweh (see Josh. 8:33–35), outsiders like Ruth and Rahab make it into the genealogies of Israel's heroes (Matt. 1:5), and Isaiah looks ahead to a day when Israel's "kindred from all the nations" will come to Yahweh. Some will even become priests (Isa. 66:18–21)!

These passages are important for our missiology. God's mission not only sends people out; it also draws people in. The life of God's people ought to exert a "gravitational pull," drawing people to encounter the God who dwells among us.

Figure 7.9. A Samaritan Passover, held in 2012

a barbecue! Ancient Israelites, like most people in human history, raised, slaughtered, butchered, prepared, and cooked their meat themselves. They would have understood, in a way we do not, that sacrifice is nearly always about food, food eaten in the context of worship and gratitude to God.

Passover also has a substitutionary dynamic. Because the firstborn will die apart from this sacrifice, there is a sense in which the animal takes their place. This helps explain the connection between the Passover sacrifice and the redemption of Israel's firstborn humans (Exod. 13:1–2, 11–16), on the one hand, and the echoes of the near-sacrifice of Isaac in both passages, on the other. These rituals take up a notion shared across the ancient Near East that the firstborn child belongs to the deity. In the ancient world, this could lead to actual child sacrifice.[50] Israel seems to have agreed with their neighbors that God owned everything and that the offering of the first and best to God was appropriate. But Yahweh dramatically transformed the ritual by refusing child sacrifice and instead demanding that the firstborn sons be redeemed through the giving of a gift to God. Such sacrifices reminded Israel their very lives were a gracious gift.

At yet another level, within Israel's sacrificial symbol system, the "life" of a being is "in the blood" (Lev. 17:14). The people's frailty and sinfulness bring impurity and uncleanness related to death, contaminating themselves

Figure 7.10. An Ethiopian manuscript painting from the treasury of the Church of Narga Selassie, Dek Island, Lake Tana, Ethiopia. The left page portrays the drowning of Pharaoh's armies in the sea.

and their worship spaces. The sacrificed animal offers its life in the place of such death, and its life, represented by the blood, can therefore work to purify people and places from sin's contamination or set apart people and places as holy.

This may explain why blood is placed on the doorway. It offers the sign of life in the face of threatening death.[51] Drawing parallels between Passover and later sacrifices in Leviticus, Morales argues that the blood set apart their homes as holy, and the inhabitants, by eating the sacrificial food, were set apart as holy as well.[52]

THROUGH THE SEA

In response to the death of the firstborn, Pharaoh finally sends Israel away. Yahweh is present with his people, leading them "in a pillar of cloud by day" and "a pillar of fire by night" (Exod. 13:21). When Pharaoh comes with his chariots and horses—the armored tanks of the ancient world—the conflict at the Red Sea becomes the last, decisive battle between the world's most powerful empire and Israel's God.

As we saw in Genesis, ancient peoples often saw the sea as representing the forces of chaos and evil. Some told stories about their gods winning great victories over the divinized sea. While the biblical authors rejected this conception in the Genesis creation story, they use that very idea to describe Yahweh's victory over the chaos of oppressive Egypt. This explains the numerous allusions to creation and new creation in the story's water imagery. As at creation and after the flood, Yahweh's breath is on the waters, creating dry ground. As at the flood, Yahweh wields the waters of chaos to bring about a de-creation designed to deal with human wickedness. At the same time, as with the flood, Yahweh's breath on the waters initiates new creation. New life begins on the far side of dangerous waters.

The Song of the Sea highlights this, ascribing victory to Yahweh the warrior (Exod. 15:2). The Song identifies Yahweh's dramatic victory as evidence there is none like him among the heavenly beings. The Song also interprets the exodus theologically. Yahweh's victory represents his redemption of his people, a metaphor that suggests Yahweh has paid the price to purchase the Israelites as his own servants (15:13). Given the new creation context, Yahweh is also depicted as creating for himself a people, a point made explicit if Exodus 15:16 ought to be translated "the people that [Yahweh] created," as Brent Strawn argues.[53] Yahweh's victory likewise earns him the title of king, as the people declare Yahweh will reign forever (15:18). Finally, the song anticipates that the fullest meaning of the exodus is found not in Israel's getting *out* of Egypt but in their being brought *to* Yahweh. This explains why the song celebrates Yahweh bringing Israel to his sanctuary (15:17). While historically speaking Israel hasn't even heard about this sanctuary yet, the Song of the Sea prepares us for how the construction of Yahweh's dwelling place will dominate the final section of the book (for more on the poetics of song in the Bible, see chap. 4).

On the Road to Sinai (Exod. 15:22–18:27)

READ EXODUS 15:22–18:27

What do these stories teach us about ourselves? Our world? God?

Exodus 15:22–18:27 recounts Israel's wandering in the wilderness as they make their way to Sinai and their climactic meeting with Yahweh. Several themes require further reflection.

GRUMBLING AGAINST GOD AND MOSES

The people repeatedly grumble against Moses, Aaron, and Yahweh. Their inability to find food or drink in the wilderness causes their protest, but their complaints go deeper. They publicly wish Yahweh had killed them in Egypt, where they (allegedly) "sat by the fleshpots and ate [their] fill of bread" (Exod. 16:3). They wonder aloud whether Yahweh is even "among" them (17:7).

Perhaps we shouldn't be too hard on them. Just recall how barren the land around Egypt was. For more than four hundred years they'd survived through access to the pharaoh-controlled Nile. They know life was hard there, but they don't know if life is possible here. Perhaps the Egyptians had it right after all.

And that is the deeper issue. As an old saying goes, it only took a day to get Israel out of Egypt, but it will take forty years to get Egypt out of Israel. These stories demonstrate that the imaginations of these physically liberated Israelites remain "sick with Egypt's disease."[54] Yahweh must confront this issue if he is going to succeed in calling this people to be a countercultural vehicle of blessing to the nations.

THE WILDERNESS SCHOOL OF ECONOMICS

Because of this dynamic, the wilderness becomes far more than a place to survive. It becomes "the workshop of Israel's becoming,"[55] a workshop in which God's people participate in "justice/righteousness team-building exercises," as Dru Johnson humorously puts it.[56] This is particularly true concerning Israel's economic imagination. Through his provision of daily bread from heaven, God welcomes Israel to his "wilderness school of economics."[57] Manna is designed to help Israel embrace a way of economic life completely counter to Egypt's exploitative economic system.

Lesson 1: Economic abundance is God's gift, and he can give it in even the most hostile circumstances. Even in the wilderness, Yahweh provides.

Lesson 2: When God gives, he includes everyone. The manna's curious properties mean that "those who gathered much had nothing left over, and those who gathered little had no shortage; they gathered as much as each of them needed" (Exod. 16:18). God's abundant generosity means there's enough for everyone.

Lesson 3: God's gifts can't be hoarded. Egypt's economy was built on hoarding. That's why Pharaoh forced the Israelites to build storage cities. Small wonder the Israelites try to turn their individual dwellings into storage tents, hoarding today's manna in case God stops giving tomorrow. But hoarded manna rots. Yahweh seeks to create an economy characterized by joyful, openhanded dependence on him, rather than one characterized by constant grasping and hoarding.

Lesson 4: In God's economy, everybody gets a break. Israel first learns about the gift of the Sabbath by Yahweh giving them twice as much manna on Friday and no manna on Saturday. Having just been liberated from a lord whose backbreaking brick work never stopped, they now find themselves welcomed into Yahweh's economy. Here, relentless, never-ending

ETHICS

Becoming Gleaners Together

Ellen Davis notes that the Hebrew word that describes Israel "gathering" manna connects this story to later laws requiring the Israelites to allow the poor to "glean" in their fields.[q] In the wilderness, *all* are gleaners in the fields of God.

work isn't even possible. The workaholics who go looking for manna on the seventh day come home empty-handed.

Yahweh tells the Israelites to put some manna in a jar and take it with them into the promised land. They'll need that reminder to follow the rest of Yahweh's economic legislation, which seeks to create a "manna economy" in the more settled rhythms of life in the promised land.

YAHWEH FIGHTS FOR HIS PEOPLE

Israel's involvement in the fight against Pharaoh was nonviolent, but in Exodus 17:8–16, the Amalekites attack Israel without cause (according to Deut. 25:17–19, they target the frailer members of the community). In response, the Israelites do indeed fight, though Exodus makes clear their victory comes through Yahweh's intervention. Whether Israel merely stands still, as at the exodus, or straps on swords and meets the enemy in battle, as in Exodus 17, they depend entirely on Yahweh to deliver them.

GOOD NEWS TO THE GENTILES AND GOOD ADVICE FROM THEM

In Exodus 18 Moses's father-in-law Jethro/Reuel visits. This visit demonstrates that Yahweh's plan to reveal himself to the world through the contest with Pharaoh has succeeded. Moses's testimony of what Yahweh had done leads Jethro to praise Yahweh as "greater than all gods" and to offer sacrifices in worship (18:11–12). Interestingly, this gentile priest then identifies areas of improvement. Jethro's advice to divide up leadership responsibilities is profound; God's people will not rely solely on a single charismatic leader but will share leadership among trustworthy, God-fearing leaders who oppose using their positions for unjust gain.

Living the Text: Exodus as Good News for the Poor

The book of Exodus has played a major role in announcing the Christian gospel as good news to the poor and oppressed. Enslaved Black people in the American South were given a false gospel of submission to a God who stood firmly on the plantation's side. Exodus introduced them to a God who fought the oppressor and liberated the people. As James Cone declared, "There is no knowledge of Yahweh except through God's political activity on behalf of the weak and helpless of the land. This is the significance of Yahweh's contest with Pharaoh, the plagues against Egypt, and the 'hardening' of Pharaoh's heart. . . . Israel's liberation came not from its own strength but solely from the power of Yahweh, who completely controls history."[58]

When Black Christians suffering under the horrendous violence of apartheid in South Africa turned to Exodus, they discovered a compassionate God "who liberates [God's people] from their oppressors." As a result, they confronted white Christian South Africans with a nonneutral God who "sides . . . with the oppressed."[59]

Figure 7.11. *Puah* by Sarah Beth Baca (2019), watercolor and ink

Christians suffering from extreme violence and grinding poverty in Latin America drew on the exodus in developing liberation theology. "The liberation of Israel is a political action," Gustavo Gutiérrez wrote. "It is the breaking away from a situation of despoiling and misery and the beginning of the construction of a just and comradely society. It is the suppression of disorder and the creation of a new order. . . . The Creator of the world is the Creator and Liberator of Israel, to whom he entrusts the mission of establishing justice."[60]

Of course, Exodus emphasizes that Yahweh's concern for Israel was based on his covenantal promises to this particular people. However, because those promises included Israel being a vehicle of blessing to all nations, the story offers a "paradigm of hope for all oppressed peoples, assuring them they have not been created to be slaves but to be free in a society that should protect and practice justice."[61]

This exodus paradigm points to the holistic nature of God's salvation. As Christopher Wright argues, at the exodus God provides multifaceted liberation:

- *political* liberation by rescuing people from an unjust political community
- *economic* liberation by rescuing people from oppressive slave labor
- *social* liberation by rescuing people from a context in which their identity as a minority rendered them vulnerable to horrific violence
- *spiritual* liberation by freeing them from enslavement to a false god and empowering them to worship/serve the one true God[62]

On one hand, some ways of reading "liberation" in Exodus problematically downplay the way Israel's liberation *from* slavery is simultaneously Israel's liberation *for* service to Yahweh. On the other hand, many Christians have downplayed the way Exodus reveals God's heart for the oppressed. But the holistic nature of God's liberation at the exodus echoes across Scripture, culminating in Jesus's declaration of "good news to the poor" in his first sermon (Luke 4:18). Jesus shows up preaching and teaching, healing sick bodies and driving out demons, feeding hungry humans and forgiving sins, and gathering communities that include social outcasts and commit to economic sharing.

Because God's mission in Jesus is exodus shaped, the church's mission in Jesus's name should be exodus shaped. Because God's mission is holistic, our mission is holistic. We announce the good news of God's kingdom in "word, deed, and sign."[63] As René Padilla says in his description of integral mission, Christian mission involves proclaiming the good news and demonstrating that good news in acts of service: "One without the other is an incomplete, mutilated gospel and, consequently, contrary to the will of God. From this perspective, it is foolish to ask about the relative importance of evangelism and social responsibility. This would be equivalent to asking about the relative importance of the right wing and the left wing of a plane."[64]

Indeed, Exodus not only announces good news to the poor; it calls God's people to become communities that embody God's good news for the poor.

How to Read Biblical Law Today

Wise Guidance for Justice, Mercy, and Mission

There might be no genre less appealing to contemporary readers than law. Contemporary legal codes seem written to confuse, requiring expensive legal help to decipher. When we turn to biblical law, some of what we find disturbs us. Many Christians have been taught to see the biblical law as the "bad news" that Jesus overturns with the "good news." All this means we come to the Torah's law collections with certain expectations: This part of Scripture will be boring at best, bad news at worst, and irrelevant to our lives as disciples in either case.

Such expectations would shock the biblical saints. The psalmist sings, "Oh, how I *love* your law! It is my meditation all day long" (Ps. 119:97). Jesus says he came to fulfill rather than abolish the law, and he teaches that heaven and earth will pass away before even a letter of the law will (Matt. 5:17–18; cf. Paul in Rom. 3:31). His teaching on the greatest commandments, enemy love, and divorce all engage and interpret Old Testament law. Paul argues that the law is both spiritual and good (Rom. 7:12, 14; cf. 1 Tim. 1:8). Indeed, Christ died in part so that the "just requirement of the law might be fulfilled in us" (Rom. 8:4). Scripture teaches us to treat the law collections as delightful resources for understanding what life in the Spirit might look like. Clearly, the law is not God's "bad news"!

Furthermore, if we read biblical law carefully, we quickly discover it doesn't sound anything like contemporary legal texts. Just compare the selection from "Rules of the Tennessee Collection Services Board" related to debt collection with a text from Exodus addressing a similar topic (table 8.1).

Table 8.1. Comparing Ancient and Modern Laws

Tennessee Collection Services Board[a]	Exodus 22:25–27
A debt collector or collection service may not use unfair or unconscionable means to collect or attempt to collect any debt. Without limiting the general application of this prohibition, the following conduct is a violation of this section: . . . (f) Taking or threatening to take any nonjudicial action to effect dispossession or disablement of property if: 1. There is no present right to possession of the property claimed as collateral through an enforceable security interest; 2. There is no present intention to take possession of the property; or 3. The property is exempt by law from such dispossession or disablement.	If you lend money to my people, to the poor among you, you shall not deal with them as a creditor; you shall not exact interest from them. If you take your neighbor's cloak in pawn, you shall restore it before the sun goes down; for it may be your neighbor's only clothing to use as cover; in what else shall that person sleep? And if your neighbor cries out to me, I will listen, for I am compassionate.

a. "Rules of the Tennessee Collection Services Board," June 5, 2018, https://publications.tnsosfiles.com/rules/0320/0320-05.20180605.pdf.

Both texts address the rights of people who borrow money and are in danger of defaulting, but the differences are substantial. Instead of the legalese of the Tennessee code, Exodus offers the plainspoken address of Yahweh. The Tennessee code creates distance through third-person address ("A debt collector may not use . . ."), while Exodus uses second-person address to make the legal demands direct and personal ("If *you* lend money . . ."). Both texts demonstrate a concern for justice and mercy for borrowers, but Exodus reasons with the listener. Instead of merely prohibiting, Exodus invites us to "feel the pain" of the poor person whose only covering from the cold has been taken. Most crucially, the (implicit) ground of authority in the Tennessee code is the faceless state; in Exodus, the reason for treating the borrower with compassion is ultimately grounded in God's compassion, which the lender ought to imitate, and it's grounded in God's just judgment, which the lender will suffer should they fail to imitate God's justice.

HISTORICAL MATTERS

Surprising Laws Then and Now

While many similarities exist between Israel's laws and those of her neighbors, the way biblical law addresses "you," offers both reasons and motivations for obedience, and blends the law into the character and story of God is fairly unique. In terms of the law in Exodus 22:25–27, ancient Near Eastern legal collections allow for quite high interest rates, ranging from 12.5 percent to 100 percent. The interest-free loans of Israel are almost unheard of.[a]

Four Strategies for Reading Biblical Law

If we allow them to, biblical laws surprise us. Here, then, are four strategies for reading biblical law collections well.

Figure 8.1. Eighteenth-century Sefer Torah showing the beginning of Genesis

1. Read in Light of the Big Story

Reading biblical law well begins with placing it within the Torah's grand story. Central to that story is Yahweh's decision to call Abraham to become the head of a family characterized by justice and righteousness (Gen. 18:19), a "kingdom of priests" through whom God would bless the nations. This plan includes God creating a covenant with Israel where they willingly embrace his way for the sake of the world. The laws of the Torah give the people just, righteous, wise guidance on how to live as God's kingdom of priests.

We need to be careful here, though. Sandra Richter argues that while God's law is intended to help Israel incarnate God's kingdom in their culture, it does not endorse every aspect of that culture.[1] God calls Israel in the midst of a subsistence agricultural economy in the ancient Near East, a patrilineal society in which extended family households overseen by male household heads represented the foundational social unit, and a political economy in which kings extended power over villages and empires extended power over smaller kingdoms. God's law seeks to help sinful, broken people within this context move toward his kingdom by seeking justice, righteousness, and holiness within that context. Torah instruction represents not "the way it is *supposed* to be" but rather "a way that it *can* be, given the ruinous situation of humanity in the world." In this sense, the law is a "compromise document."[2] Moreover, while the law often subverts Israel's culture, economy, and politics, it does not dismantle that culture, economy, and politics and replace them with something completely "other." As Richard Averbeck says, "Old Testament law is both *in* its world and *against* its world."[3]

Because of this, some laws serve as early steps in a larger, biblical trajectory. Leviticus requires landless immigrants to be well treated, but Ezekiel envisions a day when immigrants will be given plots in the land (Ezek. 47:21–23). The tenth commandment ("You shall not covet") shows that Torah's laws were never exclusively outward focused, but Jesus takes this teaching further by associating lust with adultery and hatred with murder. This trajectory concept must not be used to reject the Torah's teaching on any particular topic because "we've gotten past all that," but it does teach us to look for ways the biblical story leads God's people to love the law and lovingly pursue where the law points beyond itself toward greater expressions of the justice and righteousness in which God delights.

Reading the law within the big story also reminds us that Torah's laws are both good and weak. As Averbeck argues, "There are certain things no law can do, not even God's law. The law has never had the power to change a human heart. Only the Holy Spirit can do that."[4] That is why Deuteronomy, Jeremiah, and Ezekiel all prophesied that God would one day work directly on people's hearts so that they *could* freely and fully live out the deepest intentions of the law.

That day began when Jesus defeated the power of sin and freed us to walk by the Spirit in the newness of life. Yet we still wait for sin's final defeat when Jesus returns. Because of this, biblical law plays an important role in believers' lives. As the Reformer John Calvin argued, "by frequently meditating upon the law," Christians will be energized for obedience and "drawn away from the slippery paths of sin."[5] Close attention to the Torah's law collections can give Spirit-filled followers of Jesus the wisdom and energy to walk in step with the Spirit.

2. Read According to Genre

We need to read biblical laws as *laws*. Law as a genre is realistic rather than utopian. Biblical laws flow out of Israel's core moral ideals, but they are not idealistic.[6] The laws help God's people decide what justice requires when men beat each other up and seduce younger women, creditors oppress debtors, and widows get pushed off their land. The laws do not pretend

Israel is a place where such things do not happen. Nor do they imagine that perfect options are always available in a world like ours.

Because of this, some laws offer a moral ceiling, calling the people to aspire to the highest of ideals—"You shall love the immigrant as yourself" (Lev. 19:34 AT), for instance. Arguably more often, however, the law offers a moral floor, seeking to limit pervasive evil rather than eliminate it.

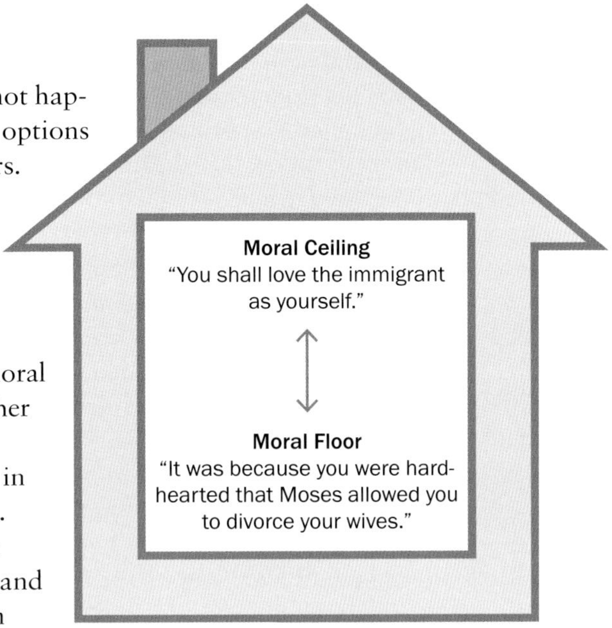

Figure 8.2. Moral floor and moral ceiling

Jesus explicitly states this principle in his teaching on divorce (Matt. 19:3–9). He begins by telling the Pharisees that divorce violates God's design for husband and wife to become "one flesh." When they ask why the law of Moses allows divorce, Jesus's reply sheds a great deal of light on the genre of law as a whole: "It was because you were so hard-hearted that Moses allowed you to divorce your wives, but from the beginning it was not so" (19:8).

Interestingly, Deuteronomy prohibits a man from remarrying his divorced wife, which scholars think provided some sort of protection for the woman.[7] In this case, then, Deuteronomy's law recognizes a pervasive problem that cannot be eliminated by legal decree. Given hard-heartedness, sometimes the best the law can do is limit damaging consequences rather than fully eliminating their causes. But as Jesus points out, obedience to such a law falls far short of God's creational ideal; the fact that the law does not say "thou shalt not" does not mean we should.[8]

ETHICS

Limiting Laws Today

Contemporary law also seeks to limit damaging consequences. The fact that large taxes on cigarettes make them expensive, rather than illegal, does not mean lawmakers think smoking is a good idea; indeed, quite the opposite. Contemporary society recognizes that unintended consequences and the lack of perfect solutions mean sometimes well-intended laws may create harm. The fact that our global free market can facilitate child labor in sweatshops *does mean* we ought to pursue laws and trade agreements that protect children, but a law simply banning all garments from the Global South might do more harm than good. We believe Christians should care about climate change, but an immediate global ban on cars and airlines would cause massive global issues. In biblical and modern law, complex and pervasive problems often require legislation that progressively limits rather than eliminates pervasive problems, at least in the short run.

THE LEGAL GENRE: THEN AND NOW

All we've said so far applies to the genre of both ancient and contemporary law. However, research on ancient law collections alerts us to differences between contemporary and ancient law. For instance, Western readers often assume ancient laws functioned as statutory law.[9] Statutory law is the primary approach to law codes in the US. Under statutory law, judges refer to specific statutes when rendering decisions. Indeed, they are bound to follow the statutory codes to the letter.

For instance, I (Michael) once attended the trial of a friend in my neighborhood who had been arrested for selling cocaine. The defense attorney, the judge, and the prosecuting attorney all appeared to want to work out a situation where my friend walked out of the courtroom that day. But when the defense attorney twice asked the judge to make a specific ruling, the judge replied, "Tennessee law does not permit me to do that." After a recess, the defense attorney tried again with the same request worded slightly differently. Same response. Finally, another lawyer in the courtroom shouted out an alternatively worded legal request that amounted to the same outcome. After pondering for a minute, the judge said, "Yes, I can do that." This is a vivid example of how, under statutory law, all legal parties are bound to follow the identified prescriptions of the legal code.[10]

Ancient law collections do not appear to have worked this way. Scholars have identified numerous law collections published by ancient monarchs, as well as ample evidence of the actual courtroom decisions rendered by ancient judges.[11] Surprisingly, the judges did not cite the law collections in their decision-making and often directly deviated from their precise legal demands.[12]

What then is the function of these law collections?[13] While scholars debate this, one prominent answer suggests they are a form of common law.[14] Under common law, judges consult written law for nonbinding precedents, rather than for binding statues they must implement to the letter.[15] Such law collections may emerge from lists of previous legal decisions[16] or include "hypothetical legal cases" that show readers what judicial wisdom looks like.[17] Given that the law collections were often published by kings, these collections may also be propagandistic demonstrations of a king's justice and wisdom.[18]

Three lines of evidence suggest that Israel's law fits this common law model rather than a statutory-law model:

1. Biblical judges are never called to "consult the lawbooks or adhere to the letter of the law." Instead, they receive generic guidance to reject bribes and do justice (see Exod. 23:6–8).[19] Similarly, the law is never used as a statutory code in narrative depictions of courtroom decisions in the Old Testament.[20]
2. Judicial decisions sometimes deviate from the law collections.[21] The author of Ruth knows the laws of the Pentateuch and shows Boaz

obeying them to a certain extent by following the gleaning laws and embracing the practice of levirate marriage. Nevertheless, the book has apparently no problem with Boaz's marriage to Ruth openly flouting Deuteronomy's law that no descendant of an Israelite married to a Moabite is ever to be welcomed into Yahweh's assembly (Deut. 23:3). In Jeremiah 34:8–22, King Zedekiah spontaneously responds to trouble in the capital by calling the people to enact a one-off release of enslaved people. The language of the text draws on the Torah's rules about the release of those enslaved for debts, and Yahweh himself says that King Zedekiah and the people were following these laws when they freed people. But Zedekiah's release differs from the Torah's laws on debt release in a number of ways.[22] Apparently both the author of Ruth and Yahweh in Jeremiah believe you can follow the law without implementing it "to the letter."

3. Numerous laws in the Torah apply to similar topics and yet appear to contradict one another in their literal implementation. This is clearest in Deuteronomy, which often essentially cites the laws of Exodus while often altering or updating them.[23]

All three of these realities would challenge the intelligibility and integrity of Scripture if these legal texts were understood as statutory laws. In a statutory-law framework, Ruth's and Jeremiah's bending of the letter of the law and the tensions between pentateuchal laws would suggest that biblical authors disagreed with and contradicted one another. However, these problems disappear if biblical law is common law instead. As the community moves from the wilderness to settled life in the promised land and then into a monarchy, Yahweh's laws offer them flexible guidance for what justice and wisdom will require in each context. All these laws demand obedience, of course—just check out the curses for disobedience in Leviticus and Deuteronomy! But understanding the law as common law suggests that the obedience required is obedience

Figure 8.3. King Hammurabi's law collection is one of the more famous law collections from the ancient Near East. The image here is of the top part of a pillar on which the law collection is inscribed. It shows Hammurabi standing before a Mesopotamian god. While Hammurabi claims to be beloved of the gods, he makes clear that he is the one who has written the law.

to the spirit of the law and to the wisdom, justice, and holiness that legal spirit teaches the people.

THE GENRE OF ANCIENT LAW IN ISRAEL AND ELSEWHERE

Some of the more unique features of Israel's law help us further understand how Israel's law collection was countercultural in its own context. For instance, while ancient Near Eastern law collections were written by kings, Israel was unique in claiming that their laws were written by Yahweh himself.[24] While legal collections were often only for the literate elite, Yahweh makes provisions for his law to be read regularly to the entire people. It thus serves as "treaty stipulations" for the entire community.[25]

Because of this, the primary place of application for many of the laws isn't the courtroom at all. Israel's laws give guidance for how the entire people should live. Many seem designed to help neighbors know how to interact with one another *without* involving judges and courts.[26] As such, we might best understand biblical law as a form of wisdom literature.[27] The laws present an understanding of what wise, just communal policy and practice might look like at a given time and place. As wisdom literature, these laws do not merely tell people what to do. They reason with readers, offering paradigmatic cases designed to instill wisdom, justice, creativity, and discernment.[28] This is deeply empowering. Israel's law treats average citizens as responsible participants in God's mission; each plays their part in becoming a community of justice and righteousness by seeking to live wisely and justly under God's good law.

We can see how understanding the genre of legal collections can make a difference by looking at a remarkable little law from Exodus 23:4–5: "When you come upon your enemy's ox or donkey going astray, you shall bring it back. When you see the donkey of one who hates you lying under its burden and you would hold back from setting it free, you must help to set it free."

Figure 8.4. Donkey in Ethiopia

From a statutory-law perspective, this text is bizarre and unhelpful. Unlike most modern statutory laws, it requires members of the community to offer help, rather than penalizing them for committing harm. It mentions no consequences for breaking the law and no responsible court for administering consequences. And it's weirdly specific. How often did Israelite men and women discover donkeys in ditches, anyway? Does the requirement to assist my *enemy's* donkey mean that I'm free to leave my *friend's* donkey in the ditch? And am I allowed to let sheep of either my enemy or my friend run off? If you see the law as giving people legal requirements to be carried out "to the letter," this law makes very little sense and certainly has little contemporary relevance.

From a wisdom-law perspective, the law is brilliant. It forces you into a miniature story, in which *you* are busy about *your* business and discover *your enemy* facing a crisis. It specifically forbids the most natural reaction and requires you to love your enemy instead. Indeed, the law refuses to allow such love to be reduced to warm, fuzzy feelings; enemy love requires concrete, practical action. The extreme precision of the case forces you to imagine countless other ways God's wisdom and justice might require you to love and serve your enemy through costly, inconvenient action.

THEOLOGICAL ISSUES

Breaking and Keeping or Cultivating and Crossing Against?

Dru Johnson's *Understanding Biblical Law* is one of the best, most accessible treatments of biblical law available. Johnson argues that the genre of biblical law suggests we need different metaphors for understanding our response to God's instructions. The typical language of "breaking the law" or "keeping the law" resonates better with a statutory-law framework. By contrast, the wisdom-law framework of the Old Testament suggests that we either "cultivate" and "tend" Yahweh's instruction (both legitimate translations for the Hebrew word *shamar*, often translated "keep"), or we "cross against" (*'avar*) or "turn aside" from them.[b]

3. *Read for What Law Seeks to Accomplish and How*

A third strategy for reading biblical law well is to try to understand what the laws are meant to accomplish and how. This principle works at both the macro and micro level. For instance, my coauthor, Dave, likes to say that if love of God and neighbor is the heartbeat of the Torah's law collections, then the Ten Commandments are the skeleton around that heart. The law collections that follow put flesh on the skeleton. We can and should ask of every law, How does this ultimately call us to love God and love neighbor? Moreover, because God's loving justice is particularly concerned with the orphan, widow, poor, and oppressed, Dru Johnson is right that we ought also to ask of every law, including "the most seemingly barbaric statutes, How might this provide a protection for the vulnerable? Or, what vulnerable group of people might this law have in mind?"[29]

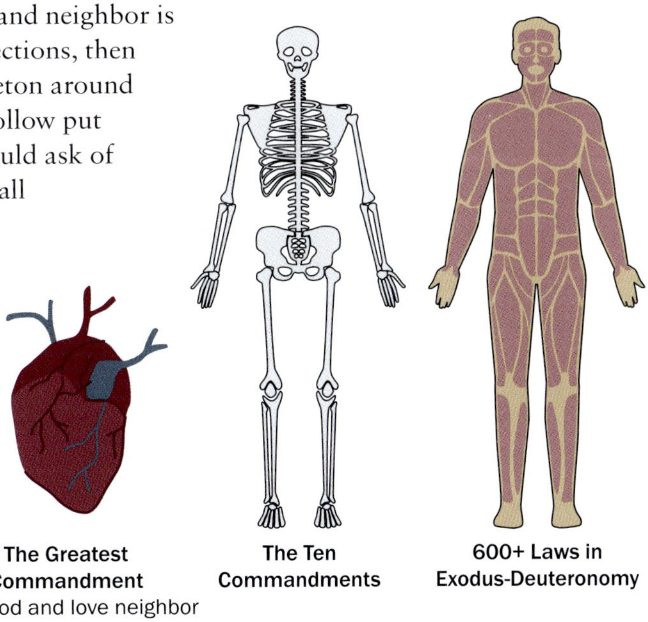

Figure 8.5. The heart, skeleton, and flesh of the law

ETHICS

Reading Israel's Law as a Paradigm

There are significant differences between participating in the life of God's people in the contemporary church and participating in the life of God's people in Israel's ancient theocracy. Christopher Wright suggests we treat Israel's laws paradigmatically, searching for analogies and comparisons between what God's law was trying to do with God's people then and there and what God might be calling us to do in our own here and now. He offers diagnostic questions to help us think through specific laws:

- What kind of situation was this law trying to promote or prevent?
- Who would have benefited from this law and why?
- Whose power was this law trying to restrict and how did it do so?
- What rights and responsibilities were embodied in this law?
- What kind of behavior did this law encourage or discourage?
- What vision of society motivated this law?
- What moral principles, values, or priorities did this law embody or instantiate?

Answering these questions about Old Testament law can then help us ask parallel questions about our own context.[c] Old Testament law provides not a blueprint to be slavishly replicated but an imagination-shaping 3D model to inspire and guide us for faithfulness today. To return to the body metaphor, exploring the Old Testament law in its entirety can help us imagine what it would look like to put flesh on God's command to love God and neighbor in our world today.

ETHICS

Goring Oxen Today

What might the Torah's teaching about the ethical obligations of owners who know their oxen are dangerous say about corporations that knowingly sell products or embrace workplace practices that hurt and even kill? What might it say about laws, lawyers, and legal frameworks that often allow those who benefit from these dangerous modern-day "goring oxen" to actively avoid liability? Imaginatively considering how the paradigm of the ox laws might speak to such situations would require thinking deeply about our own context (in America's hyperlitigious society, for instance, there may be times when we legitimately need to argue about questions of liability).

Or given that the apostle Paul was quite happy to imagine what another ox law might say about pastoral compensation (1 Tim. 5:17–18), what might this ox law say about church structures and leaders who knowingly allow abusive people to continue to serve in ministry roles, and thus allow God's people to be continually abused? What about denominations and church structures that address allegations of abuse with a concern to reduce institutional liability rather than care for victims? These instances suggest that reading the Torah paradigmatically allows its prophetic concern for the vulnerable to cut more sharply.

Thinking carefully about what the laws seek to accomplish helps us discover morally provocative aspects of seemingly obscure laws. For instance, some laws are what is known as apodictic; these are the absolute "You shall not . . ." laws. But we often find a different kind of law, known as case law, that unpacks the application of apodictic laws. These "If this happens, then . . ." laws provide the necessary moral reasoning to tease out the implications of the "You shall not . . ." commands.

For example, the apodictic law "You shall not murder" is followed by laws that distinguish premeditated murder—a capital crime that receives capital punishment—from similar offenses that must be treated differently. A person who accidentally kills someone can flee to a city of refuge established for their protection (Exod. 21:13). The owner of an ox that has gored people in the past, however, faces the death penalty if their ox kills someone (21:29). Ethically, such a law shows that it is not enough to avoid *actively* and *personally* harming a person; one is responsible for ensuring that one's behavior does not harm others indirectly, especially when a known danger exists. Taking responsibility for an ox that gores could be costly because you might have to kill an uncontrollable ox, which was the tractor of the Israelite farm. Yet, in this case, the family of the killed person can accept a ransom rather than the ox owner's death. Why? Presumably because allowing a dangerous ox to run loose is in a category related to and yet somewhat different from premeditated murder.

Reading comparatively can also help us understand what Israel's laws seek to accomplish. Both the laws of Hammurabi and the Torah forbid theft, but whereas Hammurabi's laws regularly prescribe the death penalty for property crimes, the Torah never does. Conversely, Hammurabi's laws more often allow murderers to avoid the death penalty. This comparison makes clear that biblical laws teach God's people to see life as more valuable than property and to live that value out in practical ways.[30] As Dru Johnson says, here in the Torah, "for the first time in legal history, human life was worth more than a property violation."[31]

This same background can help us imaginatively reason our way through intriguing laws like the one found in Exodus 22:2–3: "If a thief is found breaking in, and is beaten to death, no bloodguilt is incurred; but if it happens after sunrise, bloodguilt is incurred." Ask yourself, Why are there different penalties? What's the underlying logic of this law? What might be the implications of that logic?

One explanation might be that the homeowner in the house at night believes the intruder intends to kill them, whereas in the daytime, it can be assumed the person is merely seeking to steal.[32] The dramatic difference between property crimes and crimes against human life in the Old Testament means that a person who kills a thief while defending their property is guilty of murder, so long as they assumed it was their stuff, rather than their lives, that the thief was after.

The point should be clear: Read biblical laws closely and often comparatively to understand what the law seeks to accomplish.

4. When You Get Stuck, Get Help!

The fourth strategy for reading biblical law is to get help when you need it. Biblical laws can be hard to understand, and they engage a cultural world quite different from ours. Don't be surprised when you run into stuff you can't make sense of, and don't be afraid to get help when you do. Both commentaries and specialist studies can help.

For instance, the laws about sex in Deuteronomy 22:23–29 are disturbing to many readers—including us. Verse 23–24 appears to require executing a virgin betrothed to be married who has been "violated" by a man simply because that

ETHICS

Whose Barbaric Laws?

Old Testament law has a reputation for being barbaric among some readers. However, it's worth noting that the Old Testament never allowed the death penalty for property crimes, but US law certainly did: "In colonial America and continuing into the nation's early years, the death penalty was authorized for a wide array of criminal offenses," including burglary.[d] Today, stand-your-ground laws in the U.S. (which permit the use of force in self-defense without a duty to retreat) and castle doctrine (which permits the use of force, even lethal force, to defend one's home) arguably allow a much broader use of lethal force to prevent robbery than Exodus 22:2–3 does.

violation happened in a town. Meanwhile, verses 28–29 in the NIV explicitly require a single woman who is raped to marry her rapist. It's hard to see how such laws could be anything but deeply unjust.

If we turn to get help, however, scholars like Sandra Richter argue this interpretation is a poor reading of the text. Deuteronomy's description of a man sleeping with an engaged virgin in the town does not describe rape at all; rather, it describes a consensual liaison. For ancient Israelites, her not crying out in the town would have been sufficient evidence of the consensual nature of their relationship. The opposite is true of the woman "seized" in the countryside (Deut. 22:25); she is a victim of rape. The point isn't the geographical location, but the question of consent. And because this is *wisdom law* rather than *statutory law*, ancient Jewish commentary was right to clarify that if there was "evidence that there was no one who could have saved her [in the town], that she resisted, or that her life was threatened if she resisted," she would be declared innocent.[33]

Richter also points out just how seriously Scripture takes sexual violence. The woman in Deuteronomy 22:24 is apparently "expected to report the crime," and her rapist receives the death penalty. In a far cry from the way victims of sexual violence continue to be blamed today, the text goes out of its way to declare the woman completely innocent.[34]

Turning to Deuteronomy 22:28, Richter argues that the NIV is incorrect to use the language of rape at all since the juxtaposition with the prior paragraph and the parallel text in Exodus 22:15–16 make it clear this is an instance of seduction. The text ensures that a man who seduces a woman cannot leave her unmarriable, unprovided for, and potentially responsible for raising a child on her own. He must formally marry her—including paying a handsome bride-price to the father—and enter a marriage in which, unlike typical marriages, the husband could not divorce his wife. The Exodus parallel clarifies that if the woman's father found the man objectionable, he could prevent the man from marrying his daughter yet still get paid what is now essentially a fine on his daughter's behalf (22:17). Early Jewish interpretation that the daughter likewise could refuse the man likely draws out the way such laws would be applied in a wisdom framework.[35]

ETHICS

Selling Your Daughter?

Sandra Richter discusses the practice of paying a bride-price, or *mohar*. While this is often derisively considered "purchasing" a bride, this is an inadequate understanding of the practice, not least because the *mohar* "seems to have remained the woman's possession."[e] It apparently provided "insurance in the event that her husband died" and would return to her at her father's death in any case.[f]

This reminds us that seemingly problematic practices from other cultures may have meanings we simply do not understand. For instance, while working in Kenya, I (Michael) once met a man whose tribe's dowry practice required the groom to pay the dowry to the father-in-law in installments, without ever paying off the dowry completely. When I suggested this sounded exploitative, he corrected me. In his culture, to pay off the bride-price completely would signal an end to the man's relationship with his in-laws. His willingness to pay the bride-price over time signaled his desire to continue to be connected to them.

Deuteronomy's laws about sex could have been otherwise. Mesopotamian laws did expect a girl to marry her rapist, subjected the rapist's *wife* to "slave-concubinage" as payment for her *husband's* sexual misconduct, and offered "revenge-rape" of the rapist's wife as a penalty.[36] Set alongside their ancient Near Eastern counterparts, Deuteronomy's laws reflect a distinctive moral vision, one that seeks to restrain violence and to protect the vulnerable within Israel's social world.

As these examples suggest, we will often get "stuck" when we read biblical law. When we do, scholars can help us by shedding light on how the law sought to move the people toward justice in an unjust world. Ancient Israel did not discover laws that eliminated sexual violence. So far, neither have we. But their law's commitment to defending the vulnerable, including vulnerable women, summons us to continue the important work of defending people from sexual violence and bringing forceful justice on perpetrators of such violence.

Bringing It All Together: Wrestling with Laws About Slavery

Let's bring these tips for reading law well to another deeply difficult topic: slavery. Readers are rightly concerned that biblical laws do not eliminate slavery, and even more disturbingly, that biblical law's tolerance of slavery was used in the American South to justify the horrific kidnapping, enslavement, abuse, rape, and torture of Black people. Against this backdrop, we confess at the outset that there are laws in the Old Testament we wish weren't there. Here's one: "When a slaveowner strikes a male or female slave with a rod and the slave dies immediately, the owner shall be punished. But if the slave survives a day or two, there is no punishment; for the slave is the owner's property" (Exod. 21:20–21).

The reference to beating an enslaved person is nauseating. The claim that the enslaved person is the owner's "property" seems to deny that person's status as God's image bearers. How might our discussion of biblical law help us work through these issues?

First, remember that laws often seek to limit widespread, pervasive evil when eliminating such evil may not be realistic. Without leaving Exodus 21:20–21, we might notice, for example, that this text in no way recommends beating an enslaved person. It only offers guidance for what to do when such an event occurs. If we read this law carefully by paying attention to its broader context, this becomes even clearer. The immediately preceding law in verses 18–19 discusses what to do when two free men get into a fight; the text is certainly *not* promoting fighting among such men.

Figure 8.6. This illuminated Bible visually shows how the people began worshiping the golden calf even as Moses was receiving the law from God. The Bible's laws are always realistic in the sense that they recognize they are given to sinful people prone to idolatry and injustice.

It offers a way forward when such fights inevitably occur. When two free men fight, if one man kills the other, he is guilty of murder (see 20:12).[37] But if the loser in the fight gets up after a few days, then all the perpetrator must do is pay for the loss of the victim's time.

From this perspective, an enslaved person who is beaten is treated the same as a free person in all but one respect. If they are beaten to death, then the master will be "punished," or, more accurately translated, "avenged," a reference to the death penalty.[38] So in complete contrast to our first reading, this text does treat the enslaved person as fully human by demanding the life of the master who has murdered them.

What then of the reference to the enslaved person being the owner's "property"? The word translated "property" is "silver" or "money," and thus draws another connection with the case of the two free persons who fight. In that case, the only penalty for a nonlethal fight is that the one person must compensate the other person for their lost time. That does not apply in the case of an enslaved person who is beaten, because the perpetrator has already "paid for the lost time" of their crime, because the enslaved person has been unable to work in the household. But this does not suggest the text sees the enslaved person as "property," as many English translations unfortunately imply.

The laws that follow clarify further. Exodus 21:22 addresses what happens when people who are fighting injure a pregnant woman, and it includes the famous clause known as the *lex talionis*: "If any harm follows, then you shall give life for life, eye for eye, tooth for tooth, hand for hand, foot for foot, burn for burn, wound for wound, stripe for stripe" (21:23–25).

The law then returns to the question of violence being committed against an enslaved person and applies this lex talionis principle in a decidedly nonliteral way: "When a slaveowner strikes the eye of a male or female slave, destroying it, the owner shall let the slave go, a free person, to compensate for the eye. If the owner knocks out a tooth of a male or female slave, the slave shall be let go, a free person, to compensate for the tooth" (Exod. 21:26–27).

The law suggests that the lex talionis was more of a principle that the punishment should fit the crime than a directive to mutilate perpetrators (it also likely served to limit the cycle of vengeance, rather than to promote it).[39] It also corrects our earlier misunderstanding; if a person does serious harm to an enslaved person, that enslaved person is immediately set free. Here "eye for an eye, tooth for a tooth" means "If you exploit power, then you lose it."[40]

We still don't like the idea that enslaved people were beaten in the first place. But there's no reason to suspect Exodus likes it either, at least not any more than Exodus likes free men beating each other up or inadvertently injuring pregnant women. By attempting to understand what this law seeks to accomplish, it becomes clear that it is seeking to provide some justice for enslaved people who are killed or maimed and to limit the suffering enslaved people might experience in the households in which they were enslaved.

If we look to scholars for help in understanding these laws, they provide further insight. On the one hand, they help us understand more accurately what ancient slavery looked like. Slavery was pervasive in the ancient world, but such slavery was not the race-based chattel slavery of the American South, with its claim that Black people were less than human and, indeed, created for enslavement. This does not mean that ancient slavery was good, but it does mean we need to recognize the differences.

Second, ancient slavery can be divided broadly into two types: debt slavery, in which a person was enslaved to a household to pay off a debt, and chattel slavery, in which a person was permanently enslaved to a household. While these are distinct categories conceptually, the Hebrew word *'eved* covers both kinds. Indeed, *'eved* can also refer to servants, and the verbal form simply means "to work" or "to serve." Because of this, it can be unclear precisely what kind of slavery or service is implied in specific laws.

Debt slavery seems to be the primary form of enslavement in the Torah. Crucially, the Torah provided strict limits on such slavery; Deuteronomy 15:12–18 even requires that the outgoing indentured servant be laden down with the fruits of their labor, sufficient to establish them again as a free person. Indeed, the institution of debt slavery served an important function within Israel's social safety net, giving people in desperate situations a way to provide for themselves or their families. This may seem like a harsh option—and it no doubt was. However, we need to remember that the Torah depicts an Israelite community in which very vulnerable farmers work very hard

HISTORICAL MATTERS

Economic Vulnerability and Debt Slavery

In ancient Israel's subsistence agrarian economy, every harvest had to feed the family, sustain domestic animals, provide seed for the next planting, and (hopefully) yield goods for trade. A single crop failure—due to drought, floods, pests, or plant disease—could throw this delicate balance into crisis. Multiple failures could be devastating, forcing families to sell land or even themselves into debt slavery to survive. Such vulnerability was common across the ancient Near East and lies behind the Torah's strong protections for debtors, its limits on the exploitation and treatment of debt slaves, and its provisions for eventual restoration.

simply to survive. There may be little excess to provide for people when things go poorly; the system of indentured servitude allowed a household member to pay off a debt that may have allowed the rest of their household to survive. While they worked that debt off, the law tried to ensure that they were treated fairly. Christopher Wright suggests that if the law had been followed, debt slavery would have been experienced similarly to "many kinds of paid employment in a cash economy," and indeed it offered "more explicit legal and economic security than [that available to] the technically free, but landless, hired laborers and craftsmen."[41]

The law specifically forbade Israelites from taking other Israelites as chattel slaves. Unfortunately, it did allow for foreigners to be bought and sold as such slaves (Lev. 25:44–46). Again, though, this *permits* rather than *promotes* such slavery, which was extremely common in the ancient world.[42] While Leviticus 25:44–46 allows for slavery, Leviticus has already instructed Israelites to love immigrants and outsiders *as themselves*, which includes treating them "as the citizen among you" (19:33–34). This is specifically based on the people's experience of oppression as immigrants in Egypt. Taken as a whole, the Torah seems to be against chattel slavery but sees it as so pervasive that the law cannot eliminate the evil. It instead seeks to limit it, while offering principles that lead to its rejection.

Scholars can also help us understand these laws by showing how they compare to other ancient laws. Concerning enslavement, David Baker argues that, when compared to the ancient Near East, Exodus's laws are "unique in considering such abuse in terms of human rights rather than property rights."[43] Laws about slave abuse in the ancient world ensured that if an enslaved person was hurt by a free person, the master of the enslaved person was compensated. The laws treat the enslaved person as property, in other words, and ensure that that property is protected. In no case do these ancient laws appear to protect an enslaved person from their own master. That Exodus does provide such protection represents a dramatic innovation in biblical law, one that appears to be based on the biblical conviction that enslaved people, too, are made in God's image. Maybe most countercultural of all, whereas ancient laws provided harsh penalties for harboring fugitives from slavery—up to and including the death penalty—Deuteronomy 23:15–16 forbids the Israelites from returning a fugitive enslaved person to their master and instead requires that they be

ETHICS

Do unto Others as You Would Do to Your Father or Mother

Dru Johnson argues the Torah's demand to treat foreigners based on Israel's own experience as oppressed foreigners and the commands about "equal treatment of the poor, the wealthy, the native-born, and the foreigner in the marketplace, home, courts, and business" in Leviticus 19:9–37 present us with a powerful, demanding challenge: God's people are "to foster an imagination to see people *as if they were their own fathers or mothers.*" How might seeing everyone, including our enemies, as if they were our own fathers and mothers change the way Christians approach major ethical issues of our day, including immigration, policing, abortion, euthanasia, business ethics, and much more?[g]

allowed to live anywhere they choose within the land! This law alone, if followed, would undermine the entire institution of slavery.

None of this means we would prefer to live in ancient Israel (at least in relation to the issue of slavery). We would not, and we should celebrate the abolishment of slavery where it has occurred and work for its abolition in the many places where its horrors continue. However, it does mean we would prefer to live in Israel rather than in ancient societies around Israel at the time (at least if Israel followed the law).

Moreover, if we read according to the big story of Scripture, we read the laws about slavery in light of the reality that Yahweh is revealed as the one who liberated his people from slavery in Egypt. We read these texts as part of a biblical trajectory that undermines the ancient, pervasive institution of slavery altogether, not least by claiming that Yahweh's ways with Israel give the world a picture of Yahweh's heart for all people. And we read these texts in light of the other legal texts that look after the welfare of the enslaved. The Sabbath laws and prescribed feasts regularly require that all, including enslaved people, participate in days and weeks of rest. Debt servitude is time bound, and Israelite debt slaves are to be treated as workers rather than debt slaves (Lev. 25:40). Hopefully we can see how these laws sought to incarnate more and more of God's kingdom in a broken cultural context, even while recognizing that the laws do not endorse many of the broken aspects of that context.

RECEPTION HISTORY

Reading the Torah Against American Slavery

Wil Gafney details a few of the many ways the Torah condemns the "North Atlantic slave trade and ensuing slavocracy":

1. Contrary to Exodus 20:10, African slaves regularly worked on the Sabbath.
2. Contrary to Exodus 21:2, African slaves did not have the option of being freed every seven years.
3. Contrary to Exodus 21:16, slave traffickers were not put to death for kidnapping persons in order to sell those persons.
4. Contrary to Exodus 21:21, slave owners who killed their slaves were not punished.
5. Contrary to Exodus 21:26, African slaves who were maimed by their owners were not set free.
6. Contrary to Deuteronomy 15:13, freed African slaves did not receive liberally from their previous owner's livestock and other income that they helped produce prior to being freed (when and if they were freed at all).
7. Contrary to Deuteronomy 21:13, captured African women were not treated as wives and were sold as slaves after having sexual relations with their abductors.[h]

According to the Torah, all those involved in the slave trade should have received the death penalty. In 1 Timothy 1:9–10, Paul lists "slave traders" among those who are "lawless and disobedient, . . . godless and sinful, . . . unholy and profane" (NIV).

Library of Congress / public domain

Figure 8.8. United States slave trade, 1830. According to Exodus 21:16, the people involved in kidnapping and selling the enslaved deserve death.

Art Renewal Center / public domain

Figure 8.7. *Israel in Egypt* by Edward Poynter (1867)

Inaugurating a Lifetime of Meditation

We have offered tools for understanding how to meditate on Yahweh's law, as well as a strong argument for why we, like the psalmist, might long to meditate on that law "day and night." Hopefully you have seen God's heart for justice in laws that looked at first like bastions of injustice. And hopefully you have seen the grand vistas of God's law in texts that demand costly love for the immigrant, open-handed generosity to the poor, concrete acts of love for the enemy, and much more.

Exodus 19–40

Becoming a Kingdom of Priests

Orientation

The second half of Exodus focuses on Israel's encounter with God at Sinai and their preparations for life in God's house.[1] Here the Israelites discover what it will mean to become covenantal partners with Yahweh in a community that uniquely experiences his presence.

Exploration

Israel's Identity and Job Description (Exod. 19:1–20:21)

READ EXODUS 19:1–20:21

How does the law relate to Yahweh's redemption of and purposes for the people?

ISRAEL'S SPECIAL IDENTITY AND JOB DESCRIPTION

In Exodus 19–20, the people arrive at Sinai. These chapters offer essential insights into the nature of God's grace and Israel's identity and vocation. Exodus 19:3–6 is particularly important for understanding the *torah*, the "law" or "instruction" that dominates much of the Pentateuch and is often despised or misunderstood by Christian readers.

> Then Moses went up to God; the Lord called to him from the mountain, saying, "Thus you shall say to the house of Jacob, and tell the Israelites: You have seen what I did to the Egyptians, and how I bore you on eagles' wings and brought you to myself. Now therefore, if you obey my voice and keep

> my covenant, you shall be my treasured possession out of all the peoples. Indeed, the whole earth is mine, but you shall be for me a priestly kingdom and a holy nation. These are the words that you shall speak to the Israelites." (Exod. 19:3–6)

First, Yahweh's initial words make clear Israel's life begins with God's grace. Yahweh did not show up in Egypt and say, "Hey look, if you follow my rules, I might be convinced to come save you" any more than he said to Abraham, "If you obey me, I'll make big promises to you." In the Old and New Testaments, salvation begins with God's initiation and lavishing grace on people who have done nothing to deserve it. If people have read Old Testament law as a way to gain God's favor, they have misread it. Israel's life begins with God's generous promises prior to the giving of the law. Grace comes first.

Second, Exodus 19:5–6 describes Israel as Yahweh's "treasured possession." In the ancient world, a powerful king could describe a less powerful king with whom they had covenanted as a "treasured possession."[2] This meant they had a special relationship with their covenantal lord and a special role in his empire. Exodus describes Israel as likewise invited into a unique, binding, covenantal relationship with the emperor of the whole earth.

That role, however, is for the sake of the world. Israel is called to be a kingdom of priests. Just as Israel's priests served as mediators, bringing Yahweh to the people and the people to Yahweh, Exodus 19:5–6 suggests the Israelites as a whole will be mediators between God and the nations. This explains the significance of their being a "holy nation." Israel is called to a separate way of life, a life lived in dangerous proximity to Yahweh's holiness, precisely so they can mediate Yahweh to all the nations of the earth.

In the opening chapters of Genesis, humans were called to live as God's royal, priestly family members. That is at least part of what it means to be made in God's image. Exodus has already described Israel as Yahweh's firstborn son. Taken with the royal, priestly language of Exodus 19:5–6, this suggests Yahweh is calling Israel to live out the identity and job description to which all humanity is called, and to do so for the sake of humanity and creation as a whole.

Third, the way Israel will live into this identity and job description is by "listening" to Yahweh's voice (as Adam and Eve flagrantly failed to do) and "keeping" Yahweh's covenant (Exod. 19:5 AT). While Israel does not earn God's favor through obedience, there is an important "if" to Israel's covenantal identity and job description. The Ten Commandments that follow, as well as the various laws in the rest of the Torah, comprise crucial aspects of this "if." They constitute a kind of "Manifesto for a Holy Nation and a Priestly Kingdom." *If* Israel follows Yahweh's way, not least through obeying this manifesto, *then* they will fulfill their calling.[3]

This often-misunderstood dynamic is essential for understanding the Pentateuch and Scripture as a whole. While scholars sometimes differentiate the "unconditional" Abrahamic covenant and the "conditional" Sinai covenant, both covenants have elements of unconditionality and conditionality. Yahweh references the unconditional promise to Abraham when he liberates Israel from Egypt. We see the conditional element in the long list of curses Yahweh promises to send if Israel breaks the covenant in Leviticus and Deuteronomy. Israel's later experience of these curses, however, does not suggest Yahweh removes the Sinai covenant but that he enacts it. As Daniel Block says, objectively speaking, the covenant is permanent; subjectively, Israel's participation in God's mission and their enjoyment of God's blessing depend on their obedience to that covenant.[4]

This is one reason God's people understood Yahweh's law as a gift. The law is Yahweh's generous guidance for how to live the incredible life and mission to which Yahweh has called them. Carmen Imes emphasizes this good news by comparing Yahweh's law giving to the experience of worshipers elsewhere in the ancient world. Ancient peoples were "desperate to know what the gods were saying" but often received little guidance.[5] In the "Prayer to Any God," one poor worshiper at about the same time as the exodus prayed for forgiveness for their sins. But they address their prayer to the "god" and "goddess" they admit they do not know, apparently seeking to address any and every divine being that might be listening. While they admit their "many sins," they also lament that they "do not know" exactly what sins they may have committed![6]

Rijksmuseum / Gift of the heirs of Mr. J. J. Aarts / public domain

Figure 9.1. *Moses with the Tables of the Law*, woodcut by Johannes Josephus Aarts

CANONICAL CONNECTIONS

Liberated for Covenantal Life

If you think the Sinai covenant's "if" is diametrically opposed to our life with Jesus, think again. Just as Israel was objectively liberated from slavery, Christians are objectively liberated from sin and death (Rom. 6:5–7). But just as God's people in Exodus had to actively obey the covenant to subjectively experience the fullness of life associated with their mission, so must we.

That's why Paul goes on to say we who have been objectively liberated must "consider" ourselves dead to sin and alive to God, refusing to let sin rule in our bodies (Rom. 6:11). Indeed, we must proactively offer our bodies to God "as instruments of righteousness" (6:12–13). Christians have been purified by the blood of Jesus "so that we might serve the living God!" (Heb. 9:14 NIV). Israel's law, along with the ample instruction offered by Jesus and the apostles, can still offer guidance on how we should live out our identity and job description as God's "royal priesthood" and "holy nation" (1 Pet. 2:9–12).

CANONICAL CONNECTIONS

Looking Toward Leviticus

The Sinai encounter with the holy God anticipates the book of Leviticus, where Israel is taught how to approach the Holy One through sacrifice and purification, as well as by reordering every dimension of their lives—time, space, body, and community—in light of God's holiness (see chaps. 11 and 12 below).

Other comparisons to ancient literature are equally powerful. The Torah offers the only example of anybody in the ancient Near East claiming their god authored their laws. Elsewhere, law writing was the work of kings. Thousands of years before the Magna Carta took the step of placing the king under the law, Yahweh had already taken his people further, identifying himself as the law's divine source and placing everyone—including future monarchs—under its authority.

The way the whole people voluntarily embrace the covenant as a "*welcome obligation*" is likewise unparalleled.[7] Having liberated the people, Yahweh essentially says, "Okay, I've rescued you from Egypt and have an important job for you. Do you want in?" And all the people say yes! This is in stark contrast to the ancient world, in which political covenants were most often made between rulers.

Yahweh's nearness in liberation, love, and law giving does not make living near him safe, however. Having accepted Yahweh's invitation, Israel must prepare to meet with Yahweh through acts of consecration (literally, making themselves "holy"). Meanwhile, Yahweh's holy presence is accompanied by endless lightning and thunder that makes the mountains—and the Israelites—shake. Strangely, Yahweh's holiness also attracts them; for the people's safety, Yahweh repeatedly warns Moses not to let the people force their way up the mountain.

Figure 9.2. Summit of a mountain in the Sinai Peninsula of Egypt that is the traditional and most accepted identification of the biblical Mount Sinai

THE TEN WORDS

Yahweh delivers the "Ten Words" (popularly called the Ten Commandments, though never in Scripture) amid this fearsome appearance on the mountain.

The Ten Words play a unique role in Israel's law. While the rest of Yahweh's law is delivered through Moses, the entire community hears Yahweh speak the Ten Words directly.[8] They are repeated, with a few alterations, in Deuteronomy 5:1–21 and shape the legal collections of both books.[9] They play a massive role in both Jewish and Christian thought; as we saw in the previous chapter, they are like the skeleton that provides a permanent structure around the heart of biblical instruction to love God and neighbor.

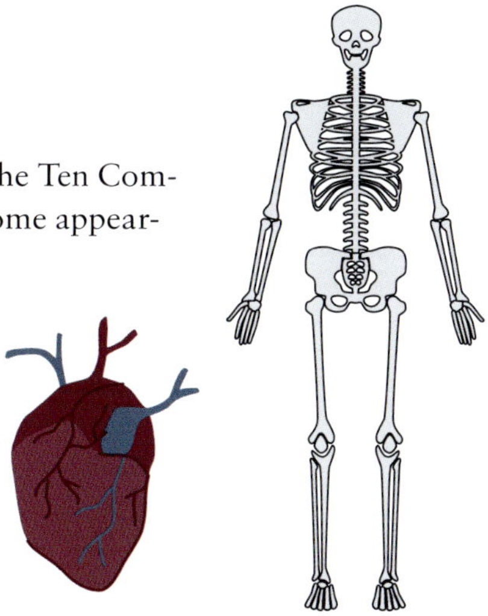

Figure 9.3. The heart and skeleton of the biblical law

Christians have often understood the Ten Words as a "revealed restatement of the natural law" and thus as timeless truths that should govern all people everywhere.[10] Such notions influence American Christians' attempts to have the Ten Words publicly displayed in schools and courthouses. On the one hand, the law does give God's people guidance for living as a kingdom of priests for the sake of the nations and guides them in ways that go with the grain of God's world. There are good reasons for thinking these words say something about God's purposes for all people everywhere.

On the other hand, public presentations of the Ten Words risk fundamentally misinterpreting them. Compare Exodus 20:2–8 to the example of a Ten Commandments monument in figure 9.4. In Exodus, the Ten Words are explicitly spoken by Yahweh *your* God "who brought you out of the land of Egypt, out of the house of slavery" (20:2). The commands that follow do not stand alone, like those of the monument, but are part of the story of *this* God rescuing *this* people. The monument omits references to the character of God as a "jealous God" who offers judgment on iniquity but steadfast love to those who keep his way. While Exodus's Sabbath command grounds the

Figure 9.4. Ten Commandments monument, Bradford County Courthouse, Starke, Florida

practice in Yahweh's work at creation and clarifies the Sabbath is both for receiving rest and giving it to others, the monument's Sabbath command is cut off from both its theological and ethical roots. To treat the Ten Words as an isolated list of dos and don'ts scrubbed of their particularity and context is deeply misguided. The Ten Words offer followers of the God who brought Israel out of Egypt a framework for living a life of covenant faithfulness in response to what God has done. Three further angles on the Ten Words help us wrestle with their meaning.

The ethos of the good neighborhood. Patrick Miller argues that the Ten Words create the "ethos" or "space" for the "good neighborhood."[11] Such commands are not burdensome requirements but invitations into a community with good, desirable boundaries.[12] Who *doesn't* want to live in a neighborhood with mandated vacations, where people tell the truth, and neighbors respect one another's marriages?[13] Imes offers the picture of a playground, with the Ten Words providing "fences" that allow children to play safely and freely.[14]

The bill of (other people's) rights. Block argues that the Ten Words may be "the world's oldest bill of rights." But "unlike modern bills of rights, the Decalogue is not interested in the addressee's rights" but in their obligation to protect the rights of others.[15] Moreover, this "bill" both protects rights and imposes responsibilities.[16]

The "opening up" of the commandments. The Torah's law collections contextualize the Ten Words in a particular time and place. The extremely compressed form of the Ten Words implies a whole host of related positive and negative behaviors. For instance, all you have to do to follow the "letter" of Exodus 20:15 is avoid stealing, but the so-called book of the covenant in Exodus 20:22–23:33 unpacks the full meaning of this command by

- providing guidance for what to do when a person inadvertently destroys another's property (22:5–6),
- providing a pathway for a person guilty of stealing to be reconciled through paying reparations (22:4),
- clarifying that the penalty for stealing people to enslave them is death (21:16), and
- positively requiring God's people to preserve the property of even neighbors who hate them (23:4–5).

The Ten Words are meant to be interpreted expansively. The Torah's law collections do precisely this, putting flesh on the heart of biblical faith (love God and neighbor) and the skeleton of the Ten Words for the *Israelites* in

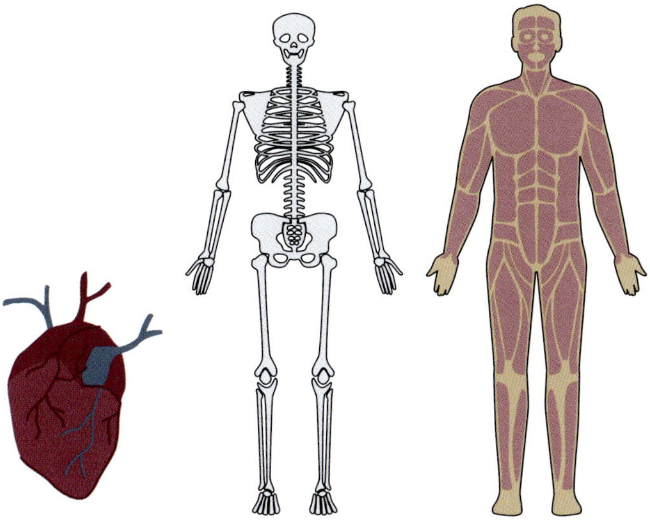

Figure 9.5. The heart, skeleton, and flesh of the law

their time and place. This suggests that the rest of the law collection ought to inspire us to imagine how *we* might "flesh out" God's way in *our* time and place.

Exploring specific commands. Central to the theological interpretation of the Ten Words is that they begin with the command to worship Yahweh alone. The good, flourishing life flows out of this initial requirement. Scholars debate, however, whether the first command means that no other divine beings exist or simply that no other beings are to be worshiped.[17]

The second commandment's prohibition of images was deeply countercultural; idols were central to worship throughout the ancient world. The rejection of idols would remind Israel that their God did not depend on the people nor could he be manipulated by them.[18] Another theological reason for the rejection of idol making is suggested by the echo of creation language in Exodus 20:4; Yahweh's purpose has always been to fill the world with living, breathing idols—humans made in the divine image.

Imes points out that the third command, the "name command," literally reads "You must not *bear* (or *carry*) the name of Yahweh, your God, in vain."[19] Drawing on the close parallel between this

THEOLOGICAL ISSUES

Theologians on the "Opening Up" of the Commandments

John Calvin argues that each command demands far more than a minimalist reading of the words might suggest and that the negative prohibitions imply corresponding positive obligations.[a] For example, Calvin interprets "Thou shalt not steal" to include a much larger range of prohibited behavior—including "selling too dear or buying too cheaply from those who are ignorant of the prices of things"[b]—as well as a whole host of positive behaviors. "Thou shalt not steal" becomes a mandate to express love for God by doing whatever we can to help both friend and foe hold on to their possessions, and to give generously to them should they fail to do so.[c]

RECEPTION HISTORY

Sabbath and the "Genesis of Liberation"

Emerson Powery and Rodney Sadler explore how enslaved Black people engaged the biblical Sabbath in their quest for liberation. Abolitionists blasted Christian slave owners for denying enslaved people a Sabbath, thus breaking God's law themselves and forcing enslaved individuals to do the same.[d] Frederick Douglass and others who were allowed a day of rest created "Sabbath schools," in which they could live "like intellectual, moral, and accountable beings," not least by pursuing literacy.[e] Others slipped away secretly "to the swamps where they were free to worship as they pleased."[f] By facilitating the "development of the early black church," the Sabbath may well mark "the birth of African American independence!"[g] Many enslaved people took advantage of the Sabbath to plan and execute their flight from slavery. As Leonard Black wrote in 1847, "We remembered what our brothers told us—when we were able to run away, to try it on some favorable Sunday."[h]

passage and the language of Israel's high priest "bearing" the names of Israel before Yahweh (Exod. 28:29), she argues that the "name command" calls the entirety of God's people to their priestly vocation: "Just as the high priest represents Yahweh to [the Israelites], so they represent Yahweh to the nations."[20] Far from merely prohibiting using God's name as a swear word, then, the name command calls us to represent Yahweh faithfully in every area of our lives.

The Sabbath command requires every Israelite to receive rest from Yahweh and to give rest to whoever depends on them in their economic life. This includes children, refugees and immigrants, the enslaved, and even livestock. Elsewhere in the Torah, the command to rest on the Sabbath day opens up to include Sabbath weeks and years that provide rhythms of worship, rest, ecological rejuvenation, and an economic reset.

The command to honor one's parents points to the need to care for them in their old age. The promise that the people's days would be long if they follow this command, however, suggests it also speaks to the need for successive generations to embrace the faith of their ancestors.

The next four commandments prohibit various forms of violence, theft, sexual misconduct, and injustice. The last commandment then shifts to the regulation of deformed desire that lies at the root of such misconduct.[21] The command against coveting cannot be externally "regulated or policed, let alone clearly observed,"[22] because it is a matter of the heart. The holiness toward which the commands aspire "requires cultivating and disciplining the heart's desires so even inner thoughts are held captive" to Yahweh.[23]

If we inquire after the positive side of the negative command against coveting, we are reminded that the command to worship Yahweh alone elsewhere in the Torah includes the command to love Yahweh, as well as the command to love the neighbor and the outsider from beyond the neighborhood's borders. Positively interpreted, the Ten Words call us to the transformation of our desires toward love of God and neighbor.

Building God's Mobile Home (Exod. 20:22–40:38)

The rest of Exodus is dominated by three major structural units with two intervening narratives (see fig. 9.6).[24] The first section, the book of the

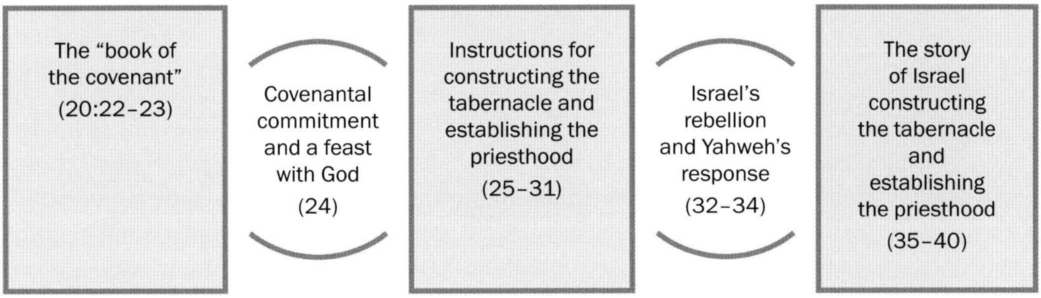

Figure 9.6. The structure of Exodus 20:22–40:38

covenant, offers a wide-ranging discussion of Torah instruction on everything from economic life, to appropriate sexual conduct, to the appropriate way to worship (because we have addressed aspects of the book of the covenant earlier in this chapter and in chap. 8, our focus in this section will be on other aspects of Exod. 20:22–40:38). The second section outlines the procedure for constructing God's mobile home (the tabernacle) and establishing the priesthood. Contemporary readers are often overwhelmed by the level of detail in chapters 25–31 and are therefore dismayed to discover chapters 35–40 essentially repeat them. The point of this repetition is apparently to underscore the importance of the tabernacle and all it represents *and* to make clear that, in the end, Israel constructed the tabernacle "just as the LORD had commanded" (see Exod. 40:16).

Between each of these sections are two important narratives: the story of Israel making a covenantal commitment and feast with Yahweh and the story of Israel's idolatrous rebellion with the golden calf and its aftermath.

COVENANTAL COMMITMENT AND A FEAST WITH GOD

After receiving the wide-ranging instructions of the book of the covenant, Moses is sent down to deliver them to the people and summon them to worship. Having heard the law, the people again universally agree to the terms of their covenant with Yahweh. The covenantal rituals that follow include both a blood rite and a meal.

As with Passover, the use of sacrificial blood speaks to the people's need for atonement if they are to live into their identity and vocation with God. Atonement "paves the way" for God to dwell with the people and the people to dwell with God.[25] But the parallels between the way Moses splashes the blood on the people and the way he will later splash blood on the priests suggest this ritual also commissions them for their vocation as a priesthood. While Israel will certainly have priests, they're also called and commissioned for service in the "priesthood of all believers."

This rite also includes a special experience of Yahweh's presence: "And they saw the God of Israel. Under his feet there was something like a pavement of sapphire stone, like the very heaven for clearness. God did not lay his hand on the chief men of the people of Israel; also they beheld God, and they ate and drank" (Exod. 24:10–11). While Exodus 33:20 states nobody can see Yahweh's face and live, in their meal with Yahweh, Israel's leaders come pretty darn close! This speaks to the profound intimacy with God that characterizes covenantal life. At the same time, the mysterious reference to their beholding God through "something like a pavement" under God's "feet" suggests that this encounter remains mediated and at a certain remove.

THE TABERNACLE

The emphasis on Yahweh's presence at the meal makes the story a fitting segue into Yahweh's instructions related to the tabernacle; indeed, if the "pavement" the elders see under Yahweh's feet suggests they glimpse God's heavenly dwelling, it makes sense to shift to instructions for making an earthly counterpart to that heavenly dwelling. The instructions for this space are lengthy, repeated, and occupy the climactic final section of the book, forcing us to ask why Exodus makes the tabernacle so central.

The tabernacle is crucial because it facilitates Yahweh's dwelling with the people of Israel (Exod. 25:8). This idea of dwelling with God is exhilarating, but Yahweh's dwelling with Israel is also essential to the larger biblical story. Yahweh had claimed he was bringing Israel *out* of Egypt and *to* himself; the tabernacle physically represents the people being brought "to" their Lord. Zooming further out, if the Old Testament is the story of Yahweh's relentless commitment to live in his good world alongside his human image bearers and to rule that good world through them, then the tabernacle plays a key role in bringing Yahweh's purposes to pass for all creation. Let's take a closer look at this uniquely Israelite structure through four different yet complementary lenses.

Tabernacle through the lens of Sinai. Morales argues the tabernacle reflects Israel's experience with God at Sinai. He observes that both (1) are divided into three-part structures representing increasing levels of holiness, (2) are especially emphasized as places from which Yahweh speaks (see Exod. 19:3; Lev. 1:1), (3) have connection to the tablets of the law (given on Sinai; stored in the tabernacle), (4) have altars "so that God is approached through" sacrifice, and (5) host manifestations of Yahweh's presence represented by clouds and fire.[26] Thus, "when the cloud of glory journeys from Mount Sinai to the tabernacle, . . . the tabernacle has become *the* mountain of God."[27]

This connection between Sinai and the tabernacle allows Israel to carry their experience of Yahweh's Sinai presence with them on their journey

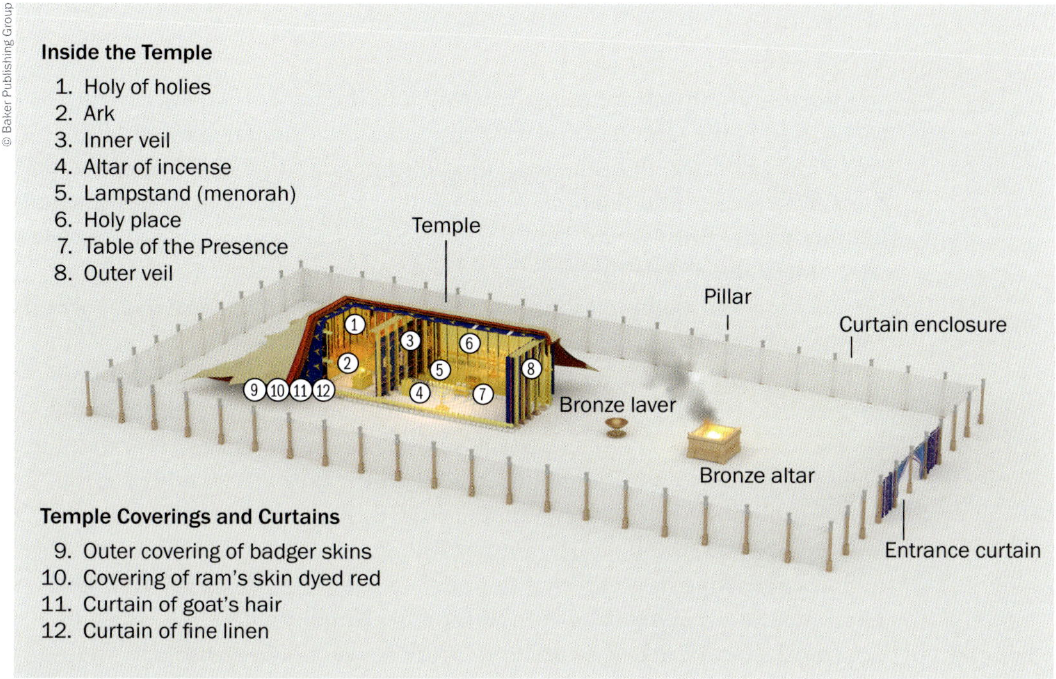

Figure 9.7. The tabernacle

toward the land.[28] Indeed, because the sights, smells, and sounds of the tabernacle evoke those experienced at Sinai, the tabernacle enables Israel to relive that Sinai experience.[29] Furthermore, the tabernacle brings this Sinai experience closer to every Israelite since it stands in the midst of the camp. As Fretheim says, "God comes down to be with the people at close, even intimate, range; they no longer need to ascend to God."[30]

Tabernacle through the lens of creation. As commentators have long noted, the tabernacle is designed as a microcosm or miniature model of the cosmos. For Robin Parry, the outer court represents the earth and sea, the holy place represents the sky, and the holy of holies stands for "God's heaven itself."[31] Morales likewise identifies similarities between the tabernacle and Eden, including cherubim guards, descriptions of priestly works, eastward-facing directions, and garden imagery (e.g., the tree-like lampstand may allude to the tree of life).[32]

Since the tabernacle's construction is also an act of new creation, numerous links connect

Figure 9.8. This image of the Eagle Nebula taken by the Hubble Space Telescope was famously called "The Pillars of Creation." In the wisdom literature, the same word used for the tabernacle's "pillars" is sometimes used to describe the "pillars" of the earth or the heavens (Job 9:6; 26:11; Prov. 9:1).

the stories of Yahweh creating the world and the Israelites constructing the tabernacle.[33] The tabernacle story also echoes the original "new-creation story": Noah's ark. In both cases, God outlines detailed building plans to a human he favors, and the human completes them "just as God/Yahweh had commanded." Both the ark and the tabernacle serve as portable sanctuaries that "carry the people through the waters/sands of chaos." Just as the waters of the flood begin to recede on New Year's Day, the tabernacle is set up for the first time on New Year's Day.[34]

The reference to the "breath" or "Spirit" of God also links these three stories. In Genesis 1's creation of the universe, the "Spirit" (*ruakh*) hovers over the waters, and in Genesis 8's postflood re-creation, God causes a "wind" (*ruakh*) to blow on the waters. With the tabernacle, however, the Spirit of God works through human artisans. Bezalel is "called by name" and "filled with the Spirit [*ruakh*] of God, in wisdom and in understanding and in knowledge of every kind of craft" (Exod. 31:3 AT). Likewise, God fills a host of other artisans with wisdom so Israel can complete the tabernacle (31:6–11). Yet these artisans' work is also made possible by the widespread participation of every Israelite "whose heart was stirred" and "spirit [*ruakh*] was willing" (35:21). They donate so much material for the construction project that Moses must tell them to stop (see 36:5–7).

Human participation in this divine act of new creation makes sense in light of Israel's vocation; they are called to participate with God in his cosmic rescue project. Their work on the tabernacle is a sharp contrast to "the demeaning work of Egypt."[35] God instigates the work, which is then made possible by generous freewill offerings and is enacted with care, creativity, a delight in materiality, and regular cycles of rest. It offers Israel a glimpse of "creation regained" and also invites them to "taste and see" the difference between work/service/worship under Pharaoh and work/service/worship under Yahweh.

At the heart of this new creation motif is Yahweh's invitation to Israel to experience more of the intimacy with the divine for which humanity was created. Morales suggests Israel as a whole is invited to dwell as close to Eden as has been humanly possible since Adam and Eve's expulsion. Of course, the reality of sin, impurity, and death means this tabernacle-enabled return to Eden falls short of humanity's full experience in Genesis. Consequently, the tabernacle encourages

THEOLOGICAL ISSUES

Kass on the Spirit and the Artist

The first people explicitly described as being "filled with the Spirit of God" after creation are not prophets, kings, or priests but artists (Exod. 31:1–6). Bezalel and Oholiab are gifted with wisdom, understanding, and knowledge to fashion God's dwelling place. Leon Kass notes the irony of artisans who likely first honed their skills under Pharaoh's overseers using those capacities for God's glory. Unlike Babel's builders who sought to "make a name" for themselves, Bezalel works "in the shadow of God," his artistry pointing beyond itself to the Creator. The tabernacle thus dignifies human creativity as a Spirit-inspired echo of God's own making. For Christian artists today, this passage affirms that creativity is not self-indulgence or self-promotion but vocation. To create faithfully, under God's Spirit and for God's glory, is to join Bezalel in transforming the stuff of this world into signs of God's dwelling with his people.[i]

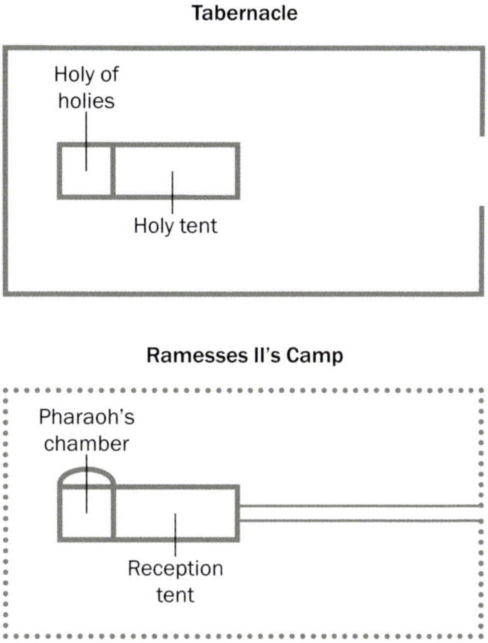

Figure 9.9. The tabernacle compared to Ramesses II's military camp Design: © Baker Publishing Group

Israel to look forward to the day when Yahweh would reclaim the entire cosmos as a sanctuary in which to dwell.

Tabernacle through the lens of kingship. A third lens for seeing the tabernacle is as Yahweh's royal residence, his earthly "palace and his base of operations."[36] The holy of holies represents his divine throne room; Hezekiah later makes this explicit in his reference to Yahweh as "enthroned above the cherubim" (Isa. 37:16). The importance of Yahweh as king emerged earlier in Exodus, and Gordon Wenham says the tabernacle's purple colors and precious metals suggest a royal setting.[37]

Joshua Berman offers another reason for seeing the tabernacle in royal terms: remarkable similarities between the tabernacle and the military tent Pharaoh Ramesses II used in his famous Battle of Kadesh.[38] Depictions of this tent and descriptions of the battle share parallels with the tabernacle story (see fig. 9.9). Some images of this war tent even picture the pharaoh in the innermost sanctuary flanked by winged, divine figures, bearing a striking similarity to the way the "wings of two cherubim" are "described as having covered the ark of the covenant's mercy seat in the tabernacle's Holy of Holies."[39]

These similarities are both architectural and theological. At the Battle of Kadesh, Pharaoh is said to fight singlehandedly against his enemies while his people stand terrified, just as Yahweh stands and fights Pharaoh on the banks of the sea while the terrified Israelites merely watch. Ramesses is

Figure 9.10. *Above*, a wall relief of Ramesses II's camp at Kadesh with a close-up of a courtyard containing the entrance to the pharaoh's tent. *Below*, a line drawing of the wall relief.

HISTORICAL MATTERS

History and the Parallels

Berman argues that parallels between the Kadesh poem and Exodus suggest that the story of the parting of the sea and the Song of the Sea in Exodus 14–15 reflect a "deliberate act of cultural appropriation," whereby the "book of Exodus claims that the God of Israel overmastered Ramesses the Great by several orders of magnitude, effectively trouncing him at his own game." Berman also observes that these close connections contribute to arguments about the historicity of Exodus by placing the likeliest dating of these biblical stories around the time when Exodus suggests Yahweh liberated the people from Egypt.[j]

CANONICAL CONNECTIONS

God's Tabernacling Presence in the New Testament

Against this background comes John's exhilarating declaration about Jesus: "And the Word became flesh and *tabernacled* among us" (John 1:14 AT). The Greek word often translated "dwelled" or "lived" in John 1:14 refers to pitching a tent and alludes to the tabernacle. In Jesus, the tabernacling presence of God has come near. In Jesus, we encounter God with us in power, goodness, and glory, guiding us by his word. In Jesus, we see the re-creation of humanity and indeed the world. In Jesus, we experience God's nearness as King of kings and Lord of lords. And in Jesus, we encounter a God willing to humble himself even unto death on a cross.

Remarkably, it is not only Jesus who embodies the tabernacle/temple; the church does as well. Paul repeatedly calls God's people to see themselves as the tangible place where God's presence can be experienced most palpably on earth (e.g., 1 Cor. 3:16; 1 Tim. 3:15). This has enormous implications for how we think about the church's identity and mission today.

even depicted as chasing his enemies into the water to kill them. In light of these parallels, Israel's tabernacle challenges Egypt's propaganda and symbolically reassures Israel of precisely what they had sung on the shores of the sea: Yahweh is a royal warrior who wins victories over even the world's greatest superpowers. Indeed, the tabernacle borrows from the Egyptian superpower's propaganda to make the point.

Tabernacle through the lens of Yahweh's holy humility. Finally, as our friend Robby Holt likes to point out, the tabernacle is an expression of Yahweh's holy humility. The great cathedrals of today and the massive temples of the ancient world seek to communicate God's grandeur and otherness. But in the wilderness, the Lord of the universe dwells in a tent. Why? Because his people live in tents. In an act of gratuitous humility, Yahweh draws near and dwells in the mobile home his people have made for him, a tent/sanctuary "on wheels," as it were. The Holy One wants to be near to his people this much: He is willing to pitch his tent beside his people's tents, joining them in their wilderness wanderings.

Bringing it all together. Seeing the tabernacle through the lenses of Sinai, creation, kingship, and holy humility helps us appreciate its theological centrality. For Israel on the move and for the Creator engaging his rebellious creation, "the tabernacle is the new definition of homeland. . . . The people become [Yahweh's] habitation. They are [Yahweh's] homeland, and [Yahweh] is their home."[40] Because this tabernacle facilitates Yahweh's purposes for bringing blessings to the nations, "this microcosm of creation is the beginning of a macrocosmic effort on God's part. *In and through this people, God is on the move to a new creation for all.*"[41]

ISRAEL'S REBELLION AND YAHWEH'S RESPONSE

In Exodus 32–34, the narrator suddenly interrupts the story of Yahweh's glorious building plans to tell us the people have been busy flagrantly breaking the first two commandments by creating a golden calf to worship. Their acts are akin to a spouse committing adultery on their wedding night[42] and thus painfully introduce the most in-depth narrative treatment of "sin, judgment, intercession, and mercy" in the Old Testament.[43] The people's rebellion and the responses of Moses and Yahweh invite us to explore vital theological themes for Exodus and the entire biblical story.

Figure 9.11. *The Ark of the Covenant Is Not of This World* by Marcellus White

Why do they want a golden calf? The people ask Aaron to "make gods" who will "go before" them because Moses's long delay on the mountain has left them wondering "what has become of him" (Exod. 32:1–2). Aaron clearly associates the golden calf with Yahweh in some way (32:4). While sometimes Israel does idolatrously trade Yahweh for another divine being, here they appear to idolatrously worship a being they *call* Yahweh but who is, according to the biblical authors, not the living Lord at all.[44] In any case, the building of the golden calf not only displaces the building of the tabernacle but contrasts with it in numerous ways. As Fretheim says,

> (1) The people seek to create what God has already provided; (2) they, rather than God, take the initiative; (3) offerings are demanded rather than willingly presented; (4) the elaborate preparations are missing altogether; (5) the painstaking length of time needed for building becomes an overnight rush job; (6) the careful provision for guarding the presence of the Holy One turns into an open-air object of immediate accessibility; (7) the invisible, intangible God becomes a visible, tangible image; and (8) the personal, active God becomes an impersonal object that cannot see or speak or act.[45]

Given Israel knows how dangerous and unpredictable life with Yahweh could be, they may also have valued being able to manipulate the idols.

Figure 9.12. Gilded bullock named "The Golden Calf," found in Byblos and dating to ca. 1700 BC

Yahweh, Moses, and the people respond. Yahweh responds by asking Moses to "leave him alone" so he can destroy Israel and start afresh in his nation-building project (Exod. 32:7–10 NIV).

ETHICS

Exodus and a Theology of Work

Exodus provides three powerful images for thinking about a theology of work: Work can be exploitative, as under Pharaoh; work can be idolatrous, as with the golden calf; or work can be a way to welcome God's presence into our world, making our world look a bit more like God's kingdom, as with the tabernacle. This is crucial for workplace discipleship. Exodus can inspire disciples to sniff out the ways we are tempted to create golden calves out of our work, giving them some of the love, trust, and service we owe to God. It can also inspire us to confront the injustices of work in our world. For instance, Exodus's brutal depiction of abusive power at work might help us identify similar injustices in a world where

- companies steal billions of dollars from American workers annually through "wage theft," whether in the form of minimum wage violations, "withholding tips or pressuring staff to work off the clock," or misclassifying workers as independent contractors while treating them like hourly employees;"[k]
- low-wage American workers saw the purchasing power of their wages decline from 1979 to 2013, even as the market grew 706 percent and CEO pay grew 1,007.5 percent.[l]

The way economic injustice occurs in Exodus in part through ethnic discrimination might likewise help us see, and confront, an American job market that continues to struggle with racism. For instance, the exact same resumes still get far fewer call backs if the names at the top are stereotypically "Black" names rather than stereotypically "white" names.[m]

But Exodus can also inspire us to "build for the kingdom,"[n] bearing witness to Christ in our work lives. As Mark Glanville says, "We bear witness to Christ by loving what Christ loves and challenging what Christ challenges" in our "offices, parents' groups, cafes, trucks, homes, factories, hospitals, [advocacy] groups," and more.[o]

When Yahweh accuses Israel of "acting perversely," he uses the same verb used in Genesis to describe humanity violently "ruining" themselves and the rest of creation (Gen. 6:11–13). Will Yahweh once again wipe out people called to be his royal, priestly family members in order to start afresh with a Noah-like Moses?

As commentators have long noticed, Yahweh's demand that Moses "leave him alone" subtly "leaves the door open for intercession."[46] As we saw in our discussion of Abraham, God desires a covenantal partner willing to engage in rigorous debate. Moses responds to the invitation. He boldly confronts Yahweh, reminding him that he brought the people out of Egypt, that the world is watching, and that Yahweh's reputation is at stake. Most importantly, he grounds his request in the promises Yahweh swore to the ancestors.

Moses's bold protest averts the immediate threat of annihilation: "And Yahweh relented over the disaster which he had said he would do to his people" (Exod. 32:14 AT). This does not mean there is no judgment, though. Moses calls the Levites to execute three thousand of their brothers, friends, and neighbors who apparently refused to turn from their idolatrous worship and come to God's side (32:26–28). While this is Moses's idea, and he may be portrayed as "somewhat *too* zealous on behalf of Yahweh,"[47] the Bible seems to see this as a desperate time calling for desperate measures. After the Israelites have willingly bound themselves to the covenantal terms, their flagrant idolatry jeopardizes the entire community's future.[48] Yahweh likewise sends a plague (32:35) and, while committing to fulfill his promise to the ancestors by bringing the people to the land, indicates he will no longer go with the people because his presence might consume them (33:1–4).

Practically, this means Yahweh is retracting the offer of the tabernacle. He will lead them to the land "from afar, but they shall not be privileged to see the symbol of [Yahweh's] presence in the midst of their camp."[49] Both

Moses and the people recognize this is disastrous. Promised lands are good as far as they go, but what matters most is Yahweh's presence. Indeed, it is Yahweh's presence that sets Israel apart *from* the nations *for* the nations (Exod. 33:16).

Moses the mediator. Moses responds by again acting as Israel's mediator. Since Moses seeks to "atone" for the people and is willing to be blotted out of Yahweh's book for their sake, Scarlata suggests he becomes the "suffering servant," the "good shepherd who lays down his life for his sheep."[50] Moses refuses to follow Yahweh's instructions to leave Sinai unless Yahweh promises to go with them (Exod. 33:15).

Yahweh "allows himself to be persuaded,"[51] both desiring and creating space for Moses's mediation. That is why he responds to Moses's requests with ever-greater displays of mercy, as we shall explore further below. Such interactions make clear Yahweh willingly enters into a genuine, responsive relationship with humanity. Intercession only works because the God to whom intercession is offered is genuinely merciful, but that mercy is exercised in part through human intercession.

The character of Yahweh. In the midst of his mediation efforts, Moses suddenly asks Yahweh to show him his glory. Yahweh responds by causing all his *goodness* to pass by Moses and announcing his divine name to him. The climax of the scene reads:

> The LORD passed before him, and proclaimed,
> "The LORD, the LORD,
> a God merciful and gracious,
> slow to anger,
> and abounding in steadfast love and faithfulness,
> keeping steadfast love for the thousandth generation,
> forgiving iniquity and transgression and sin,
> yet by no means clearing the guilty,
> but visiting the iniquity of the parents
> upon the children
> and the children's children,
> to the third and the fourth generation." (Exod. 34:6–7)

This announcement offers one of the "fullest depiction[s] of the name and nature of God within the whole Bible."[52] It is quoted at least fourteen times in the Old Testament alone.[53] Several things can be said about this climactic self-revelation.

First, Yahweh's self-description emphasizes mercy, grace, patience, loyal love, and, crucially, forgiveness. Given this text comes immediately after Israel's rebellion, we might expect an emphasis on judgment. However, this revelation of Yahweh's name/character after Israel's rebellion prioritizes Yahweh's mercy and is more saturated in the language of grace and forgiveness than any prior biblical text.[54] Similarly, Exodus 34:7 piles up language for evil ("iniquity and transgression and sin") to clarify that God will indeed forgive it all. In Exodus 3:14, Yahweh had prepared Israel to know him as "I WILL BE WHO I WILL BE"; here, Israel discovers that mercy, grace, and forgiveness stand at the heart of who Yahweh *will be*.

Second, Yahweh's climactic self-revelation centers forgiveness and grace (a thousand generations), but it does not deny Yahweh's commitment to just judgment (three to four generations). This incredibly gracious God remains committed to punishing the iniquity of entire households that violate his way (the reference to the "third and fourth generation" likely refers to all the living generations within a typical Israelite household).[55]

Nonetheless, the text does not balance Yahweh's just judgment and his mercy equally. Yahweh "forgives three things" but "only punishes one,"[56] and the "thousands of generations vastly outnumber the three to four judged generations."[57] Yahweh's character, as Matthew Lynch suggests, is "clearly imbalanced." As the apostle James would later write, "Mercy triumphs over judgment" (James 2:13).[58]

Moses responds to this revelation of God's overwhelmingly-merciful-yet-still-justly-judging goodness with worship. The Merciful One rescues the covenant Israel had broken and sends Moses back to the people with his face glowing from encountering God. Reinvigorated by their new revelation of Yahweh's character, the people finally begin the tabernacle building project. The book closes on a hopeful note, emphasizing the people's obedience and describing how the glory of Yahweh so fills the tabernacle that even Moses cannot enter it (Exod. 40:34–35; this sets up the problem that Leviticus will solve). We hear this hopeful note knowing "Israel and the church have their existence because God picked up the pieces. There was no golden period of unblemished saintliness. Rather, the people of God are from the outset the forgiven and restored community. There is a covenant—and a new covenant—because it was maintained from God's side."[59]

CANONICAL CONNECTIONS

Punishing the Next Generation Not at All!

The rest of the Torah makes clear that the reference to the "third and fourth generation" should be taken as a theological claim about the relationship between God's mercy and justice, rather than as an algorithm to determine exactly how Yahweh works in every situation. In Numbers, almost the whole generation of adult Israelites rebels against God and refuses to enter the land. Yahweh punishes their generation but does not punish the next generation at all; indeed, he gives them the land!

Living the Text: Doing Theology Alongside Exodus

Theologian Beth Felker Jones suggests that "theology is the discipline of speaking faithfully about God" so we might become "more faithful followers of Jesus."[60] One way to live the text of Exodus is by learning to "do theology" alongside this magnificent, God-soaked section of Scripture. Exodus's theological method, though, may surprise us.

We have already seen the book's strange mode of doing theology. Exodus 4–14 explores questions of divine and human agency through the complex story of both Pharaoh and Yahweh "strengthening," "hardening," and "making heavy" Pharaoh's heart. Christians sometimes act as if such storytelling is an inferior way of doing theology, one that requires us to dig out the tidy abstract doctrines buried underneath the story. But Exodus does theology, in part, by telling stories, including the story of Pharaoh's heart. The moment we surrender the story, we lose some of the theological riches it offers us.

Or consider Yahweh's self-revelation in Exodus 34:6–7. This is not the first time Yahweh has used such language to describe himself. In Exodus 20:5–6, however, he begins with a warning and puts the threat of judgment first. Only after these warnings does Yahweh mention he shows "steadfast love" to the thousandth generation of those who love him. Similarly, Exodus 23:20–21 warns the people that the "angel" that Yahweh will send before them will *not* pardon transgression. Why? Because Yahweh's "name is in him." This suggests Yahweh's "name" might be particularly prone to *un*forgiveness.

We hear these sterner self-descriptions before the debacle with the golden calf. If we take the story seriously, we come to Exodus 34:6–7 worried and perhaps even expecting "only divine wrath and judgment."[61]

This sets us up to be swept off our feet by Yahweh's amazing grace. Such grace comes through an unprecedented revelation of God's character as overwhelmingly disposed toward mercy, patience, and forgiveness. In another surprise, this revelation of God's gracious character nevertheless includes the reminder that Yahweh will "by no means clear the guilty."

For many readers, there is an irreconcilable conflict between God's love and mercy, on the one hand, and his just judgment, on the other. In Exodus, both the mercy and the just judgment are aspects of the divine goodness Yahweh allows Moses to glimpse. Strawn even suggests the poetry of Yahweh's self-description identifies Yahweh's willingness to punish as "part of the way" Yahweh keeps steadfast love.[62] After all, a God who is merciful in the sense that he is unwilling to bring just judgment on evil would have left them in Egypt. A God unwilling to justly judge sin cannot be bothered to declare good news to the poor.

These same texts also offer us an example of doing theology in relation to God's presence and knowability. On the one hand, God offers Moses a powerful, perhaps unparalleled revelation of God's character. Exodus 33:11 prepares us for this with the remarkable claim that Yahweh spoke to Moses "face to face, as one speaks to a friend," making him uniquely qualified to receive this revelation. Yet, just nine verses later, Yahweh responds to his friend's request to see his glory by telling him he is not able to see Yahweh's face because "no one can see Yahweh's face and live" (33:20 AT). Moses's unprecedented vision of God's goodness will be nothing more than a peek at God's back. One of the fullest revelations of Yahweh's character in the Old Testament is preceded by "an emphasis upon the limitation" of what even Moses can receive.[63]

By placing seemingly contradictory statements about seeing Yahweh's face side by side, Exodus shows us how the Torah does theology in relation to God's immanence and God's transcendence, his presence and absence.[64] This mysterious, paradoxical framing also prepares us to receive a revelation of Yahweh's character that juxtaposes and maintains descriptions of Yahweh that appear to us to be opposites (mercy and just judgment). These two aspects of God's character are held together through the "lyrical tension" of the text.[65] The "core confession of Yahweh's character asks us to stand in awe and wonder at the God who shows boundless mercy and who also judges the guilty."[66]

If and when Christians attempt to choose between these characteristics, we simply refuse to take the Bible seriously and instead remake God in our own image. If Scripture's depiction of God is a mosaic, then neglecting the challenging or irregular pieces may give us a God who is "simpler, more familiar, and more assimilable" to our projects and plans.[67] But such a God is a lifeless idol. It is the Bible's richer, more paradoxical portrait of God that facilitates a genuine encounter with the living Lord.

In the Old Testament, Israel consistently returns to Exodus 34:6–7, allowing different pieces of the mosaic to provide fresh angles on their life with God in different times and places. The prophet Joel called his generation to repent of their wicked rebellion and return to God "with fasting, with weeping, and with mourning," rendering their hearts and not merely their clothing (Joel 2:12–13). Why? Because God "is gracious and merciful, slow to anger, and abounding in steadfast love, and relents from punishing" (2:13). While Joel does not quote Exodus's depiction of God as punishing the guilty, he has clearly learned from Exodus that the living Lord cannot be manipulated or presumed upon. For Joel, Yahweh's character does not guarantee that the door of repentance remains open, even as he holds out hope that it does: "*Who knows* whether he will not turn and relent, and leave a blessing behind him?" (2:14). Israel's only hope is to cling to that "who knows" hope, casting themselves on the mercy of God.

Just a few prophetic books later, another group of people stake their lives on the "who knows" of God's grace: the Ninevites (Jon. 3:9). The Ninevites were the Nazis of the ancient world, yet they, too, discover Yahweh is willing to relent from judgment in the face of human repentance (see Exod. 32:14). The prophet Jonah expresses his fury at God for forgiving his outrageously unjust enemies by quoting Exodus 34:6–7's depiction of Yahweh and then hurling it in God's face as an accusation: "O Lord! Is not this what I said while I was still in my own country? That is why I fled to Tarshish at the beginning; for I knew that you are a *gracious God and merciful, slow to anger, and abounding in steadfast love, and ready to relent from punishing*" (Jon. 4:2).

Jonah gets angry at God for being too "slow to anger," too "abounding in steadfast love," too "ready to relent from punishing." Given Assyria's violence and oppression, we can't really blame him. Yet Scripture suggests the problem lies with Jonah. Jonah knows Israel has only survived because of Yahweh's superabundant mercy. He must learn Yahweh is willing to show that same mercy even to his worst enemies.

If we flip another two books over, the prophet Nahum also draws on Exodus 34:6–7. This time the prophet focuses on Yahweh's self-revelation at Sinai to remind Israel (and us) that God remains committed to just judgment. Indeed, God's just judgment is part of the gospel, the good news that God will not stand by in the face of horrific violence and oppression. Thus, the prophet Nahum introduces his vision of Yahweh's long-delayed judgment against Nineveh with a poem praising God's vengeance taken directly from Exodus 34:6–7: "A jealous and avenging God is the Lord, the Lord is avenging and wrathful; the Lord takes vengeance on his adversaries and rages against his enemies. The Lord is slow to anger but great in power, and the Lord will by no means clear the guilty. His way is in whirlwind and storm, and the clouds are the dust of his feet" (Nah. 1:2–3). Nahum recognizes what Yahweh in Exodus states: Yahweh's judgment on evil is part of what makes God good, not an aspect of God's character that challenges God's goodness.

The paradox of God's justice and mercy runs through the Old Testament and into the New Testament. Jesus's merciful self-offering justifies us by his blood so that we might be saved from the "wrath of God" (Rom. 5:9). Yet God's just judgment is still part of the good news; Jesus promises his disciples that God will "bring about justice for his chosen ones, who cry out to him day and night" (Luke 18:3 NIV). Nevertheless, the Lord delays his return precisely because he remains overwhelmingly gracious and merciful. Indeed, he is "patient with you, not wanting any to perish, but all to come to repentance" (2 Pet. 3:9).

Exodus 34:6–7 offers us a generative depiction of God's character that echoes across Scripture and is capable of transforming our life with God. The text also models a way of doing theology that allows the messy, paradoxical, complicated, and unsettling depictions of the triune God encountered in every corner and crevice of Scripture to shape and reshape our encounter with him. Christians who follow Exodus's invitation may find much that surprises, bewilders, and even bothers them about this God. Yet the witness of Scripture and the saints is that it is precisely in these moments of bewildered surprise that we, like Moses, may discover we are standing on holy ground, in the presence of the Holy One, invited to draw near.

How to Read Torah's Rituals Today

Sacred Rites and Holy Habits

Previous chapters have demonstrated that the Pentateuch is not merely a collection of stories or laws; nor is it a systematic theology treatise. The Pentateuch forms covenantal identity through a rich variety of literature and liturgy. Law structures Israel's moral and theological vision, calling a people to inhabit the patterns of God's righteousness and holiness. Narrative draws each generation into Israel's defining story, shaping imagination and self-understanding through memory and plot.[1] Song and poetry like the Song of the Sea (Exod. 15:1–18), Miriam's Song (15:21), and the Song of Moses (Deut. 32) distill these themes into emotionally charged, repeatable forms that can spark the imagination, move the emotions, and expand the perspectives of the singers/hearers.[2] Yet formation in the Pentateuch does not remain at the level of text or tune. It extends into the bodily, communal, spatial, and temporal dimensions of life through ritual and habit.[3] These practices train the body, attune the senses, and structure life with God through repeated action. Ellen Davis says, "Leviticus articulates an embodied and enacted spirituality, one that touches potentially on every aspect of human life, including our most common social behaviors, public or intimate, and our bodily functions, voluntary and involuntary."[4] Ritual and habitual behavior have a key function, together with these other modes of formation, in constructing a covenantal imagination that is storied, instructed, sung, practiced, and lived.

The book of Leviticus stands at the center of the Pentateuch. In this remarkable text, the Israelites receive instruction after instruction, mapping

Figure 10.1. Eucharistic stained-glass window in St. Michael the Archangel Parish, Findlay, Ohio

out and giving structure to the details of their lives. Hardly a waking hour of their day, a square inch of their society, or the smallest exertion of effort in their daily endeavors is left untouched by the broad scope of Leviticus's teaching. Although the concept of ritual emerges earlier in the Pentateuch—in sacrificial offerings, circumcision, Sabbath observance, and the Passover feast—it is in Leviticus that we encounter its most concentrated expression. Numbers and Deuteronomy also contain significant ritual material, but Leviticus immerses us in an intricate symbolic world where God's holiness intersects with daily life.

When we hear "ritual," many people today instinctively think of religion, or more precisely, of tedious, hollow religious routine. In some Christian traditions, there is a suspicion of ritual as being nothing more than lifeless formalism. The Torah pushes back against this notion. It insists that all of life is religious in the sense that all of life should be oriented toward the worship of Yahweh. For Leviticus, religion cannot be limited to sacrificial rites, feast days, and priestly activity. Calendars, calories, clothing, hygiene, housekeeping, and horticulture prove fertile ground for worship, for life lived before the face of God. As strange as this world may seem to modern sensibilities, rituals in Israel were foundational activities, a core mechanism of formation. Through embodied practices, Israel would come to know who they were, who their God was, and how they were to live in covenantal partnership with him for the sake of the world.

> THEOLOGICAL ISSUES
>
> **"Before the Face of Yahweh"**
>
> The Pentateuch repeatedly uses the Hebrew phrase *lipne YHWH*—literally, "before the face of Yahweh." It describes sacrifice, worship, judgment, covenant ceremonies, and communal life (e.g., Exod. 27:21; Lev. 1:3; Deut. 27:7).
>
> In the ancient world, to stand before someone's "face" meant to stand in their presence, under their attention and authority. This is relational language. Israel lives, worships, and obeys consciously before the attentive presence of their covenant Lord.
>
> Later Christian theology summarized this vision with the Latin phrase *coram Deo*—living one's whole life "before the face of God."
>
> The Pentateuch assumes no divide between sacred and secular life. All of Israel's existence unfolds before God's face.

Recovering a faithful reading of ritual texts begins with humility. Many of us are deeply formed by modern sensibilities that prioritize the cerebral and the verbal, and many popular expressions of worship emphasize the spontaneous, the spiritual, and the instantaneous. Ritual requires something different. It invites us into repetition, bodily engagement, and meaning enacted over time. It insists that what we do over and over again shapes what we love and who we become. If you are skeptical of ritual, we invite you to examine the patterns that already structure your life. Who scripts your rituals and daily habits?[5] What do your embodied practices say about what you love and believe? We also invite you to consider how much contemporary communal worship is actually scripted ritual, just a different kind. Long-time churchgoers know when they've entered the sanctuary, where to move, when to sit, when to stand, when and whether to raise their hands and say "amen." Ultimately, the Pentateuch's ritual world invites us to ask, How might the structures and practices of God's people shape us into people who love God and neighbor, who reflect God's character in every waking hour, every square inch, and every good endeavor?[6]

The Pentateuch's ritual texts are not easy reading. They can seem foreign, confusing, and even tedious. Yet their very strangeness is an invitation to grow as readers. Because most of us have little practice with this kind of literature, we need to expand our repertoire of tools. At a basic level, ritual texts ask us to read differently:

Slowly—not rushing past details, since every repetition or sequence matters

Imaginatively—picturing the sights, sounds, and rhythms of embodied practices

Repeatedly—returning again and again, since meaning often emerges over time

With guidance—learning from scholars and interpreters who have immersed themselves in these passages

Approached this way, ritual texts become less an obstacle and more a doorway. They begin to show us how ritual once formed Israel's life with God, and how it might still stretch and shape us as readers today.

To understand fully the ritual world of the Pentateuch and what the prescribed rituals are doing, we need to grasp just how enmeshed humans already are in ritual, even if we may not typically understand them as ritual. This means widening our understanding of ritual to things beyond "religious" rituals.[7]

What Is Ritual and Why Does It Matter?

We often think of rituals as events or activities. Weddings, funerals, and family traditions like birthdays or Christmas gatherings are clearly ritualized. So are institutional ceremonies such as school assemblies, graduations, and the opening of Congress or Parliament. National pledges, stock-exchange openings, and courtroom protocols likewise follow scripted patterns. Public spectacles from Olympic ceremonies to royal coronations display ritual on a grand scale, with gestures, oaths, and symbols enacting communal identity. Even the everyday rhythms of sports or civic life remind us that ritual is laced throughout ordinary experience.

Rituals are typically marked by a set of features that distinguish them from ordinary habits or spontaneous actions.[8] These include a prescribed sequence of events, symbolic bodily actions (e.g., standing, kneeling, lifting hands, or exchanging objects), and the use of set words, songs, or chants that carry communal memory and meaning. Participants may wear distinctive clothing or use designated objects, signaling the special nature of the occasion. Rituals often take place at designated times and in shared spaces, and they often involve or are witnessed by a gathered community. Importantly, rituals imbue ordinary elements like food, clothing, gestures, or space with heightened symbolic significance. Whether religious or civic, familial or cultural, they often mark a transition—such as birth, marriage, graduation, or coronation—and serve to reinforce collective identity, memory, and deeply held values.

Rituals are not confined to isolated events. Time itself can be ritualized. We mark off days, weeks, and years in patterned, symbolic ways through national holidays, religious calendars, and weekly rhythms like weekends or the Sabbath. A school week or fiscal quarter is more than a scheduling convenience; it structures expectation and behavior. The liturgical calendar transforms seasons like Advent and Lent into opportunities for communal reflection and formation. Even secular practices such as Black Friday shopping or New Year's resolution-making turn calendar dates into shared ritual experiences that shape cultural imagination for good or ill.

People, likewise, can become bearers of ritual meaning. Public figures like judges, priests, presidents, monarchs, and athletes often serve more as ritual actors than autonomous individuals in symbolic moments. Their presence and gestures carry communal significance. A graduation speaker, a best man offering a wedding toast, or a flag bearer at the Olympics is not just a person doing something; each is a role performed, often with scripted language and expected gestures. Even aside from formal ceremonies, people can take on ritual roles through repetition and tradition. Think of the family member who always carves the Thanksgiving turkey or the elder who opens every church meeting with prayer. These are not randomly chosen people performing arbitrary roles but symbolically chosen individuals performing patterned, meaningful actions that confer identity and continuity.

From this list (and it could go on and on), it should be clear that rituals permeate every area of human life: domestic, educational, political,

ETHICS

Rituals Reveal Values

Anthropologists argue that rituals reveal what a society or community values most. If this is true, it is worth sitting with. It is worth pondering, What values and things of import do Torah's rituals reveal? In our contemporary culture, where are the most highly ritualized activities? What do they reveal about what is most important to us?

economic, athletic, legal, and beyond. But what exactly makes events like birthdays and coronations, graduation ceremonies and court proceedings rituals? What do they share, and why does it matter that they are performed in these specific ways? In other words, what does a birthday party have in common with a royal coronation, and what is at stake in treating them ritually?

Across all these examples, rituals play a dual role. They reveal or highlight the significance of a person, moment, or action, and they shape/construct that significance. Anthropologists focus intense research on the first role of ritual—namely, that rituals communicate the central values of a society.[9] As anthropologist Monica Wilson argues, "Rituals reveal values at their deepest level. . . . [Humans] express in ritual what moves them most, and since the form of expression is conventionalized and obligatory, it is the values of the group that are revealed. I see in the study of rituals the key to an understanding of the essential constitution of human societies."[10]

While this is a crucial role of ritual to be aware of, we need to avoid the risk of assuming we can or should try to fully decode rituals, as if once we have discerned the seed of their cognitive meaning we can dispense with the husk of their ritual performance. Rituals don't just say things to us; they *do* things to us, and what they do cannot be fully captured through attempts at decoding or explanation. We can and should, for example, try to grow in our understanding of what the Lord's Supper ritual communicates or means, but we must always realize that *practicing* that ritual goes to work on us in ways that go beyond our attempts at explaining its meaning.

Moreover, rituals do not only reflect what we already value; it is one of the primary ways we learn what to value in the first place. Thus, ritual reveals and also *shapes* what is most valuable to humans; our desires and allegiances are forged in the fires of our rituals and practices. This insight becomes especially important when we begin to consider the relationship between ritual and habit, two deeply connected categories. To understand the power of biblical ritual, particularly in books like Leviticus, we need to explore how rituals and habits work together to shape the imagination, identity, and daily practices of a community.

Rituals and Habits

At its core, a ritual is a symbolic act, a repeated, embodied practice that communicates meaning beyond the action itself. As in the Pentateuch, rituals often take ordinary things—people, time, or events—and ascribe to them special, covenantal significance.[11] A meal becomes a memorial of deliverance. A week becomes sacred time. A priest becomes a living mediator of holiness. Rituals function as symbolic containers, holding and transmitting the deeper truths of Israel's identity and God's purposes.

Ritual/Habit Inventory

Map out a typical day in your life and list the patterns of behavior (habits, repeated activities, etc.) that structure your day—things like brushing your teeth, taking your dog for a walk, eating meals, and checking your phone.

Answer the following questions about these patterns:

- Where did this pattern of behavior originate?
- Who designed this pattern of behavior?
- For what purpose was this pattern of behavior designed?
- What underlying values does my practice of this pattern of behavior reveal?
- How is it shaping who I am and how I see the world?[a]

While all rituals are patterned behaviors, not all patterned behaviors are rituals. Many of our actions are better described as habits, repetitive routines that may lack overt symbolism but still reveal what we value and exert a formative influence. Whether or not we understand brushing teeth, checking the news, or making morning coffee as rituals, they are certainly habitual practices that, like rituals, train our attention and shape our desires over time. They form us, often without our noticing.

Habits are the repeated activities, patterns of behavior, routines, and rhythms that structure our day. James Clear, the author of the #1 *New York Times* bestseller, *Atomic Habits*, says that "a habit is a routine or behavior that is performed regularly—and, in many cases, automatically."[12] Some habits were formed in us long before we would have given any thought to them, like morning and bedtime routines, tying shoelaces, buckling seatbelts, and so on. Other habits, like eating healthy, driving a car well, and exercising, take a good deal of time and determination to establish and maintain. Still other (often bad) habits seem to take virtually no effort or determination to form and enormous determination to change; we can, for example, slip effortlessly into bad sleeping or eating patterns.

A massive and lucrative industry focused on habits has recently emerged. The self-help section of any bookstore will inevitably have many books on habits, but so too the sections on psychology and business and marketing. Why all the interest in habits? The marketing experts and self-help gurus have discovered what ritual texts of the Pentateuch have understood all along: God created humans as creatures of habit. The self-help industry knows that if we have any hope at all of changing ourselves, we will have

Figure 10.2. A saint performing the sacrament of Holy Communion, stained glass window in St. John's Cathedral in 's-Hertogenbosch, Netherlands

to contend with our habits. Marketing specialists seek to harness and even shape the habitual practices of consumers, recognizing the mysterious connection between human habits and human desires—again, an insight of which the Pentateuch is keenly aware.

Though theorists disagree on whether and where to draw the line between rituals and habits, what's important for our purposes is to recognize that both hold formative power.[13] James K. A. Smith calls attention to the "cultural liturgies" that shape us daily through embodied repetition.[14] Malls, phones, social media, and calendars form us by directing our time, desires, and sense of the good life. Such rituals and habits—such "liturgies"—deeply shape our identity.

Unlike everyday habits, which can be automatic and unnoticed, many rituals draw attention to what is being done, and they invest ordinary elements with heightened meaning. As Jay Sklar notes, rituals assign symbolic weight to specific people, times, and events within a sacred framework.[15] From this perspective, drinking a cup of coffee in the morning is habit; drinking a cup of wine in remembrance is ritual.[16] In the Torah, both habits and rituals function as instruments of divine formation. Habits are the regular, embodied practices of daily life—what to eat, how to farm, how to respond to illness and bodily fluids, how to relate to neighbors—through which God infuses holiness in the ordinary. Rituals are heightened, symbolic actions—festivals, sacrifices, washings—that mark sacred times and spaces, dramatizing Israel's identity and covenant calling. This is precisely why the Torah's ritual system matters. Its detailed instructions (what to eat, when to rest, how to sacrifice, when to celebrate) are a formative counterliturgy for Israel living in the context of the surrounding nations. Israel's ritual life was a divinely scripted pattern of meaning-making practices that sought to form a people marked by holiness, righteousness/justice, and covenant faithfulness.

In summary, the Torah addresses ritual and habitual behavior. Leviticus prescribes what the priests must do at the altar and also trains ordinary Israelites in the repeated practices of daily life. These daily and seasonal habits were every bit as essential to the Torah's formational project. Israel's life was shaped by ritual and habitual practices. Such practices provided symbolic anchors of meaning and a regime for building muscle memory for faithful living. Both were part of a covenantal rule of life meant to form God's people for living with God and for the blessing of all nations.

The Formative Function of Ritual and Habitual Practices

This section explores the Pentateuch's vision for ritual as a formative tool. We'll consider how ritual shapes covenant identity, how it conveys knowledge through the body, and how it acts as a counterformation in a world full of rival liturgies.

Rituals in the Pentateuch are intentional tools of formation. Like story, law, and song, ritual cultivates a way of seeing and being in the world. But unlike those other forms, ritual does its work primarily through the body. It integrates the physical and symbolic, the ordinary and the sacred. Through repeated, embodied actions—slaughtering animals, sprinkling blood, bathing, wearing specific garments, refraining from certain foods, resting on the seventh day—rituals inscribe covenant identity deeply onto Israel's communal life and daily rhythms. Crucially, the rituals of the Torah are not private, abstract, or optional. They are public, concrete, and central. Whether sacrifices, festivals, or regulations concerning purity and impurity, these practices function pedagogically. They shape affections, reinforce memory, cultivate reverence, and build communal coherence and identity. As Smith argues, liturgies train us to desire certain visions of the good life, often on a precognitive, heart-level plane.[17]

This formative power also makes rituals contested terrain. Just as Israel's narratives functioned as counternarratives to some of the stories of their neighbors, Israel's rituals contrast with the "cultural liturgies" of the nations.[18] The nations' rituals were rooted in idolatry, fear, manipulation, egocentrism, tribalism, economic scarcity and exploitation, and moral disorder. And they competed for the hearts and loyalties of God's people. In commanding Israel's ritual life, Yahweh counters rival visions of reality in addition to teaching theology. Rituals are formative as well as counter-formative. They resist rival identities, inscribe covenant vocation into the bones, and shape the desires of the people.

Reading the Feast of Tabernacles

Read Leviticus 23:33–43 slowly and thoughtfully at least three times. As you do, consider what practicing this ritual Feast of Tabernacles would do to and in the people of God. How might it shape their character? What might it shape them to understand about themselves, about God, and about God's world? Finally, consider this: The text says the point of this ritual of living in tents is so that Israel would "know" that their ancestors had lived in tents when they came out of Egypt. But if that's the goal, why didn't Yahweh just tell them that?

Rituals also train the senses. They help Israel perceive what they might otherwise overlook: the holiness and presence of God, the gravity of sin, the value of life, the rhythms of time, the gift of food, the sanctity of the body. These truths are taught as well as tasted, touched, seen, smelled, and heard. The smells of blood, burning flesh, and incense fill the tabernacle courts (Lev. 1:9; 2:2), signaling both the costliness of atonement and the fragrance of worship. The act of touching (laying hands on an animal; 1:4; 16:21) impresses upon the body the weight of identification. The coolness of water in ritual washings (14:8–9) and the sensation of blood being sprinkled on skin (14:14) render purification a tactile and unforgettable experience. The soundscape of Israel's ritual life would also be unmistakable: the bleating of animals, the clang of priestly instruments, the crackle of fire, the sizzling of meat, the voices of songs and liturgical words (prayers and blessings, covenant responsibilities, instructions), the sound of the bells on the priestly robes (Exod. 28:33–35). Such sounds were not background noise but part of the embodied pedagogy of worship. Taste, too, plays a role as some sacrificial offerings are consumed in sacred meals (Lev. 7:15; Deut. 12:7), allowing worshipers to participate bodily in Yahweh's provision and fellowship. The command to consume bitter herbs and unleavened bread provides ritual tastes of the bitterness of slavery and the haste of liberation (Exod. 12:8, 15–20; Num. 9:11; Deut. 16:3).

In all these ways, ritual cultivates a kind of theological attentiveness, a sensory way of knowing that is embodied, communal, and experienced. This is especially clear in the ritual calendar, which repeatedly breaks into the everyday with reminders of Yahweh's provision and calling. These rituals structure time itself around covenantal memory and hope. The Pentateuch's ritual system forms a people who are taught what is true and trained to live in truth. Though many of Israel's rituals are no longer practiced today, their formational logic remains vital. In a distracted and disembodied age, where many Christians are more shaped by digital habits and consumer rituals than by biblical rhythms, the Pentateuch challenges us to recover a vision of faith that is lived, practiced, and embodied.

How Rituals Form

Ritual and Symbol

Symbols are at the heart of ritual. Rituals work by embedding a symbolic system into the daily and communal life of a people.[19] In the Pentateuch, ritual symbols such as blood, oil, fire, water, bread, incense, and bodily fluids carry deep theological weight. They encode meaning, shaping how Israel perceives God, themselves, and the world.

Blood, for example, is simultaneously a symbol of life and death. When applied to the altar or sprinkled on individuals (e.g., Lev. 1:5; 8:23–24; 16:14–19), it marks purification, atonement, or consecration. Fire, a clear symbol of God's presence, consumes sacrifices as a visible sign of divine acceptance (9:24), while incense clouds the space, symbolizing both divine presence and concealment (16:12–13). Water, used in washings and in preparing sacrifices, signifies cleansing and boundary crossing: from common to holy, from impure to clean (e.g., 8:6; 15:13; 16:4). These are not arbitrary associations. In the Pentateuch, each symbol is part of a larger theological grammar that speaks of holiness, justice, grace, and presence.

Symbolic actions are equally significant. Laying hands on an animal (e.g., Lev. 1:4; 4:4) appears to signal identification and transfer. Eating sacred food (7:15–18) communicates participation and fellowship. Distinguishing between clean and unclean animals (Lev. 11) cultivates habits of discernment and attentiveness, not just about food, but about the nature of reality. Yearly, all Israelite households are commanded to take a seven-day camping trip at the appointed time, resting from work, offering requisite sacrifices, building a tent/booth, and dwelling in that booth for seven days (23:33–43). This camping trip is a symbolic ritual to cement into each generation the memory of God's provision during the wilderness wandering (23:43). Apparently the kind of memory Leviticus is after requires more than the Israelites simply *telling* their children that God provided for them in the wilderness; through this ritual, they have to enact it. These symbolic actions performed publicly and communally reinforce their meaning through repetition and visibility.

Ritual and Space

The ritual symbols and actions do not float in abstraction. They are anchored in a meticulously structured physical world: tabernacle courts, altars, tents, and boundaries that demarcate spheres of holiness and access. Just as ritual symbols shape perception, so too does sacred space teach Israel how to approach God. The layout of ritual geography, from the outer camp to the holy of holies, embodies a theology of presence and distance, access and boundary. Access is limited, movements are prescribed, and spatial transitions (from common to holy, from impure to clean) are often dramatized through physical acts like washing, anointing, or sacrifice. The presence of God in Israel's camp was a profound gift and a dangerous reality; rituals in sacred space shaped the people to recognize this deep in their bones.

Understanding the formative power of ritual requires attending to the spatial logic of Israel's worship. The most concentrated site of sacred space in the Pentateuch is the tabernacle. At the center of Israel's camp, it functioned as a portable Sinai, God's dwelling in the midst of his people (Exod. 25:8). Its spatial design reflected a movement from the common to the holy, from outside the camp to the most holy place. As we've seen, the tabernacle also called to mind the cosmos in general and Eden in particular, a sanctuary from which humans had been exiled but now was partially restored.[20] To move toward the most holy place was to symbolically ascend into God's presence, just as Adam and Eve once walked with God in the garden.

This symbolic ordering extends beyond the tabernacle to the entire camp. In Numbers 2, God instructs Israel to camp in concentric rings around the sanctuary. The Levites camped immediately around the tabernacle, guarding its sanctity, while the twelve tribes camped in a square formation beyond them, each with designated banners and positions. The arrangement is a visual and spatial declaration: Yahweh is at the center of Israel's life, and access to him is mediated through sacred roles and rituals. Wenham writes, "Both at rest and on the move the camp was organized to express symbolically the presence and kingship of the Lord."[21] The camp becomes a liturgical map, reinforcing Israel's collective identity as a holy people gathered around the presence of a holy God.

Importantly, this liturgical space is not static but is animated through faithful practice. Priests enter the tent daily to maintain the lamps, tend the incense, and offer sacrifices. The people gather, process, and encircle the tabernacle in festival and pilgrimage. Sacred space becomes a site of encounter and formation where divine relationship is cultivated and covenantal memory is embedded. This ordered space reflects a deeper spiritual

ETHICS

What's at the Center?

Throughout history, the center of a city has revealed the heart of a culture. In the ancient world, the center was often occupied by a temple: the dwelling place of the gods, the axis of the cosmos, the source of blessing and order. The central place of Israel's tabernacle and later the temple signaled that Yahweh, not monarch, market, or military, was the organizing presence of their life together.

This pattern continued into the medieval period, when the cathedral or church was placed at the heart of European towns and cities, not only as a place of worship but as a spatial and spiritual orientation point. Bells marked the hours, festivals shaped the calendar, and the church stood as the visible anchor of the community's life.

Vunav / Shutterstock

Figure 10.3. Cathedral of Saint Mary of the Flower in Florence

In many modern cities, that center has shifted to financial districts, sports arenas, shopping malls, or government buildings. These, too, reveal what we revere. The tabernacle's placement in Israel raises a simple but searching question: What—or who—is at the center of our life together?

movement: the journey from the outer courts of the world into the inner sanctuary of God's presence.[22]

It would be easy to read all this as reinforcing a divide between sacred and secular, that there are some places God cares about and other places he is indifferent to. That would misunderstand the Pentateuch's spatial theology. The tabernacle is not a compartmentalized "religious" space in an otherwise secular/neutral world. It is a concentrated microcosm, a portable Eden that signals God's intention for *all* creation. The spatial logic of Leviticus is not about retreating from the world but about reordering the world so that every place becomes holy ground. In this vision, Israel is called to visit holy space *and* to become a holy people who extend God's presence into every space. The spatial dynamics of the tabernacle and the camp dramatize a larger vocation: to inhabit the world as those who live before the face of God and invite others into this good life.

This ritualizing of space forms a covenantal imagination. The Pentateuch trains Israel to think theologically and, through its symbolic map, to inhabit theology spatially. Orientation matters. What the ritual instruction of the Pentateuch teaches is a truth that holds today: The things we put at the center of our life—geographically, architecturally, communally—are what we value most, and our lives orient around this core. The Pentateuch demonstrates that sacred space shapes and reveals sacred orientation.

Ritual and Sequence

The Pentateuch embeds its ritual instructions within a patterned world, reinforcing identity and memory through temporal sequences. By punctuating the lives of the people (every evening and morning, every day, every other month, every year, every seven years, every fifty years), these temporal sequences aim to structure all Israelite time. They orient Israel's time around God's saving acts, the people's movements around sacred tasks, and their gestures around embodied meaning.

Take Passover, for example.[23] Its temporal setting is exact: a very specific day and a very specific time of day, at "twilight" on the fourteenth day of the first month (Exod. 12:6; Lev. 23:5). This moment, marked by the setting sun, is not incidental; it evokes mood, urgency, and identification with the decisive night of Israel's deliverance. The ritual sequence requires forethought, as there are clear preparatory instructions (e.g., selecting a lamb, removing leaven); the rite includes a prescribed menu (lamb, unleavened bread, bitter herbs), symbolic gestures (eating in haste with staff in hand, applying blood to the doorposts), and limitations (the meal must be finished before morning). Even after Israel's initial exodus, Passover was to be repeated yearly so that each generation could enter the memory and be shaped by it. Deuteronomy integrates the Passover into a triad of pilgrimage festivals (with Weeks and Booths). As A. J. Culp notes, Deuteronomy "weaves these rites into a single commemorative fabric, making Israel's calendar into a yearlong commemoration of the exodus pilgrimage."[24] Israel's liturgical year shapes God's people to remember deep in their guts what God has done for them.

The ritual calendar of the Pentateuch structures isolated events, and it sanctifies time itself. Weekly Sabbaths (Exod. 20:8–11; Lev. 23:3), monthly new moons (Num. 28:11–15), seasonal festivals (Lev. 23), Sabbatical years (25:1–7), and Jubilee (25:8–55) inscribe sacred rhythms into time, rooting Israel's life in cycles of rest, dependence, and remembrance. These temporal cadences are intended to form

LITERARY NOTES

Sequence of Passover

The Passover is described or prescribed in the following texts: Exodus 12:1–30; 12:43–13:16; Leviticus 23:4–8; Numbers 9:1–14; 28:16–25; Deuteronomy 16:1–8.

Preparation (Before 14th Nisan)

- Choose unblemished male lamb (tenth day)
- Remove all leaven from homes
- Future observance at central sanctuary

Passover Night (14th Nisan)

- Slaughter lamb at twilight
- Apply blood to doorposts (first time only)
- Roast whole lamb; no broken bones
- Eat with unleavened bread and bitter herbs
- Eat in haste (first time only)
- Burn leftovers

Unleavened Bread (15th–21st Nisan)

- Eat no leaven for seven days
- Sacred assemblies on day 1 and 7
- Daily offerings

Commemoration

- Consecrate firstborn males
- Teach children the meaning
- Keep feast annually in Abib/Nisan

Yehoshua Halevi / Shutterstock

Figure 10.4. View of a residential apartment complex in Beitar, Israel, during Sukkoth (Booths), in which temporary wooden structures are erected on balconies as part of the ritual observance of the weeklong holiday

THEOLOGICAL ISSUES

Beginning the Year with Grace

Michael LeFebvre argues that the decision to begin Israel's year with the Passover was countercultural; the beginning of the year in other cultures coincided with planting rather than harvesting. By beginning "the year with bounty rather than with labor," Israel's calendar trained them to see the world as running on God's grace. They worked not toward God's gift but already caught up in that gift. It may also "have been a deliberate, theologically significant break from the practice of the Canaanites."[b]

a people who view time covenantally—as a gift from God, set apart for worship, service, justice, and joy. As with sacred space, there is a danger of seeing only these designated times as holy and the rest as secular or mundane, but the opposite is true: These holy days are anchors that reveal the sanctity of all time. They train Israel to inhabit every moment of every day, ordinary and extraordinary alike, as a moment with and before God.

Ritual sequencing and sacred time are pedagogical and formational. To belong to Israel was to inhabit a world where time itself was patterned by grace, where the calendar testified to God's saving acts, and remembering meant reenacting those acts in bodily form. Through repetition and ritualized time, Israel's story was preserved as well as performed, embedding covenant identity in the structural cadence of life.

Ritual and States of Purity/Holiness

The Pentateuch presents a ritual world in which people, objects, animals, and spaces fall along a spectrum of ritual status: unclean, clean, and holy (or impure, pure, and sanctified). Alongside these states, Leviticus also distinguishes between what is common (ordinary) and what is holy (set apart for sacred use), creating two overlapping axes of ritual life: clean/unclean and common/holy. These states are not primarily about hygiene, morality, or worth, but they indicate symbolic status in relation to God's holy presence. Something becomes *holy* when something *common* is set apart for sacred use. To be *clean* is to be in a fit condition for worship and participation in communal life. To be *unclean* is not necessarily sinful, but it is incompatible with approaching God or entering sacred space.

This system is most fully articulated in Leviticus, but its logic is already foreshadowed earlier in the Pentateuch. The tabernacle makes visible a pattern traced from creation to Eden to Sinai: access to God is structured, with greater restriction as one draws nearer to the divine presence (Gen. 2–3; Exod. 19).[25] Distinctions between clean and unclean animals surface in the flood narrative (Gen. 7:2), rooting Israel's symbolic worldview long before the giving of the law. What Leviticus does is make this implicit symbolic structure explicit and prescribe the rhythms and practices by which Israel is to navigate it.

Crucially, the Levitical system does not treat impurity as a static state. Regular Israelites would move in and out of impurity through the normal course of life.[26] The emphasis is not on avoiding impurity at all costs but on attending to it, recognizing its significance, undergoing the prescribed rituals of restoration, and maintaining reverence for God's holiness in the midst of ordinary life. Over time, this trained the imagination to see impurity as a normal part of embodied life that must be met with attentiveness, humility, and trust. It cultivated a consciousness shaped by rhythms of disruption and return, exclusion and reentry, loss and restoration, patterns that mirrored Israel's covenantal relationship with God.

Figure 10.5. *Sacrifice of Noah* after a woodcut by Bernard Salomon

Gift of J. Pierpont Morgan, 1917 / The MET

However, the system does not treat all impurity equally. The remedies for impurity are graded, and those gradations are themselves instructive. Some conditions require only the passage of time (e.g., Lev. 11:24–28); others require bathing or the washing of clothes (15:5–11); still others require sacrificial atonement (12:6–8; 14:1–32). In a few extreme cases, there is no remedy, and the offender is to be "cut off" from the people (e.g., 16:4; 17:10, 14). Such violations signal deliberate departure from God's holiness and order and invite expulsion or divine judgment.[27] In this way, the system teaches Israel to discern the gravity of actions and their symbolic implications.

The structure of ritual states trains Israel in covenantal consciousness; rituals are not a burdensome or arbitrary code. The categories of clean and unclean mark thresholds, those between ordinary and sacred, life and death, order and chaos. They cultivate ethical awareness: If holiness is about nearness to God, then purity becomes a metaphor for moral and spiritual readiness. The ritual world of Leviticus thus calls

THEOLOGICAL ISSUES

Not All Impurities Are Sinful, but All Sin Defiles

It's important to distinguish between ritual impurity and sin, even though the two sometimes overlap in Leviticus.

- Not all impurities are sinful. Many sources of impurity, such as childbirth (Lev. 12), menstruation (Lev. 15), skin disease (Lev. 13–14), or burial duties, are normal parts of embodied life. They require purification but carry no moral guilt.
- All sin, however, creates impurity. Sin doesn't just violate a command; it pollutes persons, spaces, and relationships, including the sanctuary itself (Lev. 16:16; 18:24–28). This pollution must be cleansed through sacrificial atonement.

This distinction allows Leviticus to uphold both the goodness of embodied life and the seriousness of sin's defiling power. In Israel's covenantal world, ritual impurity is expected and repairable, but unaddressed sin is corrosive to the life of the community and the presence of God.

RnDmS / Shutterstock

Figure 10.6. An ancient mikvah in Qumran used for ritual bathing

ETHICS

"Purity Culture" and the Bible's Purity System

In contemporary Christian usage, the word *purity* often evokes the so-called purity culture associated with late twentieth- and early twenty-first-century evangelical teaching on sexuality. This movement emphasized virginity until marriage, modest dress, and clear gender roles, often enforced through books, conferences, and symbolic tokens like purity rings. While it aimed to encourage holiness and got right that marriage is the right context for sex, it frequently reduced purity to sexual abstinence, elevated shame as a motivator, and disproportionately burdened females. Though perhaps well-intentioned, it frequently fostered shame and gender imbalance and has resulted in devastating and lasting harm in many Christian communities.

This is a far cry from the ritual purity system in the Pentateuch. In Leviticus, impurity is often natural, temporary, and symbolic. Activities like childbirth, menstruation, or burying the dead make one unclean, but they are part of normal human life. While Scripture can use the metaphor of purity to speak to moral issues, the purity system of the Torah was not primarily about moral worth but about maintaining covenant attentiveness in the presence of a holy God. Understanding this helps us read Leviticus more faithfully and more sensitively.

Israel to live in a state of constant formation through responsive, repeated reorientation to the God who dwells in their midst.

This symbolic system does not create a sacred-secular divide, as if only some aspects of life belong to God. Rather, like the design of sacred space and sacred time, it points toward the sanctification of all things. Israel is not a community with a holy core but is through and through a "holy nation" (Exod. 19:6), called to embody God's holiness in every aspect of life. The prophetic hope in Zechariah's vision is of a day when very ordinary household pots will be dedicated to holy service and when the "bells of the horses" will bear the inscription "Holy to the Lord" (Zech. 14:20–21), language once reserved only for the high priest's diadem (Exod. 28:36). In this vision, holiness permeates everything.

Sklar helpfully points out that reasons behind Israel's ritual states (impure, pure, holy) are not always made explicit, and yet their overall formative intent is clear.[28] He notes that these distinctions functioned as ongoing,

ETHICS

From Practice to Character

Rituals and habits connect closely to the ethical idea of virtues. A virtue is not just a rule you follow but a stable disposition: the capacity to desire what is good, to recognize what God requires in a given situation, and to act on it consistently. For example, a person with the virtue of justice knows what justice demands and also wants it and habitually pursues it in the complexities of daily life. Both Scripture and the Christian tradition recognize that we grow in virtue through practice, through repeated actions that train our desires. Rituals and habits, then, are schools of character. What we repeatedly do, as disciples, gradually shapes who we are.

embodied instruction and served at least three purposes. First, they were constantly reinforcing Israel's understanding of Yahweh's holiness—dwelling in a ritually holy sanctuary, served by ritually holy priests, and approached only through prescribed ritual purity. Second, they reminded Israel that they were to be a holy people, set apart to reflect God's distinctiveness in the world. Third, these laws served as physical reminders with moral implications: Like a wedding ring signifies marital fidelity, the ritual practices trained Israel to live in moral faithfulness to God. The result was that everyday activities like meals, bodily functions, and contact with life and death became occasions for covenantal mindfulness, anchoring moral identity in daily life.[29]

From Ritual to Reflection: The Enduring Instruction of Torah's Rituals

The ritual world of the Pentateuch is intricate, symbol-rich, and often foreign to modern readers. Yet when approached with attentiveness and care, these texts reveal a deeply coherent vision for life with God, one that integrates body and spirit, individual and community, time and space. Having explored how rituals form covenant identity through symbol, space, sequence, and status, we turn to the challenge and opportunity of reading these texts today. How can we honor their ancient context while discerning their enduring theological value? What might they reveal about God's heart, humanity's vocation, and the shape of worshipful life in our own time?

Reading ritual texts well today is to resist the assumption that ritual is dead religion and embrace the reality that God still shapes his people through embodied, repeated practices. Many Christians are hungry for depth but skeptical of structure, drawn to authenticity but wary of repetition. Yet the need for formative practice has never been more urgent. We are not just thinking beings but desiring beings, shaped by what we believe and by what we habitually do.[30]

In Leviticus, God scripts Israel's daily, weekly, and yearly rituals and holy habits as the backbone of a distinct identity. These rituals reveal a vision of life in which nothing is neutral, where food, time, space, and bodily rhythms all fall under the reign of God. Leviticus insists that worship is not confined to one day or one place. Every table, field, season, and interaction becomes an opportunity for faithfulness and formation. Leviticus gives Israel holy habits and covenantal rituals to form them for the sake of the nations. It integrates ethics and worship so thoroughly that the two are inseparable: "You shall be holy, for I the Lord your God am holy" (Lev. 19:2) is followed by instructions about how to treat the poor, the disabled, the laborer, the foreigner. Johnson says, "The sacrifices (grains, animals, oils) would only work as much as they had been ethically prepared in the common life of Israel. . . . The same sacrifice can be a pleasing aroma or a foul stench to God, depending on how the community has shepherded his instructions in their daily lives—farm to altar."[31] In Leviticus the ethical and the ritual, the social and the spiritual, the economic and the theological are all intertwined.[32] Worship that does not extend into everyday justice and holiness is rejected (see Isa. 1:11–17; Amos 5:21–24).

We are ritualized people, whether we recognize it or not. Even the most secular lives are filled with patterned behaviors that signal value and shape identity. A morning routine or a national holiday, a pregame chant, or a phone-checking tic—our habits reflect and reinforce what we value. The key question is, Who is scripting them? And how do they orient us to God, ourselves, our fellow humans, and our world? If we are not conscious of it, our culture will happily script our habits and rituals every day, forming us into consumers, competitors, and anxious individuals who often use and abuse our fellow creatures for our own projects, human and otherwise. The question is not whether we are being formed, but by what and for what. Our cultural liturgies shape our hearts, not by argument but on a prerational level.[33]

We are living through a crisis of attention and identity. Ours is an age of constant stimulation—images, glowing screens, sounds, interrupting notifications—an always-on culture that leaves us more distracted, more anxious, and more fragmented than ever. Mental health crises are surging. Our habits are being scripted often unconsciously by forces that neither know us nor love us. Into this noise, the Torah offers a different vision: a life patterned by rest, reverence, repetition, and holy

ETHICS

Michael's Daily Smartphone Ritual

The Torah's rituals might challenge us to explore and possibly reject the habits and rituals we often thoughtlessly embrace. I, Michael, for instance, struggle not to begin my day by checking my smartphone. My bleary eyes are lit up by the news, my work email, and a brief glance at whether anybody has validated my existence by liking my latest Substack post. This may seem like a freely chosen ritual, but this powerful supercomputer and the apps that exist on it have been provided to me by brilliant scientists and marketers whose job it is to keep me scrolling as long as possible. The algorithm on the social media app likewise is designed to captivate my attention, the workplace email means that work can haunt my thoughts outside the normal rhythms of work and rest, and the news I receive is channeled through algorithms designed to provide news that fits my worldview.

So, who are the authorities who offer me these habits? What are their goals and worldviews? What does my ritual shape me to see about the world? About myself? How does this ritual foster a certain kind of allegiance, and to what? How does it shape my orientation to time? And if the Torah were to shape my life more deeply, what kind of Torah-inspired habits and rituals might take this one's place?

attention. Long before psychologists urged mindfulness or wellness experts advocated for daily rhythms and digital detoxes, Leviticus called God's people to structure their time, train their bodies, and form their communities around presence and peace. We do not need to invent new solutions; we need to recover ancient wisdom. The Pentateuch's ritual texts invite the church today to wrestle with these issues and to ask with fresh urgency, What rituals and holy habits are capable of forming communities that can resist the liturgies of speed, anxiety, and consumption? Such communities might yet live as a countercultural people, deeply rooted in the love, justice, and holiness of God.

Figure 10.7. This contemporary visual meditation on attention, isolation, and technology was painted by Arnold Guerrero, an artist in Phoenix, Arizona. The image invites reflection on the practices that form modern life.

Leviticus 1–16

Sacrifice, Purity, and Drawing Near to God

Orientation

Approaching Yahweh

Exodus ends with a problem: God's glory has filled the tabernacle, but Moses, Israel's mediator, cannot enter (Exod. 40:34–38). If even Moses cannot enter the tent, how can this people so "prone to inadvertent error and deliberate sin" nevertheless "host the radical holiness of God"? After all, "holiness is, at its fullest intensity, almost too much for ordinary human beings to bear." On the other hand, "human sinfulness is, over time, almost too much for God to bear."[1]

Leviticus is the Torah's solution. The book addresses this holiness conundrum head-on, offering a way for Israel to draw near without being destroyed (cf. Lev. 10:1–3). Yet every approach, whether by offering, priestly service, or entry into the sanctuary, is carefully ordered and guarded. It requires not only atonement, purification, and proper approach but also a way of life and ethical action consistent with a community that bears Yahweh's name and harbors his presence in their camp. If Israel wants to host the Holy One, then they must *become* holy as *he* is holy (11:44).

High in the eastern Himalayas lies the small kingdom of Bhutan, home to one of the world's most beloved monarchs: King Jigme Khesar Namgyel Wangchuck. Known affectionately as the Dragon King, he is deeply respected by his people, not just for his position, but for his humility, wisdom, and care for the nation. He is known to walk among his subjects, visit remote villages, and engage directly with citizens. He is, in many ways, remarkably approachable. And yet, this accessibility does not eliminate the need for reverence. To formally approach the king, especially in

Figure 11.1. *The Visit of the Queen of Sheba to King Solomon* by Sir Edward John Poynter (1890)

a ceremonial or official context, one must follow clear protocols. Visitors are expected to arrive at the proper time and place, to dress appropriately, to carry themselves with respectful gestures, to speak with due respect, and in some cases, to bring a meaningful gift. One does not simply wander uninvited into the king's presence. Moreover, not just anyone is allowed an audience; those with criminal records or questionable conduct may not be granted access. The king's openness is matched by the need for honor, ethics, and following proper protocol when approaching him.[2]

This offers a helpful analogy for how the people of Israel are instructed to draw near to Yahweh in the book of Leviticus. The God who delivered Israel from Egypt invited them into covenant relationship and now graciously makes a way for his presence to dwell among them. But this divine accessibility does not mean casual familiarity. Instead, Leviticus outlines clear instructions—regarding sacrifice, purity, clothing, gestures, offerings, and conduct—so that the people may approach the Holy One rightly. God's presence is a gift, but it is also a danger if mishandled. Like approaching a revered king, drawing near to Yahweh requires preparation, reverence, integrity, and a life oriented toward holiness.

Both Ritual and Ethics: Reading the Whole of Leviticus

Leviticus may seem like a puzzling and foreign book (especially from a Western perspective), an unusual collection of ancient rituals and priestly rules. Yet, as we explored in the previous chapter, these texts form part of the Torah's formation strategy, its discipleship program.

The first half of Leviticus (chaps. 1–16), the focus of this chapter, concerns Israel's access to the divine presence through sacrificial worship, priestly mediation, and ritual purity. The first major section of Leviticus gives instructions for the five sacrifices (chaps. 1–7), consisting of instructions directed to the person bringing the offering (chaps. 1–5) and to the priest making the offering (chaps. 6–7). Leviticus 8–10 explores the institution of the priesthood and instructions for the priests. The rest of the first half of Leviticus pertains to and maps out Israel's purity system and how to deal with impurity (chaps. 11–16), including clean/unclean animals (chap. 11), cleansing after childbirth (chap. 12), skin diseases and household impurity and their remedies (chaps. 13–14), and bodily discharges and purification (chap. 15). These chapters build a system of divine approach that climaxes in the Day of Atonement (chap. 16), the high point of Israel's liturgical calendar and the reset button for the sanctuary and the people. Here, sacrifice, space, sequence, and status converge in a single ritual act of purification and atonement.

This section of Leviticus doesn't simply provide a window into ancient religious practices. It proclaims the weight of holiness, the need for mediation, the danger of presumption, and the grace of access. These themes prepare the way for Israel's covenant life, and they also shape Christian understandings of sin, sacrifice, priesthood, divine presence, and worship. Our task is to let Leviticus question our assumptions about what it means to live in the presence of God.

Leviticus is not only about rites, rituals, and sacrifices. The second half of the book focuses more on what we would call ethics than it does on ritual, although Leviticus itself sees these woven together into a seamless whole. The second half of this book continues to unpack Yahweh's command "Be holy as I [Yahweh] am holy" and is often referred to as the Holiness Code.[3] The two halves of Leviticus must not be regarded as separate or distinct from one another. The sacrificial and purity system in Leviticus 1–16 and the ethical mandates of chapters 17–27 are strands of a single covenantal tapestry.

LITERARY NOTES

Outline of Leviticus

- Regulations concerning sacrifices (chaps. 1–7)
- Ordination of the priesthood (chaps. 8–10)
- Symbolic world of purity: clean and unclean / pure and impure (chaps. 11–16)
- The Holiness Code (chaps. 17–27)

LITERARY NOTES

Leviticus as the Center of the Pentateuch

Leviticus holds a strategic place within the Pentateuch. Structurally, it is the center of the five-book Pentateuch. Theologically, it provides the most concentrated instruction for how God's people should live all of life as worship to Yahweh. Narratively, it falls at the very heart of Israel's one-year encampment at Sinai (they arrive at Sinai in Exod. 19 and do not depart until Num. 10). Thus, Leviticus is framed by covenant reception, tabernacle construction, and the eventual journey toward the promised land.

CANONICAL CONNECTIONS

Leviticus Looks Ahead

Leviticus anticipates Israel's departure from Sinai (as narrated in Numbers), life in the land (as envisioned in Deuteronomy), and a calling to be a priestly people for the sake of the world. Its vision is not confined to tents and altars but reaches toward neighborhoods, fields, relationships, and economic practices. In this way, Leviticus trains Israel—and us—to live holy lives in ordinary time.

Ritual purity (being clean, offering right sacrifice, observing sacred time) trains Israel to discern and respond rightly to the holiness of God, but this ritual attentiveness is never meant to eclipse or be separate from ethical responsibility. The second half of the book grounds Israel's ritual formation in everyday life, showing that holiness must extend from the tabernacle to the fields, homes, courts, and marketplaces, where justice, compassion, and reverence for God are to shape every relationship and decision.

Exploration

Sacrifice and the Shape of Holy Access (Lev. 1–7)

READ LEVITICUS 1–7

Read these chapters slowly, and don't skip details. When you read the rituals, resist the impulse to ask first, What does this ritual mean? Instead ask, What would this ritual do to a community that practiced it? What patterns of seeing, feeling, and living would it cultivate?

Before God can dwell with Israel, something must be done about the separation between God and humans. In the very first verses of Leviticus, Yahweh speaks to Moses from inside the tent that Moses is currently prevented from entering, and he tells Moses how God's people should bring their offering. Offerings, including sacrificial offerings that involve blood, fire, and smoke in sacred space, are part of the way the Holy One will dwell in the midst of this often-unholy people. These early chapters instruct both worshipers and priests on how to offer sacrifices properly, but they also begin to shape the moral and spiritual imagination of the covenant people.

Many assume that biblical sacrifices are bloody transactions meant to appease God's wrath, with the animal dying in the worshiper's place. Leviticus presents a different picture. Some sacrifices involve no blood at all, and even those that do are not primarily about punishment but purification and communion. As Mark Scarlata notes, the goal of atonement is to cleanse God's people and sanctuary so that relationship may continue.[4] Leviticus explains that blood atones because "the life of the creature is in the blood" (17:11 NIV). What is offered is not death but life itself. Human sin introduces death and decay into God's good creation, polluting his dwelling. The lifeblood of the sacrifice, given by divine grace, carries cleansing power: life from outside that purges death's corruption and renews holy fellowship with the living God.

The offerings described in Leviticus 1–7 are not all the same. Some are voluntary expressions of devotion or gratitude; others are mandatory acts

Wikimedia Commons / public domain

Figure 11.2. *The Sacrifice of the Old Covenant* by Peter Paul Rubens (1640)

of cleansing, reconciliation, or restitution. Some involve whole animals, some just parts, and others grain or flour. Taken together, they form a sacrificial "system" or "grammar," a pattern of making sense of the world, of drawing near, acknowledging sin, offering tribute, making peace, and seeking cleansing.[5] This is worship that engages the senses and costs the offerer something.

Unlike the sacrificial practices of the surrounding nations, the point of the sacrifices in Leviticus is not mere placation or appeasement. God is not hungry for blood or manipulated by smoke. These offerings provide a way for sinful people to enter sacred space without presumption. What may be God's demand is also his gift.

What follows is a walk through the five major types of offerings: ascension (i.e., burnt), grain, peace (or fellowship), purification, and reparation. Each plays a distinct role in Israel's liturgical life and moral formation. And each, though rooted in an ancient system, displays the same holy logic that undergirds the gospel: Access to God requires mediation, cleansing, and the surrender of self.

ASCENSION OFFERING

The burnt or "ascent" offering opens the sacrificial system with a gesture of complete devotion. Its Hebrew name means "that which goes up," a reference to the smoke rising as the entire animal is consumed on the altar. Unlike other offerings, no portion is eaten. Nothing is held back.[6] The whole creature is divided and offered to God. This act of total surrender sets the tone for everything that follows.

The worshiper brings the offering to the entrance of the tent of meeting and lays a hand on the animal's head, symbolically identifying with it, "so that it may be accepted for him to make atonement on his behalf" (Lev. 1:4 NASB). The priest then slaughters the animal and prepares it for the altar, where "he shall offer all of it up in smoke on the altar as a burnt offering, an offering by fire as a soothing aroma to the LORD" (1:9 NASB). These phrases indicate divine grace. The offering is accepted because God has provided a way for the worshiper to draw near.

Theologically, the ascension offering represents consecration. Not tied to a particular sin or impurity, it expresses a desire to live rightly before God. Worshipers come voluntarily, offering something of real value. In so doing, they acknowledge that their life belongs wholly to the Lord, who receives the offering as a "pleasing aroma." This act of worship forms a people who understand that access to God is a gift and a call. To place something on the altar, especially a costly animal raised and cared for, is to place oneself there symbolically. It's a bodily declaration of surrender, a ritual rehearsal of wholehearted devotion. Paul later echoes this posture when he writes, "Present your bodies as a living sacrifice, holy and acceptable to God, which is your spiritual worship" (Rom. 12:1).

THEOLOGICAL ISSUES

One Hand or Two?

Many readers assume that the worshiper's act of putting a hand on the animal symbolizes the transfer of sin onto it. But Leviticus describes the worshiper laying a single hand on sacrificial offerings that have nothing to do with sin. More importantly, sacrificial offerings are an offering to God, and it makes no sense to offer God a sin-laden gift.

Instead, the laying on of a single hand suggests the worshiper's identification with the offering. That identification works differently for different sacrifices. If it's a sin offering, then the worshiper is saying something like "This animal's blood brings life to purge the death that I brought into God's space through my sin." If it's an offering of thanksgiving, then the identification communicates something like "I want to give a gift and so have brought one of my flock to offer the divine king."

On the Day of Atonement, however, the priest lays two hands on the scapegoat and confesses the people's sins over it. This ritual gesture does seem to place the sins on the animal; it is telling then that what this goat does is take those sins away from God's house and God's people.

GRAIN OFFERING

The grain offering is the only sacrifice in Leviticus 1–7 that involves no blood (apart from the allowance for a nonbloody purification sacrifice for the poor in 5:11). It consists of finely ground flour, sometimes raw, sometimes baked or cooked, mixed with oil and frankincense. A portion is burned on the altar as "a food offering, an aroma pleasing to the LORD" (2:2 NIV), while the rest is eaten by the priests. It is a gift of daily substance, offered in recognition that everything—food, harvest, life itself—comes from God.

Unlike the ascension offering, the grain offering is not about atonement or cleansing. It is an act of tribute and thanksgiving, often accompanying other sacrifices or presented in fulfillment of a vow. Through it, offerers dedicate their life and work to God.[7] It may be less dramatic than offerings involving animals, but it is no less meaningful. In offering bread, the worshiper brings the fruit of labor and the basic stuff of survival. The grain offering reminds Israel that holiness is not only about dramatic acts of atonement but also found in ordinary, faithful gratitude. Worship includes not just the surrender of life but the offering of sustenance, the quiet acknowledgment that God is Lord of the field, the oven, and the table.

PEACE/FELLOWSHIP OFFERING

Like the previous two sacrifices, the peace offering is voluntary. Only part of the animal is burned on the altar; the rest is eaten, some by the priests, but most by the worshiper and their family. It is a communal meal in God's presence, a sacred barbecue that celebrates reconciliation, thanksgiving, or the fulfillment of a vow (Lev. 3; 7:11–21).

This offering expresses shalom, peace as the absence of conflict as well as fullness of life, restored relationship, and joy before God. The fat portions, considered the richest part, are burned as "a special gift of food, a pleasing aroma to the Lord" (Lev. 3:16 NLT), while the rest becomes a sacred feast. In this sacrifice, the worshiper eats part of what they've brought. The fellowship offering disciples Israel to celebrate with God in communion. Worship is joyful, embodied, and relational. In a culture where meals signify belonging, the peace offering teaches Israel that life with God includes shared celebration as well as sacrifice.

PURIFICATION OFFERING

The purification offering is often called the sin offering, but its purpose goes beyond removing guilt to include cleansing sacred space and restoring access to God. This offering is required (not voluntary like the previous sacrifices) when someone sins unintentionally or becomes ritually impure, especially when such impurity threatens the sanctuary itself. The focus is not so much on the worshiper's conscience as it is on the holy environment God shares with his people.

The ritual centers on the application of blood sprinkled on the entrance to the sanctuary, on the altar of burnt offering outside the tent, and on the altar of fragrant incense inside the tent (Lev. 4:6–7, 17–18). This blood doesn't symbolize death so much as life offered to make space for life. As Leviticus later states, "The life of the flesh is in the blood; . . . it is the blood

THEOLOGICAL ISSUES

Sharing Meals with God

The peace offering most clearly depicts a worshiper eating part of what has been offered with God. Yet in Israel's worship, meals were not confined to this one sacrifice. During festivals and corporate offerings (cf. Lev. 9:2; 23:19), burnt, purification, and peace sacrifices were often offered together, and the food consumed in God's presence became an act of shared rejoicing. The altar itself is elsewhere called God's "table" (Ezek. 41:22; Mal. 1:7, 12), underscoring that sacrifice expresses restored fellowship, a holy meal between God and his people.

that makes atonement" (17:11). In a strange and sacred paradox, shed blood becomes the very means by which death is held at bay. This offering teaches Israel that sin and impurity have consequences beyond the individual; they touch the community and even the space where God dwells. It also trains them to trust in God's provision: that life, when given sacrificially, has power to cleanse, restore, and renew covenant relationship.

REPARATION OFFERING

The reparation offering, sometimes called the guilt offering, addresses situations where wrongdoing has caused loss or damage, especially in relation to sacred things or other people. It is concerned about making things right. This offering is required, not voluntary, and involves both sacrifice and restitution. The worshiper brings a ram without blemish and, where applicable, must repay what was taken or damaged, plus 20 percent. If someone has misused something sacred, deceived a neighbor, or failed in a legal trust, they cannot simply offer a sacrifice and move on. The offense must be acknowledged, the harm repaired, and the cost borne, a concrete act that mends what was broken and signals a renewed path of trust.

This offering underscores a key truth of covenant life: Repentance includes responsibility. Ritual alone is not enough—true reconciliation requires action. The reparation offering forms a people who understand that sin is not just impurity to be cleansed but harm to be repaired, and that integrity, honesty, and restoration are holy work. At the same time, reparation requires repairing the harm done to

THEOLOGICAL ISSUES

Toxic Sin

As strange as it may seem to us, for Leviticus, one of the primary problems with sin is that it pollutes God's house. Jacob Milgrom argues that the more severe the sin, the further into God's house the deathly pollution goes. This explains why the blood from the purification offerings is placed on different parts of the sanctuary depending on the sin or impurity it is addressing; the "life" brought by the animal's blood must purge whichever part of God's house has been infected by the deathly toxicity of human sin.[a]

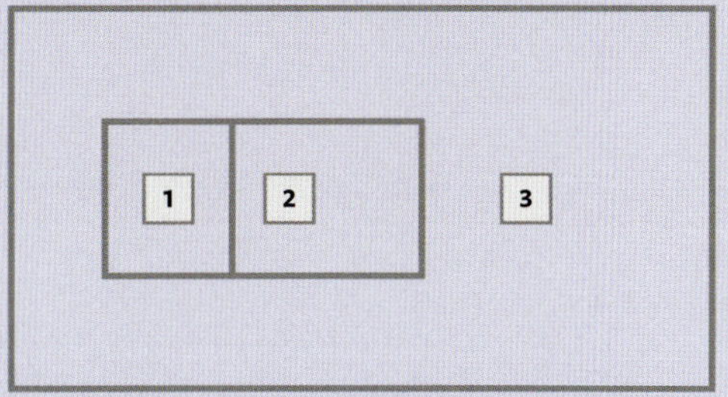

1. The Ark
Involuntary, communal violation (Lev. 4:13–21)

2. Incense Altar
Involuntary, individual violation (Lev. 4:27–35)

3. Sacrificial Altar
Brazen and unrepented violation (Lev. 16:11–19)

Figure 11.3. The toxicity of sin and its impact on the tabernacle

Based on Jacob Milgrom, *Leviticus: A Book of Ritual and Ethics*, Continental Commentaries (Fortress, 2004), 31.

Figure 11.4. A relief depicting the sacrifice of a ram (Larymna, 5th cent. BC; Archaeological Museum of Chalkis)

the neighbor and making a sacrifice to Yahweh. This makes clear that sins against one's neighbor are also sins against God. Through this final offering, then, Leviticus affirms that a person's relationship with God is bound up in reciprocal relationships with neighbors (and creation). The holiness of the sanctuary and the health of the community are bound together, and both must be tended for worship to be whole.

INSTRUCTIONS FOR PRIESTS FOR THE FIVE SACRIFICES

Leviticus 6:8–7:38 revisits the five major sacrifices, but now from the perspective of the priests, not the worshipers. While Leviticus 1:1–6:7 outlines what the offerer must do to draw near, this section details how the priests are to handle the offerings on behalf of the people: what to burn, what to eat, where to eat it, and how to treat what is holy. Portions of some offerings belong to the priests, but only under strict conditions. These instructions underscore that receiving what is offered to God is not a right but a sacred responsibility. The priests have the special role of protecting the boundary between holy and common, clean and unclean. Their careful handling ensures that God's presence can remain in the midst of the camp.

SACRIFICE AS THE LITURGICAL GRAMMAR OF COVENANT LIFE

The five sacrifices described in these first chapters of Leviticus provide the basic grammar of Israel's worship, supplying the elements that can be combined and recombined across contexts: daily offerings, festival celebrations, purification rites, the fulfillment of vows, and acts of thanksgiving or reconciliation. Just as grammar enables countless sentences to be formed from a limited set of words, these sacrifices give structure and flexibility to the liturgical life of the covenant community.

We should resist the temptation to flatten the sacrificial system into a single atonement metaphor.[8] These offerings serve multiple purposes, including consecration, thanksgiving, purification, fellowship, atonement, and restitution. They invite worshipers to be formed into a people who take holiness seriously, who rejoice in God's provision, who restore what is broken, and who trust that God has generously provided a way for sinful, frail humans to dwell with him. In this sense, Leviticus permits access to God while also training Israel to live as those who have received it.

Even today, as Christians no longer offer animal sacrifices, this "grammar of worship" can continue to shape our liturgical imagination. The surrender embodied in the ascension offering, the gratitude of the grain offering, the joy of the fellowship meal, the cleansing of the purification rite, and the justice of the reparation offering all find echoes in Christian worship and ethics. At the heart of them all is the same gracious truth: God has made a way.

One final clarification is crucial. These sacrificial offerings in Leviticus are not a blanket solution for all sin. Of the five sacrifices, only two (purification and reparation) deal with sin at all. They are designed for unintentional sins, ritual impurities, and breaches of covenant that can be acknowledged and repaired (cf. Lev. 4:2; 5:15; Num. 15:22–29). They do not cover what Numbers calls "high-handed" sins: deliberate, defiant acts of covenant rebellion (15:30–31). For such sins, there is no sacrifice. Unless God graciously and unexpectedly intervenes, the consequence is being "cut off" from the people. Not merely a legal technicality, this distinction reveals that atonement is part of a relational and moral framework. God makes a way for restoration but not for manipulation.

THEOLOGICAL ISSUES

Converting Sin Through Confession

While the sacrifices of Leviticus 1–6 are for unintentional sins, Leviticus 6 apparently (and bizarrely) includes some acts of theft and other property crimes as "unintentional." Milgrom argues that in this reparation offering "repentance converts an intentional sin into an unintentional one, thereby making it eligible for sacrificial expiation." Indeed, he suggests this ritual "bends" the "sacrificial rules in order to foster the growth of the individual conscience."[b]

Ordination and the Danger of Holiness (Lev. 8–10)

READ LEVITICUS 8–10

These chapters contain one of the few narratives in Leviticus. Read them as a single story of the ordination of the priests and the sudden crisis that follows. As you read, ask, What does this reveal about God's holiness? What does it mean to draw near rightly? How does this story shape Israel's understanding of worship and leadership?

Before the priests can serve, they must be consecrated. Leviticus 8 narrates the ordination of Aaron and his sons, following detailed commands from Exodus 29. Moses leads the ritual: The priests are washed with water, clothed in sacred garments, and anointed with oil. Sacrifices are made (a sin offering, an ascension offering, and an ordination offering), and blood is applied to each priest's right ear, thumb, and big toe, symbolizing consecration from head to toe. For seven days they remain at the entrance of the tent, fulfilling their ordination through patient obedience. The point is unmistakable: The priests themselves must be made holy before they can mediate holiness for the people.

Leviticus 9 records the priest's first official act of service. Aaron steps forward, offering the appointed sacrifices on behalf of the people. He performs everything as instructed: sin offering, ascension offering, grain offering, and fellowship offering. At the climax of the ritual, Aaron blesses the people, and fire comes out from the presence of Yahweh to consume the offering on the altar (9:24). The people fall on their faces in awe. This is the

Figure 11.5. *Nadab and Abihu*, after Hans Holbein's Bible illustrations for the *Biblia Utriusque Testamenti*

liturgical high point of Leviticus so far. The system works, God's presence is manifest, and access has been generously granted. The way to dwell with a holy God has been opened.

The next scene shatters the moment. Leviticus 10 tells the story of Aaron's sons Nadab and Abihu, who offer "unauthorized fire" before Yahweh, contrary to his command (10:1). Fire comes out again from Yahweh, but this time to consume them. The exact nature of their offense is unclear, but the result is not: Presumption in the presence of God is deadly. Holiness is not a human playground. The God who draws near is not to be approached on our own terms. "Among those who are near me I will be sanctified, and before all the people I will be glorified," God declares (10:3 ESV). The fire of Leviticus is both gift and danger.

In the aftermath, Moses instructs Aaron and his remaining sons not to mourn publicly. The priesthood continues despite the rupture, but it must do so in reverent fear. Aaron remains silent—a grief-stricken father, a consecrated servant. The episode sobers the community, signaling that holiness in the presence of God is real, weighty, and not to be manipulated.

The rest of Leviticus 10 reinforces this warning. God speaks directly to Aaron, prohibiting the use of strong drink when entering the tent of meeting. The priests must remain clearheaded and attentive to the demands of their service. Their charge is to offer sacrifices and to teach Israel to distinguish between the holy and the common, the clean and the unclean (10:10). How will they know that? The next major section in Leviticus will fill out the details of the purity system.

Together, these chapters show that priestly service is a serious call, not to be taken lightly. The priests stand in the charged space between God and the people, something like workers in a nuclear reactor, where immense energy must be handled with

ETHICS

Sacrifice, Slaughter, and the Contemporary Imagination

Readers today often recoil from the sacrificial system in Leviticus. Killing animals in this way feels strange, messy, even barbaric. That discomfort may say more about us than about the text. Peter Bray, a butcher by trade, offers an earthy, unexpected defense of Leviticus in his book *Leviticus on the Butcher's Block*. He reminds us that while biblical sacrifice involves blood, it also involves reverence and restraint. From his perspective, Leviticus teaches that animals should be killed with care, their lives honored, their bodies shared in sacred meals. Worshipers faced the cost of life head-on.

By contrast, industrial meat systems today often obscure death, desensitize consumers, and treat animals (often poorly) as mere products. Bray gently suggests that Leviticus may actually call us to a more ethical and honest engagement with the realities of animal slaughter and meat eating. Far from glorifying violence, the sacrificial system dignifies the creature, the act, and the God who gives life.[c]

precision and respect. They must be consecrated, careful, sober, and discerning.

Leviticus's Ritual World of Cleanness and Uncleanness (Lev. 11–16)

READ LEVITICUS 11–16

> As you read, notice the rhythms of clean and unclean, exclusion and restoration. Ask, What vision of holiness shapes these distinctions? How do these laws train Israel to live attentively before a holy God?

With the sacrificial system established and the priesthood consecrated, Leviticus turns to a key dimension of Israel's holiness: ritual purity. While sacrifices and priests provide a way to draw near to God, the purity system helps define who may draw near and when. Leviticus 11–15 outlines what it means to be clean or unclean, mapping how ordinary experiences like eating, childbirth, skin conditions, and bodily discharges can render a person temporarily unfit for sacred space. The priests and sacrifices introduced in earlier chapters now play a role in the diagnosis and remedy of impurity. Israel is called to live in a state of readiness to approach the Holy One and to be attentive to how that approach can be complicated and dangerous, and that means learning to navigate the rhythms of cleanness and uncleanness, as well as the remedies for uncleanness.

THE LOGIC OF THE PURITY SYSTEM

Leviticus 11–15 lays out Israel's most comprehensive instructions on ritual purity. These chapters spell out what circumstances could move someone or something from a state of cleanness into uncleanness and what purification rites were required to restore them. They do not focus on holiness or consecration (that comes later in the book, especially in chaps. 17–26). Instead, their focus is on the everyday rhythms of life in which ordinary people regularly passed in and out of uncleanness. It is crucial to remember that uncleanness is not the same as sin. Becoming unclean was part of ordinary life in ancient Israel. A woman giving birth, a man having a nocturnal emission, or a farmer handling a dead work animal was not guilty of wrongdoing. Indeed, some activities that create ritual impurity are obligatory; an Israelite whose parent has died *should* participate in the burial, and a married person *should* have sex with their spouse, even though doing so will render them unclean. Yet uncleanness matters because it disrupts access to holy space (i.e., the tabernacle). A person in a state of uncleanness cannot approach the sanctuary or participate fully in worship until they are cleansed. In this way, purity laws constantly trained Israel to recognize that

CANONICAL CONNECTIONS

Jesus and the Forces of Death

The three major sources of ritual impurity in the Torah are genital discharges, skin disease, and contact with a corpse. In each case, when a pure person encounters these, they become impure; impurity is easy to pass on.

Sibeaster / Wikimedia Commons / public domain

Figure 11.6. Mosaic of Christ and a leper

Matthew Thiessen points out that the Gospel writers systematically depict Jesus coming into contact with these powerful sources of impurity. In Mark, for instance, Jesus encounters a person with "leprosy" (1:40–45), a woman with genital discharge (5:25–34), and the corpse of a young girl (5:35–43). Contrary to all Torah-shaped expectations, however, contact with these people does not make Jesus unclean. Instead, "in each case, the ritually impure person leaves Jesus's presence purified of the source of his or her impurity." What the Gospel writers show is "that Jesus, being the holy one of God, is so powerful a force of holiness that even the three strongest sources of impurity . . . cannot withstand him. Neither can the demonic forces of impurity that run rampant on earth." This helps us to see that the Gospel writers agreed with Leviticus and the rest of the Torah that ritual purity mattered. However, they also believed that "God had introduced something *new* into the world to deal with the sources of these impurities: Jesus. By inserting a new, mobile, and powerfully contagious force of holiness into the world in the person of Jesus, Israel's God has signaled the very coming of the kingdom—a kingdom of holiness and life that through the mission of Jesus overwhelms the forces and sources of impurity and death, be they [spiritual], ritual, or moral."[d]

what happens outside the sanctuary is preparation for and impacts life in God's presence.

Why these particular sources of uncleanness? Here we need to be cautious. Some have sought a single explanation, but no theory accounts for everything. Others see the system as arbitrary and yielding no explanation at all. Both extremes miss the point. As Dru Johnson observes, "Maybe we don't need to understand how rituals work *on* us in order for them to work *in* us."[9] The system does not yield a neat rationale, but certain patterns do stand out.

One key theme is life and death.[10] God is the God of life, so anything associated with death or the loss or diminishment of life renders a person unclean. Touching the carcass of an animal, losing blood or sexual fluids, or developing a skin condition that resembles decay all symbolize death's intrusion into life. Such signifiers of death cannot stand unmediated in the presence of the God who is Life.

Another theme is boundaries and categories. Genesis 1 presents a world ordered into distinct realms (land, sea, sky), each with its fitting creatures. Mary Douglas says, "Holiness requires that individuals shall conform to the class to which they belong. And holiness requires that different classes of things shall not be confused."[11] Leviticus 11 declares clean only those animals that clearly fit their category and their realm. Animals that blur categories are unclean.

A third theme is wholeness and integrity. Animals offered in sacrifice must be without blemish and must display the full set of characteristics that mark their kind. In the same way, skin diseases, mold, or mildew signal a breach in wholeness. They represent disorder or corruption within what ought to be sound and whole.

Cloven Hooves and Cud-Chewing

In Leviticus 11:3–8, land animals considered clean for food must both chew the cud (regurgitate and rechew partially digested food) and have a cloven hoof (a hard hoof split into two distinct toes; see fig. 11.7). This distinction reflected observable traits in everyday herding life rather than modern zoological categories. Later chapters in Leviticus clarify that not all clean animals were suitable for sacrifice; only certain herd and flock animals could be offered on the altar.

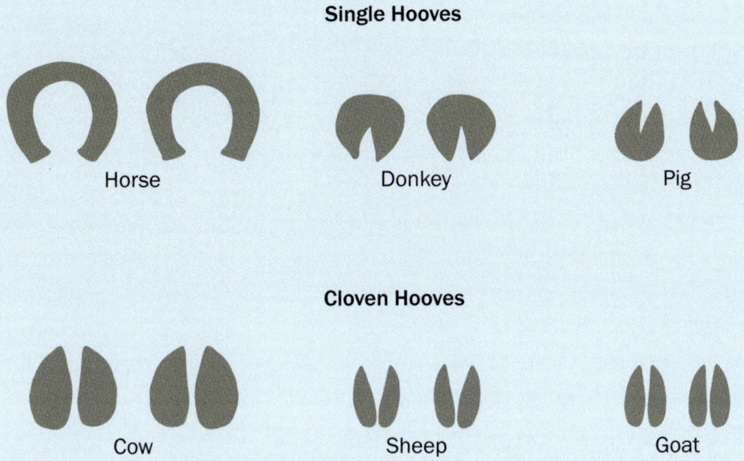

Figure 11.7. Comparison of cloven hooves and single hooves

Together, these patterns suggest that the purity system dramatizes Israel's covenantal worldview. Life is a gift to be guarded, boundaries are divinely set and not to be blurred or crossed, and wholeness reflects the perfection and integrity of God himself. Even if Israel did not always know why a given condition was unclean, the laws of purification trained them to recognize that entry into God's presence requires preparation and cleansing, even in the ordinary rhythms of life. Practicing the purity laws would help every Israelite remember the need to live a life fully oriented toward God in every area of life, even the most seemingly mundane.

CLEAN AND UNCLEAN ANIMALS

Leviticus 11 begins the purity laws with distinctions between clean and unclean animals. Like Genesis 1, the chapter organizes creatures into the realms of land, water, and sky, with a special subcategory for "swarming creatures." Within each realm, certain animals are designated clean and therefore suitable for Israel to eat, while others are unclean.

For land animals, two traits must go together: chewing the cud and having a split hoof. Cattle, sheep, and goats are clean, while camels and donkeys (chew cud but no split hoof) and pigs (split hoof but don't chew cud) are not. Water creatures must have both fins and scales (so catfish, eels, and shellfish are excluded). The unclean birds are mostly predators and scavengers but also bats (flying but not feathered) and birds like ostriches (feathered but not flying). The pattern is clear: Creatures that fit their creational kind are clean; those that blur boundaries or feed on death are not.

Contact with unclean animals does not defile unless the animal is dead. Touching or carrying a carcass, whether of an unclean creature or a clean one that died naturally, makes a person impure until evening and may require the washing of clothes. Even objects or food contaminated by such contact can become unclean, showing how death's defilement spreads through ordinary life.

Leviticus 11, then, introduces the system of purity with a survey of Israel's food and contact laws. The underlying concern is not nutrition or hygiene but Israel's participation in the symbolic order of creation. Animals that fit their category, that do not blur boundaries or bear associations with death, are acceptable. Others are not, and contact with their carcasses must be addressed through purification. In this way, daily choices about food discipled Israel to live within God's ordered creation, while even ordinary encounters with death in the barnyard or marketplace trained them to recognize that death brings uncleanness and must be set right before the God of life.

PURIFICATION AFTER CHILDBIRTH

Leviticus 12 addresses the impurity associated with childbirth. After bearing a son, a woman is unclean for seven days, followed by thirty-three days of purification. After bearing a daughter, the time periods are doubled. At the conclusion, the mother brings an ascension offering and a purification offering to the sanctuary, after which the priest declares her clean (12:6–8).

At first it may seem counterintuitive that bringing life into the world would create uncleanness. But in the world of Leviticus, the blood loss and liminality of childbirth bring mother and child close to death. As with skin disease or bodily discharge, the flow of blood signals life slipping away. The required purification rites restore the mother to wholeness and reintegrate her into the community's worship. In this way, the ritual after childbirth reminded Israel of the precariousness of life and that even life's most joyful moments take place within the shadow of death, depending on God for restoration. By marking the flow of blood

THEOLOGICAL ISSUES

Twice the Time, Not Half the Worth

The double length of time after the birth of a daughter may at first glance seem sexist, but that is anything but certain. Several explanations are possible that have nothing to do with female inferiority. Some suggest it reflects the special place of the mother-daughter bond, with extra postpartum protection for both; others point to the connection between female infants and the cycle of fertility and blood.[e] In any case, the text is not about guilt or value but about sanctifying the ordinary cycles of life and fertility within God's holy order.[f]

and the recovery of the body, the law formed Israel to see fertility as a gift sustained by God's presence and to return thanks through purification.[12]

SURFACE AFFLICTIONS ON PEOPLE, GARMENTS, AND HOUSES

Leviticus 13–14 turns from food and childbirth to the regulations for surface afflictions. The Hebrew term for these afflictions is often translated "leprosy," but it is much broader than what we know today as Hansen's disease.[13] In these chapters, the term refers to a wide range of visible surface afflictions, whether on human skin, fabrics, leather, or even the walls of houses. The concern is not medical diagnosis as such but ritual

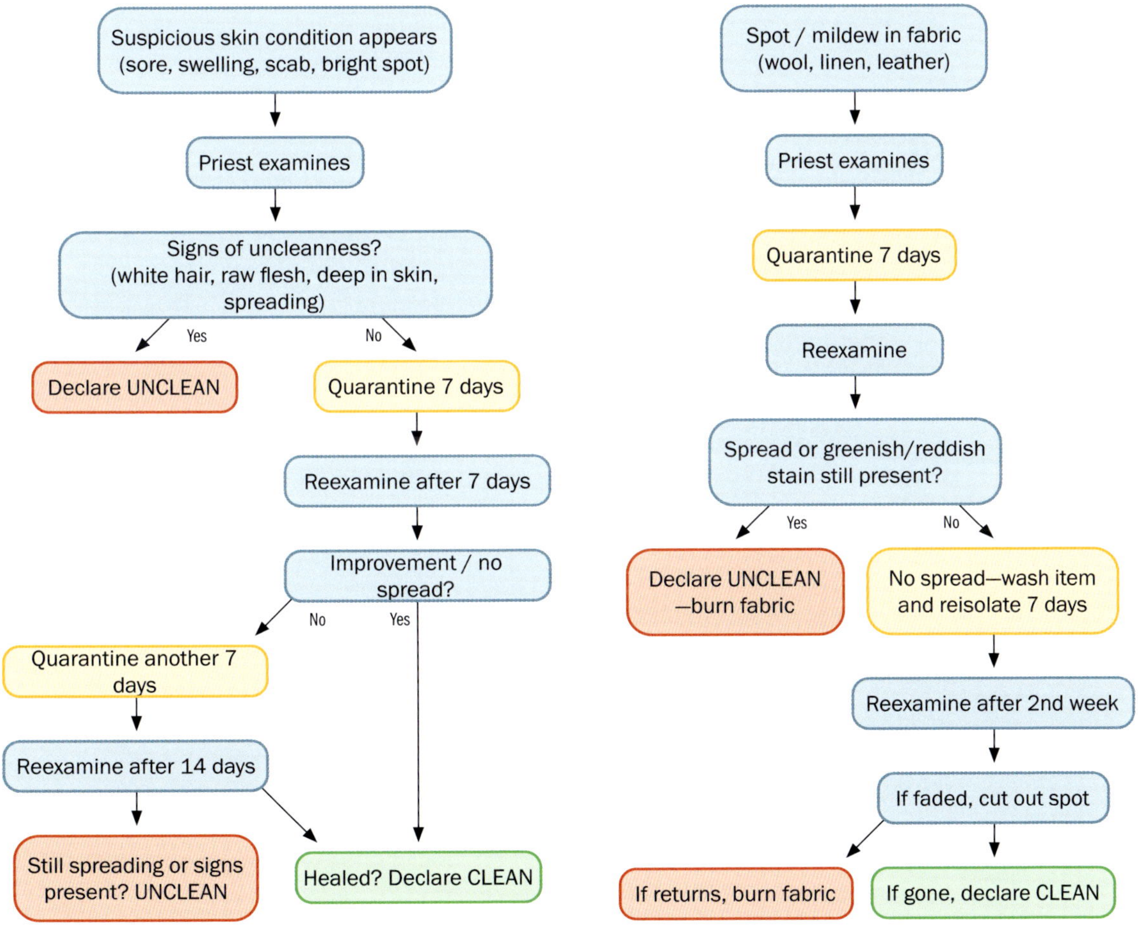

Figure 11.8. How to deal with unclean "surface afflictions" (skin diseases and fabric corruptions)

discernment: whether a visible condition signals disorder that makes someone or something unfit for contact with a holy God and his holy place.

For people, the priest functions as a dermatologist, a health examiner and diagnostician. Visible signs like swelling, scabs, white patches, raw flesh, or hair turned white trigger priestly inspection. Sometimes the result is immediate exclusion; other times the priest orders a seven-day quarantine to see if the condition spreads. A second inspection may confirm uncleanness or restore cleanness. The same pattern applies to garments and houses. A spot in fabric or leather may be washed and reexamined; if it spreads, the whole item must be burned. Priests also function as expert house inspectors; a discolored patch on a wall may lead to the removal of stones, or in persistent cases, complete demolition.

When a person with a skin condition is declared unclean, they live outside the camp, wearing torn clothes and calling out "Unclean!" to warn others (Lev. 13:45–46; this was reserved for serious, persistent cases). This exclusion dramatizes the way disorder and decay threaten the integrity of the community and the holiness of God's dwelling. If healing occurs, chapter 14 provides a path back through purification rituals.

In Leviticus's symbolic world, surface conditions represent a breach in wholeness and integrity. Skin, fabric, or stone that shows spreading decay resembles the corruption of death. The diagnosis and purification rites are about maintaining the community's integrity before God and enacting a drama of exclusion and restoration. In this way, the laws of surface conditions discipled Israel to see that disorder and decay (i.e., signs of death) have no place in God's dwelling, apparently because it is dangerous to bring the frailty of death into close proximity with the God who *is* Life. These same laws also hold out the hope of cleansing and reintegration when wholeness is restored.

BODILY DISCHARGES

Leviticus 15 addresses topics not commonly appropriate for dinner-table conversation, including various genital discharges in both men and women, some abnormal and some normal. Each of these conditions makes the individual ritually unclean for a time, and the uncleanness can be transmitted to people and objects they touch. The cleansing requirements indicate the depth of the uncleanness. An emission of semen or sexual intercourse requires bathing (and laundering, where stated) and being unclean until evening. Menstruation renders the woman unclean for seven days; anyone who touches her or what she lies/sits on must wash and is unclean until evening. Abnormal or persistent discharges (male or female) require, once the flow ceases, a seven-day waiting period, laundering and bathing, and on the eighth day bringing two birds for purification before the priest. Normal menstruation does not require a sacrifice.

At first glance, this seems to tie sexuality and reproduction, both good gifts from God, too closely to uncleanness. However, Leviticus is not associating these realities with sin or moral failure. Rather, in the symbolic system of the Torah, the loss of potential life (through semen not resulting in conception, or the shedding of menstrual blood) brings a person into contact with the shadow of death. Just as with skin disease or contact with carcasses, what is connected to death cannot simply be carried into the presence of God, who is life.

Leviticus 15:31 makes the purpose clear: "Thus you shall keep the people of Israel separate from their uncleanness, so that they do not die in their uncleanness by defiling my tabernacle that is in their midst." Everyday realities of sexuality and fertility taught Israel that God's presence is holy, that human life is fragile, and that cleansing is necessary to dwell near him. The rituals of bathing, waiting, and, when required, sacrifice would have continually discipled Israel to entrust their most intimate and ordinary bodily experiences to God, the giver and sustainer of life.

THEOLOGICAL ISSUES

What Leviticus Does Not Call Unclean

When we think today about bodily discharges that might make someone "unclean," our instincts run toward what feels most obviously polluting: human waste products like urine or excrement or even vomit. Yet Leviticus never treats these as sources of ritual impurity. Human waste is regulated only once elsewhere in the Torah and in a strictly practical way: Deuteronomy 23:12–14 commands Israel to bury excrement outside the camp, for reasons of sanitation and reverence for God's presence, not ritual purity.

These omissions are revealing. The bodily discharges that do concern Leviticus are tied not to hygiene but to the loss of potential life: semen that does not result in conception, or menstrual and pathological flows of blood. This suggests that the system of cleanness and uncleanness is not based on what seems "gross" or dirty to us, but on a deeper symbolic logic. Impurity in Leviticus consistently circles around the shadow of death and the fragility of life, reminding Israel that God must make a way for frail humans to draw near his lifegiving presence.

SUMMARY

Leviticus 11–15 presents Israel with a comprehensive program of ritual purity that involves food, birth, health, and sexuality—the ordinary rhythms of life. Each regulation underscores that uncleanness is not itself sin, but it is incompatible with approaching the God who dwelled in Israel's midst. The cleansing requirements vary in intensity, ranging from simple bathing and waiting until evening to extended quarantines and sacrificial rites, but the message is consistent: Life with God requires constant attentiveness to holiness. By weaving reminders of God's presence into eating, family life, and even bodily vulnerabilities, the teaching of Leviticus 11–15 discipled Israel to see that every dimension of existence is lived before the face of God. This steady, daily formation sets the stage for the climactic, once-a-year act of purification in the Day of Atonement (Lev. 16), when the sanctuary itself is cleansed and the whole community renewed in covenant fellowship.

ANNUAL PURIFICATION OF THE TABERNACLE: DAY OF ATONEMENT

Whereas the daily and occasional rites of purification in Leviticus 11–15 addressed individual and household uncleanness, the Day of Atonement provides a comprehensive cleansing at the very heart of Israel's worship. Leviticus 16 opens with a stark reminder: Entry into the most holy place, where God's presence rested above the ark, means certain death apart from God's prescribed ritual. Framed against the death of Aaron's sons (16:1), the chapter underscores the danger of presumption before the Holy One.

Unlike the regular purification rites, this day addresses the accumulation of uncleanness that clung to the sanctuary itself. Over time Israel's sins and impurities left behind a kind of spiritual residue at the very center of Israel's worship. Like residue on a well-used glass, impurity accumulated at the sanctuary's center; unless it was deliberately scrubbed away, it threatened to so pollute God's house that God would eventually abandon it. The Day of Atonement provided that annual cleansing, purging the most holy place, tent, and altar so that God's presence could remain among his people.

The high priest alone performs much of the rite, first offering sacrifices for his own household before making atonement for the people. Even then, the high priest must carry a censer of incense into the holy of holies so that the cloud of incense would protect him from a deadly, unmediated encounter with God's glory. At the center of the ritual are two goats: one sacrificed, its blood carried into the sanctuary to cleanse it, and the other sent alive into the wilderness, bearing Israel's confessed sins into the land of separation.

The rituals of the Day of Atonement carry a weight of meaning far beyond the mechanics of sacrifice. At their heart is the conviction that Israel's life with God is endangered by individual sin and by its cumulative effect. The blood

LITERARY NOTES

The Sequence of the Day of Atonement

The Day of Atonement was carefully ordered, with every step underscoring the danger of God's holiness and the hope of renewed fellowship:

- High priest prepares: Bathes and dresses in special linen garments.
- Sacrifice for priest and household: Bull offered as a purification offering.
- First goat ("for the Lord"): Slaughtered as a purification offering; its blood sprinkled in the most holy place, the tent, and on the altar to cleanse them.
- Second goat ("for Azazel"): The high priest lays hands on it, confesses Israel's sins, and sends it into the wilderness, bearing away guilt.
- Completion of the rites: High priest rebathes, changes garments, and offers ascension offerings for himself and the people.
- The people's participation: The community "afflicts" themselves (fasts) and refrains from work, sharing in the priest's intercession through repentance and humility.
- Final acts: The remains of the bull and goat are burned outside the camp; those who have assisted must wash before reentering.

Together, these actions removed pollution from the sanctuary and guilt from the people, securing God's presence among Israel for another year.

Lady Lever Art Gallery / public domain

Figure 11.9. *The Scapegoat* by William Holman Hunt (1854)

applied to the ark, tent, and altar do not cleanse these objects for their own sake, but because Israel's sins and impurities lodged themselves at the center of worship. By purging this pollution, the high priest renews the sanctuary as a fit dwelling place for God's holy presence.

Equally important is the goat released into the wilderness. As the priest lays his hands on the animal and confesses the sins of the people, Israel is confronted with a tangible picture of their guilt being borne away to a place cut off. The two goats, then, work together symbolically: one signifying the sanctuary's cleansing from the defilement of sin, the other signifying the removal of sin itself from the community. Only when both pollution and guilt are dealt with can the covenant relationship between God and Israel be restored.

The Day of Atonement dramatizes the gravity of God's holiness and the depth of human impurity. Even the high priest, after elaborate preparation, can enter the most holy place only once a year, and only with the prescribed rites. Meanwhile, the people humble themselves, fasting, ceasing from work, and sharing in the solemn rhythm of renewal. This annual act taught Israel that sin and impurity are not private matters but realities that endanger the whole community and the divine presence in their midst. The cleansing of the sanctuary is thus a ritual form of discipleship, an embodied confession that life with God is both gift and responsibility, sustained through continual attentiveness and periodic renewal.

THEOLOGICAL ISSUES

The Many Dimensions of Atonement

Leviticus challenges narrow definitions of atonement. If we assume that atonement is achieved only by death—the sacrifice of a life—we will miss the fuller picture. On the Day of Atonement, two goats carried distinct but complementary meanings. One goat was slaughtered, and its blood was brought into the sanctuary to cleanse it from the impurities Israel's sins had left behind. The other goat, the one that bore the people's sins, was not sacrificed, as we might expect. Instead, it was sent alive into the wilderness, carrying Israel's guilt away to a place cut off. Atonement, then, is not one-dimensional. It involves both purification and removal, both cleansing and forgiveness, so that the covenant bond between God and his people can be renewed.

The dual action of the goats also carries enduring formative power. The sacrificed goat reminds Israel that sin defiles the very center of their worship, while the scapegoat, sent into the wilderness, gives a vivid picture of sins being removed, never to return. These gestures disciple Israel to live with a keen awareness of the seriousness of sin and the mercy of God who makes continued fellowship possible. The Day of Atonement instills habits of humility, dependence, and communal solidarity, preparing Israel for the call to holiness that comes in the chapters that follow.

Conclusion

Leviticus 1–16 presents a carefully woven program for life with God at the center. Sacrifices establish the rhythms of worship, the priesthood embodies Israel's calling to mediate holiness, and the purity system touches every sphere of ordinary life. All of it culminates in the Day of Atonement, when the sanctuary itself is cleansed and the nation is renewed in covenant fellowship. Together these rituals impress upon Israel that life before the Holy One requires daily attentiveness, communal solidarity, and periodic renewal. Such rituals do not merely teach a message; the performance of such practices shapes God's people to see, know, and embody God's way in the world.

The cultivation of this way of life was not only meant to be a gift for God's people: By dwelling in their midst and inviting Israel to draw near to him, God was forming Israel to be a holy, priestly people whose life with him would radiate outward for the sake of the nations. With the tabernacle purified and God's presence secured, Israel was prepared to hear the Holiness Code (Lev. 17–27), which presses even further into what it means for every aspect of life to reflect the character of the God dwelling in their midst.

Living the Text

Contrary to all expectations, Leviticus speaks to us today. While we are not bound to perform its rituals, they remain for our instruction. Let's reflect on how instructions from the first half of Leviticus might ignite the imaginations of Christians today.

Living Sacrifice and Holy Service

Leviticus 1–10 centers on the sacrifices and the ordination of the priests, reminding us that life with God is not casual or without cost. Israel's

Figure 11.10. Mosaic of Abel and Melchizedek offering sacrifices to God

offerings came from the labor of their hands: the grain they had grown, the animals they had raised, the very fruit of their everyday toil. In a world where some of us never see the immediate, tangible results of our daily labor, and where most of us are compensated in numbers that flicker across a screen, it takes imagination to grasp what was being asked of Israel. Sacrifice meant laying before God what had occupied their time, sweat, and livelihood. Given that life in the land was extremely vulnerable for these subsistence farmers, Israel's sacrificial system called them and us to a kind of risky generosity toward God and neighbor.

Moreover, for Israel, giving was not reduced to a single tithe. In addition to their tithes, they brought firstfruits, fellowship offerings, and the regular sacrifices outlined in Leviticus 1–7.[14] The cumulative effect was that generosity, gratitude, and costly worship were part of daily life. Our giving today, too, is meant to be more than functional or mechanical. Automatic transfers and standing orders may keep ministries running, but they can bypass the formative act of deliberately presenting in the context of worship our "first and best" to the Lord to whom it all belongs. Whether or not Christians today are obligated to give a tithe of their income is the wrong question (if God expected 10 percent from subsistence farmers in ancient Israel, what might he require of us, some of the wealthiest people who have ever lived on the planet?); any and all gifts of money, certainly, but also gifts of time, energy, and presence are ways of offering ourselves before God.

The fellowship offering in Leviticus 3, especially as fleshed out in Deuteronomy, points beyond household piety to shared joy and hospitality. These meals were to include not only one's family but also the Levite, the foreigner, the orphan, and the widow (Deut. 12:7, 18; 16:11, 14). In other words, worship was incomplete if it excluded the vulnerable or confined celebration to one's own household. For the church today, this challenges both our notions of scarcity and our practices of hospitality. Do we treat our household table as a private refuge or as an altar of fellowship where God and neighbor are welcomed together? When our meals become places where rich and poor gather together to enjoy a shared abundance, we bear witness to the God who delights to dwell with his people.

The ordination of Aaron and his sons adds a final note of gravity. Leaders stand in service before God on behalf of the community, not for themselves. The tragic story of Nadab and Abihu warns against self-serving or casual approaches to God's holiness. Together, these chapters call us to recover worship as both costly and communal, to see leadership as humble service rather than self-promotion, and to embrace repeated practices that keep us attuned to God's holy presence. Whether through financial generosity, sacrificial use of our time, or shared meals that embody welcome, we are invited to live lives that are, in Paul's words, "living sacrifices, holy and pleasing to God" (Rom. 12:1).

Food and Formation

Leviticus 11 insists that eating is never a trivial act.[15] What we put into our bodies is bound up with creation, covenant, and holiness. The laws of clean and unclean animals reminded Israel that food was not simply fuel but a gift to be received with gratitude and discernment. As Ellen Davis notes, eating is "the definitive cultural act," a form of communication that shapes the eater and bears witness to the character of God.[16] By regulating what may be eaten and how and by placing meat consumption within the sacrificial system, Leviticus calls Israel to live in alignment with creation's order, respecting the life of animals and remembering that blood, the life, is God's alone.

Such discipline speaks directly into our cultural moment, where food is often abstracted from land, labor, and creatureliness. Industrial food systems encourage us to consume thoughtlessly, to take without regard for the earth or those who produce what we eat. Leviticus presses us to see food differently: as covenantal, moral, and formational. Shared meals can be occasions of holiness, testifying to God's provision and reminding us that our lives are bound up with the land and with our neighbors. Eating with attentiveness—whether by practicing gratitude, resisting waste, or making choices that honor creation and the workers responsible for producing our food—becomes a way of participating in God's holiness and bearing witness to his care for the world.

Embodied Life Before God (Lev. 12–15)

Leviticus 12–15 turns to matters we might prefer to keep private: childbirth, menstruation, bodily emissions, and skin disease. These texts signal that the vulnerabilities and rhythms of bodily life matter to God. Impurity in these cases is not moral failure, but a ritual reminder that even the most ordinary aspects of existence are lived before the face of God. Every birth, every wound, every discharge is caught up in the larger reality of God's holy presence.

This insistence that our bodies matter is a needed corrective for Christian readers, who have often divided the sacred from the ordinary. In Leviticus such divisions make no sense. Holiness encompasses eating, sexuality, illness, recovery, and work. For the church, this means that caring for bodies—our own and those of others—is not secondary to spiritual life but integral to it. How we handle sickness, how we accompany those in postpartum recovery, how we approach sexual integrity and vulnerability—all of this belongs to our life with God. Leviticus trains us to resist the temptation to privatize or spiritualize these concerns. Instead, it calls us to a holistic discipleship that honors God in the ordinary, vulnerable realities of human embodiment. As Scarlata says,

> Imagine what it would be like if we were wholly attuned to God's abiding presence in the world? What would it feel like if we lived with the understanding that everything in creation, down to its subatomic particles, was radiating with God's glory? And how would we respond if we perceived that glory in the very human being created in God's image?
>
> *The book of Leviticus invites us to explore such a world. It beckons us to experience a life where the holy God, the creator of the heavens and the earth, has come down and moved into the neighborhood.*[17]

Leviticus 17–27

Holiness, Justice, and Living with God and Neighbor

Orientation

Leviticus 1–16 established the ritual grammar of holiness. Through sacrifices, the consecration of priests, purity regulations, and the climactic Day of Atonement, Israel was to learn the basic "rules" for navigating life in God's presence. These chapters train the imagination to see and bodies to inhabit a rich, integrated, and symbolic world with Yahweh at the center. But grammar is never an end in itself. We learn grammar so that we can become fluent and converse in different circumstances. In the same way, Leviticus 17–27 takes that ritual grammar and shows Israel how to become fluent in holiness in everyday circumstances—in their families, their work, their worship, their economics, and their relationship with the land. Leviticus 17–27 is the everyday conversation of holiness, where the grammar of sacrifice and purity becomes a lived language shaping every sphere of Israel's life.

Leviticus 17–27 is often called the Holiness Code, and the title is fitting.[1] Here the call to holiness, voiced so memorably in chapter 19, "You shall be holy, for I Yahweh your God am holy" (19:2 AT), is spelled out in practical instructions that touch on every aspect of communal life. The entire community—its leaders, its calendar, and even its land—embodies the holiness of Yahweh. The second half of Leviticus makes clear that holiness is not only enacted at the sanctuary by priests and worshipers; holy worship at the tabernacle must spill out into holy living in family relationships, in business practices, in agricultural rhythms, in care for the vulnerable, and in faithful worship.

One of the most prominent features of this section is its relentless refrain: "I am Yahweh," or more often, "I am Yahweh your God." This formula occurs almost fifty times in Leviticus 17–27, punctuating laws large and small and reminding Israel that these instructions are rooted in God's own identity as the Creator of all, the liberator who brought Israel out of Egypt, and the covenant-making Lord. Just as the Ten Commandments began by recalling God's redemption of Israel from Egypt (Exod. 20:2), so too the Holiness Code grounds its vision in who Yahweh is and what he has done. To keep these laws is to commit to this God and to live in alignment with his character and reign. The call to holiness is thus not perfectionism or self-righteous separation but participation in God's holiness and mission, extending Yahweh's justice, mercy, and love into the world. Consequently, Leviticus 19:18 commands love for one's neighbor, and 19:34 extends the same love to the foreigner residing among them: "Love [the foreigner] as yourself, for you were foreigners in Egypt" (NIV).

Figure 12.1. Renanim Synagogue, Heichal Shlomo, Jerusalem, Israel

Much like the earlier chapters, Leviticus 17–27 is almost entirely law (with a short narrative interjection in 24:10–23). Remember, we should not picture "law" here as a rigid legal code restricted to courtrooms. In the biblical world, *torah* ("instruction") is formative teaching, more like covenantal pedagogy that shapes habits and identity than statutes for litigation. The Holiness Code is thus not legislation in the narrow sense, but instruction designed to form a people in covenant relationship with Yahweh.

The scope of holiness in these chapters is breathtaking. It includes dietary practice (chap. 17), sexual relationships (chap. 18), neighborliness and economic fairness (chap. 19), priestly standards (chaps. 21–22), the consecration of sacred time (chap. 23), the sanctity of God's name (chap. 24), and the Sabbatical and Jubilee years (chap. 25). Finally, blessings and curses spell out the consequences of covenant loyalty or disloyalty (chap. 26), and laws concerning vows and property (chap. 27) underline that holiness touches even voluntary commitments. From the most intimate relationships to the rhythms of the land itself, Leviticus 17–27 draws Israel's entire life into the orbit of God's holiness. These chapters insist that holiness is both God's gift and Israel's calling, a communal way of life that reflects Yahweh's presence, resists idolatry and injustice, and embodies God's love in the world.

Exploration

READ LEVITICUS 17–27

Look for "Holiness Highlights"

As you read Leviticus 17–27, watch for what we will call "holiness highlights"—moments when the steady flow of laws is interrupted by a shift in style, an explanatory note, or a summary. These passages don't add new regulations but explain or frame the laws. Identify them (e.g., 18:24–30; 20:22–26) and ask, What does this passage tell me about why holiness matters? How does it shape the way I understand the laws around it?

Holiness at the Table (Lev. 17)

Leviticus 17 is a hinge chapter, gathering up themes from the first half of the book (sacrifice, blood, food) and extending them into the daily life of the people. From here on, holiness is not just about what happens in the tabernacle but about how Israel slaughters animals, eats meals, and acknowledges that life belongs to God.

The first instruction (Lev. 17:1–9) requires that all sacrifices be brought to the sanctuary. Any Israelite who slaughters an animal elsewhere is said to be guilty of bloodshed and will be "cut off from the people" (17:4). Sacrifice, in other words, is never a private act; it is centralized so that Israel's worship remains focused on Yahweh alone and not diluted by local shrines or idolatrous practices. The next instruction (17:10–14) prohibits the eating of blood, again under penalty of being "cut off." The rationale is given in 17:11: "For the life of a creature is in the blood" (NIV). Blood is sacred because it symbolizes life and is set apart for atonement on the altar. To consume it casually would be to confuse its purpose and cheapen its power. This law ensures that even the most basic human act of eating is done in reverence to the Creator and giver of life.

The chapter also widens the scope of holiness to include foreigners living among Israel. The laws about sacrifice and blood apply to resident aliens as well as Israelites (Lev. 17:8, 10, 12, 13). Holiness is not a closed ethnic system but a covenantal reality that shapes everyone within the community.

Finally, the case of eating an animal found dead or torn by wild beasts (Lev. 17:15–16) illustrates the difference between serious violations and lesser impurities. This act requires ritual washing and temporary uncleanness but not exclusion from the community, unlike sins such as blasphemy or idolatry, which carried the penalty of being "cut off" from Israel. Israel is being taught to discern gradations of holiness: Some offenses sever covenant life; others can be remedied fairly easily.

> THEOLOGICAL ISSUES
>
> **"Cut Off"—Exclusion, Judgment, and Identity**
>
> The penalty of being "cut off" (*karat*) first appears with covenant markers like circumcision, Passover, and Sabbath (Gen. 17:14; Exod. 12:15, 19; 31:14). In Leviticus 17–27 it becomes more frequent, attached to violations such as eating blood (17:4, 9–10, 14), sexual immorality (18:29), and idolatry (20:3–6). These acts threaten Israel's covenant identity and loyalty to Yahweh and often occur in ways human courts could not see, suggesting that "cutting off" refers primarily to divine judgment.
>
> Scholars typically propose three possibilities: (1) death at God's hand; (2) exclusion from the community; or (3) loss of covenant blessings, such as shortened life or childlessness. Most favor divine judgment over human sentencing, since many of these offenses would have been impossible for courts to prove.
>
> Modern readers may find this troubling. In a cultural moment where inclusion is highly prized yet cancel culture quickly enforces exclusion, Leviticus charts a different course. "Cutting off" was not vindictive punishment but a way of safeguarding the covenant community's identity with Yahweh. It underscores that life with God could not be reduced to private choices without communal consequence.[a]

For most people today, Leviticus 17 feels distant. We do not take our food to a central sanctuary, and blood is something we mostly encounter in medical settings. For some, a rare (bloody) steak is a culinary delight rather than a cause for divine disapproval and exclusion. Yet the underlying principles remain powerful. Holiness is meant to shape everyday choices. Food is never just food but is bound up with gratitude, reverence, and justice. Life itself, symbolized in blood, is sacred and not to be treated lightly, a truth that still calls us to treat animals humanely, protect unborn human life, uphold the life and dignity of the aging and infirm, and care for vulnerable neighbors near and far. The holiness conversation that begins in Leviticus 17 continues to challenge God's people to bring every part of life, even what they eat and how they worship, into alignment with the character of Yahweh, the Creator, Redeemer, and covenant Lord.

Bodies and Boundaries (Lev. 18 and 20)

Even though Leviticus 18 and 20 are separated by chapter 19, reading them alongside one another highlights their shared themes and parallel structure. Chapter 18 lays out prohibited sexual relationships and idolatrous practices, while chapter 20 specifies the penalties for the same offenses. Together they frame the heart of the Holiness Code found in chapter 19, showing that Israel's covenant loyalty is to be lived out in the most intimate dimensions of family and community life.

Leviticus 18 opens with a long preface (18:1–5). Moses is to remind Israel that Egypt and Canaan, where they came from and where they are going, represent two alternative ways of life that only end in death. Israel is not to imitate those ways but to walk in Yahweh's statutes, which are the path of life. Three times in these opening verses Yahweh declares, "I am Yahweh your God." The same formula occurs six times in this chapter alone, anchoring Israel's ethic in God's covenant identity. Much like the Ten Commandments, these laws begin and end with the identity of Yahweh as the ground for Israel's way of life.

The chapter closes (Lev. 18:24–30) with an equally strong frame: sexual misconduct pollutes both people and land. In the biblical imagination, the land is a central character in the drama of Scripture and an active participant in the divine covenant. Just as blood pollutes the land (Num. 35:33), so illicit sexual practices defile it until the land itself will "vomit out" its inhabitants. Leviticus's treatment of this three-way relationship between Yahweh, Israel, and the land and other creatures recalls the covenantal triangle explored in chapter 2. The refrain "I am Yahweh" concludes the section, reminding Israel that both people and land belong to him.

Chapter 20 begins and ends with a similar frame.[2] The instructions are enclosed by calls for the Israelites to consecrate themselves, to be holy because Yahweh is holy (Lev. 20:7–8, 22–26). The purpose is clear and repeated: Israel must be distinct from the nations, lest the land vomit them out. These opening and closing notes make plain that the prohibitions and penalties flow from Yahweh's identity, creation's integrity, and Israel's vocation to be Yahweh's holy people; they are not arbitrary rules.

The core of chapter 18 defines forbidden sexual practices. The repeated phrase "to uncover nakedness" is a restrained Hebrew idiom for sexual intercourse, used to set clear boundaries within the household and community regarding what constitute forbidden sexual relationships within families. The list then broadens to other sexual and cultic practices: sex during menstruation, adultery, child sacrifice to Molech (a deity associated with child sacrifice), male same-sex intercourse, and bestiality. These prohibitions move from kinship

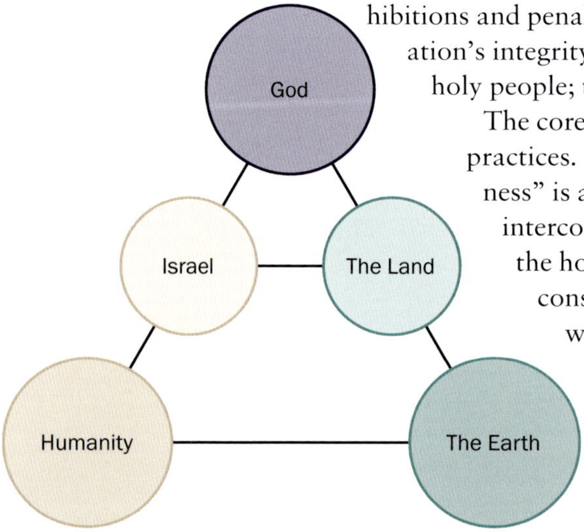

Figure 12.2. Covenantal triangle

Daderot / Wikimedia Commons / public domain

Figure 12.3. Multigenerational households in ancient Israel often shared confined living spaces, underscoring the importance of clear sexual and familial boundaries.

boundaries outward, drawing lines that safeguard the household and mark Israel off from the sexual and cultic practices of Egypt and Canaan.

While chapter 18 ends with a single sweeping penalty—"everyone who does any of these abominations . . . shall be cut off from among the people" (Lev. 18:29 ESV)—chapter 20 distinguishes between consequences. Some practices incur the death penalty: for example, Molech worship, adultery, male same-sex intercourse, sex with a woman and her mother, bestiality, and consulting mediums. Other offenses bring the penalty of being cut off, while still others result in childlessness. Why the difference in consequences between chapters 18 and 20? Scholars suggest that the two chapters address different audiences. Chapter 18 may be directed to household heads, responsible for guarding family integrity—hence the general formula of cutting off. Chapter 20, however, seems to be directed to leaders and judges, who must adjudicate offenses and enforce penalties in broader society.[3]

Why such concern with sexual boundaries? In the ancient world, the household was the basic unit of survival. Victor Matthews observes, "If we were to look for the most important theme that guided the everyday activities of the ancient Israelites, it would be family."[4] It would not be uncommon for four or five generations, often including in-laws and sometimes multiple wives and children, to live together in a single household. Such households might also include a variety of members who were not biological kin: immigrants, debt servants, an orphan who had been taken in, or workers who became attached to the household, for instance. Households could easily fracture under the weight of jealousy, exploitation, or abuse.

CANONICAL CONNECTIONS

Father and Son Abusing the Same Vulnerable Woman

The relationship between sexual boundaries, justice, and God's holiness shows up in Amos's accusation that "father and son go in to the same young woman, so that my holy name is profaned" (2:7 NRSVue). This condemnation stands alongside other accusations of blatant economic oppression, and given that the word translated "young woman" suggests someone of lower social status, it's likely that Amos is confronting sexual abuse and exploitation of a vulnerable person.[b] As Amos and Leviticus recognize, and as horrific accounts of sexual abuse in the church and broader society grievously illustrate, the violation of sexual boundaries is often both unholy and an act of egregious injustice. The law and the prophets tell us God hates and condemns such abuse, and so should we.

Genesis gives plenty of examples of how illicit sexual behavior wrecked families and jeopardized the covenant line. These laws aim to preserve the family as Israel's most vital social unit. They also protect the sexually vulnerable in patriarchal households, like stepdaughters, sisters-in-law, and others who might be targets of unwanted advances.[5] Samuel Balentine similarly argues that the prohibitions "promote healthy family units, which are essential for the covenant community that bears witness to God's presence in the world."[6]

These prohibitions emerge from a broader theological vision. Like the food laws of Leviticus 11, they assume that creation has an order marked by boundaries. To transgress those boundaries is to blur distinctions that God has built into creation and into covenant life. Moreover, these laws demonstrate a concern for procreation and fruitfulness. According to Balentine, sexual activity that destroys "seed" (incest, adultery) or produces no seed (male same-sex intercourse, sex during menstruation, bestiality) undermines God's command to be fruitful and multiply.[7] In this light, the worship of Molech is especially perverse: Child sacrifice annihilates the very fruitfulness God commands, and it tears at the heart of family life.

For modern readers, these chapters are some of the most difficult in Leviticus since they offer a more integrated vision of sexuality than the world and even the church typically promote. For Leviticus, sexuality is important, but it is not elevated over other matters. It sits alongside worship, economics, justice, and care for the land as one aspect of Israel's life of holiness. By placing sexual boundaries, the law aims to safeguard households, protect the vulnerable, and ensure that God's people walk in a way that is distinct from the nations. Holiness begins in the most basic social unit, the household, and radiates outward to the community, the land, and ultimately Israel's witness to the nations.

Love for Neighbor and Stranger: The Center of the Holiness Code (Lev. 19)

If Leviticus 18 and 20 guard Israel from the patterns of Egypt and Canaan by setting sexual and household boundaries, chapter 19 shows how holiness permeates the wider experience of daily life. As the centerpiece of

Reading Leviticus's Laws Regarding Same-Sex Intercourse Today

Leviticus 18:22 and 20:13 prohibit male same-sex intercourse and are important in contemporary debates about sexuality. They are not the Bible's only or final word on the subject, but neither are they irrelevant. However, they must be read in the context of Leviticus itself and within the broader biblical witness. The focus in Leviticus is on sexual activity between men, not on orientation, desire, the genuineness of love, or consent; nor is sexual activity between women addressed. The penalties align with those for other serious sexual violations such as adultery or incest (20:10–16), showing that Scripture treats the matter seriously but not as uniquely heinous.

While Leviticus calls male same-sex intercourse an "abomination" (*to'evah*), the same term applies to idolatry (Deut. 7:25), dishonest trade (25:16), and certain foods (14:3). Leviticus 18:26–30 uses the plural (*to'evot*) for all the sexual sins listed there. "Abomination" is a way of marking practices God forbids for his covenant people; it's not a label for a single offense. Some have argued these laws address only cultic same-sex acts tied to pagan worship, but the context places them among family and kinship boundaries, not ritual ones.

Christians have wrestled deeply and sincerely with these texts and reached different conclusions. Within the broader biblical story, we believe they reflect a consistent vision: Sexual intimacy belongs within a covenant marriage between a man and a woman. Yet one's standing before God does not depend on perfect agreement here, but on trusting Christ and his grace and walking honestly before God in light of Scripture. Because Scripture, including Leviticus, names all sexual sin as contrary to God's holiness, we all fall short of its standard of sexual holiness and should guard against hypocrisy—harshly condemning others for falling short of standards we treat lightly in our own lives—remembering that we all depend on God's extravagant mercy.

These laws raise both theological and pastoral challenges. On the one hand, they affirm that holiness extends to our bodies and sexual lives. On the other, the church has not always been a place of grace and hospitality for those seeking to live faithfully in this area. Shame, rejection, and reducing people to their sexuality have caused real harm. In our time, two distortions often appear. One treats unqualified affirmation without accountability as the loving way of Jesus; the other treats LGBTQ+ persons with fear and hostility rather than as beloved image bearers of God. Scripture calls us to a different way that holds conviction and compassion together, attending to God's boundaries without neglecting the beating heart of biblical faith: love of God and neighbor.[c]

the Holiness Code, this chapter offers a sweeping vision of communal holiness that is profoundly theological and immensely practical. Israel is summoned to avoid destructive practices and to embody Yahweh's character in ordinary interactions with family, neighbors, strangers, and even the land.

The chapter opens with one of the most memorable commands in Scripture: "Speak to all the congregation of the people of Israel and say to them: *You shall be holy, for I Yahweh your God am holy*" (Lev. 19:2 ESV mod.). This is the only place in Leviticus where Yahweh speaks to "all the congregation," underscoring that holiness is the vocation of the whole nation, not just the priests. The refrain "I am Yahweh your God" appears in the chapter fifteen times, driving home that every instruction is grounded in God's identity as Creator, Liberator, and covenant Lord. This repeated phrase keeps the focus on Yahweh's character: Holiness is not abstract morality but involves imitating God's justice, mercy, and love.

One of the remarkable features of Leviticus 19 is how many of the Ten Commandments reappear, but in rephrased or expanded form. Honoring parents and keeping the Sabbath, which are separate commands in Exodus, are paired together in 19:3. Prohibitions against idols (19:4), stealing and lying (19:11), and false witness (19:11, 16) reflect the second, eighth, and ninth commandments but are now intertwined with instructions about fair wages, honest scales, and justice in the courts (19:11–16, 35–36). Even coveting is echoed

Figure 12.4. *The Good Samaritan* by Maximilien Luce (1896)

indirectly in commands against exploitation and fraud. The Decalogue's foundational commands are not simply repeated but expanded to encompass the ordinary practices of community life.

Alongside these echoes stand many other instructions: regulations for sacrifices and offerings (Lev. 19:5–8), agricultural practices (gleaning the edges of fields, 19:9–10), fair business dealings (19:35–36), protections for the vulnerable (19:10, 33–34), and cultic prohibitions (against mixing seeds, animals, or fabrics, 19:19). The sheer diversity of laws illustrates the scope of holiness. Nothing in daily life is outside God's concern and his royal reign. Worship of Yahweh, neighborly fairness, agricultural rhythms, and ritual boundaries were all part of one coherent vision of covenant faithfulness.

The center of gravity comes in Leviticus 19:18: "You shall love your neighbor

THEOLOGICAL ISSUES

Moral, Civil, Ceremonial?

A common way of classifying Old Testament law is to divide it into three types: moral (e.g., the Ten Commandments, often considered universally binding), civil (laws for Israel's social order, sometimes seen as still paradigmatic), and ceremonial (sacrificial and ritual laws, often regarded as fulfilled in Christ and no longer applicable).

While there is some value in this approach, it can also distort how we read the Torah since not all laws fit neatly into these categories. Sabbath, for example, is usually treated as moral in the Decalogue, yet many Christians diminish its authority today. Also, Leviticus itself places laws we might classify as moral, civil, and ceremonial side by side, especially in chapter 19. Commands about honesty in business, prohibitions of idolatry, and rules about mixing seeds or fabrics are bound together within the same framework of holiness. For Israel, these were not separable domains but different strands of one integrated life before Yahweh. Finally, this framework can cause people to dismiss the "ceremonial" as irrelevant, ignoring the wisdom that these laws still offer about holiness, embodiment, worship, and community life. All of Israel's law is *torah*, God's instruction, intended to shape life in partnership with him. Therefore, we should seek the enduring wisdom these instructions reveal about God's character, God's priorities, and God's vision for human life and flourishing.

as yourself." In its original context, this command meant concrete action for the good of others, expressed in honesty, fairness, mercy, and generosity. Remarkably, the same command is extended to the resident alien in verse 34: "You shall love the alien as yourself, for you were aliens in the land of Egypt." In a world where foreigners were typically marginalized or exploited, this was revolutionary. Jesus would later identify the neighbor-love command as one of the two greatest commandments, alongside the call to love God with all one's heart (Deut. 6:5; Matt. 22:37–40). Paul calls it the summary of the law (Rom. 13:9–10), and James dubs it the "royal law" (James 2:8). In Leviticus, it comes not as an isolated maxim but embedded in a whole network of laws that protect the weak, regulate economic life, and order worship.

The Galvanizing Power of the Gleaning Laws

It's easy to rush past Israel's economic legislation, but consider for a moment one seemingly obscure set of instructions: the gleaning laws. Such laws required Israelite landowners to leave some of their profits in the field so as to create work opportunities for immigrants, widows, orphans, and the poor. Such laws allowed the most vulnerable to provide for themselves, and they also meant that Israel's "workplaces" could become sites of encounter between rich and poor, spaces of greater solidarity and connection than otherwise might be possible. Want proof? Read the book of Ruth. The gleaning laws created an opportunity for this "childless, husbandless widow from the wrong ethnicity, gender, and religion" to "provide for herself, have something to give to her family, and become a full member of the neighborhood in Israel."[d]

What would it look like for Christians today to bend their work and workplaces toward God's kingdom? What would it look like for Christians with vocational capital to leave some of *our* "profits in the field" to create opportunities for the modern day Ruths of our world?[e]

The diversity of laws in Leviticus 19 challenges privatized faith and hyperindividualist ethics. Holiness is public and communal. It embraces worship and neighbor love, household integrity and economic fairness, justice for workers and care for immigrants. And all of it is grounded in the character of God: "I am Yahweh your God." Holiness is about aligning the whole of life with the identity and reign of the God who delivered Israel from Egypt and calls them to reflect his character in the world. These seemingly strange laws and ritual instructions serve as daily reminders that Israel's life was set apart for Yahweh. They are the visual, tactile grammar of holiness. Importantly, the laws about generosity, honesty, justice, and love remain as relevant as ever. In a world fractured by injustice and self-interest, Leviticus 19 insists that holiness is a way of life ordered by love of God and neighbor.

Guarding Yahweh's Holiness in People, Things, Times, Name, and Land (Lev. 21–25)

While Leviticus 17–20 focused on the household and community as the sphere of holiness, Leviticus 21–25 shifts attention to the institutions and rhythms that shape Israel's life with God. These chapters guard the boundaries where Yahweh's holiness touches priests (21:1–22:16), sacred offerings (22:17–33), sacred time (chap. 23), God's place (24:1–9), God's own name

(24:10–23), and the land itself (chap. 25). Sometimes holiness is preserved by avoiding contamination, as with priests who must remain ritually whole or with sacred food that must not be defiled. At other times holiness is preserved by consecration, as with the festivals, Sabbaths, and Jubilee years that mark time itself as belonging to Yahweh. In both ways, the holiness grammar of Leviticus gets expressed with fluency in a lived rhythm, embedding God's presence in Israel's leaders, their worship, their calendar, and their economy.

HOLY PRIESTS, HOLY FOOD

Leviticus 18–20 focused on how all Israel was to remain holy in every aspect of life, and chapters 21–22 narrow in on the holiness required of priests. Just as the instructions for sacrifices first addressed the laity (chaps. 1–5) and then the priests (chaps. 6–7), so too the Holiness Code addresses Israel as a whole (chaps. 18–20) before turning to priestly regulations. The effect is layered: All Israel must be holy, but priests serve as a concentrated symbol of that holiness at the very center of Israel's life. Because they drew nearest to God's presence, their lives were to dramatize covenant wholeness and purity in especially visible ways.

These chapters in Leviticus divide naturally into six sections, each marked by a variation of the refrain "I am Yahweh, who makes them holy":

Mourning and marriage instructions for ordinary priests (21:1–9)
Mourning and marriage instructions for the high priest (21:10–15)
Physical limitations on priestly service (21:16–24)
Instructions for eating priestly food (22:1–9)
Who may share in priestly food (22:10–16)
Physical limitations on sacrificial animals (22:17–33)

Chapter 21 outlines the holiness of the priests themselves. Ordinary priests were limited in how they mourned and whom they could marry; the high priest was held to even stricter standards. Priests with physical disabilities or bodily blemishes could not officiate at the altar, though they still belonged to the priestly household and received holy food. Restrictions on mourning kept death, understood as the antithesis of God's life-giving holiness, away from the sanctuary. Marriage limitations modeled covenant fidelity at the very center of Israel's worship. Bodily wholeness symbolized the completeness God desired to be reflected in his holy dwelling. As Sklar notes, these laws hold priests to a higher symbolic standard because priests have a unique role in guarding the holy presence.[8]

Leviticus 22 turns to holiness in what priests handled and ate. Sacred food from offerings was reserved for priests and their households, with careful limits on who could partake and when. A priest who was ritually unclean was temporarily barred from eating until purified. The message is clear: What is consecrated to Yahweh cannot be treated as common. Food itself bore the stamp of God's holiness.

The section closes with instructions about sacrificial animals. Just as priests with physical blemishes could not serve at the altar, so too animals with defects could not be offered. Sacrifices had to be whole, unblemished, and freely given. This culminates in a purpose statement: "You shall not profane my holy name, that I may be sanctified among the people of Israel; I am Yahweh who sanctifies you, who brought you out of the land of Egypt to be your God" (Lev. 22:32–33 ESV mod.). Priests, food, and offerings together were designed to hallow Yahweh's name and act out his holiness.

Contemporary readers may find these restrictions cruel (priests forbidden to mourn), unfair (marriage limitations), or exclusionary (disqualifying priests with disabilities), but it is important to read them in context. They served an important symbolic function, preventing contact between the holy and the unclean and reminding Israel that Yahweh's holiness was absolute. In addition, the Torah elsewhere shows deep concern for widows, orphans, and those with disabilities. What we see here is a symbolic distinction tied to the priestly role, not a denial of anyone's dignity. Priests, food, and sacrifices were vivid reminders of God's holiness and of Israel's calling to reflect that holiness in all of life.

For Christians, these chapters remind us that holiness is both gift and calling. In Christ, the barriers between holy and unclean have been transformed: Jesus touches lepers, eats with sinners, and yet remains holy. He conquers the forces of death by the power of his indestructible life. He is the high priest who embodies God's holiness and makes it accessible to all. Nevertheless, the principle endures: What belongs to God is not to be treated as common. Our bodies, our worship, our resources, and our relationships are all to reflect the holiness of the God who sanctifies us.

Figure 12.5. Limestone incense altar from Megiddo (8th cent. BC)

Gary Todd from Xinzheng, China / Wikimedia Commons / CC0

HOLINESS IN TIME: ISRAEL'S CALENDAR

After focusing on priests and offerings in Leviticus 21–22, chapter 23 turns to the calendar. Just as people and sacrifices dramatize God's holiness in space, so the festivals dramatize God's holiness in time. Interestingly, the very first thing ever called holy in the Bible is not a person or place but the seventh day itself (Gen. 2:3). Genesis does not explain what it means for a day to be holy, but Leviticus 23 develops this idea in detail. Time is set apart (made holy) by stopping ordinary work, remembering, and inhabiting the time differently, so that Israel's life is rhythmically ordered around God's redemption, presence, and provision. We have already been introduced to some of the festivals that feature in Leviticus 23, but in this context, they are reframed into the calendar and integrated into the natural agricultural patterns, forming Israel to embody every moment as holy to Yahweh.

The chapter begins with the Sabbath, the weekly rhythm of sacred rest and the foundation for all the other sacred times. Sabbath trained Israel to trust God's provision, to resist endless, enslaving labor, and to experience holiness in the flow of ordinary time. Every subsequent festival builds on this pattern of sacred rest, marked by "holy assemblies" and the command to do no ordinary work.

The chapter then turns to the six yearly festivals, providing detailed instructions for what Israel could and could not do on each holy day, along with the required sacrifices and rituals. Many of these are drawn from earlier instructions in Leviticus but combined in various ways, almost like plug-and-play modules. By arranging them into the calendar, God gave Israel's rites rhythm and force that would shape the people through repeated cycles of worship and remembrance.

The first cluster of festivals fell in the spring (Lev. 23:4–22). Passover and the Feast of Unleavened Bread reenact the exodus, anchoring Israel's calendar in redemption (Exod. 12:1–2 declares that Israel's year would from that time forward begin with the month of Passover). Every year, Israel both remembered and relived its deliverance from Egypt, God's saving act that defined Israel's national identity as his covenant partners. Soon after came the Feast of Firstfruits, tied to the barley harvest (Lev. 23:9–14). Israelites were to bring the first sheaf of the harvest, and it would be waved before Yahweh, acknowledging that the land's fruitfulness was his gift. This was an act of gratitude and formation; before anyone ate of the new crop, they confessed dependence on Yahweh as provider. They gave a portion of their food back to God before they stopped to eat themselves. The Feast of Weeks, or Pentecost, came fifty days later at the wheat harvest (23:15–22). It was a festival of abundance and thanksgiving, gathering the community to celebrate God's provision. Later Jewish tradition associated this feast with the giving of the Torah at Sinai,[9] while Christians see Pentecost as fulfilled in the giving of the Spirit (Acts 2). Both associations highlight the same point: God provides not only bread for the body but also instruction and Spirit to guide his people into the way of covenant partnership for the sake of the world.

The second half of the year culminated in a cluster of fall festivals, all in the seventh month (Lev. 23:23–43), marking the end of the agricultural year.[10] The Feast of Trumpets opened the month with a solemn assembly marked by trumpet blasts as a memorial, recalling who Israel was before Yahweh. The Day of Atonement followed. We have already studied its rituals in Leviticus 16, but here it is temporally situated as the annual reset of holiness, the day when sins and impurity are purged. Finally came the Feast of Booths, a week-long harvest celebration. Israel was to live in temporary shelters as a reminder of their wilderness journey, when they depended daily on God for food and protection.[11] This festival combined joy in the land's abundance with humility about their dependence. It was a harvest feast as well as a national memory exercise. Prosperity was to be held with gratitude, not presumption.

These festivals embed memory into practices that form Israel's identity and way of life through the act of participating in God's redemptive events. Each festival rooted Israel in God's story as participants. Every generation was summoned to relive the exodus at Passover, to confess dependence on God at Firstfruits and Weeks, to enter repentance at Trumpets and Atonement, and to remember wilderness dependence at Booths. In this way, the calendar recalled history for the purpose of ritualizing time and dramatizing Israel's past so that it would become present for each new generation.

This is what sociologists call thick memory: deeply embedded and emotionally resonant collective memorial acts that shape communal identity. By participating in the festivals year after year, the whole of Israel literally embodied (enacting with their bodies and activating their senses) their story, facilitating formative muscle memory. The festivals formed Israel's imagination of who they were and trained their bodies, habits, and desires to live as God's redeemed people and partners. Time itself was covenant pedagogy, giving Israel the practices by which they remembered who God was, who they were, and how they were to live in light of that identity.

While chapter 23 focuses on weekly and yearly cycles, chapter 25 will extend the principle further with Sabbatical years and the Jubilee. Taken together, these instructions set a rhythm that stretches from every day to every week, to several times each year, to every seventh year, and finally to every fiftieth year. In this way, time itself was consecrated. Ordinary life was

CANONICAL CONNECTIONS

Feasting Our Way Through Salvation History Today

The New Testament connects some of the major events of the early church's life with Israel's feasts. In John's Gospel Jesus is specifically said to perform signs while participating in the pilgrimage feasts of Passover (2:23) and Booths (7:2–38). In the Synoptic Gospels Jesus institutes the Lord's Supper and explains the significance of his death at a celebration of Passover. In Acts the Spirit falls on the apostles during the Feast of Weeks (called Pentecost in the New Testament era).

The church's historic practice of celebrating the life of Jesus through the liturgical year thus follows in the footsteps of the Bible's own ritual calendars. While the fasting and feasting associated with the church calendar are not mandated by Scripture, Scripture does suggest that the people of God benefit from calendrical rhythms that shape us to remember the story of God in Scripture, and to learn to inhabit that story in our own lives. Worship, at its best, "does God's story." It *"proclaims, enacts, and sings God's story"* in public.[f] Embracing the liturgical year is one way to enact God's story through fasting, feasting, singing, storytelling, and more. As Sister Joan Chittister says, the "liturgical year is an adventure in bringing the Christian life to fullness, the heart to alert, the soul to focus. It does not concern itself with the questions of how to make a living. It concerns itself with the questions of how to make a life."[9] At their best, liturgical traditions ritually invite us to enter Jesus's story by also inviting us to inhabit Israel's story in the Old Testament.

constantly interrupted, recalibrated, and reoriented around Yahweh's holiness and provision.

The consecrated days/times of Leviticus reveal a timeless truth that still holds today: Our calendars form us. School years, fiscal quarters, sports seasons, and consumer holidays all tell us what matters. Black Friday and the Super Bowl may shape our lives more than Easter or Pentecost if we are not careful. Leviticus 23 reminds us that time itself ought to be ordered toward God. For Christians, these festivals find their ultimate aim and fulfillment in Jesus: He is our Passover lamb (1 Cor. 5:7), the first fruits of the resurrection (15:20), and the giver of the Spirit at Pentecost. But their formative function remains vital. Like Israel's calendar, the Christian liturgical year (including Advent, Christmas, Lent, Easter, Pentecost) trains believers to embody the story of redemption, reenacting as Christian communities Christ's death and resurrection until they sink into the body and shape habits of life.

The question is not whether our lives are formed by a calendar, but by which one. Leviticus 23 stands as a challenge today: Are our rhythms of time cultivating covenant memory, formation for mission, and holy living, or are they forming us into something else altogether?

BREAD AND LIGHT IN YAHWEH'S DWELLING (LEV. 24:1–9)

Leviticus 23 tied Israel's sacred calendar to the cycles of harvest so that agricultural life became a memorial of God's saving work. Leviticus 24 continues that theme by turning from seasonal rhythms to daily symbols. Two simple but weighty rituals bring the fruit of Israel's fields continually before God: pure olive oil for the tabernacle lamps and twelve loaves of bread for the table of the Presence. The lamps, tended regularly with oil supplied by the people, were to burn continually (24:1–4). The bread, representing the twelve tribes, was arranged each Sabbath in God's presence and renewed weekly with accompanying incense (24:5–9). These perpetual offerings extend the theology of Leviticus 23: The gifts of the land are not only celebrated at appointed times but intermingled into Israel's ongoing worship as signs of God's sustaining presence.

CANONICAL CONNECTIONS

Bread and Light

Bread and light signify God's sustaining presence elsewhere in the Bible. Manna throughout the wilderness years and Jesus's words "I am the bread of life" (John 6:35) both echo the bread of the Presence. Likewise, the lamp points forward to Israel as a light to the nations (Isa. 42:6), to Jesus as the light of the world (John 8:12), and finally to the new creation where "the Lord God will be their light" (Rev. 22:5).

Figure 12.6. *Bread of Heaven* by David Beldman (2025), broken-tile mosaic triptych

These instructions may seem small compared with the dramatic rituals of sacrifice or atonement, yet they symbolize something essential. The light testified that God's presence never flickered or failed, and Israel's vocation was to keep that light burning. The bread testified that Israel lived continually before God's face, their daily sustenance offered back to him and received as holy. Together, bread and light dramatized God's nearness. He was the source of life and the one who invited Israel to fellowship at his table.

HONORING THE HOLY NAME

The only narrative in the Holiness Code is in Leviticus 24:10–23. This stark story interrupts the flow of legal instruction: A man of mixed parentage (Israelite mother, Egyptian father) blasphemes the name of Yahweh in a quarrel. He is brought before Moses, placed in custody until God's will is revealed, and ultimately put to death. The Torah has already made clear the seriousness of honoring Yahweh's name. The Ten Commandments forbid taking God's name in vain (Exod. 20:7), and reverence for that name marked Israel's worship and life together. What this case raises, however, is a new question: How did such laws apply to foreigners living among Israel?[12] Because ethnicity was determined through someone's father, the man is Egyptian, and the people hesitate to act until God brings clarification. The divine verdict is unmistakable: Blasphemy of the holy name carried the same consequence for native-born Israelites as for resident aliens (Lev. 24:16, 22).

This episode does double duty. First, it dramatizes the weight of God's name. To blaspheme is an assault on God's covenant identity and presence. Second, it establishes the principle of equal accountability. Both native and resident foreigners[13] stand under Yahweh's rule, and his holiness is not negotiable. The passage also expands into case law. The principle of lex talionis—"life for life, eye for eye, tooth for tooth" (Lev. 24:17–21)—is reiterated as a standard of justice. Set alongside the blasphemy account, the point is clear: Reverence for God's name and fairness in human relationships belong to the same fabric of holiness.

LITERARY NOTES

Sabbath Celebrations by All the Community of Creation

Leviticus 25:1–7 beautifully demonstrates the way God's covenant purposes include nonhuman characters, including the land and animals. The passage begins by declaring that the land itself must celebrate a Sabbath to the Lord. The land is enabled to celebrate this year of rest through the obedience of humans, who refrain from organized planting and harvesting during this Sabbatical year. As the land and humans cooperate in celebrating this Sabbath, domestic and wild animals get in on the action as well. Yahweh's holy purposes here get fleshed out in ways that are good for every member of the human community, including the most vulnerable, as well as for the earth and other animal members of the ecological community.

HISTORICAL MATTERS

Life on the Edge of Subsistence

The economy envisioned in Leviticus was an agrarian subsistence economy. This means that each household depended almost entirely on its allotted land to provide food for the family, seed for the next season, fodder for animals, and a small surplus for offerings or trade. There was little margin for error. Crop failure could be caused by drought, pests, disease, or conflict, and one bad year might push a family into debt or servitude. Multiple years of crop failure could lock a family into servitude for years or even decades. In such a fragile system, the Sabbatical and Jubilee laws were safeguards, not luxuries. They protected households from permanent loss, prevented the concentration of land in a few hands, and reminded Israel that the land and its abundance belonged to Yahweh.

REST FOR THE LAND, FREEDOM FOR THE PEOPLE

Leviticus 25 widens the horizon of holy time beyond the weekly Sabbath and yearly festivals. Just as days and weeks were consecrated to Yahweh, so too were years and generations. These laws marked Israel as radically different from its neighbors, embedding trust in and faithfulness to Yahweh into the very structures of agriculture and economics.

Every seventh year, Israelites were not to sow, prune, or reap their fields (Lev. 25:1–7). The land itself was given rest, echoing the Sabbath principle of creation. Practically, this prevented the soil from being depleted by constant planting, ensuring long-term fertility. But the purpose was more than agricultural science. The land belonged to Yahweh (25:23), and Israel was to treat it as gift, not possession. Allowing the land to rest was an act of trust in God's provision and a recognition that Israel was tenant, not owner. The Sabbatical year also had a leveling effect, for its produce was to be shared freely by everyone: Israelite, servant, foreigner, and even livestock (25:6–7).

After seven cycles of seven years came the Jubilee year, the fiftieth year (Lev. 25:8–55). Trumpets sounded on the Day of Atonement to announce liberty throughout the land (25:9–10). On the very day God wiped away Israel's sins, God's people forgave one another their debts. In the year that followed, sold/leased land returned to its original family, debts were cancelled, and Israelites who had sold themselves into indentured slavery were set free.

The rationale was theological as much as economic. The land belonged to Yahweh, and the Israelites themselves belonged to him, for he had redeemed them from slavery in Egypt (Lev. 25:23, 42, 55). No Israelite could be permanently dispossessed or enslaved, because Israel already had a master who had delivered them from that kind of enslaving servitude: Yahweh himself.

Behind the Sabbatical and Jubilee years is the conviction that life, land, and people belong to God. Israel's social and economic rhythms were to resist the concentration of land in the hands of a few and the accumulation of multigenerational debt. Israelites were responsible for their lives and households, but if misfortune or hardship left them in debt or servitude and family was unable to help, the Jubilee ensured that approximately once a generation a great reset occurred. The land was restored to its families, households were protected from perpetual ruin, and Israel's covenant equality was renewed. "By ensuring that no family could ever permanently lose the farm, the Jubilee legislation aims at a just, radically countercultural economy based on a relatively equitable distribution of economic assets," as well as a society in which "social *power*" is likewise distributed widely throughout the community.[14]

The refrain "I am Yahweh your God" and the call to "fear your God" permeate these instructions (Lev. 25:17, 36, 38, 55), reminding Israel that these practices were not optional social policies but expressions of covenant loyalty. To dishonor the Sabbatical or Jubilee year was unfaithfulness to Yahweh.

The Sabbatical and Jubilee laws may sound utopian to today's readers, but there is evidence from the ancient world that kings did announce large-scale debt relief and land reform. Furthermore, the Sabbatical and Jubilee laws witness to a realistic insight: Without safeguards, economic systems tend toward inequality, exploitation, and exhaustion of the land. Ancient Israel's rhythms pushed back against both greed and despair, embedding rest and restoration into the covenant itself. From the Torah's perspective, this is good news for everyone. Modern economies have their own mechanisms for release, such as bankruptcy laws, but these often come late and benefit some more than others. By contrast, Israel's system built release into its calendar from the start. It demanded responsibility but

RECEPTION HISTORY

Jubilee and Debt Relief

The Jubilee 2000 campaign, supported by the band U2's lead singer, Bono, and others, drew directly on Leviticus 25 as a vision for global economic justice. Advocates pressed wealthy nations to cancel the crushing debts of the world's poorest countries, arguing that perpetual debt was a modern form of bondage. The effort succeeded in wiping out billions of dollars of debt (e.g., in Uganda and Mozambique), freeing resources for schools, health care, and poverty relief. Though not identical to Israel's Jubilee, the campaign showed how the biblical vision of release and restoration can still inspire movements for economic justice today.

also prevented generational poverty and unchecked accumulation. The point is not that modern societies should adopt Jubilee wholesale but that God's people are called to embody his holiness in the way they use land, wealth, and power. Leviticus 25 reminds us that the earth is the Lord's, that human life and dignity matter more than profit, and that trust in God's provision should shape even the hardest economic choices.[15]

Blessings and Curses, Consequences of Covenant Life (Lev. 26)

As we near the end of Leviticus—and with it the end of the instructions from Sinai—chapter 26 offers a fitting conclusion. It consists almost entirely of blessings for obedience, curses for disobedience, and a promise of restoration if Israel repents. Ending a covenant document with blessings and curses was common in the ancient Near East, and Leviticus 26 parallels both Deuteronomy 28 and the smaller list at the close of the Covenant Code (Exod. 23:20–33). This suggests that Leviticus 26 may have been intended not only as the conclusion to Leviticus but as the conclusion to the Sinai covenant (which began in Exod. 19).[16] The blessings and curses function as motivation to keep the covenant's terms, the blessings as the "carrot," the curses as the "stick." Yet even the "stick" is ultimately restorative: Its goal is to turn God's people back in repentance.

The blessings sketch an almost-Eden-like picture of flourishing. The land, the people, and God himself dwell together in security and abundance, with only a brief mention of enemies to remind us of life in a fallen world (Lev. 26:7–8). By contrast, the curses form a grim reversal of the blessings. Rain and harvest give way to drought and famine, peace to warfare, health and fruitfulness to disease and

CANONICAL CONNECTIONS

The Enduring Relevance of the Jubilee

Some Christians have argued that the Jubilee is irrelevant because it "never happened," but Scripture itself suggests that the Torah's jubilary legislation shaped the people of God's practice in all sorts of ways. Jeremiah 34:8–22 and Nehemiah 5:1–13 both describe God's people creatively working to free their neighbors from debts and return them to their lands; both passages are filled with the language of the Jubilee. Ezekiel imagines a new division of the land and a reinstitution of jubilary practice, but with a twist: In the future, the immigrants in Israel's midst will also be granted plots in the promised land (Ezek. 47:22). Jesus himself comes proclaiming the good news of his kingdom using the image of the year of Jubilee, which he refers to as the year of the Lord's favor (Luke 4:16–21), while the early church in Acts 2 and 4 pictures the first Christians practicing a jubilary release of their farms, fields, and houses for the sake of the community.

Figure 12.7. Painting of Jesus reading at the synagogue in Synagogue Church, Nazareth

Figure 12.8. Agriculture in Israel

death, and Yahweh's presence to his abandonment. These passages can be hard to read, and they may seem to suggest a God who is petty, angry, or vindictive. But placed in the larger biblical story, they reflect a God whose severity serves his mercy, whose judgment is aimed at renewal.

It is also important to note who the curses are directed toward. Leviticus 26 is not speaking of ordinary lapses among otherwise faithful people. The curses fall on those who decisively reject Yahweh: who spurn his statutes, abhor his rules, break his covenant (26:14–15), and persist in hardened disobedience (26:18, 21, 23, 27). Most pointedly, they turn to idols (26:30–31), pledging allegiance to other gods and abandoning Yahweh as king. Life outside Yahweh's good, true, and beautiful neighborhood is a dark and precarious place.

Yet the chapter does not end in despair. Even for those who find themselves under judgment, hope remains. If the people humble themselves and repent, Yahweh promises to remember his covenant with Abraham, Isaac, and Jacob—and to remember the land (Lev. 26:42). The God who judges is the same God who restores. Verse 46 then closes the section, marking the conclusion of the Sinai covenant with its statutes and rules.

Leviticus 26 reminds us that our choices have consequences. Following Jesus brings forgiveness and new life, but it does not erase all the ripple effects of rebellion or undo the pain that sin causes, at least this side of Christ's return. The chapter also highlights the deep bond between God, people, and land, a relationship that continues to shape how we live faithfully in the world God has made. Above all, Leviticus 26 presses us to take seriously God's promises of blessing as well as his warnings about unfaithfulness, knowing that both flow from the same covenant love.

> THEOLOGICAL ISSUES
>
> **Israel and the Land as Covenant Partners**
>
> Ellen Davis highlights how Leviticus portrays the land as an active participant in Israel's covenant life. In Leviticus 19, striking analogies connect human bodies and farmland: The edges of fields left for the poor mirror the uncut edges of beards (19:9–10, 27); newly planted trees are described as "uncircumcised" for three years (19:23); and the prohibition against prostituting one's daughter is paired with a warning not to prostitute the land (19:29).
>
> Beyond these analogies, Leviticus treats the land as a character in the biblical drama and a covenant partner with God. The land may "vomit out" its inhabitants when defiled (18:28) or rest and "enjoy" its Sabbaths when Israel is exiled (26:34–35). In this way, Israel's rebellion has consequences not only for themselves but also for creation. Exile becomes God's way of protecting the land from Israel's disobedience so that it may recover its holiness. The land is sanctified space, an extended sanctuary where God "walks about" among his people (26:12). Most strikingly, God promises, "I will remember my covenant with Jacob [and] . . . Isaac and . . . Abraham, and I will remember the land" (26:42). In Davis's words, the land appears here as Israel's original ancestor, the first covenant partner, even more steadfast than Israel itself.
>
> Together these images portray Israel's identity and vocation as inseparably bound to the land. Their bodies, their fields, and their covenantal life mirror and depend on one another.[h]

Holy Promises: Vows, Dedications, and Tithes (Lev. 27)

After the covenant blessings and curses in chapter 26, Leviticus closes with an appendix on vows, dedications, and tithes. This may feel anticlimactic, but it serves an important function: Holiness extends not only to what God commands but also to what his people voluntarily offer. The chapter outlines how individuals might dedicate people, animals, houses, or land to Yahweh, and how such dedications could be redeemed with equivalent payments. It even includes instructions for tithes from the land and herds, treating them as holy to the Lord. The valuations may seem arbitrary to contemporary readers, or the differing amounts for men and women may seem unfair. But the underlying principle is that voluntary promises matter. Once made, they carry binding weight in Israel's covenant life, because words offered to God are not casual. By ending here, Leviticus affirms that holiness is not only about obedience to rules but also about faithfulness to our own commitments. God's people are called to imitate Yahweh by honoring even their voluntary offerings, just as God is faithful to keep his covenant promises.

Living the Text: From Altar to Marketplace

Leviticus insists that worship and ethics belong together. In some corners of the church today, there is a troubling assumption that sincerity in worship is all that matters. Leviticus challenges that in at least two ways. First, God is very specific about how he prescribes worship; sincerity matters, but so does form, and in Leviticus the form of worship can even be a matter of life and death. Second, the Holiness Code insists that the conduct of God's people is just as important as the practice of their worship.

The prophets drive this point home with scathing clarity. Again and again, they condemn attempts to uphold ritual obligations while neglecting justice, mercy, and integrity (Isa. 1:11–17; Amos 5:21–24; Mic. 6:6–8). Psalms echoes the same truth:

> Who shall ascend the hill of the LORD?
>   And who shall stand in his holy place?
> Those who have clean hands and pure hearts,
>   who do not lift up their souls to what is false.
>   (Ps. 24:3–4; cf. Pss. 15; 50; 51)

Holiness, in the biblical imagination, is liturgical and ethical, priestly and prophetic.

Leviticus itself bears this out. The same God who demands pure sacrifices (chaps. 1–7) also commands honest scales (19:35–36), care for the vulnerable (19:9–10, 33–34), sexual integrity (chaps. 18, 20), and an economic way of life that is good for vulnerable humans, the land, and domestic and wild animals (chap. 25). In other words, the rituals at the sanctuary and the ethics of daily life belong together, forming a single vision of holiness that shapes how Israel worships God and treats neighbor.

Here Dru Johnson sharpens the point, arguing that in the Pentateuch, moral responsibility is woven directly into Israel's ritual life.[17] A sacrifice was not acceptable unless it had been ethically prepared in the community's daily practices. Consider whether God would be pleased with the following brought to the alter for sacrifice:

- grain harvest from a field in which the edges had not been left for the poor and foreigner to glean (Lev. 23:22)
- a bull that had gored someone (Exod. 21:28–32)
- a sheep stolen from a neighbor's flock, or oxen denied their Sabbath rest (Exod. 20:10; Deut. 5:14; 25:4)
- oil and wine from land that never received its Sabbatical rest (Lev. 25:1–7)

As Johnson memorably says, biblical law sets a "farm-to-altar" demand. The same grain, animal, oil, or wine could be either a pleasing aroma or a foul stench before Yahweh, depending on whether it was produced justly.[18]

It was not only the offerings that had to be ethically prepared. The worshiper's own life had to reflect God's holiness and righteousness. A person could not cheat a neighbor in business during the week and then expect their sacrifice to be welcomed at the sanctuary (Lev. 19:13). The prophets later make this point explicit: Sacrifices offered by people who exploit the vulnerable or practice injustice are an abomination, no matter how sincerely they are given (Isa. 1:11–17; Amos 5:21–24).

This shows that holiness was never a matter of private devotion alone. Torah fuses the individual and the community, aiming to form a people whose whole life is oriented toward God. The first half of Leviticus (chaps. 1–16) trains Israel in right worship; the second half (chaps. 17–27) presses that worship outward into relationships, economics, agriculture, sexuality, and justice. Biblical law trains Israel's moral imagination communally so that over time they learn to "smell" injustice, resist exploitation, and embody God's justice in concrete practices.[19]

The prophets, psalmists, and finally Jesus and the New Testament authors all bear out the same truth that worship acceptable to God must be joined to a righteous life. Jesus teaches that reconciliation with a brother or sister takes precedence over bringing an offering to the altar (Matt. 5:23–24), that God desires mercy rather than sacrifice (9:13; 12:7), and that even meticulous tithing must not eclipse "the weightier matters of the law: justice, mercy and faith" (23:23). He names love for God and love for neighbor as the greatest commandments (Mark 12:29–31), drawing worship and life together into one vocation. The rest of the New Testament repeats the refrain. Paul calls believers to present their bodies as a living sacrifice, holy and acceptable to God (Rom. 12:1), and James defines true religion as caring for orphans and widows in their distress while keeping unstained from the world (James 1:27). In this chorus of voices, Leviticus finds its resonance: True worship is never ritual alone but worship embodied in lives of holiness, mercy, and justice. And yet lives of holiness, mercy, and justice flow out of hearts and bodies formed by the kind of ritual and liturgical discipleship Leviticus commends.

We are often tempted to separate "religious" practices like prayer, singing, or weekly worship from the ethics of everyday life. Leviticus resists that divide. Its very structure insists that all of life is worship. To love God is to love one's neighbor, and to love one's neighbor is to honor God. That means Sunday worship cannot be severed from how we run businesses, treat employees, or care for the poor, just as for students it cannot be detached from how they approach assignments, relationships, or dorm life. Singing passionately in church or chapel while cheating on taxes, cutting corners on schoolwork, failing to use the power we have on behalf of the orphan, widow, immigrant, and the poor, or gossiping about classmates is as hollow as offering blemished sacrifices. Leviticus envisions a community that lives its whole life—at the altar, in the marketplace, in the classroom, or at the dinner table—in the presence of God, with integrity, reverence, and love.

How to Read Violent Texts Today

Wrestling Until We Receive a Blessing

The Pentateuch introduces us to our good God and announces the good news of his generous reign. So why so much blood? People commit horrific acts of violence against one another, the law prescribes punishments that strike us as extremely harsh, and God's retribution on sin is often overwhelming. Maybe most troubling of all, if "the LORD is good to everyone and everything," his "compassion" extending to all his handiwork (Ps. 145:9 CEB), how are we to explain texts like Deuteronomy 7:1–2:

> When the LORD your God brings you into the land that you are about to enter and occupy, and he clears away many nations before you . . . and when the LORD your God gives them over to you and you defeat them, then you must *utterly destroy them*. Make no covenant with them and show them no mercy.

This is one of a number of terrifying texts about Israel's conquest of Canaan that use the Hebrew word *herem*, which the NRSV translates "utterly destroy." It is a tricky word to translate, because it essentially means to dedicate something completely to God, and that does not settle the question of *how* people should do this.[1] However, texts like Deuteronomy 2:34 appear to clarify what's involved: "At that time we captured all his towns, and in each town we utterly destroyed men, women, and children. We left not a single survivor."

Such texts may appear to describe Yahweh just as the New Atheist Richard Dawkins does: a genocidal, malevolent bully.[2] Nor is it only modern

Wikimedia Commons / CC0

Figure 13.1. *Battle of Jericho* by Johann Heinrich Schönfeld (17th cent.)

people who find these texts problematic. The second-century theologian Marcion cut them out of his Bible,[3] and while the church identified him as a heretic, two centuries later Chrysostom continued to argue with Christians who saw books like Joshua as "of no use" in the life of faith.[4]

In this chapter, we consider how to read violent Torah texts as Christian Scripture. As a test case, we will use what we believe are the most difficult texts: *herem* texts such as those just quoted from Deuteronomy. Wrestling with these difficult texts will open up avenues for exploring other violent texts in the Pentateuch and Scripture as a whole. Several caveats are in order before we begin.

First, these *herem* texts aren't just disturbing *texts*; they have been used by Christians to justify actual horrific violence. Crusaders were taught to identify "Christendom" with the "Israelites of old."[5] When they arrived at Jerusalem in 1099, they imitated Joshua at Jericho by circling the city in a sacred procession, and then they massacred the city's inhabitants, including women and children. Almost immediately after, they turned to a "jubilant, intensely pious service of worship and thanksgiving in the church of the Holy Sepulchre."[6]

In 1783, the president of Yale College described George Washington as "an American Joshua" called to lead "God's American Israel" against Native American "Canaanites."[7] *Herem* texts were drawn upon to justify what one scholar calls "the most massive act of genocide in the history of the world," in which upwards of 95 percent of the Native American population died.[8] Small wonder that Robert Warrior, a member of the Osage Nation, argues that the "liberationist picture" of God at the exodus was bad news, because "the obvious characters in the story for Native Americans to identify with are the Canaanites."[9] Given this history, we may need to begin our exploration of violent texts in the Torah by joining Nehemiah in confessing our sins and the sins of our ancestors (Neh. 9:1) and then committing ourselves to work to repair the damage done in our God's name.

Second, as explained in chapter 1, we believe God calls us to continue to wrestle with these texts, refusing to let them go "until they bless us," as Esau McCaulley puts it. Such a posture requires us to be "patient with the text in the belief that when interpreted properly it will bring a blessing and not a curse."[10]

Third, this does not mean we will "solve," much less become "comfortable" with, the violence of these texts. Indeed, the Bible's own concerns with violence should warn us against ever becoming comfortable with biblical violence or the rampant violence of our world.

So how then should we approach violent texts in the Torah?

Read Within the Old Testament Context

Reading *herem* texts within their Old Testament context reveals several important features of the Torah's depiction of the conquest.

A Story of Forceful Judgment on Serious Evil

First, the Old Testament context clarifies that the conquest story is indeed a story of God's forceful judgment on serious, sustained evil. This may be the hardest pill for modern readers to swallow, but Scripture asks us to take it seriously. Genesis first mentions the conquest when God tells Abraham it won't happen for hundreds of years because "the Amorites' wrongdoing won't have reached its peak until then" (Gen. 15:16 CEB). This suggests the conquest involves God's just judgment on wickedness over a long period of time. (Of course, as the

Wikifrits / Wikimedia Commons / public domain

Figure 13.2. *Jacob and the Angel* by Carel Kneulman

RECEPTION HISTORY

Looking in the Mirror Before Pointing the Finger

Old Testament scholar Brent Strawn argues our criticism of biblical violence rings hollow when we fail to acknowledge our own:

> If we are offended by the Bible's violence, it is possible that the Bible (personified for a moment) might look back at us and say: "Who are you calling violent?" Our own brands of violence are far more graphic, more brutal, and more effective than anything the biblical authors could ever have imagined. Death by sword is one thing, but the biblical authors had no extended magazines, armor-piercing bullets, carpet bombs, biological and chemical weapons, or nuclear warheads to cause maximum damage, killing the most people with minimal physical effort. Neither did the biblical authors spend their hard-earned money and leisure time on entertaining themselves with violence. Quite to the contrary, it seems that *the Bible itself is concerned about violence* and does what it can to limit the violence it does contain in significant ways.[a]

Figure 13.3. Image of a nuclear test conducted on March 27, 1954

United States Department of Energy / Wikimedia Commons / public domain prophets teach, God's decision to justly judge the wicked can change if the people turn from their wicked ways; see Jer. 18:5–8; Jon. 3:10.)

Deuteronomy 9:4–5 reiterates the point by stating "the LORD is dispossessing" the Canaanites because of their wickedness. According to Deuteronomy 12:31, such wickedness included the Canaanites doing "every abhorrent thing that the LORD hates . . . for their gods," even burning their children in sacrificial fire. Leviticus describes the Canaanites' wickedness as polluting the land until the "ground itself vomited them out" (Lev. 18:24–30).[11] Genesis 4 depicts a polluted earth choking on the blood of human violence. Leviticus and Deuteronomy depict a community in which violence on this scale—supported and fueled by idolatrous worship—has become pervasive.

A Story of a World Gone Wrong

Furthermore, the conquest comes in a world *after* Genesis 1–11. In the Bible's earliest chapters, Yahweh nonviolently creates a beautiful world with male and female image bearers as his special caretakers and coworkers. Such a story contrasts with other ancient stories in which the gods created or arranged the world through sex and violence and often created humans to be their slaves. These stories usually gave ancient kings unique power and authority, thus divinely justifying and authorizing those most responsible for war. We should read the conquest narratives as chapters in a story about a God who created the world for flourishing and peace and who hates the violence that destroys human lives and rips at the fabric of creation. Whatever violence this God enacts or authorizes must always be understood as a "form of *counter*violence."[12]

Some scholars speak of this dynamic as God's "accommodation." In a broken world, God sometimes acts or calls his people to act in ways that *do* reflect the pursuit of justice in a concrete, messy situation, but that clearly *do not* reflect God's deepest desires for his world.[13] As we saw in Genesis 1–11, God's willingness to accommodate in this way is based in his commitment to accompany his good creation and his rebellious image bearers without wiping them out, on the one hand, or allowing violence to go unchecked, on the other. As at the flood, so presumably at the conquest: God forcefully judges with tears of grief in his eyes. Scripture invites us to see a God who gets involved with human violence only "with a heavy heart."[14]

A Story That Looks Ahead

Reading Old Testament *herem* texts also requires us to read them as chapters that precede what follows in the rest of the Old Testament story.

The conquest the Pentateuch predicts is a story of Israel gaining land, but it is knit together with the larger story of Israel losing land, as Deuteronomy anticipates. Although there is some debate about the details, evidence suggests the Torah's *herem* texts were written after the conquest and with the intent of speaking a word to those living *after* the events narrated.[15] Neither Deuteronomy nor Joshua appeared in the daily newspapers to give Israelites news from the Canaanite front.

When the story of God's judgment on the Canaanites is read in this context, its primary function is to warn Israel that they, too, will face God's just judgment should they embrace violence, injustice, and idolatry. While readers notice that *herem* texts target the Canaanites, Old Testament scholar Daniel Block points out that the Israelites appear as potential objects of God's terrifying just judgment "more than twice as often as the Canaanites" in Deuteronomy.[16] When Deuteronomy contemplates the possibility of Israel's future disobedience, it does not call the people back to the conquest project; it calls them to repent, turn toward the Lord, and follow his just and righteous way.[17]

Reading the conquest within the context of the story running from Genesis through 2 Kings reminds us that, ultimately, Israel failed to heed this warning. Yet punctuated throughout Israel's life with God is the reality that the God who judges justly is also the God of mercy who brings judgment only with reluctance and even grief.

A Story Alongside Other Stories

Reading these stories in their Old Testament context draws them into dialogue with other Old Testament texts that constrain, limit, and subvert the violence of the conquest. Deuteronomy limits *herem* warfare to the particular moment when Israel enters the land. Deuteronomy 20:10–14 requires the Israelites to offer terms of peace to their enemies

CANONICAL CONNECTIONS

Forceful Judgment and Divine Desire

The Bible is clear that God's just judgment on wickedness falls short of the triune God's deepest desire: "I have no pleasure in the death of the wicked, but that the wicked turn from their ways and live," God says (Ezek. 33:11). Peter argues that the Lord's delay in bringing "a new heaven and a new earth, where righteousness is at home" lies in God's patience (2 Pet. 3:13). Why would God be patient amid so much ungodliness? "He is patient toward you, *not wanting anyone to perish but all to change their hearts and lives*" (3:9 CEB).

Consider, too, the prophetic prediction of the end of violence in the age to come, when "nation shall not lift up sword against nation, neither shall they learn war anymore" (Isa. 2:4; Mic. 4:3). "In this way, all war In Israel's memory—whether divinely authorized or not—carries the quality of a temporary reality, a concession to current circumstances that make it necessary for the time being but not permanent."[b]

CANONICAL CONNECTIONS

The Grieving God

Few texts give us a greater glimpse of God's grief than Hosea 11:8–9. After contemplating totally destroying Israel for being bent on turning away from him, Yahweh cries out:

My heart recoils within me;
  my compassion grows warm and tender.
I will not execute my fierce anger;
  I will not again destroy Ephraim;
for I am God and no mortal,
  the Holy One in your midst,
  and I will not come in wrath.

When we read the Old Testament, we may feel that God's judgment is unimaginably harsh. We might even wish that God could just chill out and be a bit more like us. Here God tells us that our only hope is that God is *not* like us! His mercy and compassion are literally superhuman. Such mercy and compassion are humanity's only hope.

RECEPTION HISTORY

Offering Peace to the Canaanites?

Most interpret Deuteronomy 20:15–18 as requiring the Israelites not to offer terms of peace in their war against the Canaanites. However, Gerhard Lohfink—one of the world's leading Deuteronomy scholars—argues the requirement *includes* the Canaanites,[c] and Gordon Wenham says the Hebrew text can certainly be read this way.[d] Intriguingly, rabbinic literature supports this, claiming Joshua gave the Canaanites the opportunity to leave, make peace, or fight.[e] Even the book of Joshua may acknowledge something similar. Joshua 11:19 says "There was not a town that made peace with the Israelites, except the Hivites, the inhabitants of Gibeon." Since Rahab and the Gibeonites are "the only two examples of Canaanites who seek to side with Israel. . . . We can say that in the conquest, *any* Canaanite who seeks to side with Israel and YHWH is accepted."[f]

whenever they are at war with peoples other than the Canaanites, for instance.

Herem was not to be Israel's normal practice. Even without looking beyond Deuteronomy, even without reference to Jesus, attentive readers recognize that the very texts that talk about *herem* war make clear that later readers shouldn't practice it.[18] The idea that any later group of people stands in the place of "the Israelites" against their own "Canaanites" is ruled out on Torah grounds alone.

While this is often acknowledged, what is less often recognized is how subversive much of the Old Testament is in relation to war in general. Ellen Davis notes that Deuteronomy 20:5–8 requires all sorts of people to be released from the obligation to go to war—recently married people, people waiting to eat fruit from a newly planted vineyard (which could take five years!), and even those who are afraid. The cost of following these guidelines would "be high, but that is precisely the point. In detailing the several sweet, ordinary things that merit a deferment, the passage confronts us with the incalculable cost of any war. As these concessions imply, war tears at the carefully woven fabric of life in community—and not only through direct enemy attack."[19]

Even less obvious is the relationship between the Old Testament's treatment of the king and the Old Testament's subversive approach to war. There was a close relationship between royal ideology and the practice of war in the ancient world. One Akkadian myth "tells how the human king is given weapons by the gods, who confer on him not just the authority, but the *obligation* to make war."[20] Yet the Torah establishes a political economy that needs no human king at all. If the people nonetheless choose to have a king, Deuteronomy 17:15–20 forbids him from building up an army (through horses and chariots) or making extensive political alliances (through many wives).

The Old Testament's subversive approach to war does not end when Israel does get a king. In the ancient world, the "typical pattern" was "for a king to go to war for his god(s), build the god a temple, and boast about victories with warfare imagery engraved on the temple walls." In the Old Testament, however, Yahweh refuses to allow King David to build the temple precisely because of his relationship to violence (1 Chron. 22:8; 28:3). When Solomon builds the temple, no war symbolism adorns Yahweh's sanctuary walls.[21] The prophets call out nations for their violence (Amos

1), they look ahead to a great day of peace in the future (Isa. 2:4), and they occasionally advocate nonviolence against enemies in the present. When Elisha delivers the blinded army of the Arameans to the king of Israel, he tells the king not to kill them but to feed them. The violence against Israel ceases for a time because the Israelites gave a "great feast" for their enemies and sent them on their way (2 Kings 6:8–23).

Read with Awareness of Ancient Near Eastern Literature

This second point reminds us to read *herem* texts with literary sensitivity and against the backdrop of other ancient literature (the worlds "in" and "behind" the text). Doing so reveals surprising aspects of these texts.

Figure 13.4. The Meshe Stele

Reexamining "Total Kill" Language

For example, the ninth-century-BC Mesha inscription describes a Moabite king perpetrating *herem* warfare against Israel.[22] Depictions of horrendous violence and war pervaded the ancient world. When Davis compares the Bible to Assyrian king Sennacherib's boast that he "harvested [his enemy's] skulls like shriveled grain and . . . piled them into heaps,"[23] she suggests that in biblical *herem* texts "the poetry of gore is greatly muted . . . , if not absent altogether."[24]

While the "total kill" language of *herem* texts sounds genocidal to us, ancient warfare texts demonstrate that such language is hyperbolic and used to describe decisive military victory. Webb and Oeste provide a strong, lengthy argument for this perspective, offering many ancient examples:

Figure 13.5. Assyrian soldiers forcing Babylonian captives to grind bones of their family (7th–6th cent. BC, from Nineveh palace)

- Ramesses II is described as slaying "the entire force of the Foe from Khatti, together with his great chiefs and *all* his brothers, as well as *all* the chiefs of all the countries that had come with him. . . . His majesty was alone, none other with him." This text describes Ramesses singlehandedly slaying all his enemies, but historians claim that the battle it describes, the Battle of Kadesh, likely ended in a draw and certainly included more than just Pharaoh.[25]

- In the midst of a text reveling in how he made his enemy's blood "flow like waters of a river," one Assyrian governor declared, "I decisively defeated them. I annihilated them. . . . I captured those who attempted to escape." Yet just a few lines later, he acknowledges 254 of his enemies escaped.[26]
- Seti I of Egypt claimed to "kill all his enemies at one time and leave no heirs among them, but the next line says he spares some to take them captive."[27]
- Tiglath-pileser I's battle annals describe numerous conflicts with a variety of outcomes. Some enemies he looted and burnt, some he subjugated so they paid tribute, and some he could not fully defeat. Yet when the king had depictions of these battles displayed in public, he described all of them as resounding victories.[28]

Ancient parallels such as these suggest "total kill" language is hyperbolic, an admittedly disturbing way of talking about a complete military victory.

Similarly, the "total kill" language associated with *herem* warfare in the Bible is likely hyperbolic. For example, the first half of Joshua 10:20 portrays Joshua killing every single member of the military "until they were wiped out." Then the verse ends with "when the survivors had entered into the fortified towns." Here, at least, Scripture uses hyperbolic language to describe something less than annihilation. Likewise, while Joshua 10:36–37 uses *herem* language to describe Joshua leaving nobody alive "from Eglon to Hebron," just four chapters later, Caleb asks permission to go to battle against this very same Hebron because, apparently, there still were quite a few people living there.

To be clear, these stories still depict God's people going to war. People die. These texts remain disturbing. But there's ample evidence that the most disturbing language, the "total kill" language, is a hyperbolic way to describe resounding victory.

CANONICAL CONNECTIONS

What About Saul and the Amalekites?

Does the story of Yahweh rejecting Saul for leaving the Amalekite king alive in 1 Samuel 15 rule out the idea that "total kill" language is hyperbolic? Webb and Oeste say no. They point out that the narrator both affirms "*all* Amalekites *were* destroyed (except one)" (1 Sam. 15:8–9) and mentions other Amalekites later in the book (1 Sam. 27:8; 30:1–2, 18; 2 Sam. 1:1).[g] Most importantly, they observe that the hyperbolic language in Joshua describes forceful defeat and subsequent execution of kings, while 1 Samuel 15 vilifies Saul for sparing the king. They argue that, read within its context, Saul sparing the king contributes to the narrator's larger depiction of Saul acting "like the kings of nations" because he intended to use the spared king to project power and acquire honor.[h]

Reading "Total Kill" Language Alongside Other Depictions of the Conquest

"Total kill" language is neither the first nor the most common way the Bible talks about the conquest. Scripture more often speaks of the Canaanites being "driven out," often describing God or God's nonhuman agents as doing the "driving."

- "I will send my terror in front of you, and will throw into confusion all the people against whom you shall come, and I will make all your enemies turn their backs to you. And I will send the pestilence in front of you" (Exod. 23:27–28).[29]
- "See, *I* will drive out before you the Amorites, the Canaanites, the Hittites, the Perizzites, the Hivites, and the Jebusites" (Exod. 34:11; the verses that follow sound almost exactly like Deut. 7:1–2, but without the *herem* "total kill" language).
- "For *I* will cast out nations before you, and enlarge your borders" (Exod. 34:24).
- Leviticus 18:24–25 speaks simultaneously of Yahweh "casting out" the nations and "the land [vomiting] out its inhabitants."
- Deuteronomy describes the Lord "thrusting out all your enemies before you" (6:19), sending pestilence before them (7:20), and "driving out all these nations before you" (11:23).
- In Joshua 24:12, God declares it was "not by your sword or by your bow" that the people had defeated the two kings of the Amorites. Instead, God "sent the hornet before you, which drove them out before you."

Such texts undermine the idea Israel was supposed to genocidally wipe out every Canaanite. They also show that Yahweh is the primary agent behind this judgment, just as he was in relation to Sodom and Gomorrah, Pharaoh in Egypt, and the flood.

What's the Point of the Hyperbole?

Why then does the Torah include *herem* language at all? If a grieving God did involve his people in just judgment through a military action that was not about wiping out every last woman and child, why risk misunderstanding through *herem* language?

Read Deuteronomy 7:1–6 and note anything you find strange, concerning, or surprising.

Once again, attending closely to the literary nature of these texts can help. For instance, scholars suggest texts like Deuteronomy 7:1–6 may imply a metaphorical meaning for the *herem* language often translated as "utterly destroy." Thus, after calling the people to *hakharem takharim* the Canaanites, the text prohibits the people from "making a covenant" or intermarrying with them. If *herem* language meant literally killing every living Canaanite, there would be no need to prohibit intermarriage or covenant making. As Walter Moberly says, "A corpse does not raise the prospect of temptation."[30]

Moreover, the text specifically explains "what [Israel] must do with these nations: rip down their altars, smash their sacred stones, cut down their sacred poles, and burn their idols" (Deut. 7:5 CEB). Matthew Lynch says these verses tell "how the Israelites were to render the Canaanites to God"—namely, by "[tearing] down their places of worship."[31] On one reading at least, the hyperbolic language of *herem* is here explicitly defined as refusing intermarriage and destroying sacred sites (associated with child sacrifice). Earl argues that the *herem* language of 7:2a speaks to "radical separation rather than annihilation," with the verses following the *herem* language providing the content for how *herem* warfare was to be enacted.[32] The text focuses on the "destruction of idols, not image bearers."[33]

This explains why the Common English Bible (among others) translates *herem* language in Deuteronomy 7:2a and elsewhere as "place them under the ban." It captures the way the Canaanites are off limits but without implying, as neither the meaning of the word nor the context requires, literal annihilation.

Why such an extreme and even intentionally disturbing metaphor? Because Deuteronomy 7 is part of the book's larger, costly summons to wholehearted, exclusive love of and service to *this* God. *Herem* language points to a kind of "radical separation" that is, for Deuteronomy, part and parcel of "what it means to love YHWH with heart, soul and strength."[34] And everything stands in the balance. Intermarriage and Canaanite worship sites represent serious temptations to idolatry, and idolatry will lead to horrific disaster for Israel—and, because Israel is part of God's plans for the world, disaster for all humanity. *Herem* language speaks "in black-and-white terms" in order to remind "Israel that their loyalties lie with Yahweh alone. . . . The mere mention of other gods was not to be tolerated (Deut. 18:20)."[35]

Again, the Old Testament unequivocally teaches that Israel waged battles of conquest in Canaan after the exodus. But the cumulative effect of our argument thus far is that these texts were written after the fact and with the primary purpose of instructing Israel how to live in the present.

Yale University Art Gallery / Trumbull Collection

Figure 13.6. *Joshua at the Battle of Ai—Attended by Death* by John Trumbull (1839–40)

The "total kill" language in these texts is hyperbolic at least at some points, and we have good reasons for reading the most extreme *herem* language as a hyperbolic metaphor that calls Israel to give wholehearted allegiance to Yahweh. While the Torah depicts a serious military victory against the Canaanites as part of God's just judgment on sustained violence and injustice, the "total kill" language serves as a hyperbolic, metaphoric way of calling Israelites to faithfulness in the present.

Reading Conquest Metaphorically Elsewhere in the Old Testament

Is there evidence for a metaphorical interpretation of *herem* texts elsewhere in the Old Testament? Indeed, there is. First, Deuteronomy speaks at some points of a quick conquest (9:3) and other times of a conquest that will occur "little by little" (7:22). In his remarkable and highly recommended book *Flood and Fury*, Lynch calls the text's depiction of a gradual displacement the minority report and the text's depiction of a quick total destruction the majority report.[36] The book of Joshua is clear that the minority report more accurately depicts what happened: "a slow, complex, and incomplete process" in which "Israel engaged in *occasional*

HISTORICAL MATTERS

Why the Old Testament Doesn't Reconcile the "Reports" and Neither Should We

Those concerned about the difficulty in reconciling these two "reports" in factual, historical terms should recall the points we made earlier about ancient history (see the section "Three-World Reading, the Reliability of Scripture, and Questions from History" in chap. 1). Examples like Ramesses II's two differing depictions of a historical battle carved side by side remind us that the ancients did not see history writing as offering neutral, unbiased accounts of historical facts. For them, history writing was an act of "exhortation" that included historical facts but was open to the storyteller's art and theologian's agenda. As a result, the history that Deuteronomy and Joshua offer includes concerns we would call historical, but it is not bound to present them in the kind of neutral, unbiased way we would anticipate in "historical" writing. It seems they were quite content to offer two different, factually irreconcilable takes on the conquest alongside one another in order to make a theological point.

conventional warfare against major Canaanite (Late Bronze Age) strongholds."[37] In both Deuteronomy and Joshua, these two seemingly contradictory reports appear side by side, sometimes even in the same chapter.

One way to make sense of the tension between the two reports is to recognize that the majority report's *herem* language is a hyperbolic metaphor summoning Israel to total allegiance to Yahweh. Such allegiance would include costly acts of separation from Canaanites and others who might tempt the people to idolatry. But it need not include genocide, and the focus would be Israel's exclusive love of the Lord.

We see evidence for *herem* language being interpreted metaphorically elsewhere as well.

1. In his farewell speech, Joshua draws on themes from the *herem* text in Deuteronomy 7:1–5: exclusive allegiance to Yahweh, rejecting idolatry, and avoiding intermarriage with foreigners (see Josh. 23:6–12). But while Joshua utilizes Deuteronomy 7:1–5, he "doesn't yell, 'Finish the job! Kill every last one!'" Joshua interprets the *herem* command "nongenocidally" to mean separation from Canaanite religious practices, not total destruction of Canaanites.[38]
2. Second Kings 23 and 2 Chronicles 31 depict King Josiah as a particularly God-honoring leader. These texts depict him carrying out Deuteronomy 7's *herem* laws by viciously destroying *Israel's* places of idolatrous worship,[39] where *Israelites* practiced child sacrifice. Such confrontation was not without human violence; Josiah executed false priests (2 Kings 23:20). But such violence is limited and within Israel's legal context, rather than anything like literal *herem* warfare.
3. In Ezra 9, the people aggressively confront intermarriage with Canaanites (among others). Ezra and the other leaders read Deuteronomy 7 and seek to follow that *herem* text by embracing costly, difficult separation from those who might tempt the people to a way of life contrary to Yahweh's. However, the text never suggests they think Deuteronomy 7 requires them to *kill* these Canaanites. They interpreted the *herem* text metaphorically, especially in relation to intermarriage.[40]

In these texts, *herem* commands were understood as hyperbolic metaphors calling the people to "go to war" with idolatry rather than idolaters. Both Deuteronomy and Joshua recognize that in the very specific instance of the conquest of Canaan, there were also actual military battles as part of God's judgment on the Canaanites. However, we need not interpret those military battles as genocidal.

Spiritual Warfare and the Conquest

Furthermore, Numbers and Deuteronomy associate the Canaanites with the mysterious, fallen angelic beings from Genesis 6, the Nephilim. Numbers calls the giants in the land Nephilim, and it calls the Nephilim's giant descendants the Anakites (Num. 13:25–33). Deuteronomy references the Anakites/Anakim as well as other giant, demigod figures like the Emim and Rephaim. The Rephaim are dangerous "embodied spirits of the dead" according to an old Ugaritic text.[41] This gives these Canaanite enemies a "superhuman, supernatural quality." Lynch suggests there's "some overlap with the warfare Jesus wages against demonic forces in the Gospels."[42] The text's association of the temptation to idolatry with spiritual enemies may well be significant if the conquest texts were written after the fact to speak a message to their audiences.

Of course, this may seem to create new problems. Even if *herem* is (at least sometimes) a metaphor, if it's used to demonize other people groups and protect ethnic purity through banning intermarriage, that doesn't sound like good news either! This, though, is where our close reading of these metaphorical texts gets even more interesting.

THEOLOGICAL ISSUES

Prescribing and Describing

Not everything the Bible *describes* is *prescribed* or *recommended*, including much of the violence in the Old Testament. These violent texts exist because the biblical authors lived in a violent world and were unwilling to look away. We might find descriptions of such violence disturbing, but we might also find comfort in knowing God's Word does not whitewash the reality of life east of Eden.

The example of Ezra and his compatriots pressuring Israelites to divorce foreign wives seems to represent a situation where Scripture describes a practice that it does not approve. "Wasn't Ruth the Moabitess David's great-grandmother? Didn't the prophet Isaiah say that foreigners should *not* be separated from the people of God, but that those who keep covenant should be brought near instead (Isa. 56:1–8)?"[i] Didn't Malachi declare that God hated divorce (Mal. 2:16)? And didn't Ezekiel say that even the immigrant outsiders would receive a portion of the promised land if they aligned themselves with Yahweh (Ezek. 47:21–23)?

RECEPTION HISTORY

Reading Our Spiritual Enemies in the Conquest

Christians have long offered allegorical interpretations of the conquest to apply these texts to spiritual matters. For Origen, the *herem* passages summoned Christians to the "total eradication of sin. That, and only that, is what Christians hear Jesus say to them through OT *herem* passages."[j] While he believed these texts described historical events, he argued their message for later believers was spiritual: "Within us are the Canaanites," he declares in a homily on Joshua.[k] His interpretation resonates with scholars suggesting Deuteronomy and Joshua were written after the fact and with the intent of calling the people to costly faithfulness in the present.[l]

Subverting Expectations

Imagine you're a member of the original audience of Deuteronomy or Joshua. You know a conquest happened, and you know it was, in part, God's just response to serious, sustained evil. You're right about this, but you also may tend to see the story as one in which "we" are the "good guys" and the Canaanites are the "bad guys."

If we imagine such a stereotypical first audience, we discover the conquest stories seriously subvert these expectations. They trap this stereotypical hearer in their arrogance and destabilize their worldview. For example, the very beginning of Deuteronomy says God has given *other* nations *their* lands—including nations Israel often thought of as enemies—and indeed used those other nations to bring judgment on other people associated with the Canaanite "giants" (see Deut. 2:9–12, 18–23). In addition, Deuteronomy repeatedly and explicitly declares that Israel's conquest of Canaan has nothing to do with Israel's righteousness and occurs despite their waywardness, while warning Israel of similar judgment if they rebel.

Rahab serves as perhaps the most powerful example of destabilization. The book of Joshua opens on the very edge of the conquest, with God declaring, "No one shall be able to stand against you" (Josh. 1:5). But the very first Canaanite the Israelites meet is Rahab. As a Canaanite prostitute, she seems to embody the temptations Israel associated with the Canaanites. The allusion to the city of Shittim in Joshua 2:1 underscores this; the last time we heard about Shittim, the Israelites were sleeping with foreign women and, as a result, worshiping their gods (see Num. 25:1). Against our expectations, Rahab rescues the spies and demonstrates a depth of understanding of Yahweh. As a result, this "arch Canaanite" makes a covenant with Israel (apparently forbidden by Deut. 7:2) and is rescued along with her household; who knows "how many undocumented 'family' members Rahab eventually snuck into this covenant"![43] Rahab shows that Canaanites not only can become members of the community; they can serve as a paragon of Yahwistic virtue and Yahweh faith: "She extends hospitality to foreigners, protects them from harm,"[44] becomes part of Jesus's Israelite lineage (Matt. 1:5), and is held up as a hero of faith (Heb. 11:31) alongside father Abraham (James 2:23–25).

Figure 13.7. *Rahab and the Spies*, nineteenth-century wood engraving from Dalziels' Bible Gallery

Rahab destabilizes what it means to be an "Israelite" or a "Canaanite." Such destabilization continues throughout the book. After Rahab is shown to *be* an Israelite in Joshua 2, Joshua 5 shows that invading Israelites need to *become* Israelites through circumcision.

Furthermore, in a crucially important text, Joshua asks the "commander of the LORD's heavenly force," "Are you on our side or that of our enemies?" The commander answers, "Neither!" (Josh. 5:13–14 CEB). The question is not, Whose side is God on? The question is, Who will be on God's side? The book of Joshua makes clear that allegiance to Yahweh is the sole criterion for inclusion.

On the other hand, as soon as the conquest begins, we learn that those who see themselves as "Israelites" can "become Canaanite." Achan is an "Israelite's Israelite," from the line of Judah, who gets treated like a "Canaanite" because he disobeys Yahweh's commands (Josh. 7).

Taken together, Deuteronomy and Joshua demonstrate that Israel's identity has room for ethnic outsiders, including Canaanites, and they threaten exclusion for disobedient insiders like Achan. After all, Caleb, one of only two faithful Israelites in his generation, is identified by the Torah as a Kenizzite (Num. 32:12; Josh. 14:6, 14)—a group of people explicitly included among those Israel would conquer in the conquest (Gen. 15:18–21). This Canaanite, at least, not only avoided death; he inherited land and lineage in the promised land. Why? "Because he wholeheartedly followed the LORD, the God of Israel" (Josh. 14:14). In his study of outsiders in the book of Joshua, David Firth argues the book "gives far more attention to the inclusion of foreigners, especially Canaanites, than it does to their exclusion."[45]

If someone picks up these texts knowing about the conquest and expecting it to be a story of the "good Israelites" defeating the "bad Canaanites," they find that story subverted, and they are forced to consider, Am *I* wholeheartedly pledging *my* allegiance to Yahweh, obeying his commands and walking in his ways? Such questions are precisely the point of the text.

None of this denies that God commanded an actual conquest of Canaan and that the Israelites engaged in acts of war during that conquest. However, it does deny that such war necessitated literal "total kill" practices, and it also highlights the Bible's focus on summoning Israel to faithfulness to Yahweh rather than to violence. This leads us into our third strategy for reading these violent texts well.

Read with Awareness of Our Social Location—and Israel's

In chapter 1, we argued that reading the Old Testament well means engaging the world in the text, the world in front of the text, and the world behind the text. Remembering differences between our world in front of the text and their world in and behind the text can illuminate the dynamics of social location at play in these stories (and in our reading of them).

For example, when I (Michael) read these conquest stories, it is not only the violence that makes my skin crawl. It's that I see the "Israelites" playing the part of my colonizing ancestors and the "Canaanites" standing in for the Indigenous people who suffered at their hands. This has become more acute for me since moving to Aotearoa / New Zealand. When Māori and European students come together in my classroom, it can seem like Deuteronomy commends the kind of colonial violence that killed countless people and stole massive amounts of land from Māori.

We must face the horrific reality of such violence perpetrated by Christians around the world and across history, as well as how Old Testament texts have been used to justify that violence. However, what if we've misread the parallels between Israel's social location and our own? Some European colonialists read themselves as the Israelites coming against the Canaanites. Osage Nation member Robert Warrior argues Native Americans rightly read the text in the same way, with Native Americans standing in a place similar to the Canaanites. Yet enslaved Black people sang "Joshua Fit the Battle of Jericho" because they saw *themselves* as the Israelites and their white oppressors as the Canaanites. Mark Brett suggests Joshua's warfare resonates more with Māori leader Te Kooti, who "saw himself as empowered by Mosaic authority to drive out the imperial British," than with the colonialists, who identified their own program with Joshua's.[46]

Do we just pick the social location we prefer? While there's no doubt this often occurs, we should remember Ellen Davis's point: To read Scripture theologically is to read ready to hear Scripture *against* us. A close reading of the biblical texts as well as historical evidence suggests enslaved Black interpreters were on the right track.

The text relentlessly reminds us that the Israelites were the powerless ones, a ramshackle group of recently liberated slaves, on the run and underprepared. It's the Canaanites who live in military fortresses "large and fortified up to heaven" (Deut. 1:28), which is why in Numbers 13 God's people refuse to go to war with them! They're like grasshoppers facing a land of giants. It's the Canaanites who come at Israel "with all their troops, a great army, in number like the sand of the seashore" (Josh. 11:4). Most of the battles fought in Joshua are described as acts of self-defense. And when the Canaanites attack, they come with the superior military technology—the "very many horses and chariots" of iron that served as the tanks of the ancient world (11:4; cf. Deut. 20:1; Josh. 17:18).

Indeed, Deuteronomy and Joshua imply the conquest of Canaan completes the exodus from Egypt. The first battle in Deuteronomy echoes the exodus story (Deut. 2:26–30). Yahweh tells Israel he is going to give King Sihon into their hands, and the Israelites then ask King Sihon to allow them to pass through peacefully. Sihon refuses and initiates his own violent destruction. Such a battle follows the pattern of interactions with Pharaoh, but in case we had any doubts, the text tells us all this happened because God "hardened" King Sihon's "spirit and made his heart defiant" (2:30).

Figure 13.8. A stained-glass window in a French church depicting the Israelite spies carrying Canaanite grapes

The story of Joshua likewise intentionally alludes to the exodus, not least by having the people again pass through the waters miraculously. Joshua 24:6–12 recounts one seamless liberation story, beginning with God's triumph over the oppressors in Egypt, continuing through Yahweh's defense of his people in the wilderness, and culminating in his defeat of the Canaanites. Judges 6:9 "equates the Egyptian oppressors with the Canaanites that God drove out of the land."[47]

If Yahweh hardened the hearts of Canaan's kings (see Josh. 11:20), we can be sure that, as with Pharaoh, this reflects God's just judgment on long-term violence perpetrated by the powerful. This is not a story of God sending his people to wipe out powerless peasants; it is a story about God completing the exodus by defeating the last vestiges of *Egyptian* oppression.

History provides evidence for this way of telling the story. During the time of the conquest, Egypt sought "to control Canaan through a system of old-school local kings who ruled over city-states."[48] Thus "early Israel confronted *Egypt-controlled* Canaanite kings."[49] Lynch writes:

> The war stories in Joshua 9–11 emphasize the capture and killing of Canaanite *kings* at regional urban centers at major Canaanite crossroads. These were *kings* of cities, and not elders of peasant villages. . . . Killing [the thirty-one kings identified as defeated in Joshua 12], Stone notes, "would have disrupted Egypt's system of command and control and drawn the attention of the pharaoh." . . . In other words, the aims of [Israel's] campaigns were likely to demilitarize the royal strongholds to the north and south of regions where Israel peaceably settled.[50]

> Some of the existing Canaanite population who lived in rural villages and settlements dotted around the highlands were probably sympathetic to the dismantling of Egyptian control. The Canaanite city-state kings sustained their power through systemic "exploitation of village communities," and by stripping the land of its resources. The Canaanite city-states were strongholds of Egyptian colonization, set up to drain all local resources. Many locals likely said, "Good riddance!" to the Canaanite kings. . . . It is notable that the book of Joshua doesn't feature attacks on these unwalled villages or settlements and does show the willingness of some to join with Israel.[51]

There's thus no legitimate space for powerful European colonizers in the past or powerful oppressors in the present to identify themselves with Israel at the conquest, even simply in sociological terms. The Bible does not tell the story of a powerless liberated people in Exodus and then shift to the story of a powerful, colonizing people in Deuteronomy and beyond. The Bible tells a single liberation story that brings God's powerless people out of Egypt and into a land freed from oppressive Canaanite kings. Enslaved Black people were right to celebrate the conquest in song; this story ought to be good news to God's people who are experiencing violence and oppression and bad news to any, including Christians, who perpetrate such oppression.

Read in Light of the New Testament

Finally, Christians read these stories as part of the biblical story that culminates in Jesus. While the Old Testament begins to subvert human violence and warfare, nothing quite prepares us for God's decision to deal with sin and violence by willingly suffering it himself for the sake of his enemies. Jesus's life, death, and resurrection place nonviolent, suffering love for others, including our enemies, at the center of the Christian life. Our battle is not against flesh and blood but against sin, death, and the devil. Of course, humans can align themselves with these anti-God forces, and both testaments call Christians to challenge human evil when this occurs. But Christians challenge such evil by taking up our crosses and embracing self-sacrificial acts of love.

Moreover, in the New Testament, God's people no longer gather as a theocratic nation but rather gather as multicultural outposts of Jesus's kingdom amid the kingdoms of the world. The very idea that God would call a nation or state to act as God's people today the way Israel does in the Old Testament makes no sense within our redemptive-historical moment. This does not answer every question Christians might have about the use

Images of Christ's death and resurrection from the Isenheim Altarpiece by Matthias Grünewald (1512).

of force in the nations in which they find themselves, but it does prevent us from identifying any nation's use of force with that of Old Testament Israel's, and it places the practice of sacrificial love at the center of the Christian life.

Jesus does not leave the Old Testament behind, however. His call to love enemies comes from the Old Testament. The destabilizing of what it means to be "Israel" in the Old Testament anticipates the way Jesus "welcomes into his kingdom literary Canaanites and ethnic Canaanites, along with other despised foreigners, while rejecting self-righteous ethnic Israelites."[52] Just as we saw that the most troubling texts have a metaphorical application in the Old Testament, so also the New Testament marshals military language to summon us to war with both our spiritual adversaries and the sin and unrighteousness we find in our own lives. "Armor up!" the New Testament says. "Resist the enemy and his forces in the world, as well as the way they try to worm themselves into your lives!" (see Eph. 6:10–17; James 4:7). Because disciples do this in imitation of the Crucified One, in the New Testament "holy warriors are transformed into holy martyrs."[53]

Nor does the New Testament leave behind the Old Testament's commitment to justice, which includes forcefully dealing with those who perpetrate injustice. Disciples reject vengeance seeking, not because just retribution is a bad thing, but because it's *God's* thing. "Beloved, never avenge yourselves," Paul writes, "but leave room for the wrath of God. For it is written [in Deuteronomy!] 'Vengeance is mine, I will repay, says the Lord'" (Rom. 12:19). At the same time, the delay in Jesus's return gives room for more of those enemies for whom Christ died to become citizens in the Crucified King's kingdom.

Conclusion

In this chapter, we have not attempted to "solve" the problem of violence in the Torah. We have attempted to understand certain violent texts in the Torah within their broader context. These and other violent texts still disturb us, and we believe the Bible includes them in part *to* disturb us. They intend to disturb, and if we aren't disturbed, that is itself problematic from the Bible's perspective. However, we also hope by taking these texts seriously and carefully, we have opened avenues to a better understanding of even these most difficult texts as Christian Scripture, announcements of the good news of God's kingdom. Moreover, we hope our in-depth test case proves suggestive for thinking about other difficult, violent texts in both testaments.

Numbers 1–12

Preparing for the Journey Through the Wilderness

Orientation

Of all five books of the Pentateuch, Numbers may be the hardest to love. It's like the awkward relative at a family gathering—present, unavoidable, and sometimes perplexing. We tend to skim past it, assuming it is mostly lists, laws, and logistical details. Yet if we take the time to understand it, we find that this "odd uncle" has stories to tell—some strange, some beautiful, and all essential for understanding Israel's journey with God. This Orientation section will introduce the book of Numbers as a whole, before the rest of the chapter considers the opening movement in chapters 1–12.

Part of the difficulty lies in its variety. Numbers gathers together census lists, travel records, stories of rebellion, hymns, laws, prayers, and genealogies.[1] To the casual reader, it can feel like a disorganized attic or garage where every kind of object has been stored.[2] But there is method in the seeming clutter: Each piece contributes to the larger story of a people being shaped for life in covenant partnership with Yahweh. The book's English name, "Numbers," does not inspire the imagination. It comes from the Greek *arithmoi*, a reference to the two censuses that frame the book (chaps. 1 and 26). The Hebrew title, *bemidbar*, "In the Wilderness," is far more revealing. The wilderness is not only the setting of the book but also its central symbol. It is a place of testing and transformation, of loss and grace, where Israel learns who they are and who God is.

Numbers is a book about movement: spatial, spiritual, and generational. Israel moves from Sinai toward the land of promise, and along the way God moves with and among them—guiding, providing, disciplining, and dwelling in their midst. The wilderness becomes God's classroom for formation, where a liberated people learn how to live as a holy nation. If Exodus reveals God's saving power and Leviticus his holy presence, then Numbers reveals God's patient formation of his people in the long, slow work of obedience. To read Numbers well, we must be prepared for that slow, deliberate, and sometimes uncomfortable pace, because the wilderness is not a detour but part of the design.

Figure 14.1. *Mineral Bottom Road* by Jason Bouwman. In his Arabah project, Bouwman explores the desert as a place we all pass through on the way to something better. Inspired by the landscapes of the American Southwest, the project seeks to reveal beauty, hope, and blessing amid seasons of wandering.

Numbers in the Pentateuch's Story

Numbers opens at the foot of Mount Sinai, where Israel has been encamped since their liberation from Egypt. A full year has passed since the exodus, and the people have received the covenant, built the tabernacle, and learned the rhythms of worship that sustain God's presence among them. Whereas Leviticus opens with the problem that God's glory has filled the tabernacle and Moses cannot enter, by the end of Leviticus Israel's worship life has been ordered in such a way that Numbers can begin with the Lord speaking to Moses *in* the tent (Num. 1:1). The book picks up the story of what happens next: how this newly formed nation will travel from Sinai to the threshold of the promised land.

Numbers is the bridge between two defining moments. Exodus and Leviticus describe how Israel is redeemed from slavery and brought into covenant relationship with Yahweh. Deuteronomy looks forward, preparing the next generation to enter the land. Numbers narrates the long middle stretch, the testing ground between liberation and fulfillment.

Figure 14.2. *Encampment of Israelites, Mount Sinai* from *Turner Finden's Landscape Illustrations of the Bible*

After a long period of stationary instruction at Sinai, the narrative begins building toward movement. Yahweh's commands prepare Israel to break camp and set out, but for the first ten chapters the people remain in place organizing, purifying, and rehearsing obedience for the journey ahead. Not until chapter 10 does the cloud lift and the camp finally move. These opening chapters anticipate what is to come. Israel stands on the threshold of promise, poised for departure yet not quite ready to take the first step.

> Read the stories of water from the rock in Exodus 16:1–15 and Numbers 20:2–13, and of manna and quail in Exodus 16:1–15 and Numbers 11:4–9, 31–34. Note the similarities and differences. As you read through Numbers, jot down in a journal other similarities with Exodus.

Numbers exhibits intentional parallels with Exodus. We again hear of water from the rock, manna and quail, and the people's grumbling. Yet the tone and outcomes are different. In Exodus, Israel's complaints occur before the covenant; they are the cries of a newly liberated people learning to trust. In Numbers, the same actions become covenant violations. Israel's disobedience carries weight because they know better. The covenant has turned experience into responsibility. Numbers continues the great story of God's redemption but shifts the focus from deliverance to formation. It asks, What kind of people will inhabit the land of promise? The wilderness becomes the proving ground of covenant faithfulness, a setting where Israel must learn that freedom is more than release from bondage; it is the calling to walk with God in trust and obedience.

The Wilderness as a Place of Formation

Where I (Dave) am from, adventurers pack expensive gear and provisions on their backs and seek out remote places in northern Ontario, Canada, for an authentic "wilderness experience" (i.e., camping and canoeing/portaging). The "wilderness" in this context is vast expanses of dense, rugged forests on the Canadian Shield, with myriads of relatively small lakes and rivers. Equipped with the right gear, a decent knowledge of the plant and animal life, and the ability to trap and fish, a person could live quite comfortably off the land for weeks or even months (and maybe longer). This is decidedly not Israel's experience of "wilderness" in Numbers.

In the biblical imagination, the wilderness is a paradox. On the one hand, it is a place of danger, deprivation, and disorientation. On the other hand, it is the arena of God's most intimate dealings with his people. The wilderness cannot sustain life on its own. There is no water to drink, little to eat, and nowhere to plant or build. It is precisely this barrenness that makes it the perfect environment for formation. Cut off from other sources of security, Israel can only depend on the God who delivered them. This makes the wilderness not an accident in Israel's journey but part of God's

RECEPTION HISTORY

Desert Mothers and Fathers

In the third and fourth centuries AD, groups of Christians withdrew from the cities of the Roman Empire to live in the deserts of Egypt, Palestine, and Syria. Known as the desert fathers and mothers, they were not escaping responsibility but seeking radical formation. Inspired by Scripture's wilderness narratives, they believed the desert was where one met God, faced one's own demons, and learned dependence on grace.

Amma Syncletica of Alexandria, one of the great desert mothers, compared this path to a furnace in which both suffering and joy refine the soul: "In the beginning there are many battles and a good deal of suffering for those who are advancing toward God, but afterward there is ineffable joy."[a] For this fourth-century mystic, the wilderness was the place where one learns to love the world rightly.

The desert tradition reminds us that in barren places, where distractions fade and desires are laid bare, God meets his people with both challenge and grace.

Wikimedia Commons / public domain

Figure 14.3. Miniature depicting Syncletica of Alexandria, from the Menologion of Basil II (ca. 1000)

design. Yahweh brings his people into a place where they must unlearn the habits of Egypt and acquire the habits of freedom. It is one thing to be rescued from slavery; it is another to live as those who are truly free. Numbers exposes how deeply "Egypt" still lives inside Israel, how quickly the people long for the predictability of bondage rather than the risk of trust.

Throughout the book, the wilderness tests Israel's capacity for faith and obedience, revealing their frailty and God's steadfast patience. The journey from Sinai to the promised land could have taken weeks. Instead, it stretches over forty years because the formation of a "stiff-necked" people takes time. Alongside his patient faithfulness is God's discipline—often severe, always purposeful. The wilderness reveals God's sustaining grace as well as his refusal to let sin and unbelief do their destructive work. These moments of judgment can be unsettling to modern readers. They should be, but they should also remind us that divine love is not sentimental indulgence; it is a consuming holiness that will not rest until God's people are transformed. God is moving his people geographically, but he is also shaping them spiritually into a community that can bear his presence and reflect his character to a watching world.

Numbers holds these truths together: mercy and judgment, presence and purification. The same God who disciplines also provides, forgives, and leads. The wilderness becomes a mirror for our own pilgrimage, where grace and truth together form us into a people fit for God's presence.

This wilderness theme reverberates throughout Scripture. Centuries later, Jesus will be driven by the Spirit into the wilderness for forty days, reenacting Israel's story and succeeding where they failed. In the Christian tradition, the wilderness remains a symbol of formation, a place where distractions fall away, idols are exposed, and God's grace is encountered in dependence and humility. To read Numbers, then, is to enter the school of the wilderness, where God transforms a rescued people into those who live into his way of faithfulness and blessing.

Literary Design and Structure

Numbers can appear to be a disorderly compilation of genres. Yet the book's arrangement is more deliberate than it appears. Beneath its variety lies a coherent literary and theological design that holds narrative and instruction/law in creative tension. Numbers is neither a simple history nor a dry law code; it is a portrait of a people in motion guided by the word of God.

The opening and closing verses of the book frame this dynamic beautifully. "The LORD spoke to Moses in the wilderness of Sinai, in the tent of meeting" introduces the book, while its final line concludes, "These are the commandments and the ordinances that the LORD commanded through Moses to the Israelites in the plains of Moab" (Num. 1:1; 36:13). The two settings—Sinai at the beginning and the plains of Moab at the end—mark Israel's journey from promise received to promise anticipated. In both places, God speaks.

Law and narrative are woven together throughout the book. The commands of God don't come as abstract principles but are instructions spoken into concrete moments of crisis or transition. Several of the legal passages in Numbers arise precisely because the circumstances of life shift; for example, the second Passover provision (Num. 9) and the case of the daughters of Zelophehad (Num. 27; 36) show that divine instruction is responsive, meeting Israel where they are. The law in Numbers functions dynamically, as a living expression of God's faithfulness that adapts to new contexts without compromising holiness.

Scholars have proposed various ways of understanding the book's structure. Most agree that geography provides a natural framework:[3]

At Sinai (1:1–10:10): Preparation for departure
From Sinai to Kadesh (10:11–12:16): First stage of the journey
At Kadesh (13:1–19:22): Rebellion, judgment, and instruction
From Kadesh to Moab (20:1–22:1): Renewed journey
On the plains of Moab (22:2–36:13): Final preparations for entering the land

Another pattern that runs through these movements is the passing of one generation and the rise of another. Dennis Olson's structural insight captures this well. The censuses in chapters 1 and 26 divide the book into two parts—the generation of rebellion (1–25) and the generation of hope (26–36).[4] Together these structural perspectives underscore Numbers' dual focus on journey and formation. The book is about God guiding his people from one place to another and, even more, from one kind of people to another.

Exploration

Israel Prepares to Enter the Promised Land (Num. 1:1–10:10)

READ NUMBERS 1:1–10:10

Read the text straight through. Notice how often Israel does things "as Yahweh commanded." Pay attention to the ordering of the camp, the role of the Levites, and the rhythms of purity and worship. Ask, What kind of people is Israel becoming, and what kind of life is formed when God stands at the center?

The Israelites had a propensity for compromising their commitment to Yahweh and for disobeying his instruction. This will be on display later in Numbers, but in the first ten chapters it is strangely and wonderfully absent. These chapters go to great lengths to highlight Israel's obedience to the expressed will of Yahweh, intensifying the sense of hope and anticipation as Israel embarks on their journey to the promised land. Israel had been nomadic tent dwellers for more than a year, and they're finally departing for their permanent destination: a home that Yahweh had promised their ancestors over four hundred years ago!

THE FIRST CENSUS, CAMP ARRANGEMENT, AND LEVITICAL CENSUS AND DUTIES

Numbers 1–4 lay the groundwork for Israel's journey. The book's opening verse—"The Lord spoke to Moses in the wilderness of Sinai, in the tent of meeting, on the first day of the second month, in the second year after they had come out of the land of Egypt" (Num. 1:1)—answers the essential questions: who (Yahweh and Moses), where (the tabernacle in the wilderness), when (thirteen months after the exodus), and what (Yahweh spoke). Here are the great themes of the Pentateuch: revelation—God speaks; presence—God dwells with his people; and redemption—God acts on their behalf.[5]

The date ties this new moment to Israel's liberation from Egypt. Redemption has already created a new people, and God's continuing speech signals that he will guide and form them as they move toward the fulfillment of his promise. Over 150 times in Numbers God "speaks" to his people, reminding readers that revelation and presence are the lifeblood of Israel's identity. The God who once thundered from Sinai continues to commune with his people in the wilderness.

The first census. The first divine instruction is to take a census (Num. 1:1–46). Contemporary analogies, such as a head count before a family trip or a national census, miss the point. The lists of names and tallies of people in Numbers 1 are foundational for everything that follows. Before moving anywhere, Israel must be named, numbered, ordered, and claimed as belonging to God. Four theological purposes stand out for this census.

First, the census is preparation for the fulfillment of God's promise of the land. The census anticipates conquest. Israel is about to move toward the land promised to the ancestors, and the careful numbering of men of fighting age signals that God's long-delayed promise is on the verge of realization. The census thus looks backward to God's covenant with Abraham and forward to its fulfillment in the land.

Second, the census reaffirms tribal identities. The organization of the census by tribes and clans roots Israel in its ancestral story. The twelve sons of Jacob had been a fractious family, yet here their descendants are presented as one people, ordered by and obedient to the word of Yahweh. What follows will test that unity, but the starting point is a community poised for a common purpose under divine command.

Third, the census signals a fulfillment of the cultural mandate and God's promise to Abraham that he would be a great nation. The total number of men of fighting age, 603,550, implies a nation of at least two million.[6] However one interprets the numerical details, the theological message is unmistakable: God has been faithful. The Creator's call that humanity "be fruitful and multiply" (Gen. 1:28), enfolded into the promise to Abraham (12:2; 15:5), has come to fruition. A once-enslaved people has become a vast nation under the care of their Redeemer. The census testifies to divine abundance.

Fourth, the census communicates the implicit value God places on both individual and community. Some names in these lists appear nowhere else in Scripture, yet they matter enough to be recorded. Each person belongs to a family, a clan, and a tribe; each tribe belongs to the people of God. Each would be caretakers of a plot of land protected by the Jubilee laws (Lev. 25). The lists affirm both diversity and unity; the community's strength lies in each member's participation in God's covenant mission to bless the

HISTORICAL MATTERS

Why Are the Census Numbers So Large?

Numbers 1 reports 603,550 men of fighting age, a total that would make Israel's fighting force enormous, far larger than what we know of ancient armies. Because of this, scholars debate how to interpret the figures. Some take them literally, others see hyperbole or symbolism, and still others note that the Hebrew word for "thousand" (*'elef*) can also mean "clan" or "military unit." No single view has settled the discussion.

Nonetheless, the emphasis of the text is theological, not mathematical. A family of seventy in Genesis 46 has become an immense people. Whatever we conclude about the census figures, the message is clear: God has been faithful, his promise to multiply Israel dramatically fulfilled.[b]

CANONICAL CONNECTIONS

Levi's Costly Exoneration

Readers might recall that Levi has a checkered history in Genesis. In Genesis 34, Levi and Simeon exact brutal revenge on the men of Shechem for the rape of their sister Dinah. On his deathbed, Jacob curses their rash anger and wrath, prophetically foreseeing a future of violence and division for these tribes (49:5–7). However, past sins do not seal the fate of the tribe of Levi. The sword, the very instrument of their cursing (49:5), becomes the instrument of their vindication (Exod. 32:25–29) and, ironically, a means of blessing (see especially 32:29).

In subsequent history, the Levites will continue to have an honored and special role in the nation of Israel, but it is also a costly role. Unlike the other tribes, the Levites are not allotted property in the promised land, relying on the other tribes for their sustenance. In another ironic twist, although the blood from their past enemies seems to have been symbolically washed away, the hands of the Levitical priests would perpetually be bloody from sacrifices of the people. The Levites were not, however, exempt from failure and rebellion, as the incident with Nadab and Abihu (Lev. 10:1–3) demonstrates; their special calling required responsibility and obedience. The Levites' redemption is both real and costly.

HISTORICAL MATTERS

Why Thirteen Tribes?

Keen readers will notice that twelve tribes are counted in Numbers 1 even though Levi is not included, which might suggest thirteen tribes overall. The explanation lies in Israel's family story. In Genesis 48, Jacob adopts Joseph's two sons (Ephraim and Manasseh) as his own, giving Joseph a "double portion" in Israel's inheritance. In time, these two lineages function as distinct tribal groups, often called the half-tribes. Thus Levi is set apart for priestly service and excluded from the land-holding tribes, while Ephraim and Manasseh are counted separately, preserving the traditional number twelve (Num. 1:32–35).

nations. The whole world is important to God, and therefore each person is important and precious to him, whether they are fully aware of it or not.

The Levites and the sacred center. The census of fighting men ends with a note explaining that the tribe of Levi is not included (Num. 1:47–54). Their calling is different. Because of their faithfulness during the golden-calf incident (Exod. 32:25–29), the Levites are set apart for sacred service. Their work centers on the tabernacle: dismantling and carrying it, guarding its perimeter, and ensuring its holiness. In effect, they form a living boundary around God's dwelling place, shielding the tabernacle from defilement and the people from the danger of divine holiness.

Here Numbers picks up themes from Leviticus. There we learned that God's holiness is both gift and danger, life-giving yet consuming when approached carelessly. In Numbers, that theology becomes geography. The camp is arranged to embody what Leviticus expressed through ritual: holiness radiating outward from God's dwelling. At the center stands the tabernacle; around it, the Levites; beyond them, the twelve tribes. The configuration of the camp announces that Yahweh, not wealth or power, occupies the center of Israel's life. Every journey, every rest, and every act of worship or work takes its bearings from that center.

Hierarchy and order also have their place, as Numbers 2 describes. Each tribe has a role and direction. Judah is to the east, leading the march, and

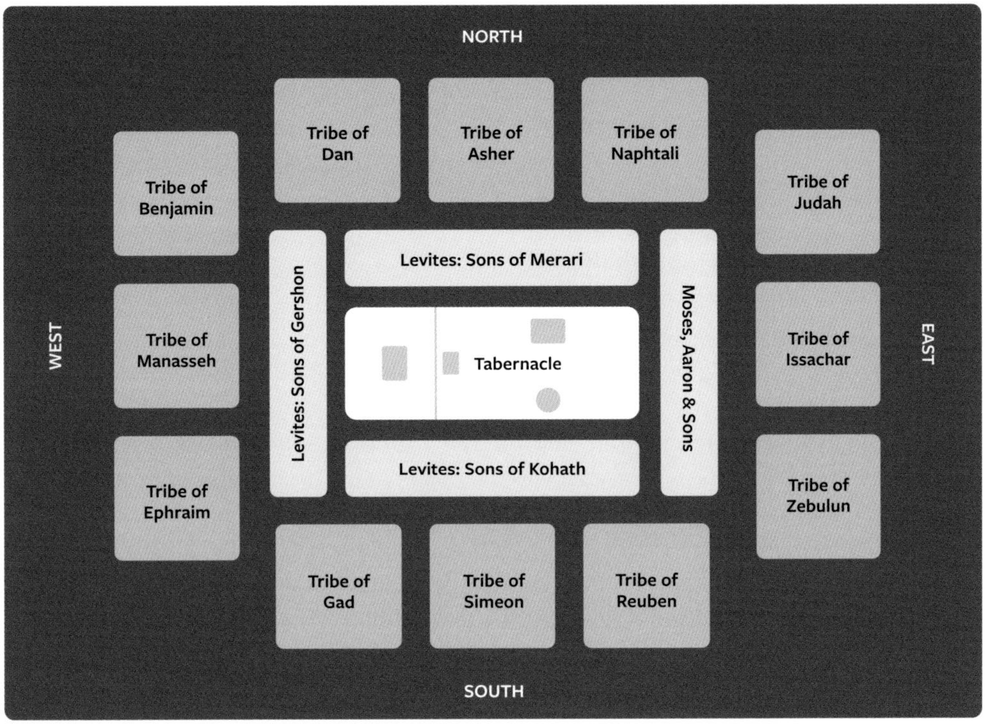

Figure 14.4. The Israelite encampment

others are arrayed according to lineage and calling. This hierarchy is not about privilege but service. Structure enables the community's flourishing and prevents chaos in a vast and vulnerable encampment. The final line of chapter 2 captures the desired result: "The Israelites did everything the Lord commanded Moses" (Num. 2:34). At least for a moment, obedience and unity prevail.

Counting what belongs to God. Numbers 3–4 turn again to the Levites, focusing on their consecration and specific responsibilities. Several new censuses highlight what belongs to God in a special way.

The Levite census (Num. 3:11–39) counts all Levite males one month and older and assigns their tabernacle duties. Together they encamp around the sanctuary, forming a protective square that embodies their mediating role. The census of the firstborn (3:40–43) links the Levites' service to Israel's redemption in

CANONICAL CONNECTIONS

The Logic of the Camp's Arrangement

The placement of Israel's tribes around the tabernacle may seem arbitrary, but it reflects both past actions and future destinies. One might expect an arrangement based on seniority, the oldest sons of Jacob taking the most prominent roles and the youngest the least. Yet God's ordering of the camp, like so much else in Scripture, overturns conventional expectations.

Judah, transformed through the Genesis narrative and richly blessed by Jacob (Gen. 49:8–12), receives the place of honor at the east side of the tabernacle, the entrance and leading position on the march. Reuben, the firstborn, forfeits preeminence through his sin with his father's concubine (35:22; 49:3–4), and his lesser placement probably reflects that loss. The arrangement also foreshadows Israel's story to come. Judah will become the tribe of kings and temple, the faithful Southern Kingdom. Ephraim, stationed opposite Judah at the rear, will later symbolize the Northern Kingdom, once prominent but eventually scattered.

In this divinely ordered camp, past and future converge in the wilderness. But neither ancestry nor position fixes destiny; the people's faithfulness will determine the shape of their future.[c]

Egypt. When God struck down Egypt's firstborn, he claimed Israel's firstborn males as his own (Exod. 13:2, 12–15). The Levites now stand in their place as substitutes for all Israel's firstborn. The duty-aged Levite census (Num. 4:34–49) focuses on men aged thirty to fifty, the years of active service. Each clan's responsibilities are described in detail, particularly those of the Kohathites since they must protect themselves while transporting the most sacred objects lest they die from direct contact with holiness. Even here, order protects life. The fourfold repetition of the phrase "as the LORD commanded Moses" in this chapter signals Israel's readiness to move under God's direction.

The first four chapters of Numbers may seem slow and uninteresting, but they are essential to the story. Israel is being prepared—militarily, liturgically, and spatially—for the journey ahead. Every person and every tribe has a place and a role. God's presence stands at the center, his holiness guarded yet accessible, his people ordered for worship and mission. The journey has not yet begun, but the people are ready, numbered, consecrated, and poised to move when the cloud lifts.

MAINTAINING HOLINESS BOUNDARIES—RITUAL AND MORAL IMPURITY AND NAZIRITE VOWS

With the camp ready to move, Yahweh turns to the readiness of the people themselves. The section in Numbers 5–6 begins with commands to remove those who are ritually unclean (5:1–4) and make restitution for sins against one's neighbor (5:5–10). It then addresses two distinctive cases: suspected adultery (5:11–31) and the taking of a Nazirite vow (6:1–21). The unit concludes with Yahweh's instruction for the priestly blessing, often called the Aaronic blessing (6:22–27).

Apart from the blessing, these chapters focus on the people's ritual and moral purity, and they echo the categories that structure the ritual world of Leviticus. Chapter 5 deals with conditions that render a person unclean (such as skin disease, contact with a corpse, or moral wrongdoing) and ensures the "cleanness" of the camp. Chapter 6 concerns holy, dedicated service expressed through the Nazirite vow.

Whereas the opening chapters of Numbers focused exclusively on men (fighting men, tribal leaders, and Levitical functionaries), these laws about uncleanness, restitution, and the Nazirite vow explicitly apply to both men and women (5:3, 6; 6:2).[7] The text thus broadens the scope of covenant responsibility to include all members of Israel's community.

Instructions for removing unclean people from the camp. The instructions in Numbers 5:1–4 ensure the ritual purity of the camp as it is on the move, but they do not repeat all the details in Leviticus for reintegrating unclean people back into the camp (Lev. 12–15). These instructions broaden Leviticus's earlier regulations. Whereas Leviticus requires removal only of those made unclean by "surface afflictions" on the skin, Numbers also excludes from the camp those with bodily discharges and those defiled through contact with a corpse. The changing circumstances and context may account for the difference. Removing only "lepers" may have been sufficient for the community camped at Sinai, but now Israel is on the move as a military camp, which may have called for a further level of ritual purity.[8] It would be logical to suppose that as Israel settled into the promised land, these laws would need further revision, perhaps relaxing the exclusion of those with a discharge and those defiled by contact with a corpse. Regardless, Yahweh is ensuring the ritual purity of the camp, and the people did just as Yahweh commanded (Num. 5:4).

The laws concerning restitution. The laws in Numbers 5:5–10 reflect instructions already given in Leviticus 6:1–7 that show a breach of faith against one's neighbor (swindling them or secretly stealing from them) is also a breach of faith against Yahweh and, thus, a defiling act. The guilt sacrifice of a ram must be offered to repair the relationship with Yahweh, and full restitution plus 20 percent must be made to restore the relationship between the guilty party and the victim. Ritual and moral impurity threaten the integrity and unity of the community, but God provides means for restoration and atonement for both.[9]

Instructions for suspected adultery. Numbers 5:11–31 is one of Scripture's most troubling passages. Olson observes that according to these instructions a husband's mere jealousy can subject a woman to a humiliating ordeal, with no reciprocal provision for wives.[10] Such texts should unsettle us, yet they invite careful engagement rather than dismissal.

First, this section extends the chapter's concern for communal purity. As with theft (Num. 5:6–10), adultery is framed as breaking faith with both spouse and God (5:12, 27), and the language of holiness and defilement permeates the entire passage. Second, the ritual's unusual specificity, conditions for initiating the test, the materials used, and the priest's exact words (unusual in Torah's rituals)[11] emphasize its seriousness and restrictiveness. The ritual was a public, priest-supervised ordeal that presumably would not be invoked lightly. In the ancient world, unfounded jealousy could easily lead to a woman's death; here, the law limits such dangers by prescribing a controlled, communal process. Third, because adultery already carried the death penalty (Lev. 20:10), the consequences here (physical affliction and exclusion) are notably less severe. This suggests the ordeal provides a moral floor not a moral ceiling; it constrains male accusation when evidence is lacking, while stopping short of irreversible punishment. Finally, this is a

Figure 14.5. *On the Way to the Ordeal* by Pieter Van der Ouderaa (1880)

form of "trial by ordeal," but unlike ordeals in other cultures, guilt here requires divine disclosure and is not susceptible to human manipulation. Nothing in the mixture itself could produce the described effects; Yahweh must step in as witness for guilt to be revealed. Innocence requires no miracle. In this sense, the ritual may protect a vulnerable woman from the whims of an enraged husband, removing judgment from private suspicion and placing it before God.

Viewed this way, the ordeal shares features with other biblical laws that restrain pervasive social evils when eliminating them may not yet be possible. It acknowledges a broken world—marriages marred by jealousy, communities vulnerable to false accusation—while placing guardrails that preserve life, restrain abuse, and entrust final judgment to God. Later biblical texts will articulate the higher moral ceiling toward which this ritual points, where love of neighbor, protection of the vulnerable, and the exposure of hidden wrongs more fully converge.

Instructions for Nazirite vows. The instructions in Numbers 6:1–21 take up the bulk of the

HISTORICAL MATTERS

What Is a "Trial by Ordeal"?

A trial by ordeal, attested in other times and cultures, is "a method of judicial proof widely used," for example, "in early medieval Europe in cases where sworn testimony and the evidence of witnesses was not thought sufficient to establish guilt or innocence."[d] Because of the lack of evidence, the accused was subject to a physical test (an "ordeal") to determine guilt or innocence. One can easily imagine how precarious such trials could be, and history attests how trials by ordeal were abused as tokens of establishing guilt. For example, the accused was forced to retrieve an object from a bowl of boiling water or grasp a red-hot iron; escaping unharmed was the requirement for innocence. Notice in these cases that a miracle is required for the accused to be deemed innocent! The trial by ordeal in Numbers 5 is different, reflecting the countercultural nature of Torah: limiting human power, slowing injustice, and protecting the vulnerable where possible.

chapter. Whereas the previous laws in this section ensure the ritual and moral purity of the camp despite defiling conditions and actions (the move from unclean to clean), the taking of a Nazirite vow would set apart individuals for holy service (the move from clean to holy). We have already learned that in the social structure of Israel, all Levites males from thirty to fifty years old were set apart for special service, and even within that tribe certain Levites (the descendants of Aaron) were dedicated for priestly service. The Nazirite vow permits any Israelite, man or woman, to enter into a status of holy service comparable to that of the priests, though the duties of priests remain distinct.[12] The meaning of the Hebrew word *nazir* is "set apart"; those who took the vow were set apart *from* (i.e., would avoid) consuming wine and any other products of the grapevine, cutting their hair, and coming in contact with a dead body, and they were set apart *to* Yahweh and were thereby "holy to Yahweh" (6:8 AT). The vow would most often be taken for a set period of time, though rarely people would take a lifetime Nazirite vow. The Nazirite calling was voluntary service for any "regular" Israelite, service that was public and costly.

Wenham says that "Nazirites were the monks and nuns of ancient Israel,"[13] and the analogy seems fitting. Each initiated their service with vows, dedicated their life to holy service, abstained from otherwise appropriate activities, and bore physical symbols of their special status. We are not told, however, *why* someone would take a Nazirite vow or the role and activities a Nazirite would perform. Samuel was probably a Nazirite (1 Sam. 1:11), and his mother Hannah's vow and his special service at the tabernacle suggest his service was in answer to prayer and involved aiding the high priest. Contemporary parallels to the Nazirite vow might be limited-term mission or ministry activity, where individuals relinquish the comforts and roles of their normal life to dedicate themselves to concentrated service.

RECEPTION HISTORY

The Ordeal That Disappeared?

About the ordeal in Numbers 5:11–31, Ellen Davis remarks, "There is no record, biblical or otherwise, of this procedure ever having been carried out," and she observes that "already in the first century, the prominent rabbi Yohanan ben Zakkai forbade it—specifically, for its failure to discourage the proliferation of *male* adulterers (Mishnah Sotah 9:9)!"[e] This early abandonment may suggest that Jewish tradition recognized the limitations of the ordeal.

Figure 14.6. *Hannah in the Temple* after a design by Jozef Israëls (1870)

HISTORICAL MATTERS

The Nazirite as Resident Pilgrim

Vineyards did not exist in the wilderness, and it would take several years for newly planted vines to produce grapes. The Nazirite instructions for abstinence from products of the vine, therefore, assume a time when Israel would be settled in the land. To be a Nazirite would involve voluntarily and symbolically "entering" the wilderness for a time.[f]

Instructions regarding the Aaronic blessing. Numbers 6 concludes with a blessing (6:22–27). Its words are probably the best-known words in Numbers, being pronounced in church services around the world to this day:

> The LORD bless you and keep you;
> The LORD make his face to shine upon you and be gracious to you;
> The LORD lift up his countenance upon you and give you peace. (Num. 6:24–26)

Yahweh himself issues the command to Aaron and his sons, the priests. The command is to pronounce blessing on the people. The actual blessing starts with the Hebrew verb "to bless" (*barakh*; 6:24) and ends with the word *shalom* ("peace"; v. 26). Having ordered the camp, appointed its leaders and duties, and safeguarded its purity, God turns from command to blessing. Through the priests he extends his presence and grace to the people. As Richard Briggs notes, the blessing does more here than close a unit; it casts a theological light over the rest of the book.[14] Its language of God's face shining and granting shalom prepares readers to look for signs of God's good presence in moments of triumph as well as in the wilderness stories that follow. Numbers will soon recount complaint, rebellion, drought, danger, and death, but the Aaronic blessing invites us to read even these difficult texts as places where God continues to meet, sustain, and form his people. It teaches us that blessing is not limited to obviously uplifting moments; it can be found within the wilderness itself.

OFFERINGS FOR THE ALTAR

Numbers 7 is the longest chapter in the Bible after Psalm 119, and it takes readers back chronologically to Exodus 40 when the tabernacle was completed (see Num. 7:1).[15] The chapter describes a twelve-day festival in which the twelve tribal leaders (who also conducted the census in Num. 1) bring to the tabernacle their offerings of silver, gold, flour and grain, incense, and various animals for sacrifice. All these offerings ensure provision for the Levitical tribe and thus the proper maintenance and function of the place of God's presence, the tabernacle. The author could have simply summarized this long chapter by saying, "and the chiefs of each tribe brought their offerings to the tabernacle on their appointed day of the festival."[16] Instead the author specifies the day of the festival on which each offering was brought, names each tribal leader, indicates a precise inventory of the offering, and concludes with the words "This was the offering of [name of the tribal leader]." Subsequent generations of readers would be excited to see their own tribe and ancestors listed here and be impressed by the generosity and participation.

A good and vital aspect of our Christian responsibility is giving, and often this comes in the form of monetary gifts, though Christians recognize this also involves the giving of time—that is, service. The tribes were not just giving stuff; each offering assumes and distinctly affirms human cultural activity/work. The silver/gold plates, basins, and dishes required the effort of skilled metalworkers, and those with expertise in making perfume produced the incense for the offerings. The flour and oil for the grain offering assumes the hard work of farmers and the careful process of cultivating grain and olives. The animal offerings are conceivable only on the basis of the domestication of animals and animal husbandry, representing years of care for each animal offered. The implication is that not only are the offerings important for proper worship but so are all the hard work and skill that go into those offerings. Christians today are likewise called to offer our *work*, as well as the produce from it, to God in worship.

The result of the offerings comes at the end of this long, repetitive chapter: The tabernacle is where Moses communicates with Yahweh and hears his very voice! These offerings, coming as they do on the heels of the Aaronic blessing, reveal the people's willing response of faith to the building of the tabernacle and God's presence among them, resulting in blessing and the facilitation of God's continued instruction.

DEDICATION OF THE LEVITES

While Numbers 7 describes the obedience and faith of the people in bringing their sacrifice, Numbers 8 describes the obedience and faith of Aaron and the Levites in performing the purification rituals. The chapter repeats their strict obedience to the voice of Yahweh (8:3, 4, 20, 21, 22). The connection between sacred offerings and priestly service may not be obvious to us, but Numbers presents the Levites as "living sacrifices" from the Israelites to Yahweh (8:9–11). Though the Levites' purification rites (sprinkling, shaving, washing, sacrifice, and the laying on of hands) are strange to us, they were a vivid public ritual of separation and dedication to sacred service (see chap. 10 for more details on the symbolism of ritual ceremonies).

By this point in the Pentateuch, we have read a great deal about the specific duties, roles, and responsibilities of the Levites. As we move closer to that highly anticipated moment when Israel will pack up camp and embark on their journey to the promised land (beginning in Num. 10:11), the Levites are finally publicly and communally ordained for their special service. Israel is one step closer to the promised land.

The chapter ends with some practical instructions about retirement age and service (Num. 8:23–26). Active Levitical service was to be from twenty-five years of age to fifty.[17] Retired Levites were given dignity by being assigned as aides to the Levites in active service. In this we might discern some contemporary implications for how Christians think through roles of retirees in our communities.

THE SECOND PASSOVER AND THE VISIBLE PRESENCE OF YAHWEH

The chronological sequence of Numbers 9 is complicated. Verse 1 sets the context of the second Passover in the first month of the second year (preceding the census in 1:1), while 9:15 recalls the glory of Yahweh filling the tabernacle after its completion (Exod. 40:34–38). Both the Passover celebration and the description of God's presence propel the story forward as the Israelites prepare to leave Sinai. Just as the first Passover marked the new reality of Israel's liberation, so the second Passover (in obedience to the divine command in Exod. 12:24) marks the beginning of their journey to the promised land.[18] Moreover, the description of the mysterious movement of the glory cloud of Yahweh reveals it as a kind of GPS navigating Israel to their destination: When the cloud moved, Israel should move; when it lingered, Israel should remain camped. In the account of the glory cloud, the status of the cloud—whether static or moving—is referred to as the "command of Yahweh" (9:18 [2x], 20 [2x], 23 [3x] AT). At Sinai Yahweh repeatedly communicates his will verbally through Moses, but here his will is communicated through divine activity. In any case, the GPS is functional and set for the promised land, Israel's bags are packed, and their bellies are full. It's time to call the people. It's time to move.

LITERARY NOTES

Chronological Loops in Numbers

The chronology of Numbers is not strictly linear. Several passages reach backward or forward in time to group related material thematically. For example, Numbers 9:1–5 describes the celebration of the Passover "in the first month of the second year," an event that actually occurred before the census in 1:1 ("the first day of the second month"). Likewise, Numbers 7 recounts the tribal offerings for the tabernacle's dedication, which belong to an even earlier moment (shortly after the events recorded in Exod. 40).

Each of these events functions uniquely in the book's sequence. The tribal offerings look back, completing the dedication of the tabernacle and linking Numbers to Exodus; the Passover looks forward, anticipating Israel's journey and testing their readiness to travel with God. These out-of-order placements are deliberate: Numbers gathers everything that prepares Israel for movement—organization, worship, and consecration—before narrating their actual departure from Sinai in 10:11.

Internet Archive / public domain

Figure 14.7. Priests in their apparel with trumpets to praise the Lord

THE SILVER TRUMPETS

Before the Israelites set out in Numbers 10, Yahweh gives instructions for making two silver trumpets. Their blasts served several functions: summoning leaders, signaling movement, and preparing for battle. Their deepest purpose, however, was remembrance. Whenever the people heard the trumpet sound, they were to recall God's words, "I am Yahweh your God" (10:10 AT). The trumpet was a sonic reminder of God's past faithfulness, intended to shape Israel's identity and strengthen their resolve for the journey ahead.

Journey from Sinai to Kadesh (Num. 10:11–12:16)

READ NUMBERS 10:11–12:16

Pay attention to the shift from careful preparation to movement, and then to complaint. Trace the pattern of grumbling, response, and intercession, and then ask, What happens when a people being formed by God begin to lose trust, and what does this reveal about the difference between faithful dependence and rebellious resistance?

DEPARTURE IN BATTLE ORDER

Everything in Numbers 1–9 anticipates the events that begin in Numbers 10. The glory cloud lifts from over the tabernacle of the covenant, and "the Israelites set out by stages from the wilderness of Sinai" (10:12). The long preparation gives way to movement. The text describes the tribes marching in the precise order Yahweh had established in Numbers 2, with the Levites fulfilling their duties as prescribed in Numbers 3.

A brief narrative interlude follows (Num. 10:29–32). Moses urges his Midianite brother-in-law, Hobab, to accompany Israel on their journey. His appeal captures the missional heart of the covenant; as Yahweh "does good" to his people, that goodness is meant to overflow to the nations (cf. Gen. 12:1–3). Whether Hobab accepts the invitation is unclear, but the story suggests that partnership with God's people brings shared blessing.

The section concludes with Moses's exclamations whenever the ark sets out and comes to rest (Num. 10:35–36):

> Arise, O Lord, let your enemies be scattered, and your foes flee before you.
>
> Return, O Lord of the ten thousand thousands of Israel.

These words balance invitation with warning. Those who align themselves with Yahweh's purposes share in his blessing, while those who oppose him meet his judgment. They also affirm the central conviction that will sustain Israel throughout the wilderness: Yahweh himself goes before them, protecting, guiding, and leading them toward the land of promise.

THREE COMPLAINTS

Nothing quite prepares us for what comes next. Well, almost nothing. Immediately after setting out from Sinai, "the people complained" (Num. 11:1). To this point in Numbers, a dominant theme has been divine instruction and human obedience. What follows in Numbers 11–12 are stories of rebellion. The steady pattern of obedience has created a sense of expectation that now begins to unravel, even as Israel's past failures linger in the background. Plus, subtle tensions are present in chapters 1–10 (the need for careful regulation, the danger of holiness, etc.), all of which suggest that this fragile order may not hold. The first ten chapters of Numbers may feel a bit like the opening scenes of a horror film: The teenagers head out for a carefree weekend of camping or the family moves into a beautiful old house. Only the smallest cues (a flicker in the lights, a curtain moving when no window is open, the sudden absence of cell service) hint that something is off. Numbers 11 is that moment when the tension finally breaks. The careful order of Numbers 1–10 unravels as complaint and chaos erupt. Chapters 11–12 record three episodes of rebellion and their consequences, stories in which the people's discontent ignites divine anger and the fragile harmony of the camp gives way.

Complaint at Taberah. The first account of complaint and punishment is brief (Num. 11:1–3), and it establishes a pattern that subsequent episodes will follow. The sequence is simple: The people complain; God's anger burns; Moses intercedes; and God's punishment ceases. The complaint itself is vague—Israel laments "their misfortunes," a reminder of the hardships of wilderness life—but their attitude betrays disbelief. Fire from the Lord breaks out at the edges of the camp, though the text does not specify whether lives are lost. The episode is a warning: Divine presence is both protection and peril.

Complaint over lack of meat. The second story is more detailed and exposes fractures in Israel's faith and leadership (Num. 11:4–35). The people nostalgically recall Egypt, not as a house of bondage but as a land of comfort (11:5, 18, 20). God exposes their complaint for what it is: "You have rejected Yahweh who is among you" (11:20 AT). Moses, too, voices a complaint, though of a different kind. Exhausted by the burden of leadership, he cries out directly to God rather than longing for Egypt. God answers the complaints differently. To Moses, he provides help: seventy elders on whom the Spirit rests to share the work of leadership. When two

Figure 14.8. *Moses Chooses the Seventy Elders* by Jacob de Wit (1736–37)

men begin prophesying outside the formal gathering, Joshua tries to stop them. Moses's response is revealing: "Would that all the LORD's people were prophets, and that the LORD would put his spirit on them!" (11:29). Numbers thus hints that the Spirit's distribution is not about protecting hierarchy but anticipating God's desire to pour out his life-giving presence broadly among his people. God answers the people's complaint by giving quail in abundance, but their indulgence ends in judgment. The episode contrasts two kinds of lament, one born of faith and the other of rejection, and it reframes leadership as shared dependence on God's Spirit rather than centralized power.

Miriam and Aaron oppose Moses. The third complaint arises from within the new leadership structure itself (Num. 12:1–16). Miriam and Aaron speak against Moses because of his Cushite wife, and they challenge his unique authority, perhaps provoked by the new outpouring of prophetic gifts among the elders (11:26–30). Yahweh intervenes directly, publicly affirming Moses as the one with whom he speaks "face to face" (12:8). Miriam is struck with leprosy, though Aaron escapes similar punishment by quickly pleading for mercy. Moses intercedes, and Miriam is healed after seven days outside the camp, symbolically bearing the impurity that rebellion against divine authority produces.

Israel is enrolled in the school of hard knocks—or, more accurately, an advanced course in the school of the desert wasteland. Each episode exposes their spiritual immaturity and resistance to trust. The question now looms: Will they emerge from the wilderness having learned from failure, or

ETHICS

Moses's Outsider Wife

Scholars debate whether Moses's "Cushite" wife refers to the Midianite Zipporah or to another wife from Cush in sub-Saharan Africa. Regardless, the most famous Israelite of all was married to an ethnic outsider, and Yahweh refuses to entertain any criticism of her. Indeed, the text suggests Yahweh's judgment includes some poetic justice in response to Miriam and Aaron's apparently ethnocentric criticisms: "Miriam experiences the ostracism she proposes" for Moses's wife, and if she is to be understood as from Africa, and thus as having darker skin, then there's further irony in God's judgment making Miriam's skin "like snow."[9]

will they be doomed to repeat it? It will soon become evident that the wilderness has many more lessons to teach.

Living the Text: Belief, Unbelief, and Lament

The Bible clearly teaches that complaint is not only permitted but also encouraged and modeled as a faithful response to suffering. Israel's songbook, the book of Psalms, contains more laments than any other kind of psalm, demonstrating that lament is an essential practice of covenant relationship. The prophets, too, are fluent in complaint, giving voice to grief and protest in the midst of injustice and loss. Even Jesus, from the cross, laments, using the words of Psalm 22: "My God, my God, why have you forsaken me?" (Mark 15:34).

Lament, when rightly directed, is not unbelief. It is faith that refuses to let go of God even in the dark. True lament is an act of courage. It tells the truth about pain and brokenness without surrendering trust in the God who hears.

But Numbers 11–12 confronts us with a different kind of complaint. Israel's murmuring is not lament but rebellion. Rather than crying out to God in hope, they long for Egypt, the very place of their enslavement. Their nostalgia is a form of unbelief, a refusal to trust that the God who redeemed them can also sustain them. Egypt becomes a symbol of misplaced faith, the false security of bondage preferred to the vulnerability of freedom.

How can we tell the difference between lament and unbelief? The difference lies in posture. Lament faces God; unbelief turns away. Lament says, "I don't understand, but I'm still talking to you." Unbelief says, "I don't trust you, so I'm turning elsewhere." The distinction can be subtle, but spiritually it is enormous.

A powerful example of faithful lament appears in Mark 9. A father brings his tormented son to Jesus and pleads, "If you can do anything,

CANONICAL CONNECTIONS

Speaking *to* God in the Book of Job

Elaine Phillips argues that recognizing the centrality of the posture of speaking *to* God helps us solve one puzzle in the book of Job. In the book, Job makes all sorts of accusations against God, yet at the end, Yahweh says Job somehow spoke rightly, whereas Job's friends did not. Phillips says the critical verse should be translated, "My anger has burned against you and your two friends because you have not spoken *to* Me in the right manner as my servant Job has" (Job 42:7–8). Job is the only character in the whole book who speaks to God. The difference between the friends and Job is not what they said, but the fact that Job lamented *to* God whereas the friends merely talked *about* him.[h]

Wikimedia Commons / public domain

Figure 14.9. *Job Confessing His Presumption to God Who Answers from the Whirlwind* by William Black (1803–5)

have compassion on us and help us." Jesus replies, "All things are possible for one who believes." The father's answer is as desperate as it is honest: "I believe; help my unbelief!" (9:22–24 ESV). This is not a polished confession of faith. It's the cry of a man whose pain is almost unbearable and in whom belief and doubt coexist. Jesus does not correct him. He receives the man's flickering faith and heals his son. God does not demand perfect belief before he acts. He honors faith, however frail, that turns toward him as the source of hope.

Wikimedia Commons / public domain

Figure 14.10. *La Madeleine* by Paul Cézanne (1868–69)

Our own age understands that father's honesty. We live in what may be appropriately called a deconstructing time, in which many are experiencing doubt, disappointment, and disillusionment with the institutions and leaders that once nurtured faith. For some, this has led to walking away from Christianity, and for others, to the painful but purifying work of stripping away false constructions to rediscover what is true. In such a time, lament may be a key practice on the faithful path forward. To lament is not to abandon faith but to practice it honestly. Numbers reminds us that lament is directed toward God.

Modern writers and artists have reminded the church of this gift. Walter Brueggemann's *The Message of the Psalms*, Soong-Chan Rah's *Prophetic Lament*, and Tish Harrison Warren's *Prayer in the Night* each recover lament as essential to resilient faith.[19] In *Just Discipleship*, Michael argues that the psalms of lament are crucial resources for becoming a church that embraces God's justice in our discipleship, and he explores how they might be recovered despite contemporary worship music's refusal to sing these justice songs.[20] A. J. Swoboda's *After Doubt* invites readers to view questioning as part of discipleship, not its failure.[21] The Rabbit Room's *Death, Grief, and Hope* and Justin McRoberts and Scott Erickson's *In the Low: Honest Prayers for Dark Seasons* extend that same vision through liturgy, poetry, and art, offering prayers and images that help believers name sorrow and hold it before God.[22]

Numbers calls us to a faith that brings its fear, anger, and anguish to God in prayer. Faithful lament keeps the conversation alive. It does not silence pain; it sanctifies it.

Lament is personal, but it is also communal. Just as Israel's complaints in Numbers were collective, so too the church is called to bring its shared griefs before God. Communities bear sorrows together: the loss of a leader, the ache of injustice, the wounds of division, the exhaustion of hope deferred. When the people of God learn to lament together in corporate worship, prayer vigils, or acts of public repentance, they resist denial and despair alike. Properly framed, communal lament becomes an act of solidarity and hope. We name our pain honestly before God and one another, believing that he still hears and still heals. By together offering our lament *to* God, we learn to resist the temptation embraced by the complainers in Numbers, who grumbled *away* from God rather than protesting *to* him.

In this sense, lament is both spiritual discipline and public witness. It trains the church to be honest about suffering and to hope stubbornly in the midst of it. The wilderness stories of Numbers confront modern readers with a searching question: When disappointment comes, where will we turn? Toward God in lament—or away from him in unbelief? The difference may be only a turn of the heart, but in that turn everything changes.

Numbers 13–36

Testing, Rebellion, and Renewal in the Wilderness

Orientation

The last chapter left Israel on the brink of a new beginning. After a year encamped at Mount Sinai where they received the law, constructed the tabernacle, and received instructions that would shape them into a worshiping community on mission, the people set out toward the land of promise. They have celebrated the first Passover since leaving Egypt, packed up camp in orderly fashion, and begun their journey under Yahweh's guidance. All appears ready, and the people have shown a genuine desire to follow Yahweh's instructions carefully. However, no sooner have they set out than cracks begin to show. The people complain about food, long for Egypt, and challenge Moses's leadership.

In Dennis Olson's terms, these chapters trace the turning point between generations: the death of the old and the rise of the new.[1] Numbers 13–25 narrates the rebellion and judgment of the exodus generation, and Numbers 26–36 describes the emergence of their children, now prepared to enter the land. The journey from disobedience to readiness is long and circuitous, marked by both judgment and grace, but through it all, God continues to guide, correct, and sustain his people.

Having been formed and ordered at Sinai, Israel stands on the edge of fulfillment. The journey that began in promise now reaches its decisive test. What unfolds next at Kadesh will define Israel's wilderness experience and the entire book of Numbers. Here, at the threshold of the land, the people's faith collapses under fear, and their refusal to trust Yahweh turns the road to promise into a forty-year detour through the wilderness.

Exploration

Forty Years near Kadesh (Num. 13:1–19:22)

READ NUMBERS 13:1–19:22

Read this section in one sitting, tracing the movement from hopeful exploration to devastating rebellion. Pay close attention to how fear, memory, and perception shape the people's response to the land. Ask, What do the spies see, and how do they interpret it? How does Israel's refusal reshape their future? What patterns of failure, judgment, and mercy emerge as they remain near Kadesh?

THE SPY MISSION AND REBELLION OF THE PEOPLE

Numbers 13–14 is the central narrative of the book. The people have come to the wilderness of Paran near Kadesh, the southern gateway into Canaan. The promised land is within sight of the camp. There Yahweh instructs Moses to send spies into the land, Israel's first foray into the territory of promise. Moses commissions one representative from each tribe to assess the condition of the land and the military strength of its inhabitants.

The spies travel through the land for forty days, returning with an abundance of its produce (Num. 13:25–26). We might imagine the Israelites waiting with anticipation as the spies approach the camp: What will their report be? The spies briefly confirm that this is indeed the good land Yahweh promised their ancestors, a land "gushing with milk and honey" (13:27 AT; cf. Exod. 3:8; 13:5; 33:3; Lev. 20:24). However, they continue their report with a much longer description of the land's formidable inhabitants and fortified cities.

Figure 15.1. From Egypt to the promised land

Sensing the crowd's fear, Caleb steps forward to strengthen the people's resolve, urging them not to delay, "for we are well able to overcome it." Ten other spies immediately contradict him: "We are not able" (Num. 13:30–31). They then mythologize the land and its inhabitants. The land itself becomes a kind of devouring monster, and its people, towering demigods (Nephilim; see Gen. 6:4) who would crush Israel like insects (13:32–33).[2] Their words are lies, which destroy the people's confidence and ultimately cost the first generation access to the land.

As chapter 14 opens, Israel stands at a crossroads. Have they learned anything from their earlier failures, or will they again choose unbelief? Their response is tragic and decisive; they raise a loud cry, weep, and grumble against Moses and Aaron (Num. 14:1–2). They claim that death in Egypt or in the wilderness would have been better than what awaits them in Canaan. Previously they longed nostalgically for Egypt (11:5, 18, 20), but now, for the first time, they resolve to appoint a new leader to take them back there (14:4). Joshua and Caleb plead with them not to rebel but to trust in Yahweh's favor, but the people respond by threatening to stone them. Only Yahweh's sudden appearance at the tabernacle stops them.

Figure 15.2. Fresco of the promised land from the sanctuary of the Greek Catholic Cathedral of Hajdúdorog, Hungary

CANONICAL CONNECTIONS

Let Yahweh's Power Be Great *in This Way*

In Exodus 33:18, Moses asks to see Yahweh's "glory." Yahweh answers by showing him his "goodness," revealing his character as one who judges justly but is overwhelmingly committed to mercy (33:19). While God's power in judgment is on full display often in Numbers, here in Numbers 14 Moses pleads with Yahweh to be true to his character as revealed on Mount Sinai, calling Yahweh to "let the *power* of the LORD be great" in *this specific "way"* (see 14:17–19): by showing mercy in the midst of judgment.

Yahweh's response is severe. From the tabernacle he announces his intent to destroy the people for their unbelief and begin again with Moses and his descendants. As in earlier crises, Moses intercedes, appealing to Yahweh's own self-revelation on Mount Sinai (Num. 14:17–19; cf. Exod. 34:6–7). True to his character, Yahweh forgives, but forgiveness does not erase consequences. Those twenty years old and older will die in the wilderness over a forty-year period, corresponding to the forty days of the spies' mission and to the people's own wish for death (Num. 14:2). The ten spies perish immediately by plague.

The story does not end there. In a final act of presumption, the people try to reverse God's judgment. Defying Moses's warning, they march into Canaan without Yahweh's presence and suffer a crushing defeat (Num. 14:40–45). This ill-fated attack displays the heart of Israel's failure: "Israel still does not take God seriously, or listen to Moses, his appointed representative."[3]

Israel has learned a terrible lesson: Rebellion leads to death. Yet even here, grace glimmers through judgment. The narrative reveals the tension between God's faithfulness and the costly consequences of sin. From the ashes of unbelief new life will emerge. The birth of a new generation will come, but only through the death of the old. Out of death, God brings renewal.[4] For forty years the Israelites will contemplate that truth as they dig graves in the wilderness sand.

INSTRUCTIONS CONCERNING OFFERINGS

Immediately following the devastating rebellion comes a section of law/instruction concerning sacrifices (Num. 15:1–29). The way these laws begin emphasizes that (1) God is determined to continue to reveal himself and his will to the people through Moses, (2) the promise of a land rich in resources is certain, and (3) beyond rebellion the people are able to please Yahweh (15:1–3).

Numbers 15 seems an eclectic mix of material (law/instruction and narrative). The chapter begins with instructions about sacrificial worship (15:1–21). It then specifies how to make sacrificial atonement for unintentional sin (15:22–29) before verses 30–31 transition to dealing with deliberate sin. A brief narrative about a Sabbath breaker follows, and the offender is executed. Contemporary readers may focus on the brutal and seemingly disproportionate nature of this punishment, but in context, the story emphasizes the gravity of deliberate sin (keeping the Sabbath is one of the Ten Commandments), and we should not miss that point.

The chapter ends with the instruction that all the people should sew tassels on the edge of their garments. Much like a wedding ring is a visible reminder for its wearer to act with integrity and fidelity in accordance with their wedding vows, the tassels are to be a constant visible reminder of who the people are, *whose* they are, and how they should conduct themselves. The final words of the chapter affirm God's character and the basis of Israel's existence and ethics: "I am Yahweh your God, who brought you out of the land of Egypt to be your God: I am Yahweh your God" (Num. 15:41 AT).

CANONICAL CONNECTIONS

Paul's Wilderness Warning

Paul's reading of Numbers in 1 Corinthians 10 is jolting. The wilderness stories, he insists, "happened to them to serve as an example, and they were written down to instruct us" (10:11). Israel's cravings, idolatry, and grumbling are warnings so that we will not desire evil as they did (10:6). Numbers is meant to sober us: Even a redeemed people, fresh from God's deliverance, can slide into unbelief and self-destruction.

Yet the warning is not the whole word. Paul pairs it with a promise: "God is faithful, and . . . with the testing he will also provide the way out" (1 Cor. 10:13). Numbers thus becomes a mirror and a shelter, a mirror exposing the ease with which God's people can fall and a shelter assuring us that God himself covers those who seek him in the wilderness.

THEOLOGICAL ISSUES

The Bible's Gift of Brutal Honesty

Brent Strawn notes that "the Old Testament is characterized by a remarkable and at times even unbearable honesty," especially about sin and suffering. While contemporary readers (and preachers!) sometimes belittle Israel for "yet again" failing, Strawn reminds us that "we only know of Israel's sins and failings because Israel was honest enough to tell us about all that."

This honesty is disruptive in the best way. Strawn cites Franz Kafka's famous line that the books we truly need are those that "come upon us like ill-fortune, . . . an ice-axe to break the sea frozen inside us." The Old Testament often works precisely like that: shattering illusions, exposing self-deception, and opening us to God's transforming mercy.[a]

Scripture's candor invites us to do the same, naming our own brokenness truthfully and trusting that God meets us not in our polished versions of ourselves but in the honest ones.

PREROGATIVES OF THE PRIESTS

Numbers 16–18 is a long section bound together by matters relating to the priesthood and legitimate roles/benefits of leadership. Numbers 16 narrates in great detail two challenges to the leadership of Moses and especially Aaron and the outcomes of these challenges. Yahweh reaffirms the legitimacy of Aaron's priestly leadership in Numbers 17, ending any further grumblings against his role. Yahweh then speaks directly to Aaron in Numbers 18, explaining how he will provide for the material needs of the Levites. Careful readers can discern how the events and instructions in this section are interconnected with previous material in Numbers.

Bain News Service photograph / Wikimedia Commons / public domain

Figure 15.3. A young boy wearing a prayer shawl with tassels, standing outside a building, East Side, New York City

The Levite Korah, along with representatives from other tribes, spearheads the first rebellion against Moses and Aaron. Korah charges that Moses and Aaron have wrongly exalted themselves above the people, saying that "all in the congregation are holy, every one of them, and Yahweh is among them" (Num. 16:3 AT). This may be true, but it does not follow that everyone has an equal role, as the opening chapters of Numbers show.

Leaders in any organization or institution are vulnerable to challenges. How they respond requires wisdom as they discern the legitimacy of the claims, keep their own egos in check, and above all prioritize the common good of their organization/institution and its constituents. Moses's response is instructive.[5] First, Moses falls on his face (Num. 16:4) in an act of worship or perhaps intercessory prayer. Second, he summons the challengers to appear publicly and in person. Third, he devises a trial by ordeal (likely in consultation with Yahweh), much like the one in Numbers 5, that would require God to intervene miraculously to vindicate Moses and Aaron. (This is not recommended for leadership

THEOLOGICAL ISSUES

God's Spacious Covenant and the Nations

Numbers 15 deliberately incorporates those not native-born ("aliens," "foreigners," "sojourners"). Foreigners appear six times (15:14, 15, 16, 26, 29, 30) and receive full standing in Israel's worship, even entering the center of the camp to bring sacrifices.

Passover laws (Num. 9:14) already welcomed foreigners, and the invitation to Hobab (10:29–33) shows this was no anomaly. Numbers 15 affirms the theme: Yahweh's covenant life is open, not closed. This inclusion reflects God's global redemptive purposes, which reach their goal in Jesus and gain further impetus in the early church's mission to the nations. The result is the multiethnic people of God that will one day stand in the new creation. Israel's worship in the wilderness thus anticipates the scope of God's saving work, wider than any one ethnicity and oriented toward the nations.

LITERARY NOTES

The Irony of a Consuming Land

There is a certain irony about the land being portrayed in this rebellion story as a beast with a mouth devouring the rebels. We should at this point recall the ten spies in Numbers 13:32 describing the promised land in similar terms.

LITERARY NOTES

Identifying the Place of "Milk and Honey"

When the rebels describe Egypt as a land gushing with milk and honey (Num. 16:13), they deliberately use language reserved for the promised land. The effect is satirical and tragic. They recast a place of crushing slavery as one of abundance and security, and in doing so deny that Yahweh will bring them to the true land of promise.

challenges today!) Fourth, Moses reminds the Levite rebels that God had already given them a special role among the Israelites; they should not despise that high calling by grasping a role that God did not intend for them.

Moses's efforts do nothing to weaken the rebels' resolve. They refuse Moses's summons and deepen their deception, accusing him of leading the people out of safety into death. Moses brings his plea to God, and when God declares judgment on the entire assembly, Moses and Aaron intercede, persuading God to limit the punishment to the instigators of the rebellion and their families (Num. 16:15, 20–21, 24).

The result is that, by a powerful and miraculous act of God, the ground "opened its mouth and swallowed" Korah, Dathan, Abiram, and their households, and fire consumes the 250 rebels who were holding the censers of incense, according to the trial by ordeal (Num. 16:30–35). This prompts all the Israelites to grumble and rebel, as they drastically misinterpret the divine judgment and accuse Moses and Aaron of killing the people of Yahweh (16:41). A divine plague breaks out, and it is only subverted by the swift action of Moses and Aaron. Aaron holds a censer of incense in

Figure 15.4. Mosaic of Aaron's staff

the middle of the assembly, atoning for the people and sparing their lives. Aaron's action prevents the plague from spreading, but only after 14,700 Israelites had succumbed to it (16:46–50).

The rebellion of Numbers 16 was directed especially at Aaron, and his swift action limits the plague's effects. In chapter 17, Yahweh devises a unique trial to confirm Aaron's special role. The twelve tribal chiefs and Aaron were to present their staffs, symbols of their leadership, to be placed in the holy place in front of the ark. Overnight, Aaron's staff alone grows blossoms and produces ripe almonds (17:8). The miracle induces fear in the people and confirms Aaron's rightful role as high priest. His staff, like the charred censers of the previous chapter (16:36–40), was to be kept in the tabernacle as a perpetual reminder to the people of the consequences of their rebellious grumbling (17:10).

Yahweh directs his instructions in Numbers 18 specifically to Aaron. He once again explains the role of the Levites (18:1–7), but the bulk of the chapter stipulates that portions of Israel's offerings and the substance of their tithes would provide for the material needs of the priests and Levites.

INSTRUCTIONS CONCERNING CLEANSING FROM DEATH'S POLLUTING EFFECTS

The chapters preceding Numbers 19 reestablish order after the chaos of rebellion, focusing on priests and Levites as guardians of holiness. Chapter 19 broadens that concern to the entire community, including resident foreigners (19:10).[6] Of all the conditions that could render a person unclean, none was more serious or more contagious than contact with death. As Leviticus teaches, death opposes the life-giving character of God and threatens the purity of his dwelling. With the rebellions in Numbers 11–16, death has entered the camp with fury. The question now is how this defilement can be undone.

Numbers 19 answers with detailed instructions for purification of those who have touched a corpse. The priest involved becomes temporarily unclean through the process, a reminder that even the means of cleansing bear the cost of impurity.[7] The instructions offer warning and grace. Warning, because those who refuse purification are "cut off" from the people, lest they defile the tabernacle (19:13). Grace, because impurity is not permanent: God provides a way for restoration and renewed fellowship. Neglecting holiness threatens the whole community, yet God's mercy ensures that life, not death, will define Israel's life with him.

THEOLOGICAL ISSUES

Death's Defilement and God's Restoring Holiness

Numbers 19 reminds us that death contaminates what God has made good. Our culture alternates between concealing death as something shameful (e.g., hiding it in hospitals, masking it with euphemisms) and glamorizing it (e.g., in violent entertainment or festivals that play with death). Numbers exposes both impulses as distortions: Death is neither trivial nor tame. Yet God provides cleansing and renewal, fulfilled in Christ, whose death and resurrection conquer defilement once for all. God's holiness is not meant to exclude but to restore, calling his people to be a community where life, not decay, defines their common life.

Journey from Kadesh to the Plains of Moab (Num. 20:1–22:1)

READ NUMBERS 20:1–22:1

> Read this section as a continuous journey narrative, noting the mixture of loss, failure, and emerging hope. Ask, How do the deaths of Miriam and Aaron and the failure of Moses shape this moment? What familiar patterns continue, and where do you see signs of renewal? How does this section mark the transition to a new generation?

DEATH AND REBELLION OF ISRAEL'S LEADERS

After the rebellion at Kadesh in Numbers 13–14, Israel has been stalled geographically and spiritually. Chapter 20 marks renewed movement toward the promised land, yet the tone is somber. The deaths of Miriam (20:1) and Aaron (20:22–29) frame the chapter, and between them Moses himself fails in obedience. These three events form a kind of obituary for the first generation of Israel's leaders.

Miriam's death is reported without comment. Though she once rebelled against Moses (Num. 12), the reporting of her death and burial suggests she died as an honored leader, completing her service alongside her brothers.[8] Aaron's death, by contrast, is directly linked to disobedience (20:12, 24). The narrative between these deaths explains why: Moses and Aaron fail to uphold God's holiness before the people.

The story begins with a familiar complaint. At Kadesh the people grumble over the absence of water, lamenting that they ever left Egypt (Num. 20:2–5). The pattern is predictable—complaint, intercession, divine response—but the outcome is unexpected. Yahweh commands Moses to take his staff, assemble the people, and speak to the rock so that it will yield water (20:8). Instead, Moses speaks to the people: "Listen, you rebels, Shall *we* bring water for you out of this rock?" Moses then strikes the rock twice. Water flows, but so does divine displeasure.

Moses's words and actions together betray a failure of trust. By striking the rock rather than speaking to it and by claiming credit for the miracle, Moses misrepresents Yahweh's holiness before the people (Num. 20:12). The one who had so often interceded for others now faces his own judgment. Neither he nor Aaron will enter the land. In the narrative logic of Numbers, the leader's failure mirrors the people's: unbelief, impatience, and presumption remain obstacles between promise and fulfillment.

Between the deaths of Miriam and Aaron comes another setback: Moses's negotiation with the king of Edom fails (Num. 20:14–21). Edom refuses to let Israel pass through their land and threatens war if Israel proceeds. Israel must detour around the territory—a reminder that the road to promise is contested and costly.

CANONICAL CONNECTIONS

When Brothers Become Barriers

In Numbers 20:14 Moses appeals to Edom for passage by invoking kinship, identifying Israel as Edom's "brother" and thus recalling their shared descent from Jacob and Esau. The appeal reaches back to the reconciliation of Genesis 32–33, where the estranged brothers met in peace. But the pattern does not repeat. Esau's descendants reject Israel's request, revealing how ancestral peace does not guarantee future cooperation.

The chapter ends with Aaron's death and the peaceful transfer of priestly authority to his son Eleazar (Num. 20:22–29). On Mount Hor, Moses removes Aaron's garments and places them on Eleazar, a literal passing of the mantle. The people mourn Aaron for thirty days, recognizing the loss of their first high priest. His death, like Miriam's, marks the end of an era. The leadership that carried Israel from Egypt to Sinai now passes away before the next stage of the journey begins.

Even faithful leaders stand under God's judgment. Moses's frustration and self-reliance in this story reveal the toll of leadership under pressure, the weariness that can erode trust even in seasoned servants of God. Yet the narrative also affirms divine faithfulness: God continues his work through a new generation. The hope of Israel does not rest on the endurance of its leaders but on the constancy of the God who journeys with his people.

DIVINE VICTORY AND MORE REBELLION

Numbers 21 opens on a hopeful note. After years of wandering, Israel again advances toward the promised land. Yet the pattern of the wilderness continues: Obedience and divine deliverance are intermingled with rebellion and judgment. The first episode records a military encounter with the Canaanite king of Arad (21:1–3). When some Israelites are captured, the people vow that if Yahweh grants victory, they will devote their enemies to destruction. God hears their plea, grants success, and the place is named Hormah ("destruction"). It is a brief but important episode of faithfulness. The people seek Yahweh's help before acting, and victory follows, a foretaste of what is possible when Israel walks in obedience.

But faith quickly gives way to frustration. As the people journey around Edom, they grow impatient and speak "against God and against Moses," complaining yet again about the scarcity of food and water (Num. 21:5). Their contempt for the daily manna brings divine judgment in the form of venomous snakes. Many people die, and once again Moses intercedes. At Yahweh's command, he fashions a bronze serpent and mounts it on a pole. Those who look at the serpent are healed. The image becomes one of the most enduring symbols in Scripture: deliverance through faith in God's provision rather than escape from consequence. The symbol also speaks a powerful word about the availability of God's salvation "*for those who*

RECEPTION HISTORY

The Bronze Snake

For centuries the bronze serpent has been associated with healing. The medical emblem of a snake coiled around a staff recalls this ancient image. Later biblical writers revisit the Numbers 21 account with new depth: Hezekiah destroys the object when it becomes an idol (2 Kings 18:4), and Jesus evokes it in conversation with Nicodemus: "Just as Moses lifted up the serpent in the wilderness, so must the Son of Man be lifted up" (John 3:14–15). In each context the meaning is the same: Life comes not from the symbol itself but from the gracious God who provides the cure.

will take advantage of it. . . . We have only to look up and live."[9]

The remainder of the chapter narrates Israel's growing momentum. At Yahweh's direction, they journey northward, and their victories over two powerful kings contrast sharply with their earlier defeat after the spies' rebellion (Num. 14:40–45). The new generation trusts God's word and experiences his deliverance. Between these accounts the people twice break into song, celebrating Yahweh's gift of water (21:17–18) and his triumph over the Amorites (21:27–30). The wilderness, once the setting for complaint, becomes a place of praise.

Together these scenes mark a turning point in Numbers. A new generation is emerging, one capable of faith and gratitude. The bronze serpent reminds them and us that healing comes by turning in trust toward God's merciful provision. The wilderness has not provided much to inspire singing, but the spontaneous composition of songs sounds a hopeful note as Israel continues its journey to the promised land. The wilderness of rebellion begins to give way to the firstfruits of renewal.

Figure 15.5. *The Bronze Serpent Raised by Moses in the Desert* by Andrea Vicentino

On the Plains of Moab (Num. 22:2–36:13)

READ NUMBERS 22:2–36:13

Read this section in one sitting, if possible, tracing the movement from blessing to failure to renewal. Pay attention to how God's purposes persist despite Israel's rebellion. Ask, How do Balaam's oracles shape Israel's identity? What happens at Peor, and why is it so devastating? How does the new generation begin to take shape as they prepare for life in the land?

BALAAM BLESSES ISRAEL

In Numbers 22–24, the Israelites have finally settled on the plains of Moab, their last stop before crossing the Jordan River into the promised land (see Josh. 3:1). The rest of the Pentateuch takes place at this location. Here, for the first time in Numbers, the narrative shifts focus away from the Israelite camp to a kind of narrative interlude that is vital for Israel's fate among the nations. With Israel unaware, sinister forces work to ensure their demise, while God is at work circumventing these evil forces.

When King Balak of Moab hears distressing reports of the Israelites' sound defeat of the Amorites (Num. 21:31–35), his people have "great dread" and "fear" of the Israelites, calling them a "horde" and saying that they are licking up their enemies as an "ox licks up the grass of the field" (22:3–4). Recognizing that no human effort will be sufficient to stop the Israelites, Balak, at great effort and cost, summons Balaam, the most renowned seer of the Middle East, to curse the Israelites.[10] What actually happens is that Balaam ends up blessing Israel instead.

The narrative of Balaam blessing Israel is a carefully crafted piece of work. Filled with irony and humor, it prophetically establishes the future blessing of Israel in the face of dark forces. However, the account also raises a number of questions for readers, ancient and modern. First, how does Balaam, a Mesopotamian diviner, know Yahweh, invoke him by name, have access to his expressed counsel, and even become filled by his spirit? The narrative does not address this, but it is clear that Balaam, not unlike Moses, is in lockstep with Yahweh. He acts only after consulting with Yahweh, and he speaks only the words given by Yahweh—facts the narrative seems at pains to emphasize. God's international purposes are again on display.

Second, why does God get angry at Balaam for going with Balak's delegation immediately after God told him to go (Num. 22:20–22)? There is mystery here, but this is not the only instance of its kind. Jacob (Gen. 32:22–32), Moses (Exod. 4:24), and Joshua (Josh. 5:13) all encounter some kind of opposition from God in the very act of attempting to do his expressed will.[11]

God is completely other, and these strange situations demonstrate that the human mind cannot always comprehend the mysteries of the divine will. It may be, as Roy Gane suggests, that, like the events at Kibroth-hattaavah when Yahweh provided quail for the people and then sent a plague while the people were gorging themselves on the meat (Num. 11:31–35), Balaam's permission to go was a test to see if he shows restraint or even resistance.[12] If this is correct, Balaam fails the test since he wastes no time in going with the Moabite princes; perhaps he cares more about his fee than discerning the divine will. This third encounter with God does one thing for Balaam. His near-death experience impresses on him that, whatever his motivations for partnering with the Moabites, he cannot circumvent the divine will. He is putty in God's hand, ready to speak God's words.[13]

Third, does Balaam's interaction with Yahweh mean he is holy—or to put it another way, is Balaam a sinner or a saint? In the Bible we encounter few impeccable saints and few irredeemable sinners. At best, we are all flawed instruments in the Redeemer's hand. While the text repeats that Balaam speaks only what Yahweh permits (Num. 22:18, 38; 23:3, 12, 17, 26; 24:2, 13), it also reveals other questionable aspects of Balaam's character. The references to his fee demonstrate Balaam's reputation as an opportunistic prophet-for-hire who will say anything for gold and glory (22:7, 17–18; 24:11–12). Moreover, he charges for divination and omen-seeking, spiritual practices that were historically prohibited for God's people. If that is not enough, the comical incident with his donkey casts Balaam as more stubborn, dull, and blind than his ass! Which raises another tricky question.

Did Balaam's donkey really talk? Our experience tells us that animals cannot speak. Talking beasts are the stuff of fairytales, children's stories, and fantasy literature, aren't they? Numbers 22:28 says Yahweh opened the donkey's mouth, and a dialogue between Balaam and the donkey follows as though it is a most natural thing. Balaam himself seems utterly unfazed by his articulate beast. Readers today might get sidetracked by this bizarre incident, but a better question than how this is possible is, What is the function of the talking donkey in this narrative? Ultimately, the incident shows the irony of the situation: Balaam the superprophet who can miraculously discern the mysteries of the universe cannot see imminent danger at the appearance of the angel of Yahweh and requires the spiritual insight of his beast of burden to perceive what is right in front of him.

LITERARY NOTES

When Animals Speak

The only talking animal in Scripture before Numbers 22 is the serpent in Eden (Gen. 3). There, the creature is *crafty*, and its deceptive words plant doubt, spark rebellion, and "open" the eyes of Adam and Eve, leading to shame, alienation, and death. In Numbers 22, the contrast is sharp. Balaam's donkey is the symbol of a notoriously stubborn, unimpressive beast. Yet this time the animal sees clearly while the human is blind. The donkey's actions alone cannot avert disaster; it must speak. And when it does, its truthful words *open Balaam's eyes* and save his life.

In Eden, listening to an animal leads humanity into death; in the wilderness, listening to an animal saves a life and returns a prophet to obedience.

Museum of Fine Arts, Houston / public domain

Figure 15.6. *The Prophet Balaam and the Angel* by John Linnell (1859)

Compare the language and themes of Balaam's oracles in chapters 23 and 24 with the promises of God to Abraham in Genesis 12:1–3. Identify and jot down in a journal as many connections as you can.

Balaam's interactions with the Moabite messengers, with God, with his donkey, and with Balak provide a relatively long and detailed preface that heightens the anticipation of the main event: Balaam's prophetic words about Israel. What will Balaam say about Israel, camped below him and ignorant of all of this? Balaam's prophetic oracles come in waves (interspersed with the building of altars and offering of sacrifices and Balak's increasing frustration). Set on high places overlooking the Israelite camp, Balaam offers four oracles (Num. 23:7–10, 18–24; 24:3–9, 15–24). The prophecies build on each other, reaching a climax in the fourth. They deliberately echo the promises Yahweh made to Abraham in Genesis 12:1–3 and reaffirmed throughout the Pentateuch—promises that Abraham's descendants will become a powerful and numerous nation, have a relationship of mutual blessing with God and the nations, and be given a prosperous and secure home in the promised land.

What is the function of the Balaam narrative in Numbers? Olson says the story is strategically positioned between the end of the first generation (chap. 25) and the beginning of the new generation (chap. 26): "Through the mouth of a foreign prophet, God blesses Israel with accolades and promises that are unsurpassed in the rest of the Pentateuch. The oracles point to a future time of well-being, strength, victory and hope."[14] Yet the placement of this story also exposes Israel's vulnerability. On the plains of Moab, between wilderness and promise, the people are unaware that spiritual forces are at work against them. Their own history of rebellion has made them fragile, and in that fragility unseen powers conspire for their ruin. The Balaam narrative reveals that God's protection extends beyond what his people can perceive. God acts above and beyond them to turn cursing into blessing. There is hope for Israel beyond the liminal space of the wilderness, and the Balaam story strengthens that hope: God will do all that he promised for his people.

NATIONAL APOSTASY

Whereas Balaam's oracles of blessing mark the highest point in Numbers, the next chapter opens with a devastating reversal. In Numbers 25 the narrative shifts from the cliffs overlooking Israel's camp (chaps. 22–24) to the camp itself (chap. 25). Previously the people had rebelled against their leaders and tested Yahweh's patience, but here, for the first time, they turn openly to another god: the Baal of Peor. There at Shittim, the last of that generation dies as they lived, defiant and unrepentant.

The narrative suggests that Israel enters into a covenant relationship with foreign nations (Moab and Midian), engages in prostitution with their women, and ultimately worships their god. A chief from the tribe of Simeon brings a Midianite woman to the center of the camp, near the tabernacle itself, where the two of them likely engage in sexual relations. Phinehas, son of the new high priest, acts decisively and impales the embracing couple with his spear. This bloody act constrains God's punishment, but not before a plague has wiped out twenty-four thousand people. There is even ambiguity surrounding the actions of Moses in this chapter; it's not clear whether he acted according to Yahweh's instructions (Num. 25:4–5). Things have spiraled out of control and the structure of the camp, society, and chain of command so deliberately established in the opening chapters of Numbers has disintegrated into chaos. Wilderness experiences are liminal spaces with the potential to affect spiritual formation. The incident with Baal of Peor reveals the dark underbelly of this truth. For the rebels who died, the wilderness was a place of spiritual deformation, a place where they aligned with false gods. The wilderness exposes where true allegiances lie.

LITERARY NOTES

Bookends of Idolatry

The only other instance of such direct idolatry in the Pentateuch is the golden calf episode at Sinai (Exod. 32), and the parallels with the Baal of Peor episode are important. In both scenes the people engage in illicit worship at the very center of Israel's life, leaders falter or stand confused, and swift judgment exposes their divided allegiance. Together the golden calf and Baal of Peor form tragic bookends around the old generation, revealing a generation unable to sustain covenant fidelity.[b]

THE SECOND CENSUS

From this lowest point in Israel's wilderness journey, Numbers 26 signals a dramatic turning of the page with the book's second census. From this point forward, complaint and rebellion disappear; conflicts are resolved through peaceful diplomacy; new laws anticipate life in the land; and not a single death is recorded.[15] The plague that claimed twenty-four thousand lives at the incident with Baal of Peor brought closure to the old, rebellious generation. The census of chapter 26, deliberately echoing the words and ordering of the first census in Numbers 1, announces a new beginning. The nation stands renewed, counted once more by name, and ready to inherit what God promised.

The total count of the second census is very near the same number of people as in the first census. The rebellion of the first generation took a costly toll, but God's sustaining hand in the wilderness has ensured the vitality of his people.[16] While the purpose for the second census seems at first glance to be identical to the first census—namely, to prepare Israel for military action—Yahweh himself says the second counting is to ensure the equitable distribution of the land (Num. 26:52–56). This census looks forward to the settling in the promised land. The chapter ends by saying that not a single Israelite from the rebellious generation was counted in this census, except Joshua and Caleb, providing what Olson calls "a programmatic summary of the structure of Numbers. The second census list is both a sign of the completed judgment on the first generation and a sign of God's promise for a new generation."[17]

INSTRUCTIONS ABOUT LAND, LEADERSHIP, OFFERINGS, AND VOWS

After the census of the new generation, Numbers 27–30 issue a series of divine instructions that may seem only loosely connected. These include laws about land inheritance prompted by the daughters of Zelophehad (27:1–11), the transfer of leadership from Moses to Joshua (27:12–23), detailed regulations for offerings at the appointed times in Israel's calendar (28:1–29:40), and laws governing

Figure 15.7. The daughters of Zelophehad

vows and the circumstances under which they may be released (30:1–16). These laws look ahead to settled life in the land, where questions of inheritance, leadership, worship, and faithfulness will shape a flourishing covenant community. What may appear to be miscellaneous laws are in fact signs that God is forming a people ready to live in the presence of their faithful King.

The dispute over land inheritance rights prompted by the daughters of Zelophehad is a subtle reminder that the tragic death of the old generation had implications for all survivors. When these brotherless daughters who lost their father and most likely their mother bring their complaint to Moses, careful readers of Numbers may expect their complaint to be like others in the book: rebellious. But this is the new generation, and this complaint is justified; it expresses a longing for future blessing in the land, with no sense of looking back to Egypt with twisted nostalgia. The daughters bring their complaint to Moses, who brings it to Yahweh, who widens the expanse of the inheritance laws to provide for brotherless daughters. This is the paradigm for how disputes and complaints should be handled in the wilderness and beyond, and it contributes to a sense of hope for life in the land. As we saw in chapter 8, biblical law offers a kind of wise, just precedent from the past that can be applied to new situations.

Similarly, God's instructions for the transfer of leadership from Moses to Joshua look ahead to Israel's continued blessing when Moses is gone. These instructions come at Moses's request when Yahweh allows him to see the promised land from afar and reminds him that he will not enter because of his rebellion. Again, we might expect Moses to protest ("My punishment is unfair") or to plead for mercy ("Forgive me and let me lead the people into the promised land"). But Israel's servant leader thinks only of the people's well-being, and he only requests that God appoint a worthy leader (a shepherd; Num. 27:17) to ensure Israel's safe passage to the land. It is a good request, and God grants it, giving instructions for how Joshua, a proven man of integrity, should take up Moses's mantle. Land for the fatherless daughters of Zelophehad and a guide for the soon-to-be leaderless nation, both from the gracious hand of Yahweh—things are looking up for this new generation!

Numbers 28–29 outline instructions for offerings associated with various days, weeks, and months of the Israelite calendar. These instructions serve several purposes in context. The ritual offerings require a substantial number of livestock and a generous amount of wine, grain or flour, and oil.[18] Yahweh is making costly demands, but these laws assume a life of overwhelming prosperity in the land and remind the people of the costly endeavor of dwelling with a holy God. Moreover, arranged as they are in this section, these offerings deliberately structure the rhythms of Israelite life.[19] Just as the instructions in Numbers 2–4 (after the first census) arrange Israelite society *spatially* to reflect the order of Yahweh, so the instructions in Numbers 28–29 (after the second census) arrange Israelite society *temporally* to reflect the same reality. The offerings provide the Israelites daily, weekly, monthly, and yearly reminders of who they are and what Yahweh had done (and was doing) for them. Both the spatial and the temporal functioned as constant memory-inducing and thereby identity-forming structures for the people.

From the regulations for offerings, Numbers 30 moves to instructions about making and keeping vows. Apart from the opening verses, which affirm that anyone who makes a vow to the Lord must fulfill it, the chapter focuses on situations in which a woman's vow may be confirmed or annulled. For today's readers, these provisions can sound uneven, reflecting a world in which men held primary economic and legal responsibility within the household. The laws do not seek to establish or promote that patriarchal structure; rather, they assume it and work within it to ensure accountability within the realities of their time. They acknowledge the communal implications of a vow: A promise made to God could carry material consequences for others in the household. The deeper concern, as Olson observes, is not hierarchy but faithfulness: "The laws in chapter 30 delineate who is ultimately responsible for any vow that is spoken. An unfulfilled vow threatened the holiness of the community, and thus it was important that the community be clear about which vows were valid and who was responsible for fulfilling them."[20] Numbers 30 connects the daily commitments of individuals to Israel's larger covenant story. Just as Yahweh fulfills his promise to Abraham and the patriarchs, so the people are called to keep their own vows with integrity before the God who keeps his.[21]

DEFEAT OF MIDIAN AND SETTLEMENT IN TRANSJORDAN

Numbers 31–32 recount challenges that the new generation faces in the wilderness, in community, and under the rule of Yahweh. Both chapters raise difficult questions, while also demonstrating that the second generation confronts such challenges in different ways than the faithless and rebellious first generation.

In Numbers 31, the Israelites undertake a divinely commanded battle against the Midianites, judgment for their role in leading Israel into apostasy with Baal of Peor. The account of the battle takes only two verses (31:7–8); it is the surrounding narrative that makes sense of the battle. The people prepare at Yahweh's command, they carry out the instructions faithfully, and the campaign ends in total success: "Not one of [the Israelites] is missing" (31:49). Within the flow of Numbers, this episode is a final demonstration of obedience. Where the earlier generation faltered, the new generation follows Yahweh's word precisely, and the result is victory rather than defeat.

Yet, this passage raises difficult questions. The killing of the Midianite men, and later of the women and boys, is disturbing and should not be explained away (Num. 31:7–11, 15–18).[22] A fuller exploration of how to read such violent texts appears in chapter 13, "How to Read Violent Texts Today," which situates the conquest within its ancient context and within the Bible's larger movement toward peace and reconciliation. Here in Numbers, it is enough to observe that (1) the killing of the women and boys is Moses's idea rather than God's, leaving a gap for a possible critique of Moses;[23] (2) the narrative likely contains the kind of hyperbole that characterizes such ancient descriptions of violence (see chap. 13); (3) the narrative portrays judgment, not conquest for gain; and (4) the narrative shows that even a divinely sanctioned war brings impurity requiring cleansing (31:19–20).[24]

This paradox—obedience that defiles—shapes the story's theological center. The campaign demonstrates that holiness is not achieved through violence and that even faithful action can leave a residue that must be cleansed. The meticulous purification rites, the measured distribution of spoils, and the offering of a portion back to Yahweh (Num. 31:50) all reinforce that lesson. God's people cannot engage in death-dealing acts, even when commanded, without confronting the moral and spiritual cost.

Israel's faithfulness in Numbers 31 is not a celebration of violence but a testimony to God's capacity to bring order out of chaos and purity out of defilement. The chapter is a warning and a reassurance; the holiness of God is unbending, yet his mercy still makes a way for a flawed people to continue the journey toward promise.

In Numbers 32 the tribes of Reuben and Gad make a request of Moses: They want to remain and settle in territory east of the Jordan River and outside the promised land. Moses interprets their request as fearful rebellion akin to the rebellion of the first generation who refused to enter the promised land because of the military might of the inhabitants (Num. 13–14). The Reubenites and Gadites clarify that they intend to send their fighting men to participate in the land's conquest; this is not fearful rebellion. Moses permits them to settle in the land east of Canaan if they remain faithful to their commitment. The tribes of Reuben and Gad have been allotted their land and have found their home. Their somewhat-limited success is a foretaste of what awaits the other tribes in the promised land.[25]

Figure 15.8. *Reuben and Gad Ask for Land* by Arthur Boyd Houghton

After the second census, God's people continue to face challenges. However, their responses to these challenges contrast with those of the faithless first generation. This alternative way of confronting and overcoming such difficulties shows us a new generation of hope.

LIST OF CAMPSITES

By the end of Numbers, the people are geographically and symbolically close to the promised land. The wilderness is fulfilling its purpose, forming a people purified by testing and prepared for promise. Numbers 33 pauses to survey the journey so far, listing the campsites from the time they left Egypt to their present location on the plains of Moab, including locations not previously mentioned. Interspersed in the list are encouragements and warnings as the Israelites begin their final steps to the promised land, their home. Chapter 33 ends with Yahweh's instructions concerning the land's inhabitants and their religious practices, as well as the equitable distribution of the land—namely, larger tribes will receive larger portions and smaller tribes, smaller portions.

MORE INSTRUCTIONS CONCERNING LAND

Numbers 34–36, the last three chapters of the book, include more instructions about land and life in Canaan and continue the hopeful note from previous chapters. After the instructions for equitable distribution of the land in chapter 33, Numbers 34 defines the boundaries of the land of Canaan that the people will divide and occupy. Yahweh then names the tribal leaders who will oversee the land's equitable apportioning. Just as he had done for the Israelite camp, Yahweh establishes just structures for life in the land. Moreover, the list of tribal leaders is one of three that appears in the book of Numbers: (1) at the outset of the journey from Sinai in Numbers 1, (2) at the borders of Canaan the first time when the people rebelled in Numbers 13, and (3) now here at the border again as Israel is ready to enter the land. These lists mark the beginning, middle, and end of the book and indicate key turning points.[26]

The instructions in Numbers 35 concern the land allotments with respect to the Levites. Because of their special role, the Levites do not receive an allotment, but they do need cities to live in and pastureland for the livestock from the people's offerings. Yahweh makes specific provisions for these, but the Levitical cities will also serve another purpose. They will be cities of refuge, scattered among the various tribes, for those who commit manslaughter (35:6). By this point in Numbers and the Pentateuch, we know the seriousness of death and its threat to the integrity of the society. Moreover, it has seemed clear that those responsible for the death of another person must forfeit their own lives. Why then does God provide places of refuge for those who have caused the death of another?

The rest of the chapter (Num. 35:9–34) distinguishes between manslaughter (i.e., death caused by another unintentionally or by accident) and murder (i.e., death caused by malicious intent). The cities of refuge were sanctuaries for those guilty of bloodshed without intent, places of mercy amid justice. Yet the taking of life, however accidental, left a mark. The manslayer was to live within the city's bounds until the death of the high priest, whose own passing signified the restoration of life and freedom. Murderers, however, would not be eligible for such protection and must receive a sentence of capital punishment. The seriousness and finality of such a sentence stipulate that a murderer may be sentenced only on the testimony of at least two witnesses. Wenham says it well: "Death, especially violent human death, pollutes the land and makes it impossible for God to dwell there. This is why homicide must be taken so seriously. An even worse disaster for the nation than a human death would be for God to forsake it (35:33–34)."[27]

Numbers ends with a second appearance of the daughters of Zelophehad, asking for additional information on their unique situation (Num. 36). Although this may seem an unusual and anticlimactic way to end the book, the circumstances of this request follow the logic of the preceding chapters. Given the boundaries of the land and its equitable distribution among the tribes (chap. 34), and given that these brotherless, orphaned females will receive a portion of the land (27:1–11), what will happen to their portion of land should they marry husbands from another tribe? Without clarity on this matter, the daughters rightly imagine a situation where their tribal possession could transfer to another tribe, such that the tribal territories become muddled and lose their integrity.[28] The daughters are asking for clarity not out of self-interest but out of the interest of the community's social and geographic integrity. The divine verdict holds freedom and order together: The daughters may marry whomever they wish, yet their inheritance must stay within their father's tribe. (As it happened, they did marry within their own clan, making the exception unnecessary but ensuring clarity for generations to come.)

The book of Numbers concludes by recalling its opening words: "These are the commandments and the rules that Yahweh commanded through Moses to the people of Israel in the plains of Moab by the Jordan at Jericho" (Num. 36:13 AT). Oh, how far the people have come since the opening verse of Numbers, where they were still camped at Sinai, fresh out of Egyptian slavery. Two details in this closing verse indicate that the wilderness story, indeed the story of the Pentateuch, is not yet resolved. Most importantly, the people are still on the "wrong" side of the Jordan; they are still in the wilderness and outside the promised land. Numbers has concluded but without the proper ending of the story. Secondly, Moses is still alive. While no one wants to hear the account of the death of Israel's beloved and long-suffering leader, as long as Moses is alive the story cannot reach its conclusion. In terms of the story of the Pentateuch, Moses will be the central actor in Deuteronomy as he and his audience take stock of where they have been, where they are, and where they are about to go with Yahweh's help.

Living the Text

Numbers follows God's people in the wilderness. Most of us will spend time in the wilderness as well. Seasons of uncertainty, loss, transition, or cultural upheaval function like wilderness spaces. They strip us down, expose our fears, and force us to ask who we trust. With its stories from long ago, Numbers offers a compass for the in-between, orienting us to how God forms his people when familiar structures fall away.

Becoming in the Wilderness

Having language for our experience often helps us discern what God is doing. In Numbers, the wilderness is a liminal space, a threshold between what was and what will be. Anthropologists were the first to explore the idea of liminality (from *limen*, "threshold"), but it's an idea that captures something deeply human and theological. Carmen Imes gives helpful examples of liminality: A couple stands poised between singleness and marriage during their wedding ceremony; a pregnant woman lives in the tension of being already and not yet a mother; a university student occupies the space between dependence and adult vocation.[29] Some liminal spaces are not chosen at all, such as a cancer diagnosis, a job loss, or adolescence. Liminality names the in-between. We are no longer what we were, but we're not yet what we will be. This is rarely an easy space to navigate. Individual wilderness seasons shape us deeply, but Numbers invites us to widen the lens: God is not only at work in private trials but also in the collective upheavals that form (or deform) his people as a whole.

Christians in the West now inhabit a liminal landscape. The collapse of Christendom has placed many churches between worlds: Old certainties have faded, and new cultural norms sit uneasily with Christian faith. For generations, the dominant Western church held cultural power; now it finds itself increasingly marginalized, misunderstood, ignored, or mistrusted. Whereas Israel entered the wilderness after a long period of oppression, the Western church is entering it after a long period of comfort and cultural power. Nostalgia may be tempting, but longing for a past that feels safer is rarely faithful. It is often simply another way of longing for Egypt. Many of the fractures now visible (e.g., tribalism, fear, defensiveness, an inability to handle difference) did not emerge overnight. They were present long before, but cultural privilege concealed them. Now hardship is exposing what comfort hid. Some of the disorientation we feel in a post-Christian age reflects patterns the Western church nurtured for generations, distortions that remained hidden when the church held cultural power but are now revealed in the wilderness.

Figure 15.9. *The Libyan Desert* by Robert Kay (1943)

Israel's wilderness nostalgia was tragically misplaced. They remembered bondage as comfort. The church's nostalgia is different but no less distorting. Many remember periods of cultural influence as seasons of faithfulness, even though that influence was often entangled with injustice and culturally accepted idolatry. Liminal experiences expose how easily we idealize arrangements God may be dismantling for our good. Like Israel, some may be tempted to long for what was. But like Israel, we are all invited to receive the wilderness as a gift, an unmasking of false security and an opening toward dependence, repentance, and renewal.

Formation or Deformation?

The wilderness can form us or deform us. The difference lies in our posture. Numbers 11–25 shows Israel pulled in two directions. Sometimes they longed for Egypt, recasting bondage as security. Other times they reached for Canaan's gods, seeking belonging and prosperity on terms that contradicted the covenant (as with Baal of Peor). These twin temptations, nostalgia for the past and assimilation to the present, turned a place meant for formation into a graveyard of unbelief.

In a post-Christian context, the church faces similar pressures. We may idealize a past that mixed real faithfulness with real injustice. Or we may drift toward uncritical assimilation, baptizing the cultural gods of our age: political absolutism and tribalism, expressive individualism, consumerism, or relevance at any cost. One looks backward in fear; the other blends in out of anxiety. Both obscure the distinctive way of righteousness and holiness that Yahweh calls his people to live.

Yet wilderness seasons can become moments of holy reorientation. They invite us to relinquish false securities, resist mirroring the surrounding culture, whether through nostalgia or accommodation, and recover God's deeper work of formation: humility, holiness, hope, courage, and love of neighbor.

Attending to the Voice That Forms

Numbers moves between two refrains. Early on, at Sinai, "Yahweh spoke. . . . And the people did as Yahweh commanded." Once the people leave the mountain, a new refrain emerges: "And the people complained." Their complaining spirit drowned out their attentiveness to God's voice. By the book's end, however, a new generation emerges, one more ready to listen, trust, and move toward God's promise. Numbers shows that formation or deformation hinges on which voice God's people listen to.

So it is in our post-Christian wilderness. The loudest voices around us, like fear, outrage, nostalgia, grievance, can easily suffocate our capacity to hear God. It is sobering how readily many Christians can articulate their political tribe's agenda, repeat cable-news talking points, or echo their favorite podcast host, yet struggle to recount the saving acts of God, the mission of Christ, or the teachings of Scripture. When this happens, outrage becomes the spirit that forms us. But outrage cannot grow love, joy, peace, patience, kindness, goodness, faithfulness, gentleness, or self-control (Gal. 5:22–23). Only the Spirit can. Others respond with anxious withdrawal, retreating into cynicism or self-protection rather than engaging with hopeful discipleship. In the noise, we forget the way of the Lamb, Jesus, who commands enemy-love (Matt. 5:44; Luke 6:27–36), cultivates integrity (Matt. 23:25–28), withdraws to hear the Father's voice so he can reenter the world with mercy (Matt. 14:23; Mark 1:35; Luke 5:16), and summons us to follow him on this cross-shaped path (Mark 8:34–35; Luke 9:23).

In a noisy world, attention is a battleground. Practices of listening and attentiveness, including Scripture meditation, listening prayer, aspects of corporate worship, and communal discernment matter because they train us to recognize and be mindful of God's presence.

Numbers invites us to become a community that listens attentively to God so that our perspective on past, present, and future is reshaped by his. The past becomes neither false nostalgia nor paralyzing shame but a testimony to God's faithfulness. The present is framed not by fear but by God's sustaining presence. And the future is not a human utopia or a return to what was but the fulfillment of God's promises. Such listening forms a people shaped by hope and by God's call, a people able to walk through the wilderness not as those who are lost but as those who are led.

Ultimately, the wilderness will either unmake us or remake us. What determines the outcome is the voice we choose to follow. For the Western church, this liminal moment may be God's severe mercy, an invitation to relinquish old idolatries, to repent of misshapen patterns, and to be formed again as a people who trust God more than the comforts they have lost.

Deuteronomy 1–11

Pledging Allegiance to the Divine King

Orientation

Deuteronomy is in the running for the "Most Important Old Testament Book Award." It brings a climactic conclusion to the Pentateuch,[1] inaugurates the story that runs from Joshua through Kings, and serves as an essential dialogue partner for the prophets.[2] It arguably stands at the center of Old Testament theology[3] and is one of the most quoted books in the New Testament.[4] When Jesus is asked about the greatest commandment, he quotes Deuteronomy (Matt. 22:37). In the wilderness, he counters the devil's temptations by citing Deuteronomy three times. Think of that! Deuteronomy provided the Lord with a one-sentence summary of his Father's way and an arsenal of weapons to resist the Evil One.

Wikimedia Commons / public domain

Figure 16.1. This image first appeared in a complete text of the Bible in Latin, produced in AD 870. This scene introduced the book of Deuteronomy.

But Deuteronomy is also strange. By the end of Numbers, everything is set for the book of Joshua, where the Israelites finally enter the promised land. All that remains is for Moses to die![5] Instead, Scripture interrupts the story to give us "these words" that Moses spoke "on the other side of the Jordan" (Deut. 1:1 AT). He starts talking in verse 5 and hardly stops till the end of the book. Many of "these words" revisit ground already explored in the Pentateuch, raising the questions, What is Deuteronomy? And what role does it play in the Torah?

What Is Deuteronomy? Why Does It Matter for How We Read It?

Scholars offer multiple lenses for viewing Deuteronomy. Each has implications for understanding what Deuteronomy offers.

DEUTERONOMY AS FAREWELL SERMON

An important clue to one lens lies in the Hebrew name of the book, *debarim*, "words." Deuteronomy mainly consists of Moses's words just before his death and the people's long-awaited entrance into the land. These words take the form of four sermons. The sermons are marked with similar language, resulting in the following overarching structure:

- First Heading (1:1–5)
  - Remember Where You've Come From: First Sermon (1:6–4:43)
- Second Heading (4:44–49)
  - Cling to Yahweh's Covenantal Way: Second Sermon (5:1–28:68)
- Third Heading (29:1)
  - Choose Life! Third Sermon (29:2–32:52)
- Fourth Heading (33:1)
  - Receive Yahweh's Blessing: Fourth Sermon (33:2–29)[6]
- Postscript: Moses's Death (34:1–12)

However, the second, long sermon can be subdivided into subsections that begin at 5:1; 6:1; and 12:1. For our purposes in what follows, we will first consider major themes in the opening of the book through the end of chapter 11, before turning to chapters 12 through 34 in the next chapter.

In Deuteronomy, Moses speaks like a passionate preacher, artfully calling his congregation to "choose life!" (30:19). Like many preachers, Moses is a consummate storyteller, embracing repetition to emphasize key points and regularly upending the congregation's expectations. Like many preachers in the Black church tradition, Moses starts singing toward the end of his message, using "music to do the ministry of proclamation" in the Song of Moses (chap. 32).[7]

Within the book's literary context, the "you" to whom Moses preaches are the Israelites preparing to enter the land. At this monumental turning point in Israel's history, Moses calls this "you" to respond to his words "today." For Moses's deuteronomic sermons, the time is now.

Yet much of Moses's preaching recounts stories from Israel's history: their liberation from Egypt, their encounter with God at Sinai (Horeb in Deuteronomy), and their wilderness wanderings. The "today" of

Deuteronomy is crucial to Moses because Israel is entering a new phase of life with God. His sermons equip Israel for their future by calling them to remember their past.

THEOLOGICAL ISSUES

Walking Backward into the Future

A famous Māori proverb is often translated as "I walk backwards into the future with my eyes fixed on my past." According to Lesley Rameka, this "speaks to Māori perspectives of time, where the past, the present and the future are viewed as intertwined"; one "does not leave the past behind; rather one carries one's past into the future."[a] Deuteronomy likewise equips the people to walk backward into their future with God, their eyes fixed on his liberating love and presence with them in the past.

One major threat Moses addresses is *forgetting*. Moses repeatedly warns the people to guard themselves in order that they might not forget—forget "the things that your eyes have seen" (Deut. 4:9); forget their covenant with Yahweh and turn to idols (4:23); forget Yahweh himself (6:12; 8:14; 32:18), not least by "failing to keep his commandments" (8:11; 26:13); forget their sad history of rebellion (9:7). Conversely, Moses calls Israel to *remember*—remember they were enslaved and Yahweh brought them out (5:15; 16:3, 12; 24:18, 22); remember what Yahweh did to Pharaoh and the Egyptians (7:18); remember their long difficult journey in the wilderness (8:2); remember their rebellion against God (9:7; 24:9); remember Yahweh himself (8:18).

A. J. Culp suggests that what makes Deuteronomy unique is not that it emphasizes memory but that it *commands* memory. The present generation must work to remember Deuteronomy's claims and, what's more, must pass on this memory to future generations. Moses's sermon is about making memory.[8]

How will Israel's sacred cultural or collective memory be carried forward from generation to generation? The rhetoric of Moses's sermon offers one answer. Moses knows most of the generation that escaped Egypt has died, yet he speaks to his audience as if *they* had been liberated from Egypt and had met with God at Horeb. Indeed, Moses even proclaims it was *not* with the ancestors that Yahweh made the covenant but with "all of us here alive today" (Deut. 5:3–5). Factually speaking, this is untrue. But this contradiction is part of Moses's strategy to cultivate a cultural memory that shapes generation after generation.[9] Moses's preaching makes Israel's past contemporary, weaving the present generation into Israel's story. Indeed, to hear Moses preach it, today, every day, *we* stand on the banks of the Jordan at the moment of decision, poised between the promise of our God-given inheritance and the fulfillment of that promise in a consummated life with him.[10] The power and urgency of these sermons increase when we recognize these sermons are Moses's last words, his deathbed challenge.

DEUTERONOMY AS DISCIPLESHIP PROGRAM

Forming lives of faithful remembering requires more than words. That's why Deuteronomy includes a program for embodied discipleship that helps God's people become the covenant partners they're called to be.

Deuteronomy does not simply tell Israel about Yahweh's great acts of liberation; Deuteronomy's festival calendar requires the Israelites to ritually reenact that liberation story. Deuteronomy does not merely offer Yahweh's guidance to Israel; it requires God's people to meditate on that instruction and to write it on memorial stones and the doorposts of their houses. Deuteronomy does not simply warn Israel not to forget; Deuteronomy teaches the people a song to sing that will bear witness against them if they do.[11]

DEUTERONOMY AS PUBLIC THEOLOGY

The English title "Deuteronomy" comes from the Greek translation of the Hebrew Bible, the Septuagint, and means "second law." This designation acknowledges Deuteronomy's massive law collection in chapters 12–26. This law collection is a *second* law because it comes after the earlier law collections in the Pentateuch and engages and adapts them. Whereas the law collections of Exodus and Leviticus are given by Yahweh at Sinai, here Moses *teaches* Yahweh's law in a new place and in a new way.

Both the stories and law collections should also be understood as a covenant. Deuteronomy even seems to intentionally mimic the political covenants formed between more powerful kings (known as suzerains) and subordinate kings within their empires (known as vassals). Gordon Wenham suggests that Deuteronomy's structures have been influenced by Hittite treaties from 1500 to 1200 BC:[12]

Hittite Treaties	Deuteronomy
Historical prologue (describing the past relationship of the two kings)	Deuteronomy 1–3
Treaty stipulations (outlining the requirements the suzerain king places on the vassal king)	Deuteronomy 4–26
Document clause (requiring the treaty document be written down and stored in a sanctuary)	Deuteronomy 27:3; 31:9–13
List of gods who witness the treaty	Deuteronomy 4:26; 30:19; 31:28 ("heaven and earth" serve as covenant witnesses, likely since no other gods are recognized by Deuteronomy)
Curses (for disobedience by the vassal)	Deuteronomy 28:15–68
Blessings (offered by the suzerain in exchange for the vassal's obedience)	Deuteronomy 28:1–14

Alternatively, many argue Deuteronomy reflects the later Assyrian treaty form. For instance, the commands to "love" God with all your heart and being, to "go after" God, to "listen to his voice," and to "fear" him are all echoed in Assyrian covenantal documents.[13] In either case, the covenantal form of Deuteronomy offers a powerful political punch; in a world where Israel was tempted to secure survival by pledging allegiance to other kings and lords, Yahweh calls Israel to pledge its sole, unswerving allegiance to him alone. No wonder Walter Brueggemann calls the book "public theology."[14]

The content of Deuteronomy resonates with the covenantal form. Old Testament scholars Dean McBride and Gordon McConville argue that Deuteronomy offers something like a constitution or a "divinely authorized social order,"[15] a "radical blueprint for the life of a people, at the same time spiritual and political, and running counter to every other social-political-religious program."[16] Yet because Deuteronomy leaves large areas of communal life unexplored and ends with a focus on Israel's future, it invites readers to imagine how the book's theological vision might be lived out in new contexts. Through its challenge to the status quo, Deuteronomy both "informs practical thinking about the organization of [society], while maintaining a vision of the kingdom of God. *The kingdom is now and not yet*."[17]

Carolyn Pressler offers another angle for understanding Deuteronomy as public theology by reading the book as "minority literature."[18] The community envisioned is not an imperial world power that could draw on the text to justify their military exploits. It is a nation Yahweh calls the "fewest of all peoples" (Deut. 7:7). Deuteronomy's grand claims depend solely on Yahweh's power rather than Israel's military or economic might. This is especially important since the powerful have sometimes misused Deuteronomy "to legitimize and motivate imperialistic aggression."[19]

DEUTERONOMY AS A MISSIONAL BOOK

Chris Wright invites us to read Deuteronomy as a missional book that summons God's people to

Figure 16.2. Image of a clay tablet with Hittite writing recording a peace treaty between the Egyptian Empire and the Hittite kingdom (mid-13th cent. BC)

HISTORICAL MATTERS

Dating Deuteronomy

Scholars continue to debate Deuteronomy's date, in large part because the book plays a major role in debates about the Pentateuch's editorial history. One major point of contention is the relationship between Deuteronomy and King Josiah. In 2 Kings 22:8, the high priest discovers "the book of the law." Since this discovery inspires Josiah to enact a series of seemingly deuteronomic reforms, some believe Deuteronomy was written, or perhaps heavily revised, during Josiah's reign.

While we believe Deuteronomy's message has roots in the historic ministry of Moses, it was clearly written after his death and was no doubt revised, edited, and adapted at different stages over the years. It may have been written down or revised during Josiah's reign. On the other hand, since Josiah's reform deviates from Deuteronomy in many ways, it is plausible that Deuteronomy was received by Josiah as he tried to resist the downward spiral toward exile that Deuteronomy warns the people about. Regardless, identifying a precise date does not strike us as particularly important for interpreting the book as Christian Scripture.

become a community capable of mediating God's blessing to the nations.[20] Deuteronomy 4:5–8 calls Israel to draw near to God and obey his way for their own sake and the sake of the nations.

> Now listen up! Just as Yahweh my God commanded me to do, I'm teaching you all the instructions and laws that you all will do in the land that you are about to enter and inherit. And you need to guard these directions and do them, because they'll be your *wisdom* and *understanding* in the eyes of all the other peoples. When they hear all these instructions, they'll say, "Surely this is a great nation, a wise and discerning people!" For what other great nation is there that has a *God so near to them* as Yahweh our God is whenever we call to him? And what other great nation is there that has instructions and laws as just as all this teaching which I'm putting right in front of you this very day? (Deut. 4:5–8 AT)

If Israel embraces God's wise, righteous, and just way, the nations "would look over the proverbial fence and be dumbstruck by (1) God's outrageously *intimate presence* among the people, and (2) the *wisdom* and *justice* of their way of life."[21] If the people of God become the joyful, just community Deuteronomy describes—a society that enfolds the orphan, immigrant, and widow into community life and orients socioeconomic structures toward the flourishing of all—nations will feel the magnetic pull of the God who makes such a life possible.

The Overarching Theme

All of this sets us up to hear Deuteronomy as an invitation to God's people to pledge their allegiance to Yahweh as their divine King. The book's form and content, its promises for blessing and warnings about disobedience, its sweeping summons to justice and its granular explorations of what justice might look like—these all seek to convince the people to make this pledge and then show them what doing so might look like.

Exploration

The Historical Prologue (Deut. 1–3)

READ DEUTERONOMY 2–3

What does Deuteronomy 2–3 communicate about the nations?

Deuteronomy 1:1–5 provides the setting for the book in terms of location (just outside the promised land), time (fortyish years after the exodus), and basic content (the words the Lord commanded Moses to speak). While the refence to Moses "expounding" this *torah* (v. 5) might suggest Moses will immediately launch into a legal collection, the preacher instead reminds the people of their history (1:6–3:29).

This historical prologue recounts Israel's first failed attempt to enter the land (Deut. 1:6–45), their more recent experience passing peacefully through the lands of one set of nations (1:46–2:23) and victoriously triumphing over another set (2:24–3:22), and finally, the tragic story of Moses's inability to enter the land (3:23–29). Moses speaks as if his audience had personally participated in all these events. Factually speaking, many hadn't. Nevertheless, by writing his audience into Israel's grand story, Moses equips the people to walk faithfully with Yahweh into their future. Several important theological themes emerge.

ISRAEL'S FAITHLESSNESS

Moses's storytelling is anything but triumphalist. He reminds Israel of their long history of rebellion, focusing on their refusal to enter the land. Yahweh had called God's people to be a kingdom of priests, but so far, Israel's faithlessness has wreaked havoc on these covenantal purposes.

YAHWEH'S FAITHFULNESS

Yet Moses makes clear that Yahweh's faithfulness is greater than Israel's failures. From ancient, childless Abraham and Sarah, Yahweh has raised up a nation "as numerous as the stars" (Deut. 1:10). Yahweh fought for

jorisvo / Shutterstock

Figure 16.3. Stained-glass window depicting Moses striking the rock and water flowing forth

THEOLOGICAL ISSUES

Yahweh as Passionate Parent

The image of Yahweh as a gentle parent is arresting. While God is neither male nor female, elsewhere Deuteronomy uses feminine, maternal imagery to describe God as the One who both "nursed" and "gave birth" to the people (32:13, 18). The Hebrew word translated "gave birth" speaks more graphically and directly to God "writhing" in labor.[b] Additionally, one of the primary descriptors of Yahweh's character in the Old Testament—that he is "merciful" or "compassionate"—may be "related to the Hebrew word for 'womb.'"[c] The prophets, too, use intimate, parental imagery for God. Hosea speaks of Yahweh as a parent who taught the people to walk and took them up in his arms. "I was to them," Yahweh declares, "like those who lift infants to their cheeks. I bent down to them and fed them" (Hosea 11:3–4). In Isaiah, Yahweh declares that Israel has "been borne by me from [their] birth, carried from the womb" (46:3). The maternal image is even more explicit in Isaiah 42:14, where God is like a woman who groans, pants, and gasps during labor.

CANONICAL CONNECTIONS

An Exodus Kind of God for All Families of the Earth

Amos 9:7 claims that Yahweh led two other occasional enemies of Israel, the Philistines and Arameans, on their own exoduses! This amazing claim suggests "Yahweh is an exodus kind of God, not just for Israel but for others."[d] In Paul's famous speech in Athens (Acts 17:16–34), the apostle argues that God has been at work among all people and places to draw people to himself, and he also creates a connection between religious truth claims spoken by pagans and the truth of the good news about Jesus.

As the gospel has spread throughout the world, people have discovered that Christianity connects with their deep aspirations and often even stories of their cultures. For instance, contemporary African theologians like Kwame Bediako and John Mbiti argue on the "basis of the oneness of God and the pre-Christian African sense of God" that pre-Christian African religious experience served to prepare Africans for the gospel.[e]

his people in Egypt and carried them through the fearsome wilderness "as one carries a child" (1:30–31).

The gift of a good land has been promised by Yahweh. Now he is bringing that promise to pass, including by fighting for his people against bigger, stronger, scarier, and better-armed enemies.

Moses's opening stories help the people see themselves as members of a people prone to faithlessness, but who have been disciplined, preserved, and prospered by the faithfulness of their divine King. Every aspect of this story should shape them to answer Deuteronomy's invitation to love and serve Yahweh.

YAHWEH'S MYSTERIOUS WAYS WITH OTHERS

There are two surprising features of Yahweh's mysterious ways with the nations here. Given the emphasis on Yahweh giving Israel the Canaanites' land, we could easily believe God's land policy is grounded in love for Israel and lack of concern for anybody else. Instead, Deuteronomy claims Yahweh has been at work with *other* nations besides Israel in *other* lands besides Canaan.

For instance, Yahweh forbids Israel from taking any territory or going to war with the Edomites, Moabites, or Ammonites (Deut. 2:4, 9, 19). These nations were enemies of God's people at various points in their history; Edom and Moab were even hostile toward Israel in their wilderness wanderings! Yet because of Yahweh's sovereign engagement with these nations, he refuses to allow Israel to invade them. Yahweh has given these occasional enemies of Israel their own land and denied his chosen people even a "foot's length of it" (2:5). This is a rare glimpse into the Old Testament's claim that Yahweh is at work among the nations in Israel-like ways.

This ought to transform the way we understand Deuteronomy's theological vision. Yahweh is at work among the nations, and the connection of peoples with their lands is part of that work (see discussion on Gen. 10–11 in chap. 3). The fact that Yahweh enables Israel to "drive out" the Canaanites provides no generalized support for God's people to drive others off their lands. Indeed, Yahweh explicitly forbids Israel from jumping to that conclusion. The mysterious hidden ways God has worked in the movements of peoples and their subsequent land claims should be respected.

We get another glimpse into Yahweh's mysterious ways with the nations in his command that Israel *should* wage war against King Sihon the Amorite (Deut. 2:24). Yahweh is "handing over" this king and his kingdom to the Israelites. Surprisingly, Moses responds to God's command by asking King Sihon to allow Israel to pass through his land in peace. Sihon refuses this peaceful offer and initiates battle instead.

Figure 16.4. *Moses Commanding the Waters of the Red Sea to Separate* by William Page (ca. 1855)

So why do the Israelites destroy King Sihon and the Amorites? Did Israel launch an offensive war at Yahweh's request or did they defend themselves against an aggressive enemy? Deuteronomy's mysterious answer comes in 2:30: "But King Sihon of Heshbon was not willing to let us pass through, for the Lord your God had hardened his spirit and made his heart defiant in order to hand him over to you, as he has now done." Such language alludes to Yahweh hardening Pharaoh's heart as part of his judgment on Pharaoh. Deuteronomy presents the conquest of Canaan as the final chapter in Yahweh's assault on Egyptian oppression, and the kings Yahweh commands Israel to defeat are described as Pharaoh-like tyrants. Their persistent wickedness leads Yahweh to "give them over" to their hard hearts as part of his just judgment on them.

The Character of God, the Calling of God's People (Deut. 4–11)

READ DEUTERONOMY 6, 8, AND 10:12–22

What are some primary themes of Moses's sermons?

Structurally speaking, Deuteronomy 4 concludes the first speech. The second and longest speech spans from Deuteronomy 5:1 to 28:68, but

Figure 16.5. *Moses Receiving the Law*, woodcut for a Dutch Bible (ca. 1465)

readers are more likely to notice the shift in style that begins in 4:1 and carries through chapter 11. These chapters contain some of Moses's most "preacherly" material. Moses repeatedly returns to Deuteronomy's primary theme: Israel's incomparable king is calling his people to pledge their undivided loyalty to him and walk in his good way. This idea is succinctly and powerfully stated in the Shema: "Hear, O Israel: The Lord is our God, the Lord alone. You shall love the Lord your God with all your heart, and with all your [being], and with all your might" (6:4–5). In many ways, Deuteronomy 4–11 simply expounds these two themes: (1) the character and action of Yahweh, and (2) the covenantal response that Yahweh demands from the people. We can therefore explore this section by asking two questions: Who is this God? And who is this people?

WHO IS THIS GOD? YAHWEH'S CHARACTER

Yahweh is one/alone. The Shema in Deuteronomy 6:4–5 can be understood as declaring either that Yahweh is God "alone" (NRSV) or that Yahweh is "one" (NIV). The translation "one" suggests Yahweh's integrity or unity of character, emphasizing Yahweh's faithfulness to fulfill his covenant promises.[22] Alternatively, both "one" or "alone" could be related to Israel's "monotheism," although many debate this term's meaning and appropriateness for describing the Old Testament's perspective. Such monotheism could be taken to mean that there simply *are* no other gods,[23] a view shared by later Jewish and Christian theology and apparently taught in texts that "deride other so-called [gods] as mere idols" (see 32:21).[24] Alternatively, the Shema could call Israel to worship Yahweh as their "one and only,"[25] ignoring and rejecting the worship of any other gods but not absolutely denying their existence.[26] "For the Lord *your* God is God of gods and Lord of lords" (10:17); as a result, "whatever 'other gods' there may be, such 'other gods' . . . should be displaced, rejected, and disregarded, since Israel's focus is to be on Yhwh alone."[27]

Moses draws on both sorts of "monotheistic rhetoric" in this portion of Deuteronomy. In 4:33–34, he asks, "Has any people ever heard the voice of a god speaking out of a fire, as you have heard, and lived? Or has any god ever attempted to go and take a nation for himself from the midst of another nation?" Moses describes Yahweh as incomparably greater than any being who has ever claimed the title "god." Nevertheless, Yahweh's superiority over other "gods" ought to lead the people to confess "the LORD is God in heaven above and on the earth beneath; *there is no other*" (4:39).

What matters most, then, is not the philosophical question of what other sorts of beings may exist, but rather that Yahweh is the Incomparable One who has covenanted with this very people. Yahweh is Israel's "one and only," because of both who he is and what he has done in their life together.

A God of love, liberation, and justice. Yahweh is Israel's "one and only" because Yahweh *loves* them (Deut. 7:8, 13; 10:15). Such love is no mere sentimentality on God's part. In ancient political covenants, the suzerain king could be said to "love" his vassals, which meant he would protect, care for, and provide for them. Yahweh certainly offers this kind of practical, "political" love to his people,[28] proving his love through his deeds, most notably by rescuing Israel from Egypt (Egypt is mentioned nearly sixty times in these eight chapters). In the immediate context of Deuteronomy, Yahweh is demonstrating his liberating love and generosity by bringing Israel safely into the good land (4:37–38; 6:3; 7:20; 8:1–20; 11:1–32). Such just acts represent the consistent character and action of a great God "who is not partial and takes no bribe, who executes justice for the orphan and the widow, and who loves the strangers, providing them food and clothing" (10:17–18). Yahweh's gift of the land to Israel both enacts just

THEOLOGICAL ISSUES

Monotheistic Rhetoric Across the Old Testament

Matthew Lynch says the Old Testament offers diverse kinds of "monotheistic rhetoric" that "entails *the expression of Yhwh's categorical supremacy, or supreme uniqueness.* That is, monotheism involves locating Yhwh in a class of his own that is uniquely distinguished from all other reality."[f] Some texts seem to deny the very existence of other gods, and others rhetorically emphasize Yahweh's supremacy. A single chapter of Deuteronomy describes other divine beings in several ways:

- as "demons" (32:17)
- as no gods at all (32:21)
- as categorically inferior to Yahweh (32:31)
- as called to bow down to and praise Yahweh (32:43)

This diversity of monotheistic rhetoric exists throughout the Old Testament. The entire Old Testament celebrates Yahweh's uniqueness and identifies a critical distinction between Creator and creation, but the texts of the Old Testament express this incomparability of the Creator in different ways.

THEOLOGICAL ISSUES

Missing the Point of Monotheism?

Some question the language of "monotheism" because descriptions of it often move in an "intellectualizing and abstracting" direction that may miss the Bible's core concerns. Moberly explains that "the term 'monotheism' does not intrinsically convey the existential dimensions conveyed by the Shema . . . —either the call for loyalty that resists alternative allegiances or a devotion to God as the one and only, as to a lover."[g] However we construe God's oneness in Deuteronomy, the "appropriate response . . . is wholehearted love and devotion," not simply intellectual recognition of a philosophical truth.[h] "Israel did not assert the oneness of her God with the dispassion of a philosopher. She praised God for being unique, incomparable, a source of embarrassment to his rivals, their master. Something precious is lost when we convert this language of hymnody into a matter of doctrine," even though, as Jon Levenson recognizes, theology must eventually do so.[i]

CANONICAL CONNECTIONS

Deuteronomy's Great Commission?

According to Chris Wright, in the so-called Great Commission (Matt. 28:18–20), Jesus paraphrases Deuteronomy's affirmations about Yahweh's universal lordship (Deut. 4:39; 10:14, 17) "and calmly applies them to himself: 'All authority in heaven and earth has been given to me' (Matt. 28:18). *The risen Jesus thus claims the same ownership and sovereignty over all creation as the Old Testament affirms for* YHWH."[j]

judgment on the "wickedness" of the Canaanites (9:5) and provides a place for Israel to live out Yahweh's justice in their community.[29]

But Yahweh's love is also not *merely* political, devoid of affection and feeling. While ancient covenants are political documents, such political documents are "based on a more primal type of relationship, one of kin."[30] Deuteronomy's covenant language draws on both the political resonances of covenants between rulers and the affective resonances of covenants between kin. Indeed, the language Moses uses for Yahweh's love for Israel is used elsewhere to describe a man's desire for a woman. For mysterious reasons, then, Moses claims the Lord of heaven and earth "took a passion to" the patriarchs and continues to set his love on their descendants.[31]

A jealous, terrifying, disciplining God. Again and again, Moses moves seamlessly from celebrating Yahweh's promises for his people to warning them against abandoning his way. If being in covenant with Yahweh is good news because of who God is, being in covenant with Yahweh is dangerous news for the same reason.

First, Yahweh is a jealous God. Because he loves Israel, he is jealous of their love. This is a distinctive feature of Israelite faith; the gods of the nations are not typically described as jealous.[32]

Figure 16.6. *Moses Giving the Law on Mount Sinai* by Gustave Doré

Deuteronomy's covenant language draws on marital and political imagery to explain Yahweh's jealousy. From Yahweh's perspective, for Israel to worship other gods would be to commit adultery, assaulting the marriage bond at the deepest level. The jealousy Yahweh feels for Israel is not a petty, selfish emotion; it is the appropriate jealousy of a spouse who expects their partner to be faithful. Likewise, ancient suzerain kings often demanded exclusive loyalty precisely because of their history with the vassal. For Israel to worship false gods would be to offer to them the loyalty Yahweh deserves because he brought the people out of Egypt.

Second, the flip side of the good news that Yahweh is near his people is the disconcerting news that Yahweh is terrifying (Deut. 5:22–27) and fearsome (7:21). Moses repeatedly reminds the people of God's nearness and his distance. When Yahweh spoke to Israel face-to-face, he did so "out of the fire," with Moses serving as an intermediary. Israel's leaders recognized their glimpse of God's glory and greatness could have turned deadly. They pleaded with Moses to be even more proactive in his mediatorial role. Yahweh approved their awe-filled response (5:28–29). God is loving and good but also jealous and overwhelming, inspiring an awe that borders on terror.

Third, the flip side of the good news that God does justice *for* Israel is the more disconcerting news that God will bring justice *on* Israel if they embrace idolatry and the injustice associated with it. Yahweh's presence includes his work as disciplinarian; in the wilderness, he disciplined the people "as a parent disciplines a child" (Deut. 8:5).

Yahweh is the creator and sustainer of life. Finally, Moses describes Yahweh as the creator and sustainer of all things (see, e.g., Deut. 4:32, 39). Yahweh is intimately involved with the land to which he is bringing the people. In a bit of preacherly poetry, Moses declares that the promised land "is a land of hills and valleys, watered by rain from the sky, a land that the Lord your God looks after. The eyes of the Lord your God are always on it, from the beginning of the year to the end of the year" (11:11–12).

Yahweh will wield his creational power to sustain an ecology of abundance if the people are faithful to the covenant. Their obedience will lead to rain in season and abundant harvests, while their faithlessness will lead Yahweh to "shut up the heavens, so that there will be no rain and the land will yield no fruit" (Deut. 11:17). As Creator and Sustainer, Yahweh is the one who can confidently set before the people life and death, blessing and cursing (see 11:26–28).

WHO IS THIS PEOPLE?

What do we learn in these chapters about who God's people are supposed to be? What struggles will they face? How will they overcome them?

A covenantal people. The Shema calls the people to pledge their allegiance to their one-and-only by loving him with all their heart, being, and might (Deut. 6:4–5). The ancient Jewish claim that a person who recited the Shema was "accepting the yoke of the kingship of heaven" is exactly right (Babylonian Talmud, Berakhot 2:2). Deuteronomy 4–11 relentlessly calls the people to an undivided, holistic faithfulness in response to the actions and character of their divine King. We can better understand this call by examining Deuteronomy's language further.

LITERARY NOTES

"With All Your Soul"?

The common translation "soul" in the Shema is misleading, since most Western readers understand the "soul" to refer to a "spiritual or immaterial part of humans, distinct from the body."[k] The Old Testament, by contrast, describes humans more holistically; the Hebrew word used here "refers to the life force" and therefore means that a person should love the Lord "with all one's vitality, vigor, energy, self-hood, inner-forcefulness, and the like. It does not mean that one should love him with some immortal and spiritual dimension of the self that is divorced from one's bodily and social identity."[l]

ETHICS

Resisting Idolatrous Political Covenants

Using language from ancient political covenants to call God's people to pledge allegiance to Yahweh alone, Deuteronomy warns against "religious" breaches through idolatry and political breaches through forming covenants with other nations. Such political covenants tempted Israel to idolatrously give the hope, trust, and service that Yahweh deserved to some other political power (see 2 Kings 16:5–20). Hosea is famous for describing Israel's idolatry as an act of adultery, but he, too, recognized that such adulterous idolatry could be deeply political. According to Hosea, when God's people went to Assyria or Egypt to make what looked like politically prudential deals, they were actually "hiring" these nations as extramarital "lovers," paying for the kind of intimacy they should have reserved for their exclusive relationship with Yahweh (Hosea 8:9). Such alliances could become a "form of conversion" to a false ideology, an ideology that involved a rejection of genuine faith.[m]

While not every political partnership represents such idolatry, Scripture asks us to consider these questions:

- Where are we tempted to partner with idolatrous political powers or ideologies in an attempt to protect ourselves?
- Do our political alliances risk becoming a sordid "affair" with false powers, not least by requiring us to compromise our Christian character or witness?[n]

THEOLOGICAL ISSUES

How Can You Command a Feeling?

Many find it strange that God would command an emotion. We see our feelings as outside of our control; they happen *to* us. But both the Bible and much contemporary science recognize that people can intentionally foster certain emotions, affections, and desires through their actions.[o] What we do shapes who we are, including how we feel. In the next chapter, we'll explore how Deuteronomy's feasts required the people to participate in rituals intended to shape their loves and affections toward Yahweh and his people.

"Love." Israel's response of love to Yahweh requires much more than warm feelings. Ancient covenantal texts demanded that vassal kings "love" the suzerain king by obediently serving him and cutting ties with other potential political allies.[33] Likewise, Israel is to love Yahweh by following his way and by severing ties with other contenders for their loyalty.

At one level, then, loving Yahweh wholeheartedly refers to the "all-consuming and incomparably demanding" task of obeying Yahweh in every area of one's life.[34] The law collection that begins in chapter 12 will show the people how to do this, whether farming in their fields or setting up a government.[35]

But the love Yahweh demands also includes "holding fast to him" (Deut. 11:22). That language is used elsewhere to describe "passion, romantic love, and sexual attraction," suggesting that "obedience *and* passionate relationship characterize the full love of God in Deuteronomy."[36] To love God wholeheartedly is to direct our desires, intentions, and actions toward him in love.[37]

"Fear." As with the command to love, Deuteronomy often unpacks the command to "fear" in terms of obedience (see Deut. 6:2, 13, 24). But fear cannot be reduced to outward actions. Deuteronomy uses the language of fear to describe the Israelites shaking in terror upon hearing God's voice from the midst of the fire at Horeb (Deut. 5:24–29). The fear-as-obedience that Yahweh desires includes a fear-as-feeling-of-terror. This suggests that English translations of "fear" with words like "revere"[38] may be misleading. The appropriate response to the good *and* loving *and* terrifying God in Moses's sermons includes gratitude, love, reverence, and, yes, at least on occasion, good old-fashioned terror. Thus, for Deuteronomy, "'love' and 'fear' are not, in fact, mutually exclusive, but complement each other."[39]

Wikimedia Commons / public domain

Figure 16.7. This nineteenth-century oil painting by Jean-Léon Gérôme, *Moses on Mount Sinai*, captures some of the terror the people felt when they saw Moses receiving the law.

"Hear . . . obey . . . swear . . . serve." Moses piles up language calling the people to listen to Yahweh, obey Yahweh, swear in his name (suggesting a "test of fidelity"),[40] and walk in his way. Moses often piles up such language to encourage obedience to the "law, commandments, statues and ordinances" of Deuteronomy.[41] For Moses, the time for such covenantal law keeping is now, today, always.[42]

Facing threats to faithfulness. In Deuteronomy 4–11, Moses calls for undivided, wholehearted loyalty to Yahweh that includes affections, thoughts, and actions. Like any good preacher, Moses also addresses the obstacles to faithfulness the people face. He emphasizes the danger of Israel turning to "serve" or "worship" other gods, and thus following after *their* death-dealing ways, as well as the danger of forgetting their history with Yahweh and their covenantal commitment to walk in *his* way. Given that Yahweh liberated Israel *from* service to Egypt *for* service to him, it would be a terrible betrayal for the people to offer their service to false gods instead. It would also prevent them from living into their calling as covenant partners in God's mission.

Why would Israel be tempted to worship false gods? The way Moses moves from Yahweh's promise of agricultural abundance to a warning about idolatry in Deuteronomy 11:14–17 suggests Israel might believe the gods of the nations provide agricultural fertility. These other gods made big promises about agricultural abundance.[43] Baal worshipers called their god "the Rider of the Clouds"[44] and claimed he caused the heavens to rain olive oil and the dry stream beds to flow with honey.[45] Baal claimed to fatten both gods and people.[46] As vulnerable, subsistence farmers, Israel depended on seasonal rains that apparently failed approximately three to four years out of every ten.[47] No wonder they were tempted to add fertility gods like Baal to the list of those they "served."

However, Dennis Olson notes that Moses takes aim at another set of false gods that are both "more insidious and more universal" (Deut. 7–10). He identifies these "gods of death" as militarism, materialism, and moralism.[48] At the center of this section is a warning to Israel about something they will be tempted to "say in their heart" (see 7:17; 8:17; 9:4 ESV).

First, when they see the military strength of other nations, they will be tempted to say in their heart, "These nations are more numerous than I; how can I dispossess them?" (Deut. 7:17–18). Yahweh calls them to reject this fear because their hope is not in their military strength. Yahweh did not choose them because they were a powerful, numerous people; they were the fewest of all peoples (7:7). They must remember what Yahweh did to Egypt. They must remember their "great and awesome" God fights for them (7:21). They must reject fear and commit themselves to walk in Yahweh's way. He'll take care of the rest.

Second, Deuteronomy 8 confronts the idol of materialism. The people are leaving behind their vulnerable life in the wilderness. Soon, they will "eat [their] fill and bless the Lord [their] God for the good land that he has given [them]" (8:10). Unless, of course, they don't and instead give into the idol of materialism, forgetting Yahweh and declaring, "My power and the might of my own hand have gotten me this wealth" (see 8:11–17).

In an all-too-familiar paradox, Moses recognizes the people may worship themselves and the gifts rather than the Giver. When they do, they will fall into a self-centered way of life that leads directly to death (Deut. 8:20). To combat this temptation, Moses reminds them their lives and land are gifts from Yahweh (8:18).

Third, in Deuteronomy 9–10, Moses warns the people not to "say in their hearts" that Yahweh gave them the land because of their righteousness (9:4). Moses reminds them not only that they are conquering the Canaanites because of *Canaanite* wickedness but also that the Israelites themselves have consistently rebelled against Yahweh since he delivered them from Egypt (9:6).

Moses summons the people to *love*, *fear*, and *serve* Yahweh. He also calls them to "guard themselves" against a series of threats to their faithfulness. Knowing about these threats is the first step to avoiding them. But does Deuteronomy offer any other tools to help the people guard themselves?

BECOMING GOD'S PEOPLE: A DISCIPLESHIP TOOL KIT

Deuteronomy 4–11 offers numerous tools for the kind of holistic, wholehearted discipleship Moses describes. First, Moses's sermons are themselves tools of discipleship. The relentless repetition of the commands to "keep/observe/do—carefully—today!"[49] attempts to drill the demand to follow Yahweh's way into even the hardest skulls. These commands also force listeners to examine whether they are adequately guarding themselves against idolatrous temptations. The book demonstrates that "the good life" is lived in line with God's creational and covenantal purposes; the alternative is death.[50] One way we are "transformed into the people of God that Deuteronomy so desperately seeks" is simply by returning to this text again and again.[51]

Second, Deuteronomy offers the law as a path to life. While most of the laws aren't discussed until chapters 12–26, Moses refers to them constantly in chapters 4–11 and reiterates the Ten Commandments in chapter 5. He also calls the people to specific moral actions in this section, most notably in Deuteronomy 10's demand that the people imitate Yahweh's loving justice: "For the Lord your God . . . executes justice for the orphan and the widow, and who loves the strangers, providing them food and clothing. [And] you shall also love the stranger, for you were strangers in the land of Egypt" (10:17–19).

Following the law is one way Israel embraces the path of discipleship. They learn the law in order that they and their children will fear Yahweh all their days (Deut. 6:2). Obeying Yahweh's just and righteous law will guide the people in ways that reflect God's good creational purposes. Because the Torah-shaped life goes with the grain of God's world, law-keeping is both "for our lasting good" and "righteousness for us" (Deut. 6:24–25).[52]

What Does "Biblical Justice" Mean?

Christians often disagree about how to define "biblical justice." As I (Michael) argue in *Just Discipleship*, one of the best ways to understand what justice *is*, is by looking at what justice *does*. For example, Scripture tells us that when Job "clothed" himself in righteousness and justice, he

- delivered the poor and the orphan,
- cared for the dying,
- caused the "heart of the widow to shout for joy,"
- served as eyes for the blind and feet for the lame,
- acted as a father for the needy,
- "investigated the court case of the one" he did not know (i.e., an outsider), and
- "smashed the fangs of the unrighteous and made them drop their prey from their teeth" (Job 29:12–17 AT).

That's what biblical justice is all about. Such justice is, as Cornel West poetically puts it, "what love looks like in public. . . . Not simply an abstract concept to regulate institutions, but also a fire in the bones to promote the well-being of all."[p] Or as Goldingay writes, justice and righteousness are most often about "the faithful exercise of power in community."[q]

This is precisely what Deuteronomy 10 describes: Yahweh demonstrates justice by loving immigrants/refugees through concrete acts, and his people are to do likewise. There are no caveats offered about what kind of refugees or immigrants are being described; Scripture calls God's people to love even their enemies. When Christians neglect the kind of justice that faithfully exercises power on behalf of the powerless and oppressed in our discipleship, we fail to be the disciples God calls us to be.

This is certainly true in relation to our care for immigrants, to whom God refers repeatedly in the Torah and beyond. While the Old Testament does not provide a blueprint for immigration policy in any contemporary nation, it does require that we love our immigrant neighbors and rules out the kind of hateful, anti-immigrant policies, practices, and attitudes so often on display in our world and, most tragically, among Christians.

Third, as we saw in Leviticus, Deuteronomy also offers disciplines, habits, and rituals to shape the people for faithfulness. While Moses assumes that changed minds lead to changed lives, he also recognizes that what we

RECEPTION HISTORY

Creating Deuteronomic Memory Through Art

Students at Carey Baptist College were invited to create artifacts as a part of a course on the Pentateuch in 2022. Sacha Olson created a vessel in the tradition of kintsugi. The cracks in the vessel symbolize creation's brokenness, while the repair of those cracks with painted gold speaks to the hope of God's new creation. The multilingual inscription of the Shema in Hebrew, te reo Māori, and English gestures toward the inclusion of "every tribe and tongue" at Christ's return. By placing the vessel on the family meal table, she sought to inspire the kind of conversations about God "on the way" that Deuteronomy inspires.

Similarly, Grace Paddison's embroidered tea towel literally weaves the Shema into the fabric of a towel used in daily kitchen work to help families weave God's way into the "fabric" of their lives. The colored threads represent six stages in Israel's story, from slavery in Egypt to a promised life in the land.

Figure 16.8. Sacha Olson's vessel

Figure 16.9. Grace Paddison's embroidered tea towel

do shapes who we are, that changed disciplines and habits affect our hearts. The passage immediately following the Shema shows this. After reiterating that the laws must be in/on the people's hearts (Deut. 6:6), Moses tells them what to do in order to get it there:

- Repeat the words of the law to their children (v. 7)
- Talk about the law constantly and everywhere (v. 7)
- Bind the words on their bodies (v. 8)[53]
- Write the words of the law in public places, including homes and the politically significant city gates (v. 9)
- Remember and retell the story of Yahweh liberating the people from Egypt and inviting them into a covenantal way of life (vv. 20–25)

In all of this, Moses points to the demanding nature of the life of discipleship; the love demanded by Deuteronomy is "an all-engaging occupation."[54]

The laws in Deuteronomy 12–26 contain other formative practices designed to cement Torah obedience and the memory of God's saving acts in the body *through* the body.[55] They provide tools for Israel to "circumcise the foreskin of their hearts," a remarkable expression that calls Israel "to discipline itself to a more intentional obedience."[56] The result? Disciples who embrace the wholehearted allegiance God demands.

Fourth, and more subtly, Moses describes the land as uniquely well-suited to shaping the people for faithfulness. Chapter 11's beautiful depiction of the land as a well-watered place that Yahweh yearly looks after includes a contrast: This land is "not like the land of Egypt . . . where you sow your seed and irrigate by foot" (Deut.

11:10). This almost certainly refers to the "labor-intensive nature of agriculture in Egypt."[57] Moses and his audience remember that slaves did most of that labor.

But they also would have noticed that this poetic depiction of the land acknowledges that it is an immensely vulnerable, fragile, and even dangerous ecosystem. Early Jewish commentators questioned whether describing the land as rain dependent was meant to celebrate the land or denigrate it.[58] After all, transporting water from the Nile to your farm may take longer, but at least the water is always there. You can always *see* the relatively stable source of your life and livelihood. In the promised land, farmers depended completely on the rain that Deuteronomy attributes to Yahweh's attentiveness. The Jewish commentator Rashbam calls such a land "better than Egypt and all other lands *to those who observe God's commands*, but *worse* than all other lands to those who do not observe them."[59] The fragile fertility of the land would force God's people to live lives of acknowledged dependence on Yahweh, lives that completely reject the self-aggrandizing, greed-saturated ideology behind a statement like "My power and the might of my own hand have gotten me this wealth" (Deut. 8:17). This is a land that fosters a glimpse of the "holy insecurity" experienced by naked, unashamed humanity in Eden,[60] and in which, as another Jewish commentator says, the commandments themselves serve as the "sole method of cultivating."[61]

HISTORICAL MATTERS

Families in Covenant

Discipleship begins in the households, "the epicenter of the covenant, the arenas in which Israel's national identity is instituted and taught." Indeed, Deuteronomy teaches that the "law should be part of the sights and sounds of a household." God's "covenant is preserved by being woven into the daily life of the family, firmly placing Israel's relationship with God at the very center of social existence."[r]

Figure 16.10. Painting of a thirteen-year-old Jewish boy putting on the tefillin for the first time (2023). Such tefillin contain passages of the Torah and represent one way some Jewish people practice the command of Deuteronomy to place the law between their eyes (Deut. 6:8).

Deuteronomy 4–11 offers God's people a discipleship tool kit, a program for helping them become a people who, in response to the incomparable love of their incomparable God, love Yahweh with all their hearts, beings, and might . . . today, tomorrow, and always.

Living the Text: Discipleship for the Whole Family and Community

Deuteronomy plays a central role in the Torah's dazzling depiction of holistic discipleship. It envisions the *whole* family and community going on the discipleship journey together. Parents talk about their faith with their children constantly, and the entire family's participation in liturgies prompts children to ask questions and receive answers. Such back-and-forth helps children understand themselves as full members of the community. When a child asks about the meaning of what God commanded *you*, the question places some distance between child and parent. The parent's response, however, places the child within the story: "*We* were Pharaoh's slaves . . . , but the LORD brought *us* out. . . . Then the LORD commanded *us*. . . . If *we* diligently observe this entire commandment, . . . *we* will be in the right" (Deut. 6:21–25).

Studies suggest 40–50 percent of youth group seniors "drift from God and the faith community after they graduate."[62] Against that background, research demonstrates that Deuteronomy is exactly right to emphasize the family's role in discipleship: "The single, most powerful causal influence on the religious lives of American teenagers is the religious lives of their parents. . . . Myriad studies show that, beyond a doubt, the parents of American youth play *the* leading role in shaping the character of their religious and spiritual lives, even well after they leave home and often for the rest of their lives."[63]

Deuteronomy anticipates the central role of conversation in family discipleship. Church attendance contributes very little to handing on the faith if that attendance is not accompanied by regular, open conversation about the faith.[64] "Parents need not only to 'walk the walk' but also regularly to talk with their children about their walk, what it means, why it matters, why they care."[65]

The quality of such conversations is important. Sociologists Christian Smith and Amy Adamcyzk argue that parents have the highest positive impact on their children's spiritual development when

- they combine "clear and implemented life standards for their children" (i.e., when they raise them as members of a faith community and with the expectations of that faith community) "with expressive emotional warmth and relational bonding";[66] and
- they foster children-focused conversations, by which they mean "children ask questions; . . . [conversations] are clearly related to children's lives; parents try to help children understand their religious faith and practices; [and] the conversations are open, not rigid or highly controlled."[67]

All of this sounds like what Deuteronomy has in mind. Deuteronomy can inspire parents to commit to gathering their families together to learn the biblical story, practice Scripture-inspired rituals, and sing Scripture-saturated songs. The Rhodes have tried to do this with their four children by committing to family devotions that include open-ended inductive Bible study with lots of space for kid Q&A and by embracing some of the rituals, feasts, and fasts associated with the Christian calendar. The Beldmans prioritize daily shared meals together (easier when their kids were younger), which incorporated prayer, Scripture reading, singing, and conversation and regularly included hospitality toward others. Resources like Justin Whitmel Earley's *Habits of the Household: Practicing the Story of God in Everyday Family Rhythms* can help families reimagine their formative practices.[68]

Furthermore, research suggests that after parents, the single most important factor in youth maturing in the faith is whether they have strong intergenerational relationships and participate in intergenerational worship. Researcher Kara Powell summarizes, "In our study of 500 youth group graduates, bringing the generations to sit shoulder to shoulder or look eye to eye was more important for long-term faith than any other youth group activity."[69] Numerous studies suggest a major contributing factor to young people leaving the faith is "the separation of the ages in churches." Those who continue on their faith journeys "often credit the influence of cross-generational relationships."[70]

The *bad* news is that youth and children's ministry often "prioritizes" young people by taking them away from older generations for youth-only programming. Young people are walking away from the family of God in part because they have spent so little time *with* the full family of God. The *sad* news is that, while some discipleship ministry likely should occur in groups divided by age, there's zero biblical justification for making that the primary focus. When God's people gather, they *all* gather. When God's Old Testament people ran a "building campaign" to construct their new "worship space"—the tabernacle—the God-given blueprints did not require nursery spaces or youth rooms. Whole families went on pilgrimages, celebrated the feasts, and listened to the reading of the law—the same law their parents were listening to (Deut. 31:12–13). The early church in the New Testament met in homes where whole families gathered at the table.

The *good news* is that churches can embrace the whole-family, whole-community discipleship that Torah depicts and research recommends. Intergenerational worship is an obvious first step; resources for doing it well are increasingly available,[71] but a lot of this stuff is obvious. Quit taking middle schoolers out of sermons, and instead ensure sermons can be heard by middle schoolers. Quit sending children to cry elsewhere; create a culture where they can see your faith by watching you worship. Be genuinely intergenerational, with all ages greeting, offering prayers, helping lead the music, or taking up offerings.[72]

Fuller Youth Institute provides a wealth of resources for doing youth ministry that partners with families and fosters intergenerational relationships. Take, for instance, the five-to-one principle, which recommends that churches have five adults engaged with every student. That bar isn't as high as it sounds: "We're talking about five adults who know a young person's name. Who pray for them. Who show up occasionally at that young person's piano recital or volleyball tournament. In other words, five adults who are on their team."[73] These are the kind of intergenerational relationships the Torah envisions with whole communities feasting, pilgrimaging, and writing God's words on the doorposts of their towns together.

Intergenerational relationships in the church are particularly important because many youth lack a healthy family context within which faith is formed, either because their parents are not believers or because of trauma in the home. Intergenerational worship and relationships allow these young people to become part of the family we all require for growth in our life with God.

The Torah depicts discipleship taking place as whole families and communities worship and journey with Yahweh *together*. Because intergenerational discipleship is God's design, it shouldn't be surprising that research shows us it works. But that same research shows that many families and churches fail to embrace this vision. May God's word lead us into greater faithfulness, as the whole family of God becomes the people we were meant to be—together!

Deuteronomy 12–34

Choosing Life, Depending on Grace

Orientation

Deuteronomy 12–34 brings the Pentateuch to a close. While Deuteronomy's second sermon runs from 5:1–28:68, major shifts exist within this section. Deuteronomy 12 introduces a lengthy, preacherly exploration of deuteronomic law. These laws "form the identity of the ideal Israel as a community of people who fear Yahweh."[1]

Deuteronomy 27:1 introduces another subsection, describing how God's people must ritually commit themselves to the laws they have received when they enter the land. Deuteronomy 28 offers a lengthy promise of blessings to the people if they follow the covenant, followed by an even lengthier warning of curses should they fail to do so.

The third speech begins in Deuteronomy 29:1 and includes crucial theological reflection on Israel's future should they fail to keep the covenant. It includes the Song of Moses. The fourth sermon (Deut. 33) is composed exclusively of Moses's farewell blessing, before the postscript in Deuteronomy 34 describes Moses's death.

It's easy to feel lost in Deuteronomy 12–34. The laws seem endless, repetitive, and occasionally off-putting. The blessings and curses sound harsh and bewildering. And in the end, the book

LITERARY NOTES

Deuteronomic Law as Exposition of the Ten Words?

Some scholars suggest that the Ten Words influenced the content and order of the laws in Deuteronomy 12–26.[a] For instance, consider the following:

- The first two commandments focus on exclusive worship of Yahweh. Deuteronomy 12:1–32 describes what this looks like by demanding the people worship Yahweh exclusively in the place he chooses.
- The Sabbath commandment structures time around a weekly day of rest that orients the people to God and is good for the community, especially the orphan, widow, outsider, and poor. Deuteronomy 14:22–16:17 structures Israel's seasonal and annual rhythms of rest so they orient the people to God and contribute to the well-being of the community, especially the orphan, widow, outsider, and the poor.
- The command not to murder gets unpacked in the laws about taking life in Deuteronomy 19–21.[b]

Figure 17.1. *Moses with the Ten Commandments* by Rembrandt (1659)

can't seem to make up its mind about whether Israel is even *capable* of following Yahweh's way.

Yet these chapters are theologically explosive. Prick the deuteronomic laws and they bleed Yahweh's special concern for his people to embrace a socioeconomic and political way of life that is good news for orphans, widows, immigrants, refugees, and impoverished members of the community. The blessings and curses that take us by surprise serve as a primary lens for the rest of the Old Testament to interpret Israel's subsequent history. And Deuteronomy's reflection on the possibly inevitable failures facing the people provide both the prophets and the New Testament writers with some of their most stunning theological images for understanding the depth of both humanity's sinful condition and Yahweh's lavish grace and abiding faithfulness to his covenant.

Exploration

Locating Allegiance to Yahweh (Deut. 12:1–14:21)

READ DEUTERONOMY 12

Consider what Deuteronomy tells the people about Yahweh's chosen place.

The law collection begins with a familiar theme: Whatever you do, don't worship the way the Canaanites do (Deut. 12:2–4). Deuteronomy 12:5–28 takes this theme in a new direction. Israel must also turn from some of their own existing practices. "You shall not act as we are acting here today, all of us according to our own desires" (12:8). Yahweh is going to do something new within the land by choosing a specific place as a "dwelling for his name" (12:11). This will become the one place Yahweh's one people will offer sacrifices, tithes, and offerings. This centralization affects much of the book's teaching. We need to ask, What's the significance of this centralization?

WHAT'S SO SIGNIFICANT ABOUT CENTRALIZATION?

Some claim that evidence from the world behind the text shows the book was written to shore up Jerusalem's political power during the reigns of

Hezekiah and Josiah.[2] Maybe centralized worship is simply a religious front for power politics. However, within the world of the text, Yahweh is Israel's only king, and Deuteronomy, like the Pentateuch as a whole, seems to have a decidedly antimonarchic and even *de*centralizing edge (see below on tithes and debt forgiveness).

Moreover, Gordon McConville believes "the place" remains nameless intentionally. Because the Hebrew word for "place" can refer both to the land as a whole and to a worshiping space within it, such language creates a "correspondence"[3] that suggests Israel will flourish in the "place" that is the land only to the extent that they faithfully worship Yahweh in the "place" he will choose.[4] At the same time, Deuteronomy's refusal to name the central place avoids binding God to any specific sacred site.

Deuteronomy repeatedly describes worship at the place where Yahweh's name has been placed as worship before or in the presence of Yahweh (e.g., Deut. 12:12, 18). Sandra Richter argues the phrase "placing the name" (see 12:21) was used to describe kings inscribing their names on monuments to "claim that monument as [their] own and to commemorate [their] great deeds." In Deuteronomy, then, this language suggests that Yahweh is Israel's conquering king, who will claim a place for him to meet with his people.[5]

The primary purpose of the centralization of worship, then, is twofold. On the one hand, centralization guards the people from temptations to idolatry and illicit forms of Yahweh-worship.[6] On the other hand, worshiping in one place helps individual tribes and families understand themselves as *one people* living under the reign of their *one* divine King through faithfulness to his *one way*.

THE DUTY AND DELIGHT OF CENTRALIZED WORSHIP

Establishing a central location for worship requires serious commitment: "Guard yourself to ensure that you do not offer your burnt offerings in any place that you see" (Deut. 12:13 AT). It also introduces practical challenges. Since Leviticus demands nearly all meat be sacrificed before being eaten, would establishing a central sanctuary mean people had to go without meat?

Deuteronomy addresses this question by allowing the people to eat meat without sacrificing it, wherever they are and whenever they desire. Meat eaten apart from the sacrificial system and far away from the sanctuary still represents "blessing" from Yahweh (Deut. 12:15). Yahweh's permissive generosity emphasizes the abundance of the good land and Yahweh's benevolence as their king. Centralized worship is not a burdensome, life-draining obligation. Nor does it mean God is less present elsewhere in the

The Yorck Project / public domain

Figure 17.2. Twelfth-century illumination on parchment by Master Hugo. The bottom panel shows Moses teaching the people the food laws, while the top panel depicts Jesus as the fulfillment of the law of Moses.

land.[7] Through the law of centralization, Yahweh invites them to live the *good life* with their *good God* in every corner of the *good land*.

In Deuteronomy 1–11, Yahweh commands the people to pursue a certain affective stance toward him through the language of love and fear. In chapter 12, Moses introduces another affective command, one that will be relentlessly repeated: You shall *rejoice* (12:7, 12, 18; 14:26; 16:11, 14; 26:11). The invitation to meet with the one God in the place he chooses is gospel—good news. You are invited to come, all of you, and rejoice with your generous, gift-giving King. If Deuteronomy serves as a constitution for the kingdom of God, then inclusive, joyful worship stands at the center of political lives lived under the Lord of heaven and earth. Moses says resisting idolatry will be tough, exacting, costly work. But here in chapter 12, he says that the resulting abundant, joy-filled life with Yahweh is worth the effort.

Deuteronomy 13 turns from this joyful depiction of a life worshiping God to the threat posed by treasonous prophets or community members. While we considered how to think about violent Torah texts in general in chapter 13, we note here the surprising possibility of *false* prophets making *true* prophesies. While accurate prediction can be an aspect of prophetic ministry (see Deut. 18:21–22), the defining feature of a prophet is that they call the people back to covenantal faithfulness.

Deuteronomy's unique emphases show up in laws about clean and unclean foods in 14:1–21. By reminding the people they are a chosen, "treasured possession" just before reminding them of the food laws, Deuteronomy suggests that the people would somehow participate in God's mission through their diet. Presumably, practicing the food laws would set them apart. For Deuteronomy, Israel's countercultural identity is missional and central to

HISTORICAL MATTERS

Creating Space for *Religious* Outsiders?

Some occasionally claim that the immigrants in Israel had to obey all Israel's laws, but Deuteronomy 14:21 indicates this is not true. While immigrants could become full members of God's people through circumcision, they could also live in the land without adopting all of Israel's religious identity (that is why they can eat "unclean" food).

their participation in God's work. Only if they remain distinct from the nations can they fulfill their purpose of drawing the nations in.

This "set apartness" is held in tension with the desire to care for the vulnerable, a consistent theme in Deuteronomy. This explains why animals that are unclean for Israelites can still be shared with outsiders (Deut. 14:21).

Learning the Joy of Life with Yahweh (Deut. 14:22–16:17)

READ DEUTERONOMY 14:22–16:17

> Imagine you're an Israelite child whose family and village follow the feast laws of Deuteronomy 14:22–16:17. What is it like to go on these feasts? What do you learn? How do you learn it?

Deuteronomy 14:22–16:17 introduces a series of laws that shape the rhythms of the people's life with God.[8] These laws structure Israel's households, villages, and political and economic institutions, but they do so primarily by structuring Israel's calendars. The liturgical, ritual patterns prescribed should shape the people to know, deep down in their bones, the joy of life lived with God and inclusive of the vulnerable in God's community.

ANNUAL AND TRIENNIAL TITHES

Deuteronomy 14:22–29 and 15:19–23 describe regular tithes the people were to bring to God. In the ancient world, tithes were taxes levied by royal or religious elites, often on peasants who were already barely scraping by (see 1 Sam. 8:15). Elsewhere, the Old Testament mainly understands tithes as contributions to the sanctuary and priests (see Num. 18:26; 2 Chron. 31:4; Neh. 13:12; Mal. 3:10). So when Deuteronomy 14:22 instructs the Israelites to bring their tithes to the central sanctuary, you can almost hear them starting to groan. They know where this is headed.

Wikimedia Commons / public domain

Figure 17.3. The potentially exploitative nature of religious offerings is captured in Pieter Brueghel's seventeenth-century painting *The Payment of the Tithes*. Imagine how the scene would change if these tithe payers suddenly discovered that God was giving them back all they owed in order to celebrate a feast!

Nothing could have prepared them for what follows in Deuteronomy's radically innovative tithes. Yes, the Israelites owe Yahweh a tenth of their harvest and the firstborn of their livestock. Yes, this tithe constitutes Yahweh's tax levied on his tenants in his land.[9] But when they reach the sanctuary, their divine King takes everything they owe him and immediately returns it to them so they can have an enormous party in his presence: "You shall *eat* the tithe of your grain, your wine, and your oil, as well as the firstlings of your herd and flock" (Deut. 14:23).

Yahweh even allows the people to sell their tithes in the villages, bring the proceeds to the sanctuary, and buy whatever they want for their feast: "oxen, sheep, wine, strong drink, or *whatever you deeply desire*. And you shall eat there in the presence of the LORD your God, and you shall *rejoice*, you and your household" (Deut. 14:26 AT).

In the ancient world, kings used tithes to exploit the people and feasts to seduce them for their own political purposes. Here, Israel's subsistence farmers find themselves invited to a feast of royal proportions, a meal in which their tithes are returned to them for their own indulgence. And no human king is present! The only host at this table is Yahweh, and his generosity—highlighted by repeated references to lavish amounts of meat and overflowing alcoholic beverages—exceeds anything Israel could have imagined.

The Israelites get to pick the menu, but Yahweh gives strong directions on the guest list. They must feast with Yahweh and alongside all Yahweh's people. That's what the reference to eating with the "household" means, since for Deuteronomy, the "household" includes multiple generations of extended family as well as refugees, orphans, widows, debt servants, and landless Levites. In an ancient context, "to be able to eat together, one must *be* kin or one *becomes* kin."[10] Deuteronomy's feasts would have strengthened kinship relationships among household members and created

Wikimedia Commons / public domain

Figure 17.4. The Sumerian Standard of Ur portrays a massive feast from the third millennium BC. The king is seated in the top panel, but the huge parade of goods in the next two panels demonstrates that kings could use royal feasts to collect goods rather than to share them.

opportunities for landless, displaced people to become attached to households, which served as the smallest and most fundamental unit in Israel's economy and society.

God's people can only experience the joy of feasting with God if they surrender their offerings to God and then come ready to party in his presence alongside the vulnerable. Such feasts shape the people to taste and see the generosity of God—literally! These occasions would also help them see one another, and especially the vulnerable, as family. At the feast, Israel doesn't simply hear God's heart for the inclusion of the vulnerable; they experience and thus create a new, countercultural family at the festival.[11]

The good news for the marginalized that begins at this feast does not end there. Generosity begins with sharing at the table and spills over to giving charitably beyond the table. Deuteronomy 14:28–29 shifts from the annual tithe feast to an alternative tithe practice every third year. In these years, the tithe is not eaten at the sanctuary but stored in the village. Why? To ensure those vulnerable orphans, widows, immigrants, and Levites who must be welcomed at the feast can "eat and be satisfied" all year long.

REST FOR THE INDEBTED

Whereas Deuteronomy 14:22–29 shows special concern for those who might fall through the cracks between Israel's households, Deuteronomy 15:1–18 turns to a challenge faced by the households themselves (as well as agrarian households the world over): the need to borrow food or seed to bridge the gap between last year's harvest and the next or to survive a crop failure. Deuteronomy envisions Israelite households addressing this need by freely lending to one another. If one

HISTORICAL MATTERS

The World's First Social Safety Net

The radical socioeconomic legislation in Deuteronomy 14 establishes what scholars recognize as the first social safety net instituted for the vulnerable funded through fixed contributions by the whole society.[c] In some ways, the modern idea that society as a whole should contribute to the well-being of the vulnerable through taxation begins here. From Deuteronomy's perspective, though, the idea of a fixed tithe for the vulnerable starts with the need to feast with the vulnerable as family.

LITERARY NOTES

Eat and Be Satisfied

Deuteronomy 4–12 frequently uses the phrase "eat and be satisfied" to describe the danger economic abundance presents to the people. "When you eat and are satisfied, guard yourself to make sure you don't forget Yahweh!" (6:11–12 AT). But here in 14:28–29, the phrase is used positively: The vulnerable "eat and are satisfied" because God's people have set aside a portion of the abundance they have received from God for their sake. The message is clear: The only safe way to pursue and experience economic abundance without falling into greedy idolatry is in the context of a community that ensures all eat and are satisfied together.[d]

LITERARY NOTES

Where Did the Poor Go?

Norbert Lohfink argues that Deuteronomy's good news for the poor becomes clearer when we notice that Deuteronomy 14:22–29 does not describe the orphans, widows, Levites, and refugees as "poor," nor does it place the category of "the poor" alongside them. This is strange since Deuteronomy does talk about "the poor" elsewhere. Lohfink believes Deuteronomy intentionally avoids placing groups like the immigrant and widow into the umbrella category of "the poor." Instead, Deuteronomy changes "the structures of society so as to provide support for those groups which . . . are not in a position to live off their own land." While eliminating the conditions that create immigrants, refugees, orphans, and widows may be impossible, Deuteronomy claims it is possible "to create a world in which one can be a stranger, an orphan, or a widow without being poor."[e] However, creating such a world is only possible if these vulnerable people are able to become family, to find a place to belong among Israel's households.[f]

household needs to offer such a loan this year, they may well need to receive one in a later year.

Just like today, ancient lending was often predatory. High interest rates were the norm,[12] and as with some predatory car dealerships, loans were often given in order to seize the collateral when the borrower inevitably defaulted.[13] Against this backdrop, Deuteronomy 15:1–18 and 23:19–20 establish a just, neighborly economy among households. Several features of this economy deserve more attention.

First, the prohibition of interest is extremely countercultural. Almost no clear parallels to interest-free lending existed in the ancient world. Second, Deuteronomy limits the harm defaulting could do to a needy borrower. All loans will be forgiven every seven years; it is "the Lord's year of debt cancellation" (Deut. 15:2 CEB). In the ancient world, kings sometimes announced debt forgiveness, but they did so sporadically, at their own whim, and often with the goal of gaining some sort of political advantage. Yahweh makes such debt release a fixed part of his economic program, changing the structure of society as a whole. Moreover, because debt relief belongs to Yahweh, it also belongs to every Israelite household; all are responsible for enacting Yahweh's release in their own households, villages, and cities.

Deuteronomy also limits debt servitude—a situation in which a defaulting household surrenders one of their members to work off a debt in the lender's household—to seven years. Moreover, in the seventh year, households not only release debt slaves but liberally provide for them from the household's flock, threshing floor, and wine press (Deut. 15:12–18). This allows enslaved people to reap some of the rewards of their labor, and it reduces the likelihood they will fall quickly back into debt.

Third, Yahweh is at the center of this radical, countercultural economy. It is Yahweh's release that gets declared every seven years (Deut. 15:2) and Yahweh's gracious gift-giving that allows them to have an abundance to lend (15:6, 7, 10). The practice of sending out the debt servant laden with good gifts imitates the way Yahweh brought the people out of slavery in Egypt (15:15; cf. Exod. 12:35–36).

Fourth, Yahweh's economic program seeks to establish and protect a relatively egalitarian economy, in which each household can claim a place to stand and a portion to steward in the land. Such an economic program resonates deeply with the vision of the Jubilee in Leviticus 25. By placing limits on debt, Yahweh limits the ability of any household to permanently lose the family farm, as well as placing limits on more powerful households seeking to permanently acquire new farms and fields.

This relatively egalitarian, neighborly way of life sits on the surface of Deuteronomy 15. The text repeatedly refers to the person in need as the "brother" or "neighbor." Such language "encourages listeners to see the neighbor as a member of a family in which they are 'linked by kinship.'"[14] Israel is being invited to a socioeconomic way of life that treats the neighbor as family, a vision that flows directly out of the family-forming feasts of the previous chapter. To put the matter more strongly, Israel is being called to place economic life at the service of communal life. As Brueggemann says, "Economic matters must yield to social reality; and the social reality is that if the needy are kept in debt, they cannot be viable neighbors."[15]

Fifth, Deuteronomy's laws recognize that a neighborly economy depends on just structures *and* community members whose hearts have been transformed by God's just generosity. A law requiring debt forgiveness could have the unintended consequence of encouraging Israelites simply to refuse to make loans in the first place. Deuteronomy 15:9 warns, "If you do that, [your poor fellow Israelites] will cry out to the LORD against you, and you will be guilty of sin" (CEB). Instead, God's people must open their hands wide through generous lending. If Israel is going to experience the just, life-giving economy God desires, they must embrace Yahweh's just structures around

ETHICS

Family Economics Today

The Torah regularly calls us to treat others as if they were our own family. What difference might it make if our moral imaginations were discipled to see others—including orphans, immigrants, refugees, citizens from "enemy" nations, our political opponents, people from other racial groups, the poor, and more—as our own mothers and brothers? Among other things, such a stance would prove revolutionary in our economic lives, because our modern economic systems tend to place all social, political, and familial life at the service of the economy. All must be offered on the altar of unending economic growth. But God calls his people to bend the way we work, earn, spend, save, invest, share, and give toward the kingdom of God and the good of the whole community. This vision does not answer all our questions about markets and other aspects of political economy, but it does call us to pursue those complicated questions in countercultural, kingdom-oriented ways. (For practical ideas on what this might look like, see *Practicing the King's Economy* by Michael Rhodes, Robby Holt, and Brian Fikkert.)

HISTORICAL MATTERS

Laws That Walk the Walk

Like other ancient law collections, Deuteronomy boasts about the lawgiver's justice in the prelude to the laws themselves. Hammurabi says his laws aided the oppressed and that the oppressed could come read the laws and be comforted. However, Lohfink points out that when we actually look at the content of these ancient law collections, we do not "discover even a single occurrence of the words 'poor' or 'oppressed.'" According to Lohfink, "there is no social legislation" in the laws of Hammurabi, Ur-Nammu, Lipit-Ishtar, or any other Mesopotamian law collection; "they never deal directly with the poor or with their rights in society."[9] By contrast, Scripture celebrates Yahweh as the just lawgiver who cares for the poor, and it provides examples of Yahweh's good laws that protect the poor and oppressed, especially in Deuteronomy 15 and 24.

Deuteronomy 24, for instance, protects the rights of borrowers (24:6, 10–13), requires day laborers to be paid promptly and fairly (24:14–15), demands justice for refugees, orphans, and widows (24:17–18), and requires farmers to go over the fields only once during harvesting so that the vulnerable can come and glean in their fields. While ancient kings talked the talk, when it comes to the poor and oppressed, Yahweh's law walked the walk.

Wikimedia Commons / public domain

Figure 17.5. *Gleaners* by Jean-François Millet (1857)

ETHICS

Justice Demands Changed Structures and Hearts

Deuteronomy joins together what some Christians put asunder: the biblical requirement to change structures *and* hearts. Dr. Martin Luther King Jr. pointed to this dynamic in his long war against racism. He recognized court-enforced desegregation could not eliminate the "fears, prejudice, pride and irrationality" preventing a "truly integrated society." The "dark and demonic" forces of injustice could only be removed when humans became "possessed by the invisible inner law which etches on their hearts the conviction that all men are brothers."[h] But King also recognized that while "the law cannot make a man love me, [it] can restrain him from lynching me and I think that is pretty important, also." Indeed, King recognized changed legal structures could even "change the habits of men . . . and through changes in habits" affect their attitudes and hearts in the process.[i] This resonates deeply with Deuteronomy's vision of a community of disciples who are *becoming* just in both their individual character and their corporate structures. (For more on what Scripture says about how disciples *become* just, see Rhodes, *Just Discipleship*).

tithing and lending. But they also need to become just people,[16] people who sacrificially give to their neighbor even when it costs them.

THE FESTIVAL LIFE OF THE FAITHFUL

Deuteronomy 16:1–17 offers Israel an annual calendar built around three pilgrimage festivals (Passover / Unleavened Bread, Weeks, and Booths). As we saw in Leviticus 23, scholars argue these festivals are ritual reenactments of Israel's history.[17] The embodied actions associated with these pilgrimages are part of Deuteronomy's memory-making program of discipleship (Deut. 16:3, 12). They shape the people to know that their corporate lives depend on God's grace.

Deuteronomy's calendar repeatedly emphasizes the joy of life with God and the importance of bringing the whole community to the pilgrimage party. Such feasts require significant commitment. Without a supermarket, prep time begins months beforehand, and the party itself requires lengthy time away from homes and fields. These annual rituals would give the community a special time to step away from everyday workloads and social hierarchies in order to experience God and God's goodness *together*. They would help Israel orient the entirety of their socioeconomic life toward love of God and neighbor. As the Dutch economist Bob Goudzwaard once memorably said, "The horizon of Israel's economy is the feast."[18]

A Constitutional Vision for a Just People (Deut. 16:18–19:21)

Scholars describe Deuteronomy 16:18–18:22 as a sort of "constitutional proposal,"[19] including God-given guidelines for judges, kings, priests, and prophets. Deuteronomy 19 further explores political structures by demanding that the people

1. establish cities of refuge to which a person who has accidentally killed someone may flee to avoid being killed in revenge,
2. honor the ancestral boundaries of the family farms Yahweh has bequeathed to Israel's households, and
3. enforce the provided guidelines for witnesses in court.

Much of this material is related to the remarkable command in Deuteronomy 16:20: "Justice, and only justice, you shall pursue, so that you may live and occupy the land that the Lord your God is giving you."

While Deuteronomy 16:18–18:22 focuses on leaders, the whole people ultimately bear responsibility for pursuing Yahweh's just way.[20] The system of judges, king, priests, and prophets provides something like a system of "checks and balances,"[21] but the people themselves play a central role in establishing Yahweh's justice in the land.

In other ancient societies, kings wrote the laws, appointed judges, maintained a special relationship with the gods, and often at least technically owned the land. Priests were often in their pockets, and prophets served as yes-men in their courts. By contrast, in Deuteronomy, Yahweh writes the law and enters the covenant directly with the whole people. Yahweh raises up prophets and chooses priests, and the people themselves are involved in appointing "judges and officials" (Deut. 16:18). Since Yahweh is the people's king, Israel doesn't need a human king at all. If they choose to have a king, the people must select one from among the Israelites and under Yahweh's guidance (17:15). Even then, Deuteronomy severely limits the monarch. He cannot amass weapons for his military (represented by horses), economic power (represented by silver and gold), or international alliances (represented by marriage to many women from nations that worship other gods) (17:16–17). This is a bit like saying to Americans, "Okay, you can have a president, but they can't live in the White House, serve as commander in chief of the military, draw a salary, or veto legislation." Those activities are what it *means* to be the president! What's left, then, for this deuteronomic king?

LITERARY NOTES

No Poor Among You? Or the Poor You Will Always Have with You?

Some claim that Jesus's statement "The poor you will always have with you" (Matt. 26:11 NIV) means Christians shouldn't be *too* concerned about poverty, because there will always be poor people. Given that interpretation, it's interesting to discover Jesus is alluding to Deuteronomy 15:11, which calls Israel to shape their economic life around care for the poor: "Since there will never cease to be some in need on the earth, I therefore command you, 'Open your hand to the poor and needy neighbor in your land.'" When we realize that just seven verses earlier Deuteronomy boldly declares, "There will be *no* poor among you" (15:4 ESV), though, matters become somewhat confusing.

We can understand this tension in two ways. First, "no poor among you" in Deuteronomy 15:4 could envision the possibilities if Israel obeys God's way, while Deuteronomy 15:11 recognizes they will fail to do so.[j] Alternatively, 15:4 could mean there need be no *permanently poor* people among you. Read this way, 15:11 guides the people on how to address temporary poverty in such a way as to fulfill that vision. Neither interpretation commends apathy regarding persistent poverty—quite the opposite. Likewise, the One who declared "good news to the poor" (Luke 4:18) certainly did not intend to convince his disciples they should care less about the poor.

We might reflect further on Jesus's claim in light of the fact that the poor are often *not* "with" others in all sorts of ways. In Jesus's day, the economically poor and socially marginalized were often excluded. Today, the poor are increasingly segregated from other economic classes in workplaces, schools, neighborhoods, and some churches; "in nearly every area of public life, 'rich and poor Americans today are less likely to know one another and to share the same social spaces' than they were even fifty years ago."[k] But in both Deuteronomy and Jesus's vision, the poor should be "with" God's people. Jesus's statement does not justify an apathetic shrug about the plight of the suffering; it offers a scathing indictment of our failure to embrace God's economic vision.

Figure 17.6. Relief depicting the Assyrian King Ashurbanipal, who called himself the "king of the world," relaxing in his garden. The head of an Elamite king hangs from a tree on the far left (645–635 BC).

CANONICAL CONNECTIONS

Laws That Indict

Solomon becomes famous for acquiring the very wealth, women, and military might Deuteronomy forbids with the exact result Deuteronomy predicts: a heart turned away from Yahweh and a life lived in defiance of Yahweh's way. However, nearly all Israel's kings are judged and found wanting by Deuteronomy's rigorous rejection of ancient Near Eastern statecraft. These kings are judged failures even if they presided over politically and economically "successful" regimes in the world's eyes.

Figure 17.7. *King Solomon in Old Age* by Gustave Doré (1866)

According to Deuteronomy 17:18–20, the king's sole job is to keep "a copy of this law" with him and read it "all the days of his life." Why? So that "he may learn to fear the LORD his God, diligently observing all the words of this law and these statutes, neither exalting himself above other members of the community nor turning aside from the commandment." The one Torah text that allows for a king insists that the king be completely countercultural, rejecting the militaristic, acquisitive power politics that characterized ancient kings and standing alongside, rather than above, his fellow Israelites.

Israel's "constitutional proposal" shapes them for their vocation to mediate God's blessing to the world by embodying God's justice and righteousness.

Miscellaneous Matters (Deut. 20–25)

READ DEUTERONOMY 20:19, 22:6–7, AND 25:4

What do these laws teach us about God? About our world? About ourselves?

Deuteronomy 20–25 covers a wide variety of topics, including how to wage war (Deut. 20); issues related to marriage, family, and sex (see 21:15–21; 24:1–5; 25:5–10); justice and care for the vulnerable (see 23:15–16); and ritual purity (see 22:9–12; 23:9–14). Overarching themes and structures are difficult to discern, in part because Deuteronomy, like Leviticus, recognizes connections between topics we tend to separate.

One theme in this section that we have not yet explored is the law's concern for creation. Deuteronomy includes numerous laws seeking the good of the entire community of creation.

Figure 17.8. Using oxen in agricultural work in Spain (1966)

- *Limits on ecological destruction during war.* Fruit-bearing trees played a special role in ancient Israel's life, in part because they served as an important food source. They also were treasured because they could take five to six years to begin bearing fruit, and up to twenty before reaching full maturity.[22] Small wonder, then, that attacking fruit trees was a popular strategy during war.[23] Deuteronomy 20:19 prohibits Israel from practicing such ecological warfare.
- *Treating domestic animals as coworkers.* The prohibition on muzzling an ox while it treads out grain recognizes that the ox serves as something of a "partner-worker in the family business" and thus has "a right to eat of the fruits of the land while engaged in agricultural production" (Deut. 25:4).[24] In an environment in which families could face a sixty-day shortage of food in the lean period just before harvest, allowing an ox to consume five to seven pounds of grain every day it worked in the field would be very costly. "Yet God commands Israel to allow the beast . . . to benefit from the fruit of its labors. *Even when that benefit and joy cut into the farmer's profits . . . or even his essential food supply.*"[25]

Such laws suggest humans are called to engage "creation on behalf of Yahweh and in ways that reflect his love for it."[26]

Concluding the Law in Liturgy (Deut. 26)

READ DEUTERONOMY 26

> Imagine that you are performing the worship ritual described in chapter 26. Imagine the sights, smells, sounds, and feelings you encounter as you engage in it. Consider, What might this ritual be shaping you to know? To believe? To feel?

Deuteronomy 26 closes the law collection by returning to the theme of wholehearted worship at Yahweh's chosen place. The text offers a particularly intimate depiction of a liturgical performance of Deuteronomy's theology and ethics. The lengthy script the worshiper speaks—which Gerhard von Rad identified as a sort of mini-creed—allows us to "listen in" on this paradigmatic act of worship.

- *Yahweh's generous gift*. Yahweh's good gifts are the primary theme; the Hebrew verb for "give" (*natan*) occurs six times in Deuteronomy 26:1–11.[27] Furthermore, the liturgy reinforces Israel's total dependence on Yahweh's generosity. The statement "A wandering Aramean was my ancestor" points to Jacob's precarious position. Israel started out as a homeless, vulnerable people who became easy prey to the Egyptians (26:6–7).

  Yahweh's *grace* preserved them in their homelessness, made them a great nation even as sojourners in Egypt, rescued them from oppression when they cried out, and brought them into this "land flowing with milk and honey." The ritual reenactment of the exodus through the pilgrimage to the sanctuary and the liturgical references to "our" affliction in Egypt weave successive generations into this foundational story. At the climax of this rite, the formerly homeless worshiper arrives at Yahweh's home and declares with their body, words, and gifts, "It's all *grace*, *God's* grace, grace *alone*!"
- *The people's "pledge of allegiance" in response*. The liturgy likewise allows the people to pledge their allegiance to Yahweh in response (Deut. 26:13). Brueggemann suggests this "mutual giving and receiving of promises of fidelity" remind us of wedding vows.[28]

  The firstfruits of the harvest play a special role in this declaration. Subsistence farmers face their hardest days just before the harvest. Until the harvest is fully gathered, their crops and lives remain vulnerable. The ritual interrupts farmers at this critical moment, requiring they journey to the sanctuary to make this declaration while offering the first portion of their partially harvested crop. Such a liturgy requires the farm family to perform an act of holy, hopeful dependence on Yahweh.
- *The poor and vulnerable at the center*. Finally, this liturgy encapsulates the way Deuteronomy centers justice and inclusion for the poor in Yahweh's covenant community. The worshiper brings firstfruits to God before they even know if the full harvest will pay off, and they are called to feast with the landless Levites and immigrants among them before they leave (Deut. 26:11). The context of 26:13–15's liturgical declaration is the setting aside of the triennial tithe to provide

for the poor. Such social safety nets are holy portions that provide for the marginalized (26:13). Yahweh has brought the people out of homelessness and into a good home in his presence. As a result, hospitality becomes a hallmark of God's kingdom, required by the law and enacted through Israel's worship.

The law collection ends by reminding the people of its goal: a community that embraces its identity and job description as Yahweh's holy, treasured people (Deut. 26:18–19). Such a people will serve as Yahweh's vehicle of blessing to the very ends of the earth.

Figure 17.9. From the Leningrad Codex, one of the oldest complete manuscripts of the entire Old Testament (early 11th cent.)

Blessings and Curses (Deut. 27–29)

Deuteronomy 27–29 shifts away from the law collection but stays focused on liturgical practices that foster faithfulness. Moses's second speech climactically closes with a covenant enactment performance that includes writing the law on stones (27:3), making sacrifices and celebrating at feasts (27:5–7), and ritually reciting curses for disobedience (27:11–26; 28:15–68) and blessings for obedience (28:1–14).[29]

The blessings and curses worry us. The blessings can feel like a mechanical "prosperity gospel," while the brutality of the curses borders on the incomprehensible. However, such lists would be expected by Deuteronomy's audience. Blessings and curses commonly featured in the covenantal form Deuteronomy adapts.[30] Moreover, carefully exploring Deuteronomy's blessings and curses reveals several important theological insights.

First, looking specifically at the curses in Deuteronomy 27, many of these prohibitions relate to actions that could remain hidden

Figure 17.10. During the ceremony of blessings and curses, half the Israelites were to stand on Mount Gerizim, while the other half stood on Mount Ebal. This image captures the view of Mount Ebal from Mount Gerizim in 2013.

("Cursed be anyone who strikes down a neighbor in secret"; 27:24). One purpose of such curses, then, "is to remind Israel that Yahweh sees and knows what happens when nobody else is watching."[31]

Second, while the curses greatly outnumber the blessings, Deuteronomy's blessing section is far more extensive than those of ancient parallels. Some ancient covenant treaties lack any blessing section at all.[32]

Third, there is an ironic aspect to the curses. They hint at a reversal of Israel's fortunes; instead of "growth and greatness . . . , [they] will wither away to insignificance" and eventually be expelled from the land. They will suffer "plagues once laid on the Egyptians" and experience a reverse exodus out of the land and into captivity.[33] The irony is that Israel will only receive this judgment if they idolatrously seek the blessings Yahweh has already promised from other gods or powers. All Israel has to do is serve the Lord "with gladness of heart for the abundance of everything" (Deut. 28:47).

Fourth, a paradoxical tension emerges in Deuteronomy 28. On the one hand, the blessings and curses are conditional: "*If* you will only obey," the result is blessing, "but *if* you will *not* obey," the result is cursing (28:1, 15). On the other hand, verse 47 is most naturally read as stating that because Israel *will not* serve Yahweh, they *will* experience the curses. The "grammatical shift" in verses 45–48 suggests the curses have moved from possibility to "a declared state of fact that will happen in the narrated future."[34] This raises the question, Is obedience a genuine possibility? Deuteronomy's surprising answer emerges more fully in the chapters that follow.

Well-Worn Repetitions and Surprising Paradoxes (Deut. 29–33)

READ DEUTERONOMY 30–32

> Consider, How do these chapters address the question raised in the previous ones? Namely, Is obedience a genuine possibility?

Moses's third and fourth sermons repeat and reiterate well-worn deuteronomic themes pertinent to the covenant Moses establishes with the people in Moab.

Once again, Moses returns to their "origin story," beginning with the ancestors and lingering over poetic depictions of Yahweh's miraculous provision in the wilderness (Deut. 29:5–8; 32:10–14). His storytelling emphasizes Yahweh's character as perfect, just, and faithful. Yahweh is the "Most High" who is sovereign over all nations (32:8). Not only was Yahweh the only god responsible for Israel's flourishing (32:12); he is the only God at all (32:39).

Second, Moses again invites God's people to enter that story, to bind themselves to it, through faithfully entering and obeying Yahweh's covenant.

Because of who Yahweh is and what Yahweh has done, Moses calls the people to choose "life and the good" rather than "death and disaster" (Deut. 30:15 AT).

Third, Deuteronomy again casts a radically inclusive vision for covenantal life. The entire community, including children, women, and ethnic outsiders, is invited to become the people who inherit the promises made to Abraham (Deut. 29:10–13). By requiring the people to regularly read the entire law during the Feast of Booths, Deuteronomy 31:10–13 seeks to enfold future generations into the covenantal, God-fearing family.

Yet these chapters also offer a series of surprising new theological paradoxes. Right in the middle of Moses's familiar summons to obey the law, he drops this bombshell: "But to this day Yahweh has not given you a heart to understand, or eyes to see, or ears to hear" (Deut. 29:4 AT). How can Moses say Israel lacks the moral hardware—the heart, eyes, or ears—necessary to obey the law? This seems to contradict both what Moses has said so far and what he's about to say. Right after telling the people they don't have what it takes because God hasn't given it to them, he calls them to obey a law that is "not too hard for" them. "No," Moses continues, "the word is very near to you; it is in your mouth and in your heart for you to observe" (30:11–15; cf. 29:10–15).

Similar apparent contradictions run throughout these sermons. Yahweh calls the people to "choose life" (Deut. 30:19) right before telling Moses the people definitely won't because of their inclination and giving the people a convicting song to sing when they inevitably fail (31:16–32:47). Yet even though the song puts Israel's future failures in the past tense, Moses offers it to the people as a warning to choose life and follow Yahweh's way (32:45–46). And the song is not Moses's last word. Moses's last words are lengthy blessings pronounced on the whole people, culminating in an announcement that Israel has received the promise and attained the blessed life in God's land (33:28–29a).

So which is it? Is Israel's failure inevitable? Are the people able to follow Yahweh's way? Or is there something deeply dysfunctional about their ability to follow the law? And if failure is inevitable, if their hearts are unable to obey, what will happen to Yahweh's plan to bless the nations through his people?

Some commentators downplay these tensions by emphasizing one side or the other of the apparent contradictions.[35] Others rightly recognize the contradictions create a meaningful theological paradox. This paradox is on

LITERARY NOTES

Which Covenant in Moab?

Deuteronomy 29:1 references a covenant made in Moab "in addition" to the covenant at Horeb. Scholars differ on how to understand this. Some understand the Moab covenant as all that Deuteronomy has been saying since chapter 5, so that the Moab covenant is simply a "second and expanded version of the same Sinai/Horeb covenant."[l] Alternatively, Dennis Olson sees the covenant of Moab as referring to what comes next in Deuteronomy 29–32. He argues that Deuteronomy uses this Moabite covenant to address Israel's likely suffering due to the covenantal failures anticipated in 28:45–48.[m] Richard Nelson offers something of a mediating position, seeing the references to the covenant in Moab as looking "both ways, referring to previous material and summarizing it, while simultaneously pointing forward and initiating what follows."[n]

full display in the carefully constructed passage in Deuteronomy 30:1–10. A central feature of the text is the wordplay created through repeated use of the Hebrew word *shuv*, meaning "turn, return, repent." Below are sections of the text in the NRSV, with adaptations in brackets and forms of the word *shuv* set in bold.

> [When/if][36] all these things have happened to you, the blessings and the curses that I have set before you, [and when/if] you [**return** them to your heart] among all the nations where the LORD your God has driven you, and **return** to the LORD your God, and you and your children obey him with all your heart and with all your [being], just as I am commanding you today, then the LORD your God will [**return**] your fortunes and have compassion on you, [**returning**] you again from all the peoples among whom the LORD your God has scattered you. . . . *Moreover, the LORD your God will circumcise your heart and the heart of your descendants, so that you will love the LORD your God with all your heart and with all your [being], in order that you may live.* . . . Then you [shall surely **return**, and you will listen to the voice of] the LORD, observing all his commandments that I am commanding you today. . . . For the LORD will [**return** to] delight in prospering you, just as he delighted in prospering your ancestors, when you obey the LORD your God by observing his commandments and decrees that are written in this book of the law, because you [**return**] to the LORD your God with all your heart and with all your [being].

As Ryan O'Dowd points out, "Israel turns, Yahweh turns to Israel, and Yahweh turns Israel toward himself."[37] This mutual turning will result in God's people one day living precisely because they love and obey Yahweh with all their hearts (20:2, 6, 10). The transformation that will make this possible stands at the center of the passage: Yahweh will circumcise the people's hearts. The heart surgery Yahweh had called Israel to perform in 10:16, he now promises to perform all by himself.[38]

This may be the Torah's most powerful depiction of Yahweh's generous commitment to bring blessing to the world through humans who bear his image and live in line with his way. Yahweh's mercy and grace have been on display since Genesis 3:14–21, climaxing in Yahweh's revelation of his overwhelmingly merciful character to Moses at Mount Sinai. Yet here we discover something new. Yahweh is so committed to humans that he will perform heart surgery to ensure they can serve as his covenantal partners. Apparently "only God can create obedience," and Deuteronomy 30:6 announces the good news that he will.[39] Deuteronomy 30:1–10 thus recognizes that the obedience of God's people ultimately depends on Yahweh's intervening grace.[40]

At the same time, the profound "paradox or tension between divine grace and Israelite repentance" ought to be sustained rather than eliminated.[41] While God's gracious action dominates, human agency remains present. For instance, Deuteronomy 30:1 could be translated "*if* all these things have happened," raising the possibility that Israel will follow God's law and avoid catastrophe. Whether one translates Deuteronomy 30:1 as "if" or "when," the first step in the process that leads to Yahweh's heart surgery is repentance.[42] Most tellingly, by making both Yahweh and Israel the subject of verbs for "turning," Moses shows that "human responsibility and divine action fit together."[43]

As we argued in chapter 1, reading the Pentateuch well requires us to recognize that "mystery is the lifeblood of theological reflection."[44] Quantum physics can tell us that light acts like both a particle and a wave, but it cannot tell us how. Deuteronomy simultaneously offers the people a good law that can be followed *and* the prophetic promise that God will do whatever it takes—including heart surgery—to ensure that the people become a community that "chooses life" in line with Yahweh's way. But Deuteronomy cannot resolve this paradoxical mystery, which is closely connected to the theological question of divine sovereignty and human responsibility. Instead, Deuteronomy simply creates "a mosaic of paradoxes and juxtapositions that work theologically with some of the most basic and ultimate issues of theology and faith."[45]

Ultimately, we are called to marvel at the goodness of our mysterious God, to draw near the dizzying heights of the "secret things [that] belong to the LORD our God." Having marveled at such secret mysteries, we find ourselves called by Deuteronomy to turn to the "revealed things [that] belong to us and to our children," not least by seeking to walk in the Lord's way (Deut. 29:29).

HISTORICAL MATTERS

Dating the End of Deuteronomy

Deciding how to interpret Deuteronomy 29–33 is complicated by the fact that many scholars believe this portion of Deuteronomy was written *after* the exile.[o] From this perspective, while these chapters read like a *prophetic prediction* of failure, in fact they actually emerged as a *reflection* on the people's historic experience of exile.[p] This is a possibility, but of course, Deuteronomy's prediction of failure need not depend on the people's experience of exile. The Torah is fully aware of God's people's tendency to rebellion.

CANONICAL CONNECTIONS

The Unfolding Mystery of the Heart

While the Old Testament often seems to assume people can follow God's law,[q] Deuteronomy 30:6's claim that Yahweh must intervene at the heart level gets picked up and expanded throughout Scripture. Just as in Deuteronomy, Jeremiah first calls the people to circumcise their own hearts (Jer. 4:3–4). Then, in the aftermath of exile, he looks ahead to a day when Yahweh would create a new covenant with his people, inscribing his law on their hearts and forgiving their sins (31:33–34). While Jeremiah and Deuteronomy emphasize repentance, the prophet seems to have been inspired by Deuteronomy to go beyond Deuteronomy in portraying Yahweh as unilaterally offering forgiveness and moral transformation.[r] Ezekiel goes further, promising Yahweh will give Israel a "new heart" altogether (Ezek. 36:26). God's gift of an "organ transplant" gives the people hearts of flesh so they can follow Yahweh's way.

Jesus explicitly claims to launch Jeremiah's "new covenant" (see Luke 22:20; cf. 2 Cor. 3:6; Heb. 8:8–13; 9:15). Kyle Wells argues that Paul believed Deuteronomy 30:1–10 had come true through Jesus.[s] Reading Deuteronomy alongside Jeremiah and Ezekiel taught Paul that true circumcision "is a matter of the heart" (Rom. 2:29). He believed such heart circumcision occurred through union with Christ. This divine gift transforms God's people, liberating them from enslavement to sin and death. Yet perhaps *because* Paul had been discipled by the paradoxes of Deuteronomy, Jeremiah, and Ezekiel, he recognizes this heart circumcision does not make obedience automatic. Humans with hearts circumcised by the Spirit are called to "walk in newness of life" (Rom. 6:4), proactively refusing to "let sin exercise dominion in [their] mortal bodies" and instead offering those bodies as "slaves to righteousness for sanctification" (6:12, 19).

Photo by Szilas in Museum of Fine Arts Ghent (MSK) / public domain

Figure 17.11. *Moses Sees the Promised Land* by Christian Rohlfs (1912)

Arriving at the End (Deut. 34)

Deuteronomy brings the Torah to a close with the tragic story of Moses's death and a final statement on Moses's unique position in Israel's life. Whoever wrote the final words of Deuteronomy could confidently state, "Never since has there arisen a prophet in Israel like Moses, whom the LORD knew face to face" (Deut. 34:10).

It's a heavy ending. Moses is dead, the people's new leaders will not rise to his level, and though the book is confident the people will soon enter the land, literarily they remain outside. Yet perhaps this heavy ending holds out a deeper hope. For Ellen Davis, Israel's position outside the land suggests that "what binds Israel to God" is not the land but the history of Yahweh's deliverance and subsequent giving of covenantal instruction.[46] This anticipates what the people would have to learn: Life with God can continue even in exile.

Moreover, Deuteronomy's claim that no prophet had yet risen to Moses's stature does not eliminate Moses's prophecy that Yahweh *would* "raise up" a prophet like him to whom the people would listen (Deut. 18:15). It merely confirms that the prophecy had not been fulfilled within the horizons of Deuteronomy. To read the Torah as Christian Scripture is to recognize this promise has been fulfilled in Jesus (Acts 3:22–26). He is the one Moses wrote about "in the law" (John 1:45), the one who "is worthy of more glory than Moses" (Heb. 3:2–3). Deuteronomy's demand that God's people listen to the voice of Yahweh so that they might become vehicles of God's blessing to the nations ultimately points us to and prepares us for the Father speaking over Jesus of Nazareth: "This is my Son, whom I love. Listen to him!" (Mark 9:7 NIV).

Living the Text: Deuteronomy's Economic Vision Today

While Deuteronomy's vision does not provide a straightforward blueprint for contemporary Christian communities, it does offer a God-authorized paradigm for imagining how to pursue God's kingdom today. As such, Deuteronomy has a great deal to say about economic life. The book suggests

God's people must be ready to love their neighbors and practice economic justice and mercy at several different levels:

- God's people include the poor and marginalized in the community's feasts.
- God's people provide food for the most vulnerable through emergency aid (triennial tithe).
- God's people bend the way they run the family business toward the vulnerable through the gleaning laws. These laws require family farms to leave profits in the field, creating space for the vulnerable to provide for themselves through work.
- God's people practice just generosity in relation to other households through interest-free loans. In doing so, they pursue a more just economic structure.
- Finally, the Sabbatical and Jubilee years prescribe an economic way of life that's good for the land and all of its nonhuman inhabitants, ensuring no Israelite family ever permanently loses access to the primary social and economic asset within the community: the family farm. They thus confront multigenerational poverty, in part by placing limits on multigenerational affluence.

In other words, the Torah's vision of economic justice and generosity includes everything from emergency food aid to the structural rearrangement of society so that economic life contributes to ecological flourishing and every human has a socioeconomic place to stand and portion to steward.

The Torah's spectrum of economic activity looks somewhat like the "relief–rehabilitation–development" continuum described by Brian Fikkert and Steve Corbett in their book *When Helping Hurts*:

- In the relief phase, Christians offer urgent, temporary emergency aid to alleviate immediate suffering in the wake of a crisis.
- In the rehabilitation phase, Christians walk alongside people and communities as they work back toward their precrisis state.
- In the development phase, Christians advocate for and participate in a community's ongoing process of mutual change—including structural change—in which all move closer toward God's vision for the community.[47]

While many Christians act generously toward the poor, we often fail to holistically live out God's just and generous way. Deuteronomy calls us to think expansively about how we might bend the entirety of our economic lives—the way we give, work, invest, save, lend, share, and vote—toward an economy where the poor are fed, the unemployed are welcomed into workplaces, families can invest in their futures, the land and all creatures flourish, and our society's structures interrupt multigenerational poverty.[48]

Notes

The endnotes for each chapter appear first, followed by the notes to the sidebars for that chapter.

Chapter 1 How (and Why) to Read the Pentateuch Today

1. Brent A. Strawn, *The Old Testament Is Dying: A Diagnosis and Recommended Treatment* (Baker Academic, 2017), 53n98.
2. Richard Dawkins, *The God Delusion* (Random House UK, 2016), 31.
3. See Michael Gryboski, "Christians Must 'Unhitch' Old Testament from Their Faith, Says Andy Stanley," *Christian Post*, May 9, 2018, https://www.christianpost.com/news/christians-must-unhitch-old-testament-from-their-faith-says-andy-stanley-223818/.
4. See Kevin J. Vanhoozer, introduction to *Dictionary for Theological Interpretation of the Bible*, ed. Kevin J. Vanhoozer, Craig G. Bartholomew, Daniel Treier, and N. T. Wright (Baker Academic, 2005), 20–25.
5. See Craig G. Bartholomew, *Introducing Biblical Hermeneutics: A Comprehensive Framework for Hearing God in Scripture* (Baker Academic, 2015), 18.
6. Esau McCaulley, *Reading While Black: African American Biblical Exegesis as an Exercise in Hope* (IVP Academic, 2020), 21.
7. Ellen F. Davis, "Losing a Friend: The Loss of the Old Testament to the Church" *Pro Ecclesia* 9, no. 1 (2000): 77.
8. Herman Bavinck, *Reformed Dogmatics: Abridged in One Volume*, ed. John Bolt (Baker Academic, 2011), 147.
9. Bavinck, *Reformed Dogmatics: Abridged*, 168.
10. John Calvin, *Institutes of the Christian Religion*, trans. Henry Beveridge, 1.13.1, https://www.ccel.org/ccel/calvin/institutes.iii.xiv.html, accessed November 28, 2023.
11. Terence E. Fretheim, *The Suffering of God: An Old Testament Perspective*, Overtures to Biblical Theology (Fortress, 1985), 5.
12. Fretheim, *Suffering of God*, 8.
13. Fretheim, *Suffering of God*, 8.
14. See Terence E. Fretheim, *What Kind of God? Collected Essays of Terence E. Fretheim*, ed. Michael J. Chan and Brent A. Strawn (Eisenbrauns, 2015), 78.

15. See Daisy Dobrijevic, "The Double-Slit Experiment: Is Light a Wave or a Particle?," *Space*, March 23, 2022, https://www.space.com/double-slit-experiment-light-wave-or-particle.

16. Chad Orzel, "What Has Quantum Mechanics Ever Done for Us?," *Forbes*, August 13, 2015, https://www.forbes.com/sites/chadorzel/2015/08/13/what-has-quantum-mechanics-ever-done-for-us/.

17. Christopher Seitz, "Canon and Conquest," in *Divine Evil? The Moral Character of the God of Abraham*, ed. Michael Bergmann et. al. (Oxford University Press, 2011), 293.

18. The phrase "further up and further in" comes from the final volume in C. S. Lewis's Chronicles of Narnia, *The Last Battle* (The Bodley Head, 1956). See particularly chap. 15.

19. See C. John Collins, *Reading Genesis Well: Navigating History, Poetry, Science, and Truth in Genesis 1–11* (Zondervan Academic, 2018), 34–50.

20. Jane B. Reece, Noel Meyers, Lisa A. Urry, Michael L. Cain, Steven A. Wasserman, Peter V. Minorsky, et. al, *Campbell Biology: Australian and New Zealand Version*, 10th ed. (Pearson Australia, 2015), 4.

21. V. Philips Long, *The Art of Biblical History* (Zondervan Academic, 1994), 17–30.

22. See Herman Bavinck, *Reformed Dogmatics*, vol. 2, *God and Creation*, ed. John Bolt, trans. John Vriend (Baker Academic, 2004), 496.

23. Matthew J. Lynch, *Flood and Fury: Old Testament Violence and the Shalom of God* (IVP Academic, 2023), 85.

24. Origen raised these questions already in the third century; cf. Michael LeFebvre, *The Liturgy of Creation: Understanding Calendars in Old Testament Context* (IVP Academic, 2019), 118.

25. See Collins, *Reading Genesis Well*, 94.

26. Collins, *Reading Genesis Well*, 245–63.

27. See John H. Walton, "A Historical Adam: Archetypal Creation View," in *Four Views on the Historical Adam*, ed. Matthew Barrett (Zondervan Academic, 2013), 116.

28. Gordon J. Wenham, *A Guide to the Pentateuch*, vol. 1 of *Exploring the Old Testament* (IVP Academic, 2003), 15.

29. John Goldingay, *Genesis*, Baker Commentary on the Old Testament: Pentateuch (Baker Academic, 2020), 5. See also C. John Collins, "A Historical Adam: Old-Earth Creation View," in Barrett, *Four Views on the Historical Adam*, 148–55.

30. Terence Fretheim, *Exodus*, Interpretation: A Bible Commentary for Teaching and Preaching (John Knox, 1991), 9–10.

31. See Craig Bartholomew, *The Old Testament and God*, Old Testament Origins and the Question of God 1 (Baker Academic, 2022), 176.

32. Bartholomew, *Old Testament and God*, 177.

33. See Richard S. Hess, "The Ancestral Period," in *Behind the Scenes of the Old Testament: Cultural, Social, and Historical Contexts*, ed. Jonathan S. Greer, John W. Hilber, and John H. Walton (Baker Academic, 2018), 187–93; David A. Falk, "The Egyptian Sojourn and the Exodus," in Greer, Hilber, and Walton, *Behind the Scenes*, 194–200; Joshua Berman, "Was There an Exodus?," *Mosaic*, March 2015, https://ideas.tikvah.org/mosaic/essays/was-there-an-exodus; Bartholomew, *Old Testament and God*, 444–51.

34. John H. Walton and Andrew E. Hill, *Old Testament Today*, 2nd ed. (Zondervan Academic, 2013), 24.

35. Walton and Hill, *Old Testament Today*, 24.

36. LeFebvre, *Liturgy of Creation*, 60.

37. Joshua Berman, *Inconsistency in the Torah: Ancient Literary Convention and the Limits of Source Criticism* (Oxford University Press, 2017), 20.

38. Berman, *Inconsistency in the Torah*, 25.

39. Berman, *Inconsistency in the Torah*, 25, 28. Scholars refer to this as the historiographic, the theological, and the literary dynamic (see Long, *Art of Biblical History*, 70–71).

40. Edward Delman, "How Lin-Manuel Miranda Shapes History," *The Atlantic*, September 29, 2015, https://www.theatlantic.com/entertainment/archive/2015/09/lin-manuel-miranda-hamilton/408019/.

41. Wenham, *Pentateuch*, 4.

Chapter 1 Sidebar Notes

a. Lisa M. Bowens, *African American Readings of Paul: Reception, Resistance, and Transformation* (Eerdmans, 2020), 297.

b. For more, see T. Desmond Alexander, *From Paradise to the Promised Land: An Introduction to the Pentateuch* (Baker Academic, 2012).

c. Kwame Bediako, *Jesus in Africa: The Christian Gospel in African History and Experience* (Regnum Africa, 2004), 78–82.

d. See Jerry Hwang, *Contextualization and the Old Testament: Between Asian and Western Perspectives* (Langham, 2022), 49–50.

e. See Kwame Bediako, *Jesus and the Gospel in Africa: History and Experience* (Orbis Books, 2004), 78–82.

f. Andrew Walls, *The Cross-Cultural Process in Christian History* (Orbis Books, 2002), 80.

g. See Bediako, *Jesus in Africa*, 120–21.

h. Andrew F. Walls, *The Missionary Movement in Christian History: Studies in the Transmission of the Faith* (Orbis, 1996), 29.

i. See quote and discussion in LeFebvre, *Liturgy of Creation*, 124–25.

j. Collins, *Reading Genesis Well*, 238, 258–64.

k. Collins, *Reading Genesis Well*, 123, 141–47.

l. Collins, *Reading Genesis Well*, 95.

m. "Infographic: You Have More Time for Bible Reading Than You Think," Crossway (website), November 19, 2018, https://www.crossway.org/articles/infographic-you-can-read-more-of-the-bible-than-you-think/.

Chapter 2 Genesis 1–3

1. See Joseph Blenkinsopp, *Creation, Un-Creation, Re-Creation: A Discursive Commentary on Genesis 1–11* (T&T Clark, 2011), 1–3.

2. See Todd L. Patterson, *The Plot-Structure of Genesis: 'Will the Righteous Seed Survive?' in the Muthos-Logical Movement from Complication to Dénouement* (Brill, 2018), 14–18.

3. See "ברך [*brk*] II," in *The Hebrew and Aramaic Lexicon of the Old Testament*, ed. Ludwig Koehler, Walter Baumgartner, and Johann J. Stamm, trans. and ed. Mervyn E. J. Richardson (Brill, 1994–99), 1:160; and John N. Oswalt, "בָּרַךְ [*bārak*]," in *Theological Wordbook of the Old Testament*, ed. R. Laird Harris, Gleason L. Archer Jr., and Bruce K. Waltke (Moody, 1980), 1:132.

4. Richard Bauckham, *The Bible and Ecology: Rediscovering the Community of Creation* (Baylor, 2010).

5. See similarly Catherine L. McDowell, *The Image of God in the Garden of Eden: The Creation of Humankind in Genesis 2:5–3:24 in Light of the Mīs Pî, Pīt Pî, and Wpt-r Rituals of Mesopotamia and Ancient Egypt*, Siphrut 15 (Eisenbrauns, 2015), 207.

6. Gordon J. Wenham, *Genesis 1–15*, Word Biblical Commentary (Word Books, 1987), 3–4, quoted in J. Gordon McConville, *Being Human in God's World: An Old Testament Theology of Humanity* (Baker Academic, 2016), 17.

7. Jon D. Levenson, *Creation and the Persistence of Evil: The Jewish Drama of Divine Omnipotence* (Princeton University Press, 1994), 114–17.

8. G. K. Beale, *The Temple and the Church's Mission: A Biblical Theology of the Dwelling Place of God*, New Studies in Biblical Theology 17 (InterVarsity, 2004), 29–80; McDowell, *Image of God*, 207.

9. See J. Richard Middleton, *A New Heavens and a New Earth: Reclaiming Biblical Eschatology* (Baker Academic, 2014), 45.

10. McDowell, *Image of God*, 204, 207.

11. McDowell, *Image of God*, 125–26, 132.

12. See J. Richard Middleton, *The Liberating Image: The Imago Dei in Genesis 1* (Brazos, 2005), 99–104.

13. The phrase "every square inch" alludes to a similar claim made by the Dutch theologian and statesman Abraham Kuyper in a speech in 1880.

14. Ellen F. Davis, *Scripture, Culture, and Agriculture: An Agrarian Reading of the Bible* (Cambridge University Press, 2009), 43.

15. See Moshe Weinfeld, "Sabbath, Temple, and the Enthronement of the LORD," in *Mélanges bibliques et orientaux en l'honneur de M. Henri Cazelles*, ed. Mathias Delcor and André Caquot (Neukirchner Verlag, 1981), 501–12.

16. Abraham Joshua Heschel, *The Sabbath: Its Meaning for Modern Man* (Farrar, Straus & Giroux, 1995), 29.

17. Victor H. Matthews and Don C. Benjamin, *Old Testament Parallels: Laws and Stories from the Ancient Near East*, 4th ed. (Paulist Press, 2016), 26–32.

18. See F. J. Mabie, "Chaos and Death," in *Dictionary of the Old Testament: Wisdom, Poetry & Writings*, ed. Tremper Longman III and Peter Enns (IVP Academic, 2008), 42.

19. Although it could also sum up what has gone before. McDowell argues it both sums up and shifts to the next section (McDowell, *Image of God*, 203).

20. See C. John Collins, *Reading Genesis Well: Navigating History, Poetry, Science, and Truth in Genesis 1–11* (Zondervan Academic, 2018), 168.

21. Dru Johnson, *The Universal Story: Genesis 1–11* (Lexham, 2018), 37.

22. Colin E. Gunton, *The Triune Creator: A Historical and Systematic Study* (Edinburgh University Press, 1998), 86. Gunton makes this argument throughout.

23. Gunton, *Triune Creator*, 189.

24. On "serving and preserving," see Mark Brett, *Indigenous Rights and the Legacies of the Bible: From Mabo to Moses* (Oxford University Press, 2024), 188–89.

25. R. W. L. Moberly, *From Eden to Golgotha: Essays in Biblical Theology* (Wipf & Stock, 2018), 5.

26. Carmen Joy Imes, "Helper: You Keep Using That Word for Women," *Christianity Today*, August 30, 2022, https://www.christianitytoday.com/ct/2022/august-web-only/womens-rights-leadership-old-testament-using-word-helper.html.

27. Mary L. Conway, "Gender in Creation and Fall: Genesis 1–3," in *Discovering Biblical Equality: Biblical, Theological, Cultural, and Practical Perspectives*, 3rd ed., ed. Ronald W. Pierce, Cynthia Long Westfall, and Christa McKirland (IVP Academic, 2021), 40.

28. Conway, "Gender in Creation and Fall," 41.

29. Conway, "Gender in Creation and Fall," 40.

30. See John Goldingay, *Genesis*, Baker Commentary on the Old Testament: Pentateuch (Baker Academic, 2020), 65.

31. Dru Johnson, *What Hath Darwin to Do with Scripture? Comparing the Conceptual Worlds of the Bible and Evolution* (IVP Academic, 2023), 56.

32. Phyllis Trible, *God and the Rhetoric of Sexuality*, Overtures to Biblical Theology (Fortress, 1978), 108.

33. Trible, *God and the Rhetoric of Sexuality*, 115.

34. See Andrew T. Abernethy and Greg Goswell, *God's Messiah in the Old Testament: Expectations of a Coming King* (Baker Academic, 2020), 12–13.

35. Goldingay, *Genesis*, 79–80.

36. Abernethy and Goswell, *God's Messiah*, 13.

37. Gordon J. Wenham, *A Guide to the Pentateuch*, vol. 1 of *Exploring the Old Testament* (IVP Academic, 2003), 23.

38. Gerhard von Rad, *Genesis*, trans. John H. Marks, Old Testament Library (Westminster, 1972), 93.

39. Walter Brueggemann, *Genesis*, Interpretation: A Bible Commentary for Teaching and Preaching (Westminster John Knox, 2010), 42.

40. John H. Walton, "A Historical Adam: Archetypal Creation View," in *Four Views on the Historical Adam*, ed. Matthew Barrett (Zondervan Academic, 2013), 92.

41. See Gunton, *Triune Creator*, 189–90.

42. The following options are derived from Bruce Wells, "Death in the Garden of Eden," *Journal of Biblical Literature* 139, no. 4 (2020): 642–55.

43. Moberly, *From Eden to Golgotha*, 18.

44. Wells, "Death in the Garden," 642.

45. See similarly Von Rad, *Genesis*, 97.

46. Gunton, *Triune Creator*, 174.

47. H. Daniel Zacharias, "The Land Takes Care of Us: Recovering Creator's Relational Design," in *Theologies of Land: Contested Land, Spatial Justice, and Identity*, ed. K. K. Yeo and Gene L. Green (Cascade, 2021), 88–95.

48. Bruce K. Waltke, with Cathi J. Fredricks, *Genesis: A Commentary* (Zondervan, 2001), 18.

49. Claus Westermann, *Genesis 1–11*, Continental Commentaries (Fortress, 1990), 85.

50. Beverley Moana Hall-Smith, "Whakapapa (Genealogy), A Hermeneutical Framework for Reading Biblical Texts: A Māori Woman Encounters Rape and Violence in Judges 19–21" (PhD diss., Flinders University, 2017), 32, https://flex.flinders.edu.au/file/c9dc7eb3-a137-4757-8bdc-65b197d75886/1/ThesisHall-SmithJune.2017.pdf.

51. Wayne Manaaki Rihari Te Kaawa, "Re-Visioning Christology Through a Māori Lens" (PhD diss., University of Otago, 2020), 76 (emphasis added), https://ourarchive.otago.ac.nz/handle/10523/10210.

52. Te Kaawa, "Re-Visioning Christology," 85.

53. H. Daniel Zacharias, "Land Takes Care of Us," 72.

54. See Pā Henare Arekatera Tate, "Towards Some Foundations of a Systematic Māori Theology" (PhD diss., Melbourne College of Divinity, 2010), 36–38, published subsequently as *He Puna Iti I te Ao Mārama: A Little Spring in the World of Light*, 2nd ed. (Oratia Media, 2021).

55. Te Kaawa, "Re-Visioning Christology," 143.

56. See Jerry Hwang, *Contextualization and the Old Testament: Between Asian and Western Perspectives* (Langham, 2022), 167.

57. Te Kaawa, "Re-Visioning Christology," 143.

58. Zacharias, "Land Takes Care of Us," 70.

59. Hwang, *Contextualization and the Old Testament*, 174.

60. Christopher J. H. Wright, *The Mission of God: Unlocking the Bible's Grand Narrative* (IVP Academic, 2006), 395.

61. Zacharias, "Land Takes Care of Us," 82.

62. Christopher N. Johnson, "Past and Future Decline and Extinction of Species," The Royal Society, accessed April 12, 2024, https://royalsociety.org/topics-policy/projects/biodiversity/decline-and-extinction/.

63. William P. Brown, *Seeing the Psalms: A Theology of Metaphor* (Westminster John Knox, 2002), 165.

Chapter 2 Sidebar Notes

a. See John H. Walton, *Genesis 1 as Ancient Cosmology* (Eisenbrauns, 2011), 180.

b. McDowell, *Image of God*, 148–52.

c. See L. Michael Morales, *Who Shall Ascend the Mountain of the Lord? A Biblical Theology of the Book of Leviticus*, New Studies in Biblical Theology 37 (IVP Academic, 2015), 41.

d. Morales, *Who Shall Ascend*, 102.

e. Jon D. Levenson, *Sinai and Zion: An Entry into the Jewish Bible* (Harper, 1987), 143.

f. Ronald Hendel, *Genesis 1–11: A New Translation with Introduction and Commentary*, Anchor Yale Bible 1A (Yale University Press, 2024), 128–29.

g. See Goldingay, *Genesis*, 45.

h. See John Frederic Kilner, *Dignity and Destiny: Humanity in the Image of God* (Eerdmans, 2015), 17–36.

i. Martin Luther King Jr., "Peace on Earth," sermon delivered at Ebenezer Baptist Church, December 24, 1967, https://www.upaya.org/2012/12/peace-on-earth-dr-martin-luther-king-jr/.

j. Karen Teel, *Racism and the Image of God* (Palgrave Macmillan, 2010), 72.

k. William P. Brown, *The Ethos of Creation: The Genesis of the Moral Imagination in the Bible* (Eerdmans, 1998), 45.

l. See Brett, *Indigenous Rights*, 188–89.

m. Bauckham, *Bible and Ecology*, ix.

n. See Andrew Picard, "Be Fruitful and Multiply, Reclassify the Earth and Dispossess It: The Political Utility of Gen 1:28 in Colonial New Zealand," in *Rereading the Bible in the Aftermath of Colonisation: To Conquer and Subdue the Earth*, ed. Brian Kolia, Emily Colgan, and Michael Mawson (Routledge, forthcoming).

o. Al Wolters, *Creation Regained: Biblical Basics for a Reformational Worldview*, 2nd ed. (Eerdmans, 2005), 44.

p. Abernethy and Goswell, *Messiah*, 21–31.

q. See, e.g., Susan Grove Eastman, *Paul and the Person: Reframing Paul's Anthropology* (Eerdmans, 2017), 74–81.

r. Istan Czachesz, "From Mirror Neurons to Morality: Cognitive and Evolutionary Foundations of Early Christian Ethics," in *Metapher-Narratio-Mimesis-Doxologie: Begründungsformen frühchristlicher und antiker Ethik*, ed. Friedrich Wilhelm Horn, Ulrich Volp, and Ruben Zimmermann, Wissenschaftliche Untersuchungen zum Neuen Testament 356 (Mohr Siebeck, 2016), 274.

s. Ellen F. Davis, *Opening Israel's Scriptures* (Oxford University Press, 2019), 371.

t. Collins, *Reading Genesis Well*, 232.

u. Collins, *Reading Genesis Well*, 135.

v. In writing this section, I have been most helped by S. Joshua Swamidass's very active website www.peacefulscience.org; John H. Walton, *The Lost World of Genesis One: Ancient Cosmology and the Origins* (IVP Academic, 2009); Matthew Barrett, ed., *Four Views on the Historical Adam* (Zondervan, 2013); William Lane Craig, *In Quest of the Historical Adam: A Biblical and Scientific Exploration* (Eerdmans, 2021); and Johnson, *What Hath Darwin to Do*.

w. Robin A. Parry, *The Biblical Cosmos: A Pilgrim's Guide to the Weird and Wonderful World of the Bible* (Cascade Books, 2014), 47.

Chapter 3 Genesis 4–11

1. Gerhard von Rad, *Genesis*, trans. John H. Marks, Old Testament Library (Westminster, 1972), 108.

2. Gordon J. Wenham, *Genesis 1–15*, Word Biblical Commentary (Word Books, 1987), 104.

3. See Mark S. Smith, *The Genesis of Good and Evil: The Fall(out) and Original Sin in the Bible* (Westminster John Knox, 2019), 68.

4. Smith, *Genesis of Good and Evil*, 69.

5. See Mari Joerstad, *The Hebrew Bible and Environmental Ethics: Humans, Nonhumans, and the Living Landscape* (Cambridge University Press, 2019), 58–65.
6. Matthew J. Lynch, *Portraying Violence in the Hebrew Bible* (Cambridge University Press, 2022), 30.
7. Nahum M. Sarna, *Genesis*, JPS Torah Commentary (Jewish Publication Society, 2001), 40.
8. Sarna, *Genesis*, 40.
9. See Willem A. VanGemeren, "The Sons of God in Genesis 6:1–14: An Example of Evangelical Demythologization?," *Westminster Theological Journal* 43 no. 2 (1981): 320–48.
10. Smith, *Genesis of Good and Evil*, 75.
11. Amy Kalmanofsky, *Dangerous Sisters of the Hebrew Bible* (Fortress, 2014), 124.
12. See Matthew J. Lynch, *Flood and Fury: Old Testament Violence and the Shalom of God* (IVP Academic, 2023), 68–76.
13. Von Rad, *Genesis*, 115–16.
14. For an overview, see Tremper Longman III and John H. Walton, *The Lost World of the Flood: Mythology, Theology, and the Deluge Debate* (IVP Academic, 2018), 51–87.
15. Longman and Walton, *Lost World of the Flood*, 61.
16. Longman and Walton, *Lost World of the Flood*, 61.
17. For what follows, see "Stories of Atrahasis," in Victor H. Matthews and Don C. Benjamin, *Old Testament Parallels: Laws and Stories from the Ancient Near East*, 4th ed. (Paulist Press, 2016).
18. Gordon J. Wenham, *A Guide to the Pentateuch*, vol. 1 of *Exploring the Old Testament* (IVP Academic, 2003), 28.
19. Lynch, *Flood and Fury*, 97.
20. Lynch, *Flood and Fury*, 79–81.
21. See Ellen F. Davis, *Opening Israel's Scriptures* (Oxford University Press, 2019), 23.
22. Daniel I. Block, *The Triumph of Grace: Literary and Theological Studies in Deuteronomy and Deuteronomic Themes* (Wipf & Stock, 2017), 98.
23. John Goldingay, *Genesis*, Baker Commentary on the Old Testament: Pentateuch (Baker Academic, 2020), 126.
24. Walter Moberly, *The Theology of the Book of Genesis*, Old Testament Theology (Cambridge University Press, 2009), 120.
25. Wenham, *Genesis 1–15*, 190.
26. Lynch, *Portraying Violence*, 81.
27. Lynch, *Portraying Violence*, 74.
28. Lynch, *Portraying Violence*, 81.
29. Leon R. Kass, *The Beginning of Wisdom: Reading Genesis* (University of Chicago Press, 2006), 174.
30. Terence E. Fretheim, *The Pentateuch*, Interpreting Biblical Texts (Abingdon, 1996), 83.
31. See David M. Goldenberg, "What Did Ham Do to Noah?," in *"The Words of a Wise Man's Mouth Are Gracious" (Qoh 10,12)*, ed. Mauro Perani (De Gruyter, 2005), 257–65.
32. Goldenberg, "What Did Ham Do," 29.
33. Wongi Park, "The Blessing of Whiteness in the Curse of Ham: Reading Gen 9:18–29 in the Antebellum South," *Religions* 12, no. 11 (2021): 11.
34. Amanda Beckenstein Mbuvi, *Belonging in Genesis: Biblical Israel and the Politics of Identity Formation* (Baylor University Press, 2016), 66.
35. Mbuvi, *Belonging in Genesis*, 95.
36. Mbuvi, *Belonging in Genesis*, 43.
37. Frank Crüsemann, "Human Solidarity and Ethnic Identity: Israel's Self-Definition in the Genealogical System of Genesis," in *Ethnicity and the Bible*, Biblical Interpretation Series 19, ed. Mark Brett (Brill, 1996), 63.
38. Mark McEntire and Wongi Park, "Ethnic Fission and Fusion in Biblical Genealogies," *Journal of Biblical Literature* 140, no. 1 (2021): 32.

39. Mbuvi, *Belonging in Genesis*, 89.
40. Crüsemann, "Human Solidarity," 69.
41. Crüsemann, "Human Solidarity," 69.
42. Craig Bartholomew, *The Old Testament and God*, Old Testament Origins and the Question of God 1 (Baker Academic, 2022), 8.
43. Fretheim, *Pentateuch*, 84.
44. Rubén Rosario Rodríguez, *Dogmatics After Babel: Beyond the Theologies of Word and Culture* (Westminster John Knox, 2018), 188–89, discussing Luis Pedraja, *Jesus Is My Uncle: Christology from a Hispanic Perspective* (Abingdon, 1999).
45. Dru Johnson, *What Hath Darwin to Do with Scripture? Comparing the Conceptual Worlds of the Bible and Evolution* (IVP Academic, 2023), 117.
46. Wenham, *Genesis 1–15*, 244.
47. Walter Brueggemann, *Genesis*, Interpretation: A Bible Commentary for Teaching and Preaching (Westminster John Knox, 2010), 99.
48. J. Richard Middleton, *The Liberating Image: The Imago Dei in Genesis 1* (Brazos, 2005), 225.
49. Crüsemann, "Human Solidarity," 72.
50. Chico Harlon and Amanda Coletta, "Residential Schools Banned Native Languages. The Cree Want Theirs Back," *Washington Post*, July 27, 2022, https://www.washingtonpost.com/world/2022/07/27/canada-first-nations-indigenous-language-cree/.
51. Mbuvi, *Belonging in Genesis*, 92.
52. Laura Romig, "2/13: Linguistic Diversity and Language Loss," Language Learning and the World, Brown Center for Language Studies, accessed February 13, 2026, https://sites.google.com/brown.edu/languagelearning-and-the-world/explorations/213-linguistic-diversity-and-language-loss.
53. Douglas Bax, "The Bible and Apartheid, 2," in *Apartheid Is a Heresy*, ed. John W. de Gruchy and Charles Villa-Vicencio (Eerdmans, 1983), 117.
54. Mark Rathbone, "Reframing the Tower of Babel Narrative for Economic Justice Within the South African Context," *HTS Theological Studies* 72, no. 3 (2016): 2.
55. Mbuvi, *Belonging in Genesis*, 69.
56. Mbuvi, *Belonging in Genesis*, 75–76.
57. Mbuvi, *Belonging in Genesis*, 105.
58. Mbuvi, *Belonging in Genesis*, 106.
59. Safwat Marzouk, *Intercultural Church: A Biblical Vision for an Age of Migration* (Fortress, 2019), 118.
60. Marzouk, *Intercultural Church*, 119.
61. Willie James Jennings, *Acts*, Belief (Westminster John Knox, 2017), 27.
62. Marzouk, *Intercultural Church*, 137.
63. See further Michael J. Rhodes, *Just Discipleship: Biblical Justice in an Unjust World* (IVP Academic, 2023), 214–34.
64. Jennings, *Acts*, 157 (emphasis added).

Chapter 3 Sidebar Notes

a. See C. John Collins, *Reading Genesis Well: Navigating History, Poetry, Science, and Truth in Genesis 1–11* (Zondervan Academic, 2018), 192.
b. See Longman and Walton, *Lost World of the Flood*, 145–50.
c. Isaac Watts, "Joy to the World."
d. David M. Goldenberg, *The Curse of Ham: Race and Slavery in Early Judaism, Christianity, and Islam* (Princeton University Press, 2003), 1.
e. See "Scientific Racism," available at https://guides.library.harvard.edu/scientificracism.
f. Park, "Blessing of Whiteness," 2.
g. Quoted in Park, "Blessing of Whiteness," 6.

h. Park, "Blessing of Whiteness," 4.

i. See Beth Baker, "Race and Biology," *BioScience* 71, no. 2 (2021): 119–26, https://academic.oup.com/bioscience/article/71/2/119/6101069.

j. See Mbuvi, *Belonging in Genesis*, 73.

k. See Mbuvi, *Belonging in Genesis*, 72.

l. Mbuvi, *Belonging in Genesis*, 69.

m. Johnson, *What Hath Darwin to Do*, 115.

n. Crüsemann, "Human Solidarity," 72.

o. Middleton, *Liberating Image*, 225.

p. Von Rad, quoted in Crüsemann, "Human Solidarity," 72.

q. Crüsemann, "Human Solidarity," 72 (emphasis added).

Chapter 4 How to Read Old Testament Narrative and Poetry Today

1. Joshua Berman, *Inconsistency in the Torah: Ancient Literary Convention and the Limits of Source Criticism* (Oxford University Press, 2017), 28.

2. For a more specific treatment of narrative reliability and history, see V. Philips Long, *The Art of Biblical History* (Zondervan, 1994). On the importance of poetry as conveying truth, see Craig G. Bartholomew and Ryan O'Dowd, *Old Testament Wisdom Literature: A Theological Introduction* (IVP Academic, 2011), chap. 3.

3. See "The Shaping of Space," in Shimon Bar-Efrat, *Narrative Art in the Bible* (A&C Black, 1989), 184–96.

4. For the discussion here, see Robert Alter, *The Art of Biblical Narrative*, rev. & updated ed. (Basic Books, 2011), 114–30; Meir Sternberg, *The Poetics of Biblical Narrative* (Indiana University Press, 1985), 186–229; Adele Berlin, *Poetics and Interpretation of Biblical Narrative* (Eisenbrauns, 1994); Bar-Efrat, *Narrative Art in the Bible*; and Rachel Toombs, *Reading the First Five Books: The Invitation of the Pentateuch's Stories* (Baker Academic, 2024), 23–50.

5. Toombs, *Reading the First Five Books*, 23–50.

6. For the discussion here, see Bar-Efrat, *Narrative Art in the Bible*, 13–46; Berlin, *Poetics and Interpretation*, 43–82; Yairah Amit, *Reading Biblical Narratives: Literary Criticism and the Hebrew Bible* (Fortress, 2001), 69–92; Toombs, *Reading the First Five Books*, 75–98; on reticence, see Alter, *Art of Biblical Narrative*, 114–30.

7. For the discussion here, see Alter, *Art of Biblical Narrative*, 114–30; Sternberg, *Poetics of Biblical Narrative*, 186–229.

8. Toombs, *Reading the First Five Books*, xiv.

9. Leon Kass is especially adept at drawing out this quality of the literature of the Torah. For the discussion here, see Leon R. Kass, *The Beginning of Wisdom: Reading Genesis* (University of Chicago Press, 2006); Kass, *Founding God's Nation: Reading Exodus* (Yale University Press, 2021). See also Walter Brueggemann, *Genesis*, Interpretation: A Bible Commentary for Teaching and Preaching (Westminster John Knox, 2010); Gordon J. Wenham, *Story as Torah: Reading Old Testament Narrative Ethically* (Baker Academic, 2004).

10. For the discussion here, see Amit, *Reading Biblical Narratives*, 103–14; Toombs, *Reading the First Five Books*, 51–76.

11. For the discussion here, see Alter, *Art of Biblical Narrative*, 88–112; Sternberg, *Poetics of Biblical Narrative*, 365–72.

12. See Bar-Efrat, *Narrative Art in the Bible*, 143–84.

13. Calum Carmichael has done foundational research on the dynamic between narrative and law in his *The Laws of Deuteronomy* (Cornell University Press, 1974); Carmichael, *Women, Law, and the Genesis Traditions* (Edinburgh University Press, 1979); and Carmichael, *Law and Narrative in the Bible: The Evidence of the Deuteronomic Laws and the Decalogue* (Cornell University Press, 1985). His work has spawned further reflection, both critique and development of his ideas; see Bernard M. Levinson, "Calum M. Carmichael's

Approach to the Laws of Deuteronomy," *Harvard Theological Review* 83, no. 3 (1990): 227–57.

14. On righteousness and holiness, see further the Orientation section of chapter 5.

15. See Patrick D. Miller's essay "Poetry and Interpretation," in *Interpreting the Psalms* (Fortress, 1986), 29–47.

16. A. J. Culp, *Memoir of Moses: The Literary Creation of Covenantal Memory in Deuteronomy* (Lexington, 2020); see especially his chapter on song/poetry (175–90).

17. For the discussion here, see Robert Alter, *The Art of Biblical Poetry* (Basic Books, 2011).

Chapter 4 Sidebar Notes

a. Ellen Davis, "The Way of Manna: Culture and Agriculture in the Hebrew Bible," lecture at Villanova University, October 4, 2012, YouTube, 1:07:02, https://youtu.be/_MhuqUUJ1mg?feature=shared (emphasis added).

b. Alter, *Art of Biblical Narrative*, 47–62.

c. Craig S. Keener, *The Gospel of John: A Commentary* (Hendrickson, 2003), 1:586, 590, 668.

d. James Kugel, *The Idea of Biblical Poetry: Parallelism and Its History* (Johns Hopkins University Press, 1981); Adele Berlin, *The Dynamics of Biblical Parallelism* (Indiana University Press, 1985).

e. See James K. A. Smith, "The Intelligence of Love," *Christian Century* 138, no. 5 (2021): 30–35.

Chapter 5 Genesis 12:1–25:11

1. Abraham Joshua Heschel, *God in Search of Man: A Philosophy of Judaism* (Farrar, Straus & Giroux, 1976), 66.

2. N. T. Wright, *Paul and the Faithfulness of God*, Christian Origins and the Question of God 4 (Fortress, 2013), 795.

3. Leon R. Kass, *The Beginning of Wisdom: Reading Genesis* (University of Chicago Press, 2006), 12.

4. Paul Borgman, *Genesis: The Story We Haven't Heard* (InterVarsity, 2001), 56–114.

5. Gordon J. Wenham, *Genesis 1–15*, Word Biblical Commentary (Word Books, 1987), 279.

6. My (David) understanding of this text has been profoundly affected by Robert Guerrero's sermon "Three Altars and a Fourth," a talk given at the 2023 Surge All Region Gathering, Roosevelt Community Church, Phoenix, AZ, January 11, 2023, available at Surge Network Podcast, https://podcasts.apple.com/us/podcast/robert-guerrero-at-2023-surge-all-region/id1141126741?i=1000599614946.

7. Robert Alter, *The Five Books of Moses: A Translation with Commentary* (Norton, 2004), 64.

8. Wenham, *Genesis 1–15*, 298.

9. Borgman, *Genesis*, 65.

10. Borgman, *Genesis*, 66.

11. Borgman, *Genesis*, 67.

12. The promises are, admittedly, ambiguous: God will establish her offspring, who will increase and multiply but be at odds with others (Gen. 16:10–12; cf. 21:18).

13. Borgman, *Genesis*, 72–73.

14. Borgman, *Genesis*, 90.

15. Borgman, *Genesis*, 89.

16. Borgman's chapter on this matter is excellent: Borgman, *Genesis*, 103–14.

Chapter 5 Sidebar Notes

a. See Wenham, *Genesis 1–15*, 256–57.

b. *Genesis Rabbah* 14.6, in H. Freedman and Maurice Simon, eds., *Midrash Rabbah* (Soncino, 1961), 1:114.

c. Munther Isaac, *From Land to Lands, from Eden to the Renewed Earth: A Christ-Centered Biblical Theology of the Promised Land* (Langham Monographs, 2015), 377.

d. "With God on Our Side," by Bob Dylan, track 3 on *The Times They Are A-Changin'*, Columbia Records, 1964.

e. Graham Paulson and Mark G. Brett, "Five Smooth Stones: Reading the Bible Through Aboriginal Eyes," *Colloquium* 45, no. 2 (2013): 206–7.

f. Jerry Hwang, *Contextualization and the Old Testament: Between Asian and Western Perspectives* (Langham, 2022), 78–82.

g. Gordon J. Wenham, *Genesis 16–50*, Word Biblical Commentary (Word Books, 1994), 7–8.

h. Delores S. Williams, *Sisters in the Wilderness: The Challenge of Womanist God-Talk* (Orbis Books, 2013).

i. Marcel Poorthuis, "Hagar's Wanderings: Between Judaism and Islam," *Der Islam (Berlin)* 90, no. 2 (2013): 220–44.

j. Jon Levenson, *The Death and Resurrection of the Beloved Son: The Transformation of Child Sacrifice in Judaism and Christianity* (Yale University Press, 1993), 140–41.

k. Levenson, *Death and Resurrection*, 134, 174–75.

l. Ellen F. Davis, *Biblical Prophecy: Perspectives for Christian Theology, Discipleship, and Ministry* (Westminster John Knox, 2014), 34.

m. See J. Richard Middleton, *Abraham's Silence: The Binding of Isaac, the Suffering of Job, and How to Talk Back to God* (Baker Academic, 2021).

Chapter 6 Genesis 25:19–50:26

1. J. Gerald Jantzen, *Abraham and All the Families of the Earth: A Commentary on Genesis 12–50*, International Theological Commentary (Eerdmans, 1993), 99, quoted in Paul Borgman, *Genesis: The Story We Haven't Heard* (InterVarsity, 2001), 125.
2. Borgman, *Genesis*, 124–25.
3. Walter Brueggemann, *Genesis*, Interpretation: A Bible Commentary for Teaching and Preaching (Westminster John Knox, 2010), 221.
4. Brueggemann, *Genesis*, 206–7.
5. Adapted from Brueggemann, *Genesis*, 211–13.
6. Leon R. Kass, *The Beginning of Wisdom: Reading Genesis* (University of Chicago Press, 2006), 436.
7. Kass, *Beginning of Wisdom*, 436.
8. Kass, *Beginning of Wisdom*, 461.
9. Kass, *Beginning of Wisdom*, 461.
10. Kass, *Beginning of Wisdom*, 463.
11. Kass repeatedly highlights the theme of transmission. He applies this to Abraham's legacy, the structure of marriage and family, and the generations of Isaac and Judah; Kass, *Beginning of Wisdom*, 288, 325, 377, 530.
12. Gordon J. Wenham, *Genesis 16–50*, Word Biblical Commentary (Word Books, 1994), 316–18.
13. Brueggemann, *Genesis*, 350.
14. Brueggemann, *Genesis*, 352.
15. Although Joseph gives his sons Hebrew names, some ambiguity remains about how these names reflect Joseph's posture toward family and faith, on the one hand, and toward Egypt and empire, on the other.
16. Brueggemann, *Genesis*, 334.

17. Michael J. Rhodes, *Just Discipleship: Biblical Justice in an Unjust World* (IVP Academic, 2023), 239.

18. Kass, *Beginning of Wisdom*, 517.

19. Ellen F. Davis, *Preaching the Luminous Word: Biblical Sermons and Homiletical Essays* (Eerdmans, 2016), 2. See also her chapter on Genesis 1 in Davis, *Scripture, Culture, and Agriculture: An Agrarian Reading of the Bible* (Cambridge University Press, 2009), 42–65.

20. See later in this chapter (2 Kings 4:42–44), where Elijah instructs a man to feed one hundred men with twenty loaves of bread—the bread was multiplied to feed them all with some left over.

21. Brueggemann, *Genesis*, 356.

22. Rhodes, *Just Discipleship*, 263. In this section, I am indebted to Michael's excellent work.

23. Rhodes, *Just Discipleship*, 263–64.

Chapter 6 Sidebar Notes

a. Kass, *Beginning of Wisdom*, 389.

b. *Baker Encyclopedia of the Bible*, ed. Walter A. Elwell (Baker, 1988), under "Teraphim."

c. Walter Brueggemann, "A Fourth-Generation Sellout," in *The Collected Sermons of Walter Brueggemann* (Westminster John Knox, 2011), 164–67.

Chapter 7 Exodus 1–18

1. Nahum M. Sarna, *Exploring Exodus: The Origins of Biblical Israel* (Schocken Books, 1996), 2.

2. Walter Brueggemann and Tod Linafelt, *An Introduction to the Old Testament: The Canon and Christian Imagination*, 3rd ed. (Westminster John Knox, 2021), 89–90.

3. L. Michael Morales, *Who Shall Ascend the Mountain of the Lord? A Biblical Theology of the Book of Leviticus*, New Studies in Biblical Theology 37 (IVP Academic, 2015), 76.

4. See Carmen Imes, "Exodus and the Exodus," session 1 of *Exodus Overview*, BibleProject, https://bibleproject.com/classroom-alpha/education-videos/session-1-exodus-and-exodus/.

5. See Craig G. Bartholomew, *The Old Testament and God* (Baker Academic, 2022), 224, 233.

6. Terence Fretheim, *Exodus*, Interpretation: A Bible Commentary for Teaching and Preaching (John Knox, 1991), 26.

7. See Judy Fentress-Williams, "Exodus," in *The Africana Bible: Reading Israel's Scriptures from Africa and the African Diaspora*, ed. Hugh R. Page Jr. et al. (Fortress, 2010), 82.

8. See Renita Weems, "The Hebrew Women Are Not Like the Egyptian Women: The Ideology of Race, Gender, and Sexual Reproduction in Exodus 1," *Semeia* 59 (1992): 30.

9. Jacqueline E. Lapsley, *Whispering the Word: Hearing Women's Stories in the Old Testament* (Westminster John Knox, 2005), 76.

10. Imes, "Exodus and the Exodus."

11. Imes, "Exodus and the Exodus."

12. Leon Kass, *Founding God's Nation: Reading Exodus* (Yale University Press, 2021), 43.

13. Fentress-Williams, "Exodus," 83.

14. Imes, "Exodus and the Exodus."

15. Sarna, *Exploring Exodus*, 37.

16. Sarna, *Exploring Exodus*, 41.

17. Sarna, *Exploring Exodus*, 41.

18. Fretheim, *Exodus*, 55.

19. Mark Scarlata, *The Abiding Presence: A Theological Commentary on Exodus* (SCM, 2018), 48–49.

20. See Sarna, *Exploring Exodus*, 52.

21. Bartholomew, *Old Testament and God*, 4.

22. Brevard S. Childs, *The Book of Exodus*, Old Testament Library (Westminster, 1974), 201.

23. T. Desmond Alexander, *Exodus*, Apollos Old Testament Commentary (Apollos, 2017), 155.

24. Alexander, *Exodus*, 167.

25. Ellen F. Davis, *Opening Israel's Scriptures* (Oxford University Press, 2019), 47.

26. See Bartholomew, *Old Testament and God*, 217–18.

27. Ellen F. Davis, *Scripture, Culture, and Agriculture: An Agrarian Reading of the Bible* (Cambridge University Press, 2009), 70.

28. Davis, *Scripture, Culture, and Agriculture*, 68, 71, 73.

29. Scarlata, *The Abiding Presence*, 16.

30. Davis, *Scripture, Culture, and Agriculture*, 68.

31. Herodotus, *Histories*, 2.37 (quoted in Bartholomew, *Old Testament and God*, 214).

32. Or at least partially divine; see Bartholomew, *Old Testament and God*, 233–37.

33. Emily Teeter, *Religion and Ritual in Ancient Egypt* (Cambridge University Press, 2011), 51.

34. Bartholomew, *Old Testament and God*, 234.

35. Ellen Morris, "Propaganda and Performance at the Dawn of the State," in *Experiencing Power, Generating Authority: Cosmos, Politics, and the Ideology of Kingship in Ancient Egypt and Mesopotamia*, ed. Jane A. Hill, Philip Jones, and Antonio J. Morales (University of Pennsylvania Museum of Archaeology and Anthropology, 2013), 33.

36. Bartholomew, *Old Testament and God*, 224.

37. See Sarna, *Exploring Exodus*, 68–78.

38. See Alexander, *Exodus*, 141–42.

39. Fretheim, *Exodus*, 108.

40. Carol Meyers, *Exodus*, New Cambridge Bible Commentary (Cambridge University Press, 2005), 71.

41. Alexander, *Exodus*, 145.

42. Fretheim, *Exodus*, 132.

43. See Kass, *Founding God's Nation*, 157.

44. See John H. Walton and Andrew E. Hill, *Old Testament Today: A Journey from Ancient Context to Contemporary Relevance*, 2nd ed. (Zondervan, 2014), 89.

45. Fretheim, *Exodus*, 106–8.

46. Fretheim, *Exodus*, 107, 110.

47. Mishnah Pesachim 10:5, https://www.sefaria.org/Mishnah_Pesachim.10.5?lang=bi.

48. Nyasha Junior, "Exodus," in *Women's Bible Commentary*, 20th anniversary ed., ed. Carol A. Newsom, Sharon H. Ringe, and Jacqueline E. Lapsley (Westminster John Knox, 2012), 61.

49. Kass, *Founding God's Nation*, 170.

50. See Jon Levenson, *The Death and Resurrection of the Beloved Son: The Transformation of Child Sacrifice in Judaism and Christianity* (Yale University Press, 1993), 3–54.

51. Fretheim, *Exodus*, 138.

52. Morales, *Who Shall Ascend?*, 81.

53. Brent A. Strawn, *The Old Testament: A Concise Introduction* (Routledge, 2020), 65.

54. Davis, *Scripture, Culture, and Agriculture*, 70.

55. Carmen Joy Imes, *Bearing God's Name: Why Sinai Still Matters* (IVP Academic, 2019), 18.

56. Dru Johnson, *Understanding Biblical Law: Skills for Thinking with and Through Torah* (Baker Academic, 2025), 108.

57. See Michael Rhodes and Robby Holt, *Practicing the King's Economy: Honoring Jesus in How We Work, Earn, Spend, Save, and Give*, with Brian Fikkert (Baker Books, 2018), 110–11.

58. James H. Cone, *God of the Oppressed* (Orbis Books, 1997), 59.

59. Gary S. D. Leonard, ed., *The Kairos Documents* (Ujamaa Centre for Biblical and Theological Community Development and Research, 2010), 3.4.1, pp. 24–25, https://www.kairospalestine.ps/index.php/about-kairos/kairos-palestine-document.

60. Gustavo Gutiérrez, *A Theology of Liberation: History, Politics, and Salvation*, ed. Sister Caridad Inda and John Eagleson (Orbis Books, 1973), 88.

61. Enrique Nardoni, *Rise Up, O Judge: A Study of Justice in the Biblical World*, trans. Sean Charles Martin (Hendrickson, 2004), 67.

62. Drawn from Christopher J. H. Wright, "Biblical Paradigms of Redemption: Exodus, Jubilee, and the Cross," in *Transforming the World? The Gospel and Social Responsibility*, ed. Jamie A. Grant and Dewi A. Hughes (InterVarsity, 2009), 71–74.

63. See Bryant L. Meyers, *Walking with the Poor: Principles and Practices of Transformational Development*, 2nd ed. (Orbis Books, 2011), 68–69.

64. Quoted in Robert Chao Romero, *Brown Church: Five Centuries of Latina/o Social Justice Theology and Identity* (IVP Academic, 2020), 159.

Chapter 7 Sidebar Notes

a. See David A. Falk, "The Egyptian Sojourn and the Exodus," in *Behind the Scenes of the Old Testament: Cultural, Social, and Historical Contexts*, ed. Jonathan S. Greer, John W. Hilber, and John H. Walton (Baker Academic, 2018), 194–200.

b. Fretheim, *Exodus*, ix.

c. M. Daniel Carroll R., *Christians at the Border: Immigration, the Church, and the Bible*, rev. ed. (Brazos, 2013), 55, emphasis added.

d. Jorge Pixley, "Exodus," in *Global Bible Commentary*, ed. Daniel Patte and Teresa Okure (Abingdon, 2004), 18, emphasis added.

e. Shay Dawson, "Harriet Tubman," *National Women's History Museum*, https://www.womenshistory.org/education-resources/biographies/harriet-tubman.

f. L. Juliana M. Claassens, *Mourner, Mother, Midwife: Reimagining God's Delivering Presence in the Old Testament* (Westminster John Knox, 2012), 76.

g. Claassens, *Mourner, Mother, Midwife*, 74.

h. Scarlata, *The Abiding Presence*, 35–36.

i. "The Canon of the Epiphany" 9.1, cited in Alexander Pokhilko, "The Contemplation of Christ and Salvation in the Liturgical Canons of St. John Damascene" (PhD thesis, University of Durham, 2004), 103.

j. This is a major theme of Morales, *Who Shall Ascend?*

k. Origen, "Letter to Gregory," *New Advent*, accessed June 10, 2025, https://www.newadvent.org/fathers/0415.htm.

l. See Andrew F. Walls, *Crossing Cultural Frontiers: Studies in the History of World Christianity*, ed. Mark Gornik (Orbis Books, 2017), 32.

m. Walls, *Crossing Cultural Frontiers*, 32.

n. Walls, *Crossing Cultural Frontiers*, 31.

o. Walls, *Crossing Cultural Frontiers*, 32.

p. Matthew Schlimm, "Reparations in Exodus," in *Reparations and the Theological Disciplines: Prophetic Voices for Remembrance, Reckoning, and Repair*, ed. Michael Barram, Drew G. I. Hart, Gimbiya Kettering, and Michael J. Rhodes (Lexington, 2023), 4–6.

q. Davis, *Scripture, Culture, and Agriculture*, 74–75.

Chapter 8 How to Read Biblical Law Today

1. See "Sexual Violence Against Women and the OT Law," Scott Rae in dialogue with Sandra Richter, *Think Biblically*, August 18, 2020, https://www.biola.edu/blogs/think-biblically/2020/sexual-violence-against-women.

2. Dru Johnson, *Understanding Biblical Law: Skills for Thinking with and Through Torah* (Baker Academic, 2025), 49.

3. Richard E. Averbeck, *The Old Testament Law for the Life of the Church: Reading the Torah in the Light of Christ* (IVP Academic, 2022), 77, emphasis added.

4. Averbeck, *Old Testament Law*, 23–25.

5. John Calvin, *Institutes of the Christian Religion* 7.12–13, trans. Henry Beveridge, Christian Classics Ethereal Library, accessed February 4, 2026, https://www.ccel.org/ccel/calvin/institutes.iv.viii.html.

6. Averbeck, *Old Testament Law*, 76.

7. See Richard D. Nelson, *Deuteronomy: A Commentary*, Old Testament Library (Westminster John Knox, 2002), 286–89.

8. Johnson, *Understanding Biblical Law*, 76.

9. See Joshua A. Berman, *Inconsistency in the Torah: Ancient Literary Convention and the Limits of Source Criticism* (Oxford University Press, 2017), 107–17.

10. This paragraph is adapted from Michael J. Rhodes, *Just Discipleship: Biblical Justice in an Unjust World* (IVP Academic, 2023), 180.

11. Bernard S. Jackson, *Studies in the Semiotics of Biblical Law* (Sheffield Academic, 2000), 115.

12. Joshua A. Berman, *Created Equal: How the Bible Broke with Ancient Political Thought* (Oxford University Press, 2008), 84.

13. For options, see Jackson, *Semiotics of Biblical Law*, 115–16; Raymond Westbrook, *Law from the Tigris to the Tiber: The Writings of Raymond Westbrook*, ed. F. Rachel Magdalene and Bruce Wells (Penn State University Press, 2021), 1–16.

14. Berman, *Inconsistency in the Torah*, 145–47.

15. See Berman, *Inconsistency in the Torah*, 110, 114.

16. Westbrook, *Law from the Tigris*, 8–10.

17. Averbeck, *Old Testament Law*, 74–75.

18. See Berman, *Created Equal*, 84.

19. Dale Patrick, *Old Testament Law* (John Knox, 1985), 191–93.

20. See Michael LeFebvre, *Collections, Codes, and Torah: The Re-Characterization of Israel's Written Law* (Bloomsbury, 2006), 31–54.

21. LeFebvre, *Collections*, 31–54.

22. See Rhodes, *Just Discipleship*, 182–84.

23. See Berman, *Inconsistency in the Torah*, 171–83.

24. Jeremiah Unterman, *Justice for All: How the Jewish Bible Revolutionized Ethics* (Jewish Publication Society, 2017), 21.

25. Berman, *Created Equal*, 84–85.

26. See Jackson, *Semiotics of Biblical Law*, 71–74.

27. Jackson, *Semiotics of Biblical Law*, 70–92.

28. See John Barton, *Ethics in Ancient Israel* (Oxford University Press, 2014), 145–48.

29. Johnson, *Understanding Biblical Law*, 42.

30. Unterman, *Justice for All*, 25–29.

31. Johnson, *Understanding Biblical Law*, 38.

32. Carol Meyers, *Exodus*, New Cambridge Bible Commentary (Cambridge University Press, 2005), 194.

33. Jeffrey H. Tigay, *Deuteronomy*, JPS Torah Commentary (Jewish Publication Society, 1996), 207.

34. Sandra L. Richter, "Rape in Israel's World . . . and Ours: A Study of Deuteronomy 22:23–29," *Journal of the Evangelical Theological Society* 64, no. 1 (2021): 66–67.
35. Richter, "Rape in Israel's World," 69.
36. Richter, "Rape in Israel's World," 71.
37. Note that here, too, there are caveats about intentionality (vv. 13–14).
38. David L. Baker, *Tight Fists or Open Hands? Wealth and Poverty in the Old Testament* (Eerdmans, 2009), 125–27.
39. See Meyers, *Exodus*, 193.
40. Dru Johnson, "The Key Biblical Principle for Police Reform? Humane Imagination," *The Biblical Mind*, July 10, 2025, https://hebraicthought.org/police-reform-biblical-imagina tion/.
41. Christopher J. H. Wright, *Old Testament Ethics for the People of God* (IVP Academic, 2004), 333.
42. Baker, *Tight Fists*, 118.
43. Baker, *Tight Fists*, 129.

Chapter 8 Sidebar Notes

a. Baker, *Tight Fists*, 252–66.
b. Johnson, *Understanding Biblical Law*, 59.
c. Wright, *Old Testament Ethics*, 323.
d. Matthew T. Martens, *Reforming Criminal Justice: A Christian Proposal* (Crossway, 2023), 325.
e. Richter, "Rape in Israel's World," 69.
f. Walter C. Kaiser, "מָהַר, (*māhar*)," *Theological Wordbook of Old Testament*, ed. R. Laird Harris, Gleason L. Archer Jr., and Bruce K. Waltke (Moody, 1980), 492.
g. Johnson, *Understanding Biblical Law*, 174.
h. This numbered list is from Wil Gafney, "Reading the Hebrew Bible Responsibly," in *The Africana Bible: Reading Israel's Scriptures from Africa and the African Diaspora*, ed. Hugh R. Page Jr. et al. (Fortress, 2010), 49.

Chapter 9 Exodus 19–40

1. Language drawn from L. Michael Morales, *Who Shall Ascend the Mountain of the Lord? A Biblical Theology of the Book of Leviticus*, New Studies in Biblical Theology 37 (IVP Academic, 2015), 76.
2. See Carmen Joy Imes, *Bearing God's Name: Why Sinai Still Matters* (IVP Academic, 2019), 31–32.
3. See Nahum M. Sarna, *Exploring Exodus: The Origins of Biblical Israel* (Schocken Books, 1996), 130.
4. Daniel I. Block, *The Triumph of Grace: Literary and Theological Studies in Deuteronomy and Deuteronomic Themes* (Wipf & Stock, 2017), 132–33.
5. Imes, *Bearing God's Name*, 33–34.
6. Imes, *Bearing God's Name*, 34.
7. Patrick D. Miller, *The Way of the Lord: Essays in Old Testament Theology* (Eerdmans, 2007), 57.
8. Imes, *Bearing God's Name*, 40.
9. See Miller, *Way of the Lord*, 17–36.
10. Jennifer Herdt, "Natural Law in Protestant Christianity," in *The Cambridge Companion to Natural Law Ethics*, ed. Tom Angier (Cambridge University Press, 2019), 156.
11. Miller, *Way of the Lord*, 51.
12. Miller, *Way of the Lord*, 52.
13. Robby Holt, personal communication, 2023.
14. Imes, *Bearing God's Name*, 35.

15. Daniel I. Block, *How I Love Your Torah, O Lord! Literary and Theological Explorations in the Book of Deuteronomy* (Cascade Books, 2011), 32.
16. Jon D. Levenson, *The Love of God: Divine Gift, Human Gratitude, and Mutual Faithfulness in Judaism* (Princeton University Press, 2016), 16.
17. See Matthew J. Lynch, "Monotheism in Ancient Israel," in *Behind the Scenes of the Old Testament: Cultural, Social, and Historical Contexts*, ed. Jonathan S. Greer, John W. Hilber, and John H. Walton (Baker Academic, 2018), 340–48, and the discussion of the Shema under "Who Is This God? Yahweh's Character in Deuteronomy 4–11," in chap. 16 below.
18. Mark Scarlata, *The Abiding Presence: A Theological Commentary on Exodus* (SCM, 2018), 160.
19. Imes, *Bearing God's Name*, 49.
20. Imes, *Bearing God's Name*, 51.
21. See Bob Goudzwaard and Craig Bartholomew, *Beyond the Modern Age: An Archaeology of Contemporary Culture* (IVP Academic, 2017), 153–57.
22. Terence Fretheim, *Exodus*, Interpretation: A Bible Commentary for Teaching and Preaching (John Knox, 1991), 238.
23. Scarlata, *The Abiding Presence*, 169.
24. This way of exploring the structure has been deeply influenced by Fretheim, *Exodus*, 202.
25. See T. Desmond Alexander, *Exodus*, Apollos Old Testament Commentary (Apollos, 2017), 471.
26. See Morales, *Who Shall Ascend?*, 95–100.
27. Morales, *Who Shall Ascend?*, 98.
28. Morales, *Who Shall Ascend?*, 95–96.
29. Morales, *Who Shall Ascend?*, 98.
30. Fretheim, *Exodus*, 264.
31. Robin Parry, *The Biblical Cosmos: A Pilgrim's Guide to the Weird and Wonderful World of the Bible*, illustrated by Hannah Parry (Lutterworth, 2015), 148.
32. See Morales, *Who Shall Ascend?*, 102.
33. See Jon D. Levenson, *Creation and the Persistence of Evil: The Jewish Drama of Divine Omnipotence* (Princeton University Press, 1994), 84–86.
34. Fretheim, *Exodus*, 269.
35. Ellen F. Davis, *Scripture, Culture, and Agriculture: An Agrarian Reading of the Bible* (Cambridge University Press, 2009), 143.
36. John H. Walton, "Interactions in the Ancient Cognitive Environment," in Greer, Hilber, and Walton, *Behind the Scenes*, 352.
37. Gordon J. Wenham, *A Guide to the Pentateuch*, vol. 1 of *Exploring the Old Testament* (IVP Academic, 2003), 76.
38. But see Sarna, *Exploring Exodus*, 196–200, for evidence of other parallels.
39. See Joshua Berman, "Was There an Exodus?" *Mosaic*, March 2015, https://ideas.tikvah.org/mosaic/essays/was-there-an-exodus; and Michael M. Homan, "The Tabernacle in Its Ancient Near Eastern Context," TheTorah.com, March 6, 2018, https://www.thetorah.com/article/the-tabernacle-in-its-ancient-near-eastern-context.
40. Judy Fentress-Williams, "Exodus," in *The Africana Bible: Reading Israel's Scriptures from Africa and the African Diaspora*, ed. Hugh R. Page Jr. et al. (Fortress, 2010), 87.
41. Fretheim, *Exodus*, 271.
42. Walter R. Moberly, "How May We Speak of God? A Reconsideration of the Nature of Biblical Theology," *Tyndale* 53, no. 2 (2002): 198.
43. Scarlata, *The Abiding Presence*, 210.
44. On the two kinds of idolatry, see M. Daniel Carroll R., *The Book of Amos*, New International Commentary on the Old Testament (Eerdmans, 2020), 75–77.
45. Fretheim, *Exodus*, 280–81.

46. Brevard S. Childs, *The Book of Exodus*, Old Testament Library (Westminster, 1974), 567.

47. Fretheim, *Exodus*, 288, emphasis added.

48. Fretheim, *Exodus*, 289.

49. Umberto Cassuto, *A Commentary on the Book of Exodus*, trans. Israel Abrahams (Magnes, 1967), 426.

50. Scarlata, *The Abiding Presence*, 217.

51. Childs, *Book of Exodus*, 567.

52. Moberly, "How May We Speak of God?," 193.

53. Matthew J. Lynch, *Flood and Fury: Old Testament Violence and the Shalom of God* (IVP Academic, 2023), 229.

54. Moberly, "How May We Speak of God?," 200.

55. See Scarlata, *The Abiding Presence*, 224.

56. Brent A. Strawn, *The Incomparable God: Readings in Biblical Theology*, ed. Collin Cornell and M. Justin Walker (Eerdmans, 2023), 37.

57. Lynch, *Flood and Fury*, 230–31.

58. Lynch, *Flood and Fury*, 231.

59. Childs, *Book of Exodus*, 580.

60. Beth Felker Jones, *Practicing Christian Doctrine: An Introduction to Thinking and Living Theologically*, 2nd ed. (Baker Academic, 2023), 13.

61. Moberly, "How May We Speak of God?," 198.

62. Strawn, *The Incomparable God*, 41.

63. Moberly, "How May We Speak of God?," 198–99.

64. See Jerry Hwang, *Contextualization and the Old Testament: Between Asian and Western Perspectives*, (Langham Global Library, 2022), 191–93.

65. Strawn, *The Incomparable God*, 41.

66. Lynch, *Flood and Fury*, 229–30.

67. Collin Cornell and M. Justin Walker, "Introduction," in Strawn, *The Incomparable God*, xvi.

Chapter 9 Sidebar Notes

a. See Miller, *Way of the Lord*, 134–35.

b. John Calvin, *Institutes of the Christian Religion, 1536 Edition*, trans. Ford Lewis Battles (Eerdmans, 1995), 26.

c. Calvin, *Institutes, 1536*, 26.

d. Emerson B. Powery and Rodney S. Sadler Jr., *The Genesis of Liberation: Biblical Interpretation in the Antebellum Narratives of the Enslaved* (Westminster John Knox, 2016), 107.

e. Powery and Sadler, *Genesis of Liberation*, 113.

f. Powery and Sadler, *Genesis of Liberation*, 117.

g. Powery and Sadler, *Genesis of Liberation*, 124.

h. Quoted in Powery and Sadler, *Genesis of Liberation*, 115.

i. Leon Kass, *Founding God's Nation: Reading Exodus* (Yale University Press, 2021), 515–19.

j. Berman, "Was There an Exodus?"

k. Chris Hacker, Ash-Har Quraishi, Amy Corral, and Ryan Beard, "Wage Theft Often Goes Unpunished Despite State Systems Meant to Combat It," CBS News, January 24, 2023; updated June 30, 2023, https://www.cbsnews.com/news/owed-employers-face-little-accountability-for-wage-theft/.

l. See Jonathan Tran, *Asian Americans and the Spirit of Racial Capitalism* (Oxford University Press, 2022), 223–24.

m. Janice Gassam Asare, "New Research Reveals Resumes with Black Names Experience Bias in the Hiring Process," *Forbes* (April 17, 2024), https://www.forbes.com/sites/janicegassam/2024/04/17/new-research-reveals-resumes-with-black-names-experience-bias-in-the-hiring-process/.

n. This language comes from N. T. Wright and Michael Bird, *Jesus and the Powers: Christian Political Witness in an Age of Totalitarian Terror and Dysfunctional Democracies* (Zondervan, 2023), 7.

o. See Mark Glanville, *Improvising Church: Scripture as the Source of Harmony, Rhythm, and Soul* (IVP Academic, 2024), 45.

Chapter 10 How to Read Torah's Rituals Today

1. A. J. Culp, *Memoir of Moses: The Literary Creation of Covenantal Memory in Deuteronomy* (Lexington, 2020), 117–40.
2. Culp, *Memoir of Moses*, 175–90.
3. On the embodied nature of rituals, see Dru Johnson, *Human Rites: The Power of Rituals, Habits, and Sacraments* (Eerdmans, 2019), 13–19.
4. Ellen F. Davis, *Opening Israel's Scriptures* (Oxford University Press, 2019), 63.
5. We are indebted to Dru Johnson for this notion of inquiring into the origin of rituals and who "scripts" our rituals; Johnson, *Human Rites*, 9.
6. See the helpful little books by Lexham Press: Bruce Riley Ashford, *Every Square Inch: An Introduction to Cultural Engagement for Christians* (2015); Benjamin T. Quinn and Walter R. Strickland II, *Every Waking Hour: An Introduction to Work and Vocation for Christians* (2016); David W. Jones, *Every Good Thing: An Introduction to the Material World and the Common Good for Christians* (2024).
7. See, e.g., Tish Harrison Warren, *Liturgy of the Ordinary: Sacred Practices in Everyday Life* (InterVarsity, 2016).
8. Catherine Bell, *Ritual: Perspectives and Dimensions* (Oxford University Press, 1997), 138–70. A case can also be made that ordinary habits may be reimagined and reconceived as holy rituals, as is argued by Warren, *Liturgy of the Ordinary*.
9. Gordon J. Wenham, *A Guide to the Pentateuch*, vol. 1 of *Exploring the Old Testament* (IVP Academic, 2003), 83.
10. Cited in Wenham, *Pentateuch*, 83.
11. Jay Sklar, *Leviticus: The Lord's Holy People Living Out His Holy Character*, Zondervan Exegetical Commentary on the Old Testament 3 (Zondervan Academic, 2014), 47–48, esp. his emphasis on people, time, and events as focal points of ritual.
12. James Clear, *Atomic Habits: An Easy & Proven Way to Build Good Habits & Break Bad Ones* (Avery, 2018), 6.
13. Dru Johnson discusses the relationship between habits and rituals in his thought-provoking book *Human Rites*, 1–9.
14. James K. A. Smith, *Desiring the Kingdom: Worship, Worldview, and Cultural Formation* (Baker Academic, 2009), esp. 89–128.
15. Sklar, *Leviticus*, 47–48.
16. Habits may take on the appearance or even function of a ritual. For instance, drinking morning coffee may well become a ritual prescribed by an authority if you've been shaped by a thousand "best part of waking up" Folger's commercials.
17. Smith, *Desiring the Kingdom*, 25–27.
18. Again, Smith, *Desiring the Kingdom*, 75–88, is most helpful in this regard.
19. Mary Douglas, *Purity and Danger: An Analysis of the Concepts of Pollution and Taboo* (Routledge, 1966), esp. chaps. 1–2.
20. E.g., L. Michael Morales, *Who Shall Ascend the Mountain of the Lord? A Biblical Theology of the Book of Leviticus*, New Studies in Biblical Theology 37 (IVP Academic, 2015), 39–108.

21. Gordon J. Wenham, *Numbers: An Introduction and Commentary*, Tyndale Old Testament Commentary 4 (InterVarsity, 2015), 64.

22. L. Michael Morales, "The Tabernacle: Mountain of God in the Cultus of Israel," *Interpreter: A Journal of Latter-day Saint Faith and Scholarship* 37 (2020): 97–140 (Article 9), https://scholarsarchive.byu.edu/cgi/viewcontent.cgi?article=1351&context=interpreter.

23. I am indebted to the chapter "Sedimenting Memory: Ritual as Memory Vector" in Culp, *Memoir of Moses*, 141–73.

24. Culp, *Memoir of Moses*, 141.

25. Morales, *Who Shall Ascend?*, 75–107.

26. Sklar, *Leviticus*, 24–25.

27. Sklar, *Leviticus*, 40–42.

28. See Sklar, *Leviticus*, 25–26.

29. Sklar, *Leviticus*, 26.

30. Smith, *Desiring the Kingdom*, 37–73.

31. See Dru Johnson, *Understanding Biblical Law: Skills for Thinking With and Through the Torah* (Baker Academic, 2025), 90.

32. Christopher J. H. Wright, *The Mission of God: Unlocking the Bible's Grand Narrative* (IVP Academic, 2006), 373–74.

33. Smith, *Desiring the Kingdom*, 17–73.

Chapter 10 Sidebar Notes

a. See Johnson, *Human Rites*, 135–46.

b. Michael LeFebvre, *The Liturgy of Creation: Understanding Calendars in Old Testament Context* (IVP Academic, 2019), 22–23.

Chapter 11 Leviticus 1–16

1. Ellen F. Davis, *Opening Israel's Scriptures* (Oxford University Press, 2019), 64.

2. See Ministry of Foreign Affairs, *Handbook on Protocol Practice* (Royal Government of Bhutan, 2020), https://www.mfa.gov.bt/wp-content/uploads/2021/06/Handbook-on-Protocol-Practice.pdf; Amarit (Aim) Charoenphan, "A Meal with His Majesty," Medium, October 7, 2024, https://medium.com/theaim/a-meal-with-his-majesty-c3a4f6a9b3c5.

3. Christopher J. H. Wright, "Leviticus," in *New Bible Commentary*, ed. D. A. Carson, R. T. France, J. A. Motyer, and G. J. Wenham, 4th ed. (InterVarsity, 1994), 122.

4. Mark William Scarlata, *A Journey Through the World of Leviticus: Holiness, Sacrifice, and the Rock Badger* (Cascade Books, 2021), 32, 34.

5. We have been greatly helped by the teachings of Alastair Roberts on the sacrificial system, such as his discussion "The Levitical System for the Uninitiated" in "No. 34: A Return to Ireland," *The Anchored Argosy*, Substack, June 6, 2024, https://argosy.substack.com/p/34-a-return-to-ireland.

6. Although Lev. 7:8 says that the hide/skin of the animals of the ascension offering would be given to the officiating priest.

7. Gordon J. Wenham, *The Book of Leviticus*, New International Commentary on the Old Testament (Eerdmans, 1979), 72.

8. Scarlata's discussion on atonement in Leviticus and the New Testament is worthwhile reading; see Scarlata, *Journey Through the World of Leviticus*, 29–37.

9. Dru Johnson, *Human Rites: The Power of Rituals, Habits, and Sacraments* (Eerdmans, 2019), 53.

10. See Jacob Milgrom, *Leviticus: A Book of Ritual and Ethics*, Continental Commentaries (Fortress, 2004), 12–13.

11. Mary Douglas, *Purity and Danger: An Analysis of the Concepts of Pollution and Taboo* (Routledge, 1966), 53.

12. Jay Sklar, *Leviticus: The Lord's Holy People Living Out His Holy Character*, Zondervan Exegetical Commentary on the Old Testament 3 (Zondervan Academic, 2014), 345–46.

13. See Wenham, *Book of Leviticus*, 194–97.

14. The instructions for tithing do not appear until Lev. 27:30–33 and then are expanded in Num. 18 and Deut. 12, 14, and 26.

15. In this section we are indebted to the exceptionally insightful work of Ellen F. Davis, *Scripture, Culture, and Agriculture: An Agrarian Reading of the Bible* (Cambridge University Press, 2009), 80–100; Davis, *Opening Israel's Scriptures*, 61–71.

16. Davis, *Scripture, Culture, and Agriculture*, 94.

17. Scarlata, *Journey Through the World of Leviticus*, 4, emphasis added.

Chapter 11 Sidebar Notes

a. Milgrom, *Leviticus*, 30–33.

b. Milgrom, *Leviticus*, 51.

c. Peter J. Bray, *Leviticus on the Butcher's Block: Trimming Away the Fat to Reveal a Misunderstood Biblical Book* (Wipf and Stock, 2025), 42–51.

d. Matthew Thiessen, *Jesus and the Forces of Death: The Gospels' Portrayal of Ritual Impurity Within First-Century Judaism* (Baker Academic, 2020), 178–79.

e. See Wenham, *Book of Leviticus*, 187–88.

f. See the helpful discussion of these instructions in Samuel E. Balentine, *Leviticus*, Interpretation: A Bible Commentary for Teaching and Preaching (John Knox, 2002), 100–103.

Chapter 12 Leviticus 17–27

1. In fact, Lev. 27 is often seen as appended material and not part of the Holiness Code; also, some debate whether Lev. 17 belongs to the Holiness Code or with the section that precedes it. See Gordon J. Wenham, *The Book of Leviticus*, New International Commentary on the Old Testament (Eerdmans, 1979), 6–8.

2. The opening and closing frames of chaps. 18 and 20 provide clear examples of the "holiness highlights" introduced at the beginning of this chapter.

3. Samuel E. Balentine, *Leviticus*, Interpretation: A Bible Commentary for Teaching and Preaching (John Knox, 2002), 157.

4. Victor H. Matthews, "Family, Children, and Inheritance in the Biblical World," in *Behind the Scenes of the Old Testament: Cultural, Social, and Historical Contexts*, ed. Jonathan S. Greer, John W. Hilber, and John H. Walton (Baker Academic, 2018), 403.

5. Jay Sklar, *Leviticus: The Lord's Holy People Living Out His Holy Character*, Zondervan Exegetical Commentary on the Old Testament 3 (Zondervan Academic, 2014), 513.

6. Balentine, *Leviticus*, 158.

7. Balentine, *Leviticus*, 158.

8. Sklar, *Leviticus*, 598–600.

9. Babylonian Talmud, Shabbat 86b; cf. the festival liturgy, which names Shavuot "the season of the giving of our Torah."

10. Wenham, *Book of Leviticus*, 305.

11. Wenham in *Book of Leviticus*, 305, believes the extra sacrifices signal that the Feast of Booths was the most important of the fall festivals.

12. Sklar, *Leviticus*, 656.

13. Sklar, *Leviticus*, 656, notes that laws such as blaspheming do not apply to foreigners outside the covenant community.

14. Michael J. Rhodes, *Just Discipleship: Biblical Justice in an Unjust World* (IVP Academic, 2023), 164.

15. Rhodes, *Just Discipleship*, 178.

16. Sklar, *Leviticus*, 712.

17. Dru Johnson, *Understanding Biblical Law: Skills for Thinking With and Through the Torah* (Baker Academic, 2025), 89.
18. Johnson, *Understanding Biblical Law*, 89–98.
19. Johnson, *Understanding Biblical Law*, 90–92.

Chapter 12 Sidebar Notes

a. See Wenham, *Book of Leviticus*, 241–43.
b. Sklar, *Leviticus*, 513.
c. For further reading, see Preston Sprinkle, ed., *Two Views on Homosexuality, the Bible, and the Church* (Zondervan, 2016).
d. Michael Rhodes and Robby Holt, *Practicing the King's Economy: Honoring Jesus in How We Work, Earn, Spend, Save, and Give*, with Brian Fikkert (Baker Books, 2018), 139.
e. For more ideas on what this might look like, see Rhodes and Holt, *Practicing the King's Economy.*
f. Robert E. Webber, *Ancient-Future Worship: Proclaiming and Enacting God's Narrative* (Baker Books, 2008), 38–39.
g. Joan Chittister, *The Liturgical Year: The Spiraling Adventure of the Spiritual Life* (Nelson, 2009), 4.
h. Ellen F. Davis, *Opening Israel's Scriptures* (Oxford University Press, 2019), 77–81.

Chapter 13 How to Read Violent Texts Today

1. Daniel I. Block, *The Triumph of Grace: Literary and Theological Studies in Deuteronomy and Deuteronomic Themes* (Wipf & Stock, 2017), 507.
2. See Richard Dawkins, *The God Delusion* (Random House UK, 2016), 31.
3. Christian Hofreiter, *Making Sense of Old Testament Genocide: Christian Interpretations of Herem Passages* (Oxford University Press, 2018), 248.
4. Quoted in J. Gordon McConville and Stephen N. Williams, *Joshua*, Two Horizons Old Testament Commentary (Eerdmans, 2010), 109n27.
5. Hofreiter, *Making Sense of Old Testament Genocide*, 169–70. Hofreiter's close, nuanced discussion is worth reading in full.
6. Hofreiter, *Making Sense of Old Testament Genocide*, 180.
7. Ellen F. Davis, *Opening Israel's Scriptures* (Oxford University Press, 2019), 130.
8. David E. Stannard, *American Holocaust: The Conquest of the New World* (Oxford University Press, 1993), x.
9. Robert Allen Warrior, "Canaanites, Cowboys, and Indians: Deliverance, Conquest, and Liberation Theology Today," in *Native and Christian: Indigenous Voices on Religious Identity in the United States and Canada*, ed. James Treat (Routledge, 1996), 95.
10. Esau McCaulley, *Reading While Black: African American Interpretation as an Exercise in Hope* (IVP Academic, 2020), 21.
11. Brent A. Strawn, *Lies My Preacher Told Me: An Honest Look at the Old Testament* (Westminster John Knox, 2021), 50.
12. McConville and Williams, *Joshua*, 112, emphasis added.
13. William J. Webb and Gordon K. Oeste, *Bloody, Brutal, and Barbaric? Wrestling with Troubling War Texts* (IVP Academic, 2019), 16.
14. McConville and Williams, *Joshua*, 121.
15. McConville and Williams, *Joshua*, 2.
16. Block, *Triumph of Grace*, 497.
17. Christopher Seitz, "Canon and Conquest: The Character of the God of the Hebrew Bible," in *Divine Evil? The Moral Character of the God of Abraham*, ed. Michael Bergmann, Michael J. Murray, and Michael C. Rea (Oxford University Press, 2010), 300.
18. As suggested by Jewish interpretive practices; see Anthony Milner, *A Theology of Genocide? Reading Deuteronomy 20* (Sheffield Phoenix, 2021), 98.

19. Davis, *Opening Israel's Scriptures*, 123.

20. John C. Collins, "The Agonistic Imagination: The Ethics of War in Deuteronomy," in *Worship, Women, and War: Essays in Honor of Susan Niditch*, ed. John J. Collins, T. M. Lemos, and Saul M. Olyan (Brown University Press, 2015), 185–86, emphasis added.

21. Webb and Oeste, *Bloody, Brutal, and Barbaric?*, 300–301.

22. See Block, *Triumph of Grace*, 509.

23. Douglas S. Earl, *Reading Joshua as Christian Scripture*, Journal of Theological Interpretation Supplements 2 (Eisenbrauns, 2010), 92–93.

24. Davis, *Opening Israel's Scriptures*, 131.

25. Webb and Oeste, *Bloody, Brutal, and Barbaric?*, 144.

26. Webb and Oeste, *Bloody, Brutal, and Barbaric?*, 145.

27. Webb and Oeste, *Bloody, Brutal, and Barbaric?*, 146n29.

28. Webb and Oeste, *Bloody, Brutal, and Barbaric?*, 147–48.

29. See Earl, *Reading Joshua*, 108.

30. Walter R. Moberly, *Old Testament Theology: Reading the Hebrew Bible as Christian Scripture* (Baker Academic, 2013), 61.

31. Matthew J. Lynch, *Flood and Fury: Old Testament Violence and the Shalom of God* (IVP Academic, 2023), 132–34.

32. Earl, *Reading Joshua*, 109.

33. Lynch, *Flood and Fury*, 134.

34. Nathan MacDonald, "One God or One Lord? Deuteronomy and the Meaning of 'Monotheism'" (PhD thesis, University of Durham, 2001), 153, 140, http://etheses.dur.ac.uk/3806/.

35. Lynch, *Flood and Fury*, 130.

36. Lynch, *Flood and Fury*, 118.

37. Lynch, *Flood and Fury*, 123.

38. Lynch, *Flood and Fury*, 135–36.

39. Lynch, *Flood and Fury*, 134–36.

40. MacDonald, "One God or One Lord?," 147.

41. Lynch, *Flood and Fury*, 172–73.

42. Lynch, *Flood and Fury*, 177–78.

43. Lynch, *Flood and Fury*, 109–11.

44. Lynch, *Flood and Fury*, 109–11.

45. David G. Firth, *Including the Stranger: Foreigners in the Former Prophets*, New Studies in Biblical Theology 50 (IVP Academic, 2019), 44.

46. Mark G. Brett, *Political Trauma and Healing: Biblical Ethics for a Postcolonial World* (Eerdmans, 2016), 245.

47. Lynch, *Flood and Fury*, 157–60.

48. Lynch, *Flood and Fury*, 157.

49. Lynch, *Flood and Fury*, 160 (emphasis added).

50. Lynch, *Flood and Fury*, 164. Lynch quotes Lawson Stone, "Early Israel and Its Appearance in Canaan," in *Ancient Israel's History: An Introduction to Issues and Sources*, ed. Bill T. Arnold and Richard S. Hess (Baker Academic, 2014), 161.

51. Lynch, *Flood and Fury*, 165–67. Lynch quotes Ann E. Killebrew, *Biblical Peoples and Ethnicity: An Archaeological Study of Egyptians, Canaanites, Philistines, and Early Israel, 1300–1100 B.C.E.* (Society of Biblical Literature, 2005), 33.

52. Webb and Oeste, *Bloody, Brutal, and Barbaric?*, 323.

53. Slightly adapted from Stephen B. Chapman, "Martial Memory, Peaceable Vision: Divine War in the Old Testament," in *Holy War in the Bible: Christian Morality and an Old Testament Problem*, ed. Heath Thomas, Jeremy Evans, and Paul Copan (IVP Academic, 2013), 66.

Chapter 13 Sidebar Notes

a. Strawn, *Lies My Preacher Told Me*, 49–50.
b. Chapman, "Martial Memory, Peaceable Vision," 62.
c. Gerhard Lohfink, "*ḥāram*; *ḥērem*," in *Theological Dictionary of the Old Testament* (Eerdmans, 1998), 5:196.
d. Gordon J. Wenham, *A Guide to the Pentateuch*, vol. 1 of *Exploring the Old Testament* (IVP Academic, 2003), 137.
e. See MacDonald, "One God or One Lord?," 139n70.
f. William Ford, "The Challenge of the Canaanites," *Tyndale Bulletin* 68 (2017): 181, https://doi.org/10.53751/001c.29433.
g. Webb and Oeste, *Bloody, Brutal, and Barbaric?*, 212.
h. Webb and Oeste, *Bloody, Brutal, and Barbaric?*, 204–30.
i. Lynch, *Flood and Fury*, 140.
j. Hofreiter, *Making Sense of Old Testament Genocide*, 249.
k. Origen, *Homilies on Joshua* 1.6, in Hofreiter, *Making Sense of Old Testament Genocide*, 67.
l. Hofreiter, *Making Sense of Old Testament Genocide*, 250.

Chapter 14 Numbers 1–12

1. Jacob Milgrom, *Numbers*, JPS Torah Commentary (Jewish Publication Society, 1990), xiii; Raymond Brown, *The Message of Numbers: Journey to the Promised Land* (InterVarsity, 2002), 16.
2. The idea of Numbers as the "junk room" of the Pentateuch is attributed to Julius Wellhausen; see Mary Douglas, *Thinking in Circles: An Essay on Ring Composition* (Yale University Press, 2008), 43.
3. Gordon J. Wenham, *Numbers: An Introduction and Commentary*, Tyndale Old Testament Commentary 4 (InterVarsity, 1981), 17–18; Wenham, *A Guide to the Pentateuch*, vol. 1 of *Exploring the Old Testament* (IVP Academic, 2003), 104.
4. Dennis T. Olson, *The Death of the Old and the Birth of the New: The Framework of the Book of Numbers and the Pentateuch*, Brown Judaic Studies 71 (Scholars Press, 1985). See also Ronald B. Allen, "Numbers," in *The Expositor's Bible Commentary*, ed. Frank E. Gaebelein (Zondervan, 1990), 2:675.
5. On revelation and redemption, see Brown, *Message of Numbers*, 26–28.
6. Roy E. Gane, *Leviticus, Numbers: From Biblical Text . . . to Contemporary Life* (Zondervan, 2004), 496. For a thorough summary and evaluation of the various views on the numbering, see Gane, *Leviticus, Numbers*, 495–99; Wenham, *Numbers*, 68–76.
7. Olson, *Numbers and the Pentateuch*, 35.
8. Gane, *Leviticus, Numbers*, 520.
9. Olson, *Numbers and the Pentateuch*, 34.
10. Olson, *Numbers and the Pentateuch*, 36–37.
11. Wenham, *Numbers*, 90.
12. Wenham, *Numbers*, 98.
13. Wenham, *Numbers*, 96.
14. Richard S. Briggs, *Theological Hermeneutics and the Book of Numbers as Christian Scripture* (University of Notre Dame Press, 2018), 231.
15. Brown, *Message of Numbers*, 60.
16. Olson, *Numbers and the Pentateuch*, 45.
17. There seems to be a discrepancy between these instructions in Num. 8 with those of Num. 4, which indicate that the age of duty is from thirty to fifty years old. It may be that the number here in Num. 8 includes a five-year training period, and scholars have proposed other explanations for the discrepancy. See Wenham, *Numbers*, 110n75.
18. Olson, *Numbers and the Pentateuch*, 51.

19. Walter Brueggemann, *The Message of the Psalms: A Theological Commentary* (Augsburg, 1984); Soong-Chan Rah, *Prophetic Lament: A Call for Justice in Troubled Times* (IVP Books, 2015); Tish Harrison Warren, *Prayer in the Night: For Those Who Work or Watch or Weep* (IVP Books, 2021).

20. Michael J. Rhodes, *Just Discipleship: Biblical Justice in an Unjust World* (IVP Academic, 2023), 81–102.

21. A. J. Swoboda, *After Doubt: How to Question Your Faith Without Losing It* (Brazos, 2021).

22. Douglas Kaine McKelvey, ed., *Death, Grief, and Hope*, vol. 2 of *Every Moment Holy* (Rabbit Room, 2024); Justin McRoberts and Scott Erickson, *In the Low: Honest Prayers for Dark Seasons* (Baker Books, 2025).

Chapter 14 Sidebar Notes

a. Amma Syncletica, in *The Sayings of the Desert Fathers: The Alphabetical Collection*, trans. Benedicta Ward (Cistercian, 1975), 230–31.

b. See the helpful discussion in Peter Altmann and Caio Peres, *Numbers: An Introduction and Commentary*, Tyndale Old Testament Commentaries 4 (IVP Academic, 2024), 75–78.

c. Olson, *Numbers and the Pentateuch*, 22–23.

d. Sarah Foot, "Ordeals," in *The Oxford Dictionary of the Christian Church*, 3rd ed., ed. F. L. Cross and E. A. Livingstone (Oxford University Press, 2009), 1194.

e. Ellen F. Davis, *Opening Israel's Scriptures* (Oxford University Press, 2019), 96.

f. Brown, *Message of Numbers*, 50.

g. Altmann and Peres, *Numbers*, 166.

h. Elaine A. Phillips, "Speaking Truthfully: Job's Friends and Job," *Bulletin for Biblical Research* 18, no. 1 (2008): 31–43, https://doi.org/10.2307/26423727.

Chapter 15 Numbers 13–36

1. Olson divides Numbers into two halves framed by its censuses: chaps. 1–25 recount the death of the first generation; chaps. 26–36 narrate the rise of the new; Dennis T. Olson, *The Death of the Old and the Birth of the New: The Framework of the Book of Numbers and the Pentateuch* (Scholars Press, 1985).

2. See Olson, *Numbers and the Pentateuch*, 79.

3. Gordon J. Wenham, *Numbers: An Introduction and Commentary*, Tyndale Old Testament Commentaries 4 (InterVarsity, 1981), 139.

4. On the theme of the death of the old generation and the birth of the new, see Olson, *Numbers and the Pentateuch*, 87–89.

5. For the following on Moses's response, we are indebted to Olson, *Numbers and the Pentateuch*, 103–4.

6. Olson, *Numbers and the Pentateuch*, 119–20.

7. Wenham, *Numbers*, 163.

8. Olson, *Numbers and the Pentateuch*, 124.

9. Carol Bechtel Reynolds, "Life After Grace: Preaching from the Book of Numbers," *Interpretation* 51, no. 3 (1997): 274, https://doi.org/10.1177/002096439605100305.

10. Gordon J. Wenham, *A Guide to the Pentateuch*, vol. 1 of *Exploring the Old Testament* (IVP Academic, 2003), 114.

11. Olson, *Numbers and the Pentateuch*, 144.

12. Roy E. Gane, *Leviticus, Numbers: From Biblical Text . . . to Contemporary Life* (Zondervan, 2004), 693.

13. Gane, *Leviticus, Numbers*, 693.

14. Olson, *Numbers and the Pentateuch*, 151.

15. Olson, *Numbers and the Pentateuch*, 159–60.

16. Olson, *Numbers and the Pentateuch*, 162.

17. Olson, *Numbers and the Pentateuch*, 163.

18. According to Wenham, the minimum number of sacrifices in a year (not including other sacrificial offerings that could be made; see Num. 29:39) would amount to the following: 113 bulls, 32 rams, 1,086 lambs, over a ton of flour, and the equivalent of 1,000 bottles of oil and wine. See Wenham, *Numbers*, 220.

19. On this important insight, see Olson, *Numbers and the Pentateuch*, 170–73. Also take note of the connection that Olson makes between the structure of the offerings in Num. 28–29 and the creation story in Gen. 1 (170).

20. Olson, *Numbers and the Pentateuch*, 175.

21. Wenham, *Pentateuch*, 117.

22. According to Olson, these women were presumably killed because of their participation in the sexual activity related to Baal of Peor and the male children because they were potential enemy warriors (Num. 25); Olson, *Numbers and the Pentateuch*, 178.

23. Peter Altmann and Caio Peres, *Numbers: An Introduction and Commentary*, Tyndale Old Testament Commentaries 4 (IVP Academic, 2024), 333.

24. Wenham, *Pentateuch*, 118.

25. Wenham, *Pentateuch*, 118.

26. Olson, *Numbers and the Pentateuch*, 188–89.

27. Wenham, *Pentateuch*, 120.

28. Wenham, *Pentateuch*, 120.

29. Carmen Joy Imes, *Bearing God's Name: Why Sinai Still Matters* (IVP Academic, 2019), 16–18.

Chapter 15 Sidebar Notes

a. Brent A. Strawn, *The Incomparable God: Readings in Biblical Theology*, ed. Collin Cornell and M. Justin Walker (Eerdmans, 2023), 387–88.

b. Olson, *Numbers and the Pentateuch*, 153 (see 153–55 for the parallels between these two events).

Chapter 16 Deuteronomy 1–11

1. Gordon J. Wenham, *A Guide to the Pentateuch*, vol. 1 of *Exploring the Old Testament* (InterVarsity, 2003), 123.

2. See J. G. McConville, *Deuteronomy*, Apollos Old Testament Commentary (IVP Academic, 2002), 20.

3. Brevard S. Childs, *Introduction to the Old Testament as Scripture* (Fortress, 1979), 204.

4. Wenham, *Pentateuch*, 123.

5. Brent A. Strawn, *The Old Testament: A Concise Introduction* (Routledge, 2020), 63.

6. This description follows Strawn, *The Old Testament*, 63–64.

7. See Luke Powery, *Dem Dry Bones: Preaching, Death, and Hope* (Fortress, 2012), 23–25.

8. A. J. Culp, *Memoir of Moses: The Literary Creation of Covenantal Memory in Deuteronomy* (Lexington, 2020), 33.

9. Alan Kirk and Tom Thatcher, *Memory, Tradition, and Text: Uses of the Past in Early Christianity*, Semeia Studies 52 (Society of Biblical Literature, 2005), 6.

10. Culp, *Memoir of Moses*, 39.

11. See Culp, *Memoir of Moses*, 109.

12. See Wenham, *Pentateuch*, 125–26.

13. See Ellen F. Davis, *Opening Israel's Scriptures* (Oxford University Press, 2019), 108–9.

14. Walter Brueggemann, *Deuteronomy*, Abingdon Old Testament Commentaries (Abingdon, 2001), 19.

15. S. Dean McBride Jr., "Polity of the Covenant People: The Book of Deuteronomy," *Interpretation* 41, no. 3 (1987): 231–37.

16. McConville, *Deuteronomy*, 21.

17. McConville, *Deuteronomy*, 50, emphasis added.

18. Carolyn Pressler, "Deuteronomy," in *Women's Bible Commentary*, 20th anniversary ed., ed. Carol A. Newsom, Sharon H. Ringe, and Jacqueline E. Lapsley (Westminster John Knox, 2012), 89.

19. Pressler, "Deuteronomy," 89.

20. Christopher J. H. Wright, *Deuteronomy*, Understanding the Bible (Hendrickson, 1996; repr., Baker Books, 2012).

21. Michael J. Rhodes, *Reimagining Biblical Politics: What Scripture Says About Public Life and Why It Matters* (Baker Academic, 2026), 19.

22. See Richard D. Nelson, *Deuteronomy*, Old Testament Library (Westminster John Knox, 2004), 89; McConville, *Deuteronomy*, 141.

23. Peter C. Craigie, *Deuteronomy*, New International Commentary on the Old Testament (Eerdmans, 1976), 169.

24. Especially in Isa. 40–48. See Matthew J. Lynch, "Mapping Monotheism: Modes of Monotheistic Rhetoric in the Hebrew Bible," *Vetus Testamentum* 64, no. 1 (2014): 53, https://www.jstor.org/stable/43894098.

25. Walter R. Moberly, *Old Testament Theology: Reading the Hebrew Bible as Christian Scripture* (Baker Academic, 2013), 20.

26. Jon D. Levenson, *The Love of God: Divine Gift, Human Gratitude, and Mutual Faithfulness in Judaism* (Princeton University Press, 2016), 11.

27. Moberly, *Old Testament Theology*, 20.

28. Levenson, *The Love of God*, 36–37.

29. J. G. McConville, *God and Earthly Power: An Old Testament Political Theology; Genesis–Kings*, Library of Biblical Studies (T&T Clark, 2006), 89.

30. Levenson, *The Love of God*, 29.

31. Levenson, *The Love of God*, 41.

32. Patrick D. Miller Jr., "God and the Gods: History of Religion as an Approach and Context for Biblical Theology," in *Divine Doppelgängers: YHWH's Ancient Look-Alikes*, ed. Collin Cornell (Penn State University Press, 2022), 26.

33. Moshe Weinfeld, *Deuteronomy and the Deuteronomistic School* (Eisenbrauns, 1992), 81–83.

34. Nathan MacDonald, "One God or One Lord? Deuteronomy and the Meaning of 'Monotheism'" (PhD thesis, University of Durham, 2001), 265, http://etheses.dur.ac.uk/3806/.

35. Levenson, *The Love of God*, 14.

36. Dennis T. Olson, *Deuteronomy and the Death of Moses: A Theological Reading* (Fortress, 1994), 51.

37. J. Gordon McConville, *Being Human in God's World: An Old Testament Theology of Humanity* (Baker Academic, 2016), 54–55.

38. See, e.g., CEB and NET at Deut. 6:13, 24.

39. Bill Arnold, "The Love-Fear Antinomy in Deuteronomy 5–11," *Vetus Testamentum* 61, no. 4 (2011): 567, https://www.jstor.org/stable/41309096.

40. Jeffrey H. Tigay, *Deuteronomy*, JPS Torah Commentary (Jewish Publication Society, 1996), 80.

41. Brent Strawn, "Keep, Observe, Do—Carefully—Today! The Rhetoric of Repetition in Deuteronomy," in *A God So Near: Essays on Old Testament Theology in Honor of Patrick D. Miller*, ed. Brent Strawn and Nancy R. Bowen (Eisenbrauns, 2003), 215–40, here 216–17.

42. Strawn, "Keep, Observe, Do," 240.

43. See Tigay, *Deuteronomy*, 114.

44. *Corpus des tablettes en cunéiformes alphabétiques découvertes à Ras Shamra-Ugarit de 1929 à 1939*, ed. Andrée Herdner (Geuthner, 1963), 3.14, 8–23 = *Die keilalphabetischen Texte aus Ugarit*, ed. Manfried Dietrich, Oswald Loretz, and Joaquin Sanmartin (Ugarit-Verlag, 2013), 1.2, 4.

45. *Corpus des tablettes en cunéiformes alphabétiques* 6.3, 3–9.

46. *Corpus des tablettes en cunéiformes alphabétiques* 1.4, 7.
47. Albino Barrera, *Biblical Economic Ethics: Sacred Scripture's Teachings on Economic Life* (Lexington, 2013), 31.
48. Olson, *Deuteronomy and the Death of Moses*, 52–53.
49. See the essay of this name by Strawn, "Keep, Observe, Do."
50. See Michael J. Rhodes, *Formative Feasting: Practices and Virtue Ethics in Deuteronomy's Tithe Meal and the Corinthian Lord's Supper*, Studies in Biblical Literature (Peter Lang, 2022), 136.
51. Strawn, "Keep, Observe, Do," 238.
52. See McConville, *God and Earthly Power*, 79.
53. Culp, *Memoir of Moses*, 159–64.
54. MacDonald, "One God or One Lord?," 266.
55. See Rhodes, *Formative Feasting*, 135.
56. Brueggemann, *Deuteronomy*, 130.
57. Rhodes, *Formative Feasting*, 143.
58. Tigay, *Deuteronomy*, 112.
59. Tigay, *Deuteronomy*, 112.
60. Phyllis Trible, *God and the Rhetoric of Sexuality* (Fortress, 1978), 108.
61. Tigay, *Deuteronomy*, 113. See Ellen F. Davis, *Scripture, Culture, and Agriculture: An Agrarian Reading of the Bible* (Cambridge University Press, 2009), 76.
62. Kara Powell, "Preventing Teenage 'Faith Drift,'" *Leadership Journal*, July 7, 2016, https://www.christianitytoday.com/pastors/content/preventing-teenage-faith-drift/; also August 13, 2018, https://karapowell.com/2018/08/preventing-teenage-faith-drift/.
63. Christian Smith and Amy Adamczyk, *Handing Down the Faith: How Parents Pass Their Religion on to the Next Generation* (Oxford University Press, 2021), 1–2.
64. Smith and Adamcyzk, *Handing Down the Faith*, 71–72.
65. Smith and Adamczyk, *Handing Down the Faith*, 33.
66. Smith and Adamczyk, *Handing Down the Faith*, 62–65.
67. Smith and Adamczyk, *Handing Down the Faith*, 5.
68. Justin Whitmel Earley, *Habits of the Household: Practicing the Story of God in Everyday Family Rhythms* (Zondervan, 2021).
69. Powell, "Preventing Teenage 'Faith Drift.'"
70. Holly Catterton Allen, Christine Lawton, and Cory L. Seibel, *Intergenerational Christian Formation: Bringing the Whole Church Together in Ministry, Community, and Worship*, 2nd ed. (IVP Academic, 2023), 150.
71. See chap. 10 in Allen et al., *Intergenerational Christian Formation*.
72. Allen et al., *Intergenerational Christian Formation*, 177.
73. Powell, "Preventing Teenage 'Faith Drift.'"

Chapter 16 Sidebar Notes

a. Lesley Rameka, "Kia whakatōmuri te haere whakamua: 'I Walk Backwards into the Future with My Eyes Fixed on My Past,'" *Contemporary Issues in Early Childhood* 17, no. 4 (2016): 387, https://doi.org/10.1177/1463949116677923.
b. See Pressler, "Deuteronomy," 102.
c. Carol Meyers, *Exodus*, New Cambridge Bible Commentary (Cambridge University Press, 2005), 123.
d. Brent. A. Strawn, "What Is Cush Doing in Amos 9:7? The Poetics of Exodus in the Plural," *Vetus Testamentum* 63, no. 1 (2013): 122.
e. See Kwame Bediako, *Theology and Identity: The Impact of Culture upon Christian Thought in the Second Century and in Modern Africa* (Fortress, 1999), 436.
f. Lynch, "Mapping Monotheism," 50.
g. Moberly, *Old Testament Theology*, 35.

h. MacDonald, "One God or One Lord?," 153.

i. Jon D. Levenson, *Sinai and Zion: An Entry into the Jewish Bible* (Winston, 1985), 63.

j. Christopher J. H. Wright, *The Mission of God: Unlocking the Bible's Grand Narrative* (IVP Academic, 2006), 403.

k. Moberly, *Old Testament Theology*, 21.

l. Levenson, *The Love of God*, 70.

m. Jerry Hwang, *Hosea: A Discourse Analysis of the Hebrew Bible*, Zondervan Exegetical Commentary on the Old Testament 24 (Zondervan, 2021), 187.

n. Derived from Michael J. Rhodes, *Reimagining Biblical Politics: What Scripture Says About Public Life and Why It Matters* (Baker Academic, 2026).

o. See Arnold, "The Love-Fear Antinomy," 569.

p. Cornel West, *Brother West: Living and Loving Out Loud* (Smiley Books, 2010), 23.

q. John Goldingay, *The Theology of the Book of Isaiah* (IVP Academic, 2014), 21.

r. Caryn A. Reeder, *The Enemy in the Household: Family Violence in Deuteronomy and Beyond* (Baker Academic, 2012), 19–20.

Chapter 17 Deuteronomy 12–34

1. Caryn A. Reeder, *The Enemy in the Household: Family Violence in Deuteronomy and Beyond* (Baker Academic, 2012), 19.

2. Richard D. Nelson, *Deuteronomy*, Old Testament Library (Westminster John Knox, 2004), 147.

3. J. G. McConville, *Deuteronomy*, Apollos Old Testament Commentary (IVP Academic, 2002), 219.

4. McConville, *Deuteronomy*, 83.

5. See Sandra L. Richter, *The Deuteronomistic History and the Name Theology: leshakken shemo sham in the Bible and the Ancient Near East*, Beihefte zur Zeitschrift für die alttestamentliche Wissenschaft 318 (De Gruyter, 2002), 183–216.

6. Nelson, *Deuteronomy*, 146–50.

7. See Peter Altmann, "Making the Meal Sacred in the Old Testament: Complexities and Possibilities for Christian Appropriation," in *Sacrality and Materiality: Locating Intersections*, ed. Rebecca A. Giselbrecht and Ralph Kunz (Vandenhoeck & Ruprecht, 2016), 131.

8. See further Michael J. Rhodes, *Formative Feasting: Practices and Virtue Ethics in Deuteronomy's Tithe Meal and the Corinthian Lord's Supper*, Studies in Biblical Literature (Peter Lang, 2022), 87–132.

9. Sandra L. Richter, "Environmental Law in Deuteronomy: One Lens on a Biblical Theology of Creation Care," *Bulletin for Biblical Research* 20, no. 3 (2010): 355–76, here 360, https://doi.org/10.2307/26424450.

10. Georg Braulik, *The Theology of Deuteronomy: Collected Essays of Georg Braulik, O.S.B.*, trans. Ulrika Lindblad (D & F Scott, 1998), 51.

11. Rhodes, *Formative Feasting*, 105.

12. David L. Baker, *Tight Fists or Open Hands? Wealth and Poverty in the Old Testament* (Eerdmans, 2009), 257.

13. See Roland Boer, *The Sacred Economy of Ancient Israel* (Westminster John Knox, 2015), 159–60.

14. Walter J. Houston, *Contending for Justice: Ideologies and Theologies of Social Justice in the Old Testament* (T&T Clark, 2006), 183; internal quotation from Nelson, *Deuteronomy*, 199.

15. Walter Brueggemann, *Money and Possessions*, Interpretation: Resources for the Use of Scripture in the Church (Westminster John Knox, 2016), 45.

16. For more on this and other biblical examples of how God's people might become just, see Michael J. Rhodes, *Just Discipleship: Biblical Justice in an Unjust World* (IVP Academic, 2023).

17. See A. J. Culp, *Memoir of Moses: The Literary Creation of Covenantal Memory in Deuteronomy* (Lexington, 2020), 141–59.

18. Bob Goudzwaard, lecture given at Redeemer University, Hamilton, Ontario, 2014.

19. Nelson, *Deuteronomy*, 213.

20. J. G. McConville, *God and Earthly Power: An Old Testament Political Theology; Genesis–Kings*, Library of Biblical Studies (T&T Clark, 2006), 94.

21. Nelson, *Deuteronomy*, 213–14.

22. Philip J. King and Lawrence E. Stager, *Life in Biblical Israel* (Westminster John Knox, 2001), 96.

23. Richter, "Environmental Law in Deuteronomy," 367.

24. Michael Rhodes and Robby Holt, *Practicing the King's Economy: Honoring Jesus in How We Work, Earn, Spend, Save, and Give*, with Brian Fikkert (Baker Books, 2018), 142.

25. Richter, "Environmental Law in Deuteronomy," 372, emphasis added.

26. Rhodes et al., *Practicing the King's Economy*, 142.

27. Christopher J. H. Wright, *Deuteronomy*, Understanding the Bible (Hendrickson, 1996; repr., Baker Books, 2012), 270.

28. Walter Brueggemann, *Deuteronomy*, Abingdon Old Testament Commentaries (Abingdon, 2001), 250.

29. See Melissa D. Ramos, *Ritual in Deuteronomy: The Performance of Doom*, The Ancient World (Routledge, 2021), 130.

30. Wright, *Deuteronomy*, 280.

31. Wright, *Deuteronomy*, 277.

32. See McConville, *Deuteronomy*, 402.

33. Wright, *Deuteronomy*, 282.

34. Dennis T. Olson, *Deuteronomy and the Death of Moses: A Theological Reading* (Fortress, 1994), 122.

35. Jeffrey H. Tigay downplays the extent of Israel's inability to obey in *Deuteronomy*, JPS Torah Commentary (Jewish Publication Society, 1996), 275–76, 283–84; J. G. Millar argues that Deut. 29 calls Israel to "do all that she can to obey, knowing that ultimately she is doomed to fail." Millar, *Now Choose Life: Theology and Ethics in Deuteronomy* (Eerdmans, 1999), 174.

36. On "when" versus "if," see McConville, *Deuteronomy*, 426.

37. Ryan O'Dowd, *The Wisdom of Torah: Epistemology in Deuteronomy and the Wisdom Literature* (Vandenhoeck & Ruprecht, 2009), 95.

38. Paul A. Barker, *The Triumph of Grace in Deuteronomy: Faithless Israel, Faithful Yahweh in Deuteronomy* (Paternoster, 2004), 150.

39. Dennis T. Olson, "How Does Deuteronomy Do Theology? Literary Juxtaposition and Paradox in the New Moab Covenant in Deuteronomy 29–32," in *A God So Near: Essays on Old Testament Theology in Honor of Patrick D. Miller*, ed. Brent Strawn and Nancy R. Bowen (Eisenbrauns, 2003), 209.

40. See Barker, *Triumph of Grace in Deuteronomy*, 176–77.

41. O'Dowd, *Wisdom of Torah*, 94–97.

42. A point emphasized by Tigay, *Deuteronomy*, 284.

43. Barker, *Triumph of Grace in Deuteronomy*, 148.

44. Herman Bavinck, *Reformed Dogmatics: Abridged in One Volume*, ed. John Bolt (Baker Academic, 2011), 147.

45. Olson, "How Does Deuteronomy Do Theology?," 202.

46. Ellen F. Davis, *Opening Israel's Scriptures* (Oxford University Press, 2019), 126.

47. Brian Fikkert and Steve Corbett, *When Helping Hurts: How to Alleviate Poverty Without Hurting the Poor . . . and Yourself!* (Moody, 2014), 99–101.

48. See Rhodes et al., *Practicing the King's Economy*.

Chapter 17 Sidebar Notes

a. See Georg Braulik, "The Sequence of the Laws in Deuteronomy 12–26 and in the Decalogue," in *A Song of Power and the Power of Song*, ed. Duane L. Christensen (Eisenbrauns, 1993), 313–35.

b. Braulik, "Sequence of the Laws," 322.

c. See Baker, *Tight Fists*, 248.

d. Rhodes, *Just Discipleship*, 63.

e. Norbert Lohfink, "Poverty in the Laws of the Ancient Near East and of the Bible," *Theological Studies* 52, no. 1 (1991): 44–45.

f. Derived from Rhodes, *Formative Feasting*, 105.

g. N. Lohfink, "Poverty in the Laws," 37.

h. Martin Luther King Jr., *Where Do We Go from Here: Chaos or Community?* (Beacon, 2010), 107.

i. Martin Luther King Jr., "Speech on Receipt of Honorary Doctorate in Civil Law," University of Newcastle upon Tyne, November 13, 1967, https://www.ncl.ac.uk/congregations/honorary/martinlutherking/.

j. Jeremiah Unterman, *Justice for All: How the Jewish Bible Revolutionized Ethics* (Jewish Publication Society, 2017), 74.

k. Rhodes, *Just Discipleship*, 48, quoting Jonathan J. B. Mijs and Elizabeth L. Roe, "Is America Coming Apart? Socioeconomic Segregation in Neighborhoods, Schools, Workplaces, and Social Networks, 1970–2020," *Sociology Compass* 15, no. 6 (2021): 7–9, https://doi.org/10.1111/soc4.12884.

l. Olson, "How Does Deuteronomy Do Theology?," 202.

m. See Olson, "How Does Deuteronomy Do Theology?," 205–7.

n. Nelson, *Deuteronomy*, 339.

o. McConville recognizes this possibility even while arguing that the core of the book is pre-monarchial (*Deuteronomy*, 39). See also Olson, "How Does Deuteronomy Do Theology?," 205.

p. Walter Brueggemann, "The Travail of Pardon: Reflections on *slḥ*," in Strawn and Bowen, *A God So Near*, 285–87, 294.

q. Carol Newsom, "Models of the Moral Self: Hebrew Bible and Second Temple Judaism," *Journal of Biblical Literature* 131, no. 1 (2012): 11, https://muse.jhu.edu/article/470021.

r. See Brueggemann, "The Travail of Pardon," 292.

s. Kyle B. Wells, *Grace and Agency in Paul and Second Temple Judaism* (Brill, 2015), 272.

Index